AMERICAN POLITICS

POLICIES, POWER, AND CHANGE

FOURTH EDITION

Kenneth M. Dolbeare
University of Massachusetts, Amherst

Murray J. Edelman
University of Wisconsin

D. C. HEATH AND COMPANY
Lexington, Massachusetts ■ Toronto

Cover photograph by Owen Franken/STOCK, BOSTON.

PREFACE

This is the fourth edition of a book originally conceived and written in the late 1960s. We are relieved to note that its two most distinguishing features — its political-economy framework and its critical nature — have stood the test of more than a decade.

Our framework integrates politics and government with the private economy and its dynamics. The influence of economic conditions on politics and public policy could hardly be clearer than it is today. Neither politics nor economics can be understood separately, and the connections between them must be made explicit, rather than left to the coincidental combination of courses from several departments or a happy intellectual leap by a determined student.

This book is critical, not in the sense of being a negative polemic or proceeding from an alternative ideology, but rather in the classical liberal arts sense. To be critical is to be self-conscious about one's own values, assumptions, and way of thinking; to clarify concepts and rigorously examine evidence; and to look beyond the way that institutions and events present themselves in search of underlying causes and relationships. With this sort of critical approach, people learn analytical and evaluative skills and not just facts. On this basis, we frankly encourage readers to make judgments and interpretations, and we state some of our own in the last two chapters.

This edition reflects some substantive changes over previous editions. Extensive material has been added on the nature of current economic problems and their implications for politics and public policy, as well as on the concept of national security and the changing American foreign and military policies surrounding it. Expanded materials on the U.S. energy problem and policies link together economic and foreign policies. A chapter new to this edition considers how the nation's political agenda is managed by powerful policy planning groups. In addition, there are new sections on the "new right" and, of course, the election of 1980.

Other substantive changes have been made to the descriptions of institutions and processes. The chapter on the Constitution, for example, has been expanded to include a detailed analysis of the document itself. The chapter on the Supreme Court now contains a lengthy case study: a description of how the key 1973 abortion case came to the Court, how it was argued and decided, an edited text of the Court's opinion, and a brief analysis of its reception and impact. New materials have also been added to the discussion of political socialization. The contents of what was previously a chapter on symbolism have been adapted and redistributed to those areas in the book where they have immediate relevance. Thus, the important themes of symbolic reassurance are fully integrated with our developing analysis, as in the revised chapter on American values and ideology. The material on public opinion, political parties, voting, and interest groups has been considerably expanded. Finally, we have tried to raise vital questions about the U.S. political system, direct evidence at those questions, and then answer them. We hope that this makes the book more direct and readable.

This fourth edition is accompanied by an excellent Student Handbook, prepared by Robert Sahr of Purdue University. We think that it will be of great assistance in providing students with opportunities to digest and work with the concepts and evidence contained in the book. There is also a very useful Instructor's Guide, prepared by Janna Merrick of St. Cloud State University, which has been thoroughly updated to fit with this edition. Professor Merrick has more experience teaching with this book than anyone else we know and is ideally qualified to provide instructors with test questions and other assistance.

We want to acknowledge the immensely helpful reviews of the previous edition provided by Andrew T. Cowart, State University of New York at Stony Brook; Joan De Bardeleben, Colorado State University; Judith Elmusa, Suffolk University; James Masuda, University of Kansas; Robert A. Poirier, Northern Arizona University; and Joan Rothschild, University of Lowell. Valuable research assistance for the fourth edition was provided by Joe Peschek of the University of Massachusetts and David Crapo and James Zaffiro of the University of Wisconsin. As always, we invite comments and suggestions from teachers and students.

K.M.D.

M.J.E.

CONTENTS

PART 2
Problems and Policies

PART 3
Contrasting Reactions to Policy Patterns

PART 4
Institutions and Processes: The Role of Elites

PART 5
Institutions and Processes: The Roles of Nonelites

PART 6
Power Structure and Political Change

PART 1

THE AMERICAN POLITICAL ECONOMY: DESIGNING AN APPROACH

WHY AND HOW
TO STUDY POLITICS

Why are we here? Where are we going? These questions may occur to students confronting a new textbook as well as to Americans facing multiplying social problems. *American Politics*, properly used, will help to explain why our political system works as it does, what difference its workings make to people and problems, and where *it* is going. If successful, it should also help readers to ask the right questions and either to get what they want or to reconstruct the system so they can. This is not a book for those who think they can avoid or transcend the effects of politics. Moral dilemmas and the failures and successes of human efforts to build a decent world deserve our best understanding and active responses. We think this book can help.

Our primary purposes are to help people see their political system more clearly, to develop their skills of *analysis* and *evaluation*, and to enable them to act more effectively to gain their ends in politics — whether through, around, or in spite of the established political system. To do these things honestly forces us to look critically at many of the revered institutions and values of the United States, to challenge some familiar myths, and to depart from some of the standard approaches of academic political science.

Naturally, this book is biased. Every textbook is. There is no such thing as a "neutral" or "objective" textbook. Some books may appear neutral or objective because they say things we have heard many times before. That is, they reiterate dominant beliefs and familiar interpretations, whose familiarity causes us to respond favorably. But this is to say only that we have not *recognized* the biases that lie hidden in those orthodox points of view or that reside unconsciously in our minds and shape our responses. The most scrupulously "neutral" authors must select certain facts, present them within a particular conceptual framework, suggest ways of interpreting them so that they become meaningful, and so on. At every stage, the authors' assumptions and preferences — in short, their biases — determine what will be presented as truth to their readers. The best that authors can do is to declare frankly where they stand and to warn their readers to be skeptical — one purpose of this introduction.

But if all books are thus biased, why read any except those we agree with? What can a serious reader expect to gain from a biased book? This brings us to a vital point. We believe that it is possible, even necessary, to be both honestly critical and frankly biased without sacrificing intellectual quality, rigor, or utility. The key lies in our conviction that readers must become independent thinkers and in our determination to provide them with the tools to do so. A critical stance that points up the culture-bound, parochial, self-congratulatory, or otherwise limiting elements of standard American beliefs is absolutely essential for this purpose. Only thus can people begin to analyze where power is located and how and for whose benefit it is used.

Finally, becoming a truly independent person requires that one make repeated value judgments — about particular policies and practices, about the political system itself, and about alternatives to both. Change is constant, and more drastic changes appear to lie ahead. Choices must be made, and conscious action taken, to shape the future. To do these things, people must learn to identify their present values and preferences and to ask the right questions about both the present and the future so that they can effectively further the values they conclude are desirable. A substantial portion of this book is devoted to presenting these questions systematically and to exploring their implications and possible answers. Therefore, although we readily acknowledge the biases of this book, we argue that such biases are functional — in fact, necessary — for the purpose of forcing questions to the surface and equipping the reader to become a truly independent thinker.

Thus, this is not the usual civics book. But neither is it a mere polemic, another in the long series of attacks on things American. It is a set of tools and questions, applied to the real world of American politics, to enable readers to gain a better understanding of the political system and of themselves — in short, to help them decide what they want and how to get it. The purpose of understanding what is happening in politics, and why, is to be able to judge and then to act. Of course, all understandings, judgments, and actions are not equally sound. Some are clearly better than others in terms of factual accuracy, human values, or both. Our task is to find the ways of understanding, judging, and acting that can lead to a more just and decent society.

This book may be difficult in spots. If the writing is at fault, we are to blame. More often, we think, the difficulty is due to the complexity of the subject matter and to misconceptions and incapacities produced by the dominant American ideology, which not only teaches that all is well and need not be examined closely, but also erects verbal and conceptual barriers against doing so. We must establish factual points thoroughly, on the basis of data and other evidence where possible; thus, there are many tables and charts in this book. To meet a high standard of proof, some precise definitions and carefully detailed considerations are essential. Because we must comprehensively synthesize and interpret a vast body of material — the totality of the American econopolitical system and process — repeated conceptual clarification is necessary. For all these reasons, we ask that readers respond to difficult sections by trying a little harder. The end product — understanding how and why the system works as it does, and for whom, and what can be done about it — is surely worth the trouble.

Chapter 1 begins to spell out what is involved in our twin goals of *analysis* and *evaluation*. *Analysis* means factual description, accompanied by *explanation* (what caused facts to be this way, what dynamics lie behind apparent reality) and *interpretation* (the meaning or implications of the factual situation). At some point interpretation begins to shade into *evaluation*, the act of making value judgments about the factual situation. Such judgments must be based on *standards*, necessarily value-based, that are clear and defensible. The first two sections below set forth some key definitions that are important tools of analysis; these sections also explore the problem of standards for evaluation. Next, we caution readers against some of the most often encountered obstacles to rigorous analysis and evaluation. Finally, we summarize our major points and give a preview of the plan of the book.

Tools of Analysis

Let us begin by briefly illustrating why a careful approach is essential; we will use a problem that will remain with us throughout the book. Then we can move on to develop the necessary tools of analysis.

The United States is a capitalist society. This pronouncement is one of the most meaningful statements that can be made about American politics. It is not a very startling or original observation, but Americans react to it in sharply contrasting ways. Most people never understand its implications. Others are so shocked by the discovery and its implications that they believe that there is nothing more to be said. Much recent talk about American politics falls into the latter category, interpreting all political attitudes, behavior, institutions, processes, and prospects exclusively in terms of the (bad) characteristics of capitalism.

Neither of these two responses satisfies the demands of sophisticated political analysis. Both result from a lack of understanding of the interrelationship of economic, social, cultural, and ideological factors in shaping politics. These two types of intellectual failure define our task in this book. We must develop concepts, methods, and other tools of analysis that enable us to transcend these responses to the point of understanding, for example, how much of our politics is traceable to the capitalist nature of the American social order and how much is due to other factors.

What does it mean that the United States is a capitalist society? First, it means that the productive resources of the society — farms, factories, mines, and so on — are all owned by private individuals or corporations and operated so as to produce profits for those owners. Services such as transportation, advertising, communications, and the like are also privately owned and operated for profit. Most people are not owners and must earn their livelihoods by working for those who are.

Next, it means that the social structure is shaped in important ways by patterns of wealth and income distribution created by that economic system. A relatively few people — mostly owners, but also some salaried managers and other persons — receive a large share of all the wealth and income produced. A larger group of people with especially useful skills — engineers, lawyers, accountants, salespeople — also receive a substantial proportion. A still larger number of people, mostly blue-collar workers and minorities, receive a smaller proportion of income. They are not highly skilled and hold those jobs that are both low paying and most likely to be eliminated during economic recessions. Status and power in the society are distributed in the same stratified manner, thereby giving rise to a class system.

A capitalist society also has certain cultural and ideological characteristics. The values of the society support kinds of behavior that are consistent with the economic system and social structure. Individual self-seeking, materialism, the work ethic or profit motive, and respect for private property are both basic American values and necessary principles of behavior in a capitalist society. The characteristic American way of thinking is also (but less obviously) consistent with a capitalist social order. It assumes the continuity of existing patterns of ownership, social structure, and values and unconsciously tries to fit all it sees or imagines into that mold. It asks only questions that are answerable in these terms and employs only words that express attitudes appropriate to such a society. For example, it looks at higher education chiefly as a means to prepare young people for jobs and income in a technological society. It either cannot imagine other purposes or considers them uneconomical "frills" — or possibly even subversive.

Finally, although all societies generate self-congratulatory and justifying ideologies, that associated with a capitalist society has certain special features. It holds that economic activity is separate from (and morally superior to) politics. And it teaches that human nature itself is the basis of capitalism: people are naturally competitive and self-seeking, and thus capitalism is the "natural" economic system. American ideology includes many other beliefs as well, as we shall see in a later chapter, but the outlooks just identified are especially linked to the capitalist nature of the American system.

All these economic, social, cultural, and ideological characteristics play significant parts in our politics. They are not the only major factors in politics, of course. But they are often so familiar as to pass unrecognized or so much a part of our way of thinking as to control our perceptions and judgments. How do we identify precisely the parts played by different factors in our politics? Clearly, we must cast our analytical net wide enough to include all major causal factors — and we must be alert enough to see them after we have caught them. Part of the answer lies in some careful definitions.

Preliminary Reflections on Politics

In order to live together on a continuing basis and to achieve their various goals in life, people seek and employ power in ways that affect the lives of their fellows. In other words, they engage in politics. They erect governments to maintain order, further mutual goals, and promote general well-being. Around and within the framework of that government, they continue to seek their individual and group goals. People can no more live without politics in this sense than they can forego food, love, or other basic human needs and desires. Politics is the activity by which they define themselves, seek their goals, maintain a context that allows them to pursue those goals, or defend what they have already gained. For many people, of course, politics serves all of these purposes.

In the broadest sense of the term, political activity occurs whenever an individual or group brings resources of power to bear not only on government, but also on any other individual or group whose behavior it desires to change. If tenants withhold rent in order to induce a landlord to make needed improvements on a building, they are, in a general sense, engaging in political activity. Regardless of how often, or seldom, individuals employ their own political resources to influence the actions of others, they cannot escape the consequences of political decisions. If only as consumers of the political products generated by the actions of others, we are all in politics, whether we like it or not, inevitably and permanently.

Because war has been a continuing fact of history, politics has always had life-or-death importance for at least some people. With the advent of nuclear weapons, politics has come to have such meaning for practically everybody. But it is not only in relation to other countries that politics has life-or-death significance. The more powerful elements in a society prescribe the behavior that in their eyes is consistent with the established order of things and fix punishments for those who break the rules. Further, thousands of men are hired and equipped with weapons to enforce such codes of behavior. For those whose situations and/or preferences make them able and willing to accept the rules, the political preferences they reflect and the power exercised to enforce them create no great problems. For those not satisfied with the status quo, however, the same rules may serve as apparently unjust obstacles to desired change. But violation of the rules, or even talk of the justice of doing so, often brings swift retribution in the form of imprisonment, physical injury, or death.

Politics is also routine. At every hour of the day, in practically any activity in which an individual engages, he or she is affected by the consequences of politics. Consider so prosaic an act as driving to a drugstore to buy a pack of cigarettes. The driver (licensed by the state) gets into the car (licensed and registered with the state; fitted with safety devices according to federal specifications; sold at prices reflecting the manufacturer's response to federal antitrust laws, labor-management relations practices, and interstate commerce rate controls; and taxed by federal, state, and local governments). He or she drives (according to local and state ordinances and subject to local traffic officers) to the drugstore (where the state-licensed pharmacist is closely regulated as to the hours he or she may do business and the prescriptions he or she may sell to customers) and buys (with federal currency) the cigarettes (which have been the subject of extensive federal testing for danger to health, carry a required warning to users, and are taxed by both federal and state governments).

The point is that the relationship of the individual to politics never ends. And every instance of contact with politics implies a prior history of conflict and governmental choice made in keeping with the preferences of those with the greatest amount of power at a particular time or over a particular issue. Thus, the individual exists in a world shaped by the decisions of others, and not even the most determined effort to extricate oneself from such effects can be successful.

Key Definitions: Politics, Power, Legitimacy, Authority

Politics is a process (1) in which power is employed to gain rewards and (2) through which the interests of broad segments of the population are affected. We like the shorthand phrasing of a leading political scientist who characterized politics as "who gets what, when, and how." [1] This is a wide-ranging definition (which we shall have to refine shortly), for it points well beyond "government" or "the state" to focus on other holders of power in the society and the ways they achieve their goals and affect others' lives.

Nothing is more tedious, or more important, than precise definition of what we are talking about. This is particularly true of the emotion-laden subject of politics. We have deliberately adopted a distinctive definition of politics in order to employ the widest possible, and least ideologically shaped, frame of reference for our inquiry. But even at the risk of tedium, we must spell out in detail what is implied by our definition and how it differs from the more familiar and more limited (and more self-congratulatory) definitions usually employed.

We believe that we must include in our definition extragovernmental activity that bears on who rules, who benefits, and how change comes about, because government is only one of several channels through which vital goals are obtained. The use of government therefore implies change or confirmation of preexisting patterns of benefits — either of which is of vital concern to political participants. Fundamentally revealing uses of power are more often prompted by the question of *whether* government should act in a given area than by *the way in which* government is to act. For example, the "natural" residential pattern in most areas is one of racial segregation. Neighborhood schools thus tend to be enclaves of whites or minorities. Some like this situation, but others do not. Should there be national governmental involvement in this area? Some will gain and some will lose in either event. The consequences for ordinary people, who inevitably feel the impact of this struggle in one form or another, may be very great — and eminently a product of politics.

Further, a concern for the nature of problems and the character of extragovernmental activity will alert us to the processes by which an issue becomes recognized as a possible subject for political debate or governmental action. Some matters are routinely understood as appropriate for governmental action, some (such as poverty and racial discrimination) are seen as such only at very late stages, and some (such as nationalization of major industries and compensation for victims of crime) not at all. Sometimes a subject initially appears quite outside the range of "practical" political consideration, but after a period of years moves into the field of political debate and finally takes a place among the policies of government. This was the case, for example, with medical care for the aged and, more recently, with the guaranteed annual wage or "negative income tax."

Throughout the period when some political actors are trying to move a subject from the unthinkable stage to the stage of debate and even action, many forces are at work to shape opinion about whether the issue

---

[1] Harold Lasswell, *Politics: Who Gets What, When, How* (New York: McGraw-Hill, 1936).

should be a subject for government and, if so, what should be done about it. These shaping forces reach deep into the underpinnings of our politics. Our understanding of what is proper for government action, for example, is strongly affected by the cultural values and assumptions we have acquired while growing up.

But these values and assumptions are not coincidental: somebody or something has taught them to us. The result is that some participants in politics — usually those who do not need governmental protection or might be hindered by it in some way — are better able than others to gain their ends. Nevertheless, some issues and problems do elicit public attention and are acted upon by government. Which issues do this, and why, and under what conditions? And when they do, who acts how to shape our understanding of the nature of these issues? What is at stake?

The temptation is strong to try to understand too much, to treat almost every event and pattern of social and economic activity as if it had political implications. The fact is, of course, that almost everything does. But we must exclude much of this activity in order to cope concretely with some of it. We shall limit ourselves to matters that have a direct and immediate relation to the present character or future prospect of government action. Our definition of politics then becomes: *the process by which power is employed to affect whether and how government will act on any given matter.*

Power is the possession of resources, ranging from money and prestige to official position, that cause other political actors to modify their behavior and to conform to what they perceive the possessor of the resources prefers. Such resources need not be tangible; what counts is others' perceptions of one's resources. They need not actually be mobilized and employed in any particular situation, because others may act in anticipation or expectation. Indeed, much politically significant behavior occurs because of "voluntary" conformity with the perceived expectations of others.

One of the major resources of power, of course, is *legitimacy*. Legitimacy is a status conferred by people generally on the institutions, acts, and officials of their government. When people believe that their government is the right one — that it works properly and for desirable ends — they place their trust in it and grant it their obedience. Elected officials, bureaucrats, and law enforcement personnel all acquire some of this special status by virtue of their institutional positions. We then say that the government has *authority*. This authority enables higher officials, at least, to exert considerable influence over what people believe, to draw support for their actions, and (under normal circumstances) to shape the agenda of politics so as to gain their ends more easily.

But legitimacy is a fluid and intangible attribute. It can be undermined by frequent requests for uncritical support, actions inconsistent with expectations or traditions, and extreme misconduct. It may be withdrawn by a segment, or even by most, of the people. Under such circumstances, voluntary compliance with the acts of government and normal cooperative routines may cease. *Authority* then has been lost. If this occurs among a large proportion of the population, people in government may have to fall back on outright coercion to achieve their ends. The shift to this form of power, of course, means that the political system is close to breakdown.

Thus, politics is a vast interactive process of power applications, which, although sometimes unintentionally, nearly always has consequences for others. From our early acquisition of ideology to the present process of defining a "problem" for government, we are subject to the effects of past and present power. Fortunately, our limited definition of politics as those uses of power that bear directly on whether or how government will be employed makes it unnecessary to trace the entire web of power transactions in society. The delineation of what bears "directly" on the use of government will not always be clear-cut. But we shall try, by holding on to what is tangible and demonstrable, to keep our definition manageable.

Standards of Evaluation

Analysis — explaining how and why governmental policies take the form they do and what difference that makes to people and problems in the society — is an interesting and important task. But it is only a preliminary for the person who wants to be more than a passive consumer of the products generated by the power and activity of others. One must decide whether a particular policy is good or bad, whether the political system is working well or not, and whether and how to seek improvements. To do this on a sound basis may seem to require more knowledge and greater wisdom than any person can really expect to develop. But this problem, too, can be rendered manageable.

Several simplifying approaches can make it possible for a person to judge and to act in politics in a responsible and still timely manner. One does not need to be intimidated by the fact that some scholars spend a lifetime studying particular governmental procedures or narrow subject areas. It is often enough that there be some solid evidence, especially if it pertains to the performance of government with respect to problems with which one is familiar. People can specialize in certain areas of the greatest interest to them. And they can avoid being diverted by rhetoric, ideology, or elaborate explanations about how the procedures of government operated to prevent accomplishment of their goals.

But perhaps the most important act in preparing oneself for sound evaluation in politics is clarification of the standards to be used in making judgments. Often, the standard applied contains the judgment within itself. For example, a standard that emphasizes maintaining established procedures or traditions is likely to lead to a status quo–supporting judgment. So is a standard that emphasizes what is "practical" or "pragmatic" under the circumstances of today's power distribution. Today's procedures, of course, promote the interests and preferences of those who hold the balance of power now. What is "realistic" is what they can permit to take place without serious danger to their own predominance. In both cases, therefore, the use of such standards inevitably directs judgments toward minimal changes, which have the effect of supporting the basic outlines of today's power distribution.

On the other hand, standards that emphasize efficiency or economy in the solution of problems are likely to lead to severe judgments of the need for drastic change, often at the cost of important human values. Useful standards require explicit specification of the relative priorities to be assigned to each of several desired results. In the case of "equality," for example, it must be clear whether one means equality in the formal, legalistic sense or in the actual social and economic conditions of individuals. In the case of "democracy," it must be clear whether one means merely full participation in civil rights or also consistency between popular needs and desires and the products of governmental action.[2]

The key to all evaluation, however, is one's personal political philosophy, which each of us must construct and apply. This is easier said than done, of course. Developing one's own view of *what should be* is even more difficult and frustrating than understanding *what is* in politics. Most people can acquire facts about their political system, although they sometimes do so in the fashion of spectators at a game or passive memorizers in the classroom rather than as analytical, purposeful, and independent persons. Relatively few people make the effort to survey, self-consciously and comprehensively, alternative ends and means in politics and to arrive at their own set of standards and goals for political action. But not to do so is to commit oneself in advance to a passive role in the processes that determine the shape of the future. In effect, it means acquiescence in the decisions of those now in power about what is best for themselves, and perhaps for others. The person without an independent basis for analysis and evaluation in politics must be somebody's pawn, and the only remaining question is *whose*.

Centuries of reflection and writing by the great political theorists have not produced agreement among them, or among their respective followers, for reasons that are by now obvious to readers. But analysis of their work reveals remarkable consistency in the kinds of problems they found it essential to face. Because these problems also accord with our view of the intellectual issues involved, we shall use some classic categories to indicate the central questions that must be faced by a student of politics seeking to establish his or her own independent judgmental framework. Each individ-

---

[2] We deliberately avoid giving an "authoritative" definition of democracy at this point, because that definition is not only value-based, but also the subject of a continuing political and cultural struggle. For a full discussion, see Chapter 20.

ual must answer three basic questions, however temporary those answers may be, in order to evolve an independent political stance.

■ *1. What Is the Nature of People and of Their Relationship to Their Society and Environment?* To some extent these are factual questions, but for the most part we must simply assume or speculate — which means that our answers are more or less frank expressions of our value preferences. Some assume that human nature is fundamentally good — that a human being is essentially a cooperative, rational creature. If so, governing processes should be designed to maximize openness and participation in confidence that the right decisions will be made. Others assume that people in general are selfish, emotional, likely to pursue short-range interests, and subject to demagogues, but that some people possess superior talents. According to these assumptions, a strong government run by the talented few is necessary to civilize people and to maintain order and justice in the society. In other words, a whole series of conclusions and preferences is built on one's assumptions about human nature.

Assumptions must also be made about the character of society and the extent to which both people and their society are incapable of, or resistant to, change. For some, "society" is a term with real meaning — an independent entity with a life of its own, distinct from the people who happen to make it up at any given time. Such people are likely to value the "needs of the society" above any particular member's preferences. But some device for ascertaining those needs must be found. The net result is likely to be a form of government dominated by a relative few of the better-qualified persons in the society. A less mystical use of the term "society" is as a synonym for all, or a majority, of the individuals who happen to be present at any moment within the nation's geographical confines. According to such usage, the needs of the society and majority preference are one and the same, and an entirely different decision-making process is suggested.

Another set of assumptions concerns the extent to which people are irretrievably the product of something innate within their nature or, alternatively, the product of their environment. If the latter is true, they can be improved (at least to some extent, but with accompanying risks) through manipulation of the environment. If the former is true, of course, such efforts are both hopeless and potentially very dangerous.

Which of these sets of alternative assumptions is better or more soundly based? At the moment, there seems to be no way in which a case for one or the other can be conclusively established or "proved." There are scraps of evidence regarding aspects of these issues, but they often can be used to support contrasting and equally plausible interpretations. People are therefore forced to adopt what seems to them the most reasonable set of assumptions. Because this is just another way of expressing one's preferences, such position-taking tells the listener or reader little about human nature, but a great deal about the speaker's or author's political values.

■ *2. What Are the Proper Goals of Social and Political Life, and in What Order of Priorities and at What Cost Should They Be Sought?* This is the area in which evidence is of least assistance. People must answer these questions in response to their own preferences and with only their personal values for guidance. Such questions are rarely put so bluntly, of course: they arise in the context of familiar concepts for the establishment of priorities among familiar and generally shared goals. For example, the concept of "freedom" carries several alternative meanings. To some it may mean freedom from governmental interference, leading them to seek severe limitations on the activities of government. To others, it may mean freedom to do what one could if only the handicaps of poverty and ignorance were removed. This stance would lead them to seek broad expansion of the social welfare activities of government.

The concept of "equality" is equally pliable according to one's preferences. It may mean the right to use one's talents, whatever they may be, in the pursuit of one's goals. Or it can be expanded slightly to include the right to at least a minimal education and standard of living. Or it can be broadened still further to signify that all persons are entitled to full social and economic parity with one another.

Economic equality is a much more ambitious goal than mere political equality, but even within the latter concept there is room for considerable difference of viewpoint. In the eighteenth century some defined political equality in terms of suffrage — the right to vote — which was granted only to males who owned a certain amount of property. More recently, sharp controversy has developed about whether this generally agreed-upon goal requires the observance of "one man, one vote" at all levels of government. The fact that people who strongly subscribe to the goal of political equality can sincerely argue that some people should have more votes than others indicates that there is wide room for disagreement even when the basic goal is shared "in principle." Thus, it is determining the specific content of familiar terms that is critical in building one's own independent framework. No definition is necessarily preferable or "correct," for no person is the ultimate arbiter of the meanings of words. They mean for each citizen what he or she says they mean, and that is why there is bound to be disagreement in politics.

These differences in meaning may become apparent only when an issue arises that requires the concept to be put into practice (or "operationalized"). At other times, generalized agreements on the undefined concept of "freedom" or "equality" or "justice" may create the illusion of consensus. A similar illusion may be fostered by the widespread acknowledgment of these goals, despite sharply differing views as to which should be given first priority. Once again, the illusion is dispelled only when it is sought to actually *do* one or the other.

Consider the dilemma of the person who subscribes strongly to both "liberty" and "equality": at some point, he or she will have to decide which is paramount, because they frequently conflict. In order to provide equality for some, it may be necessary to limit the liberty of others to do as they wish with their property or their talents. If equality is defined as rough parity of opportunity to compete for the goals of life and if it is a paramount goal, one must reluctantly conclude that in this instance liberty must be limited. But if one holds to a more restrictive view of equality or considers liberty to be deserving of first priority, this would be an utterly wrong way for government to act. The same type of problem is involved in recent controversies over the proper priority rankings of "justice" and "order," two goals readily acknowledged as vital by all. To some, nothing is more important than order and tranquility; to others, the rights and privileges that are components of justice deserve precedence.

When neither specific meanings nor priority rankings have been established for these concepts, they are not much more than glittering generalities in citizens' minds. As such, they are aspects of ideology; we tend to believe that since all right-thinking people share the same views, all that needs to be done to resolve conflicts is to sit down and "reason together." Or we may believe that our leaders' views are the same as ours because they use these words in their explanations or exhortations. Clearly, these concepts offer us nothing but symbolic satisfactions and complacency until we undertake to define their specific content and relative valuations.

■ *3. What Means — Institutions and Processes — Offer the Best Prospects of Reaching the Goals We Establish, Given Our Assumptions About Human Nature?* In other words, how can we get from specific assumptions about human nature to the characteristics of the good life? What logically consistent and empirically practicable means are there for reaching the goals desired? This is the area where we should be able to get the most assistance from factual knowledge about the workings of political institutions and processes. In seeking to establish some coherent connection between the nature of human beings and the realization of their goals in life, we have for guidance considerable evidence about how particular institutions work and why. We know, for example, that all members of the House of Representatives are not equally influential in determining the provisions of new statutes, and we would not rest our hopes for goal attainment on the illusion that they are. Thus, one of the first necessities in this area is to become familiar with the basic facts and processes that determine how the political system presently works and to use this understanding to establish certain landmarks around which value preferences are to be exercised.

A second requirement in this area, as we suggested above, is logical consistency. If human beings are irrational and selfish, for example, one can hardly expect to achieve equality for all through political mechanisms that are highly responsive to individual preferences. The nature of each set of institutions and processes depends on the characteristics of the people

who design and operate them and in turn shapes the kinds of goals that
can be attained through them. This is a crucial point: the nature of people,
the character of institutions and processes, and the goals that can be realized are interdependent in politics. When we study institutions and
processes, we do so realizing that they have been structured by the values
and natures of the people who created and animate them and also knowing
that their character determines in major ways the nature of the goals that
can be achieved through them. Because this is so, we must organize our
personal political positions to take this interdependence into account.

This is not to say that we must proceed consecutively from a definition
of human nature to a vision of an ideal world and finally to institutional
tinkering necessary to link the two together. Most political thinkers probably start with certain highly valued goals and some convictions about
what does and does not work in the real world and then seek to fill in the
gaps more or less consistently and adequately. Nor do all the possible
questions and problems in these three areas have to be resolved before a
personal framework becomes functional. It is enough to be aware of the
interdependencies among them and, therefore, to perceive what is at stake
when considering one area in apparent isolation and to see the implications
that findings or assumptions in one carry for the others. What is important
is to begin to build a map in one's mind of what is, can be, and ought to be
in politics. This, in turn, will make it possible to respond rationally and
selectively to the urgings and pleadings of others and to shape one's own
independent course in politics.

Problems in Analysis and Evaluation

It is time to become more rigorous about how one seeks to achieve understanding of a subject like politics, so embedded in emotions, patriotic
loyalties, threats, and symbolic diversions. How can we assure ourselves
that the understanding we acquire consists of valid interpretations and not
merely uncritical projections of our assumptions, hopes, or fears about
American politics? How do we avoid being unconsciously trapped in our
own assumptions, as are the men in the "Last Laugh" cartoon? We shall
consider some of the technical problems of data collection and interpretation as they arise in later chapters. The more serious problems of nonob-
jectivity and misinterpretation, however, are conceptual in character. Let
us try to identify some of them.

Culture-Bound or Ideological Premises and Assumptions

We are all more or less captives of our culture and products of years of
indoctrination in its values and assumptions about what is right and good:
what is, is right. And what exists in the United States is necessary, desir-

"The Last Laugh." (*Source:* Reprinted by permission of Russell & Volkening, Inc., as agents for the author. Copyright © 1972 by Fernando Krahn.)

able, or at least the best that is practical given all the circumstances. These initial (and often subconscious) premises, to say nothing of social or official pressures to adhere to them or the economic self-interest we may have in endorsing the status quo, cause even sophisticated observers to introduce approving evaluations into their supposedly objective "descriptions."

Every person who would be an objective analyst must go through a process of wrenching loose from such premises, assumptions, and conceptual blinders. The process is a lengthy and difficult one, for ideology reaches deep into the culture — into stereotypes (or "pictures in the mind"), symbols, even the language we use. Positive images are conjured up in most of us by such phrases as "Constitution," "free enterprise," "the rule of law," "free speech," and the use of such terms to describe what exists may lead us to believe that reality fits into such "good" patterns. Sometimes reality may indeed be what the words implicitly suggest, but reality is not determined by the words or assumptions used to describe it. Reality has its own independent set of characteristics and causes, and it may bear little resemblance to what the familiar words urge us to believe. If we are diverted from objective perception by symbols, stereotypes, and loaded words, we may never come to know reality as it is.

The Nature of Evidence

What do we need to know in order to say that a political institution or process works in a particular way? We cannot accept assumptions or speculations, exhortations about how they *should* work, or the self-serving assurances of their sponsors. No matter how hallowed and revered the authority that prescribes or declares how things work, we cannot accept such characterizations as truth. Instead, we must demand precise specification of who actually did what, when, and with what effects. We must be able to say with confidence that thus-and-so is the way the Congress works or that voters respond to factors X, Y, and Z in deciding which candidates to support. To be able to do so, we must have enough data on hand for a comprehensive characterization — one that leaves no gaps to be filled by ideology-affected assumptions.

When we have achieved exhaustive and accurate descriptions, we are ready to attempt explanation: Why do people do what they do in politics? Again, we rest primarily on factual evidence — on cause-and-effect relationships that are demonstrable to us or at least are inferable from the evidence — rather than on other people's explanations or wishful thinking. It is tempting, once one adapts to exclusively data-based analysis, to assume that the collection of empirical data is all-important and that we can accurately come to know and understand politics and the political process simply by building up larger amounts of more concrete and rigorous data. In seeking explanation for empirically identified patterns of behavior, however, analysis must be aided by theory. In this sense theory means hypotheses (informed guesses about causes, which can be tested against available evidence) reflecting experience and sophistication about politics. In order to arrive at hypotheses, we must employ our knowledge of the wide range of possible causes, the many forces at work within a context, and the structure of relevant power relationships.

The Focus of Analysis

We must look comprehensively at the acts of all (or at least most) of the powerholders who are active in any given area and not direct our analyses exclusively at the acts or words of leaders or the official decisions, laws, and regulations of organs of government. The easiest way to observe and to analyze politics is to look at the public acts and words of political leaders, on the assumption that they make the key decisions and set the goals their followers accept. Political leaders act in public. One of their chief functions is to make a strong and widespread impression. Because they have a stake in being dramatic, they make good copy for journalists. Journalistic accounts of politics consist very largely of descriptions of the statements, actions, and interactions of political leaders.

But the political analyst who confines his or her attention to leaders is likely to be led astray at every turn. If there is a riot, such a person assumes that ringleaders or outside agitators must have "caused" it. The social scientist looks deeper: at the social, economic, and political conditions that explain the willingness of rioters to engage in violence, to follow leaders who advocate it, and to ignore potential leaders who counsel patience or peaceful courses of action.

Another pitfall is the assumption that everything important in politics and policy formation takes place in the formal institutions and organs of government. A high proportion of decisions are made outside the corridors of government buildings, though their outcomes are closely tied to people's assumptions about how great the political power of the participants is. Even the actions that can be observed taking place within governmental institutions often convey a very superficial or misleading notion of what is going on. One reason formal government acts can be misleading is that they are frequently not put into practice. Almost twenty years after the Supreme Court had declared racial segregation in public schools unconstitutional, it still existed in a very high proportion of American classrooms. What goes on in courts, legislatures, bureaus, and United Nations meetings certainly has to be observed. But merely observing it usually reveals little about its meaning. To understand the significance of formal governmental actions, the political analyst has to observe many other activities as well. And he or she must have in mind a theoretical framework that describes how the observed activities are related to one another.

Summary and Preview

In this chapter we first stated our purposes: to help develop skills of *analysis* and *evaluation* — the capabilities that enable people to make independent critical judgments and to take purposeful action to gain their ends in American politics. Then we set forth some vital tools of *analysis* by defining four central concepts: politics, power, legitimacy, and authority. These concepts will be important components in our efforts to describe as objectively as possible how things work and why. Next, we looked at what is involved in *evaluation*, at the task of clarifying and defending the standards to be used. We saw that this is ultimately a matter of examining one's own basic political assumptions and goals. Finally, we identified some of the characteristic problems that people frequently encounter in political analysis and evaluation. Most of these problems were seen to be in our own heads, in the way that we *think* about politics. In Chapter 2, we complete our approach by sketching the outlines of the American political economy — the integrated economic-social-political system that shapes the context and gives dynamics to American politics.

In each of the chapters in Part 2, we examine what the U.S. government has actually done with regard to a particular problem in the last few years. By looking at the actual outcomes of public policies and by asking who was affected and in what ways by a government action, we shall understand for whom government works. We believe that the performance of government can best be measured by results, and that is why we focus on the consequences of governmental actions. Our questions in Part 2 will be: Who wins and who loses as a result of this policy? What effect did this policy have on the problem or goal involved?

Once we can recognize who gets what from government policies and how people and problems are affected, we shall be in a position to ask why this is so. Our inquiry proceeds in two ways. First, in Part 3 we look at contrasting ideological justifications and challenges to these outcomes. What values, assumptions, and goals are apparent in these policies and their effects? The orthodox American ideology, dominant for decades, pervades the practices of government and the words and actions of leaders. Challenges to the validity or propriety of this established ideology are also apparent, however, from both the left and right. The contrasts between these sets of beliefs are sharp, and they raise some vital questions of fact and interpretation for us as analysts. They also, quite obviously, indicate some of the reasons for continued conflict in American politics today.

Then, in Parts 4 and 5, we turn to an analysis of power and decision-making. We look not just at the institutions of the national government, but also at the structure of power in the society generally. Much of what is done by government institutions reflects needs and preferences flowing from the economic or social structures of the society.

In effect, we will be using our knowledge of the consequences of public policies as a kind of prism through which to look at power and decisionmaking. We can see far more clearly how power is distributed and used in this way than we can by focusing on elections or politicians' rhetoric, and it is undeniably better than merely describing how government institutions work in isolation. Many benevolent assumptions and democratic myths may be exposed as false, but that is both necessary and proper in an accurate political analysis. Where we know the long-term patterns of benefit and burden from government policies — who consistently wins and loses — and we find that the beneficiaries have the apparent power to shape decisions as they wish, we have a solid basis for inferring that they in fact do so for their own benefit. This is the primary focus of analysis in this book.

A final and important feature of our approach is its concern with the process of political change, a concern that culminates in the two chapters of Part 6. Why do we try to discover who rules and for whose benefit, except to ask whether, and if so how, this situation should be changed? And yet very few analyses of American politics systematically explore the conditions and actions that permit, promote, or impede change in this society. Our analysis, from the outset, is undertaken from the perspective of these findings' implications for change. In Part 6 we first reach some conclusions about the structure of power in the United States. Then we propose a general theory of change and apply it to our present circumstances to forecast possible changes in the United States in the next decade. This is a potentially controversial endeavor, but we think that it is a necessary and desirable sequel to the analysis undertaken earlier. Moreover, it should be both rigorous and provocative enough to enable readers to test their skills of independent political judgment.

THE AMERICAN
POLITICAL ECONOMY

2

What you see in the social order depends on what you
are looking for; how you understand the world depends
on the *concepts* (images and expectations) you already
hold as you undertake your inquiry. All concepts *reflect assumptions and suggest conclusions.* For example,
many people conceive of "politics" as a distinct com-
partment of social life, set apart from "economics" and
"society." "Politics" has to do with Democrats and
Republicans, the President on television, and occasional
elections. People choose their leaders, thereby shaping
policy directions, and that is "democracy." "Economics" involves a complicated system of production and
distribution within which one tries to find satisfying
work and adequate income; it seems to work mechanically, impersonally, and, on the whole, better if government keeps "hands off." "Society" is an independent
area with distinct forces at work: people have unequal
status and prestige, mostly as a result of differences in
talent and effort. Customs and values from the past
are steadily modified by changing relationships within

the family, between racial and ethnic groups, and between men and women.

An older — and newer — conceptual approach is to see economic and political life, as well as society and culture, as one integrated whole. All areas are connected to one another so closely that they become mutually supportive and interdependent (more technically, "coherent"). In the eighteenth century people such as the framers of the Constitution regularly thought and talked in terms of a single economy-government-society unit, within which they saw the economy as the principal source of social dynamics — whether of strife or of tranquility. We use their term, *political economy*, to refer to the web of political and social institutions and human activity that are interwoven with the contemporary economy. We include not just government and politics, but society and culture as well. However, we do *not* mean to suggest that these areas are *merely* reflections of economic conditions or forces. Each area has independent characteristics and causes of change that affect all the other areas. But rather than seeing the areas as either reflections or causes, we want to stress their continuing *relationship* and the centrality of economics to all.

What difference does it make how we conceive of the interaction between economy and government? In social analysis the most useful concepts are usually those that take the most factors into account. And we want to be able to look beyond mere facts in search of *relationships* and *explanations*. The compartmentalized approach to politics and economics obscures many such vital connections, while the integrated political-economy approach is deliberately inclusive.

We consider the political-economy concept valuable and rewarding, but it will not always be easy to think (or write or read) in that framework, because we all are so used to the idea of separate compartments. It will take deliberate effort for each of us to abandon our familiar habits of thought. In this chapter, for example, we shall characterize our present political economy in a preliminary way. But this material should not evoke images of "government" managing "the economy," which would represent a return to the two-compartments concept. Instead, we should be searching for interests, trends, power, and potential actions wherever they exist within the single entity under analysis. Our focus will shift from one sector of the political economy to another. But our entire inquiry will proceed within this integrated conceptual framework.

The first part of this chapter describes the American political economy, not only to sketch the background context of American politics, but also to illustrate how the concepts used in analysis shape *what you see* and *the range of possible interpretations* you might reach. The second part draws on this description and its implications to explain more fully what is at stake in the basic questions ("Who rules?" and "What difference does it make?") that will guide our analysis in this book. What we are proposing is suggested by both our broad definition of politics and everyday common sense: that we should look at our whole social order together — economics, society, culture, and politics — in order to fully understand politics. This apparently simple premise carries important implications, some of which may be controversial. So it will be necessary to spell out our approach carefully.

The Structure of the American Political Economy

It is becoming increasingly standard to characterize the American economy as having two parts, or sectors. One sector is composed of massive and often multinational corporations and banks, a few of which dominate national and world industries or markets. The other sector is made up of a much larger number of small businesses, mostly retail and service-providing, and is characterized by real competition and the operation of market principles. To this orthodox view, we shall add two factors. First, we shall explore separately the nature of the integration between government and the two sectors — the needs of each and the supports and services that flow from government in response. Second, we shall treat the government as an additional part, or sector, and explore its consumption, investment, and other fiscal and monetary activities. Most of our effort in this chapter will be conceptual, oriented toward painting a broad picture of the American political economy today. Step by step, we shall fill in the details in later chapters.

The (Multinational) Corporate and Banking Sector

The basic character and workings of the American political economy are shaped by wealthy, service-demanding, and often multinational corporations. Perhaps the most obvious characteristic of the individual units in this system is sheer size. The General Motors Corporation is often used as an example. In economic, political, and social terms, it is comparable only to the more important nations of the world. Its annual sales receipts are larger than the combined general revenues of the eleven populous northeastern states: New York, New Jersey, Pennsylvania, Ohio, Delaware, Massachusetts, and the other five New England states.[1] It has 1,300,000 stockholders and more than 700,000 employees in 46 countries. Although General Motors is the largest of the great American corporations, it is not

---

[1] Richard J. Barber, The American Corporation (New York: E. P. Dutton, 1970), pp. 19–20. Unless otherwise indicated, all data in this and the next two paragraphs are from this source.

distinctively different from several others. Here is a government lawyer's characterization of Standard Oil of New Jersey:

> With more than a hundred thousand employees around the world (it has three times as many people overseas as the U.S. State Department), a six-million-ton tanker fleet (half again bigger than Russia's), and $17 billion in assets (nearly equal to the combined assessed valuation of Chicago and Los Angeles), it can more easily be thought of as a nation-state than a commercial enterprise.[2]

These two companies, and a handful of others like them, dominate the American economy in sales, assets, and profitability. In part, this is because two, three, or four giants so dominate key markets that competition is replaced by tacit cooperation. For example, the aluminum market is shared entirely by Alcoa, Reynolds, and Kaiser; more than 95 percent of automobiles are manufactured by General Motors, Ford, and Chrysler; more than 90 percent of telephone equipment by Western Electric; more than 75 percent of steel by U.S. Steel, Bethlehem, and Republic; and 90 percent of copper by Anaconda, Kennecott, Phelps Dodge, and American Smelting. Nor are these proportions unique. Concentration is particularly high throughout the industrial core of the economy — manufacturing, finance, utilities, transportation, and communications; from two to four firms share upwards of 70–80 percent of the markets in such areas.[3]

In proportion to the total economy, the largest corporations account for the lion's share of assets and profits. For the last twenty years, *Fortune* magazine has been reporting the sales, assets, and profits of the 500 largest American nonfinancial corporations according to their sales ranking. Table 2.1 lists the top twenty for 1979. In general, these companies have grown faster and have absorbed larger proportions of sales and net income than have other companies. But the performance of the top 500 as a whole is even more striking: having accounted for about half of all industrial sales in 1954, these corporations were by 1975 (and still are today) responsible for two-thirds of all such sales. Their share of all industrial earnings rose from two-thirds to three-quarters in the same two decades.[4]

Of equal importance is the multinational scope of these giants. All of the biggest — but, of course, not all even of the "Fortune 500" — are global in character (that is, they have plants or other major facilities in more than one country). The top twenty listed in Table 2.1 include thirteen of the top twenty companies in the *world*. Many of these corporations have more economic resources than most of the nations of the world. More than 300 U.S.-based corporations conduct business all over the world; investments

---

2 Ibid., p. 20.
3 William Shepherd, *Market Power and Economic Welfare* (New York: Random House, 1970), pp. 152–153.
4 *Fortune* 41 (May 1975), p. 241.

Table 2.1
The Top Twenty U.S. Industrial Corporations, 1979 (ranked by sales; $ in millions)

Rank 1979	Rank 1978	Company	Sales[a] ($000)	Assets[a] ($000)	RANK	Net Income ($000)	RANK	Employees NUMBER	RANK
1	2	Exxon (New York)	79,106,471	49,489,964	1	4,295,243	1	169,096	9
2	1	General Motors (Detroit)	66,311,200	32,215,800	2	2,892,700	3	853,000	1
3	4	Mobil (New York)	44,720,908	27,505,756	3	2,007,158	4	213,500	6
4	3	Ford Motor (Dearborn, Mich.)	43,513,700	23,524,600	5	1,169,300	11	494,579	2
5	5	Texaco (Harrison, N.Y.)	38,350,370	22,991,955	6	1,759,069	6	65,814	50
6	6	Standard Oil of California (San Francisco)	29,947,554	18,102,632	7	1,784,694	5	39,676	113
7	9	Gulf Oil (Pittsburgh)	23,910,000[a]	17,265,000	8	1,322,000	9	57,600	63
8	7	International Business Machines (Armonk, N.Y.)	22,862,776	24,529,974	4	3,011,259	2	337,119	5
9	8	General Electric (Fairfield, Conn.)	22,460,600	16,644,500	10	1,408,800	8	405,000	3
10	12	Standard Oil (Ind.) (Chicago)	18,610,347[a]	17,149,899	9	1,506,618	7	52,282	75
11	11	International Telephone & Telegraph (New York)	17,197,423	15,091,321	12	380,685	42	368,000	4
12	13	Atlantic Richfield (Los Angeles)	16,233,959	13,833,387	13	1,165,894	12	50,341	80
13	14	Shell Oil (Houston)	14,431,211[a]	16,127,016	11	1,125,561	13	36,384	129
14	15	U.S. Steel (Pittsburgh)	12,929,100	11,029,900	15	(293,000)	492	171,654	8
15	18	Conoco (Stamford, Conn.)	12,647,998	9,311,171	17	815,360	17	40,502	111
16	16	E.I. du Pont de Nemours (Wilmington, Del.)	12,571,800	8,940,200	19	938,900	15	134,200	13
17	10	Chrysler (Highland Park, Mich.)	12,001,900	6,653,100	26	(1,097,300)	493	133,811	14
18	19	Tenneco (Houston)	11,209,000	11,631,000	14	571,000	24	107,000	21
19	17	Western Electric (New York)	10,964,075	7,128,324	24	635,898	21	168,000	10
20	23	Sun (Radnor, Pa.)	10,666,000	7,460,600	23	699,900	19	40,065	112

Source: Reprinted by permission from the 1980 Fortune Directory; © 1980 Time, Inc.
[a] Because dollar totals are in millions, these figures represent billions of dollars.

abroad in 1975 totaled over $70 billion.[5] In the last decade there have been sharp increases in these corporations' overseas employment, sales, and profits. More than 20 percent of all corporate profits are currently derived from abroad. For many large U.S. corporations, the international network — exports, imports, and production and sales in foreign countries — is thus crucial not only to the size of profit margins, but also to the very question of profitability itself.

But nonfinancial corporations are only one component of the dominant sector of our political economy. The nation's largest banks are one of its most potent sources of leverage over the entire system. Even the largest corporations must borrow to finance expansion and growth. And banks' profits depend on making such loans at the most advantageous risk-to-earnings-rate ratio. Only 220 banks account for practically all lending in the United States. And a mere nine banks, six of them associated with the Rockefeller-Morgan group and all in New York City, accounted for more than 26 percent of all commercial and industrial lending by U.S. banks in 1973. About half of this money is lent to global corporations. One authority estimates that 90 percent of the entire indebtedness of the U.S. petroleum and natural gas industry, three-quarters of that of the machinery and metal products industry, and two-thirds of that of the chemical and rubber industry is held by the same nine New York banks.

In the process of making loans, banks make judgments about the management and activities of prospective debtor-corporations and also gain influence over them in such other ways as obtaining positions on their boards of directors in exchange for loans. The more loans they make, the more their interests are associated with those of the major corporations. In recent decades banks have loaned larger and larger proportions of their deposits, a phenomenon that contributes both to greater influence and shared interests and to dependence on conditions that facilitate repayment of such loans. In 1950, for example, the large New York banks had loans outstanding of about $10 billion, or less than 40 percent of their deposits; in 1974 their loans totaled $79 billion, or more than 84 percent of their deposits.[6]

The other major components of this sector — insurance companies, other investment trusts (real estate, mutual or pension funds, and the like), and utilities — have in common domination of their fields or markets, ownership or control over vast sums of money or capital investment, and close ties to the banks and corporations just described. Together, the relatively few — but giant — units in this sector account for the overwhelming

---

[5] Data in this and the next paragraph are drawn from Richard J. Barnet and Ronald Muller, "The Negative Effects of Multinational Corporations," in David Mermelstein, ed., *The Economic Crisis Reader* (New York: Random House, 1975), pp. 153–155.

[6] Harry Magdoff and Paul M. Sweezy, "Banks: Skating on Thin Ice," in Mermelstein, *Economic Crisis Reader*, p. 200.

preponderance of the total economy's sales, assets, and profits. In a basic and compelling way their needs for profit, secure investment opportunities, and general economic and social predictability create the context and establish the leading priorities for all actions by major American institutions, both private (corporations, trade associations, unions) and public (Congress, the President, the political parties).

The Competitive Sector[7]

The contrast between the corporate-banking sector and the competitive sector is sharp and growing in every dimension. The number of businesses in this sector has been estimated at around 250,000. Many are started, and more fail, every year. Production is usually on a small scale, and markets are local or regional. Typical examples are repair shops, restaurants, independent drug and grocery stores, cleaners, and other service-providing businesses. Nearly one-third of the U.S. labor force is employed in this sector, approximately the same number as in each of the other two sectors.

While the largest corporations and banks dominate markets and thus achieve relative control over supplies, costs, prices, and profits, the situation of the competitive firms is normally the opposite. The market is real; suppliers and purchasers come and go, prices fluctuate widely, and unpredictability reigns. Profit margins are often narrow and highly unstable. Employment is irregular, and many workers are marginal and/or part-time (minorities, many women, students, and so on). Wages are substantially lower than in the corporate-banking sector, and very few firms are unionized. Incomes are inadequate and constantly in need of supplementation, increasingly from some governmental source.

The corporate-banking and competitive sectors also differ markedly in their respective needs for services and supports from the national government. The size, scope, market domination, and profitability of units in the corporate-banking sector make it possible for them to encourage unions, survive recessions, and wield massive influence over governmental policy. At the same time, their international interests require extensive diplomatic and military support. They need an educated work force, elaborate scientific and technological research and development, and a network of governmental programs to ensure stability of demand (unemployment insurance, welfare, social security, and the like). And their size enables them to avoid the burdensome aspects of controls and regulations that also help ensure stability and predictability.

For the fragmented and relatively powerless competitive sector, on the other hand, governmental policy is much more often oppressive. Taxes are

---

[7] This section and the following are derived from James O'Connor, *The Fiscal Crisis of the State* (New York: St. Martin's Press, 1973), pp. 13–18.

a greater burden, for example, and demand-assuring spending is of lesser benefit. Prices cannot be raised to compensate for increased taxes, nor are as many ways available to defer or conceal income. Unemployment and welfare benefits reduce the number of workers willing to work for the lowest wages, and minimum-wage laws also push pay levels up. Education and other services are of much less value to this sector, in which highly skilled workers are largely unnecessary and employment tends to be short-term. A large military is of little direct benefit, and research and development are irrelevant.

These differences in the character and interests of the two sectors, and the resulting contrast in their costs and benefits from governmental policies, are not readily recognized. A widely promulgated and almost as widely shared set of beliefs holds that (1) all business is essentially the same — competitive and dependent on market forces; (2) government should normally keep "hands off" the activities of the "private economy"; and (3) public services and social insurance benefits are aimed exclusively at people in need. That points (1) and (3) are inaccurate and that (2) is deliberately and regularly violated — due to the character and needs of the corporate-banking sector — are only the beginning of our reconceptualization of the U.S. political economy.

The State as a Sector of the Integrated Political Economy

Part of the reason for the corporate-banking sector's dominance over the competitive sector is the massive size of the units in the former, which enables them to control markets, withstand bad times and other threats, and exert powerful influence over public policy. Thus, the state (considering national, state, and local governments as a unit for the moment) might appear to be a potential rival of the corporate-banking sector. This is in some respects true: the sheer magnitude of revenue raised and expenditures made does place the state squarely on a par with the corporate-banking sector. The federal budget for 1980 alone called for an income larger than the *combined* total sales of the top twenty corporations listed in Table 2.1. And expenditures ($650 billion) equaled about one-third of the total gross national product (the sum of all goods and services produced) estimated for the same year.

But for two major reasons, the state is not an economic *rival*, but an effective *ally* of the corporate-banking sector. First, "the state" is thoroughly fragmented into independent and sometimes competing units, each responsive to a particular constituency. This is as true of the federal government as of the more obviously independent states, cities, counties, towns, and villages.

Second, the key unit, the federal government, is heavily influenced — if not dominated — by the corporate-banking sector. Full demonstration of this point requires detailed analysis, which is undertaken in later chapters. Basically, however, many of the crucial decisions that shape governmental taxing, spending, fiscal or monetary actions, and other economy-related policies are made in one or more of the following ways:

1. By the corporate-banking sector directly, such as decisions to buy or not buy municipal or state bonds, or decisions on the part of the World Bank to lend or not lend, and on what terms;

2. Jointly by the corporate-banking sector and governmental officials, operating through an agency of the government, such as the Federal Reserve System;

3. By corporate-banking-sector managers who are temporarily governmental officials in most cases, such as in the U.S. Treasury, the Office of Management and Budget, and other agencies;

4. By governmental officials and decisionmakers who, though not actually part of the corporate-banking sector, recognize that unless its needs are served, there will be serious unemployment or such other undesirable consequences as tax cuts to spur business investment or create new jobs;

5. In response to developments within the economy as a whole that trigger preexisting commitments on the part of the national government, such as unemployment insurance benefits.

In many respects, in other words, *the national government is the corporate-banking sector by another name.* (Jules Feiffer, a noted political cartoonist, makes the same point.) We shall explore how taxing and spending policies benefit business at the cost of others in Chapter 5; how governmental supports, subsidies, and regulations sustain big business, and

(*Source:* By permission of Jules Feiffer © 1975. Dist. Field Newspaper Syndicate.)

the nature of various business influences on governmental decisionmaking in Chapters 10 through 17. Here we shall sketch the integration of the federal government in the larger political economy in general conceptual terms. If it is true that money talks, it should be the starting point.

The amount of money expended by all levels of government in the United States has risen steadily since World War II and now amounts to about $800 billion, or nearly 40 percent of the gross national product. During this period, state and local governments' expenditures have more than doubled; the sources of their income are derived not only from local taxes, but also from substantial transfers by the federal government ($80 billion in 1979) and, of course, borrowing from banks and other investors. As we have said, the large and loosely connected set of enterprises that constitutes the state employs about one-third of the entire U.S. labor force. Clearly, no treatment of our political economy would be complete without consideration of all this activity.

One way to grasp the nature of the state's impact on, and its close connection to, the rest of the economy is to consider the national budget. Of the nearly $650 billion in estimated expenditures for 1980, about 1 percent is for maintenance of the government itself, such as upkeep of buildings, salaries of civilian employees, and the like. About 27 percent is required for maintenance of the military establishment. Much of this $175 billion is designated for purchases of weapons and other supplies, and a significant proportion of the corporate-banking sector is engaged almost exclusively in such production. The relationship between expenditures and employment here is so direct, according to a study analyzing the 1965–1970 period, that each billion dollars in additional purchases created 75,000 jobs.[8] Presumably, the same ratio applies to reductions; if so, the military cutbacks of 1969–1970 were alone responsible for the subsequent 2 percent rise in the unemployment rate.

Another major component of federal expenditures is social security payments to retired or disabled workers. Of course, these workers and their employers pay taxes over an extended period of time to cover a large proportion of these costs; nearly a third of all federal income is derived from such taxes. A similar partially tax-supported expenditure is unemployment compensation. Such payments obviously help significantly to maintain the purchasing power of millions of people.

Interest payments to banks and investors who hold U.S. Treasury bonds and other securities represent a different sort of tie to the other sectors of the economy. Roughly 10 percent of the budget is devoted to such interest payments. The U.S. government is the single most secure investment banks and other investors can find, because its taxing capability (as well as its capacity to print money) represents complete assurance of

---

[8] Richard P. Oliver, "Increase in Defense-Related Employment During Vietnam Buildup," *Monthly Labor Review* 93 (February 1970), p. 3.

its ability to repay except in the direst emergencies. This helps explain why banks and investors have been willing to finance and refinance a federal debt now nearing $600 billion. It also suggests that other borrowers will find it difficult to obtain needed loans when the U.S. Treasury is seeking them, as it must whenever there is a *deficit* — more expenditures than revenues in a given year — in the federal budget. The U.S. Treasury often has to seek more than $50 billion in loans to cover the deficit in the national budget. This sum is in effect diverted from other potential borrowers, such as cities and corporations, which then have trouble paying their debts or increasing their capabilities.

A final category of government expenditure is devoted to building roads, financing railroads, operating the mail service, supporting agriculture, conducting scientific research and development, operating and supporting schools, and the like. Some of these functions are performed by state and local governments using federal funds. These numerous and diverse direct services are often understood as efforts to help people generally or as the result of pressures from various specific interests. But they may also be understood, in conjunction with the other supporting efforts of government, as providing the *infrastructure* — underlying but necessary building blocks — on which businesses can build to become profitable. The fact that the costs are public and the profits private leads to the assertion that the general public has made vast social investments in order that a few people can enjoy substantial profits.[9]

How It Works: A Case Study

Continuing to focus on money, let us illustrate how the corporate-banking sector interlocks with the national government to determine the integrated political economy's most basic directions. The Federal Reserve System was created by Congress in 1913 and empowered to regulate the nation's money supply. This is an immensely significant power. By managing the amount of money in circulation and thus (indirectly) nationwide interest rates, the Federal Reserve Board (Fed) can affect the whole economy. By rapidly increasing the money supply and thus lowering interest rates, it can give the economy a major push, in effect speeding up all its buying, selling, production, and other transactions — and increasing employment. By slowing the rate of increase in the money supply, it can have the opposite effect — raising interest rates and forcing cutbacks, credit crises, and unemployment.

The Fed's powers do not give it complete control; no single entity could exercise total authority over an economy as complex and interna-

---

[9] For a full version of this argument, see O'Connor, *Fiscal Crisis,* and Michael Best and William Connolly, *The Politicized Economy* (Lexington, Mass.: D. C. Heath, 1976).

tional as ours. But they are sufficient, for example, to completely offset the effects of a tax cut intended to spur the economy, such as the anti-recession tax cut of $23 billion in 1975. Refusal to make loans or release reserves to other banks to do so can drive states and cities into default and bankruptcy. Or the extension of massive credit to a failing bank can keep it afloat long enough to preserve the stability of the rest of the banking system. *All of these actions were taken in the period from 1974 to 1976.* More immediately, there is no question but that the most vital aspects of the daily lives of all Americans — jobs, living costs, taxes, credit — are profoundly affected by Fed actions.

In light of the vast scope of the Fed's power and its impact on business and personal lives, it might be expected that there would be some form of public accountability and control over those who make such fateful decisions. There is, but it is so indirect that one can accurately say that the nation's money supply is managed by the nation's bankers. *How and in whose interests they do so, and their priorities with regard to the con-flicting goals of full employment and low inflation,* are matters of continuing controversy.

The Fed is headed by a seven-member Board of Governors, appointed by the President to seven-year terms and subject to confirmation by the Senate. All major banks are members of the Federal Reserve System, and their needs are served by twelve Federal Reserve Banks in various parts of the country. Banks are, of course, profit-oriented enterprises, whose goals are to make as many loans as possible at the highest possible interest rates — and then to see that those loans are repaid in money of the same or higher value (that is, with as little inflation as possible). No matter how decisions are made or who makes them, a system made up of banks that have such needs and interests will be concerned about preserving the profitability of banks by limiting inflation.

The key decision-making unit of the Fed is the Federal Open Market Committee (FOMC), which consists of the chairman, the other six governors, and five of the twelve presidents of Federal Reserve Banks. This group meets every Friday to decide on Fed policy for the next week with regard to buying and selling government securities (Treasury bonds and notes). If the Fed *buys,* it pays by crediting the selling banks with new reserves in their accounts at the Fed, a transaction that in effect creates new money. The selling banks, which are only the very largest, are now able to make more loans themselves; their borrower banks in turn can make more loans. As this new money circulates, the economy picks up speed. If the Fed *sells* government securities, it reduces the reserves in the biggest banks, makes money more difficult to acquire, pushes interest rates up, and slows the economy down. The meetings at which such decisions are made are completely secret, and the Fed does all it can to mask its strategy in the complex securities market so that it can work its will effectively.

Who are the members of the FOMC? Chiefly private bankers with experience in the largest banks of New York and Chicago (and often with the Treasury Department as well), some career Federal Reserve bankers, and usually one or two corporate executives. The present chairman is Paul Volcker, former president of the New York Federal Reserve Bank and before that associated with both the Chase Manhattan and the U.S. Treasury.

What is the significance of the banking background of FOMC members? At the very least, it suggests a special concern for a stable currency ("hard money") and prevention of inflation at almost any cost. Volcker, for example, in 1979 raised interest rates and member bank reserve requirements to their highest levels in modern history in an effort to hold down American inflation and stabilize the dollar. In doing so, he willingly risked contributing to recession and unemployment. But he was only following precedents set by other chairmen before him. In 1975 Chairman Arthur Burns fought against increasing the money supply to combat the recession, despite the pleas and arguments of many in business and in Congress that the Fed was thereby threatening the economy with still more recessionary pressure and even more unemployment. *Business Week*, a journal known neither for sensationalism nor for special sympathy to working people, in 1975 published an analysis of the Fed under the title "Burns: Architect of the Worst Recession?"[10] At about the same time, Representative Wright Patman, long-time chairman of the House Banking Committee, described the FOMC as "one of our most secret societies. These twelve men decide what happens in the economy. . . . In making decisions they check with no one — not the President, not the Congress, not the people."[11]

The FOMC's secrecy and power have persisted, and the Fed has stood firm against the economy-spurring actions of the rest of the federal government. It is *able* to do so because it is an independent agency, subject to none but the most indirect control by elected officials. And it *wants* to do so because its decisionmakers are bankers and others who think as they do. In effect, the Fed is a "public" agency run by leading members of the "private" banking industry in accordance with their own view of what is desirable.

Society and Culture

How do we conceive of social structure in the United States? What values and ideology do we expect to find at various points within it? What are the possible causes of such conditions? In important ways these are

---

10 *Business Week*, 21 April 1975, p. 106.
11 Quoted in *Parade* 26 (October 1975).

empirical (factual) questions that we shall want to pursue at later points in this book with the best data and other evidence that we can find. But they are first *conceptual* issues: if we do not conceive of them as important questions to ask, we shall never seek factual answers to them. For example, the 1950s and early 1960s were a time when the United States was thought to be an essentially middle-class and affluent society that had reached "the end of ideology" — that is, a society in which all conflicting demands had been satisfied and harmony prevailed. The outbreaks of the later 1960s and early 1970s, of course, drastically altered this conception.

A harder look at American society would reveal a highly stratified (unequal, hierarchical, with a few at the top and many at the bottom) system of wealth, income, status, and (probably, but we do not know yet) power. A very few people indeed enjoy the lion's share of the rewards of the American economy, but most people have trouble making ends meet. Let us imagine a social pyramid that measures *people* horizontally and their *income* vertically — that is, many people with relatively low income at the base and few people with high income at the top. Imagine further that this pyramid has its base at the bottom of this printed page and is scaled so that the largest number of people in any income category does not exceed the width of this page. In this carefully scaled American social pyramid, about 85 percent of all American households would be included within the size of this page, with the great bulk ranging between incomes of $5,000 and $25,000 and substantial proportions being below the "minimum budget" and "poverty" lines. But the *top* of the pyramid would extend about *forty feet* beyond the top of the page![12]

Let us examine basic data regarding income, wealth, and occupation as a way of sharpening our image of American society. Table 2.2 presents

Table 2.2
Distribution of Income, 1972 and 1976

Families (%)	Income, 1972 (%)	Income, 1976 (%)
Top 5	14.4	14.2
Top 20	41.6	41.0
Next 20	23.5	24.1
Middle 20	17.4	17.6
Lower 20	12.0	12.0
Bottom 20	5.5	5.4

Source: U.S. Bureau of the Census, *Current Population Reports*, Series P-60.

---

[12] U.S. Bureau of the Census, *Current Population Reports*, Series P–60, 1976. The "poverty" and "minimum budget" levels are established annually in accordance with changing cost of living data and vary also with age and family size.

recent breakdowns of *income received* before (and, essentially, *after*) taxes, by fifths of American families. The top fifth receives more than twice as much as its proportion of the population and nearly eight times as much as the lowest fifth; the latter receives only about one-quarter of its proportional share. Moreover, these patterns are constant: they endure essentially unchanged not only for the 1970s, but for the entire twentieth century as well, regardless of tax policies. Both in distribution shares and continuity, these patterns are quite similar to those of other advanced industrial countries. Canada and Great Britain are skewed somewhat more favorably toward the two lower fifths, while France and Germany are tilted slightly toward the highest 20 percent.[13]

But *wealth* patterns (all assets owned, minus all debts and liabilities) show an even more sharply elongated pyramid. Table 2.3 shows that 61 percent of American households own less than $10,000 worth of property (including houses, cars, stocks and bonds, personal property, and so on) for a total of 7 percent of the nation's wealth. A mere 2 percent at the top own 43 percent of such assets. These patterns remain constant over time; we use 1962 data here because they were carefully developed from the most reliable sources, and all indications are that this distribution pattern remains the same today.

The attribution of social status within American society is a complex phenomenon that we shall explore in more detail later, but it is usually thought to be generated by a person's income, wealth, occupation, education, and other, less tangible characteristics. Education beyond high school is still an experience known to only about a quarter of the adult population, with ratios of such opportunity very limited at the lower levels of family income and rising sharply at the higher levels. Even in the mid-1970s, when postsecondary education rates were at their highest, well below half

Table 2.3
Distribution of Wealth, 1962

Wealth	Households (%)	Total Wealth (%)
Over $100,000	2	43
$25,000–$100,000	15	32
$10,000–$25,000	23	18
Less than $10,000	61	7

Source: Dorothy Projector and Gertrude Weiss, *Survey of Financial Characteristics of Consumers* (Federal Reserve Board, 1966).

Note: Although dollars are 1960 dollars, the *ratios* of wealth-holding remain the same in 1980.

[13] Organization for Economic Cooperation and Development, "Income Distribution in OECD Countries" (Paris: OECD, 1976).

of all high school graduates went on to some form of further education, and most of these were from higher-income categories.[14]

Occupational characteristics of the population are consistent with wealth, income, and occupational levels. Table 2.4 shows the breakdown as of 1970, when only 27 percent of the work force was in the higher-paid managerial or professional categories and 71 percent in clerical, sales, service, and manual work. Little additional analysis is needed to recognize that women and minorities have lower-status occupations (and education, wealth, and income). Women are concentrated in the clerical and service categories, while minorities, on the other hand, are in service, manual, and farm work.

Thus, the image of the American social structure that emerges is one of stratification and inequality in all the relevant categories. Of course, this pattern may be a totally random product of differences in talent, effort, or luck. But the fact of its existence at least poses such questions as its relative permanence across generations, whether and how it may be related to the economic system, and whether and how it may translate itself into political power. Our posing of the political-economy concept, in which society and economy are connected and together affect politics, brings such questions up for analysis. We shall explore these issues in depth later, but we may note now that recent studies show a very close link between the top strata of the society and positions of institutional leadership in the economy and government. In analyzing a total of 5,416 persons at the highest levels of corporate, government, media, foundation, law, university, and civic/cultural institutions, political scientist Thomas Dye found that (by his carefully developed definitions) 30 percent of such people came

Table 2.4

Occupations of the Labor Force

Occupation	Male	Female	All	Nonwhite % of All
Managers, officials, proprietors, farm owners	17	5	13	4
Professional-technical	14	15	14	7
Clerical and sales	13	42	24	7
Service workers	7	22	12	23
Manual workers	47	16	35	14
Farm workers	3	1	2	12
Total	100	100	100	100

Source: Historical Statistics of the United States; Statistical Abstract, 1970.

---

14 U.S. Bureau of the Census, "Social and Economic Characteristics of Students," Current Population Reports: Population Characteristics (October 1973).

from the 1 percent of the general population that makes up the "upper class." Another 60 percent came from the 21 percent of the population that constitutes the "upper-middle class," and only 3 percent from the 78 percent of "middle and lower classes." Only two nonwhites were found among these more than 5,400 top elites. And despite the fact that women make up 40 percent of the work force, very few are included in this body of leaders; those who are made it by means of family wealth.[15]

What kinds of values and ideology and other cultural characteristics are found at different levels in this social hierarchy? Our conceptual approach requires us to consider that there may be different, probably conflicting, values and ideology between the uppermost leadership elites and the great bulk of the population, and particularly distinctive attitudes among minorities and women. Again, we shall explore these possible differences later, against a background of the systematically communicated orthodox American values and ideology that sustain and justify our political system. But the suspicion grows that there may be an empirically demonstrable connection among where people are located in the social pyramid, what their values and ideology are, what their relationship to the economic system is, and how they think and act in politics. Such conceptualization helps to focus our basic questions more sharply.

Questions that Shape Later Analysis

By arguing that we should try to cast our analytical net as widely and as skeptically as possible, we affect the kinds of interpretation that we might ultimately reach. If we reject the idea of separate compartments for "politics," "economics," and "society," we force ourselves to be alert to their interconnections — and we might find some. If we are skeptical about familiar images of an affluent, classless, conflict-free society, we might find reasons to doubt each of these. But we do not think this means that our approach is biased, except in its commitments to scope and skepticism — our ways of transcending ideology in search of truth. What should distinguish an analysis that claims to be trustworthy is a *framework and approach* whose components are made clear *and* which permit contrasting interpretations to be tested against the evidence. In other words, *are conclusions left open by the assumptions and procedures of the inquiry?*

We think that this is the case here and that this can be demonstrated by posing alternative answers to the two major questions — Who rules? and What difference does it make? — that will shape our inquiry throughout the book. These possible alternative answers should be kept in mind as we progress in each chapter, and when we reach Chapter 20, we shall try to summarize the evidence and draw conclusions.

---

[15] Thomas Dye, *Who's Running America?* (Englewood Cliffs, N.J.: Prentice-Hall, 1979), pp. 170, 173, 176.

Who Rules?

The first basic question is, stated simply: Who rules? What configuration of powerholders effectively shapes the actions of the U.S. government? Three alternative answers in the form of models are frequently urged: (1) power is located chiefly in governmental offices, whose incumbents respond to a mix of public and interest-group pressures; (2) power is extracted from both public and private resources by an establishment that seeks to shape popular preferences into forms that can be used to support its own basic goals and the system itself; and (3) power is derived from private economic resources by a relatively few persons who influence government in their interest, using it to promote popular acquiescence, discourage resistance, or both. Shorthand terms for the first and last models are "pluralism" and "ruling-class."

■ *Pluralism.* The pluralist interpretation denies that there is either a deliberate purpose or a unified power structure behind the making of national policy — except for those instances when practically the entire population is of a single mind on an issue. The pluralist model holds that each area of public policy involves distinctive problems and separate sets of political agents and forces, such that each action undertaken by government is the result of a unique process of interaction. Accordingly, each action can be understood only by focusing on the particular circumstances and idiosyncratic features of the policy-making processes and individuals involved. In other words, policies vary unpredictably in substance, depending on what the people in office perceived, sought, and did and on the complex of forces and circumstances that happened to exist at the time. By implication, if the public had strong preferences otherwise, or if the officeholders were different, or if the institutional mechanisms of government were different, the end results would also be different. This interpretation contains at least five major elements, each of which makes some necessary assumptions about the economic and social setting in which American politics takes place.

1. Government's independent resources give it the decisive balance of power within the society and make it the mechanism through which all other spheres of activity may be managed. Government responds principally to popular preferences expressed in elections and secondarily to the pressures of organized interests. Thus, it can become an arbiter between conflicting interests or an agent of the general will, essentially in accordance with the people's wishes.

2. The power of government is parceled out into so many component branches, agencies, committees, and offices that every significant interest within the society is able to gain access and affect the course of government action.

3. Government is an arena within which the various interests in the society contend with one another for often conflicting goals. Public officials, because they control the use of decisive (governmental) power, must be at the center of these conflicts. They serve as brokers, mediating the differences among competing interests and helping them to find the necessary compromises. This is a broadly representative process because practically every citizen is or can be represented by one or more groups and can thereby have his or her interests weighed in the process of policy-making. Conflicting pressures are applied to officials in roughly the same proportions that they are felt within the society. Divisions within the society are in effect translated into negotiable claims and adjusted; officials certify the accommodations through their authoritative support for one or another public policy.

4. These accommodations are reached through a set of well-established procedures that ensure fairness and opportunity to all; all groups share a commitment to making such a process a continuing reality. Compromises that are just and acceptable to all do not occur by accident; they develop because of strict adherence to principles of procedural due process. These procedures call for full and fair hearings, consideration for others' points of view, and self-limitations if the larger system might otherwise be endangered. Each interest has an investment in preserving a setting in which it can be confident of receiving fair treatment; therefore, all act to protect the fairness and openness of the procedures by which decisions are made.

5. The brokerage role played by public officials in reaching accommodations, and the residual choice-making role the situation permits them, means that the public exercises meaningful control over the general direction of public policy through elections. Further, the system as a whole amounts to a stable, satisfied equilibrium of groups and individuals. The officials who serve as mediators of conflicting claims are either elected or directly responsible to those who are. The wide availability and equal weighting of the vote therefore allows the people to choose at least the broad priorities of the government. The entire political system, though with some acknowledged imperfections and time lags, is thus tuned to popular preferences. Realistically, this is about what one can expect of "democracy" under contemporary circumstances.

■ *Establishment Orchestration.* This interpretation accepts the pluralist model for minor decisions, though with less optimism about government's mediating group conflict in the public interest and more emphasis on special interests' success at achieving their goals. On major issues, however, involving the basic structure of the economic and political order and the permanence of the established patterns of distribution of wealth and social status, a more unified power structure comes into being. Various holders of power coalesce to form a coherent and nearly single-minded force capable of managing major sources of private power, the government, and the general public alike.

The "glue" that holds this coalition together and enables it to work so effectively in defense of the status quo comes from two primary sources. One is the class-originated shared values and interests of the establishment, itself consisting of a circulating group of persons moving freely among the upper echelons of the economic, social, and political systems. These people are accustomed to holding and exercising power from their "command post" positions. Their life experiences and current interests have bred in them a strong commitment to orthodoxy and defense of the integrated economic and political structure. They see these values as synonymous with the public interest, not as self-serving.

The other source is the willingness of the general public — or at least the majority of its visible, audible, and active members — to endorse and support the actions of the major officials of their government. This acquiescence has many sources: faith in the institutions established by the Constitution, lack of alternatives, apathy, political party loyalties, hopelessness, fear of coercion. One of its major sources, however, is the wide dissemination of effective inculcation of the familiar American political values and ideology — itself one of the major achievements of the establishment. From twelve or more years of schooling to patriotic rituals and media messages, the individual lives in a context of symbolic assurances, materialism, racism, and benevolent rationalizations about how the government does and should operate. Embedded in this body of myth are the clear grounds of establishment dominance. At least some fragments of this belief system become implanted in people's minds, available to be drawn on in times of stress by the status- and legitimacy-exuding establishment.

Under ordinary circumstances, few major issues arise. Most public policies and private practices fit snugly within the approved contours of the established economic, social, and political systems, and special interests are free to seek their narrow ends within this context. When conditions change and more basic questions are forced to the fore, the establishment begins to rally to the defense of the systems that have served it so well. Despite some disagreements about the best way to preserve the basic framework of the status quo (by yielding in the direction of greater equality or by "standing firm"), a consensus usually emerges without much direct consultation. Action then occurs on many fronts simultaneously to mobilize public support for particular forms of governmental action to meet and "solve" the crisis. Taking their cues from the actions of the uppermost echelons, many lesser officials and associated elites (mayors, police officers, chambers of commerce, and the like) institute similar (or more drastic) policies and manifest their support for the system-preserving program.

What looks like a consciously synchronized and coordinated movement may be no more than an elaborate follow-the-leader game. And what appears to be slavishly ideological mass support may be no more than silence. But the establishment seems to have managed the situation, and by so doing it improves its chances of succeeding again the next time — unless the social situation reaches a point at which open opposition destroys the harmonious image. Then the issue becomes the capacity to apply coercion to some without losing the public acquiescence and cooperation necessary to make the system operable.

■ *The "Ruling Class."* This interpretation views power as tightly concentrated in private hands and public impact on policy as negligible. According to this model, economic resources are the paramount sources of power, and those relatively few persons who own or control them are in a virtually unchallengeable position of power. They set the operative values and priorities in their own private interest. They can direct the actions of people in government and, through control of the foundations, universities, and mass media, shape the attitudes of the general public. Normally they provide only general direction, but when necessary they can and do assert specific control over governmental action. A principal tool for thus managing the society (and in some respects, the world) for their own benefit is physical coercion. Although efforts are made to present this use of power publicly as necessary and desirable, the lower classes in particular are kept aware of the ready availability of police and other military forces frequently used against them.

There is in this view a distinct structure of power — a more or less definable and self-conscious group of individuals, sometimes labeled "the ruling class." This group uses its extragovernmental resources to control nominations, elections, and governmental decisionmaking, not necessarily by dictating specific decisions, but by maintaining boundaries within which action may proceed unrestricted and beyond which rejection is swift and drastic. The motivations of this group are almost exclusively economic: maximization of the profits of the corporate economy. All areas of governmental activity are subject to that overwhelming goal. Nor is the need for governmental support limited to a desire to defend established domestic prerogatives. Because of the pressing need of the economy for new opportunities to invest surplus capital, this economic class exerts control over government to ensure profitable opportunities in the developing nations.

Which of the models is correct and/or what refinements or combinations of models should be made are questions that can be answered only after all the evidence has been examined. But it seems clear that our conceptual framework and approach are broad enough and free enough of ideological assumptions that *any one* of these might be found to be correct. Our strategy for deciding *which* one, as we noted earlier, is to focus first on the consequences of public policies — at the pattern of burdens and benefits established over time and (in Part 3) at reactions to these results. Then, in Parts 4 and 5, we move to analysis of who holds power and how decisions are made. With these two types of evidence assembled, we should be able to decide which general model of "Who rules?" is correct.

What Difference Does It Make?

The second basic question that shapes our inquiry throughout the book builds on the first: What difference does it make? For example, does our answer to "Who rules?" bear upon the character of American democracy or the probable directions of change in the near future? Most Americans share a belief in representative democracy and believe also that our system, though improvable, amounts to a rough approximation of that kind of democracy. But what if the evidence leads us to conclude that the patterns of who wins and who loses through public policies are *not* in the interests of majorities of people? What if we find that, over and over again, the interests of a relative few at the top of the economic and social pyramids instead are reflected in public policies? And suppose that analysis of power and decisionmaking leads similarly in the direction of choosing one of the two latter models of "Who rules?" Clearly, we would be faced with the problem of why so many Americans had the wrong idea about our system or perhaps of modifying our definition of "democracy" to fit what we actually found to exist. Along the same lines, our estimation of the probable directions of future change would be very different if we concluded that the ruling-class model is correct than if we believed that popular wants and needs play a decisive role in shaping public policies in the United States.

Summary

We have tried to design an approach that encourages both *scope* and *skepticism* as aids in getting beyond tunnel vision, assumptions, and ideology toward some approximation of reality. We started by stressing the concept of *political economy* — the integration of economy, politics, society, and culture into one coherent social order whose nature and dynamics are powerfully affected by the character and needs of the economic system. By looking at the components of the American political economy, we began to see some of the connections that lace the social order together. We tried to cite bits of data on key points so that we would not rely on familiar images or stereotypes for our analysis. At this stage, of course, all that was intended was a beginning sketch of an *approach*, not the full characterization that must await filling in with various kinds of evidence.

But laying out our approach in this way helped to further explain the nature and implications of the two basic questions that will guide our inquiry from this point forward. "Who rules?" raised three alternative answers, or models, each of which is a possible conclusion given our approach. "What difference does it make?" was seen to lead to greater understanding of American democracy and prospects for change.

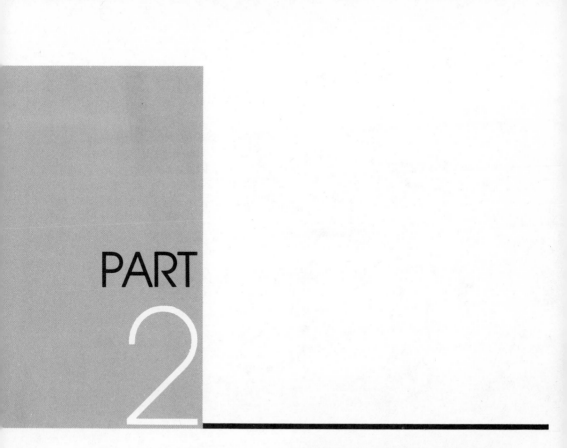

PART

2

PROBLEMS
AND POLICIES

THE WORLD CONTEXT OF U.S. ECONOMIC AND FOREIGN POLICY

3

The beginning of the 1980s appeared to confront policy-makers with an array of economic problems unequaled in scope, complexity, or importance since the Great Depression of the 1930s. Nor were these problems merely domestic in character. The interpenetration of the American economy with the rest of the industrialized, capitalist world and, secondarily, with the Third World meant that American economic problems were partly international in their origins (as well as in their consequences) and only partly subject to American control. The problems that were principally domestic in character seemed to defy all efforts at control by conventional means. Moreover, as such problems ate away at American resources, strength, and self-confidence, national security itself seemed to be at stake.

Economic security and national security can only be understood together, of course, because the search for the former helps to define the goals and priorities of the latter. In this chapter we look at world economic problems and at the way they affect American economic and foreign policy. In a final section we examine the problems posed by the actions of oil-exporting countries and the international oil industry. In the next two chapters we shall take up two other crucial components of the economic security–national security problem — U.S. economic problems and policies (particularly energy policy) and the military and other policies involved in implementing our understanding of "national security."

The World Economy: Problems and U.S. Priorities in the 1980s

The world emerged from World War II totally dominated by the American economy. No other national economy could come close to matching American wealth or productivity and thus the power of that economy to design the framework for world economic activity. But because the U.S. economy needed trading partners and investment opportunities, it was in its interest to help other capitalist countries rebuild their shattered economies. One price such nations paid was seeing their former colonies penetrated by American business and made dependent on American rather than European banks and corporate investors. Another price was general American *hegemony* (influence capable of shaping the basic actions of other countries and people): the U.S. dollar became the world's basic currency; multinational banks and corporations sprang up throughout Europe; and the United States insisted on policing the world, particularly by mobilizing forces against the Soviet Union. The United States experienced two decades of prosperity and influence unparalleled in world history.

But then, slowly at first but with rapidly increasing speed, the pillars of American dominance were undermined. American economic and military strength began to wane, in part for self-generated reasons, to the point that by the mid-1970s, the United States was increasingly vulnerable. The process was probably inevitable and in any event represents only the prologue to our present context. Its first manifestation was Soviet development of nuclear capability, which resulted in a new balance of power. The process continued as newly technological and highly productive economies were built in Europe and Japan. For a while, the key status of the dollar enabled American corporations and banks to operate around the world with a cushion of capital and credit. But by the early 1960s, European banks were flooded with dollars. Both European and Japanese products were competing favorably all over the world. And all the industrialized capitalist countries were creeping up on the U.S. lead in total output, income, exports, and other key economic indicators. By 1980, six countries were ahead of the United States in per capita income.

The United States clearly faces a new world in the 1980s. Understanding that world and the new limitations it places on American goals and policies is as essential as it is difficult. One way to begin is to distinguish *three* "worlds" and to examine changing conditions in each. The first is the industrialized, capitalist world, including the United States, Western Europe, and Japan. Mutual dependence on closely linked markets and investments does not prevent competition for relative advantage among major sectors of this economy, and the United States is here a kind of "first among equals."

The second world is made up of the socialist countries. In the case of the Soviet Union and Cuba, economic relations are clearly subordinate to the renewal of the cold war. Embargoes and boycotts, for example, are used in an effort to turn trade into a weapon. The threat perceived from these countries is used to justify expanded military expenditures and to mobilize Americans to endure sacrifices and reduced standards of living. The situation with respect to Eastern European nations is not as tense, but neither are (or were) economic relations as important. With regard to China, economic relations probably will expand rapidly as a means of aiding a major counterweight to the Soviet Union. All of these relationships are dominated by the renewed confrontation between the United States and the Soviet Union, which will be analyzed in Chapter 5.

The rest of the world is usually imprecisely labeled the *Third World* — a term that blurs many vital distinctions, including wealth, level of development, culture and history, and past or present relationships with developed countries. We use the term to emphasize the contrast with the relatively well-defined and more equal relationship of the United States with countries in the other two arenas. In the Third World the weight of U.S. economic and political power may be heavy or light, brutal or subtle, depending on a variety of factors.

The Capitalist World

Two conditions define the industrialized, capitalist world of the 1980s: interdependence and crisis. Interdependence — the interweaving of investment, trade, and other forms of economic activity so that each country's prosperity depends on the health of all the others — can be seen in several ways. One is the way in which the gross national product, or GNP (the total of all the goods and services produced in a country), of the major countries moves up or down in concert. Growth was high and sustained for many years in the 1960s. Some countries enjoyed greater success than others, and occasionally one (usually Japan, sometimes West Germany) would spurt ahead. But for the most part, all moved together — downward in 1974 (when all but Japan had negative growth), upward again, and then dropping as the 1980s began.

Another measure of interdependence is the extent of investment in other countries. In 1978 U.S. corporations had direct investments abroad of about $170 billion. Most of that was in the industrialized world, but nearly one-third was in the Third World. Conversely, foreign corporations and individuals had about $41 billion invested in U.S. land and industries.[1] Also in 1978, worldwide production of components for shipment, assembly, and sale in distant markets was common. The Ford Fiesta offered for sale in the United States, for example, contains major components manufactured in three cities in West Germany, five cities in England, one city each in Northern Ireland, Belgium, France, and Spain — and is finally assembled in Spain, West Germany, or England.[2]

The key to both the interdependence and the prosperity generated in the post–World War II world is the new role of exports. In the case of West Germany, for example, exports represented over 20 percent of the entire gross national product throughout the 1970s. For the other major nations, this figure was somewhat lower; for such countries as Holland, Belgium, and Denmark, it was much higher. Exports represented only 7 percent of the U.S. GNP, but even this relatively low proportion amounted to three times the entire value of the production of the U.S. domestic automobile industry, generally considered the cornerstone of the U.S. economy.

Two other facts will help to highlight the importance of export trade. First, GNP consists of *both* goods and services, but the latter by their nature cannot be exported. Thus, if we consider only the production of goods, mainly manufacturing and agriculture, exports account for 20 percent in the United States, 45 percent in Italy, and 75 percent in Canada of all that is produced. Second, trade levels fluctuate more widely than GNP, acting to raise it when they are rising and to depress it when they are dropping. The GNP of the advanced countries thus appears to be becoming more and more dependent on trade exchanges.

A crisis in the capitalist world was building before the staggering rise in oil prices that occurred in 1973–1974 and again in 1978–1979. Economic growth had slowed, and American inflation was beginning to be felt elsewhere; unemployment was climbing steadily. Spurred by the oil price increases, inflation exceeded 20 percent in Japan and Britain in 1974 and 1975; Italy and France were not far behind. By the end of the decade, growth was declining again, and inflation and unemployment were both rising. In this context another round of oil price rises — adding up to a twelvefold increase, from about $2 per barrel to $24 per barrel during the 1970s — posed a serious threat of still lower growth and more inflation.

One great danger was the prospect of restrictions on the exports and trading that are so crucial to the entire capitalist world. In countries where unemployment is rising, inflation is eroding real wages, and energy costs are rising, both workers and industry often seek help from their national governments by urging passage of import restrictions to protect against foreign goods entering their markets. Import restrictions can take several

---

[1] U.S. Department of Commerce, *Survey of Current Business*, August 1979, pp. 15, 38.
[2] *New York Times*, 3 February 1980, Section 12, p. 17.

forms, including tariffs, quotas, prohibitions, and conditions pertaining to the sending country's acceptance of exports in exchange. The situation has been rendered more acute by some governments' practice of subsidizing exports to make them more competitive in foreign markets. All the major capitalist countries pledged not to impose restrictions, but all were under pressure from local businesses to help save them from foreign competition that hurt their sales and profitability. If they yielded to such temptations, of course, retaliation by foreign governments could set off a ruinous trade war. Short of that, certain advantages might be gained by some industries in more powerful countries, such as the United States, by insisting on complete elimination of all restrictions regardless of their importance to another nation's economy.

Another major danger was the instability of the international monetary system — the set of arrangements between banks and governments whereby the exchange values of various currencies are maintained. Stable exchange rates are vital to carrying on all international transactions and particularly to the level of trade. If sellers cannot be sure of the value of the currency in which they will be paid, they are much less likely to sell. The results, of course, are lower profits and growth and greater unemployment. When one nation's economy seems very strong, its currency may serve as the international standard, as did the U.S. dollar for so long. Exchange rates may be fixed in relation to such a standard — that is, all countries' currencies are set at a specific ratio to the dollar by their governments. In time of economic instability, however, when no standard is generally accepted, exchange rates are permitted to float, or vary, depending on the actual trading between buyers and sellers in the currency markets.

Three forces threaten monetary stability in the early 1980s. One is the volatility given to the floating exchange values by uneven rates of growth and inflation in the major countries. In this situation the currency from the "stronger" economy with higher growth and lower inflation may become more attractive to sellers and investors, thereby pushing the value of all other currencies down by comparison with it.

A second factor is closely related, but has independent power as well. This is the prospect of massive speculation (buying or selling currencies in the expectation that they will soon rise or fall in value, with obvious self-fulfilling possibilities if many people do the same thing). Multinational banks and corporations, or even very wealthy individuals, can cause currency-exchange levels to rise or fall sharply in this way, with possible great profit to them, but certain disaster to international trading levels over the long run.

Finally, there is the great difficulty involved in the vast transfer of cash from oil importers to oil-producing nations. Perhaps $100 billion of surplus money in the hands of the oil-exporting nations would have to be "recycled" back to importing nations somehow so that they could continue to purchase their vital oil. For all these reasons, at the beginning of the

1980s the capitalist world was looking anxiously at its troubled monetary system and hoping that it would hold. Many investors feared (or hoped) that it would not, however, and the price of gold, the "currency of last resort" that always seems to hold its value, shot upward in unprecedented fashion — adding still another strain to the world economic system.

It might appear that the capitalist world has everything to gain from close cooperation. But neither avoidance of all import restrictions nor stable exchange rates, even though they are in the long-run best interest of the entire capitalist world, can automatically be anticipated. The crux of the question is what national governments actually do. And behind that, in turn, is the fact that some sectors of world capitalism stand to gain from every restriction or fluctuation and to lose from their removal or control. The struggle for comparative advantage is reflected in the behavior of national governments, some of which in effect profit from endangering the whole. By danger, of course, we mean not only the threat of economic collapse, but also the social unrest that accompanies even severe dislocations.

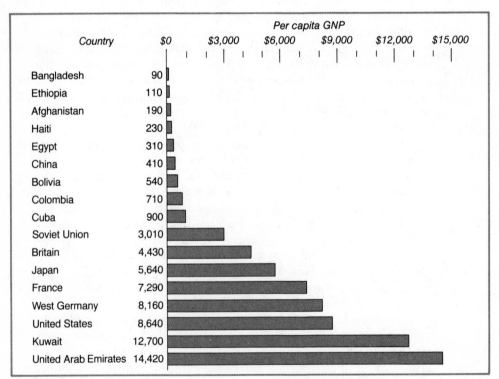

Source: *World Bank Atlas* 1978, p. 30 (1977 data)

Figure 3.1 Gross national product, per capita, selected countries (1977 data; $ U.S.). (*Source: World Bank Atlas*, 1978, p. 30. Used by permission.)

None of the tensions within world capitalism, however, should be allowed to obscure the contrast between the advanced industrialized nations as a whole and the Third World. This contrast is apparent in the vast gap in wealth and standard of living between the two areas, as well as in the relationship between them. The Third World is in debt to the bankers of world capitalism; its natural resources are for the most part still owned or exploited by foreign corporations; and it is increasingly unable to support itself, chiefly for these reasons. The term *dependence* very considerably understates this relationship, as we shall now see.

The Third World

Two conditions characterize the Third World today: dependence and crisis. The contrast between the Third World and the developed countries is stark and may be portrayed first by a comparison of the per capita gross national product of various countries (Figure 3.1). Such a comparison may be misleading, however, because there is no assurance that the distribution of income in a country is anywhere near equal — that is, that *per capita* GNP means anything. All we can say is that *if* the total product were divided equally, these are the sums that would accrue to each citizen.

A more revealing comparison relates several factors, such as per capita income, population, growth rate, and overall prospects. Figure 3.2 does so in three categories, following the World Bank's breakdown and its projection of comparisons between 1970 and 1980. The poorest countries are those in which per capita income is less than $200 per year. In these countries the period 1969–1973 (for which these figures were compiled)

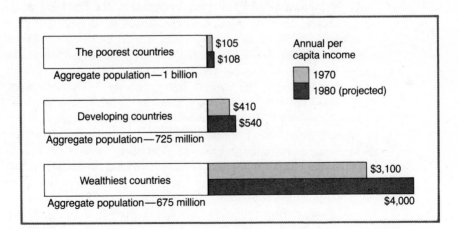

Figure 3.2 The distribution of wealth. (*Source: New York Times*, 24 August 1975, pp. 3–13. © 1975 by The New York Company. Reprinted by permission.)

saw almost no growth at all — only 0.5 percent. In other words, more than seventy countries with over 1 billion people made almost no progress whatsoever in what were boom times for the rest of the world! People in this part of the world (mostly India and Africa) were living in hunger, squalor, and hopelessness about the future.

In the "middle-income" countries populations are somewhat smaller, and average incomes are more than $400 per year. There are great disparities *within* each country, but the annual growth rate as a whole was over 4.5 percent for this period. These are the countries of Latin America and other specially aided nations, such as South Korea and Taiwan; one can say that they are the most fully incorporated into the American sphere of world capitalism. According to the World Bank's data, however, even those countries took a step backward in the capitalist/energy crisis of the mid-1970s.

The wealthiest countries (here defined as the Western European nations and the United States, but not the socialist countries) enjoy per capita incomes more than seven times as high as those of the middle-income countries. And it is virtually inevitable that the rich will get richer and the poor poorer. In effect, one-quarter of the world's population has three-quarters of the world's income, investment, and services and most of its research skills. Because these are the essential ingredients of progress, future progress can only expand the gap between nations.

What is the U.S. interest, or stake, in the Third World? It may be more subtle, and is certainly less purely economic, than many have alleged. Two quite tangible kinds of interests must first be acknowledged. One is the need for scarce natural resources possessed by Third World countries. In Figure 3.3, which shows vital materials and their sources, Third World nations are prominent. Demand for oil is thus only one of the factors that makes the Third World's allegiances crucial to the capitalist world.

A second tangible interest is represented by the amount of American investment in Third World countries, which by 1978 totaled about $45 billion. Returns on such invested capital are much higher from Third World countries than from the industrialized nations, and higher proportions are returned to the United States each year. Thus, even though less than a third of foreign investment is in the Third World, it plays a disproportionate role in producing profits for American owners.

These two sets of interests — crucial resources and existing investments — account in large part for American policies toward the Third World. But the importance of resources and investments varies from country to country, and some of the American stake in the Third World must be attributed elsewhere. At the time of maximum American effort in Vietnam — an effort that may have marked the threshold between the old and the new world orders — little in the way of either resources or investments there could explain American actions. The missing ingredient appears to be a posture toward the Third World as a whole, whose com-

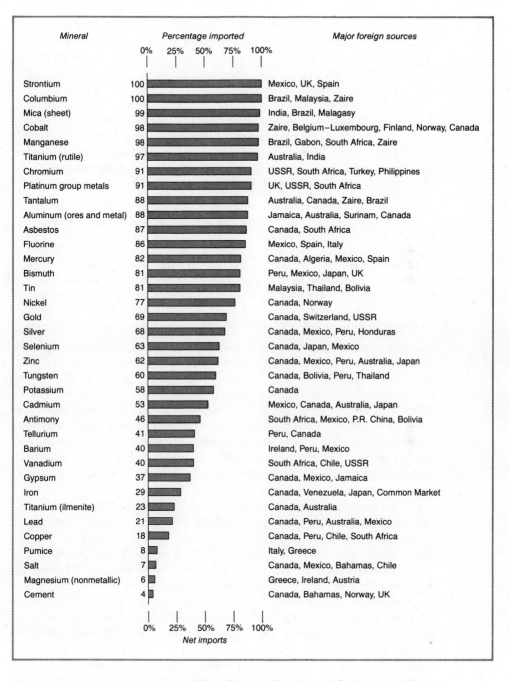

Mineral	Percentage imported	Major foreign sources
Strontium	100	Mexico, UK, Spain
Columbium	100	Brazil, Malaysia, Zaire
Mica (sheet)	99	India, Brazil, Malagasy
Cobalt	98	Zaire, Belgium–Luxembourg, Finland, Norway, Canada
Manganese	98	Brazil, Gabon, South Africa, Zaire
Titanium (rutile)	97	Australia, India
Chromium	91	USSR, South Africa, Turkey, Philippines
Platinum group metals	91	UK, USSR, South Africa
Tantalum	88	Australia, Canada, Zaire, Brazil
Aluminum (ores and metal)	88	Jamaica, Australia, Surinam, Canada
Asbestos	87	Canada, South Africa
Fluorine	86	Mexico, Spain, Italy
Mercury	82	Canada, Algeria, Mexico, Spain
Bismuth	81	Peru, Mexico, Japan, UK
Tin	81	Malaysia, Thailand, Bolivia
Nickel	77	Canada, Norway
Gold	69	Canada, Switzerland, USSR
Silver	68	Canada, Mexico, Peru, Honduras
Selenium	63	Canada, Japan, Mexico
Zinc	62	Canada, Mexico, Peru, Australia, Japan
Tungsten	60	Canada, Bolivia, Peru, Thailand
Potassium	58	Canada
Cadmium	53	Mexico, Canada, Australia, Japan
Antimony	46	South Africa, Mexico, P.R. China, Bolivia
Tellurium	41	Peru, Canada
Barium	40	Ireland, Peru, Mexico
Vanadium	40	South Africa, Chile, USSR
Gypsum	37	Canada, Mexico, Jamaica
Iron	29	Canada, Venezuela, Japan, Common Market
Titanium (ilmenite)	23	Canada, Australia
Lead	21	Canada, Peru, Australia, Mexico
Copper	18	Canada, Peru, Chile, South Africa
Pumice	8	Italy, Greece
Salt	7	Canada, Mexico, Bahamas, Chile
Magnesium (nonmetallic)	6	Greece, Ireland, Austria
Cement	4	Canada, Bahamas, Norway, UK

Net imports

Figure 3.3 U.S. mineral imports, 1978. (*Source:* Data from U.S. Bureau of Mines.)

ponents are the desire for a favorable investment "climate" throughout the world, aspects of basic American ideology, and our conception of national security needs. These factors are often inseparable, and in illustrating one we illustrate the others.

U.S. governmental policies have consistently sought to promote conditions that would render private investment in the Third World profitable and relatively safe. The definition of a good investment climate is stability, determination to repay, and capacity to sell something for dollars so as to be able to repay. American policies designed to foster such favorable climates have as their central theme the efficacy of private enterprise. In the words of one moderate authority on economic policy:

> To representatives of the less developed nations, it must seem that the United States never tires of citing the advantages — real and imagined — of an economic system based on private enterprise. The main advantages of private investment cited by American policymakers were: first, private investment is more "flexible," presumably referring to the relative absence of governmental "red tape." Second, private investment is "non-political," presumably referring to a supposed absence of interference in domestic affairs by private investors. And third, private investment often carried with it technical knowledge and managerial skill.[3]

U.S. trade and tariff policy, however, was never adapted to make it easier for Third World nations to *either* repay development loans or undertake their own development. Protections against agricultural products (the most common Third World product) remained high, and Third World countries found it difficult to obtain markets and hence dollars for their own development. Private investors, on the other hand, could earn substantial profits from Third World investments if they kept ownership or control of the commodities produced and arranged their sales themselves. In addition, of course, their investments would be insured by the U.S. government.

This combination of exhortation and policy may be merely ambiguous or simply self-serving — as the Third World often suggests. But there is undeniably a significant ambiguity in the general ideological posture from which Americans view the Third World. Although procapitalism and anticommunism are paramount, there is also a strand of altruism, of the desire to help others enjoy the good things Americans see themselves as possessing.

This mixture of motives is readily visible in the annual debates over, and actual uses of, "foreign aid." Each year since World War II, the U.S. government has extended from $3 to $7 billion in military and economic assistance, much of it to Third World countries. Among the general public and to some extent in Congress, the issue is seen as altruism versus "giveaways" that benefit us little in return. Actually, of course, the amount

---

[3] David A. Baldwin, *Economic Development and American Foreign Policy* (Chicago: University of Chicago Press, 1966), p. 19.

the United States so expends represents a diminishing proportion of the GNP (now less than 0.5 percent); the United States is approximately tenth among nonsocialist countries in the proportion of GNP devoted to foreign aid. In other terms, we spend only about one-third as much on foreign aid as we do on toilet articles and preparations. What we do spend is devoted almost entirely to military assistance to client states (countries whose viability, economically or militarily or both, depends on American assistance), such as South Korea or Taiwan. Thus, in practice, there is little altruism and much anticommunism in the extension of aid. National security interests permeate the policies that are ostensibly intended to promote Third World development.

This sense that national security is at stake in a generalized manner everywhere in the Third World is based on the premise that such countries are either "ours" or "theirs." Needless to say, such a premise is emphatically rejected by the nationalist countries of the Third World. But it remains a factor among American policymakers, many of whom (particularly in the area of foreign policy) either have had or still have close ties to the business world.

From the perspective of the Third World, the great gap in wealth and the developed world's lack of assistance are the major issues of our times. Despite nationalistic rivalries, racial differences, and vast distinctions in wealth and development, Third World nations as a whole have begun to question the very premises of an international order characterized by the distributions and prospects of the present world. So far, only the most minimal efforts at financial or other assistance have been made by the developed world, except in furtherance of its own profitability or security interests. And conditions of life are steadily worsening.

Two lines of approach to the developed world have recently been taken by Third World countries. One is use of the leverage that possession of crucial natural resources provides to redistribute wealth. The obvious example is oil; other such maneuvers may follow. The problem with this approach is that success requires a delicate balance of power between the major world blocs. If the United States had not been weakened by the Vietnam War and if the Soviet Union had not been available for support, it is doubtful that the OPEC actions of 1973–1974 would have been so successful. Moreover, as we have seen, there were substantial benefits to be gained by major segments of the capitalist world economy in that situation. And the oil price rise may in time be damaging to Third World nations embarking on energy-utilizing development, far beyond the willingness of Arab governments to compensate through loans.

The other approach is to insist, at the United Nations and elsewhere, on greater assistance — with no strings attached — from the developed world. The drawback of this route is that the industrialized countries can simply refuse; unless concerted Third World action (such as expropriations or refusal to repay loans) is backed up by Soviet military power, very little can be done about such refusals. Only when the conditions of

(*Source:* Rius-Siempre, Mexico)

the Third World are understood as relevant to the conditions and prospects of the industrialized countries is there likely to be serious cooperative effort. Some problems are indeed global and threaten all nations. But here again, there are great disparities in how such problems are understood and hence in the solutions sought.

The Capitalist World and the Third World: Contrasting Problems and Solutions

Definitions of both problems and solutions differ sharply between these worlds; the "facts" simply do not have the same meaning everywhere. There is little doubt that conditions in the world are such that the entire world population faces substantial threats to its very survival. The first problem is the sheer number of people in the world and the ever-increasing rate of expansion of that number. If the present rate of increase continues, more people will be added to the world's population *each year* by the middle of the next century than were added in the first *fifteen hundred years* of the Christian calendar.

The world's population, 200–300 million in the year 1 A.D., took sixteen centuries to double. It doubled again in the next two hundred years and again in only one hundred years. The next doubling took less than half a century, making world population in 1975 about 4 billion people. It is predicted that the world's population will be over 6 billion by the year 2000. According to all estimates of available and prospective food supply, the world cannot begin to feed such numbers of people.

And not only food will be in short supply. Various mineral resources are estimated as so limited that dates of probable exhaustion can be calculated. New reserves or substitute resources may be found, and price rises may preserve supplies for longer periods than are forecast. But such costs will probably mean hardship, and more likely destitution, for those who depend — as does most of the world — on the products of these resources. Energy resources alone will pose a severe crisis: coal will last only somewhat longer than oil and gas, and new sources must be found.

The depletion of natural resources is not limited to certain scarce minerals, however. It extends to the air we breathe and to the ecological balance of nature itself. Industrial production has led to waste, environmental destruction, and pollution to such an extent that some forms of life have been extinguished, and the means by which nature reestablishes itself have been endangered. The prospect is the loss not of amenities by a few wealthy people, but of air and water by the many.

A number of "futurist" writers, and particularly the business-and-foundation-financed Club of Rome studies, have articulated world capitalism's definition of these problems. They see a "population crisis" and an "energy crisis," both global in character, which mandate (1) limits on population, (2) stable or reduced standards of living, and (3) worldwide cooperation to manage the remaining resources and their usage.

But definitions and solutions of this sort present some serious problems. From the perspective of the Third World, for example, the problem is not overpopulation, but maldistribution of wealth. To urge limitation of population on people whose infant mortality rates are very high and whose livelihood depends on labor-intensive means of cultivation or production is to ignore the basis on which whole peoples now survive. To stabilize their standards of living at submarginal levels is to hand them death certificates; without growth, they and their children have no future. To advocate worldwide cooperation sounds very much like incorporating them into a system intended to serve the needs of profitability on the part of the capitalist world's corporations and banks — a system that clearly works for the developed world at the cost of Third World suffering.

What are the assumptions behind the three basic prescriptions? One basic assumption is that the capitalist world system is desirable, permanent, or both. A "population crisis" exists only to the extent that there are more people than can now be fed by capitalist agribusiness. In other words, food is grown as long as it can be profitably sold under circumstances of multiple profit-taking (fertilizer, mechanized equipment, transportation, and so on). Moreover, food is grown in volumes limited by the need to maintain profit-producing prices. Those who cannot pay such prices must go without. The Third World nations have for the most part been discouraged from engaging in diversified agriculture because it was desirable to keep them focused on one-crop production for sales in world markets — to enable them to repay loans and to keep the developed world well supplied with needed resources. Finally, evidence indicates that rates of population increase are highest in the poorest countries and lowest in the richest countries. The surest route to reduced birth rates is thus not pious exhortation, but steadily increasing standards of living.

The prescription for austerity involves a similar number of assumptions — or hypocrisy, as the Third World charges. To limit growth at this stage is to freeze a situation in which the United States, for example, with 6 percent of the world's population, enjoys between 40 and 50 percent of its resources and productivity. Unless Third World economies are not only allowed but encouraged to grow, their populations face mounting starvation. Citing an "energy crisis" as a reason to restrict growth assumes that production of oil and gas must be limited to those levels that maximize prices to those able to pay at all, that the oil industry's monopoly must be preserved and extended to other sources of energy as well, and that alternative sources can be developed only privately.

World organization and cooperation are therefore in the interests of some and at the expense of others, due to the extremely unequal distribution of wealth. The Third World understandably suspects that its people are considered expendable. Thus, even global problems, however staggering in their implications, do not necessarily give rise to agreed-upon definitions or solutions. Instead, they merely exacerbate already tense relations among conflicting interests.

The Impact of OPEC

The Organization of Petroleum Exporting Countries (OPEC) was formed in 1960 as a result of growing nationalism and a temporary drop in oil prices and revenues to producing countries. Saudi Arabia and Iran, the two largest producers, were closely linked to the United States, and the oil companies still held considerable leverage in most producing countries. OPEC's early years, therefore, showed little of its recent militance. As nationalism increased and the relative power of the United States waned, however, the producing countries began to take over a larger share of the role formerly played by the "seven sisters" — the seven major oil companies (Exxon, Royal Dutch/Shell, Mobil, Texaco, British Petroleum, Standard Oil of California, and Gulf).

This role, which consisted of control of the *price* and the *supply* of oil in the world markets, became defined in three related ways.[4] First, the seven companies controlled most of the sources of oil in the world and managed what was made available for sale very carefully. These "majors" were all "integrated" companies whose operations ranged from exploration through transportation and refining to marketing. There were thus no "middlemen" to be considered. Independent companies involved in any of the separate functions were tolerated as long as they adhered to the

---

[4] For a full discussion, see the two leading works on this subject: John M. Blair, *The Control of Oil* (New York: Pantheon, 1977), and Robert Engler, *The Brotherhood of Oil* (Chicago: University of Chicago Press, 1977).

patterns set by the majors; if they did not, the vast resources of the majors would be applied competitively to force the "independents" back in line or out of business.

Second, starting in 1928 the seven majors adopted a series of "as is" agreements to stabilize their operations and relationships with one another. They agreed to accept one another's existing shares of the market in various countries and thus to prevent price-cutting. Any major increasing its share of the market at the expense of another major (as opposed to one of the many then existing smaller companies) actually paid a penalty to the affected company. But the important achievements were the agreement on pricing and the spirit of cooperation and trust developed over years of working together under explicit and tacit agreements of this sort.

Third, because the majors so dominated the field in terms of assets, experience, and technology, they were able to shape and control the post–World War II expansion into the new oilfields of the Middle East, Latin America, and Africa. Their close working relationships with Western governments shaped those governments' policies and ensured private (rather than the oft-proposed public) development of the new fields. And the majors moved to establish equally close working relationships with ruling elites wherever the much more cheaply available new oil was to be produced. For years, the total growth of world production was maintained at a steady 9.5 percent per year, with stable prices and substantial profits.

OPEC began to come of age in the early 1970s. Not only was the United States clearly unable to exert the influence it had in the past, but also new oil discoveries in Libya set a new pattern for government–oil company relationships. Libya granted concessions to some of the larger independent producers rather than to the seven majors. Untroubled by the agreements the majors had among themselves, the independents paid higher proportions of revenues to the Libyan government and produced oil as quickly as they could. The revolutionary government that came to power in 1969 raised prices further and cut back on production. Because 55 percent of Libyan oil was produced by independents as opposed to 15 percent for other OPEC countries, the majors had no choice but to follow Libya's demands.

Other factors that stimulated OPEC ambitions were the continuing rise in world demand and the leveling off of U.S. production that occurred about the same time. The leaders in seeking a larger share of the ownership of producing facilities and control over wellhead prices were the more "radical" countries (Libya, Iraq, Algeria, and Venezuela), but the others soon followed. By September 1973 (before the Arab-Israeli war of that year), the price per barrel of Saudi Arabian crude oil (the standard measure for OPEC pricing) had risen to $3.01, an increase of 60 percent since 1970.

In late 1973 the anti-Israel members of OPEC forced through an "embargo" against shipments of oil to the United States and other countries aiding Israel. The embargo had almost no effect in preventing oil from reaching such countries, however. Iran sharply increased its production and shipments; Saudi Arabia had stockpiled supplies through previously increased production in anticipation of war and embargo; and other producers, including Middle East countries, let oil "leak" around the embargo. U.S. imports for the period of the embargo maintained their steady growth pattern, month after month. But there were spot shortages and gasoline lines all over the United States. The prices of both gas and home-heating oil *did* rise dramatically. Apparently, the major oil companies acted extremely conservatively and rationed their ample stocks of oil through the transportation, refining, and marketing systems very slowly. An often voiced, less charitable view is that the majors saw and took the opportunity to drive independents out of business, eliminate environmental and other objections to new production, and raise their profits substantially.

In any event, by the end of the embargo in March 1974, a new relationship between OPEC and the world had been created. The price of Saudi crude was up again and would reach $11.25 per barrel by the end of the year. Vast sums of money began to flow from the oil-consuming nations to the OPEC countries, which created severe problems for oil-importing Third World countries and threatened the stability of the international monetary system. The major oil companies no longer dictated prices or production allocations or levels, and in some cases they even lost ownership of facilities. Their share of OPEC production began to drop steadily, as state-owned companies began to take over production.

But the major oil companies were not thrown on the defensive so much as to prevent them from working out a new relationship with their former clients in OPEC. For one thing, they had been able to pass along all the price increases of crude oil to their consumers, apparently with some increment for their own refining and marketing services as well, for oil company profits rose dramatically in 1974–1975. Also, every price rise by OPEC also increased the price for all the other oil owned by the majors everywhere else in the world. With no increase in exploration or extraction costs and no effort on their part, the major oil companies thus received much higher revenues for the oil they chose to produce. They also retained their control over the postproduction stages of the business and substantial influence within the OPEC nations — if only because of the mutuality of interest between them.

OPEC countries were quick to point out that their resources had been exploited for years without much return to them. They noted that in exerting control over price and supply, they were only doing what the major oil companies had been doing for years. They sought to find ways to use their surpluses to assist other Third World countries, but without much success. As their prices rose steadily in the period 1975–1978, they pointed out (accurately) that their prices had not kept pace with world inflation and the reduced value of the dollars they received for their oil.

In fact, at the beginning of 1979 the real price of oil was 27 percent *below* the level of five years earlier — a fact that OPEC nations used repeatedly to deny that they were responsible for world inflation.[5]

The OPEC price decisions of 1979 set about to restore members' real income with a vengeance. By the year's end, Saudi crude was at $24 per barrel. It was likely to climb steadily further as regular reviews of world conditions were agreed upon and ways of linking revenues to inflation levels to create an inflation-proof system were sought. As world demand began to slacken in the face of these staggering costs, OPEC's focus turned to controlling production levels in order to avoid the greatest danger that suppliers had always struggled with: oversupply, or "glut," of oil.

The new price levels presented immense new problems for the rest of the world. Industrial countries faced massive balance-of-payments deficits (more money paid for imports than earned through exports) and new inflationary pressures. Their people faced lower standards of living. Oil-importing Third World countries had even greater problems. They lacked the cash to pay for oil and were faced with the possibility of having to default on debts to developed countries' banks, with resulting danger to some of the world's largest banks. Their people, already struggling, faced drastic cutbacks in services and standards of living. Most of all, international bankers doubted the capacity of the world monetary system to "recycle" billions of dollars from the OPEC countries back to their debtors without threatening the stability of that system. At some point, they feared, the whole world economy would simply collapse.[6]

The situation in 1980 was one of leveling demand, controlled production, and massive numbers of dollars flowing back and forth in the world. Table 3.1 shows comparatively that the United States is OPEC's largest customer, consuming over 30 percent of its production. But U.S. demand for OPEC oil has actually been dropping, and world demand has leveled off. Non-OPEC countries that are important producers include the United States, the Soviet Union, Mexico, Canada, and the West Indies. Not all of these countries export their oil, but the United States gets about 20 percent of its imports from the latter three sources.

The members of OPEC are listed in Table 3.2, along with the production proportions that were obtained in 1978 (the last year in which Iranian production was stable). Saudi Arabia has taken up most of the slack caused by Iran's lower production, but even though total OPEC production is estimated at 3.1 million barrels per day *less* in 1980 than in 1978, there have been no shortages. Indeed, predictions were for a glut rather than a shortage in the 1980s.

A summary of the massive financial problem created by OPEC's price

---

[5] *New York Times*, 26 February 1980, p. D15.
[6] See *Business Week*, 19 November 1979, pp. 176–179, for a special section, "The Petro-Crash of the '80s."

Table 3.1

World Oil Demand and Projected Supply (millions of barrels per day)

Demand	1978	1979	1980 (est.)
United States	18.8	18.4	17.8
Japan	5.3	5.5	5.4
Europe	14.4	14.7	14.1
Others	13.5	13.7	14.4
Total	52.0	52.3	52.0
Projected supply			
OPEC			28.8
Natural gas liquids			3.1
From Communist countries			1.3
Non-OPEC			19.0
Total			52.2

Source: New York Times, 14 January 1980, p. D1. © 1972/79/80 by The New York Times Company. Reprinted by permission.

Table 3.2

OPEC Members and Oil Production, 1978

Country	Barrels/Day (millions)	Total (%)
Saudi Arabia	8.3	26.0
Iran[a]	5.2	19.0
Iraq	2.6	9.0
Kuwait	2.1	8.0
Venezuela	2.2	7.0
Nigeria	1.9	6.6
Libya	2.0	6.6
United Arab Emirates	1.8	5.6
Indonesia	1.6	5.0
Algeria	1.2	3.7
Qatar	0.5	1.6
Gabon	0.2	0.6
Ecuador	0.2	0.6
Total	31.9	100.0

Source: Reproduced by permission from *Petroleum Intelligence Weekly,* copyrighted 1979 by Petroleum & Energy Intelligence Weekly, Inc.

[a] Iranian production has been uncertain since the 1979 revolution, and others, notably Saudi Arabia, produced more in alternating fashion. But these are the basic proportions when all members are producing.

Table 3.3 How Petrodollars Flow Through the World's Economies

Consuming Countries Buy this Much Oil from Abroad . . .ᵃ

Estimated 1979 Oil Imports	Billions of U.S. Dollars
U.S.	$ 61
Japan	40
Germany	22
France	19
Italy	18
Netherlands	14
Britain	12
Other industrial countries	16
Brazil	7
India	4
South Korea	3
Other developing countries	26
Total	$242

. . . and OPEC Collects this Much in Returnᵇ

Projected 1979 Revenuesᵈ	Billions of U.S. Dollars
Saudi Arabia	$ 62.3
Kuwait	21.0
Iraq	20.6
Iran	20.5
Nigeria	16.7
Venezuela	14.7
United Arab Emirates	13.6
Libya	13.1
Indonesia	12.0
Algeria	10.5
Qatar	3.6
Ecuador	2.4
Gabon	1.7
Total	$212.7

OPEC's Surpluses Flow into Eurocurrency Markets . . .ᵇ

Projected Surplus for 1979 after Expenditures and Transfersᵉ	Billions of U.S. Dollars
Saudi Arabia	$12.5
Kuwait	12.3
Iraq	9.3
United Arab Emirates	5.5
Libya	2.5
Iran	2.0
Nigeria	1.9
Qatar	1.6
Total	$47.6

. . . and then Out in the Form of Eurocurrency Lendingᶜ

Net Eurocurrency Bank Loans	Billions of U.S. Dollars	Net Eurocurrency Bank Loans	Billions of U.S. Dollars	Net Eurocurrency Bank Loans	Billions of U.S. Dollars	Net Eurocurrency Bank Loans	Billions of U.S. Dollars
Mexico	$ 8.0	Venezuela	$ 4.6	Spain	$ 3.5	Poland	$ 2.0
Brazil	5.5	Algeria	3.0	Italy	3.0	East Germany	1.0
South Korea	3.5	Indonesia	1.7	France	2.2	Other East bloc countries	1.5
China	3.5	Other OPEC countries	2.7	Norway	1.0		
Argentina	2.0			Britain	0.9		
Taiwan	1.2			Other European countries	2.0		
Other non-OPEC developing countries	10.0					Total	$62.8

Source: *Business Week*, 19 November 1979, pp. 176–177. Used by permission. ᵃData from Central Intelligence Agency, BW estimates. ᵇData from Chase Manhattan Bank, BW estimates. ᶜData from Morgan Guaranty Trust Co., BW estimates. ᵈIncludes oil exports plus investment income. ᵉFor other OPEC countries, expenditures and transfers exceed all revenues.

increases appears in Table 3.3, which shows the sources of the $242 billion paid for imported oil and which OPEC countries received how much for that oil in 1979. Much of this money is spent by OPEC countries directly or for their own development, but some is left over as surplus. It goes to European banks for "recycling" as loans to Third World countries so that they can pay for imported oil and other necessities for their own development. In addition to the problem caused by the rapid movement of such massive sums, the "Eurocurrency" loans are putting Third World countries deeper and deeper in debt. But the latter have no choice, because they must have oil; whether they can repay their debts is another question, however, and more loans may be sought to do so. Much as the bankers might like to make such loans so as to employ their OPEC surpluses, they may feel that repayment is so unlikely as to make it unwise. At some point, bankers worry, the system will simply stop working.

U.S. ECONOMIC PROBLEMS AND POLICIES

4

Although the United States is still the world's strongest economy, the 1980s seem to present U.S. policymakers with each of the capitalist world's problems in an especially complex form. In this chapter we will look at five problems and their political implications in turn: (1) inflation, (2) unemployment, (3) the near bankruptcies of several major cities and even states, (4) debt and capital formation, and (5) economic growth. Then we shall examine the policies available for coping with them and will conclude with a case study of a sixth problem that affects all of the others: energy.

Five Leading Problems

Inflation

Inflation is a general rise in the prices of goods and services such that the *real* value, or purchasing power, of money is reduced. Three dollars are necessary today to buy what two dollars bought yesterday. More specifically, what cost $1.00 in 1967 cost $2.30 in 1979. The year 1979 saw the worst inflation in the United States in thirty-three years (13.3 percent), and most forecasts envisioned only marginal improvement (if any) in the near future. On the average, real wages, or purchasing power, dropped 5.3 percent after wage and salary increases were counted.

The blame for inflation is variously attributed, depending on one's ideology; economists do not begin to concur on one or two reasons. Conventional wisdom identifies three types (or causes) of inflation, and we shall add two more that are often suggested regarding the inflation of the 1980s.

■ *Demand-Pull Inflation.* An excess of money in the hands of consumers bids up the prices of goods in what is called demand-pull inflation. This may happen during periods when consumer goods are scarce, such as wartime, or as a result of government's spending in excess of its revenue — in which case it is injecting new money (or increased demand) into the economy. Many people see such federal budget deficits as a primary cause of inflation, and much political energy is mobilized to force balancing of the national budget (see the section on the "tax revolt" in Chapter 9). It is not clear, however, just how much of the impetus to inflation comes from such a source. At the very least, the relationship between a federal budget deficit and the total GNP must be considered; when this is done, the record peacetime deficits of the Carter administration show up as only half as large as those of the Ford administration.[1] Some part of the pressure for balanced budgets may come from people who are less concerned about inflation in the abstract than they are about their own taxes and governmental services to other people.

■ *Cost-Push Inflation.* This type of inflation occurs when the rising costs of production (raw materials, interest on loans, wages, and the like) force producers to charge more for their products. Assertions often made about rising costs are that they are due to wage increases, government regulations, and/or increased energy costs. But average wage increases have fallen well short of the rate of inflation, and only about one-fourth of the ongoing American inflation is usually attributed to the rise in energy costs. Government regulation adds at most 0.5 percent, and some argue that the figure should be much lower. Again, it seems that other reasons must be involved.

■ *Profit-Push Inflation.* In this type of inflation, those producers or investors who have sufficient control over the market for their products or capital to flourish seek to make more profit by raising prices or by maintaining them at an artificially high level when other prices are declining. In profit-push inflation, of course, a noncompetitive market situation is

---

[1] *U.S. News & World Report*, 18 October 1979, p. 36.

assumed. As we shall see later, this is the case for many American industries, dominated by a few large corporations. Thus, the prospect of this form of inflation, while new, is real.

■ *Declining Productivity.* When productivity (the amount of goods and services produced per hour of working time) does not increase enough to offset increases in wages and other costs, the cost per unit produced will necessarily be higher. To maintain profit margins, the business must charge higher prices to the consumer. Figure 4.1 compares productivity rates and inflation rates in consumer prices. From 1948 to 1965 productivity increased an average of well over 2 percent per year. This period was also one of remarkable price stability; with the exception of two Korean War years, price increases averaged less than 2 percent per year. Rates of increase in productivity began to drop in 1965, however, and productivity actually declined in 1974 and again in 1979. Simultaneously, inflation took hold, and prices increased 130 percent from 1967 through 1979.

■ *Inflation Psychology.* This type of inflation arises when people become convinced that inflation will continue and act accordingly. Such an attitude helps to spur inflation in a kind of self-fulfilling way. People buy now, even at high prices and at the cost of going further into debt, because they

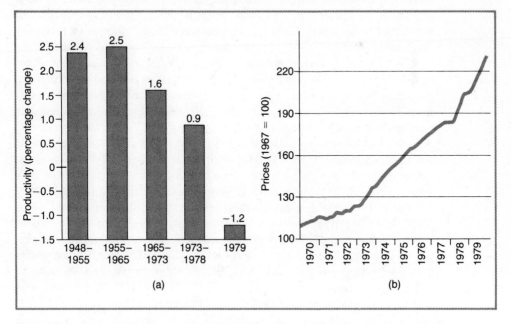

Figure 4.1 Falling productivity, rising prices: (a) Labor productivity growth in nonfarm business (percentage change); (b) Consumer prices, all items (1967 = 100). (*Source:* Data from Bureau of Labor Statistics; *New York Times,* 3 February 1980. © 1972/79/80 by The New York Times Company. Reprinted by permission.)

fear that prices will be higher in the future. Manufacturers and retailers court these fears and continue to raise prices, and the cycle goes on.

In addition to the major causes of inflation, other factors contribute to a lesser extent. For example, some fuel is added by government commitments to expand military expenditures by 4 or 5 percent in real (after inflation is taken into account) terms during each of the next several years. Even the weather can contribute substantially to inflation, by determining the size of the grain harvest that is so central to world agricultural prices.

Combinations of any of the types of inflation mentioned above are also possible. For example, producers may use slight rises in the costs of production as grounds for large price increases. Or a period of inflation may be initiated by one form of inflation, such as governmental spending in excess of revenues for a sustained period (such as the Vietnam War) and prolonged by one or more of the other forms.

What are consequences of inflation? The first and most damaging impact is on the standards of living of millions of ordinary people. Every dollar previously saved or currently earned can buy less than half of what it did only twelve years before. A graphic illustration of price rises for the ten-year period ending in mid-1979 is provided in Table 4.1. Both middle-class and working-class people find that they must fundamentally alter their styles of living. With the greatest price rises coming in such necessities as housing, energy, food, and health care, many families can manage only by cutting down or eliminating "basics" they have taken for granted for years.

While nearly everybody suffers from inflation, people do not suffer equally, and some do not suffer at all. In the case of demand-pull inflation, for example, the need for more workers to produce more goods may result in a sudden increase in the availability of jobs and/or higher income for people who are usually unemployed or poorly paid. This is the case during periods of heavy military expenditures; since World War II, unemployment has dropped below 4 percent only during the Korean and Vietnam wars. Since periods characterized by this type of inflation are apparently the only times such people experience full employment or decent incomes, they may be said to benefit. Some workers, usually those in the unionized fields (less than 20 percent of the labor force), may be able to stay ahead of inflation. But those whose incomes are derived from ownership of corporate stock stand the best chance of staying ahead of inflation, since profits and stock value are quite likely to rise in value faster than the rate of inflation. As real wages dropped in the years 1974–1975, however, the spending power of corporate profits rose 24 percent.[2]

---

[2] *Economic Report of the President, 1975* (Washington, D.C.: U.S. Government Printing Office, 1975).

Table 4.1

Consumer Prices — the Results Since 1969

	Typical Price 10 Years Ago	Typical Current Price	Percent Increase
Semiprivate hospital room, per day	$47.00	$134.00	185
Regular gasoline, 10 gallons	$3.48	$9.68	178
New house, median price	$25,600.00	$64,000.00	150
First-class postage, 1 ounce	$.06	$.15	150
Hamburger, per pound	$.62	$1.54	148
Physician's office fee	$6.75	$14.60	116
Tuition, room, board at state university, per year	$1,117.00	$2,346.00	110
Week's food for family of four	$36.90	$77.50	110
New car	$3,400.00	$6,910.00	103
Tooth filling	$7.40	$14.15	91
Loaf white bread, per pound	$.23	$.43	87
Man's haircut	$2.50	$4.25	70
Cigarettes, per pack	$.37	$.62	68
Local bus ride	$.30	$.50	67
Woman's skirt	$7.50	$12.00	60
Eggs, per dozen	$.53	$.81	53
Man's suit	$109.00	$128.60	18

Source: Reprinted from U.S. News & World Report, 1 October 1979, p. 45. Copyright 1979 U.S. News & World Report, Inc.

Note: During this same 10-year period, the consumer price index increased by 99 percent.

Businesses may benefit from inflation individually or for brief periods generally, but it is a threat to them also. Major corporations and banks, for example, most need predictability and stability. They must be able to plan ahead. If profits are to be ensured, return on investments must exceed the rate of inflation. If loans and other investments made this year are repaid ten years from now in money of substantially lower value, they will return insufficient real profits to investors — and soon there will be no willing investors. Similarly, businesses must be confident that their investments in plant and equipment today will lead to sales at prices that will mean real profits tomorrow. Thus, it is not so much the prospect of inflation itself (which can be planned for), but the prospect of uncertainty — uneven or unpredictable rates of inflation — that is most troublesome to business and financial interests.

Finally, inflation, if prolonged, is likely to have an unsettling effect on broad segments of the population. Those who have fallen behind economically, and even those who by dint of special efforts have managed to stay even, begin to feel the pressure and to express resentment of the economic and political system that has permitted such conditions. Over a prolonged period, their resentment may give rise to rejection of that system and action to fundamentally change it. One study of the period 1963–1973 found that of forty countries whose inflation reached 15 percent in that period, thirty-eight "abolished their democratic institutions in one way or another."[3]

Unemployment

As the 1980s began, the United States led the capitalist world in unemployment rates and prospects. Unemployment was back above 6 percent and was predicted to go to 8 percent or more as efforts to control inflation were felt throughout the economy. For specially affected groups it was much higher; in the case of black male teenagers, for example, it was estimated at 40 percent.

In stark terms, an unemployment rate of 8 percent means that about 8,500,000 people are out of jobs. But what *that* really means, in human and large-scale economic terms, is not so easily characterized. To begin with, the official figures drastically underestimate the actual number of jobless people. Such figures include only those people known to government agencies (unemployment compensation and employment offices) to have been searching for work in the previous four weeks. They do not include people who are "underemployed" or are working at part-time or other jobs well below their capacities because they cannot locate anything else. They do not include workers who have given up looking for jobs because they have been unsuccessful for so long or people who are doing other things (such as attending school) because they have no job expectations. The U.S. Department of Labor estimates the total number of people in these latter categories as roughly identical to the number of those officially unemployed. If one includes various other categories of people who might well seek jobs if they were available, such as older people, students, and housewives, unemployment rises to around 25 percent.[4]

Next, considering only the official figures for the moment, we must recognize that it is not the same 8,500,000 people who are unemployed all year. People find jobs and are laid off throughout the year. Thus, the actual number of persons unemployed at some point during a given year is around 25,000,000.[5] The impact of such a rate of unemployment, there-

---

[3] *New York Times*, 3 February 1980, Section 3, p. 1.
[4] Bertram Gross and Stanley Moss, "Real Unemployment Is Much Higher Than They Say," in David Mermelstein, ed., *The Economic Crisis Reader* (New York: Random House, 1975), pp. 32–37.
[5] *Boston Globe*, 10 July 1975.

fore, is spread widely throughout the population. And for every person who actually experiences some unemployment, many others live in fear of it.

Unsurprisingly, the people who feel the effects of unemployment most acutely are the marginal workers — minorities, the unskilled, many women, and others. One study has shown, for example, that whenever the national unemployment rate rises 1 percent, it really rises more than 2 percent for black heads of poverty-line families and only about 0.5 percent for white heads of families earning $25,000 or more. Nor are such losses made up for by either unemployment compensation or welfare. The same study shows that low-income families recovered only about 31 percent of lost earnings from all assistance programs combined, including food stamps.[6]

The human costs of unemployment are much more difficult to characterize. Millions of people live on the margins, often without much food or hope; millions more exist just above that level, fearing that at any time they may sink below it. Prolonged high unemployment also has important large-scale economic effects. Consumer demand decreases, which may force cuts in production and more unemployment. Stability and profitability require that unemployment be held roughly constant at a rate that provides for adequate demand and yet keeps workers available and willing to work for relatively low wages. Another effect involves the national budget. For each 1 percent increase in the unemployment rate, the federal government suffers the loss of about $1.5 billion in income tax revenue. Because it must simultaneously pay out about $3.5 billion in unemployment compensation and welfare, the net cost per 1 percent unemployment is $5 billion.[7] There remains, of course, the fact — and the fear — that continued high unemployment may lead to serious social unrest. Clearly, nothing could be more "destabilizing" than that prospect.

Governmental Fiscal Crises and Bankruptcies

The close integration of national, state, and city governments' budgets with the rest of the economy is dramatically illustrated by the spread of fiscal crisis in these bodies in the mid-1970s. Major cities, such as New York, Cleveland, and Chicago, and several smaller cities actually underwent partial reorganization at the hands of creditor banks. Some hard-pressed states, particularly in the Northeast, also took drastic action to convince creditor banks that they were determined to pay their debts and stave off bankruptcy. The reasons for the crisis at all governmental levels are similar, although the federal government has greater and different resources than the states and cities do and thus is far less vulnerable.

---

6 *Monthly Labor Review*, June 1975, p. 30.
7 *Boston Globe*, 10 July 1975.

In all cases governments' commerce-promoting and service-providing commitments have risen steadily in the past decades. As we have noted, much of this activity seems generated by the needs of the corporate-banking sector and in effect provides the infrastructure for its stability and profitability. The construction of elaborate port facilities, highways, and airports; the guarantee of housing or other loans; and tax concessions to attract business both spur business directly and underwrite the general level of prosperity. Health and educational services help maintain the kind of work force necessary to a technological society. All these services, as well as such direct income- and consumer-demand-maintaining services as unemployment compensation and welfare, are also desired by the general public or important segments of it. Neither business needs nor public desires alone account for the magnitude of government commitments. Taxes were seldom sufficient to support such enterprises, and many were financed by extensive borrowing — on the assumption that revenues would continue to rise to cover repayment costs.

By the mid-1970s, however, the condition of the economy had changed drastically, and the impact was immediately felt by governmental budgets. The federal government experienced a sharp decline in revenues and an increase of expenses such that budget deficits began to set new records each year. Lower revenues resulted from reduced individual income and declining productivity in industry; higher expenses resulted from inflation (itself capable of adding $10 billion to expenditures in a single year), new obligations for unemployment compensation and welfare, and another round of new military weapons purchases.

But the federal government can always continue to borrow or simply to make new money by means of its deficits, even though such practices generate new waves of inflation. The states and cities have no such capacity: they must find the money to pay their creditors (employees, vendors, contractors, bondholders) in hard cash. Furthermore, their hard-pressed taxpayers have much greater capacity simply to reject the new taxes that would generate new revenues. As recession shrinks their revenues and inflation raises costs, states and cities approach a point at which only new borrowing can make up the difference. But lenders increasingly doubt their continuing ability to pay and demand both higher interest rates and greater assurance of state/city determination to repay. The result is cutbacks in many public services, layoffs of employees, and the threat or reality of default and bankruptcy.

As states and cities approach this threshold, investing banks and others begin to withdraw from such investments entirely — in effect making bankruptcy, even on the part of cities that could pay their debts under conditions of ordinary investor confidence, a self-fulfilling prophecy. Creditors begin to wrangle among themselves and in court about who gets paid first from the limited available assets. Banks around the world are threatened with the loss of some of their major assets in the form of state and city bonds, and their own stability is in turn called into question.

Worst of all, life in such states and cities becomes more and more austere, and public services steadily decline. Former public employees search fruitlessly for jobs along with thousands of others. And for every one hundred public employees who are laid off, another seventy-five employees of private businesses lose their jobs as a result of reduced buying power in the area, fewer contracts with governments, and the like. Other job losses result from the generally lower level of business activity throughout the area. These are, of course, only the general trend in the fiscal crisis that stalks the 1980s.

Debt and Capital Formation

Even if the economies of the world were healthy, there would still be cause for concern over the related problems of vast outstanding debts, overextended banks, and the lack of capacity to generate the new capital necessary for future growth. As the situation stands in the early 1980s, these factors may be the most threatening of any we have surveyed.

The late 1970s represented a period of recovery from the recession of 1974–1975, the worst period for the American economy in forty years. The recovery, however, was financed largely through great expansion of debt. In 1978 *Business Week* described it as

> a new debt economy, a credit explosion so wild and so eccentric that it dwarfs even the borrowing binge of the early 1970s. . . . In the three years of the new debt economy, corporate debt has risen 36 percent to slightly more than $1 trillion, . . . while total debt in the economy has risen 42 percent to $3.9 trillion. More ominous is that consumer installment debt is up 49 percent to $300 billion.
>
> Overall, for every $3 owed in 1974, the U.S. now owes $4, a growth in debt far faster than the growth of the U.S. economy, even when inflation is counted in economic growth.[8]

Unless these massive debts continue to be paid, this country's whole economic structure is threatened. Any major default could set off a chain reaction that would endanger the entire world economy.

The squeeze is focused particularly on the banking system — the financial core of the nation and world's economies. Because the ratio of loans to deposits is high, many banks run the risk of insolvency if their borrowers fail to pay promptly. In some cases banks themselves have suffered losses from speculation in currency markets (such as the Franklin National Bank, the nation's twentieth largest, which failed in 1974). As

---

[8] *Business Week*, 16 October 1978, p. 76.

"And so, extrapolating from the best figures available, we see that current trends, unless dramatically reversed, will inevitably lead to a situation in which the sky will fall." (*Source:* Drawing by Lorenz; © 1972, The New Yorker Magazine, Inc.)

these pressures multiply, banks become increasingly cautious, making it more and more difficult for borrowers to obtain loans or credit.

The inability and/or reluctance of banks to lend to any but the most credit-worthy corporate borrowers, coupled with heavy indebtedness throughout the economy, poses problems for future growth, for growth depends upon the availability of investment capital. If profits are consumed by debt payments and savings are used to pay debts or to buy in anticipation of inflation, relatively little capital will be available to build the new plants and other facilities that are required for increased productivity and continued competitiveness in world markets.

Economic Growth

Each of the four problems just surveyed is relevant to the question of future growth of the economy. To pay the mounting totals of debt, create new jobs, make profits, and pay taxes, expansion in the total of goods and services produced must continue. This is a matter of necessity, not of choice. Once capitalist principles and today's conditions are acknowledged, growth is the only solution — despite obstacles and despite the fact that more growth will create new problems and worsen some existing ones. The same or lower total output simply will not generate enough to do all the things necessary to keep the economy going.

But inflation reduces real growth, makes planning difficult, and discourages investment. Unemployment reduces production, claims a larger share of federal tax revenues for compensation and welfare, and adds to budget deficits. State and city fiscal crises result in reduced services, additional unemployment, and increased taxes. Debt reduces new capital for investment, reduces confidence, and threatens stability. As all these conditions worsen together, they reduce or prevent economic growth. To restore profits and growth for the long term is a major task. Possible actions include development of various tax incentives for investment, drastic reductions in government services and hence taxes, and government loans or guarantees for failing corporations. All of these proposed solutions, however, favor businesses at the expense of working people and are likely to add to social unrest and opposition.

No matter how the problem was analyzed at the start of the 1980s, forecasts of the economic future were grim. Analysts of varying ideologies all saw high inflation, rising unemployment, and probable recession.[9] The President's 1980 Economic Report made the same predictions and accordingly modified targets for control of inflation and unemployment. Moreover, the effects of these various economic problems were being felt very differently by different sectors of the economy. The automobile industry was undergoing very hard times, with Chrysler requiring special federal assistance to survive. But the oil industry was simultaneously reporting record earnings and profits, with Exxon setting a record profit in 1979 at $4.26 billion.

None of this analysis is intended to suggest that capitalism is necessarily about to collapse. We do think that these problems add up to unprecedented difficulties constituting a crisis period. What is implied for politics is a period of *transformation*, one in which governments will take on new roles with respect to economic activity and face major problems in coping with the social unrest likely to accompany economic pressures and dislocations.

Policies for "Managing" the Economy

In the confident days of the late 1950s and 1960s, economists and policymakers believed that government could indeed "manage" the economy to produce substantial growth, low inflation, and general prosperity. Most of this confidence was lost amid the intractable problems of the 1970s, however, and the issue became whether or not a new depression could be avoided. The policy tools available seemed not only modest in the context of the problems involved, but also based on economic theories that were

---

[9] *New York Times Magazine*, 30 December 1979, p. 12 (a survey of twenty leading economists of various political viewpoints).

no longer relevant to conditions. Two major questions arose: Would the known tools *work*, assuming that they were applied and retained long enough? Who would have to bear the burden of reducing inflation and restoring profitability, everybody equally or primarily lower-middle and working-class people? With these questions in mind, let us look at some of the traditional policy tools.

Monetary Policies

These are basically the kinds of policies the Federal Reserve System applies to the money supply as well as the Treasury's power to print more or less new money than the total amount that has worn out in a given period. One advantage of this type of remedy is that it seems to be impersonal. That is, conscious choices about who is to suffer from efforts to prevent inflation do not appear to be being made. By using only contraction or expansion of the monetary supply as a tool, government in effect lets the workings of the private economy determine who shall bear the inevitable burdens that result from slackening of demand and reduced investment. Normally, of course, this approach translates into unemployment for millions of people at the lowest levels. Another apparent advantage is the limitation on governmental intrusion into the workings of the economy: monetary policies are relatively slight and indirect thrusts and are felt by various sectors of the economy only after being transmitted by the standard sources of guidance — the supply of and demand for money. But perhaps for these reasons, monetarists concede that the effects of such policies are not immediate. Under ideal conditions they take from six to nine months to have measurable consequences and sometimes longer before their effects are significant. And in an economic situation in which rapid expansion of debt in effect creates new money, they may not work at all.

Fiscal Policies

These have somewhat more direct and immediate effects on the economy. The various forms of fiscal policy all have to do with the way the government manages its own finances — that is, how much money it raises in taxes, how much it spends, and for what. The fiscal-policy approach to stabilization and growth was originated by the English economist John Maynard Keynes. Writing in the 1930s, Keynes argued that it is possible for a capitalist economy to become stabilized at low or depression levels of productivity and employment and that the key to both levels and fluctuations lies in the amount of total consumer demand being generated in the economy. Because the budgets of modern governments are primary sources of impact on the private economy, Keynes urged the conscious use of government expenditure-revenue policies to promote or decrease demand and thereby spur or retard the economy.

Such policies could take the form of large budgetary deficits or surpluses, tax reductions or increases, expenditures for new projects such as public works, or cancellation of such projects already under way. The first item in each of these pairs would stimulate demand; the second would contract it. To spur the economy, government should, according to Keynes, cut consumers' taxes, run a budget deficit, and invest heavily in public-works projects. When these ideas were first introduced, resistance to the unorthodoxy of a deliberately unbalanced government budget and to purposeful government intervention in the private economy ran high. But avoidance of a depression since 1946, despite anti-Keynesian rhetoric and practices, has gradually made such policies accepted as part of the role of government. Who gains and who loses from fiscal policy actions depends on the specific actions taken (whose taxes are cut or raised, by what relative amounts, and so on). The apparent impossibility of generating a budget surplus led to widespread rejection of Keynesianism as a means of controlling inflation. One of the reasons why budget surpluses are so difficult to obtain is that many programs constitute binding obligations on the government that must continue to be funded, plus the new commitment to several years of increased military spending.

Income Policies

These represent the third more or less conventional approach, reserved as yet for what are perceived as "emergency" conditions. They assume that circumstances (inflation, profit levels, and the like) require direct government controls over wages and prices to produce the desired economic conditions quickly and effectively. This means that the government must make not only an annual estimate of the direction in which the economy should be guided, as under the Keynesian system, but also a conscious choice of the segments of the economy that should gain or lose proportionally in profits or income during the year. Controls are then applied in such a way as to accomplish the wage and/or price increases or decreases that will bring this about. Clearly, this type of policy involves direct and extensive government management of the economy. Though practiced in wartime, it was unprecedented in the peacetime United States before 1971. Moreover, it is widely believed by economists that such controls "don't work." Some argue that wages are held down effectively by employers' refusals to pay more, but that prices are not subject to such restraints. Instead, price rises, if and when challenged by government authorities, can often be justified by a variety of bookkeeping methods purporting to show higher production costs. Others argue that whenever controls are lifted, severe dislocations occur as prices and wages rapidly seek their "natural" levels. Almost all agree that the problem of checking and policing prices and wages is an impossible one to solve.

What is distinctive about each of these types of economy-managing policies? We have seen that they reflect increasing degrees of government "intervention" in the economy. They are also distinguishable by the assumptions on which they are based and by the degree of choice on the part of government as to who will gain and who will lose from their effects. The first two — monetary and fiscal policies — assume the same "package" of economic problems. For example, both see inflation, low unemployment, and active growth as comprising one set of consistent symptoms: of an active, booming economy in which the problem is to dampen expansion so that inflation does not get out of hand. Both see depression or recession, high unemployment, and low growth as typical of the opposite or stagnating end of the business cycle. The problem in such a situation is to get the economy growing again. Each type of policy has a remedy for each package of characteristics or problems, and the remedies differ chiefly in the aggressiveness with which they use government as an instrument for that purpose. Fiscal policies are the more aggressive, but both make major use of the workings of the private economy (properly stimulated by government) for the purpose of bringing about the desired result.

The 1970s, however, did not conform to the assumptions of monetary and fiscal theory. Inflation was associated with high unemployment and low growth, an unprecedented combination. That it was not a demand-pull inflation was particularly serious because the remedies prescribed by each theory (intended to reduce or stimulate demand) were rendered counterproductive or contradictory. A remedy designed to combat inflation would do so by promoting unemployment and further impeding growth. And a remedy designed to counter unemployment and spur growth would do so only by promoting inflation. Any action by policymakers in accordance with either theory would only make part of the existing problem worse.

An incomes policy, of course, is not necessarily bound to any particular assumptions about the economy. It simply asserts governmental control over the economy. It is a much more direct and complete control system, in which the government's degree of choice about who wins and who loses is much greater. Those who believe, for whatever reason, that a minimum of government control over the economy is desirable tend to be opposed to an incomes policy. But so do those who suspect that if it is applied at all, it will be applied in the interests of the corporate-banking sector. In 1971–1972, under the Nixon administration's incomes policy, corporate profits surged to a record annual rate.

Other Policies

Nothing *requires* the national government to do anything to remedy the difficulties of the economy. In our view, government is not an independent choice-making vehicle, but rather the agent of those who can in any given instance mobilize enough influence to bring about action. And experience tends to show that the corporate-banking sector enjoys the most such influence. A judgment that prolonged recession is relatively desirable could thus make government inaction a deliberate economic policy, involving just as much choice as any of the other, more aggressive policies. The losers in such a case would probably be workers forced to undergo extended unemployment and reduced real wages and the smaller businesses of the competitive sector unable to maintain their prices or borrow money.

At the heart of this issue is the question of a "trade-off" between inflation and unemployment. Most economists believe that inflation can be controlled by permitting or forcing unemployment. If there is enough unemployment for a long enough time, they say, prices will simply have to stop rising and will level off or even drop. But disagreement is bitter over whether inflation *should* be stopped by letting workers suffer. Conservative economists and businesspeople tend to believe that high unemployment is a price that must, when necessary, be paid. Liberal and radical economists, on the other hand, believe that it would be better to live with a certain amount of inflation.

The argument centers on the meaning of the official term *full employment*. Originally, the term referred to workers' jobs and was defined as a proportion of unemployed (say, 3 percent) accounted for by workers normally changing jobs or being temporarily displaced by the advent of new technologies. Recently, however, unemployment rates of 4 and then 5 percent have been characterized as full employment, as the definition's focus shifted from workers' jobs to the level of unemployment that would maintain price stability and hold inflation down. Needless to say, this definition is a continuing subject of controversy.

Radical economists tend to see recessions as periodically necessary and often encouraged by government inaction or prorecession policies. Periodic recessions are not only inevitable, in their eyes, but also functional for a capitalist economy in that they discipline labor by halting claims for higher wages — thereby reducing labor's share and increasing the corporate share of total output. Because it is always easy for government to do nothing, its actual cooperation in such policies is not always recognized as such.

Conservative ideology regards government inaction as the only appropriate "remedy" for economic problems. Those who believe in a laissez-faire, or "hands-off," role for government, consistent with traditional assumptions about the separation of the economy and the government, insist that the only correct policy is for government to watch the economy work out its own problems. The resulting, perhaps longer, recession may work hardships on workers and competitive-sector businesses, but that outcome is taken as necessary to allow the economy to resume its supposedly self-regulating operation. It is also possible, of course, that government inaction — for whatever reason — may lead to a semipermanent recession or even a collapse of the sort experienced in the Great Depression of the 1930s.

None of these "remedies" addresses the problems of restoring investment and expanding productivity in a direct way. Some economists and policymakers believe that a coherent national approach involving all of these plus taxing and other policies will be necessary to cope with today's problems. A start toward the goal of national economic planning has been made, with the support of liberals and many of the largest corporations and banks, in the form of the Humphrey-Hawkins Act of 1978 (the Balanced National Growth Act). Although currently without enforcement powers or real mandates, the act takes a step in the direction of setting specific goals and coordinating government policies to achieve them. To plan adequately, a great deal of information would have to be collected from businesses, and recommendations would have to be made for harmonizing government taxation, expenditures, and other activities with those intentions. To administer such a plan would require extensive governmental capacity to control the allocation of resources, the availability of labor, and perhaps the kinds of products manufactured, as well as the more familiar wage and price controls.

Predictably, there is considerable opposition to this kind of national economic planning. Some see it as undesirable government intervention into what should be private economic decisionmaking — or, in other words, as the final disappearance of a free-market, private-enterprise system. Others see it as the final stage in the takeover of the state by the corporate-banking sector, or a kind of economic fascism. This unfamiliar but increasingly visible alliance of right and left may be able to prevent more such planning and control. But the advocates of national economic planning argue that there is really no alternative, that the complexity of the economy and the depth of its problems require comprehensive management in this fashion. And among its advocates are the very corporations, banks, and liberal politicians whose alliance has been the source of most government policy for the post–World War II years.

The issues we have posed are whether — and if so, how — the nation can avoid a depression comparable to that of the 1930s and which sectors of the economy will pay the price of such efforts. Policy choices in the next several years will play an important (though perhaps not a controlling) part in determining the outcome. And those choices in turn depend on questions of ideology, power, and preference.

Energy: A Case Study

The policy problem of energy may be stated simply: to ensure an adequate supply at reasonable prices. But our everyday experience teaches us that achieving these goals is far from a simple task. In this case study we approach the problem of energy in the same manner as we analyze other policy areas: first we identify the elements of the problem, then describe national government policies, and finally assess their consequences. Although we consider some energy alternatives, we focus primarily on oil because oil and its control are central to the energy problem and fully representative of its complexity.

The Nature of the U.S. Energy Problem

The essence of the U.S. energy problem lies in inefficient use of energy, fostered and encouraged over decades by relatively inexpensive and available energy and the determined sales efforts of utilities, manufacturers, and energy suppliers. The demand for energy rose steadily as more people used less efficient private automobiles to travel longer distances and bought more home appliances and air conditioners. Industry led the way with the continuous development of energy-using labor supplements. Some energy sources now appear so limited that their exhaustion can be predicted, others are increasingly high priced, and still others seem to pose serious safety and other risks. Furthermore, the flow of energy from foreign sources may be interrupted during international crises. Thus, at the outset of the 1980s, an adequate supply of energy at reasonable prices had not been ensured or achieved.

Several dimensions of the energy problem are revealed in Table 4.2. The sharply rising demand for energy can be seen in the near doubling of the total supply between 1960 and 1978. Proportionally, the increase in demand is larger for residential and commercial uses than for transportation or industrial use. But transportation stands out as the most profligate usage. Nearly one-quarter of all energy consumed is in the form of gasoline, usually powering low-mileage cars with few occupants.

Oil supplies about half of all U.S. energy usage, followed by natural gas. Coal, the most plentiful U.S. resource, supplies only about 20 percent of current needs. Production of coal from underground mines actually declined as energy usage mounted from 1960 to 1978 and companies turned to the more profitable strip mines to expand total production. Coal is also the only U.S. energy source that is exported. Nuclear reactors provide only a small share of total energy requirements, although they account for about 13 percent of the fuels used to produce electricity. The growing use of electricity in homes, stores, and industry has been one of the major reasons for the steepness of the U.S. demand curve. In addition, the need for

Table 4.2

U.S. Energy Usage, 1960–1978

	1960	1970	1978
Total supply[a]	44.08	66.82	78.01
Usage by purpose:[a]			
Transportation	11.23	16.76	20.59
Residential and commercial	14.37	23.77	29.30
Industrial	18.48	26.29	28.13
Usage by source:[a]			
Oil	20.39	30.38	38.04
Natural gas	12.82	22.52	20.24
Coal	11.12	15.05	15.11
Nuclear	0.01	0.24	2.98
Hydro, other	1.67	2.72	3.47
Population[b]	180.00	203.80	218.10
Number of cars	61.70	89.20	117.10
Energy consumption per $ of GNP[c]	59.80	62.10	56.30
GNP[d]	737.00	1,075.00	1,386.00

Source: Reprinted with permission from *National Journal*, 21 July 1979, p. 1200.

[a] Usage expressed in "quads" (quadrillions of British thermal units, BTU).
[b] Figures in millions.
[c] BTU per (constant) 1972 dollar of GNP.
[d] In constant 1972 dollars.

electricity has provided a steady market for coal as well as the only market for hydro and nuclear power. Despite unavoidable inefficiencies in producing electricity, about 30 percent of U.S. fuel consumption is committed to it.

The focus on oil comes about because of its versatility of use as well as its role in transportation. Although almost half of all oil is used in automobiles and trucks, substantial shares go to heat homes, stores, and businesses, and some is used for the production of electricity. The demand for oil doubled between 1960 and 1978, as Table 4.3 shows. But U.S. production did not keep pace. Instead, the more profitable imported oil began to account for larger and larger proportions of U.S. total usage. Imports quadrupled between 1960 and 1978, and their share of total usage more than doubled, from less than 20 percent to more than 40 percent. American domestic production peaked in the early 1970s and actually declined for several years. By the late 1970s, it was rising again as the Alaskan fields began to produce and price controls were lifted. But U.S. dependence on foreign sources for 40 percent of vital oil supplies was the chief concern of most policymakers in the 1980s.

Other energy sources besides oil contributed to the character of the energy crisis of the 1970s and early 1980s. Nuclear power was increasingly

Table 4.3
Oil Consumption and Sources (millions of barrels per day)

(a) Consumption Patterns, 1960–1978

Year	Consumption	U.S. Production	Imports	Imports as % of Consumption
1960	9.7	8.0	1.8	19
1964	10.8	8.8	2.3	21
1968	13.0	10.6	2.8	22
1970	14.4	11.3	3.4	24
1972	16.0	11.2	4.7	29
1974	16.2	10.5	6.1	38
1976	17.0	9.7	7.3	43
1978	18.7	10.8	7.9	42

(b) Sources of Imports, 1979

Country	Millions of Barrels per Day	Country Share as % of Total
Saudi Arabia	1,309,200	16.7
Nigeria	930,000	11.9
Libya	632,500	8.1
Venezuela	597,700	7.6
Algeria	591,400	7.6
Virgin Islands	451,200	5.8
Canada	428,000	5.5
Iran	387,500	5.0
Mexico	355,900	4.5
Indonesia	347,200	4.4
United Arab Emirates	244,300	3.1
Netherlands Antilles	203,900	2.6
Trinidad and Tobago	169,700	2.2
23 other nations	1,177,500	15.0

Sources: (a) Robert Stobaugh and Daniel Yergin, eds., *Energy Future: Report of the Energy Project at the Harvard Business School* (New York: Random House, 1979). The 1978 figures are from *National Journal*, 21 July 1979, p. 1200; (b) Reprinted from *U.S. News & World Report*, 28 November 1979, p. 34. Copyright 1979 U.S. News & World Report, Inc.

challenged as unsafe, and the future of that source was called into question by its own rising costs and the Three Mile Island near tragedy of 1979. Although the Carter administration insisted on projecting a larger role for nuclear generation of electricity in the coming years, the behavior of potential users reflected general public concern for safety. Table 4.4 compares

Table 4.4

The Market for Nuclear Reactors

	1970	1971	1972	1973	1974	1975	1976	1977	1978	1979
Orders	14	21	38	38	34	4	3	4	2	0
Cancellations	0	0	6	0	9	10	5	10	11	11

Source: *New York Times*, 16 March 1980, p. E11. © 1972/79/80 by The New York Times Company. Reprinted by permission.

orders for nuclear reactors by utilities in the United States with cancellations for the period 1970–1979. Moreover, the actual share of steadily rising electricity production borne by nuclear power dropped in 1979, partly because of Three Mile Island's shutdown and partly because of repairs on other reactors. But the long-term prospect no longer looked promising for new reactors in the United States. While antinuclear groups might feel satisfaction, those concerned with future electrical power needs did not share it.

Nor is coal without difficulties as a partial solution for the energy crisis. It is plentiful but hard to remove from antiquated underground mines without serious danger to the miners involved. It is harder still to transport without building major new systems. And strip-mining, while profitable, creates environmental and ecological problems. Significantly, increased use of coal will apparently depend on requirements and/or assistance for large users such as utilities to convert from oil to coal.

The overall relationship between American energy sources and uses is summarized in Figure 4.2. Each source is traced to its ultimate usage, and the patterns revealed sketch the outlines of the American economic success story as well as its current vulnerability. As oil prices rise sharply, for example, every essential activity is affected, and inflationary pressures are felt directly and indirectly by everybody. Thus, there is both celebration and anxiety in the fact that the United States, with 6 percent of the world's population, consumes 30 percent of the world's energy annually. American agricultural production, using only 3 percent of all U.S. energy, provides not only the basic food for the country, but also about 20 percent of the total value of U.S. exports. But by the time food processing, distribution, and cooking are added, the food cycle actually uses about 17 percent of all U.S. energy.

The evidence is clear that greater efficiencies in energy usage and significant conservation began to occur in 1978 and 1979. Table 4.2 shows that although U.S. gross national product rose substantially (as did population), energy usage per dollar of GNP actually declined almost 10 percent since 1970. Predictions about usage and depletion, and the related problem of economic growth, began to be revised in the light of changed behavior by both businesses and consumers. In the five years between 1968 and

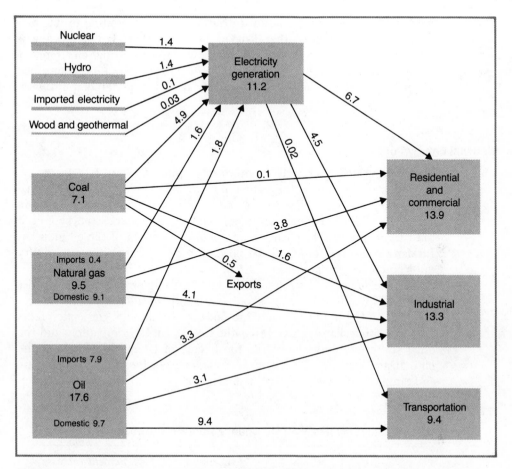

Figure 4.2 U.S. energy — sources and uses, 1979 (units are millions of barrels of oil per day or their equivalent). (*Source:* Data from U.S. Department of Energy, *Monthly Energy Review.*)

1973, energy consumption rose 22 percent and the GNP only 17 percent. But in the five years between 1973 and 1978, energy consumption rose only 5 percent and the GNP 12 percent. Clearly, the impact of higher prices was reshaping lives.[10]

The effects of the "energy crisis" are not felt equally by all, of course. Increased energy costs take from four to six times as large a bite out of the incomes of poor people as they do from higher-income people. Energy cost increases, including only home uses and gasoline, were estimated to result by 1985 in major reductions in the standards of living of all but the highest-income strata of the American population. This estimate does not

---

[10] *New York Times*, 20 January 1980, p. E20.

include the time-consuming and frustrating periods of waiting in line during gasoline "shortages" that may or may not be real, but are always followed by substantial price increases and record-setting oil company profits. Percent changes in profits for 1979 for the leading oil companies, in their order of sales among *all* American nonfinancial corporations, were as shown in Table 4.5.

National Energy Policy

Despite repeated rhetorical commitments from 1973 on to "energy independence" programs, the actual policy achievements of the national government through 1979 were modest. While responsibility may lie in part with a timid, conflict-ridden, or inept government, some part of it must be credited to the character and political strength of the oil industry. Insofar as organized international power can be measured, the oil industry must be ranked competitively with all but the largest nation-states.

To begin with, the sales of the eighteen largest U.S. oil companies totaled $275 billion in 1978, about one-eighth of all goods and services produced.[11] Oil profits amounted to one-tenth of all U.S. corporate profits and were rising sharply. Exxon was the world's largest corporation, and the other six majors were among the top twenty of the world. In short, the oil industry was, and still is, a major component of the American economy and cannot be seriously affected without shaking the whole economic order.

Table 4.5
Oil Companies' Profits, Percent Change from 1978 to 1979

	Earnings in Millions of Dollars	*Percent Increase over 1978*
Exxon (1)	4,295	+ 56
Mobil (3)	2,010	+ 78
Texaco (6)	1,759	+106
SoCal (7)	1,785	+ 64
Gulf (8)	1,322	+ 68
Standard (Ind.) (12)	1,507	+ 40
Atlantic-Richfield (15)	1,166	+ 45
Shell (16)	1,126	+ 38
Conoco (18)	815	+ 81
Sun (25)	700	+ 69

Source: New York Times, 19 March 1980. © 1980 by The New York Times Company. Reprinted by permission.

---

[11] Data in this and the following paragraph are drawn from *U.S. News & World Report,* 5 November 1979, pp. 26–27.

The major oil companies have diversified significantly in the last several years. They have moved into other energy industries and into a wide range of other fields as well. For example, oil companies own about half of all coal reserves and control most of the major coal-producing companies; coal output by oil company firms is expected to reach 50 percent by 1985. Synthetic fuels (oil or gas equivalents made from coal, or shale oil) are also dominated by oil companies. They own 44 percent of U.S. uranium reserves and control considerably more; in addition, three of the top five uranium producers are oil companies. Finally, the oil companies control key stages of the solar energy-producing process.

One of the reasons for diversification outside the energy field is the oil companies' need to make use of available cash. Another reason is a sense of the need for expansion to render companies stable over the long term. These activities are summarized in Table 4.6.

Table 4.6

Branching Out — the Oil Empires (ten oil firms and how they're diversified)

Exxon Corporation
Coal—Carter Mining and Monterey Coal
Uranium, copper, zinc—Exxon Minerals
Solar energy—Solar Power, Daystar
Electric motors—Reliance Electric
Information systems—Vydec, Qwip Systems
Graphic fibers—Graftex
Real estate—Friendswood Development

Mobil Corporation
Coal—Mount Olive & Staunton Coal
Retailing—Montgomery Ward
Packaging—Container Corporation of America
Solar energy—Mobil Tyco
Real estate—Reston Development
Printing—W. F. Hall

Texaco, Inc.
Coal, uranium, real estate—Texaco Ventures

Standard Oil of California
Coal, uranium, geothermal—Chevron Resources
Minerals—American Gilsonite (50 percent interest)
Coal—AMAX (20 percent)
Synthetic fibers—Vectra

Gulf Oil Corporation
Coal—Pittsburg & Midway Coal Mining
Uranium, chemicals—Harshaw Chemical; Millmaster Onyx

Shipping—American Heavy Lift Shipping (75 percent)
Hardware—Hutchinson-Hayes International

Standard Oil (Indiana)
Copper—Cyprus Mines
Solar energy—Solarex (20 percent)
Computer circuits—Analog Devices (15 percent)

Atlantic Richfield
Coal, copper, aluminum—Anaconda
Solar energy—Northrup and ARCO Solar
Publishing—The Observer (Britain)

Shell Oil Company
Coal—Seaway Coal

Conoco, Inc.
Coal—Consolidation Coal

Sun Company
Coal—Elk River Resources
Health care—Becton, Dickinson (34 percent)
Shipbuilding—Sun Shipbuilding & Dry Dock
Real estate—Radnor
Trucking—St. Johnsbury Trucking; Milne Truck Lines
Food stores—Stop-N-Go and Mr. Zip
Electronics—Audio Magnetics
Data processing—Applied Financial Systems

Source: Reprinted from *U.S. News & World Report,* 5 November 1979, p. 27. Copyright 1979 U.S. News & World Report, Inc.

The oil industry does not rely on its size and significance to the economy for defense of its interests. A vast lobbying system is deployed in Washington, D.C., with close grass-roots alliances in the home districts of congressional representatives. The American Petroleum Institute alone has a $30 million budget and 500 employees and can put many more lobbyists into the field when conditions warrant. About $75 million per year is invested in oil's lobbying effort.[12] Thirty-seven senators (including nine members of the key Finance Committee) and sixty-one representatives own oil and gas company stock. Many more receive campaign contributions, totaling $3.5 million in 1978. The same nine members of the Senate Finance Committee, for example, received more than half a million dollars in contributions from oil companies in 1974–1976. The committee chairman, Senator Russell Long of Louisiana, personally owned more than $1 million in oil company stocks. In 1979, as pressure to do something about oil company profits and energy problems seemed to be rising, the oil industry had no fewer than 133 political action committees operating to influence (and make campaign contributions to) senators and representatives. In 1974 the total number of committees was exactly twelve.[13]

In the face of these legally mandated disclosures of close linkages between the oil industry and Congress, it is tempting to see the President as the representative of consumers, taking a strong stand against the self-serving efforts of big oil. But this suggestion is probably both unfair to the Congress and naive. Executive-branch policies have generally followed the interests of the oil companies, not just in the 1979 deregulation of domestic oil prices. The Interior, Commerce, Defense, Treasury, and State departments have always been sympathetic to oil industry needs, in part because of effective lobbying, but also because incumbent officials are often "on-leave" oil industry executives.

This is the context in which national energy policy is made — some of it clearly contrary to oil industry preferences and all of it in a complex and time-consuming manner. In the immediate postembargo months of 1973, President Nixon sought legislation to speed up the Alaska pipeline, allocate fuels, invest in energy research, and decontrol prices on new natural gas. The first two were enacted, but not the latter. In 1974 Nixon added requests for reorganization of federal energy bureaus, and Congress complied. But urban Democrats blocked decontrol of gas prices, and in 1975, when a bill to set strip-mining controls was passed, President Ford vetoed it.

In 1975 Ford sent Congress a thirteen-part Energy Independence Act. Emergency authorizations for fuel allocations, production and economy

---

[12] Data in this paragraph are drawn from a study by *U.S. News & World Report*, 7 May 1979, pp. 59–60.

[13] For a full discussion, see *Congressional Quarterly Weekly Report*, 3 November 1979, p. 2455 ff.

standards, and conversions from oil and gas to coal were enacted to increase the President's standby powers. But Ford's requests for natural gas deregulation, new energy taxes, and support for synthetic fuels were rejected. Instead, Congress passed a bill setting standards for strip-mining, which Ford again vetoed. He resubmitted some of the same proposals in 1976, but no significant actions were taken by Congress that year except authorization to produce oil from federal lands formerly held in reserve for the navy.

Early in his presidency, Jimmy Carter proposed a major new energy program. In a speech to the nation on April 18, 1977, he declared, "Our decision about energy will test the character of the American people and the ability of the President and Congress to govern this nation. This difficult effort will be the moral equivalent of war." (Critics promptly seized upon the acronym for the last four words and dubbed the program MEOW.) The program included extension of natural gas controls with a higher price ceiling, higher gasoline taxes and crude oil taxes, a "gas guzzler" tax on low-mileage cars, mandatory efficiency standards for home appliances, and power for the President to force conversion from oil and gas to coal use. Nothing was enacted from this list in 1977, although the Congress did create the new Department of Energy that Carter had requested and enacted a comprehensive Clean Air Act that tightened standards on cars while postponing antipollution deadlines for cities and businesses.

Not until the final day of the 1978 session was action taken on the administration's 1977 proposals. Then Congress established a schedule for price increases and eventual decontrol of natural gas and allowed tax credits for energy-saving devices and solar energy equipment. Carter's proposed early deadlines for conversion to coal were lengthened to set 1990 as the date for compliance. States and utilities were required to consider and/or to provide information about energy-saving measures rather than to implement them. Carter's proposed taxes on industrial use of oil, on domestic oil, and on gasoline were all rejected. Nothing in the package substantially changed the basic stance of national policy or intruded upon consumption patterns.

In 1979, with dependence on foreign oil still high and a new "shortage" of gasoline frustrating motorists, President Carter took some extraordinary steps. After retiring to Camp David for ten days to consult with advisers and citizens, he emerged to announce, in a speech on July 15, a major new energy program. He linked the failure to cope with the energy crisis with a moral and spiritual crisis in the nation, saying,

It's clear that the true problems of our nation are much deeper — deeper than gasoline lines or energy shortages. Deeper, even, than inflation or recession. . . .
So I want to speak to you tonight about a subject even more serious

than energy or inflation. I want to talk to you right now about a fundamental threat to American democracy. . . .

The threat is nearly invisible in ordinary ways. It is a crisis of confidence. It is a crisis that strikes at the very heart and soul and spirit of
our national will.

We can see this crisis in the growing doubt about the meaning of our
own lives and in the loss of a unity of purpose for our nation.

The erosion of our confidence in the future is threatening to destroy
the social and the political fabric of America. . . .

Energy will be the immediate test of our ability to unite this nation.

And it can also be the standard around which we rally. On the battlefield of energy we can win for our nation a new confidence, and we can
seize control again of our common destiny. . . .

The energy crisis is real. It is worldwide. It is a clear and present
danger to our nation. These are the facts and we simply must face them.
What I have to say to you now about energy is simply and vitally important.

The proposals that were central to the new program included a "windfall tax" on oil company profits from newly decontrolled domestic oil
production. Because lifting price controls meant that the oil companies
would derive almost twice the revenue per barrel of domestic oil, with no
change in production costs, their new profits were viewed as a "windfall"
to be shared. Some of the proceeds of this tax were to be used to promote
conservation by utilities and business and to help poor people pay the
increased energy costs. The major use of windfall tax revenues, however,
was to fund a new Energy Security Corporation that would invest heavily
in the development of synthetic fuels, particularly liquefied and gasified
coal, oil shale, and ways of removing natural gas in "unconventional"
locations. Some moneys were to be allocated to mass transit and solar
energy development. An Energy Mobilization Board was also proposed,
with power to override certain federal, state, and local laws and eliminate
delays in constructing new energy projects.

As might be expected, these proposals met heavy opposition in the
Congress. The oil industry was particularly opposed to the size of the
windfall profits tax, and the Senate Finance Committee set to work to
weaken its initial provisions. With oil prices rising steadily, no one could
estimate the size of profits or tax revenues that would be at stake. The
figures that Congress did work with were slightly more than $1,000 billion
in extra new income from decontrolled domestic production for the oil
companies in the decade of the 1980s, and the tax was set to produce $227
billion for the government. Aid to the poor was to take 25 percent of this
sum, energy development and mass transit were to get 15 percent, and 60
percent was reserved for business and personal income tax reductions.
Synthetic fuel development was enacted at much more modest levels and
without the independent new corporation proposed.

The Consequences of National Energy Policies

It seems fair to say that in the 1970s the national government accomplished nothing that contributed significantly to easing the energy crisis. The major favorable development — a substantial slackening of demand and a slowing of imports — occurred in 1979 and resulted from sharply rising prices, a kind of rationing by price, for which the government can claim credit only through its inaction. And the conservation achieved was disproportionately through reductions in energy use by those least able to pay. Indeed, perhaps the most significant consequence of all was the impact of higher energy prices on the standards of living and lifestyles of all Americans below the most affluent levels.

By government "policy," we mean both action and conscious choices not to act over a period of time; the latter must be understood in practical terms as a form of policy. In the case of energy policy, such patterns of inaction in the face of repeated proposals and opportunities are clear. Thus, we may add to the results of U.S. government policy at least some proportion of the record earnings and profits of the major oil companies, some share of the inflationary pressure that threatened the economy in the 1980s, and some part of the responsibility for U.S. dependence on imported oil and resulting imperatives for U.S. foreign policy.

The oil companies' record earnings and profits from decontrolled domestic production made possible, in turn, the windfall tax — the largest tax ever to be applied to a single industry. These revenues were potentially the source of many new energy-related initiatives on the part of the government. The oil companies' earnings and profit levels were also a tribute to their strategic role in the economy and their political power.

The inflationary surge of the 1970s was not even principally fueled by oil price rises. All energy increases, including indirect ones such as energy-cost-increased prices of manufactured products, totaled less than one-third of the American inflationary pressures of the late 1970s. But it was convenient to blame OPEC for whatever was happening in the United States, and public officials from the President on down were eager to do so.

The consequences of the American government's acquiescence in the major oil companies' new partnership with the OPEC countries were threefold: (1) steadily increasing prices for consumers, (2) new commitments to defend militarily (against a variety of possible enemies, including nationalist movements) American oil interests in the Persian Gulf area, and (3) threats to the international monetary system (and the American dollar) described at the close of the previous chapter.

It was difficult in the early 1980s to ascribe benign intent or consequences to American energy policy. Instead, both acts and omissions appeared to be reflective first of oil company power and influence and second of a general commitment to assuaging the loudest complaints through rhetorical and symbolic gratification.

NATIONAL SECURITY: ISSUES, POLICIES, AND CONSEQUENCES

5

As the previous chapters have suggested, national security is a complex concept with several dimensions. It is not just a calculus of military capabilities compared with those of potential enemies. It is made up also of economic needs (raw materials, energy, investment and sales opportunities, and so on), ideological and psychological pressures (anticommunism, human rights, hopes and fears about ourselves and our government), and our evolving historical context (other countries and world problems as they have developed). People disagree sharply about what the national security interests of the United States are and what they require in the way of government policy. But a large number of major government policies are enacted to serve our "national security," with literally life-and-death consequences for millions of ordinary citizens.

In this chapter we explore what the concept of "national security" has meant in the United States since World War II and what conflicts exist over its proper meaning for public policy today. Then we take up the major issues and policies involved in both the *strategic* and *substrategic* categories of government actions to serve our national security interests. By *strategic*, we mean the ultimate problem of winning (or preventing) all-out war with the Soviet Union. Reduced to its essence, this category primarily involves military power and its use, but a number of other factors are also necessarily involved. By *substrategic*, we mean all the other ways of implementing national security interests, in whatever arena. Clearly, the two categories are connected in that actions in the latter may escalate to the threat or fact of nuclear war. But the understanding of national security has many dimensions, and the character and range of policies is much more diverse in the second category, such that it makes analytic sense to differentiate them. Finally, at the end of the chapter, we assess some of the consequences and implications of these policies for ordinary citizens in the United States.

National Security: Continuity and Change in a Complex Concept

National security involves a *relationship* with forces outside the country; that relationship maximizes, or makes very high, the probability that (1) the integrity and way of life (political and economic) of the country will be preserved, and (2) the economic and ideological needs and cultural values of the country will be realized. Forces outside the country include the power and policies of other countries and world conditions, problems, and events. These forces are continually changing, so that national security is an ongoing problem involving uncertainty and controversy. Moreover, national security can never be *ensured*; the best one can hope for is its probability to be *very high*, or *maximized*. But again, uncertainty and disagreement inevitably surround how far it is possible or desirable to raise or maximize such probabilities and to what level, with what sacrifices of other goals, and so on.

One relatively simple way to seek national security is to try to develop and deploy massive military power. If a country has such a preponderance of power, it may be able to work its will in the world and to feel secure. With such military power in reserve, it may prefer to have other countries act in its behalf and/or to manipulate economic and other incentives in such a way as to gain its ends without actually using its military forces. Where there is a rough parity of military power, however, a variety of mutual interests and compromises must be relied upon to create a context in which stability and national goals are equally realizable.

One argument in the United States today is over the issue of whether American military *supremacy* can be ensured or restored, in the context of other circumstances, values, and goals, or whether Soviet power and other world conditions dictate a new definition of national security that emphasizes military *sufficiency*. The latter position means the capacity to inflict upon the Soviet Union an unacceptable level of destruction even if it should start a war, plus the ability to promote a more limited version of U.S. interests elsewhere by other means. People differ in their perceptions of the USSR's power and intentions, of the goals of the rest of the world's governments and peoples, of what the United States *can* do, and of what they think it *should* do, in furtherance of "national security." Other countries are also understandably confused as to what Americans *think* is, and what *actually* is, vital to American security interests and therefore worth the risk of nuclear war. Let us try to understand the current controversy in the United States from a historical perspective.

At the close of World War II, the conventional wisdom was that German aggression occurred because of the military weakness of potential opponents. Military preparedness, it was therefore assumed, would be the key to peace and stability in an uncertain and amoral world. It was only a short step to the conclusion that the national security of the United States required military supremacy over the obvious enemy, the Soviet Union. Because the United States held exclusive nuclear warfare capability for several years, military supremacy was established without much effort. Under this umbrella, the United States could reconstruct the world pretty much as it desired. Not surprisingly, the United States emerged as the dominant economic and political force of the world in the 1950s and early 1960s.

But military supremacy is an elusive and frustrating goal. For several reasons it can never be finally ensured. And, paradoxically, the more it is sought, the more it may recede. At any moment, a potential enemy may reach a scientific breakthrough that enables it to achieve military supremacy through technology. Or such a nation may drastically alter the strategic situation through a sudden diplomatic success, subversion, or other means. The more a nation seeks assurance of security by military means, the more it must commit its resources to weapons, research and development, procurement of multiple attack and defense systems, alliances with the governments of other nations, economic and military support for such governments if necessary, and anticipatory intelligence and subversion activities throughout the world. Every such act, of course, provokes the potential enemy to undertake or expand similar activities, and these in turn reduce the first nation's security and require countering moves. But nearly three decades of cold war marked by the continuing threat of nuclear annihilation, combined with the fear of communism, made such commitments almost unquestioned among American policymakers.

The achievement of security through such means thus presents inevitable and apparently unending difficulties. On the one hand, it may be costly to the point of financial, if not moral, exhaustion. On the other, it may be so provocative that it causes the enemy to do as expected: to attack first in the fear that its survival depends on such a move. In the early years of the post–World War II period, however, the risks *and* the alternatives seemed equally limited. One after the other, American presidents endorsed a "world policeman" role under the American nuclear umbrella.

The Truman Doctrine

In March 1947 President Truman announced what has come to be known as the Truman Doctrine: "We cannot allow changes in the status quo by such methods as coercion, or by such subterfuges as political infiltration." This declaration was made in the context of the Greek civil war, in which a highly authoritarian government sought to suppress a revolution that enjoyed considerable popular support, but had strong local Communist components. For more than two years, British troops had fought on the side of the Greek government they had set up, finally achieving a measure of stability despite continued official corruption and severe inflation. The British, however, were unable to keep up their efforts; their own financial situation was so desperate that they had no alternative but to withdraw their troops. The United States proceeded to take over support of the Greek government's campaign by supplying weapons, military advisers, and substantial amounts of money. The decision to intervene was perceived by the President as essential to American security, given the context of a global struggle between contrasting ways of life, and it has come to be understood in these terms ever since.

The commitment in Greece was a major turning point in American foreign policy. It effectively marked the beginning of the period when national security concerns led to the use of Third World nations, particularly those on the perimeter of the Soviet bloc, as buffer states, with prevention of the spread of communism seen as more important than the nature of the government or long-term economic development. Ultimately, Greece and Turkey were incorporated into the North American Treaty Organization; despite massive military and economic assistance, however, their financial conditions and general economic levels remained low. In the 1960s continued dissatisfaction led to several changes in the makeup of the government in Greece. Apparently still acting to promote national security, American policymakers tended to support the more conservative factions in each case.

The Korean War of 1950–1953 provides an Asian illustration of this early stage of American policy. South Korea was considered crucial as another testing ground of what was assumed to be Soviet expansionism. Experts now differ about the extent to which the two crises were instigated or encouraged by the Soviet Union. In the case of Greece, it seems clear that the Soviet Union had declined to help because it considered the revolution a hopeless cause.[1] And it is also apparent that the belligerent threats of the South Korean government to invade the North may have contributed to the North's decision to send its armies south. In any event, this aggressive act triggered American involvement. When the American army appeared to be pushing toward the Chinese border, the Chinese too

---

[1] Based on a quotation from Joseph Stalin reported in Milovan Djilas, *Conversations with Stalin* (New York: Praeger, 1962), p. 164.

became involved. The war then settled into a long-term stalemate. Nearly two decades after the end of the war, South Korea had received such massive economic assistance that it was becoming a showcase of economic growth. The government, however, had made little progress toward more democratic organization or operation.

As the perceived Communist threat became global, the Eisenhower administration set about to tie as many Third World nations as possible to the United States through alliance treaties. Alliances modeled on the NATO pact were formed with Turkey, Iran, Iraq, and Pakistan (CENTO) and, together with Britain and France, with Thailand and Pakistan directly and Laos, Cambodia, and South Vietnam by informal extension (SEATO). Bilateral defense treaties were undertaken with the Philippines and Taiwan. Pursuant to these various treaties, considerable military assistance was extended. Similar help was made available when the key neutralist nation in the world, India, was engaged in border skirmishes with the Chinese. Ironically, the major use of American military assistance occurred not in defense against Communist attack, but in small wars between nations allied with the United States, such as Pakistan and India.

The Eisenhower Doctrine

When the containment policy was rendered obsolete in the late 1950s by the development of indigenous popular movements all over the world, the United States faced new difficulties in serving its security interests. Any independence movement in an African or Asian colony or any revolutionary movement in Latin America might serve as a route to power for Communists. Almost without considering the limits of propriety or capability, the global approach to security was extended once again to cover such possibilities: the Eisenhower Doctrine in effect served notice that the United States might see its security at stake and act accordingly not only in the internal conflicts of nations with which we had alliances, but also where violence either seemed to threaten or else occurred elsewhere in the world.

The meaning of this commitment is illustrated by the situation in Lebanon in 1958, when marines landed in and occupied the country for four months. The cause of the disorder was an effort by Lebanon's incumbent anti-Communist president to change the country's constitution in order to serve another term in office. Arab nationalists, supported by aspiring Lebanese politicians, had formed a powerful coalition in opposition. Calls for the violent overthrow of the government came from Egypt and Syria, but UN observation groups could find no major foreign sources of arms or men behind the opposition. There was undeniable fighting, however, and it seemed to be part of a trend toward revolutionary disorder throughout the nations of the Middle East. At the height of the fighting, the president abandoned his efforts to succeed himself, but nevertheless called for American assistance. The marines had been alerted for months and landed the next day. Soon the U.S. forces, armed with atomic howitzers, numbered seven thousand men. President Eisenhower told Americans in a television address that the situation was like the Greek civil war and various Communist conquests of the early 1950s and that American troops were required to defend Lebanese sovereignty and integrity. They did so by acceding to the election of a new president, whereupon the fighting died away.

But a precedent had been set for the involvement of U.S. troops in the internal affairs of Third World nations, even in cases where the opposition to the local government came not from Communists, but from indigenous nationalist forces. This precedent was much recalled in 1965, when American marines landed in the Dominican Republic. In this instance there was no solid evidence of Communist involvement in the revolution, but the American embassy thought there was, and President Johnson acted accordingly. The consensus of experts now, however, is that the embassy was either hysterical or acting as the agent of the conservative military forces that were ultimately installed in power with U.S. help. In any event, the U.S. commitment to a global view of its security needs, reaching into the internal affairs of Third World nations, began to appear more like a determination to use force to prop up any government that could be induced to request U.S. intervention.

The leading example of American policy under this global definition is, of course, the Vietnam War. Escalating slowly but steadily from the dispatch of the first U.S. advisers in the early days of the cold war, the American commitment finally became one of maintaining an unpopular government against an indigenous revolutionary movement that enjoyed not only widespread popular support, but also the active assistance of a neighboring Communist country. To make matters worse for the United States, the site of this insurrection was dense jungle on the Asian mainland, ten thousand miles from the United States. Neither a half million U.S. troops nor bomb tonnages exceeding those dropped by all sides during World War II succeeded in halting the progress of the revolutionary movement.

The use of military force is often an indication that other forms of power have failed to achieve the ends sought. In the mid-1970s a seemingly unending series of revelations about covert intelligence operations suggested that the scope of American involvement in other nations' internal affairs was far greater than these relatively isolated military interventions would indicate. The Central Intelligence Agency (CIA) was acknowledged to have undertaken a variety of deliberate efforts to subvert governments and even to assassinate leaders over a thirty-year period and on every continent. Much of the rationale for these interventions was the single unifying concern that unless the United States acted decisively, Communist penetration would succeed in gaining control of the government and produce a new ally for the Soviet Union or China.

Another factor in all of these bold assertions of American power is the importance of domestic politics in the formulation of foreign policy. Few policymakers have been willing to give their opponents any grounds for charging them with weakness in "standing up to the Communists." The dynamics of domestic politics seem to lead decisionmakers to take the strongest possible stances against even remote contingencies that might lead to Communist gains. Chagrin at "losing" Cuba is no doubt partly responsible for this bellicosity, but so is an undifferentiated conviction that the security interest of the United States is intimately involved in the domestic difficulties of small nations anywhere in the world.

After the Vietnam War

In retrospect, the assertion of such a world-policeman role involved the United States in a variety of interventions in Third World countries (economic, intelligence, and military) and led almost inevitably to the national disaster in Vietnam. But the lessons of that experience remained unclear to many American policymakers and perhaps to people generally. Was the world really that much different, or did U.S. policymakers' mistakes just lead to a period of national uncertainty, isolationism, and lack of confidence and willpower? Did we have to adjust to a new role amid new world conditions, or could we restore ourselves to preeminence by means of sacrifice and assertion of our interests and renewed power? At stake was a definition of "national security" and a set of policies to implement it — and, of course, the quite real risk of nuclear annihilation.

One clue to policymakers' understanding may be seen from the opening paragraphs of the Atlantic Council's 1977 study of American security. The Atlantic Council, formed in the early 1960s, is made up of business and government leaders and reflects a relatively "internationalist" position in foreign affairs. Here is its version of the national security problem in the late 1970s:

> In the nuclear age, in an increasingly crowded and interdependent world, security is not a matter merely of military strength. Security also involves a combination of many other factors, including domestic as well as foreign ones: political, economic, social and psychological. It is the combination of these factors which Communist doctrine calls the "correlation of forces." The West cannot afford a narrower view.
>
> Nor can security be limited to any specific geographic area. Its ramifications are global.
>
> So long as the Soviet Union's policy is based on the extension of world-wide Communist totalitarianism, it will be necessary for the United States and its allies to maintain military strength, both nuclear and conventional, adequate to deter the use or threat of armed aggression against any of them. That strength is also necessary to provide the time, however long, for the leaders and peoples of the world progressively to eliminate the causes of wars.

The resulting period of détente will not mean the end of conflict and struggle between the two camps. The conflict is not, as Soviet propaganda has so long alleged, between "Communism" and "Capitalism." While agriculture and industry in the West have achieved unparalleled and widespread prosperity under private enterprise and both have stagnated under totalitarian bureaucracy, that is not the real conflict. Rather it is that between "Freedom" — the right of the individual to worship God in his own way, to choose his own government and form of government, his own economic and social system, his own means of seeking a better life — and "Totalitarianism" — the subordination of the individual to all-pervasive bureaucracy under dictatorship. . . .

Over-all, it [security] means working together to defend, develop and promote freedom, human dignity, rights and opportunity. These values have a global reach as wide as humanity itself and may yet provide the ultimate weapon in the battle for men's minds. Dynamic pursuit of these values can give us, in President Kennedy's words, "an alliance based not on fear but on hope," and provide confidence and an inspiring sense of purpose.[2]

It should be kept in mind that these paragraphs were written in 1977, not 1947, and that this is one of the more "forward-looking" organizations concerned about foreign policy. Other organizations endorsed more rigid and aggressive stances toward the Soviet Union. The Committee on the Present Danger, for example, a body of 141 military, industrial, and opinion leaders, strongly opposed all efforts at arms limitations and called for greatly expanded military capabilities.

The policies of the Carter administration in 1979 and 1980, uncertain as they appeared, nevertheless embodied a clear movement toward restoring American military supremacy and capacity and intent to intervene in other countries where we felt our interests to be involved. Domestic needs, such as the desire to divert people from economic problems or to restore the legitimacy of a discredited government or simply to mobilize people to undergo sacrifice, may have contributed to the renewal of anti-Communist bellicosity. No doubt the Soviet Union's invasion in the winter of 1979–1980 of neighboring Afghanistan contributed to this movement and perhaps served as a convenient opportunity. Even the tragic end to three decades of massive support for the Shah of Iran was turned to advantage in the form of patriotic mobilization. But behind these and other salient events, the commitment to expand military capability and return to earlier definitions of "national security" had already been made. The military's rising share of the national budget, for example, had been made a commitment as far back as 1978.

---

[2] Excerpt from *The Growing Dimensions of Security: The Atlantic Council's Working Group on Security.* Joseph J. Wolf, Rapporteur; Harlan Cleveland and Andrew J. Goodpaster, Co-Chairmen. Published with the Support of the Rockefeller Brothers Fund and the Lilly Endowment, Washington, D.C., November 1977, pp. 1, 4. Used by permission.

At least some important aspects of the world, however, were different in the 1980s from what they had been as recently as the early 1960s. The Soviet Union had achieved essential parity with the United States in number, destructive capacity, and deliverability of nuclear weapons. Third World countries were determined to both maintain their independence and, where possible, make up for centuries of exploitation by the developed countries. American allies in the capitalist world were more independent and much more doubtful of American capability, judgment, and leadership in the world. Whether a definition of national security that emphasized military supremacy and interventionism could be restored in such a world was at least open to serious doubt. As we shall see, policies implemented in both strategic and substrategic categories reflected the intent to do so — and the difficulties and dangers involved in such an effort.

The Strategic Level of National Security

The United States and the Soviet Union now have about 14,000 strategic (long-range) nuclear weapons aimed at each other.[3] The explosive power of the approximately 9,200 nuclear warheads deployed by the United States is between 3,500 and 5,000 *million* tons of high explosive, while the USSR's 5,000 warheads would generate the equivalent of between 6,000 and 9,000 *million* tons of high explosives.[4] The inclusion of so-called tactical nuclear weapons brings the total of U.S. and Soviet warheads up around 60,000.[5] Strategic nuclear warheads each carry as much as 500 times the destructive power of the original atomic bomb dropped on Hiroshima, Japan, in 1945.[6] The total from all nuclear weapons today would equal from 1 to 1.5 *million* Hiroshima bombs.[7] The 1979 Yearbook of the Stockholm International Peace Research Institute declares:

> A nuclear world war in which all, or a significant fraction, of these weapons were used would almost certainly:
>
> - destroy all the major cities in the Northern Hemisphere;
> - kill the bulk of the urban population in the Northern Hemisphere by blast and fire, and the bulk of the rural population by radiation; and
> - kill many millions in the Southern Hemisphere by radiation from fallout.
>
> The long-term consequences of a nuclear world war are unpredictable but may include:

---

[3] William J. Lanouette, "SALT II — Preserving the Balance of Terror," *National Journal*, 16 June 1979, p. 990.

[4] Frank Barnaby, "World Arsenals in 1978" (Annual Report from the Stockholm International Peace Research Institute), *Bulletin of the Atomic Scientists*, September 1979, p. 21.

[5] Ibid.

[6] Lanouette, SALT II, p. 991.

[7] Barnaby, "World Arsenals in 1978."

- a change in the global climate;
- a serious reduction in the ozone layer; and
- severe genetic effects from radiation.

No one can say that human life would survive these effects. Nevertheless, the nuclear arsenals are still being quantitatively increased.[8]

The strategic weapons involved include land-based intercontinental ballistic missiles (ICBMs) launched from underground concrete silos ("hardened sites") that protect them from attack; submarine-launched ballistic missiles (SLBM) launchable from submerged vessels stationed around the enemy's coast; various other missiles, such as the American self-powered "cruise missile"; and bombs that can be delivered by long-range aircraft. Each missile can be equipped with several warheads, called multiple independently targetable reentry vehicles (MIRVs), which can hit widely separated targets after reentering the earth's atmosphere from space. According to the Strategic Arms Limitation Treaty (SALT II) draft of 1979, the United States and the Soviet Union had deployed the following strategic weapons as of June 1979:

Weapon Systems	USA	USSR
ICBMs	1,054	1,398
SLBMs	656	950
Long-range bombers	300	140
MIRVed ICBMs	550	608
MIRVed SLBMs	496	144
Total MIRVed missiles	1,046	752

The Soviet Union has been deploying MIRVed missiles at the rate of about 150 per year and is expected to reach a total of 820 MIRVed ICBMs by 1985.[9] According to current plans, by 1985 the United States will add about 144 more MIRVed SLBMs on the new Trident submarines, plus 160 cruise missiles on 80 B-52 bombers. This arsenal will enable the United States to deliver about 10,000 MIRVed nuclear warheads — 1,600 by cruise missiles, another 1,600 by land-based ICBMs, and about 6,400 by SLBMs. Another 4,000 single warheads will be deliverable by the remaining ICBMs, SLBMs, and bombers.

The planning and assumptions that accompany the development of this destructive capacity are in some ways more important than the technical characteristics of the weapons themselves. One crucial distinction is that between "deterrence" and "counterforce" strategies.

---

8 Ibid.
9 Ibid., p. 23. All data in this paragraph are from this source.

Deterrence

The principle of deterrence holds that no nation will launch a "first strike," or "preemptive strike," against another if it knows that the attacked nation will still have the capability to retaliate by causing unacceptable levels of destruction. If all major antagonists believe that about one another, mutual deterrence will take effect, and relative peace (or a "balance of terror") will reign. This is sometimes called "mutually assured destruction" (MAD). Second-strike capability requires that the necessary missiles be located so that they cannot be destroyed by the prospective enemy in a first-strike attack. All missiles at above-ground locations and all heavy bombers not actually in the air are potentially applicable only to first-strike use and thus serve to provoke rather than to deter. Even ICBMs at hardened sites now may be vulnerable to accurate first strikes with heavy new warheads, and deterrence is coming to depend more exclusively on submarine capabilities. In computing second-strike capability, of course, planners must provide for the defensive capabilities of an alert enemy, particularly through its antiballistic missile (ABM) system. Although ABMs have yet to be proved effective, the possibility always exists that some incoming missiles might thus be rendered ineffective.

And so strategic planners must calculate the destructiveness of their second-strike capabilities, which they aim at cities and industrial areas rather than at military targets. Part of the problem for American planners is that the Soviet Union perceives itself as threatened by both the United States and China and deploys separate sets of missiles in the two directions. In any event, the rough balance struck in the early 1970s gave the Soviet Union a slight lead in the total number of ICBMs in hardened sites and the United States a slight lead in submarine-based missiles. The United States, however, had more than 1,000 ICBMs in place, and the Soviets had almost 600 missiles in submarines; neither side was short.

What does this stock of missiles and warheads mean in terms of second-strike capability? According to Defense Department estimates, 200 nuclear warheads landing on major Soviet targets would kill 52 million people (21 percent of the population) and destroy 72 percent of Soviet industrial capacity. In addition, millions would be injured or homeless, the physical environment contaminated, and social organization thoroughly disrupted. We may take this as representing an "unacceptable" level of destruction, sufficient to deter Soviet policymakers from launching a surprise attack on the United States. Assuming that five times the required number of missiles must be launched from protected land sites and from under the sea to ensure that 200 missiles penetrate Soviet air defenses and reach their targets, it still appears that the United States possessed enough nuclear armament to destroy the Soviet Union several times over. The reverse was also true, of course. No matter how large the U.S. strategic forces grow, not even an American surprise attack could prevent the Soviet Union from launching a prohibitively destructive second strike from its protected sites and submarines.

The clear capacity to destroy each other several times over, in conjunction with the soaring costs of such weapons, led in 1972 to a Soviet-American agreement to limit future offensive weapons development. In effect the United States and the Soviet Union agreed in the so-called Strategic Arms Limitation Talks (SALT) to freeze their respective weaponry at existing levels. Only strategic arms were involved, but limits on both offensive and defensive systems were set for a five-year period, and both sides were committed to efforts to extend the limits to other kinds of armaments and for longer periods.

Counterforce

A counterforce strategy is one that aims at the military capabilities of the enemy, hoping to achieve a first strike that knocks out its capacity to retaliate. Even if retaliatory capacity is only greatly reduced, the enemy might capitulate rather than suffer further devastation in a war it could no longer win. In such a strategy very precise targeting and accurate delivery of an overwhelming number of warheads on all forms of the enemy's retaliatory capacities are required; cities and industrial areas are less vital targets. In the late 1970s both sides developed much more precise delivery systems and began targeting them on each other's ICBM sites and other military targets.[10] Emphasis began to shift from deterrence to counterforce, greatly increasing the risk of nuclear war. What was still lacking, despite enormous research and development efforts, was the ability to detect and to destroy submerged submarines and/or to effectively destroy enemy missiles at harmless distances. Without high levels of confidence in one or the other of these capabilities, a counterforce or first-strike strategy would still be risky — unless it appeared that the other side was about to launch one.

It is clear at least that the MAD concept is being seriously challenged, in part by the development of more and more sophisticated and accurate delivery systems. Strategies have in effect changed to fit with the technological developments in weaponry. And more sophisticated weapons and delivery systems are on the way: the American MX missile system and maneuverable reentry vehicles (MARV) will ensure that "virtually no military target would be invulnerable."[11] The MX missile system involves constructing as many as 10,000 miles of concealed railways or roads so that missiles can be moved from one site to another. Their mobility greatly reduces the chance that they could be destroyed, and missiles could be deployed so that a potential enemy would know neither their location

---

10 Ibid., pp. 24–25.
11 Ibid., p. 24.

nor their number (arms-control limitations would thus be unverifiable as well). The missiles to be used would be advanced models capable of carrying twenty high-precision MARV warheads.[12] The MARV development means the addition of guidance systems to each warhead such that accuracy is greatly increased, to within thirty feet after journeys of thousands of miles. Such capabilities are needed only to strike military targets, of course; countercity weapons can have much less precise accuracy levels.

The cost of this renewal of the arms race is mounting rapidly. Each new weapon or delivery system carries a larger price tag, and each investment adds further to inflationary pressures. The Stockholm International Peace Research Institute estimates world military spending at an annual rate of more than $400 billion, or nearly $1 million a minute, an increase of about 50 percent over the past two decades.[13] The new MX missile system is alone estimated at $40 billion over the next five years (critics charge that it will be $100 billion). In 1978 NATO countries agreed to increase their military spending by at least 3 percent per year in after-inflation terms, and the United States moved in 1980 to increase its commitments 50 percent beyond the current level.

The combination of risks and costs, together with acquiescence in the MAD concept, made possible the first SALT treaty in 1972. In 1975 talks began on a second version to extend arms limitations into the 1980s, and the SALT II draft was finally completed in 1979. Even before its terms were known, however, opposition was mounted by people convinced that the United States should not accept the fact of nuclear parity with the USSR and that the Soviets were determined to confront the United States with overwhelming superiority at some future time. The terms of SALT II amounted to a freeze of certain categories of weapons at essentially existing parity levels, but allowed expansion in the newer categories. The question of ratification of the treaty in the U.S. Senate appeared to be a very close one, even with the Carter administration's commitment to five years of increased military spending at the rate of 4.5 percent per year. The whole matter was shelved at least temporarily when the Soviet Union invaded neighboring Afghanistan.

Substrategic Aspects of National Security

Within the general context of a continuing struggle with the Soviet Union for influence and control, particularly in the Third World, a variety of other policies are implemented in the name of American national security.

---

[12] Robert C. Aldridge, *The Counterforce Syndrome: A Guide to U.S. Nuclear Weapons and Strategic Doctrine* (Washington, D.C.: Transnational Institute, 1978), p. 28. Data in the remainder of this paragraph are drawn from this source.

[13] Barnaby, "World Arsenals in 1978," p. 18.

Some are directly related to countering Soviet moves or blocking its needs. Others project American power and interests in the Third World, and still others may be intended to serve domestic purposes. Let us consider several of these policies in turn.

Sale of Military Arms

The worldwide arms trade in the late 1970s was well over $20 billion annually. The largest suppliers were the United States (47 percent), the Soviet Union (27 percent), and France (11 percent).[14] NATO countries accounted for 70 percent of all arms exports; Warsaw Treaty Organization countries, for 27 percent. Third World countries bought 70 percent of the arms sold, the leading purchasers in 1978 were Iraq, Israel, South Korea, Saudi Arabia, India, and Libya. The Middle East absorbed 47 percent of the total, while 17 percent went to the Far East and 12 percent to sub-Saharan Africa.

The United States has exported arms under three different programs. The Military Assistance Program, phased out in 1980, was a direct military aid program that transferred arms without payment from the recipient countries. Most U.S. arms transfers in the 1950s and 1960s were made under this program. From a high of $4.2 billion in 1973, however, the program was steadily reduced until its termination. Its replacement is the Foreign Military Sales program, whereby foreign governments buy arms directly from the U.S. government. Modest orders from 1967 to 1971 jumped annually to $10 billion in 1974 and $14 billion in 1980.[15] Because many orders are for the most modern weapons, large backlogs of unfilled orders develop; more than $40 billion was outstanding in 1979. When the Shah of Iran was overthrown in 1979, his revolutionary successors canceled $10 billion in orders for arms. In 1974 alone, the Shah had signed agreements worth more than $4.6 billion, more than 40 percent of all U.S. weapons sold that year to the entire world. From 1974 to 1976, the Shah invested more than $7.4 million per day on U.S. arms for his military forces.[16] The other major purchasers in the late 1970s were Saudi Arabia, Israel, and Egypt.

The third category of arms transfers is commercial arms sales in which foreign governments buy directly from U.S. corporations. Sales of this sort were rising sharply in the late 1970s, despite some congressional restrictions, to more than $1 billion per year. In addition, U.S. corpora-

---

14 Ibid., p. 19. All data in this paragraph are from this source.
15 Weapons for the World Update and Weapons for the World Update II (New York: Council on Economic Priorities, 1979).
16 Max Holland, "The Myth of Arms Restraint," International Policy Report, May 1979 (Washington, D.C.: Center for International Policy), p. 5.

tions participated in a variety of licensing and coproduction agreements whereby weapons or weapon components could be produced or assembled in purchasing countries.

The American corporations enjoying the largest arms sales in the late 1970s tended to be the same ones year after year: of the top ten recipients in 1976, for example, eight were in the top ten for 1977. They were dependent on foreign military sales for between 25 and 30 percent of all their business.[17] The leading American arms exporter is the Northrop Corporation, which regularly approaches 20 percent of all foreign military sales. Its chief product is the F-5 aircraft, the most widely deployed in the non-Communist world, a multipurpose fighter that has been through thirty-nine different model configurations in the twenty years that it has sold more than 3,450 planes worth more than $3 billion.[18] Not including unfilled orders, foreign countries held in 1980 F-5s in the following numbers:

Taiwan	363	Vietnam	47
Iran	309	Brazil	42
South Korea	276	Morocco	24
United States	145	Ethiopia	23
Canada	115	Philippines	22
Saudi Arabia	114	Singapore	21
Norway	108	Malaysia	20
Turkey	108	Venezuela	20
Netherlands	105	Chile	18
Greece	77	Libya	18
Switzerland	72	Indonesia	16
Jordan	71	Kenya	12
Spain	70	Yemen	12
Thailand	57	Total	2,285

Source: New York Times, 4 February 1980, p. D1. © 1980 by The New York Times Company. Reprinted by permission.

President Carter came into office with a pledge to halt spiraling American arms sales, but apparently found it difficult to do so. Total arms transfers increased each year of his administration, although some categories were reduced and some recipients limited. Some $4.5 billion was granted to Egypt and Israel alone on the occasion of their agreeing to the Camp David Mideast peace treaty. After Iran is excluded from the comparison, sales to Mideast and South Asia increased 141 percent between 1977 and 1980. After inflation is taken into account, arms exports to 98

[17] Weapons for the World Update II, p. 31.
[18] New York Times, 4 February 1980, pp. D1, D3.

percent of the Third World market increased more than 85 percent from 1977 to 1980.[19]

Part of the reason for continued increases in arms sales is the felt need to support "friendly" governments, regardless of their character or intended uses for new weapons. To some extent, furnishing weapons is an entry toward greater influence in another country: once the weapons are purchased, instruction in their use becomes necessary, spare parts are needed, and American assistance may become a semipermanent factor. In addition, the income from arms sales helps with the U.S. balance-of-payment problems. A final factor to be considered is the powerful influence the arms industry wields. In any event, it seems unlikely that the American role as the largest arms supplier in the world will change much in the near future.

Nuclear Proliferation

One of the most serious, and growing, threats to national security is the spread of nuclear weapons throughout the world. The technology is now so widely understood that one pressing concern is that terrorist groups may construct or acquire nuclear weapons. Many Third World countries have the fuel-reprocessing, plutonium-separating, or uranium-enriching facilities that are essential to weapons-grade nuclear production. Plutonium, for example, is now made in twenty-two countries.[20] India is the most recent country to explode a nuclear device, joining China, Britain, France, the Soviet Union, and the United States in the "nuclear club." Israel and South Africa may already have done so, and Pakistan, Brazil, Argentina, South Korea, and Taiwan are moving in that direction at varying rates of speed. West Germany, Italy, Japan, and Belgium all have nuclear capacity, if not the current intent.

France and West Germany have been particularly active in selling facilities and technical assistance to other countries, filling the gap left by American reluctance to help expand nuclear weapon capabilities. Efforts to prevent proliferation now appear to depend more on political agreements than on economic or technical barriers, which means that the danger of accidental or "small war" nuclear explosions is increasing all the time. Underground nuclear test explosions occurred at the rate of about one per week in the late 1970s, and China has conducted at least twenty-five tests in the atmosphere. Most of the more than 1,200 known nuclear explosions were made after the Partial Test Ban Treaty of 1963, and the Non-Proliferation Treaty has not been much more successful. But these remain the only means of controlling the prospect of the spread and ultimate use of nuclear weapons.

---

[19] All data from Holland, "The Myth of Arms Restraint," p. 1.

[20] Data in this and the following paragraph are drawn from Barnaby, "World Arsenals in 1978," p. 20.

Intelligence Gathering and Covert Operations

American policies with respect to gathering information and covertly affecting events in other countries, particularly Third World countries, came under heavy criticism in the early 1970s. Many Third World countries alleged that from the overthrow of the Iranian government and installation of the Shah in 1953 to a variety of "destabilizations" and repressive support for right-wing dictatorships in the 1960s and 1970s, the American Central Intelligence Agency (CIA) was intimately involved in promoting regimes favorable to U.S. penetration. American policymakers, media, and opinionmakers regularly brushed aside such charges, until the post-Vietnam revelations began to surface. When they did, the American public learned that even the political left's most imaginative charges were only a pale shadow of everyday practice.

From a series of books by former CIA personnel, investigatory articles by a number of reporters, and sober inquiries by House and Senate intelligence committees, a picture of CIA operations in the 1950s through the 1970s began to emerge. Intelligence gathering was conducted through means including "cover" provided by diplomatic, business, journalistic, and academic status, subversion by local government personnel, and outright theft or manipulation — as well as by various forms of surveillance. Governments were created or unmade by management of local elites, rebellious military officers, media, and interest groups. A Senate inquiry detailed a bizarre series of assassination plots against Third World leaders, encouragement of military coups and attempted coups in "friendly" countries, and financial and military support for dissident movements in other countries.

All of these revelations added up to an indictment of the practices employed by a nation holding itself out to be the world's leading democracy. When it was learned that systematic spying and some of the other techniques were applied to Americans in the United States as well, the CIA and other intelligence agencies underwent severe criticism. But soon concern shifted to the possible "demoralization" of the CIA and other intelligence services, the quality of the intelligence being provided to key policymakers, and the "chartering" of their operations to free them for long-term functioning. Legislative charters were intended to provide guidelines within which agencies could operate, but some critics charged that they were essentially legitimations of the criticized practices of the past. And, under conditions of renewed hostility toward the Soviet Union, proposals were made to "unleash" the CIA and restore its freedom for clandestine action.

Assistance to "Friendly" Governments and to American Companies Doing Business There

In addition to the sale of arms for use against external enemies, the United States has provided non-Communist governments with a variety of forms of economic aid, equipment, and training for the maintenance of internal order and support for American corporations and banks doing business in their countries. Each of these programs runs in the billions of dollars annually.

Economic aid flows to recipient countries through up to twelve different programs, some of them funded and controlled directly by the United States and some of them multilateral agencies in which the United States has the dominant fiscal and decision-making role. Total expenditures by the United States range from $4 to $7 billion per year and are concentrated in a relatively few specially favored countries, such as South Korea, Chile, Brazil, Taiwan, the Philippines, Indonesia, and the Middle East. Direct aid is administered through the U.S. Agency for International Development (AID), the Food for Peace Program, Military Assistance Program, and the Peace Corps. Multilateral agencies providing assistance include the Export-Import Bank, the World Bank, the Asian Development Bank, and the International Monetary Fund, each of which is funded and controlled up to 33 percent by the United States. Other agencies providing loans and guarantees include the U.S. Commodity Credit Corporation, Housing Guarantees, and Overseas Private Investment Corporation.

Only the first four of these programs (Aid, Food for Peace, Military Assistance, and the Peace Corps) are subject to congressional control; the rest are provided through multilateral, and essentially independent, or executive, agencies. In some celebrated cases, such as South Korea, even where direct American assistance has been held at then current levels, multilateral and independent-executive agencies have increased their contributions. By 1975, the share of aid to South Korea subject to congressional control had dropped to 13 percent of the nearly $1.5 billion worth of assistance provided. At the same time, South Korea was maintaining the fifth largest army in the world.[21]

Equipment and training for the maintenance of internal order ranks with nuclear sales in level of controversy. Particularly during the Kennedy and Nixon years, the United States began providing friendly Third World countries, many of them right-wing dictatorships, with sophisticated police equipment and began training their security forces in methods of counterinsurgency warfare. Critics argued that the United States was "supplying repression" and gaining the enmity of national liberation movements around the world. Advocates argued, as did an under secretary of state in 1971:

Effective policing is like "preventive medicine." The police can deal with threats to internal order in their formative states. Should they not be prepared to do this, "major surgery" would be needed to redress these threats. This action is painful and expensive and disruptive in itself.[22]

---

21 Center for International Policy release, 2 January 1978.
22 U. Alexis Johnson, "The Role of Police Forces in a Changing World," *Department of State Bulletin*, 13 September 1971, p. 282.

"Major surgery" is, of course, military intervention, and "preventive medicine" ranges from surveillance and interrogation to police terror and assassination squads.

The principal programs by which internal-order equipment and training are made available include the Public Safety Program of the Agency for International Development, the International Narcotics Control program, the Military Assistance Program and its successor, Military Sales program, the International Military Education and Training Program, a vast commercial police-supply system, and the CIA-supported International Police Chiefs Association. By 1975, the Office of Public Safety (OPS) had distributed $200 million worth of arms and equipment to foreign police organizations and trained more than 7,500 senior officers at U.S. police schools; hundreds of foreign police were trained in bomb and other assassination techniques at a CIA-staffed school.[23] Dissolved in 1975, the Office of Public Safety transferred many of its functions to the Narcotics Control program, which distributed $142 million in the next three years to the same recipients and for the same purpose as had the Office of Public Safety.[24] Training of foreign police is actually provided in the same Washington building that once housed the OPS-supported International Police Academy. The United States Drug Enforcement Agency employed at least sixty-four former CIA agents in 1975.[25]

Assistance to American businesses wishing to do business in potentially turbulent foreign countries is provided by a variety of services from the State, Commerce, Labor, and Treasury departments in Washington and abroad. Additional help comes from the Overseas Private Investment Corporation, which provides insurance against losses caused by war, revolution or insurrection, expropriation, or inability to bring profits back to the United States. Much of this insurance goes to giant multinational corporations: between 1974 and 1976, 41 percent of all insurance went to only eleven companies, all of them high on the Fortune 500 list of largest U.S. corporations and the top-fifty list of banks and utilities. Any losses would in effect be made up by U.S. taxpayers. Supporters argue that such insurance is necessary to encourage multinationals to exploit the Third World.

Human Rights

The subject of the status of any protection for human rights around the world rose to considerable public visibility in the mid-1970s. This surge was due in part to the continuing efforts of private human rights groups such as Amnesty International and public agencies such as the United

---

[23] *Washington Post*, 8 October 1973, citing Office of Public Safety records; for a full report based on documents obtained under the Freedom of Information Act, see Michael T. Klare, *Supplying Repression* (New York: Field Foundation, 1977).

[24] Klare, *Supplying Repression*, p. 25 ff.

[25] *Washington Post*, 19 February 1975, cited in Klare, *Supplying Repression*, p. 27.

Table 5.1

U.S. Military and Economic Aid to Selected Human Rights Violators,
Fiscal Years 1973–1978 (current dollars, in millions)

Country	*Fiscal Years 1973–1977*				
	MILITARY AID GRANT	MILITARY SALES CREDITS	TOTAL ARMS SALES	TOTAL ECONOMIC AID	NUMBER OF MILITARY TRAINEES
Argentina	2.2	134.0	98.6	—	689
Brazil	3.4	230.7	258.3	93.3	1,062
Chile	2.5	27.4	146.6	226.7	1,391
Ethiopia	53.2	46.0	200.6	111.0	736
Indonesia	107.9	54.7	91.8	634.2	1,272
Iran	0.3	—	15,677.3	5.4	—
Philippines	124.4	60.0	194.7	383.5	1,460
South Korea	601.1	552.4	1,333.1	487.0	2,741
Thailand	229.4	74.7	220.3	91.4	2,655
Uruguay	9.0	12.0	16.9	22.8	717
Totals	1,133.4	1,191.9	18,238.2	2,055.3	12,723

Source: Michael T. Klare, *Supplying Repression* (New York: Field Foundation, 1977),
p. 9. Used by permission.

Nations Commission on Human Rights to expose and end such practices
as torture, assassination, arbitrary imprisonment, and unlimited police
harassment of dissidents. It was also owed in part to the failure of American policy in Vietnam and to a general revulsion at revelations concerning
brutal practices condoned, supported, or actually undertaken by the United
States in Third World countries for the previous decades.

In any event, evidence about U.S. involvement in denials of human
rights was painfully available. One example is provided by a comparison
of those governments ranked highest on the list of systematic violators of
human rights by Amnesty International, the International Commission of
Jurists, and the United Nations Commission on Human Rights and those
governments regularly high in military and economic aid from the United
States. Table 5.1 presents such a comparison for the years 1973–1977.

Against this background, American policy began to change. Congress
enacted provisions in the Foreign Assistance Acts of 1973 and 1974 and in
the International Development Act and the International Security Assistance of 1975 setting limits to support for governments that were consistent
human rights violators. Congress established an office in the State Department to report on the status of human rights in all countries for which aid
was proposed and asserted the power to limit economic and military aid
to flagrant violators. Despite the opposition of the Kissinger State Department, military and economic aid to Korea was temporarily cut, and military
aid to Chile ended in 1976.

The Carter administration moved quickly to seize the initiative on human rights issues, in part because of candidate Carter's campaign pledges. Human rights were declared to be the "cornerstone" of American foreign policy, and past interventions and transgressions by the United States, its allies, and Communist or nationalist governments were all criticized. Contemporary human rights violations were used as a basis for reducing or delaying American assistance in some cases. Congress continued to press for stronger action in 1977, including requirements that U.S. representatives on multilateral aid agencies (such as the World Bank) vote against loans to governments that were consistent violators of human rights.

By 1978, considerations of national security needs were reducing administration enthusiasm for actual implementation of human rights limitations on economic and military aid to "friendly" governments. The State Department developed a number of criteria and mechanisms intended to insert national security priorities and high-level review into the process of making judgments about such actions. In the summer of 1978, for example, the U.S. government–chartered Export-Import Bank decided against a $300 million loan to Argentina, one of the most notorious human rights violators, which was to be used for purchase of heavy equipment from the Allis-Chalmers corporation. After an organized campaign by Allis-Chalmers, its workers, other multinationals doing business in Argentina, and Argentine business and government officials, the administration ordered approval in September 1978.

Since that time, the issue of human rights has been primarily a rhetorical device rather than a practical reality in U.S. governmental policy. On occasion, human rights principles are used to pressure a reluctant Third World government toward more liberal policies that might make it more acceptable in the eyes of its own people over the long term. And President Carter referred to human rights as "the soul of our foreign policy" as late as December 1978. But economic and military aid began to increase in 1978 to the worst human rights violators as well as to other "friendly" governments. At the same time, a number of human rights–oriented liberals in Congress were defeated for reelection, and other liberals began to worry about an apparently deteriorating national security situation in the world.

In some highly visible cases, such as Chile, direct U.S. government aid was supplanted by multilateral assistance and private loans. When military aid was banned by the Congress, private bank loans to Chile increased more than 500 percent over the previous year. From the CIA-initiated overthrow of President Allende in 1973 to the end of 1978, private loans from multinational banks totaled $1 billion, nearly all of it from U.S. banks and much of it organized by David Rockefeller of Chase Manhattan. The human rights barriers to action in the national interest as perceived by administration policymakers were thus circumvented and a process of erosion in the principles themselves begun.

The Rapid Deployment Force (RDF)

During the height of the period of revelations about CIA and other covert operations in Third World countries, general concern for human rights, and public anti-interventionist attitudes (roughly 1974–1977), the United States engaged in no direct military actions anywhere in the world. Where American interests were seen to be involved, such as in Angola in 1975 and Zaire in 1976–1977, active support was provided for other Third World governments to use their forces in our behalf. But in some cases no surrogates were willing to intervene, despite U.S. efforts to mobilize them, as in the revolution in Nicaragua in 1977–1979. Some trusted regional stabilizers either collapsed (Iran) or became less capable (Brazil), and the Carter administration became concerned about U.S. capacity to promote national security interests in the Middle East, Africa, Asia, and Latin America.

In 1978 a general return to the earlier world policeman role, with concurrent restoration of U.S. power and prestige, was apparently decided upon by U.S. policymakers. The forms this role would take included both a harder line against the Soviet Union, backed up at the strategic level, and a new willingness to intervene in Third World situations, for which expanded capabilities would be necessary. In both cases popular support would have to be mobilized. The first steps were the campaign to get NATO countries to agree to the positioning within their territories of nuclear missiles that are not tactical but offensive — that is, capable of striking the Soviet Union. NATO countries agreed in 1978 to increase their military budgets in real terms for a period of years and in 1979 to accept installation of 572 U.S. missiles.

In 1979 attention turned to the need to develop a Rapid Deployment Force (RDF) of 100,000 men with the capability to be landed in any part of the world within a matter of hours. Without such a force, it was argued, the United States would not be able to defend its interests and friends around the world.[26] The budget for the coming fiscal year was modified to include the costs of developing transportation and manpower for such a large force.[27] All of these commitments had been publicly made before the seizure of U.S. hostages in Iran or the Soviet invasion of Afghanistan in late 1979. Nevertheless, the latter events helped greatly to mobilize popular support for greater military capabilities and their readier use. Public opinion was further mobilized by the 1980 release of a Pentagon staff report declaring that the U.S. means of repulsing a Soviet attack on Iran or the Persian Gulf area would be the use of tactical nuclear weapons

---

[26] For President Carter's major speech on this subject, see the New York Times, 2 October 1979. The speech was delivered in the context of an essentially manufactured "Cuban crisis" and before the Iranian seizure of U.S. hostages and the Soviet invasion of Afghanistan.

[27] New York Times, 26 October 1979.

(*Source:* By permission of Jules Feiffer © 1980. Dist. Field Newspaper Syndicate.)

and by the President's declaration that the Gulf was a region vital to American national security that would have to be defended "by any means necessary, including military force."

Staffing the Military

During the Vietnam War, as in all major wars, the armed forces obtained their manpower through conscription, or "the draft." At first the Selective Service System operated as its name suggests, classifying men in such deferred categories as physically or mentally unfit, fathers, students, essential workers, and so forth and selecting for service those who had no grounds on which to be deferred. The inequity resulting for people who were too poor to go to college and thus be deferred for four years as a student, plus the wide variation in classifications and practices among the nation's 4,000 local draft boards, led to many complaints against the system. The basis of selecting men for actual service was therefore changed to a lottery, in which birth dates were given numbers and an annual drawing assigned priorities for the draft according to the order in which those numbers were drawn. At the end of the war, when the size of U.S. armed forces was reduced, the draft was replaced by a "voluntary military," in which pay and other incentives were relied upon to produce men in sufficient numbers.

Concern about the viability of such a voluntary military began to be voiced in the mid-1970s. Some of the military services, most often the army, were not able to fill their quotas despite substantially increased salaries, promises of training during and after service, and guarantees regarding type and location of service. All of the services had difficulty attracting persons of sufficient educational backgrounds to handle modern weapons systems and keeping a core of well-trained manpower. Critics pointed to the fact that there were more than twice as many blacks in the armed forces than in the population. We were employing a mercenary army of the otherwise unemployable poor and black strata of our society, they charged, and it was unjust. Some military officers and their supporters in Congress also felt it was an unworkable situation.

A return to the draft was proposed by President Carter in 1980, this time with the lottery system, but without the symbols that provoked opposition (the variable local boards and draft cards, for example). He argued that it was necessary to ensure readiness to meet Soviet challenges and that no immediate inductions into military service were contemplated. Critics asked whether the new draft was not really intended to produce larger and better-quality military manpower, perhaps at lower expense than would be required to attract similar personnel at market wage levels. Others charged that the real purpose was mobilization of the general public — to convince Americans that the nation faced an emergency situation justifying sacrifices and to continue using the threat of war to divert people from serious economic problems at home. Some attention was focused on the issue of whether women as well as men should be required to register, and a number of court suits appeared inevitable, no matter what decision was finally made. But much more attention centered on the meaning that reinstituting the draft held for the future of national security policy generally.

The Consequences of National Security Policies

We will now attempt to identify the effects of the policies just examined in the order in which they have been described and also to assess the domestic consequences of the same policies. These may be more important than effects overseas in many cases, and domestic concerns may indeed be the primary sources of national security policies from the outset. Certainly domestic factors figure importantly in the crucial act of defining "national security," and we conclude by looking at some continuing issues in regard to that concept.

At the strategic level, the decision to abandon the Strategic Arms Limitation Treaty and to develop and deploy new missile systems clearly renders the superpower relationship less stable. The nuclear balance of terror, or mutually assured destruction, seems to be less balanced and less assuring. A new version of the arms race will apparently have to run its course until both sides believe that such balance and assurance is the only possible outcome. Most destabilizing of all is the development of counterforce or first-strike capabilities rather than deterrence weapons. When both sides believe that the other might be able to eliminate their retaliatory capability with an overpowering first strike, each will be tempted to act first — and nuclear war will be a constant prospect.

Was the newly unstable arms race forced upon the United States by new developments in Soviet military power, as some argue, or did the American desire for military supremacy rather than parity trigger it? Was the American action a defensive one, partially in response to the Soviet invasion of Afghanistan, or an offensive policy designed to force the Soviet Union back and to restore American dominance over the Persian Gulf and the rest of the Third World? To a considerable extent, the answer would depend on one's definition of "national security," which in turn would depend on one's basic values and ideology. We shall have to defer such considerations until Chapters 8 and 9. But it is clear that the new military commitments and renewed spending would change U.S. priorities significantly in the 1980s. The lead sentence in a New York Times business section article on the fiscal 1981 budget summarized the change: "Love it or loathe it, the military-industrial complex is back in business."[28]

At the substrategic level, it seems clear that arms sales to Third World countries have made small wars more likely — wars that could easily escalate into larger wars. Arms sales, about half of them by the United States, continued to rise during the 1970s despite rhetorical efforts to limit them. One result was that even small countries often possessed the means to wreak widespread destruction, and both terrorists and liberation forces could count on a ready supply of powerful modern weapons.

An even greater danger to peace, both in the Third World and with respect to the two superpowers, was generated by the proliferation of nuclear weapons and weapon-making capability. Commercial rivalries and opportunities prevented efforts to limit the spread of the necessary technology and other facilities from being successful. In 1980 many countries were knocking at the door of the nuclear "club," and the world was that much more dangerous.

American intelligence gathering and covert operations, freely employed in the Third World and elsewhere during the 1960s and early 1970s, seriously damaged the reputation of the United States in two major ways. One was the undermining of American moral leadership, including skepticism about our commitments to the principles of democracy and the self-determination of nations. The other was the growing concern about American capability to gather and interpret information in a timely manner so as to be able to respond rationally and purposefully to events in the world. The United States seemed to be caught unprepared more and more often and to overrespond afterward in ways that worried its major allies.

Nor was the reputation of the United States enhanced by its economic and military assistance to many of the world's more repressive governments.

---

28 New York Times, 30 January 1980, Section 3, p. 1.

Popular movements seeking to rid their countries of dictatorial regimes found their rise to power blocked by American-supplied arms and American-trained (and often directly advised) police and military forces. When the power of masses of ordinary people finally succeeded, as in Iran and Nicaragua, the new governments were naturally hostile to the United States. Many suspected that, like Chile, they would be the target of American efforts to mount a counterrevolution if possible and/or to cut off loans and trade with the rest of the world.

In this context the Carter administration's human rights policy was understandably met with skepticism, if not cynicism, in most of the Third World. Continued aid to right-wing regimes provided a basis for continued doubt. The principal achievement, and possibly the real intent, of the human rights policy was to bring greater support for the U.S. government from its own people. Americans could feel better about their government's conduct of foreign affairs when such a principle was said to be paramount. And the government needed a renewal of legitimacy after the events of the 1960s and early 1970s.

The consequences of the increase in military spending and emphasis on the Rapid Deployment Force seemed to be similar. Americans generally rallied to the support of their President and their national prestige as the country seemed to be taking a firmer stand against the Soviet Union and others. The President's declaration of intent to defend the Persian Gulf as vital to American interests met with approval from all but a few policy-makers and opinion leaders.

There was little doubt that conscription would be essential to staff the armed services if they were to be expanded and upgraded. The revival of the draft, however, was less successful as an effort to mobilize support, further the sense of national emergency, and create a mood of willingness to sacrifice. Draft-age people, particularly college students, were divided on the issue, although their elders generally acquiesced.

The domestic consequences of implementing these national security policies can be seen chiefly in terms of financial impact and secondarily perhaps in the attitudes and feelings of people generally. Domestic production for military use hit $60 billion in fiscal 1978 and is programmed to rise steadily. In the mid-1980s, when total Department of Defense budgets reach $175 billion, production and research and development contracts should exceed $100 billion. Much of this expenditure is concentrated year after year in a few large companies, which then become substantially dependent for their sales and profits upon military policies and budgets. Their workers and their geographic regions become similarly dependent. The pattern of military production contract awards for the top ten suppliers in fiscal 1978 is shown in Table 5.2. The table reveals not only the continuing award of contracts to the same companies, but also that in many cases these companies have become dependent on such contracts for as much as 80 percent of their business. In the case of Grumman Corpora-

Table 5.2

Top Ten Military Contractors, Fiscal 1978

Rank in 1978	Rank in 1977	Company	Contracts (in $, millions)	Percentage of Company's Total Sales
1	8	General Dynamics Corp.	4,153.5	47
2	1	McDonnell-Douglas Corp.	2,863.3	69
3	3	United Technologies Corp.	2,399.8	38
4	2	Lockheed Corp.	2,226.4	64
5	5	General Electric Co.	1,786.4	9
6	16	Litton Industries Inc.	1,557.1	43
7	4	Boeing Company	1,524.9	28
8	9	Hughes Aircraft	1,488.6	NA
9	11	Raytheon Co.	1,306.7	40
10	7	Grumman Corp.	1,180.0	80

Source: *100 Companies Receiving the Largest Dollar Volume of Military Prime Contract Awards, Fiscal Year 1978* (Washington, D.C.: Department of Defense, 1979).

tion, which set the latter mark, the 80 percent total actually represented a decrease — from 91 percent in 1977 and 99 percent in 1976. Grumman is the largest private employer on New York's Long Island (Nassau and Suffolk counties), with a work force of 19,500 people, more than 12 percent of the manufacturing work force. The future of this entire region is thus intimately bound up with Grumman's success or failure in receiving contracts from the Defense Department.[29]

In addition to the dependence on military spending of some of the largest companies and their workers and regions, the country as a whole is affected by the nature and level of such spending. Each increase in military spending, even though funneled through a relatively small number of companies, has the effect of reducing unemployment while increasing inflation and the gross national product. It also has the effect of reducing revenues available for other programs, particularly (given the fixed nature of many entitlements, such as agricultural subsidies, veteran's payments, social security, and so forth) domestic social programs. When the effort was made to balance the fiscal 1981 budget, for example, nearly all of the billions cut were to be taken from domestic social programs.

The attitudes and feelings produced in people by these policies are highly volatile and only partly traced by opinion polls. In general, the polls always show increased support for firm actions in times of crisis. But military spending is generally not popular while there are economic and social problems at home, and increases under such conditions have to be

---

[29] For a full analysis, see the Council on Economic Priorities *Newsletter*, 12 December 1979, from which these data were drawn.

justified by creation of a sense of emergency or threat. The draft, in particular, is not popular, except with the older generations that associate the draft with the patriotic fervor and mass sacrifices of World War II.

At the same time, people feel deeper anxieties and hope for solutions that preserve the American way of life for themselves and their children. The returning day-to-day threat of nuclear annihilation is a major psychic burden for many people. They also are aware, sometimes very painfully, of pressing social and economic problems at home, solutions to which are deferred or made impossible by the expenditures and partial mobilization involved in the new arms race. But they generally subscribe to the often repeated view that only American military power restrains the Soviet Union and preserves the good life at home.

The issue thus comes back to the point with which we began: the definition of the concept of "national security" itself. If the definition is cast primarily in military terms, particularly in regard to maintaining military supremacy and a world policeman role, then sacrifices and unsolved problems at home may be required for our national security. If the definition is expanded to include concern for social unrest and disintegration at home or the danger of a change of the social order toward a more authoritarian form, then a balance might be in order among military sufficiency, limited use of power in behalf of vital interests only, and new efforts to rebuild our own society.

INCOME DISTRIBUTION: INEQUALITY, POVERTY, AND WELFARE

6

Income and wealth are paramount goals of individual economic and political activity in the United States. It is hardly news that some people are more successful than others. This is due to a variety of factors, including individual talents and opportunities, the systematic effects of government policies, and the nature of economic forces in a highly industrialized capitalist society. In fact, the combination of factors may be different for each individual. *Patterns* of distribution of income and wealth, however, offer a means of analyzing the social consequences of all these factors taken together. Patterns of distribution of income and wealth are a kind of snapshot of the results of many public policies and the way they have combined with "private" forces to shape individual attainments.

As we have seen, many government policies serve to allocate economic benefits and burdens among segments of the population. But some policies bear more directly than others on who has how much spendable income at any given moment. By focusing on such policies as taxation, subsidies, and welfare — areas in which the actions of government bear directly on the vital income-and-wealth goals of all individuals — we should be able to see clearly for whom government works.

This chapter therefore operates on two levels of analysis. First, and rather briefly, we sum up the combined effects of public policies and private forces in this crucial area by analyzing the basic patterns of distribution of income and wealth in the United States. Second, we explore in some detail those government policies that bear most directly on such distribution. In separate sections we look at taxation, subsidies to different sectors of the population, and welfare. The larger problem addressed by the chapter is that of income inequality and its sources, but a major subsidiary problem is poverty and its alleviation by various means — chiefly welfare. We conclude with an analysis of the alternatives to, and probable future of, the nation's welfare programs.

Patterns of Income and Wealth Distribution

We begin this analysis with three basic facts. (1) The United States is a sharply stratified society in which a very few people receive very large proportions of income and wealth, the majority share a relatively modest proportion, and a substantial number receive very little indeed. (2) This pattern has persisted for at least the last sixty years and has changed only negligibly in the last decades; indeed, recent change has tended to widen these gaps rather than to close them. (3) Income inequalities are closely related to *sources* of income (those who gain their income from stocks and dividends and from capital gains are at the top, and wage earners at the bottom, of the scale), *sex* (men earn more than women in the same jobs, and women are disproportionately concentrated in the lower-paying jobs), and *race* (nonwhites earn less than whites with comparable education in comparable jobs and are highly concentrated in the lower-paying jobs). Poverty and racism are so closely linked in the United States that it is very difficult to talk about them separately; we do so chiefly for the sake of analytical clarity.

The Basic Patterns

Figure 6.1 presents data on the distribution of income for 1977; the pattern it illustrates has prevailed at least since the early years of this century. Stratification — that is, inequality — is evident and may be summarized in a variety of ways. The top 20 percent of the population, for example, earns more than three times as much as the bottom 20 percent. And the top 20 percent earns more total dollars than the bottom 60 percent, though the latter group includes more than three times as many people! The data for unrelated individuals reveal even greater disparities. The meaning of these figures in human terms, of course, is that a substantial number and pro-

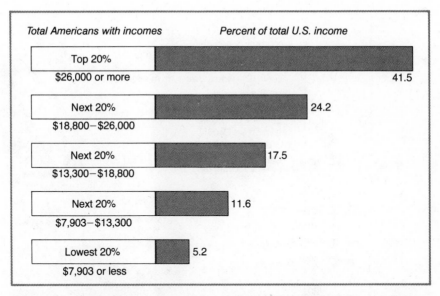

Figure 6.1 U.S. incomes, 1977. (*Source:* Data from Bureau of the Census, *Current Population Reports*; *AFL-CIO American Federationist* 85, September 1978, p. 14. Used by permission.)

portion of Americans live in poverty or near poverty. The precise number depends on a series of definitions and calculations, which we shall explore in a later section; by any reasonable assessment, however, at least 27 million persons, or 13 percent of the population, are at or below the poverty level.

Wealth — financial resources not derived from income — is even more concentrated at the top of the social and economic pyramid. The top 1 percent of adult wealth holders own more than 25 percent of all personal property and financial assets in the country.[1] The top 5 percent of family units hold more than 40 percent of all wealth. Most of this wealth is in the form of financial assets (stocks, bonds, mortgages, and the like), real estate, and business capital equipment. Using data from a survey of American households, one major study found that the top 1 percent held 31 percent of the nation's wealth and 61 percent of all corporate stock; the top 20 percent was found to hold 76 percent of all wealth and 96 percent of all corporate stock.[2]

These distribution patterns are well summarized in Figure 6.2, from *Business Week*. Not known for exaggeration, the editors of *Business Week* nevertheless declare flatly: "Personal holdings of wealth, to a much greater extent than shares of income, are dramatically concentrated at the top of the population heap."[3] In the same article, the editors note that this

---

[1] James D. Smith, Pennsylvania State University, cited in *Business Week*, 5 August 1972, p. 54.

[2] Dorothy Projector and Gertrude S. Weiss, *Survey of Financial Characteristics of Consumers*, Federal Reserve Board, 1962, pp. 110–114.

[3] *Business Week*, 5 August 1972, p. 54.

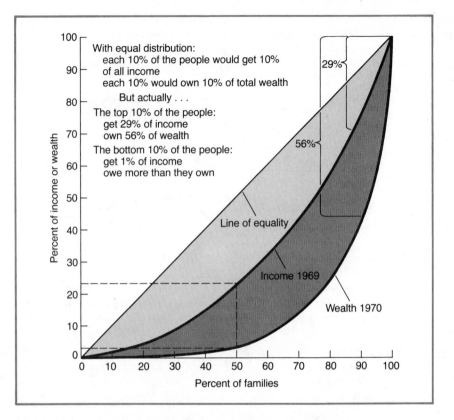

Figure 6.2 U.S. income is shared unevenly, but wealth distribution is more unequal. Percentages of income and wealth recipients are plotted on the horizontal axis; percentages of income and wealth, on the vertical axis. Both are expressed in cumulative form. The dashed lines show that the bottom 50 percent of income recipients, for example, drew 23 percent of personal income in 1969, whereas the bottom-half wealth holders in a 1970 survey accounted for only 3 percent of net worth. (*Source: Business Week*, 5 August 1972. Used by permission.)

pattern of wealth holding persists by virtue of inheritance and that the rich, by virtue of their headstart, get richer faster than others can rise. Citing a study of the top 1 percent of wealth holders — "the rich" — the editors estimated that $326 billion in corporate stock and a total of $753 billion in all was held at this level.[4]

The Permanence of These Patterns

Again in the words of *Business Week*, ". . . income distribution seems to be one of the few real constants in the U.S. system."[5] In the twenty years

---

[4] Ibid., p. 55.
[5] *Business Week*, 1 April 1972, p. 56.

between 1950 and 1970, the share of the national income received by the poorest 20 percent of Americans rose only from 4.5 to 5.5 percent, and the economic recession of the mid-1970s again decreased that share by cutting into the family incomes of the poor.[6]

At the same time, the share of national income received by the top 20 percent dropped only 1 percent, from 42.6 percent in 1950 to 41.6 percent in 1970. The middle three income fifths remained the same during this period. The continuity of these basic patterns could hardly be clearer. Moreover, though all real incomes have been rising, the gap between rich and poor has actually widened in absolute terms. Citing a recent study, *Business Week* reported that from 1949 to 1969, "the gap between average real incomes of the poorest and richest fifths of the population widened from less than $11,000 to more than $19,000 in constant 1969 dollars."[7]

Nor has there been any closing of the wealth gap. The share of national wealth held by the top 1 percent did drop during the Great Depression and in World War II, but since that time it has been widening again. Starting at 32 percent in 1922, it dropped to 28 percent in 1933 and as low as 21 percent in 1949, but it was back up to 26 percent by 1956 and is now probably higher than that.[8] On the other hand, the poorest 25 percent of Americans have no net worth at all; their total debts equal or exceed their "assets."[9]

The Sources of Income and Wealth Disparities

The most obvious source of income differentials is the way in which people gain their income. Those who earn their income from wages and salaries, while they are many in number and earn a much larger dollar total than others, are concentrated at the lower income levels. At the higher income levels, the source of income is much more likely to be stock dividends and capital gains (increases in the value of property held). Of those receiving more than $100,000 per year, for example, 67 percent of all dollars were derived from dividends and capital gains.[10] This is another way of saying that the concentration of wealth (financial assets that give rise to dividends and capital gains) in a few rich people results in sharp income differences.

---

[6] Irwin Garfinkel and Robert D. Plotnick, "Poverty, Unemployment, and the Current Recession," mimeographed (University of Wisconsin, Institute for Research on Poverty, 1975), p. 2.

[7] *Business Week*, 1 April 1972, p. 56.

[8] Robert J. Lampman, *The Share of Top Wealth-Holders in National Wealth* (Princeton, N.J.: Princeton University Press, 1962), p. 24.

[9] *Business Week*, 1 April 1972, p. 56.

[10] U.S. Internal Revenue Service, *Statistics of Income, 1966: Individual Income Tax Returns*, tables 7, 11, and 19. Cited in Frank Ackerman et al., "Income Distribution in the United States," *Review of Radical Political Economics* 3 (Summer 1971), p. 28.

Income and wealth are related in many and obvious ways, some of which are mutually reinforcing. Theoretically, it is possible that the patterns we have identified could be permanent, but that the particular persons or families composing each level could vary over time. In other words, people who were in the top fifth in one period could be in the second or middle fifth twenty years later. Or people whose families were once at the bottom could rise until they reached the top fifth. But the evidence we have examined so far makes this very unlikely. Those who were rich in one time period appear likely to be even richer in the next time period, because the sources of great fortunes are types of wealth holdings that are handed down within families or transferred only to others with great wealth. Only a few very unusual or fortunate individuals appear likely to rise to the levels of the great incomes within one or two generations, and the amount of mobility between the lower fifths may not be much greater. As we are about to see, other factors also work to hold people at their existing levels of income-earning capacity.

A second major cause of income differentials is the occupations of income earners. Professionals, managers, and other white-collar workers earn substantially more than blue-collar, service, and farm workers. Both categories tend to be self-perpetuating. The former requires more education; hence a white-collar family is likely to have greater financial resources and the social status or upward identification that makes college education appear appropriate for its children. In other words, white-collar families are likely to produce white-collar children. Conversely, people enter blue-collar occupations in part because their parents held such jobs, were relatively poor, and could offer neither the money nor the social support necessary for further education and occupational mobility.

There is considerable doubt about the usefulness of education in increasing occupational mobility for the poor. An eminent sociologist found that (1) schooling does not go very far toward compensating black children for the educational disadvantages with which they start;[11] (2) schools do not narrow the gaps between social classes by enabling the poor to earn more money later in life;[12] and (3) the methods we use to finance public education subsidize higher-income groups at the expense of those with lower incomes.[13] Despite a great deal of mythology, occupational mobility remains limited.

Another major cause of income differences is sex. Culturally imposed limitations on educational opportunities and career expectations and systematic discrimination in both employment and wage or salary levels have

---

[11] James S. Coleman et al., *Equality of Educational Opportunity* (Washington, D.C.: U.S. Government Printing Office, 1966).

[12] Christopher Jencks et al., *Inequality* (New York: Basic Books, 1972).

[13] W. Lee Hansen and Burton A. Weisbrod, "A New Approach to Higher Education Finance," mimeographed (University of Wisconsin, Institute for Research on Poverty, Discussion Paper No. 64, 1970).

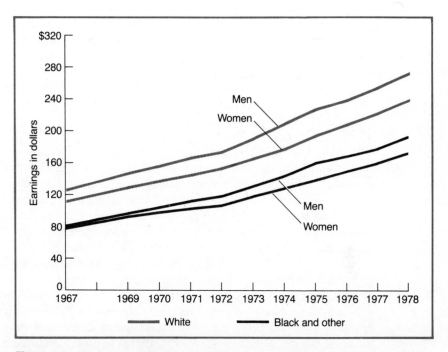

Figure 6.3 Median usual weekly earnings of wage and salary workers who usually work full time, in current dollars, by sex and race, May 1967–May 1978. (*Source: Monthly Labor Review*, August 1979, p. 35.)

combined to limit severely the income-producing capabilities of women. The result is that women find many jobs closed to them and are paid less than men for comparable work when it is available.

But the single greatest and most enduring cause of income differentials — one that persists across time and despite individual efforts to fulfill the requirements of mobility within the society — is racism. Nonwhite Americans have always been among the last hired and the first fired; they are systematically excluded from educational and other opportunities; and they are paid less for every job than equally or less well educated whites in the same jobs. The effects of sex and race on income are summarized in Figure 6.3. Here we come a little closer to understanding the human dimensions of the discrepancies in income between groups of people. The wages of white men are greater than those of nonwhite men. The wages of women trail those of men within races, so that nonwhite women are the lowest paid of all. Thus race combines with sex to create a self-perpetuating cycle of income limitation for the majority, while special sources of income provide a vastly greater level of income for the favored minority.

In this context the question with which we began becomes even more crucial. How do governmental policies affect income distribution? Do they contribute to greater equality or to increased inequality? Left alone, the private economy appears likely to work toward considerable (perhaps increasing) inequality. But it is not yet clear whether governmental policies accelerate that process, control it, or retard it and how this comes about. It is to these issues that we now turn.

Taxing and Spending

The U.S. government raises and spends roughly $270 billion per year. Nearly all of this amount is raised through taxation, mostly in the form of individual and corporate income taxes. It is spent on a wide variety of functions, the major items now being national defense, social security, and interest on the national debt. The U.S. government is, in effect, a massive transfer agent, drawing money from certain people and activities and transferring it to other people and activities to fulfill public purposes.

The act of raising and spending sums of this size has profound consequences for the economy as a whole and for the individuals involved at both ends of the process. *It is no exaggeration to say that government taxing and spending policies quite literally determine the income level at which most Americans live.* We do not mean merely that these policies make differences of from $500 to $1,000 in a person's net income, though that is the case for some; in many cases these policies are the difference between spendable income and no income or between comfort and hardship or poverty. This is because tax provisions may determine whether a business will be profitable, whether it will be expanded or contracted, whether it will enter a new line of production or marketing, and so on. Spending decisions may create new jobs, terminate others, provide or foreclose educational or economic opportunities of various kinds, and the like.

Stakes this high are likely to arouse sharp value conflicts and much controversy. At every stage of the taxing and spending process, it must be decided who is to pay and on what basis and who is to receive and for what specific purposes. The result is a vast array of inducements and rewards, penalties and punishments, which have — and are *designed* to have — the effect of shaping the economic behavior, attitudes, and opportunities of nearly everybody in the society. If people fail to see this, it is because they do not look at the totality of the process, the pattern of benefits and burdens, and the values, purposes, and applications of power they represent. We shall survey only a few representative illustrations of the major tendencies of taxing and spending policies.

Taxation

How should a tax system be designed? In reality, principles of equity become enmeshed with plain political expediency. The basic principle of equity on which the national tax system is grounded is that of *progressive*

Table 6.1

Shares of National Income, Before and After Federal Income Tax, 1962* (percentages)

	Bottom 20%	Next 20%	Middle 20%	Second 20%	Top 20%	Top 5%
Before tax	4.6	10.9	16.3	22.7	45.5	19.6
After tax	4.9	11.5	16.8	23.1	43.7	17.7

Source: Edward C. Budd, Inequality and Poverty (New York: W. W. Norton, 1967), pp. xiii, xvi. Used by permission.
* Family units and unrelated individuals combined.

income taxation. This means that people are to be taxed in accordance with their ability to pay; it assumes that the people with the most income can afford to pay at higher rates than those with limited incomes. Thus, rates vary from zero on the lowest incomes to more than 50 percent on the highest. If the system actually worked this way, the higher-income brackets would have their share of national income reduced, and the poorest would gain ground in relative terms.

But this does not happen. Table 6.1 shows that in the 1960s changes in the share of national income received by the various income fifths as a result of the "progressive" income tax were very slight. The poorest fifth of the population, for example, gained only three-tenths of 1 percent, while the highest fifth lost less than 2 percent. Another study conducted in the 1970s and aimed specifically at poverty-level people found that those with incomes under $4,000 gained only 1.4 percent of the national income (from 5.0 percent to 6.4 percent) when after-tax income was compared with before-tax income. Those earning over $15,000 dropped 2.4 percent, from 37.7 percent to 35.3 percent.[14] This taxing arrangement clearly has very little redistributive effect, no matter how it is calculated. Other studies show that nonprogressiveness has been characteristic of the tax system since its inception more than a half century ago.[15]

The Department of the Treasury reported in 1978 that the 1.4 percent of American taxpayers with incomes of more than $50,000 receive almost one-third of the $84 billion provided by special-treatment provisions of the tax code.[16] Why does this happen, and what does it mean for the distribution of income and wealth in the country? Essentially, it means that the income tax is progressive in name or image only; people think it is

[14] S. M. Miller, "Income Redistribution and Economic Growth," Social Policy 2 (September–October 1971), p. 36.
[15] Gabriel Kolko, Wealth and Power in America (New York: Praeger, 1962), p. 34.
[16] New York Times, 13 February 1978, p. D1.

something that in most respects it is not.[17] What, then, does this system do, and how? One answer is that by means of a package of tax exclusions, deductions, exemptions, credits, write-offs, and reductions — most of which are applicable only to large corporations or the very rich — the privileged are allowed to pay sharply reduced shares of the tax load. The burden must then be shifted elsewhere, and the only alternative is the individual wage- and salary-earning taxpayer.

Examples of tax-avoiding exemptions include the opportunity to deduct a proportion of the value of resources drawn from the earth (the oil industry's famous "depletion allowance"), the opportunity to deduct sums invested in new equipment ("investment credits"), and reduced rates on certain kinds of income (such as income gained from the rise in value of stocks and real estates, or "capital gains"). This list could be multiplied at great length. Such selective advantages elicit periodic outcries against "tax loopholes" and calls for tax reform, but new loopholes are created more often than old ones are closed.

The attack on loopholes has produced a number of spectacular illustrations of apparent inequities. In one study, the *real* tax rate was found to be the same for families earning $50,000 per year as for families earning $5,000 a year, because of the variety of deductions open to the higher-income people.[18] An under secretary of the treasury admitted to Congress that people earning between $7,000 and $20,000 per year pay a higher proportion of their incomes to the federal government than do the richest 1 percent of Americans. Each year many taxpayers with large incomes pay no taxes at all. In the fiscal year ending June 1974 the 160,000 Americans with annual gross incomes of at least $100,000 were able to save a total of $7.3 billion as a result of preferential tax provisions; the same loopholes cost the government a total of $52.8 billion that year. And because of the tax advantages granted for home ownership and for certain kinds of business expenses, persons with identical net incomes can bear very different tax burdens. A wage earner who lives in a rented house, for example, pays much more than a person who lives in his or her own mortgaged house and earns the same amount from an increase in the value of stocks.

Another kind of inequity is special opportunities for businesses to reduce their taxes. Some companies making large profits have very low rates.

---

[17] Note that only the federal income tax makes any pretense of being progressive. State and local governments raise more revenue than does the federal government, and do so primarily from the property tax and/or sales tax. Both of these are regressive, in the sense that they take about the same absolute amounts from each taxpayer — or, in effect, a much larger proportion from the relatively poor than from the affluent. When state and local taxes are combined with the federal income tax, the effect is to eliminate any vestige of progressiveness from the total American tax system.

[18] Jack Newfield and Jeff Greenfield, "Them That Has, Keep: Taxes," *Ramparts* 10 (April 1972), p. 34.

In 1974 the cleaning women who worked for Exxon paid a higher proportion of their incomes in federal taxes than did the corporation, whose
first-quarter profits increased 38 percent that year.[19] In the case of the oil
industry, this situation is made possible by depletion allowances and
generous credit for a variety of business expenses. Other industries benefit
from opportunities to deduct new investment from their tax obligations
or to increase their allowable deductions for depreciation of equipment
by large sums; in both cases profits can be large but taxes minimal.
According to a congressman who studied the subject, seventeen major U.S.
corporations paid no federal income tax in 1976, although taken together,
they had a worldwide income of $2.5 billion.[20] In 1946 the corporate
income tax brought in almost half of all federal revenue; in 1978 it accounted for only 16.1 percent.

Tax-avoidance advantages are justified by appeal to long- and/or short-
range social goals. For individuals such goals include the encouragement
of property ownership and investment and rewards for hard work, thrift,
willingness to take business risks, and the like. For large corporations the
theory is that increased investment and higher profits will lead ultimately
to more jobs and faster economic growth. Each type of tax advantage has
powerful defenders in and out of government; in addition, each network
of support normally succeeds in retaining or expanding its particular
advantage.

Very little study has been done of the overall effects of the entire
pattern of tax advantages. In a major study released in 1972, however,
the Joint Economic Committee of Congress introduced the concept of
"tax expenditures," or "tax welfare payments."[21] This outlook views tax-
avoidance opportunities as costs to the government — money the government would otherwise have raised. One of the committee's consultants
estimated that some $73 billion a year was being "distributed" by such
avoidance opportunities. In other words, loopholes and other tax forgive-
ness provided some people with untaxed income. The 6 million families
with annual incomes of $3,000 or less got only $92 million of these benefits,
and families with incomes of less than $15,000 per year (more than 70
percent of all families) received only 25 percent. By contrast, the three-
tenths of 1 percent of families with incomes over $100,000 per year received
15 percent of such untaxed money.[22] In effect, the committee argued, the
Congress was voting the nation's richest citizens annual "welfare" payments
amounting to tens of billions of dollars.

---

[19] *The Economist,* 6 April 1974, p. 48.
[20] *Moneysworth,* May 1978, p. 3.
[21] U.S. Congress, Joint Economic Committee, *Economics of Federal Subsidy Programs*
(Washington, D.C.: U.S. Government Printing Office, 1972).
[22] William Proxmire, *Uncle Sam: The Last of the Bigtime Spenders* (New York: Simon
& Schuster, 1972), p. 181.

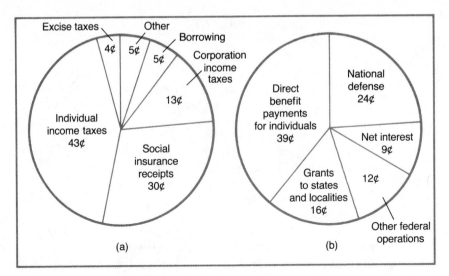

Figure 6.4   The budget dollar — fiscal year 1980 estimate: (a) Where it comes from; (b) Where it goes. [*Source:* U.S. Office of Management and Budget, *The United States Budget in Brief for Fiscal Year 1980* (Washington, D.C.: U.S. Government Printing Office, 1979.]

Spending

Let us focus on the other side of government's activities as a "transfer agent" and ask who gets what the government spends. Figure 6.4 summarizes the sources of federal revenues and one kind of breakdown of expenditures. Once again, principles of equity compete with long- and short-range social goals and sheer political expediency. The broad patterns of expenditure are shown in Table 6.2. Income security outlays grow as more workers qualify for social security benefits. Military expenditures are the second largest item.

Within these classifications by function, of course, government is actually engaging in many different activities. In the case of national defense, it is paying salaries to military and civilian employees, buying supplies, conducting research, and doing countless other things. In the case of foreign aid, it is transferring money to other countries in the form of grants or loans or export goods. Under commerce and transportation, it is making grants to the states for road building. Under education, it is transferring funds to local school districts for a variety of purposes. Under social security, it is paying elderly citizens directly from a trust fund created by the payments of working people and their employers over several decades. Under veterans' benefits, it is supplying services and making payments to veterans out of the general tax revenues. It is also paying interest on the national debt, incurred for the most part in World War II, but greatly increased since then, to banks and investors who hold such investments. Under general government expenses, it is paying its own officials

Table 6.2

Percentage Distribution of Federal Budget Outlays, by Function

Function	1960	1965	1970	1972	1973	1974	1975	1976	1977	1978	1979[a]
National defense	49.0	40.1	40.0	33.0	30.1	28.9	26.2	24.4	24.2	23.3	23.2
Income security	19.8	21.7	21.9	27.5	29.5	31.3	33.3	34.8	34.2	32.4	32.2
Health	.9	1.5	6.7	7.5	7.6	8.2	8.5	9.1	9.6	9.7	10.0
Veterans' benefits and services	5.9	4.8	4.4	4.6	4.9	5.0	5.1	5.0	4.5	4.2	4.1
Education, training, employment[b]	1.1	1.8	4.4	5.4	5.1	4.6	4.8	5.1	5.2	5.9	6.2
Commerce and housing credit	1.7	.9	1.1	.9	.4	1.4	1.7	1.0	(z)	.7	.6
Transportation	4.4	4.9	3.6	3.6	3.7	3.4	3.2	3.7	3.6	3.4	3.5
Natural resources and environment	1.7	2.1	1.5	1.8	1.9	2.1	2.2	2.2	2.5	2.4	2.3
Energy	.5	.6	.5	.6	.5	.3	.7	.8	1.0	1.3	1.7
Community and regional development	.2	.9	1.2	1.5	1.9	1.5	1.1	1.3	1.6	2.4	1.8
Agriculture	2.8	3.3	2.6	2.3	2.0	.8	.5	.7	1.4	1.7	1.3
Net interest	7.5	7.3	7.3	6.7	7.0	8.0	7.1	7.3	7.5	7.9	8.7
Revenue sharing[c]	.2	.2	.3	.3	3.0	2.6	2.2	2.0	2.4	2.1	1.8
International affairs	3.3	4.4	2.2	2.0	1.6	2.1	2.1	1.5	1.2	1.3	1.5
General science, space, and technology	.7	4.9	2.3	1.8	1.6	1.5	1.2	1.2	1.2	1.0	1.1
General government	1.1	1.3	1.0	1.1	1.1	1.2	1.0	.8	.8	.8	.9
Administration of justice	.4	.4	.5	.7	.8	.9	.9	.9	.9	.8	.9
Undistributed offsetting receipts	−1.3	−1.2	−1.3	−1.3	−2.8	−3.7	−2.0	−1.9	−1.7	−1.6	−1.8

Source: U.S. Office of Management and Budget, *The Budget of the United States Government*, annual. Cited in *Statistical Abstract of the United States* (Washington, D.C.: U.S. Government Printing Office, 1979), p. 257.

[a] Estimated.
[b] Includes social services.
[c] Includes general purpose fiscal assistance.

and employees and conducting day-to-day business. And, finally, it is simply transferring a portion of its revenues to the states to use as they wish.

The broad totals thus do not reveal the specific uses or, in many cases, the recipients of government money. It is very difficult, as the Congress has learned over and over again, to tell exactly who gets how much from government spending. Frequently, the various operating arms of a single agency do not even know what one another are doing, and the secretaries of cabinet-level departments can only guess at the real beneficiaries. The inability or unwillingness to identify systematically the actual recipients of federal funds, of course, may permit more benevolent interpretations than are really justified. Without clear evidence to the contrary, we usually assume that the funding-program intentions have been met.

But this is often not the case. One area in which some investigation has been conducted is housing and urban renewal.[23] The Housing Act of 1949 pledged decent housing for all, and more than $10 billion has been spent on urban renewal. Urban renewal has destroyed some 400,000 housing units that once housed the poor, but only 20,000 units of public housing have been built in their place. More often, urban renewal has meant systematic exclusion of nonwhites and the construction of business or civic center facilities for use by entirely different classes of people. The real beneficiaries must be identified as the construction industry, real estate brokers, downtown businesses, and suburban dwellers — not those in need of housing or the original residents of the area.

It seems likely that similarly tracing the consequences of government expenditures intended to benefit the general public or the poor would show the real beneficiaries to be investors, builders, and other major units of the private economy. Where data are available on the usage of public services provided by government, such as education, health care, research information, and the like, the beneficiaries tend to be middle- and upper-class persons rather than the lower-class or poor people for whom such services are often said to be provided.

Another way to examine the purposes and beneficiaries of federal spending is offered by the Joint Economic Committee of the Congress.[24] Applying its concept of "tax expenditures" to the spending side of governmental fiscal activity, the committee identified three other kinds of "subsidies" being provided by the government. Subsidies are payments or other assistance, not for services the recipients provide the government, but for the support of the ordinary and necessary business activities of private (mostly profit-making) companies or individuals. Thus, governmental purchase of military goods would not be considered a subsidy by this definition; only payments and other assistance for which the government got nothing in return would qualify. Even with this limited definition, the committee

---

[23] Ibid., pp. 191 ff.
[24] Joint Economic Committee, *Federal Subsidy Programs.*

found about $25 billion per year being distributed in cash, goods, or services to private businesses and individuals. We will describe briefly each type.

■ *Cash Subsidies.* These are direct payments from the U.S. Treasury, running upward of $13 billion per year, designed to increase the profits or reduce the losses of various businesses. Cash subsidies also make up for airlines' losses, support construction of merchant shipping, send students to college, and support a wide variety of other activities. In order to protect farmers against price drops due to increasing production, the government instituted a program of supporting prices by purchasing some foods and paying farmers *not* to produce others. Once again, however, it is the largest farms that receive the overwhelming proportion of such subsidies; small family farms get very little assistance of this kind. One percent of all farms got 18 percent of all cash receipts in the 1960s, for example, while half of the farms in the country accounted for only 12 percent. In 1969, 396 farms received government checks for more than $100,000; 25 giant farms received checks ranging from $360,823 to $4,370,657. For the most part, the big winners from the price and crop-control programs are the cotton, wheat, and feed-grain growers of California, Arizona, and Mississippi.

■ *Credit Subsidies.* These are low-interest loans for housing, farming, rural electrification, education, veterans' needs, hospital construction, and purchase of military supplies and guarantees of privately issued loans for an even wider variety of business activities. If the government makes a low-interest loan itself, it loses a proportion of the usual interest rate and thus, in effect, subsidizes the recipient by that amount. If the government guarantees or insures payment of a loan that is privately issued, it is using its credit to obtain something for the borrower that he or she could not otherwise obtain.

■ *Benefit-in-Kind Subsidies.* These are services provided by government to private companies or persons for which they would otherwise have to pay in some way. Grants of public lands, absorption of much of the cost of running the Postal Service or moving certain kinds of mail, airport construction, grants of the use of government-owned machinery, research and development services, information gathering and other analytical services, and the like are of benefit to some, but not to all. In fact, the committee found, most of the recipients of these services are profit-making firms. If not provided by government, the services would have to be paid for by such firms at the cost of lower levels of profit.

Much of the expenditure we have identified, and all the tax advantages, appear to benefit the wealthier segments of the population. In effect, we have described the relationship between government and the top of the income-and-wealth pyramid. In the next section, which focuses on the problem of poverty, we examine the relationship between government and the bottom of the income-and-wealth pyramid.

Poverty and Welfare

Who Are the Poor?

The extent of poverty in the United States depends on the definition used, and the definition always incorporates an arbitrary decision as to how few goods and services people must have available to them in order to be called poor. Since 1964 the official definition of the "poverty line" has been based on cash income and the number of persons in the family; that figure has been adjusted periodically as the cost of living has risen. In 1979 the poverty line was $6,700 for an urban family of four and $5,700 for a rural family of four. As Figure 6.5 shows, a very large number of Americans live in poverty — almost 25 million in 1977. The number declined substantially in the 1960s, partly as the result of the "War on Poverty" of those years, but it remained close to 25 million throughout the 1970s, rising somewhat during the economic recession of 1974–1976.

A 1975 Brookings Institution study proved that every 1 percent increase in the national unemployment figures means a 4 percent increase for low-income groups.[25] But not all the poor are unemployed. In 1977, 3.1 million workers, or 5.8 percent of all people who worked all year at full-time jobs, earned less than $5,000.[26]

One observer points out that "the Other America" of poor people can be viewed as an underdeveloped nation within the United States. As such, it would be exceeded in population, among the underdeveloped nations of the world, by only six nations. He continues:

> Of 19 Latin-American republics, only Brazil and Mexico were larger than our own "nation" of the poor. In Africa, only Nigeria had more people. All the rest of some 35 underdeveloped African countries had far fewer. There was no country in the Middle East as large; Egypt with 28 million came closest of the thirteen countries in that area. Our own internal "nation of the poor" has twice as many people as Canada. As a matter of fact, a separate nation of American poor would constitute the fifteenth largest nation of the world.[27]

The Bureau of Labor Statistics publishes three levels of budgets — imaginatively termed "lower," "intermediate," and "higher" — for families living in urban areas. These budgets are intended to represent the cost of

25 New York Times, 30 October 1975, p. 39.
26 Anne M. Young, "Median Earnings in 1977 Reported for Year-Round Full-Time Workers," Monthly Labor Review (June 1979), pp. 35–39.
27 John C. Donovan, The Politics of Poverty (New York: Western Publishing Company, 1967), p. 96.

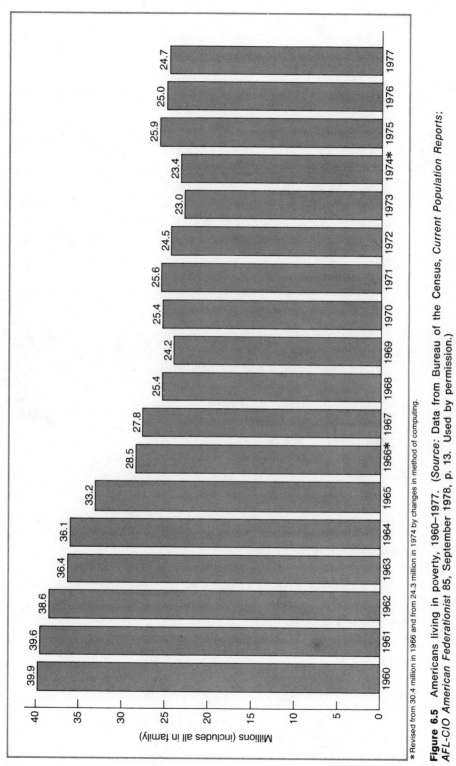

* Revised from 30.4 million in 1966 and from 24.3 million in 1974 by changes in method of computing.

Figure 6.5 Americans living in poverty, 1960–1977. (*Source:* Data from Bureau of the Census, *Current Population Reports; AFL-CIO American Federationist* 85, September 1978, p. 13. Used by permission.)

Table 6.3

Characteristics of the Poverty-Level Population

Age				Race			
		NUMBER	%			NUMBER	%
Under 16	(1971)	9,917,000	38.8	White	(1971)	17,780,000	69.6
	(1973)	8,665,000	37.7		(1973)	15,142,000	65.9
	(1974)	9,320,000	38.4		(1974)	16,290,000	67.1
16–64	(1971)	10,990,000	43.0	Non-	(1971)	7,780,000	30.4
16–65	(1973)	10,955,000	52.3	white	(1973)	7,831,000	34.1
16–65	(1974)	11,632,000	48.0		(1974)	7,970,000	32.9
Over 64	(1971)	4,652,000	18.2				
Over 65	(1973)	3,354,000	14.6				
Over 65	(1974)	3,308,000	13.6				

Residence (in numbers of families)				Residence (in numbers of families)			
		NUMBER	%			NUMBER	%
Northeast	(1971)	916,000	17.3	Central cities	(1971)	1,781,000	33.6
	(1973)	877,000	18.2		(1973)	1,753,000	36.3
					(1974)	1,827,000	35.8
North Central	(1971)	1,191,000	22.4	Suburbs	(1971)	1,189,000	22.4
	(1973)	1,005,000	20.8		(1973)	1,086,000	22.5
					(1974)	1,246,000	24.4
South	(1971)	2,356,000	44.4	Outside	(1971)	2,333,000	44.0
	(1973)	2,143,000	44.4	metropolitan	(1973)	1,990,000	41.2
				areas	(1974)	2,036,000	39.8
West	(1971)	840,000	15.8				
	(1973)	803,000	16.6				

Sources: U.S. Bureau of the Census, *Current Population Report*, Series P-60, no. 98 (January 1975); no. 99 (July 1975).

living at these levels. The lower-level budget for an urban family of four in 1978 was $10,112, considerably higher than the "poverty line." By the former standard, between 40 and 50 million people were below the lower level and living in poverty.

The only available data on the poor use the official government definitions, however, and it is on these that our analysis must rest. The characteristics of the nation's poor in the early 1970s are outlined in Table 6.3.

More than half the poor were either children or the elderly; of the working-age population, most were women. Thus, children, the elderly, and women comprised about 80 percent of all poor persons. Nonwhites accounted for only about 11 percent of the nation's population, but 33 percent of the poor; nevertheless, almost seven out of every ten poor persons were white.

Some other facts about the poor are worth noting.[28] In the early 1970s only 12 percent of all poor people who did not work were physically able to hold jobs, and most of these were mothers with small children. Only 1.5 percent of all nonworking poor people were able-bodied men. Thus, the poor — even those who were physically able to work — either could not find jobs for which they were qualified or were paid such low wages that they were unable to avoid poverty. One study, conducted by the Senate Subcommittee on Employment, Manpower and Poverty in 1971, found that more than 30 percent of all inner-city residents were paid less than the $80 per week required for a family of four to stay above the poverty line. Many of the families above the poverty line managed by having two or more working members. The subcommittee identified twenty-two large cities where at least a third of the inner-city labor force was paid less than $80 per week.

Why are these people poor? Many factors contribute to poverty, but the two major ones are unemployment (or subemployment, which is defined as work at a part-time job or a job that pays less than one is qualified for) and racial discrimination. Unemployment among the poor usually runs well above the national average. Lacking education and skills, the poor are among the last hired and the first fired as the economy expands and contracts. For blacks the unemployment rate in 1978 was about 12 percent, as opposed to 6 percent for whites. For young nonwhites, figures over 35 percent are common in most large cities. As the Senate subcommittee survey documents, low pay and a shortage of jobs reduce the likelihood that the poor can help themselves. Clearly, much of the explanation for low income and poverty is structural in character: that is, it has to do with the characteristics of the economic system and the racial biases of the society, rather than with the personal failures that might be attributed to the poor.

In one sense, low income and poverty are consequences of the combined workings of the private economy and government policies for the last hundred years. For many years, slavery was enforced and defended by governments at all levels. After the Civil War, many public policies defended the rights of employers and promoted the opportunities of various businesses, while only a few aided workers or minorities. The dominant ethos of laissez faire ("hands off") in the private economy limited the capacity of government policy to benefit low-income people,

---

[28] The data in this paragraph are drawn from U.S. News & World Report, 14 August 1972, pp. 23–25.

though it did not inhibit self-interested actions on behalf of wealthy individuals or large corporations. Not until the Great Depression did federal social welfare programs seek to deal comprehensively with the problems of low-income persons.

BILLS SWAMP NONWELFARE COUPLE

Laurie Johnston

Beulah and Ralph Watkins did not know that a pothole lay ahead of their 1965 Oldsmobile as they were driving home through Queens Village after church and Sunday dinner at the home of friends.

"A river of rain was hiding that hole," Mrs. Watkins recalled in her bright, wry manner as she described an incident at Springfield Boulevard and Murdock Avenue. "My head hit the roof of the car twice, and I'm still going to the doctor for neck treatments."

The jolt was enough to break the couple's grasp, once again, on their personal will-o'-the-wisp — financial solvency. As with countless blue-collar families who struggle to keep within their meager budgets, such things as a hidden pothole, a leaky roof or a steep medical bill can plunge them into red ink and desperation.

At the age of 59, Mrs. Watkins is not old enough for Medicare or quite poor enough for Medicaid, despite her chronic kidney disease and diabetes. "I have to go and fight with the clinic for some kind of reduced rate," she said.

In addition, the day she missed from work cost her half of the $60 a week she still earns doing part-time housework on Manhattan's Upper East Side — commuting nearly three hours a day.

Mr. Watkins, who is 68, gets a $58.94 monthly union pension as a retired plasterer and $212 in monthly Social Security payments. He needs a hernia operation, but he still owes $60 from three months in the hospital after stomach surgery last year.

"Every month, I think I can pay that bill," he said, "but some emergency always comes up."

In search of "some green and a little space," the couple left Harlem 10 years ago for an $18,500, three-bedroom house near the Queens Village-Hollis boundary. They were the fourth black family on their street.

Mrs. Watkins was making $80 a week as a full-time housekeeper, plus extra for serving at parties. Her husband earned at least $150 a week. Their daughter, Linda, was at Emma Willard Academy, a fairly exclusive girls' school in Troy, N.Y., on a scholarship. They themselves were able to pay for "about $1,000 worth of singing lessons" for her over the years, and she now sings with the Harlem Chorale.

The decade has left the family shaken, still proud and confirmed in a basic blue-collar belief: that society places more potholes in the precarious upward path of the struggling than it does for either the affluent or the indigent.

"We were always trying to better our lot," Mrs. Watkins said. "No gimmicks, just hard work. Welfare is degrading, but the working people who are not on welfare are caught in a tight economic squeeze. We're really being used. They keep us poor to keep others rich.

"Even the clinic says we must be doing all right — don't we have our own house?"

"I helped build the city," said Mr. Watkins, who now has Parkinson's disease, "East Side, West Side, the Bowery to the Bronx. I paid income tax, too." With a short laugh, he added, "I considered myself middle income. Now I'm not even working poor.

"But when the property tax goes up for Mr. Rockefeller, it goes up for me too. Ten years ago we paid $104 a month on this house. Now we pay $150, but I think only about a third of it goes to pay off the mortgage. The rest is for taxes and sewers and all that."

Mr. Watkins, self-supporting since he dropped out of the seventh grade, came to New York in 1926 from Virginia. Mrs. Watkins, who is from Louisiana, finished the ninth grade and "always wished for more."

Linda, 24 years old, attended Barnard College on a scholarship, dropped out and now need only complete summer school to get a bachelor's degree in anthropology from Columbia.

"But what can you do with it without a Ph.D.?" she said. "And I'm tired."

In the carpeted living room, on the baby grand piano, a gift from a wealthy employer, an Emma Willard graduation picture shows a very "finishing school" Linda with straightened hair.

Recalling those days, she remarked: "That was a nice interlude — very plush and I wasn't used to that — even though I had to repeat English and history because I was so badly educated in Harlem."

Now Linda wears her hair Afro-style and talks longingly of a future in Senegal. But she has a 4-year-old son, Charles, from a broken marriage to a Columbia student who is now disabled. Charles lives with his grandparents during the week, and the family's most immediate worry is how to keep the boy in a city-sponsored day-care center so his grandmother can go on working.

The day-care center families are convinced that H.R.1, the Federal welfare reform bill passed by the House and now before the Senate, takes aim — as usual — at them, despite proposed Social Security increases.

"The new bill is designed to do away with the kind of center Charles is in," Mrs. Watkins said. "It won't be for community children, only for people on welfare, so the welfare families can work."

As a taxpayer, Mr. Watkins does not grudge pensions for policemen and firemen — "those fellows gamble their lives for us" — but he sometimes wishes he had worked for the city instead of for private contractors. And he wishes the *city would come up with some tax relief "to help us maintain and hang on to our property."*

He once thought he could sell his house "for a few thousand more than we paid," since he built a patio and added other improvements. Now it needs paint, gutters and leaders, and he can no longer do the work himself. The collapse of the old heating system last year put him $1,000 in debt for a new one.

The assumptions on which the New Deal programs were structured are of crucial importance. They not only still shape the pattern of government action in regard to poverty, but also help to explain the present character of poverty and the nature of American attitudes toward ameliorative action. The basic purpose of the New Deal social legislation was to protect individuals against hazards beyond their control — both natural and biological hazards (aging, blindness) and economic hazards (unemployment, disability through accident on the job). The assumption was that if individuals were given certain minimal assurances of economic security, a revived and prosperous economy would do the rest.

Thus, the basic approach was a series of *social insurance* programs (a federal system of old-age, survivors', disability, and health insurance and a federal-state system of unemployment insurance) for which working people and their employers would pay throughout their working lives. Men and women in eligible occupations were entitled to benefits, the amounts of which were based chiefly on their earnings while employed.

Supplementing these systems, on what was assumed to be a temporary basis, were *public assistance*, or "welfare," programs assisting the blind, disabled, elderly, families with dependent children, and others; these programs were administered by the states, but utilized federal funds to a great extent. They were expected to "wither away" as an expanding economy drew more and more people back to work and social insurance programs were expanded.

Under a strictly temporary program of government employment, many new public works — bridges, highways, public buildings, and the like — were built. The rights to form unions and to engage in collective bargaining were also protected by new laws. The final major component of this package of policies was minimum-wage legislation, which required employers in certain fields to pay at least the specified minimum hourly wage to all employees.

Throughout, the assumption was that the minimum needs of the population could be met adequately by the workings of a reasonably prosperous economy, provided only that some minimum protections were legally established. There was no provision for assistance to those who did not work, except under stringent conditions. Due to fear that the incentive to work might otherwise be weakened or that moral damage

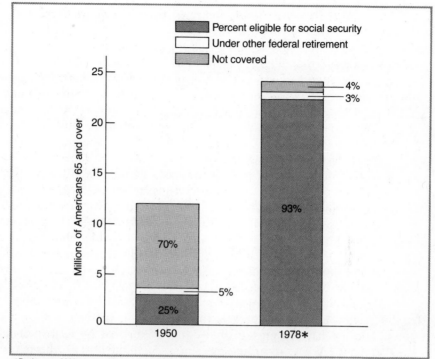

Figure 6.6 The growing number of Americans protected by social security. (*Source:* Data from Social Security Administration; *AFL-CIO American Federationist* 86, February 1979, p. 22. Used by permission.)

might be inflicted, public assistance programs required that disability or destitution be proved as conditions for receiving aid.

The social insurance programs, chief among which is social security, have for the most part fulfilled expectations. About 138 million people now contribute to social security, and more than 90 percent of the population aged 65 and over is eligible for monthly social security benefits, as Figure 6.6 shows. A very large proportion of employed people now have protection against loss of income from several important causes. In 1971, 8 million people received $5.2 billion in unemployment compensation. The benefits, which are not adequate to enable most people to support themselves without further income, are paid only to those who have previously paid into these funds.

The public assistance programs, however, have not lived up to expectations. There has been no "withering away"; instead, the numbers of people in need of such assistance have steadily increased, and the costs of these welfare programs have multiplied rapidly. The most dramatic rise has occurred in the large cities, in the category of Aid to Families with Dependent Children (AFDC). Between 1961 and 1979, the number of families receiving AFDC increased from 916,000 to 10,420,721. Most of this increase occurred in the years after 1967, as a result partly of inflation and economic recession and partly of amendments to the law and court decisions that liberalized eligibility and benefits. In New York City in 1975, almost 11 percent of the population was on AFDC; the figure in Boston was 14.5 percent and in St. Louis and Baltimore more than 15 percent.[29] The total number of persons on welfare in the nation in 1973 was over 25 million, and the total costs for public assistance exceeded $21 billion.

At the beginning of 1974, a somewhat more generous kind of welfare program went into effect for the aged, the blind, and the disabled — three classes of recipients some conservatives and some legislators regard as more deserving than the women and children under AFDC who are not destitute due to disability. The new Supplemental Security Income Plan (SSI) guarantees an income floor of $2,500 for a couple, both federal and state governments contributing to the payment. If a recipient works, the SSI contribution is reduced by half the amount she or he earns; people earning more than about $6,000 a year are not eligible for SSI benefits. If a recipient has "unearned" income, such as social security benefits, the SSI contribution is reduced by the full amount of such benefits. Recipients do not have to prove inability to work or that no relative could support them (AFDC recipients must prove both, at least in theory). But most people claiming SSI benefits lose their eligibility for food stamps. The makeup of the welfare population is similar to that of the poverty-level population, for obvious reasons. Nearly 60 percent are children, and another 19 percent are their mothers; these stark proportions suggest the contribution of AFDC to the rising costs of the program. Another 16 percent are aged, and 9 percent are blind or disabled. Less than 1 percent of welfare recipients are able-bodied men. Figure 6.7 summarizes public welfare expenditures.

The costs of welfare shot up in the 1960s for several reasons. One was that the number of eligible families and children increased. Another was that the level of payments increased. Between 1965 and 1970, payments rose 19 percent. According to one set of experts, the most important reason was that welfare was used as a means of reducing discontent and as a direct response to urban rioting.[30] In any event, the greatest increase occurred between 1965 and 1970. During the 1960s the population increased 13 percent, but the welfare rolls went up 94 percent, and the number of families receiving AFDC more than doubled. Still, many poor

29 Mitchell I. Ginsberg, "New York's Welfare Problem," *New York Times*, 28 October 1975, p. 33.
30 For an elaboration of this point, see Frances Fox Piven and Richard A. Cloward, *Regulating the Poor: The Functions of Public Welfare* (New York: Random House, 1971).

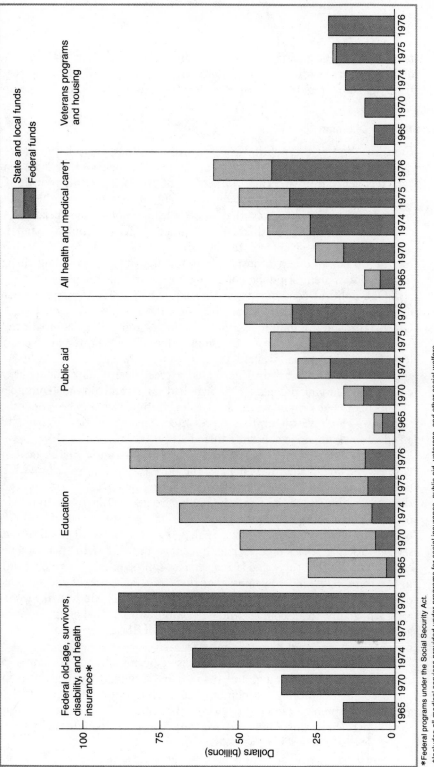

*Federal programs under the Social Security Act.

†Includes all medical services provided under programs for social insurance, public aid, veterans, and other social welfare.

Figure 6.7 Social welfare expenditures under selected public programs, 1965–1976. [*Source:* Chart prepared by U.S. Bureau of the Census; data from U.S. Social Security Administration; *Statistical Abstract of the United States, 1978* (Washington, D.C.: U.S. Government Printing Office, 1979), p. 326.]

people do not qualify for welfare payments. And the kinds and amounts of benefits vary greatly among the states. In 1973 AFDC benefits for a family of four ranged from $375 per month in Alaska to $60 in Mississippi.

The Current Policy Dilemma

From one end of the political spectrum to the other, there is intense dissatisfaction with AFDC. Some resent its cost and believe that it discourages recipients from working. Others point to its failure to provide aid for many who need it, the inadequate benefits it provides, and the repressive administrative practices that control the number and behavior of claimants and stigmatize them in the process. Its unpopularity and ineffectiveness have given rise to several forms of supplemental "welfare reform." They all deserve consideration, for they imply far-reaching change in the whole system of public policy toward low-income people.

One political consequence of the unrest of the 1960s was enactment in 1964 of the Economic Opportunity Act, the so-called War on Poverty. Chiefly through community action agencies established in approximately 1,000 communities, programs providing educational, vocational, medical, legal, and other social welfare services were initiated. By 1972, it was apparent that this "war" had generated a great deal of talk and political controversy; several programs that had had an impact on small numbers of the poor, but only a relatively small investment of money and other resources — an investment that represented experimentation rather than an effort to eliminate or substantially reduce poverty.

The number of poor people did decline significantly in the next six years, even though the investment in the poverty program was always relatively small. Most program funds of the War on Poverty were cut back sharply or eliminated in the late 1960s. Some of the more important programs that have continued offer "in-kind" services — benefits to the poor in forms other than money. Such services are justified politically on several grounds: that some recipients cannot be trusted to spend money as they should; that some goods and services can be offered more efficiently in the form of in-kind programs; that these programs benefit the suppliers of the commodities and services offered; and that they are less likely than are cash grants to discourage the poor from working. Though there is good reason to doubt the validity of most of these arguments, in-kind benefits have increased sharply in recent years.

The least effective in-kind programs have been such "social services" as counseling, family planning, and manpower training. Resented by many poor people as demeaning or pointless, counseling is now stressed less than are efforts to prepare the poor for work. Attempts at "rehabilitation rather than relief" have done more to frustrate the poor than to help them, especially in a time of high unemployment.

Some in-kind programs do provide necessities. For example, people certified as eligible by a local welfare agency receive food stamps. In 1979 a four-member family qualified for stamps if its income was under $6,504 a year. The surplus commodity–distribution program gives food to recipients directly, but a balanced diet is difficult to achieve because the program is designed primarily to dispose of farm surpluses rather than to meet recipients' needs. A national school lunch program provides lunches free or at reduced prices to children certified by local officials as unable to pay the full price.

While they help a great deal, these programs also present problems. Because of the "means test" requiring people to prove that they are poor, they stigmatize recipients. Some localities choose not to participate, which is especially likely to hurt the rural poor. A study published late in 1972 found that half of the country's 25 million poor people were still going hungry; 43 percent were getting no federal help with food.[31] Meanwhile, some critics of the food stamp program were concerned in the middle 1970s that it covered too many people; demands were made that the program be cut back to eliminate from eligibility anyone with an income above the poverty line.

Everyone over sixty-five is covered by the Medicare program, which pays some, but far from all, the costs of medical services. The program has been of substantial benefit to the elderly, both poor and middle class, but covers only about 40 percent of their health costs. Far more controversial has been Medicaid, which offers a federal subsidy to the states for medical aid to the poor of all ages. Because of rising costs, Congress has sharply cut back both the quality of Medicaid benefits and the number of people eligible for them. Medicaid has spawned abuses by some physicians who pad their costs and refusals to participate by others because it pays less for their services than does Medicare.

There are other in-kind programs. Federal housing assistance rose sharply in the 1960s, but helped the working poor more than it did welfare recipients, and it did not go far toward meeting the overall housing need. Legal aid has also been useful, but politically controversial and trivial in comparison to the demand. In some cases it provided the interesting spectacle of lawyers paid by one government agency (the Office of Economic Opportunity) to challenge in court the denial by other government agencies of benefits to the poor.

Under such programs as Headstart and Upward Bound, poor children have been given special educational opportunities to try to compensate for the disadvantages with which they start their educational careers. A Comprehensive Employment and Training Act (CETA) funds full-time temporary jobs to train people in skills needed in the private sector. Federal funds also provide summer jobs for young people in large cities.

Though every significant sector of the American public is dissatisfied with the motley set of welfare programs in effect, and especially with the rise in the welfare rolls, there are sharp differences over what to do

---

[31] *New York Times*, 27 October 1972, p. 22.

about it. The effort that has received most attention has been to provide work incentives for AFDC recipients. In 1967 the law was amended to provide small payments for participation in job-training programs and to enable welfare recipients who find jobs to retain some of their welfare benefits if their total incomes remain low. Experience with the WIN (Work Incentive) program was disappointing; it did little either to encourage job training or to provide jobs for people on welfare. In 1971 the WIN program was made compulsory for every able-bodied person on AFDC aged sixteen or over, except some specifically exempted groups, such as mothers of children under the age of six. The 1971 amendments also encouraged the states to force recipients to work by providing more federal funding and making funds available for a relatively small number of public-service jobs.

Opponents of this emphasis on "workfare" are convinced that it will continue to be ineffective because only a very small percentage of recipients are physically able to hold jobs. Also, research has demonstrated that welfare recipients are already eager to work if they can only find jobs.[32] The basic problems, according to opponents, are high unemployment and the number of jobs paying so little that those who hold them remain poor. It is, they argue, the failure of the economy to provide enough jobs and to pay adequate wages that creates the need for welfare, not individual laziness or the character of the welfare programs. According to this view, the chief function served by work requirements is psychological: they serve to create and reinforce the belief that welfare recipients do not want to work.

Those who see the problem as primarily economic rather than psychological and who do not like to vest arbitrary power over recipients in bureaucrats favor automatic "income maintenance" programs, under which a minimum income is guaranteed to all American families. An approach winning support from some conservatives, as well as many liberals, would establish a "negative income tax" — an arrangement whereby families with incomes under the poverty line would receive money from the government in amounts sufficient to maintain a subsistence standard of living. As a work-incentive provision, the grants would be decreased by *less* than a recipient earns so long as his or her total income is under a fixed amount. Some favor allowances to families for the support of children. Another income-maintenance proposal would ensure government jobs to those unable to find work in the private sector.

Behind all these elaborate proposals, of course, is the stark fact that the transfer of about $10 billion would raise *all* of the nation's poor above the poverty line.[33] Meanwhile, the very concept of a poverty line that

---

[32] Cf. Leonard Goodwin, *Do the Poor Want to Work? A Social-Psychological Study of Work Orientations* (Washington, D.C.: Brookings Institution, 1972).

[33] Sar A. Levitan, Martin Rein, and David Marwick, *Work and Welfare Go Together* (Baltimore and London: Johns Hopkins Press, 1972), p. ix. For recently published

distinguishes the poor from the nonpoor is also under attack. Poverty can be defined as the inability to enjoy goods and services available to many others, regardless of the absolute amount one has. In this sense it is gross *inequality* that defines poverty, making it a social as well as an economic condition.

Social Policy and Income Distribution

Average family incomes have grown larger in the period since World War II, even after being adjusted for price increases, but this improvement is partly the result of an increase in the number of workers per family, especially the number of working women. Also, because the growing participation of women (one result of the feminist movement) in the labor force comes largely from middle- and upper-middle-income families, it will increase the income spread between the rich and the poor.[34] Since the 1960s there has been a significant decline in poverty and in income differences based on race, color, and region, due partly to governmentally provided or subsidized medical care, food, housing, and other in-kind services. However, the average earnings of women declined relative to those of males in this period because most women entered low-paying jobs.[35]

At the same time, neither the War on Poverty nor other economic policies have significantly reduced *inequality* in income or in wealth. It seems unlikely that any set of antipoverty policies will do that, partly because they have only limited effects in raising the income of the poorest section of the population, partly because they often help the affluent more than the poor. A reduction in inequality is possible only if increased public expenditures that benefit nonelites are financed by tax reforms that impose higher tax rates on people with high incomes. Because public officials typically assume that they must limit expenditures for health, welfare, and education programs and must keep effective tax rates for the wealthy low, a set of policies that would make for greater equality has not been regarded as politically feasible.

Summary

Income and wealth are distributed very unequally, with the most affluent 5 percent of the population receiving close to 20 percent of national income

accounts and evaluations of American welfare policy, see this book and also Bruno Stein, *On Relief: The Economics of Poverty and Public Welfare* (New York: Basic Books, 1972).

[34] Robert H. Haveman, "Poverty, Income Distribution, and Social Policy: The Last Decade and the Next," *Public Policy* 25 (Winter 1977), p. 15.

[35] Sheldon H. Danziger and Robert J. Lampman, "Getting and Spending," *Annals of the American Academy of Political and Social Science* 435 (January 1978), pp. 30–31.

and the poorest 20 percent receiving about 5 percent. These shares have not changed significantly in fifty years. Neither a federal income tax that is supposed to redistribute income to favor the disadvantaged nor governmental spending patterns have narrowed the gap between rich and poor.

By the government's definition, about 25 million Americans are poor. The number declined during the War on Poverty of the 1960s, but did not show any clear trend upward or downward in the 1970s. Governmental social security and assistance in cash and in goods and services prevent a far larger number of people from sinking below the poverty line.

THE STATUS OF
RACIAL MINORITIES

7

Racial minorities — blacks, Native Americans (American Indians), Chicanos and Puerto Ricans, Asians, and others — are at the bottom of the American social and economic pyramid. That this is the case because of centuries of often deliberate and systematic discrimination and exploitation by both governmental and private forces can be stated bluntly today, although to do so would have seemed extreme or provocative only a decade ago. In the last twenty years, primarily because of the insistence of minorities themselves, there has been growing recognition of the status of minorities in the United States. Some of the many resulting governmental and private efforts to enhance their opportunities have been effective, and in several ways minorities' progress has been significant.

But such progress has also served to bring into focus the depth and complexity of the problem of racial minorities in the United States. Racism is deeply embedded in American culture and erects barriers far more difficult to surmount than those faced by European immigrant groups in the past. Moreover, governmental undertakings to assist minorities have run up against serious obstacles rooted in the character of American society itself. Even the best-intentioned public policies can do only so much in a capitalist and property-conscious society to advance the economic and social status of an entire group promptly and substantially. We have not yet approached those boundaries, but even the modest acts undertaken so far have generated considerable — and sometimes violent — resistance from a great many people. Finally, some members of each racial minority seek not only full participation in the existing American system, but also legitimacy and autonomy for the perspectives, values, and way of life of their culture. In effect, they seek to live in their own way, even though it may be inconsistent with the values and practices of other groups.

This chapter, therefore, focuses both on the conditions of minorities today and on the problem exposed by efforts to improve those conditions — the gap between minorities' needs and goals and what American society offers them. The policies that brought about the present situation will be briefly reviewed. After characterizing minorities' conditions, needs, and goals, we will examine current policies and their consequences.

U.S. Minorities and Four Centuries of Public Policies

What have governments done with respect to nonwhite races on the American continent — and why? And what have their acts meant for not only the affected minorities, but also the dominant society? For each minority, we will touch only on certain basic policies to illustrate generalized and long-established practices.

Indians

When Columbus "discovered" America, there were probably about 1 million persons living on the North American continent. Believing that he had reached India, Columbus mislabeled those he met "Indians"; this was to be the first of many instances of Europeans' failure to understand native Americans except on their own terms. The "Indians" of the time were highly diverse peoples, but they shared the beliefs that land is a resource for all to share and that human beings should live in harmony with nature, appropriating only those animals needed for food and clothing. As waves of land-hungry white settlers arrived, the Indian was introduced to the concepts of private ownership of land and the use of nature for commercial purposes such as fur trapping. Indian lands were "bought," acquired by means of governmental decrees or soon violated treaties, or despoiled by the hunting and trapping of commercially oriented whites.

By 1840, Indians had been displaced from practically all their lands east of the Mississippi. In some cases broken treaties were accompanied by forced marches (or "removals"), in which thousands of Indians were resettled farther west by whites who wanted their remaining lands. In a series of "Indian Wars," thousands of Indians were killed, injured, or rendered homeless to make first the South and then the West available for commercial and homesteading opportunities. On the Great Plains, millions of buffalo were slaughtered by white hunters for commercial purposes, depriving the Indians of their major source of food and hides. Indians were confined to reservations on then unwanted lands and caught between the Army's urge to exterminate them completely and the Bureau of Indian Affairs' preference for simply managing their affairs and making "good Americans" out of them.

By 1900, displacement, removals, wars, and disease had reduced the Indian population to one-sixteenth its original size. Reservation schools enforced the dominant society's customs and religions, thus preventing Indians from knowing their own heritage. Not until 1924 was the right to vote extended to Indians, and other forms of political redress have been unavailable or ineffective. Many treaties made over the years were broken to serve the needs or desires of governments and private economic interests.

Blacks

The first blacks arrived on the American continent in 1619 and were sold as slaves in Virginia. Slavery was incorporated into the legal structure of the southern colonies somewhat later in the seventeenth century. Jefferson's proposal to abolish slavery found no place in the Declaration of Independence's glowing language about the rights of men, and the Constitution specifically provided for representation based on slave-holding and for protection of the slave traffic for a period of years. Slavery was too important to the economic and social structure of the South, and too fully in accord with general beliefs in the North as well, to be seen as inconsistent with the assumptions and goals of either document.

The abolition of slavery, accomplished during the Civil War, did little to change the practical effects of previous policies. The war was justified as a means of preventing the spread of slavery to the new western states — that is, of keeping the territories free for the wage-earning white working man. The Emancipation Proclamation was thus a tactical act of warfare as well as a principled policy. The Fourteenth and Fifteenth amendments to the Constitution were intended as much to build the political strength of the struggling Republican party as to ensure freedom for blacks. The swift passage of Jim Crow segregation laws, whose constitutionality was confirmed by the Supreme Court in the famous case *Plessy* v. *Ferguson* (1896), officially and legitimately subjected black people to a condition only abstractly better than slavery.

Official segregation continued to be the law of the land until 1954, when a well-orchestrated legal campaign by blacks finally led the Supreme

Court to rule segregated education unconstitutional. The federal government practiced segregation in the armed forces until after World War II. Aside from these official policies, governments at all levels condoned or practiced systematic discrimination against blacks. Educational systems not only were segregated and unequal, but also actually taught that blacks were inferior; other agencies and activities of governments were almost equally "white only."

Chicanos

Spanish explorers, settlers, and missionaries were the first whites to enter New Mexico, Texas, and California in the late sixteenth, seventeenth, and eighteenth centuries, respectively. Contacts with the surrounding Indians of the Southwest and with Mexico, where the Spanish had intermarried with Aztecs and other Indians, led eventually to a mixed Spanish-Indian-Mexican population in these areas. In some cases vast landholdings existed in relative isolation.

And then came the Anglos, or English-speaking North Americans. The influx of Americans into Texas was followed by the acquisition of the entire Southwest in the Mexican War. The people now known as Chicanos, or Mexican-Americans, owe their status as Americans chiefly to this conquest, particularly to the Treaty of Guadalupe Hidalgo in 1848. The treaty confirmed all existing land titles as it granted the ostensible subjects of Mexico living in those areas American citizenship, but in the words of one historian, "Mexicans quickly became the Negroes of the Southwest."[1] Although they were not officially slaves, they were not far from slavery, living in conditions of peonage and officially condoned discrimination. Land was taken from them, stock stolen, voting rights denied, and physical violence employed to intimidate and prevent efforts at redress.

The discovery of gold in California led to the rapid Anglicization of that territory, and once again the Mexican-origin population was displaced and reduced to near-peonage. In both law and practice, the Republic and then the State of California aided the rapid private exploitation of a captive population while denying them effective redress. Not until the advent of mass farming techniques and the resulting need for cheap labor were Mexican-origin people in demand, and then only as the lowest form of laborers. Whenever they were not needed, Mexicans and Mexican-origin people were uprooted from their homes and deported.

The Mexican-origin population of New Mexico and Arizona was incorporated into the American system somewhat later. Lack of resources or of opportunities for development kept rural areas essentially unchanged until the end of the nineteenth century, and in some cases later. At that

---

[1] Paul Jacobs, Saul Landau, and Eve Pell, *To Serve the Devil: Volume 1, Natives and Slaves* (New York: Random House, 1971), p. 237.

time, a somewhat modernized version of the familiar process began. In time family land titles were completely replaced by Anglo ownership, and Anglo forms of organization were imposed on whole communities.

Puerto Ricans

The Puerto Rican population, concentrated principally in major East Coast cities, is the other major, though smaller, group of Spanish-speaking Americans. The island of Puerto Rico was also acquired by conquest, in the Spanish-American War of 1898. Although legally American citizens since 1917, Puerto Ricans have suffered from the same officially condoned and systematic peonage and discrimination as have Chicanos. The lack of economic opportunities on their native island has led many to seek jobs in New York, Philadelphia, and Boston, where until quite recently they were ignored by governments at all levels.

Asians

Asians have been subject to governmental policies that, though inconsistent, have always condoned private discrimination and exploitation. In the nineteenth century, for example, thousands of Chinese were imported as cheap labor to build railroads; when no longer needed (and when white workers' demands that they be prevented from undercutting wage levels led to riots and lynchings), they were excluded by law in 1882. The same exclusion applied to Japanese after 1907. California's land laws prevented Asians from acquiring title to property for many years. And during World War II, the federal government uprooted American citizens of Japanese descent from their homes and businesses to relocate them in camps in Utah and Nevada, fearing that they might be disloyal.

Summary

Why has there been a consistent pattern of discriminatory public policies toward racial minorities? Neither economic necessity nor racism is a sufficient answer in itself, though both are major factors — independent but mutually reinforcing. It is not necessary to speculate on which is more important or whether economic interests lead to an increase of racism. It is enough to see that neither could function without the other. A recent history sums up four centuries of American policy as follows:

> The colonizers came to the New World believing that colored people were inferior, and used that ideology to justify the enslavement of blacks, the killing of Indians and Mexicans, and the importation of Oriental labor for work considered unfit for whites. The identification of colored skin with evil, with the devil, with inferiority, infused the entire culture of the Anglo-Saxons during the first centuries of colonization.
>
> In each case, the racism coincided with economic need for slave labor

and for land. At the same time, racist attitudes were institutionalized as laws, religion, and everyday practice. Each school child learned, along with the principles of republicanism and democracy, about the inferiority of colored people. Ministers explained to their flocks that slavery was God's will.

Racist law and racist behavior became an integral part of American culture. . . . Racist attitudes not only made whites feel superior by virtue of their skin color; it also made all colored, colonized people feel inferior because of their skin color.[2]

As this passage implies, it is not only minorities who experience the consequences of racially discriminatory public policies. Dominant groups are also deeply affected, both in the circumstances of their individual and social lives and in the ideology and mythology they accept. Belief in the superiority of whites and the "natural" inferiority of other races can come to serve as an underlying principle of social order. Without a myth of this kind, no discriminatory public policy can long persist, and the institutionalization of the myth in such policies serves in turn to sustain it. If today most whites concede that they are not biologically superior to other races, they still tend to believe that they are socially, economically, and/or culturally superior. And some members of racial minorities have also come to believe in the supremacy of whites and white culture. Once established, this myth penetrates all levels of society and serves to justify subordination as well as supremacy. Many in the dominant society do not even realize that their actions reflect such assumptions. They may believe that they are merely "following the rules" or being "realistic" or "practical." Yet their actions are essentially racist because they cannot escape assumptions.

But the effects of racial myths are the least visible consequences of American policies toward minorities. More readily apparent are the actual social and economic conditions of such minorities today.

The Contemporary Circumstances of Minorities

That minorities share low levels of education, income, and employment is increasingly clear from research (see Figure 7.1). We shall not undertake an exhaustive catalog here, in part because the conditions, attitudes, and behavior of minorities are discussed at appropriate points elsewhere in this

---

[2] Ibid., p. xxi.

Figure 7.1 Socioeconomic characteristics of white, black, and Spanish-origin population, 1975. [*Source:* U.S. Department of Commerce, *Social Indicators, 1976* (Washington, D.C.: U.S. Government Printing Office, 1977), p. xxxix.]

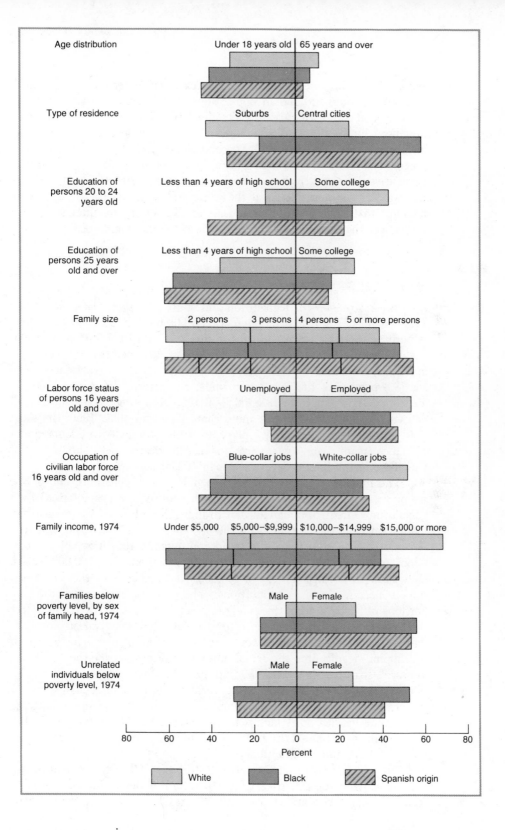

| Age distribution | Under 18 years old | 65 years and over |

| Type of residence | Suburbs | Central cities |

| Education of persons 20 to 24 years old | Less than 4 years of high school | Some college |

| Education of persons 25 years old and over | Less than 4 years of high school | Some college |

| Family size | 2 persons | 3 persons | 4 persons | 5 or more persons |

| Labor force status of persons 16 years old and over | Unemployed | Employed |

| Occupation of civilian labor force 16 years old and over | Blue-collar jobs | White-collar jobs |

| Family income, 1974 | Under $5,000 | $5,000–$9,999 | $10,000–$14,999 | $15,000 or more |

| Families below poverty level, by sex of family head, 1974 | Male | Female |

| Unrelated individuals below poverty level, 1974 | Male | Female |

80 60 40 20 0 20 40 60 80
Percent

White   Black   Spanish origin

book. We shall touch only on certain basic characteristics of the black, Spanish-speaking, and Indian populations, emphasizing in each case those features that are distinctive to each minority. Not all the deprivation experienced by minorities is accounted for by the social and economic gaps visible in these data, however. To concentrate exclusively on the tangible aspects of minority status is to ignore the important point that minorities' difficulties derive partly from less tangible factors, particularly the distinctive way each minority looks at the world. Thus, in a sense the characterizations that follow are preliminary to the effort to understand the differences that distinguish minorities from the dominant society.

Blacks

As the nation's largest minority, blacks have for many years set the pace in minorities' struggles for recognition and status. In 1976 blacks comprised 11.8 percent of the American population. The black population as a whole is both younger and increasing at a faster rate than the white population: the black population increased at the rate of 19.6 percent between 1960 and 1970, compared to 11.9 percent for whites. In 1970 blacks accounted for 13.8 percent of the population under age fifteen. Increasingly, blacks are concentrated in the cities: in 1970 they comprised 21 percent of all center-city residents, a rise of more than 4 percent since 1960; the same year, blacks accounted for 27 percent of all center-city residents under fifteen years of age. Twenty-five major American cities, only seven of which are in the South, have more than 100,000 blacks.

The migration patterns of black people, which constitute one of the major social phenomena of the twentieth century, are characterized by a general movement from agricultural to industrial jobs and also by a movement away from the South toward the big cities of the North and Midwest. Between 1960 and 1970, as the trend continued, three cities (New York, Chicago, and Los Angeles) all had net gains of more than 100,000 blacks. New York drew a net increase of 435,000 black residents. Other cities had similar increases in black proportions. The dramatic increases in the proportions of blacks are not due solely to black immigration; they also reflect the exodus of whites from the central cities. This observation does not undermine the basic point, however: the proportion of blacks in the South is dropping steadily, and the actual number of blacks outside the South has increased sharply. Between 1960 and 1970, the number of blacks in the Northeast increased by 43 percent; in the North Central states, by 33 percent. There is no escaping the implication that these migration patterns are combining with other factors to concentrate the black minority in the nation's major cities. This fact has profound import for future urban, transportation, and welfare policies.

But perhaps the most distinctive feature of black peoples' lives in the United States is the extent to which they trail whites in income, employment status, and educational attainments. In Chapter 6 we noted the gaps between the median incomes of white and black men and the extent to which white and black women trailed both. There are many more blacks at the lowest levels and a substantial number of whites (but almost no blacks) at the very highest income levels. In the case of women the curves are more similar: most women of both races are concentrated at the lowest pay levels, and only a very few white women are at the highest ranks.

Tables 7.1 and 7.2 provide background information about the non-European American ethnic groups and compare them with the white pop-

Table 7.1
Population and Distribution of American Ethnic Groups, 1970

	Popu-lation	% in North-east	% in North Central	% in South	% in West	% Urban	% Rural Nonfarm	% Rural Farm
Chinese	431,583	27	9	7	57	97	3	<1
Japanese	588,324	7	7	5	81	89	9	2
Filipino	336,731	9	8	9	74	85	13	1
Hawaiian	99,958							
Korean	69,510							
Mexican	4,532,435	1	8	37	53	86	13	2
Puerto Rican	1,429,396	81	9	4	5	98	2	<1
Cuban	544,600	32	6	52	10	98	2	<1
American Indian	763,594	6	19	25	50	45	49	6
Black	22,549,815	19	20	53	8	81	17	2
White	178,107,190	25	29	28	17	72	23	6

Source: U.S. Census Bureau, 1970.

Table 7.2
Nativity, Education, Income, and Unemployment of American Ethnic Groups, 1970

	% Foreign-Born	% Not U.S. Citizens	Median Years School (25+)	% High School Gradu-ates	Median Family Income	% of Families Below Pov-erty Line	Unemployment Rate MALE	Unemployment Rate FEMALE
Chinese	47		12.4	58	$10,610	10	3.0%	3.7%
Japanese	21		12.5	69	12,515	6	2.0	3.0
Filipinos	53		12.2	55	9,318	12	4.7	4.7
Hawaiian	1		12.1	53			5.1	5.6
Korean	54		12.9	71			3.6	5.4
Mexican	18	11	8.1	24	6,962	24	6.1	8.9
Puerto Rican	1	< 1	8.7	23	6,165	27	5.6	8.7
Cuban	82	62	10.3	44	8,529	13	4.3	7.3
American Indian	2		9.8	33	5,832	33	11.6	10.2
Black	1		9.8	31	6,067	30	6.3	7.7
White	5		12.1	54	9,961	9	3.6	4.8

Source: U.S. Census Bureau, 1970.

ulation. It is apparent that blacks, Indians, and Spanish-speaking Americans are the largest and the poorest of these groups, and so our analysis focuses chiefly on them.

In recent years sexual inequality in employment has been more serious than inequality based upon color. Between 1962 and 1972, both racial and sexual inequalities decreased, but sexual inequality was greater at both the start and the end of the period. Sexual inequality is lower for blacks than for whites.[3]

Black-white differences in educational attainment remain substantial. In 1977, 36.1 percent of all persons over the age of twenty-four had completed four years of high school, but only 28.4 percent of blacks in that age bracket had done so. In the same year, 15.4 percent of all Americans had completed four or more years of college, but only 7.2 percent of blacks had done so.[4]

Spanish-Speaking Americans
(Primarily Chicanos and Puerto Ricans)

The second largest American minority group is loosely classified as Spanish-speaking. We treat this group as a racial minority here for the powerful reason that it consists primarily of persons who identify themselves as Mexican-Americans, or Chicanos, referring to their mixed Spanish, Mexican, and Indian origins. Some Puerto Ricans, too, trace their origins to the mixture of Spanish, West Indian, and black strains. But analysis is rendered difficult by the fact that nearly all Spanish-speaking persons are officially classified by the Census Bureau as white. Their only readily identifiable shared characteristic is the propensity to speak Spanish as their native, home, or family language. And, as we shall see, Spanish-speaking Americans also share another characteristic — a certain level of poverty and deprivation.

Table 7.3, an official Census Bureau table, shows the breakdown of Spanish-speaking people into major categories, of which the Mexican, or Chicano, is by far the largest. Including those "other Spanish" who are probably Mexican in origin, the number of Chicanos approaches 6.5 million. Puerto Ricans number approximately another 1.5 million, perhaps more. Most Chicanos live in the five southwestern states (Texas, California, New Mexico, Arizona, and Colorado) and to some extent in the Midwest, south of and including Chicago. Most Puerto Ricans are, as we have said, located in the coastal cities of the Northeast.

---

[3] David L. Featherman and Robert M. Hauser, "Trends in Occupational Mobility by Race and Sex in the United States, 1962–1972," mimeographed (University of Wisconsin, Institute for Research on Poverty. Discussion Paper 239–74, November 1974).

[4] Statistical Abstract of the United States, 1978, p. 143.

Table 7.3

"Spanish-Origin" Population, 1969 and 1974 (in thousands)

| | | United States | | The Five Southwestern States | | Southwest as % of U.S. |
		NUMBER	PERCENT	NUMBER	PERCENT	
Mexican	1969	5,073	55.0	4,360	79.2	85.9
	1974	6,455	59.8	5,453	86.3	84.5
Puerto Rican	1969	1,454	15.8	61	1.1	4.2
	1974	1,548	14.3	62	1.0	4.0
Cuban	1969	565	6.1	82	1.5	14.5
	1974	689	6.4			
Central or South American	1969	556	6.0	170	3.1	30.6
	1974	705	6.5		12.8	28.8
Other Spanish	1969	1,582	17.1	835	15.2	52.8
	1974	1,398	13.0	806*		
Total		9,320	100.0	5,507	100.0	59.7
		10,795	100.0	6,321	100.0	58.6

Source: U.S. Census Bureau, Current Population Reports, Series P-20, No. 267.

* Cuban, Central or South American, and Other Spanish are all combined into one category, "Other Spanish," for 1974 data on Southwest.

Black and Spanish-Speaking Americans: Some Comparisons with Whites

By undertaking special analyses, the Census Bureau has finally begun to sort out the characteristics of minority groups, certain of which are particularly worth noting. For example, 51 percent of white workers held white-collar jobs in 1974, while only 32 percent of Spanish-origin workers and 29 percent of blacks held such jobs. The unemployment rates for Spanish-origin persons and for blacks were almost twice those for whites. Spanish-origin families had achieved a median income somewhat above that of blacks, but well below whites'. Figure 7.2 presents some basic comparative information on incomes. It shows, for example, that the median income of Spanish-origin families, though about $1,000 higher than that of blacks, was still barely 70 percent that of whites in 1976.

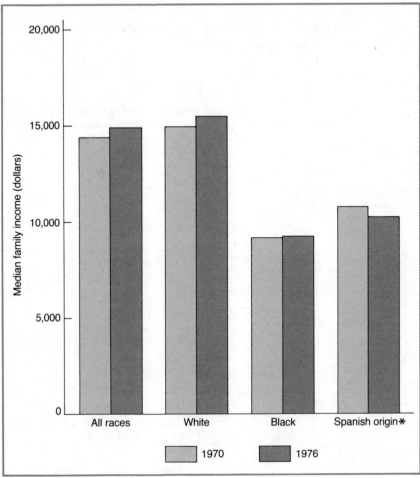

*Persons of Spanish origin may be of any race.

Figure 7.2 Median family income in 1976 and 1970, in constant 1976 dollars, by race and Spanish origin. [*Source:* U.S. Department of Commerce, Bureau of the Census, *Current Population Reports: Consumer Income*, Series P-60, No. 118 (Washington, D.C.: U.S. Government Printing Office, 1978), p. 46.]

Twenty-three percent of all Hispanic families are poor, compared to 9 percent for the general population. Incomes of Hispanic males average $4,000 a year less than for the average American worker.[5] By 1995, Spanish-speaking Americans will be the largest ethnic minority group, but it is an extremely disadvantaged minority.

Table 7.4 shows that whites receive substantially more schooling than do either blacks or people of Spanish origin; sexual inequalities are signifi-

---

[5] *AFL-CIO American Federationist* 86 (December 1979), p. 28.

Table 7.4

Educational Attainment of Population by Ethnic Group, Race, and Sex, March 1974 (percentages)

Years of School Completed	Men			Women		
	SPANISH ORIGIN	WHITE	BLACK	SPANISH ORIGIN	WHITE	BLACK
Less than 4 years of high school	62.2	37.7	60.0	64.0	37.1	55.7
4 years of high school	22.4	32.6	26.1	25.3	40.1	30.1
1 year or more of college	15.5	29.7	13.9	10.7	22.8	14.2

Source: *Monthly Labor Review* 98 (February 1975), p. 67.

cant, but less marked. In a series of tests of specific accomplishments, such as reading level, black and Spanish-origin children regularly scored below Oriental Americans and those American Indians who were tested. That the former groups averaged three full grades below white children may indicate that the tests are oriented toward whites, that minority children are badly educated, or both.[6]

Indians

Lack of agreement about who qualifies as an Indian and absence of concern for the question until very recently make it impossible to say precisely how many Indians now live in the United States. Estimates range from 600,000 to 1 million. The best estimate is probably that of the Bureau of Indian Affairs (BIA), which puts the number of Indians on reservations at about 450,000, with at least another 200,000 or so living in cities. In recent years there has been substantial migration from reservations to the cities, partly as a result of federal programs aimed at reducing the reservation population (and its landholdings). More than 112,000 Indians, or from one-tenth to one-sixth of the total Indian population, migrated to the cities in the period 1952–1970, when such programs were in effect. Los Angeles is thought to have the largest number of urban Indians (about 60,000), followed by San

---

[6] Tetsuo Okada et al., *Dynamics of Achievement: A Study of Differential Growth of Achievement Over Time.* Tech. Note No. 53 (National Center for Educational Statistics, U.S. Office of Education, 1968).

Francisco–Oakland, Dallas–Fort Worth, Oklahoma City, Minneapolis–St. Paul, Phoenix, Cleveland, Chicago, and New York.

The economic and social conditions of Indians are probably the worst of all American minorities. The average annual income per Indian *family* is about $1,500 per year; unemployment is very high, reaching ten times the national average in some areas. U.S. Census reports show that about 60 percent of families living on Indian reservations were below the poverty line in 1973. The life expectancy of Indians is one-third less than the national average, incidence of tuberculosis among Indians is eight times the national average, infant mortality rates are twice the national average, and the suicide rate is double that of the general population. According to Senator Edward Kennedy, 50,000 Indian families (that is, nearly half of all Indian families) live in unsanitary, dilapidated dwellings; many live in huts, shanties, or abandoned automobiles. Those who migrate to the cities often find that they are untrained for employment and unable to adapt to urban life. The average educational level for all federally educated Indians is under five years, and dropout rates are twice the national average in both federal and local public schools.

A recent Senate subcommittee study examined the history of, and current policies toward, Indian education and issued a scathing indictment of such policies and their underlying purposes.[7] It not only found failures of education to lie at the root of current Indian conditions, but also — far more important — declared the whole approach to education to exemplify what is wrong with American policy toward Indians. In a sense this report is applicable to the dilemma facing all racial minorities; a brief review of it may highlight the problem to be dealt with in the next section.

In its opening sentences the subcommittee report declares: "A careful review of the historical literature reveals that the dominant policy of the Federal Government toward the American Indian has been one of forced assimilation which has vacillated between the two extremes of coercion and persuasion. At the root of the assimilation policy has been a desire to divest the Indian of his land and resources."[8] Referring to the federal statute dividing reservations into 160-acre parcels so that Indian families would learn about property ownership and become successful farmers — which resulted in the sale or abandonment of much of the acreage because such principles were totally inconsistent with Indian culture — the subcommittee states:

> During the 46-year period it was in effect it succeeded in reducing the Indian landbase from 140 million acres to approximately 50 million acres of the least desirable land. Greed for Indian land and intolerance for

---

[7] U.S. Senate, Subcommittee on Indian Education, *Indian Education: A National Tragedy — A National Challenge*, 91st Cong., 1st sess.

[8] Ibid., p. 9.

Indian cultures combined in one act to drive the American Indian into the depths of poverty from which he has never fully recovered.

From the first contact with the Indian, the school and the classroom have been a primary tool of assimilation. Education was the means whereby we emancipated the Indian child from his home, his parents, his extended family, and his cultural heritage. It was in effect an attempt to wash the "savage habits" and "tribal ethic" out of a child's mind and substitute a white middle-class value system in its place.[9]

The subcommittee's basic points are that racism and economic interests have combined to place Indians at the very bottom of the socioeconomic pyramid and that the only route by which they are allowed to rise out of poverty and degradation — education — has required that they abandon everything unique to their culture. In other words, the purpose of education has been to remake the Indian into a person whose attitudes and goals are consistent with white capitalist American society. Naturally, Indians resisted such "education" and instead fought a continuing battle to maintain their cultural heritage and integrity.

Probably the most serious attack on Indian integrity and culture has been the practice of removing large numbers of Indian children from their families. A recent study found that twenty times as many Indian as non-Indian children are placed in foster care or put up for adoption, often only because the Indian family is poor and also, the study found, because Indian children are "marketable": there are long waiting lists of whites who want to adopt them. In 1978 Congress tried to remedy this situation by passing an Indian Child Welfare Act that will let Indian tribal courts decide child-custody cases.[10]

The situation is not very different for most other minorities, although the process is somewhat less visible. "Progress," in the sense of the increasing capacity to earn income and gain status in the dominant society, has been available only for certain individuals among minorities and only at the cost of abandoning the distinctive features of their cultures. Unless they give up, at the very least, those values and habits of thought that are inconsistent with competitive individualism and materialistic self-seeking, they will not succeed in American economic life. How much of a cost does this represent? Clearly, some minority-group members would gladly pay the price in order to gain the material and other benefits of full participation in American society. But for others the cost is too high. The gap between the values and habits of mind of their cultures and those of the dominant society is too great, or they prize their own values and cultures too highly to give them up. We will explore the nature of this gap and the distinctiveness of certain minority views in the next section.

---

9 Ibid.
10 *New York Times*, 25 December 1978, p. 1.

The World Views, Values, and Goals of American Minorities

We use the term *world view* here to denote (1) the understanding of the world that is characteristic of a given minority — that is, how it sees the workings of American society — and (2) *the way in which that minority culture thinks* — that is, the concepts, language, and habits of mind that characterize its customary thinking process. The latter is of primary importance. Every culture takes certain things for granted, attaches particular meanings to words, employs specific concepts, and thus tends to think in particular ways. Understandably, these ways of thinking are consistent with the kind of society that has given rise to them; they embody the values that underlie the social order and provide its members with an understanding of what life is about.

It goes without saying that different cultures do not all employ the same ways of thinking. We will explore the basic values of the dominant American orthodoxy in some detail in Chapter 8. For the moment, we need only note certain familiar characteristics of the world view widely shared within American society. It is founded on individualism and the sense that it is natural for individuals to compete and to seek to satisfy themselves through material gain. It assumes that all people will or should want to amass a certain amount of property with which to render their economic situation more secure. It takes for granted that human beings have to struggle against nature and other obstacles until they master or are mastered. It analyzes situations and problems by means of tangible evidence, or "hard facts" that must be related to one another step by step to "prove" that something is or is not true. And it assumes that white skin, Western culture, and the Judaeo-Christian religious tradition are superior to all other brands.

This world view is characteristic of nearly all nonminority Americans. It is characteristic also of many members of racial minorities, because they too are subject to the pervasive influences of American culture — its educational system, mass media, public rhetoric, and official practices. But it is *not* shared by at least some members of each of these minorities. Within each minority, some hold to the distinct way of thinking characteristic of their own culture. In a variety of ways they have resisted assimilation into the world view and habits of thought of the dominant society. On occasion, this may take the form of an exaggerated attachment to peripheral aspects of the minority's heritage or even of efforts to rediscover a long-forgotten indigenous culture. It may be quite deliberately calculated as a response to the pervasiveness of the dominant culture and as a means to draw other members of the minority away from the values and ways of thinking that lead to assimilation into the dominant society. For the most part, such adherence to elements of an independent minority culture appears odd or incomprehensible only to those who subscribe fully to the dominant world view and are impatient with all else. In any event, there are significant numbers of Indians, Chicanos, and blacks whose world views and ways of thinking contrast sharply with those of the dominant culture.

What is distinctive about minority world views? To begin with, they consciously reject many things — basic values, assumptions, preferences, and the like — that the dominant society simply takes for granted. Individualism, competition, materialism, the concept of struggling against nature, the concept of private property, and many other basic principles of the American social order are completely rejected by some or all of the three minority cultures we have been discussing.

The Indian World View

The distinctiveness of the Indian world view is apparent in two excerpts from We Talk, You Listen, a major work by Indian spokesman Vine Deloria, Jr. He first points to some basic differences in the ways that Indians and white Americans conceive of human nature and of individualism:

> The vital difference between Indians in their individualism and the traditional individualism of Anglo-Saxon America is that the two understandings of man are built on entirely different premises. White America speaks of individualism on an economic basis. Indians speak of individualism on a social basis. While the rest of America is devoted to private property, Indians prefer to hold their lands in tribal estate, sharing the resources in common with each other.[11]

This view of land and the concept of human life as inextricably bound up with nature are major distinguishing features of the Indian world view. Peoples are to live in harmony with nature, to preserve and restore it, to be part of its ecological balance — not to struggle against it or exploit it for commercial purposes. Deloria contrasts the Indian view with whites' developmental mania as follows:

> The Indian lived with his land. He feared to destroy it by changing its natural shape because he realized that it was more than a useful tool for exploitation. . . . All of this understanding was ruthlessly wiped out to make room for the white man so that civilization could progress according to God's divine plan.
>
> In recent years we have come to understand what progress is. It is the total replacement of nature by an artificial technology. Progress is the absolute destruction of the real world in favor of a technology that creates a comfortable way of life for a few fortunately situated people. Within our lifetime the difference between the Indian use of land and the white use of land will become crystal clear. The Indian lived with his land. *The white destroyed his land. He destroyed the planet earth.* (Italics in original.)[12]

---

[11] Vine Deloria, Jr., We Talk, You Listen (New York: Macmillan, 1970), p. 170.
[12] Ibid., p. 186.

The distinctiveness of the Indian world view also extends to ways of know-ing. Indian understanding does not depend on logic or evidence, but instead on a sense of wholeness with nature and on intuitive or mystical insight. Relative isolation has made it possible for some Indians to pre-serve substantial portions of their indigenous culture, and it stands in sharp contrast to the dominant society in a variety of ways.

The Chicano World View

In many respects the Chicano world view is grounded in similar concepts. This is understandable in light of the close bond between Chicanos and their Indian forebears; the Indian heritage is stronger than the Spanish heritage among Chicanos. And a deliberate effort is being made by some Chicanos to recapture the unique combined heritage and to employ it as a means of uniting "la Raza" into a more effective force. Special emphasis is placed on the sense of brotherhood and community that should and once did exist among Chicanos and the need to reject Anglo values in order to realize these ideals again. In his *Chicano Manifesto*, for example, Armando Rendon declares:

> Our ideals, our way of looking at life, our traditions, our sense of brother-hood and human dignity, and the deep love and trust among our own are truths and principles which have prevailed in spite of the gringo, who would rather have us remade in his image and likeness: materialistic, cultureless, colorless, monolingual, and racist. Some Mexican-Americans have sold out and become agringandos, . . . like the Anglo in almost every respect. Perhaps that has been their way of survival, but it has been at the expense of their self-respect and of their people's dignity.[13]

There is no ambiguity in Rendon's insistence that Chicanos should reject the thought of assimilation into the dominant society:

> The North American culture is not worth copying: it is destructive of personal dignity; it is callous, vindictive, arrogant, militaristic, self-deceiv-ing, and greedy; . . . it is a cultural cesspool and a social and spiritual vacuum for the Chicano. The victims of this culture are not merely the minority peoples but the dominant Anglo group as well; everything that passes for culture in the United States is symptomatic of a people so swept up in the profit motive and staying ahead of the Joneses that true natural and humanistic values may be destroyed without their knowing it.[14]

This strong antipathy to Anglo society and its values is in part intended to provide a sense of identity and personal worth to enable Chicanos to better withstand the assimilative pressures of the larger society. But it is also intended as a rallying point around which several minorities can join forces. The Chicano emphasis on community leads to the idea of a multiminority

---

[13] Armando Rendon, *Chicano Manifesto* (New York: Macmillan, 1971), p. 46.
[14] Ibid., p. 178.

cultural pluralism, in which all minorities would have status and legitimacy equal to that of the dominant society. Few steps have been taken to put such an idea into effect, though there have been some tentative overtures, particularly between Chicanos and Puerto Ricans.

The Black World View

Blacks are obliged to look harder than other minorities for their independent cultural heritage because they have undergone a longer and heavier exposure to the dominant culture and its social system. But for those blacks who have either rejected or become frustrated by integration, the task is accomplished relatively easily. In many respects that heritage has been maintained intact, but misunderstood as such by whites and by those blacks who accepted white world views and values; in others it has been rebuilt out of the life of the ghettoes and the need of millions of blacks for a sense of personal worth and self-respect. In any event, many blacks share a unique understanding of the white world and of what is necessary to change it in such a way that blacks can live in dignity and comfort.

The "Black Power" era of the mid-1960s, which marked an important stage for the black movement, was partly a result of recognition by many black leaders that the mobilization and ultimate liberation of black people required change at the cultural level. In their eyes it was necessary for blacks to reject the dominant society's values and to learn to see themselves as worthy because of, and not in spite of, being black. Blacks were the first to see that integration meant integration *on the white society's terms.* To maintain one's own identity, it is necessary to avoid being subject to another's definitions; this in turn requires clear understanding and commitment to distinctive values. Stokely Carmichael made these points in 1967:

> How much easier it is to keep a man in chains by making him believe in his own inferiority! As long as he does, he will keep himself in chains. As long as a slave allows himself to be defined as a slave by the master, he will be a slave, even if the master dies. . . .
>
> Black Power attacks this brain-washing by saying, WE WILL DEFINE OURSELVES. We will no longer accept the white man's definition of ourselves as ugly, ignorant, and uncultured. We will recognize our own beauty and our own culture and will no longer be ashamed of ourselves, for a people ashamed of themselves cannot be free.[15]

Speaking before Third World audiences, particularly Latin Americans, Carmichael regularly emphasized the role played by independent cultures in the process of change. In this regard both language and symbols become

---

[15] Stokely Carmichael, "Black Power and the Third World," *Readings in U.S. Imperialism,* ed. K. T. Fenn and Donald C. Hodges (New York: Herder & Herder, 1971), p. 351.

vitally important; a people who would be free must not subscribe to those of their oppressors:

> When African slaves were brought to this country, the Anglo saw that if he took away the language of the African, he broke one of the bonds which kept them united and struggling. Africans were forbidden to speak to each other in their own language. If they were found doing so, they were savagely beaten into silence.
>
> Western society has always understood the importance of language to a people's cultural consciousness and integrity. When it moves into the Third World, it has moved to impose its own language. . . .
>
> The white man hardly needs to police his colonies within this country, for he has plundered the cultures and enslaved the minds of the people of color until their resistance is paralyzed by self-hate. An important fight in the Third World, therefore, is the fight for cultural integrity. . . .
>
> One of our major battles is to root out corrupt Western values, and our resistance cannot prevail unless our cultural integrity is restored and maintained.[16]

Summary

Certain common themes are evident in these various calls for cultural independence from the dominant American world view and values. Resistance to the overwhelming pressure of the dominant society's values is urged by all, and all insist that assimilation is offered only at the price of abandoning what is distinctive and worthwhile in minority cultures. Each insists that its own culture and world view has important contributions to make to a reconstructed version of the larger society. Indians would probably seek merely to be left alone to pursue their own ways, but the other minorities appear to recognize that their status and legitimacy depend on changes in the dominant culture and social system. Chicanos tend to envision a genuine cultural pluralism. Those blacks who emphasize the uniqueness of black culture tend to do so as a prelude to more far-reaching change, including revolution itself — which many see as necessary to eliminate racism.

Thus, the dilemma for minorities becomes somewhat clearer. Not only are the dominant world view and values promulgated forcefully and variously, but they also pervade the policies that seek to aid minorities. The cost of acquiescence in them is loss of cultural integrity and of the uniqueness of one's heritage. And yet this is the only (though still uncertain) route to "progress" for minorities. The gap that we have been seeking to understand is not just social and economic. It is also a gap in self-definition, between one identity and another. Minority persons must

---

16 Ibid., pp. 353–354.

in effect choose between the world views and values of the culture and communities in which they grew up and those of an alien and often cold society that forces them into a competitive enterprise in which the cards are stacked against them. Thus, deprivation is not measured by mere facts and figures concerning income and employment. Indeed, those are precisely the kinds of measures that are valued chiefly by the dominant society. Important as they are in terms of sheer physical survival, they do not measure the pain and desperation that are felt as one's very identity and way of thinking are cast aside. Nor can public policies conceived within the dominant culture and system go very far toward alleviating such deprivation. As we shall see, such policies can create a better life for certain individuals, but whether they can do so for minorities as a whole, and without exacting the cost of cultural submission, remains doubtful.

Minority-Related Policies of the 1960s and 1970s

We come now to the larger problem posed by the current status of racial minorities in the United States. It involves the sharp contrast between the *limits* set by the dominant culture and econopolitical system and the *needs and goals* of minorities. The limits are defined by the dominant society's perceptions of the "problem" of minorities, its options within the established framework of laws and property rights and the basic premise of individualistic self-help, and the odds against its doing *anything*, given the many powerful defenders of the status quo who oppose significant advances for minorities. The needs and goals of minorities involve both vast advances in tangible social and economic conditions of life and, for many, the desire for true cultural pluralism and legitimacy.

Bases for the Policies

The policies of the 1960s and 1970s were based on assumptions characteristic of the dominant society. Central among these was the belief that the poverty and low status of minorities were the products of lack of opportunity and thus could be alleviated by providing better educational and vocational opportunities. A related belief was that discrimination in such areas as housing, employment, and voting operated to reduce individual opportunities. Faith in legal remedies for such discrimination was widespread. Thus, one primary response to minority demands and pressure in the 1960s was a series of civil rights acts providing legal remedies for various forms of discrimination against individuals. The other was a set of new educational and training programs (the War on Poverty) designed to enable minorities to compete more successfully for employment and, hence, income.

The premise underlying such beliefs and programs is that the economic system can and does provide ample jobs and income opportunities and that if minority-group individuals were only qualified, they would be able to raise themselves through their own efforts. But this approach would at best require a long, slow process of upgrading skills, finding jobs, and eliminating discrimination on a case-by-case basis. Quite possibly, the jobs might not exist, or only a very few individuals might qualify for them, or broad-scale discrimination might prove impervious to individual attacks. It is even more likely that substantial proportions of minority persons would be unaffected by such programs or discouraged by the time and effort required for self-help against such entrenched odds.

Not all of the burden of bringing about change fell on public policies, of course. The enactment of highly visible civil rights acts and the institution of the much publicized War on Poverty also had the effect of symbolizing a change in national sentiment. One result was a greater willingness on the part of private businesses to hire at least some minority-group members. Educational institutions developed minority-recruitment programs, and various governmental and private agencies initiated hiring and other aid programs directed specifically at minorities. In place of unconcern and lack of interest, there appeared in many instances at least a superficial sensitivity to advancing the status of minorities. At the same time, the new statutes and programs led to greatly increased expectations on the part of minorities in general and to deep resentment on the part of lower- and middle-class whites of the "special favors" being granted to minority groups, apparently in response to pressure from minority-group members.

Thus, the dilemma reproduces itself over and over again. Limited public policies do create opportunities for a relatively few individuals. But the process is slow at best and dependent on the speed with which the private economy is able to absorb new workers. And the fanfare with which the new programs are instituted leads minorities to expect real assistance (and to become frustrated when it is not forthcoming) and creates the impression among whites that massive efforts are being made by their government to raise minorities above them on the socioeconomic ladder.

Consequences of the Policies

It is in this context that the consequences of the programs of the 1960s and 1970s must be analyzed. That there has been progress cannot be doubted, but it has not been substantial. Nor is it clear whether the visible advances are due to public policies or to broad private response to the militant pressures generated by minorities during that period.

Progress can best be measured in terms of the advancement of blacks, because of their numbers and relatively higher visibility as a deprived minority. Apparently dramatic progress occurred in the 1960s. In 1959 the median family income of blacks was only 51 percent that of whites, but in 1972 it had jumped to 60 percent. If both husband and wife were working, the median family income for blacks under thirty-five was 89 percent that of whites.[17]

Some qualifications must be registered, however. For one thing, the income advances appear to be due in large measure to the fact that more black women were working. In the North and West, for example, where the greatest advances were made, the number of young black families in which husband and wife both worked almost doubled between 1960 and 1970. Black women were working at considerably higher rates than were white women in 1970: 63 percent of black wives held jobs, while 52 percent had year-round jobs; only 54 percent of white wives worked at any time, and only 36 percent had year-round jobs. Moreover, the earlier figures are drawn from a period of particularly high black unemployment, higher proportions of southern residence, and lower educational levels generally. Thus, the real advance between 1960 and 1970 was probably less than the data seem to indicate.

In the 1970s the economic climate was not favorable for blacks. Unemployment rates rose faster than for the general population; for black teenagers they reached levels between 35 and 45 percent. In the last three months of 1979, even before the 1980 recession began, the unemployment rate among black heads of household was 24 percent, according to a survey conducted by the National Urban League.[18] The median income of black families fell back to 59.5 percent of white income, or $9,242, in 1976; in 1969 it had been 61 percent. Thirty-one percent of blacks were below the poverty line in 1977, compared to 22 percent of Hispanics and 9 percent of the total population.

How much of these developments should be attributed to governmental policies? At the height of the War on Poverty, less than $3 billion per year — little more than 1 percent of the federal budget — was invested by the federal government. The civil rights acts of the 1960s were enforced by a mere handful of attorneys in the Justice Department, although a series of successfully tried cases constitutionally legitimated the acts themselves. With the advent of the Nixon administration, funding for the War on Poverty dropped substantially, and much of the thrust toward school integration was undermined by the President's opposition to busing for racial equality. The steep rise in unemployment in the middle 1970s, in conjunction with a decline in the efforts of the federal government to combat poverty, increased the proportion of the population below the poverty line. The recession was especially hard on minorities, as Table 7.5 makes clear. In March 1974, 10 percent of black males who wanted to

---

[17] Data on income in this section are drawn from U.S. Census Bureau, *Differences Between Incomes of Whites and Negro Families by Work Experience and Region: 1970, 1969 and 1959,* Series P-23, no. 39 (Washington, D.C.: U.S. Government Printing Office, 1971).

[18] *Wisconsin State Journal,* 3 August 1980.

Table 7.5

Unemployment Rates by Ethnic Origin, Race, Years in School,
and Sex, March 1974

	Men			Women		
Years in School	SPANISH ORIGIN	WHITE	BLACK	SPANISH ORIGIN	WHITE	BLACK
Less than 4 years of high school	8.4	6.7	11.3	12.0	8.9	11.8
4 years of high school	6.0	3.8	9.0	8.5	5.0	9.3
1 year or more of college	4.5	2.5	7.8	5.7	3.5	5.2
Total	7.2	4.3	10.0	9.8	5.6	9.5

Source: Monthly Labor Review 98 (February 1975), p. 67.

work could not find jobs. At every educational level there was substantially higher unemployment among blacks and people of Spanish origin than among whites, with the disparities somewhat greater for men than for women. Between 1969 and 1976, the number of black poor increased by 10 percent, and in 1969 it was about three times the rate for whites; in 1976 it was almost three and a half times the white rate.

The minorities continue to have a much worse health record than do whites. A report of the U.S. Public Health Service showed that in spite of improvement in the state of Americans' health, in the 1970s the death rate for blacks and Indians was much higher than for whites. The infant mortality rate was nearly twice that for whites, and for people between the ages of twenty-five and forty-four, the death rate of blacks was almost two and a half times the white rate.[19]

The extent of real progress, even in socioeconomic terms, appears to remain an open question. Achievements to date appear fragile and perhaps temporary and so far limited to the advancement of a relatively few individuals. Achievements appear to depend on the mobilization and militance of minorities themselves, but the massive efforts of minorities in the 1960s may have been a unique, unrepeatable episode. If the various business, governmental, and educational initiatives of the 1960s were merely short-term responses to ghetto riots and other violent confrontations, the costs of "progress" will ultimately be seen as very high. Nor will the situation then appear promising for other minorities or for those among all minorities who seek legitimacy and equal status for their own cultures and lifestyles.

[19] *Madison Capital-Times,* 5 December 1979.

PART
3

CONTRASTING REACTIONS TO POLICY PATTERNS

JUSTIFYING THE STATUS QUO: IDEOLOGY AND SYMBOLISM

8

We have now analyzed a number of problems and examined a variety of government policies. Patterns of consequences have become apparent: the same groups of people, mostly blue-collar workers, women, and minorities, are at the bottom in every instance. Even though together they make up a large majority of the population, they bear the brunt of inflation control, make the least income, experience repeated unemployment, and suffer the effects of discrimination on the basis of sex, race, and ethnicity. Government policies give priority to the needs and goals of the corporate-banking sector and its owners and managers; only secondarily (and relatively recently) have the interests of the large majority been directly reflected in policy outcomes.

Despite these inequities, most people appear basically satisfied with the American system and what it does. Only relatively few challenge the system in any fundamental way, although (as we shall see in the next chapter) such challenges generate much of the conflict and change that characterize our politics today. Of course, the American system delivers many things that many people want or think they want. But two other important factors are also at work to justify the status quo, partly by encouraging people to want whatever they get and partly by discouraging opposition in a variety of ways. One is *ideology*, and the other is *symbolism*. This chapter considers each of these in some detail.

Ideology

Ideology is the collection of beliefs the members of a given society hold about how their government works, or should work, and why. Such beliefs may be articulated fully or may be merely implicit in the ways people live their lives. They may vary somewhat between the highest and lowest *strata*, or levels, of the population. And they may be held with varying degrees of intensity. But whether factually correct or not, and however expressed, such mental images serve as a kind of lens through which people see and a set of cues with which they make judgments about their political world. Both perceptions and values thus contribute to one's ideology, which is normally acquired very early in life from family and schooling. It is reaffirmed in a variety of ways as one grows older — by the media, the rhetoric of politicians, and the beliefs and actions of other people. That it fits reality in a sense may be only coincidental, for ideology has a life and continuity of its own and in effect shapes "reality" accordingly.

In most societies one particular belief system is predominant. The United States is no exception. Indeed, the depth and strength of the orthodox American ideology are so great that some people do not even recognize it as ideology. Their beliefs about politics and government seem so natural and self-evident that they can imagine no other possibilities; they are convinced that they see only the truth and nothing else. This total short-circuiting of independent analysis is the supreme achievement of an ideology.

American orthodoxy, for example, insists that wealth and income are distributed roughly in accordance with individual talents and effort and that nearly everybody is or could be reasonably affluent in this highly productive system. Such disparities as may exist do not affect the distribution or usage of political power. Thus, the American political system is democratic, works well, and regularly produces policies that are appropriate to the problems in question or at least are the best accommodation possible under the circumstances.

The Functions of Ideology

Three primary functions of ideology are worth noting here. First, ideology affects our perception of problems. Because we are used to thinking in certain ways and because we habitually make certain assumptions, we tend to "understand" new problems only in a particular (limited and narrow) context. Second, ideology not only explains why policies take the form they do, but also justifies (or condemns) these patterns. It may do so on the grounds of the rightness (or wrongness) of the political system that produced them, the structure of power that animates that system, or the basic values underlying it. Third, ideology serves broadly to organize people and to provide them with a coherent sense of the relationship among themselves, their values, and the workings of their government.

■ *The Perception of Problems.* What is a "problem"? Clearly, how we understand the character and causes of problems relates directly to what we regard as acceptable ways to solve them. Is the pollution of air and water, for example, such a drastic threat to the enjoyment of life or to the long-term ecological balance of nature that severe measures should be taken to control the industrial sources of pollution? Or is it a necessary price to be paid for the continued expansion of the economy and the provision of jobs for a growing labor force? One's answer depends only partly on objective facts. Part of the "answer," probably some of the "facts," and certainly much of the "solution" depend on one's ideology.

Thus, our understanding of a problem involves much more than its "objective" characteristics; it is a direct outcome of our values and ideology. For example, the American orthodoxy tends to see each problem in isolation, as if it had no roots in our social structure, economic practices, or basic values. Another ideology — a version of radicalism — sees problems as connected to one another and to the underlying conditions and structures of the society and economy. Such divergent ideologies would give rise to very different understandings of the nature of the problem and thus to very different prescribed solutions.

■ *Explanation-Justification.* Ideology does not affect just what we see and understand in the world around us; it simultaneously implies that what we see conforms to either our hopes or our fears. Things not only *are*, but are also *good* or *bad*, because ideology teaches us to understand them in both dimensions at the same time. By relating newly perceived events to long-established and deeply held convictions and by insisting that the former are consistent with the latter, ideology filters all events through a particular perceptual screen. In the view of the dominant ideology, for example, the rightness of the American political system and the propriety of our basic political values make it likely that public policies will benefit the society as a whole.

■ *Organization of People.* What does it mean to shape what people see and whether they see a given phenomenon as good or bad? Clearly, it implies at least organization of and potentially control over those people. By providing a coherent understanding of their world, ideology organizes people and molds them into particular relationships with other people, government, and events. People need not be aware of what is happening to them, nor is it as if they were marching in a column of thousands in response to explicit orders from their leaders. But they are organized in the sense that they see and think the same things at the same time as do many other people. In the case of the dominant ideology, the experience of most individuals implicitly reinforces (and rewards) acceptance of American orthodoxy, and political leaders explicitly call for behavior in accordance with it. Thus, ideology becomes a powerful instrument of social control on behalf of those people or interests served by its teachings. It is easier and more effective if people voluntarily behave in ways that are congenial to the existing social order; coercion can then be held to a minimum. A challenging ideology may similarly organize people's lives and serve many of the same functions on behalf of group leaders. In both cases people perceive and behave in certain ways and believe in their acts and perceptions because they consciously or unconsciously hold a particular ideology. And everybody holds some ideology, in greater or lesser degree. The only question is which ideology and how it affects understanding and action.

Political Values: The Building Blocks of Ideology

Political values are the most fundamental beliefs that people hold about what is right or wrong in politics. They are the building blocks for thinking about how political systems should be organized and why. We shall touch upon five political values that have had major impact on American political thought and practice. The first four of these are recognizable as the American version of *liberalism*. Liberalism was a system of thought articulated forcefully in seventeenth-century England, partly in defense of the new middle class of merchants and tradesmen. It had a profound effect on the American colonists, their Revolution, and the Constitution and remains potent today.

■ *Individualism.* The focal point of political thought in the United States is the individual; all other relationships and values follow from this base. The individual is the basic unit of politics, and the political system is erected for the individual's benefit. Individuals are viewed as naturally competitive, their competition leading to personal fulfillment and social progress. The principal goals of political life have to do with providing a suitable context for the individual's satisfaction and happiness. Self-fulfillment is sought and principles of government are deduced from assumptions about what is needed to serve the individual's needs. In the mideighteenth century, for example, the chief impediment to individual self-attainment seemed (with good reason) to be governmental power wielded by royal or aristocratic authorities. The principal means of ensuring individual opportunity, therefore, was a firm set of limitations on the power of government and an equally determined laissez-faire approach to the role of government in the society and economy.

■ *The "Natural Rights" of the Individual.* As part of their entitlement on earth, due them solely by virtue of their existence, individuals have certain rights. These are (1) the right to property — to be secure in the possession of goods and land, to be able to rely on the value of money, and to be able to collect debts owed; (2) the right to life and liberty, in the sense that one cannot be deprived of either without being granted the due processes of law (hearing, trial, fair procedures, and so on); (3) the right to participate, to some degree at least, in the decisions of government; and (4) the right to equality, whether defined as equal treatment before the law or as equality of opportunity.

Although property rights are only one of several natural rights, political thinkers and practical politicians have frequently tended to elevate them to first priority and sometimes to exclusive entitlement. The problem is, of course, that property rights often conflict with other natural rights, particularly equality; thus, the issue of priority is crucial. The deep and bitter conflict over slavery may serve to illustrate this point and to demonstrate the power and ascendancy of property as an American political value. None of the framers of the Constitution seriously doubted that slaves were property, to be provided for as such. The early debates over limited slavery versus emancipation foundered on the appropriate amounts of compensation (the propriety of which was never questioned) for the loss of property. The Abolitionists were bitterly resisted by most northerners, at least partly because of the antiproperty implications of their position. And when emancipation came, it was as a limited expediency in the course of a difficult war. In this sequence of events relatively few voices were raised on behalf of granting equality priority over property, and it was only the commitment to preserve the Union that finally mobilized the use of force.

This conflict between property and other natural rights is real and recurrent — in debate over the progressive income tax, social security, poverty programs, and the regulation of the economy generally. But such conflict is anticipated and feared by those who hold property far more than actual inroads on their possessions would seem to justify. The framers and the early Federalists feared attacks on property and radical redistribution of wealth if majorities were allowed to work their will through the political system. Consequently, they built in a series of restraints on the power of government.[1] In justifying this principle, they developed and promulgated the idea of "majority rule *and* minority rights." By minority rights, of course, they meant property rights. But the two are logically

---

[1] For a full presentation of the framers' ideas, one should examine the *Federalist Papers,* available in many inexpensive editions.

inconsistent: no political system can provide both majority rule and minority rights in the absolute sense. An effective limit on majority rule on behalf of minority rights means that there is no real majority rule. Conversely, if majority rule succeeds in working its will in all cases, the system cannot always be protecting minority rights. Nevertheless, most Americans subscribe to both principles and acknowledge such limitations on the power of majorities — testimony, perhaps, to the success of the Federalists in establishing their view as an integral component of American political ideology.

■ *Limited Government.* At least as far as eighteenth-century thinkers were concerned, a necessary corollary to individualism and natural rights (in which property rights hold primacy) is the principle of limited government. If rights flow to individuals from the laws of nature, then government is the creation of those individuals. Its powers must be consistent with their natural rights and must have been conferred on it by the collectivity of individuals who together possess all powers. Its sphere of action is defined both by the limited scope of the powers granted to it and by the inviolability of the rights of individuals.

In this view government is a marginal and semi-illegitimate enterprise. Regardless of the fact that the society (or collectivity of individuals) has no other agent capable of acting on behalf of the whole, each effort to employ government for particular purposes is viewed with suspicion, and its necessity and propriety are challenged. To be sure, this principle may be most often invoked to prevent governmental action deemed undesirable and forgotten when favorable action is sought.

■ *Materialism and the Business Ethic.* Since the earliest days of this nation, observers have repeatedly commented on the special disposition of Americans to seek private economic gain. Acquisitiveness and profit seeking are sometimes related to a so-called Protestant ethic, based on the belief that ultimate salvation depends on striving and attainment in this world. National celebration of such motivations reached its height at the end of the nineteenth century, in the days of Horatio Alger and the robber barons. Although it would be little more than caricature to attribute such motivations to most Americans today, it is clear that the United States is a business-oriented society. The underlying value system strongly supports such capitalist principles as the value of consumption by individuals, the measurement of the propriety and desirability of new ventures by their profitability, and the measurement of individual achievement by the accumulation of wealth.

These values and motivations, broadly shared, affect the criteria used to determine the priorities and programs of government. Because private profit and consumption are valued so highly, public expenditure is suspect. Government outlays for such public purposes as schools, hospitals, and welfare may be seen as "spending" and therefore undesirable, while corporate expenditures for new and perhaps unnecessary consumer products are "investments" and therefore good. Government action may be judged from a kind of tradesman's vantage point, in which short-range questions of profitability dominate. Can the Postal Service be run as a business and bring in enough income to balance its costs? Will the proposed bridge earn enough income to pay off the cost of building it in a fixed period?

■ *Racism.* Almost equally long-lived and pervasive in American society is the assumption of white supremacy. Originating in Western culture centuries ago, the sense of superiority of the white race has been an animating feature of Americans and their governmental policies throughout our history. Until very recently, neither the American Indian nor the Afro-American was thought fit for full citizenship. Recent scholarship indicates that nearly all the major leaders at the time the Constitution was framed, as well as in subsequent periods, held white-supremacist assumptions.[2] However unconscious such notions may have been, they were instrumental in shaping policies that massacred Indians, oppressed slaves, and built a sometimes unrecognized racist strain into the American value system.

After centuries of official action in accordance with these premises, it is not surprising that those who seek evidence of the degradation of the nonwhite races are readily able to find it. Efforts to remedy the work of centuries, however, run up against denials of personal responsibility and failure to perceive the racist bases of existing policies as well as normal resistance to change. Most Americans do not understand the extent to which subtle and not-so-subtle racial barriers have served to prevent the nonwhite poor from rising via the routes taken by the immigrant poor of the nineteenth and early twentieth centuries. Given such widespread and deep-seated racism, it is not difficult to see why the limited governmental steps taken have nevertheless been highly controversial and why the tangible signs of change are so few.

Many important factual questions can be asked about all these values, of course. We do not know which groups or strata within the society actually held or hold them, how widely shared or intensely felt they are, or whether people who assert them actually act on them. These are questions we shall attempt to answer later.

The Values Applied in Practice

The dominant political belief system holds that the values just described (with the exception of racism, of course) are realized on a day-to-day basis in American politics. In part, this is the natural function of a nation's

---

[2] Thomas F. Gossett, *Race: The History of an Idea in America* (New York: Schocken Books, 1963).

political ideology. In effect, ideology is a kind of mental map that tells people how to harmonize what they see with their strongly held convictions about what is good. Because it is simplifying and reassuring, it is also seductive and frequently unconscious. It tends to be strongest among those who have had the most formal education, possibly because their economic interests and social positions act to reinforce what they have heard so often and in so many different forms in the educational process. Others, particularly those who experience more contrast between the ideology and the realities of daily existence, may be less likely to adopt it uncritically.

But because of such ideology-induced confidence, those few who (however accurately) believe a given policy to have disastrous implications will have great difficulty gaining support from a majority of their fellow citizens. Or ideology may serve to divert or frighten people so completely as to distort consideration of various problems. American anti-communism in the post–World War II decades was apparently strong enough to dominate policymaking and suppress dissent. We shall illustrate two components of the dominant American political ideology in the paragraphs that follow.

■ *The Ideology Holds that the Basic Political Values of the United States Are Reflected in the Structure of the American Government and that the Resulting Political System Is Democratic in Character.* The core political values — individualism, limited government, natural rights (with property rights ascendant over equality and other human rights), and procedural regularity — are patently manifest within the Constitution and the government it created. Ideology holds that the institutional forms of these principles will operate as if controlled by an unseen hand and will deliver the results considered appropriate by those who subscribe to that set of values. The interplay of presidential and congressional power is seen as yielding a mechanistic (and therefore appropriate) product; the decision of the Supreme Court is seen as representing a higher law's mandate, not the preferences of five or more judges. In short, ideology suggests that the translation of values into institutions and powers has achieved a nonpartisan, depoliticized apparatus that works to the benefit of all.

Next, the ideology holds that this structure creates a situation that allows full play to the "natural" workings of human capacities and wants and of the economic market, which will result in the greatest good for the greatest number of people. Thus, the established political values are seen as manifested in a particular set of institutions; these institutions interact in a mechanical manner, and the result is the furtherance of a natural order in which talent and effort are rewarded and the incompetent and slothful carried along by the successful.

The teachings of ideology with respect to the structure and operations of government are that all will benefit equally, or at least substantially, from such procedures. But it seems clear that the character of the institutional setup and the principles on which it frequently operates neither benefit all equally nor leave results to chance. It works to the advantage of those who are situated so as to be able to seize opportunities for gaining power and influence. Separation of powers, distribution of powers between nation and states, and the protection provided for property rights, for example, make it very difficult to enact laws that change the status quo. The principle of laissez faire means that people with private economic power are free to use that power as they see fit, and it is difficult (and perhaps wrong in any event) for others to try to use government to control such activities. If government works mechanically, of course, nobody should be aggrieved about its actions, because they are inherent in the (good) design of the American governmental structure itself. Thus, it turns out that nothing is responsible for the advantages secured by those with economic or social power except their own talents in the free and open struggle for individual achievement.

Perhaps even more important than the manner in which basic political values are related to the structure and operations of government, is the way in which the ideology equates the values and the nature of American government with democracy. Democracy is good; the United States is good; the United States is a democracy; democracy is what we experience in the United States. Circularity and poor logic are no obstacles for a powerful ideology, and it may be fruitless — perhaps unpatriotic — to try to unravel the relationships here. What has apparently happened is that the ideology has adapted to the powerful appeal of democracy in the last two centuries and has interpreted American values and institutions in this light. Thus, the commitment to private property and individualism becomes a characteristic of democracy. Or, the institution of judicial review, originally designed to frustrate popular will expressed through the elected legislature, comes to be seen as a vehicle for expression of the democratic values of civil liberties. A statute outlawing political participation by people with a particular viewpoint becomes democratic because it preserves the "freedom" of the "democratic" electoral process. A natural tendency to believe that what we have is good, if not ideal, leads to favorable (democratic) interpretations of whatever we have.

We are not arguing that the governmental system of the United States is necessarily undemocratic, though we may appear to be taking a harsh view of some much revered things. We are saying that the acts of *assuming* that American institutions are democratic and of *defining* "democracy" as what exists in the United States are essentially *ideological* in character. In both cases "American" and "democratic" become synonymous — testimony to the power of ideology to suggest conclusions rather than leaving them to the judgment of the observer.

It is the social-control aspect of American ideology — its capacity to disarm analysis and provide benevolent interpretations — that is so significant to contemporary American politics. Few, if any, Americans are fully captured by all the characteristics of ideology we have touched on, but practically everyone is influenced by at least some of them. In the next section, we shall discuss forms of ideology held even by some scholars and students of American politics.

■ *The Ideology Holds that the Process of Political Decisionmaking in the United States Consists of Negotiation and Compromise Among Many Factions and Groups and that the Product Is a Reasonable Approximation of Both Democracy and the Public Interest.* In the next few paragraphs we shall characterize the generally accepted view of the American political process, sometimes termed "democratic pluralism."

To begin with, the system is considered to be open to all those who wish to take the time and trouble to participate. For the most part, Americans actually do participate through the vehicle of voluntary associations, organized around the ethnic, religious, occupational, social, economic, political, or other interests that are of concern to them. A single citizen may belong to several such groups. These groups articulate the needs and desires of the people at all levels of the society, but particularly with reference to government.

In organizing support among the population and presenting their claims on the government, groups come into conflict with other groups. Each group's efforts to achieve its goals are likely to call into play another group with different or opposing goals in the same field. This is sometimes termed "the principle of countervailing powers." The various interested groups then engage in an elaborate process of negotiation, bargaining, appeals to principle and popular support, pressures on decisionmakers, and finally compromise. Because each group represents a significant segment of opinion and probably has access to some source of power within the governmental structure, it can usually delay, if not completely frustrate, an extreme demand made by another group. This means that each group is induced to compromise on a solution that falls short of its full goals; if it does not, it may end up with nothing.

Harmonious handling of conflict through compromise is also promoted by the informal rules for group goal seeking. Each group is assumed to be sufficiently concerned with the fairness and openness of the process (because the attainment of its goals depends on getting a fair hearing from the others) to commit itself to defending the procedures of decisionmaking. Above all, parties to the goal-seeking process should be willing to see one another's problems and also to compromise at a point short of not only their own goals, but also absolute disaster for one another. This is also sound strategy, since those who happen to win today may be on the losing side tomorrow, in which case they can expect the same consideration from their new opponents. Thus, the informal rules promote compromise and help to build a shared feeling of mutual approval for the decision-making system itself. One's opponents, after all, are people who play the game by the rules and are entitled to respect for their views and for the demands placed on them by their constituencies. Those who do not accept the rules are not playing the right game or are cheating and are properly censured by all the regular players. When the regular groups do find themselves in disagreement, or at other moments when major decisions must be made, the basic outlines of national policy are determined by popular elections. In this way the day-to-day activities of group goal seeking are channeled; groups devote themselves to working out the details of policies decided on by the mass electorate.

Groups perform many functions within the social and political orders. They serve as a major means of representation, providing people with a sense that their voices are heard in the halls of government by means other than the familiar geographical or party systems of representation. Thus, a citizen who belongs to the minority political party in his or her state or congressional district can nevertheless feel represented in government by the efforts of interest groups that seek to further his or her goals. In discharging this representative function, groups also root the citizen more thoroughly in the society — giving him or her a sense of place, status, and fulfillment. And in a reciprocal manner, groups give public officials a means of knowing what the people want and need and a way of communicating back and forth that makes for more responsive government.

The pattern of group activity in politics has other consequences. People who participate in groups acquire the tolerance for others and respect for fair procedures that help to support a democratic system. They may also belong to two or more groups whose interests are occasionally in conflict. For example, a woman may belong to both the League of Women Voters and the Catholic Church. If the league seeks to take a position contrary to that of the Church on birth control issues, the citizen may be "cross-pressured" to take a much less extreme position on the issue than she otherwise would have. At the same time, her influence within each organization helps to lead it to a less extreme position. This "cross-pressured," or cleavage, effect, multiplied many times over for many issues, helps to keep the political system on an even keel by reducing the extremity of pressures on it. The process is both democratic and in the public interest. It is democratic because everybody has a chance to be heard, the procedures for "playing the game" are known and observed, and a general consensus based on compromise and tolerance emerges before the decision is cast into final form. It is in the public interest chiefly because it does represent a consensus that everybody can accept and that is therefore very likely to be in harmony with the experience and capacity of the system and responsive to the problem in question.

The five paragraphs above sum up a very large body of analysis, interpretation, and self-congratulation by journalists, academics, and the general public. Most of it, however pretentiously set forth, is little more than a restatement of the dominant ideology. Taken together, these two major components of the dominant ideology are characterized by a very strong commitment to the established order. In particular, they emphasize over and over again the necessity and propriety of following the rules. Sometimes insistence on procedural regularity is raised to the level of a basic political value and given a label such as "legalism." The importance to Americans of formal written provisions, and of the law generally, has often been noted by observers; the major role played by lawyers in the governing of this society also rests on this procedural-legal bias. Beneath the stress on established rules and legalistic procedures, of course, lies a basic conviction that actions taken in the private sphere are best and should take precedence over (if not be protected against) public policies. Thus, the orthodox ideology says in effect that if policies are developed by the established rules of the political system, they must be appropriate. Further, if they maximize people's opportunities to gain their ends by private rather than governmental means, they are good. This view makes it almost unnecessary to examine the actual consequences of policies. Their merits can be determined from the circumstances of their enactment and from the extent to which they leave people free to gain their ends by private means.

The Implications of American Orthodoxy

So far, we have analyzed the American orthodoxy as a set of specific values and ideological beliefs held by Americans. We have seen how political images and beliefs are rooted in basic values and have examined the nature of each. Now it is time to note again how fully American beliefs are fused with capitalist values and to ask what this orthodoxy means for our politics.

How much of our orthodoxy is capitalism by another name? Individualism, materialism, competition, the work ethic and profit motive, property rights, and the primacy of private economic activity are clearly capitalist principles. The concepts of limited government, contractualism, and legalism are applications of capitalist principles to the political system. Study the advertisement on the Capitalist Liberation Front carefully to see how deeply rooted and connected capitalism and American values and ideology are typically said to be. Some American values may have had other origins and independent support, but have become intertwined with capitalism throughout our history. Racism, a prime example, relegates minority groups to artificially low levels of employment and income and both divides workers and diverts them from making more effective demands for larger shares of wealth and income. Some early capitalist values are honored only rhetorically by the corporate-banking sector, as a kind of "cover" for its use of government on its own behalf. Perhaps the best way to conceive of the American orthodoxy is as capitalism with certain modifications, ambiguities, and accompanying cultural idiosyncrasies. A capsule characterization, however, would have to emphasize the continuing overlap and parallel with capitalism.

The Capitalist Liberation Front

SOME DAYS, things look bleak. In the worldwide propaganda war our adversaries often seem to steal the headlines. They advance; it seems we decline. They seem to encircle us more tightly.

Except.

Except that the ideas of human liberty and full personal development were never so attractive—or so within the reach of so many human beings—as at present.

Is there a word more exciting to the human race today than "liberation"? Or "do your thing"? Or "individual liberties"? Or "self-determination"? Or "opportunity to be one's self"? Without such conceptions, capitalism would not be possible. These conceptions are the very soul of everything we mean by "free enterprise." These are *our* ideas.

The energy of capitalism is in the human heart. Its name is *liberty*. This is what critics of capitalism have always misunderstood.

In the highest form of flattery, even our enemies embrace our words: in national "liberation" fronts; in "Free" Republics; in "democratic" socialisms. More significant than that, the dreams of the peoples of the world—of billions of individuals—are, at bottom, *our* dreams. Dreams of the fully developed, cooperative, open, free individual.

The critics of capitalism misunderstand. They neglect three features in the human soul.

The number one desire of the human heart is not equality but *liberty*. Equality is an indispensable condition; we are committed to equality. But the further point, the focal point of human aspiration, is *liberty*. No other system, but ours alone, is the system of *liberty*: That deepest human energy of all is ours. Others, as we do, bring equality but we alone deliver *liberty*.

Secondly, the system of free enterprise is *value-giving*. For millenniums, oil lay useless and undesirable beneath the earth. Oil would have no value apart from the industry that capital invented. It was our inventiveness, our exertion, and our creation that in living memory made oil a precious mineral. And so, also, for many other raw materials that today have value. Capitalism is *wealth-creating*—and also *wealth-conferring*. It is true that we "exploited" some nations earlier; but we have also made them wealthy beyond their dreams. Capitalism in its abuses does at times "despoil" the earth. But in its imagination and its practicality it gives humble things values the human race never saw in them before. Capitalism has *enriched* the earth, seeing in it possibilities hidden there by its Creator, evoking marvels and miracles men had never seen before.

Thirdly, capitalism is *transformative*. It has the good of the human race at heart. And so in its unfolding capitalism transforms the world—and in the process transforms itself as well. It has given health to millions who would not have lived before; fed more millions than were ever fed before; built schools and universities for larger proportions of the race than had ever been educated earlier; and distributed higher standards of comfort and amenities, not only for an aristocracy but for ordinary workers and for many of the poor, than the world had ever dreamed of. More precious than all of these, capitalism has taken as its bride—and cherished—political democracy.

If capitalism is surrounded, it is surrounded like the yeast in dough. What capitalism stands for is what is deepest in the human soul. And what eventually, irresistibly, bursts forth: *human liberation*, for the solitary self; for every brother, every sister; and for societies and institutions everywhere.

Rumrill-Hoyt, Inc.

ADVERTISING/PUBLIC RELATIONS · NEW YORK CITY · ROCHESTER · BUFFALO · HOLLYWOOD (FLA.)

(*Source: Fortune*, May 1975, p. 90. Used by permission of Rumrill-Hoyt Advertising, Inc.)

What does this orthodoxy mean for our politics? The *strength* of its influence clearly has several important results. Most Americans are unaware how specific their values and beliefs are, partly because they are rarely challenged effectively. Thus, they consider their values and beliefs natural, inevitable, and self-evident. This stance can lead to failure to understand others' feelings and opinions and to impatience with or intolerance of those with other views. Because the orthodoxy exists at such a deep level that it is not always recognized, those who depart from it may appear mentally or morally defective. They can then be imprisoned, hospitalized, or otherwise ostracized legally and with general approval of such actions.

The *shared character* of at least the major elements of the orthodoxy has other implications. We do not argue that all sectors of the population hold the orthodox values and beliefs to the same degree; as we shall see, there are levels at which only certain basic elements of it are observed and some where other views predominate. But most Americans share the values and beliefs discussed in this chapter to some degree. This means that prominent public officials can draw support for their actions by manipulating revered symbols. They do not have to justify their acts exclusively, or even primarily, in terms of their merits. Instead, they can claim that their acts conform to the values of individualism or preservation of the economic system. In short, the broadly shared character of the orthodoxy facilitates social control. It causes people to believe in and support their leaders, almost without regard to what those leaders are actually doing.

The *content* of orthodoxy, in conjunction with its strength and shared character, has certain additional implications. Capitalism becomes insulated from critical evaluation because most Americans do not perceive the economic system in those terms and, in any event, believe it to be both good and inevitable. Nationalism is enhanced because many Americans come to feel that our system is clearly superior to all others. Some may carry their belief to the point of messianism, a feeling that it is our moral mission to bring the blessings of our (capitalist) system to the rest of the world. Those who willfully oppose and reject our system — for example, Communists or socialists — are thus seen as evil and inevitable enemies.

This characterization may seem harsh or exaggerated. We do not believe that it is; at least, it is thoroughly grounded in the interpretations of generations of reputable American scholars. It is more likely that such reactions are the result of a lifetime of uncritical acceptance of orthodox values and beliefs, to a greater or lesser degree. The strength and character of this orthodoxy also suggest one reason why radicalism has not been very successful in the United States. As we shall see, even radicalism has often been unable to extricate itself from the scope of this pervasive belief system.

Symbolism

Another vital support for the status quo is found in the way that symbolism diverts people, reassures them, creates wants and needs, and deflects or undermines thrusts toward change. There is no direct relationship between the *fact* or even the *perception* of deprivation and rationally calculated *action* to change that situation. Even if people accurately understand the causes of problems, they may not even consider acting to solve them. Politics is simply not that logical or rational. Indeed, politics is not understandable merely as a series of rational decisions and purposeful actions to produce intended results. Many actions are unforeseen or unintended, and so are many results. What seems logical or likely often simply does not occur. One of the most powerful reasons why this is true is discoverable in the part played by symbols in politics.

The Scope and Importance of Symbolism

■ *The Nature of Symbolism.* Government does not just reflect the will of some of the people. It also *creates* public wants, beliefs, and demands that all have powerful impact on who gets what in politics. If some of the major demands and beliefs of mass publics are evoked by what the government does and by what public officials say, talk of responsiveness to the will of the people means less (or more) than meets the eye.

Governmental actions and rhetoric can reassure people and make them apathetic, or it can arouse them to militant action. And the messages that reassure or arouse can be either accurate or misleading. Because controversial policies always hurt some people, the temptation is strong for public officials to be reassuring; officials are naturally eager to be reassured themselves and to believe that what they do is in the public interest. Even if political symbols are misleading, therefore, they need not be deliberately deceptive. Indeed, the most powerful political symbols are disseminated by people who believe in them themselves.

Public officials can win mass support for actions that would elicit protest and resistance if undertaken by private groups. If private gas and electric companies could raise their rates whenever they pleased, without any pretense of governmental supervision, any company that substantially raised its rates every year or two would certainly evoke massive protests and demands for public ownership or tight regulation.[3] But few people protest publicly when state public utilities commissions permit precisely the same rate rises. The blessing of a government agency reassures consumers and wins support for actions that would otherwise be resented.

---

[3] This is precisely what happened in the late nineteenth century, giving rise to the existing state and federal regulatory laws.

If the wealthy, as private individuals, forced the poor or middle class to give them a substantial part of their earnings, resistance would be massive and immediate. Yet governmental tax and subsidy policies that have exactly this effect are perceived as reasonable, even though particular taxes or subsidies are criticized by scattered interests. If private individuals forced millions of young men to leave home, submit to strict discipline, kill others, and be killed themselves, such "slavery" would be regarded as intolerable. But when legitimized by duly enacted draft laws, it is not only tolerated by most, but regarded as highly desirable and even necessary.

The point is that official governmental acts and statements are rarely *simple* in their impacts or their meanings. Almost never are their consequences clear and certain. Economists conclude that public utility laws typically do little to keep gas and electricity rates low. But it still seems likely to most people that the rates would be even higher without governmental regulation. Low tax rates for oil producers force other taxpayers to subsidize an affluent group, but the subsidy is justified on the grounds that it enlarges a vital national resource — and it probably does. In such cases the financial costs to large numbers of people are high (though they are largely or completely hidden), the method of calculating them is complex, and their fairness is difficult for most people to judge. By contrast, the symbolic benefits — protection of the consumer, promotion of national security — are easy to see and to understand, even though they often turn out to be trivial, misleading, or nonexistent when studied carefully.

The legitimacy of government — the belief that public officials represent the will of the people — therefore confers a mystique that can reassure people even when they have reason to be wary or alarmed. And it can arouse people to endure severe sacrifices due to wars or regressive taxes even if they have little to gain. In such cases the facts are difficult to recognize or analyze, and anxious people want very much to believe that the government knows how to handle the economic, military, and other threats they fear, but cannot cope with as individuals.

Not all public policy is symbolic or based on deliberate or unintended mystification, of course. The impacts of many governmental acts on people's everyday lives are so clear that there is little question whether they help or hurt. People in a slum neighborhood who want a playground or a traffic light know when they are getting what they need. The farm corporation that gets several hundred thousand dollars in "price-support" subsidies knows precisely how public policy boosts its profits. To the taxpayer, of course, this same public policy may be invisible or perceived as an aid to the small family farmer or a desirable way of enhancing the nation's food production.

The key question, then, is under what conditions the acts of government become symbolic and help *create* beliefs, wants, and demands in mass publics. The question is both a highly practical one for the citizen or lobbyist and an intriguing one for the student of government; public policies have symbolic effects under conditions that we can identify, at least within rough limits. Because political symbolism is a *systematic* phenomenon, we can learn to understand and perhaps control it.

■ *Symbol Analysis.* Analysis of political symbolism allows us to see some things that are not otherwise obvious and to evaluate or judge them in a new way. People's satisfaction or dissatisfaction with government does not depend only on how much they get. It depends even more on what society, and especially the government itself, cues them to expect, want, and believe they deserve. Corporate farm interests made rich by a price-support program are often dissatisfied if they do not also get tax breaks, such as rapid depreciation allowances. Most of the poor, taught by schools, welfare workers, and governmental policies to feel inadequate for not having made money in a "land of equal opportunity," docilely accept meager welfare benefits and sometimes degrading "counseling" on how to live their lives. They may feel lucky if their benefits are raised ten dollars a month. In both these cases it is people's *expectations*, rather than how much they get, that chiefly influences how satisfied or how demanding they are. In both examples, and in thousands of others, government helps shape expectations rather than simply responds to them. Indeed, government acknowledges "the voice of the people" largely by influencing what that voice says.

The study of political symbolism necessarily focuses on *change* and the attitudinal and behavioral conditions of change. Symbols evoke either *change* or *reinforcement* of what people already believe and perceive. It becomes essential to know, for example, how a governmental action or statement may change beliefs or perceptions. A poll may show that virtually all Americans are convinced that the Chinese People's Republic is their eternal enemy and its people enslaved and hostile. But these poll results reflect a response to particular stimuli and not necessarily to a stable state of affairs. More important than such a snapshot poll is the way such results change after the President of the United States visits China and the television networks broadcast pictures of beautiful Chinese cities and friendly-looking people. Such changes gain momentum as Chinese leaders visit the United States and businesspeople start to envision profitable trade. Statistics on support or opposition to the President are less important than what kinds of *change* in support will take place if unemployment rises or prices decline. Statistics on attitudes, in short, are not "hard data," important in themselves. They are, rather, a way of learning something about how governments and other social groups evoke changes in the direction, intensity, or stability of attitudes. The symbolic perspective is a dynamic one.

Every mode of observing and interpreting the political scene has normative implications. It crudely or subtly suggests that the system, and particular aspects of it, are good or bad, right or wrong. Here, too, the symbolic perspective makes a difference. The conventional view of the political process sees public policy as reflecting what the people want — as expressed in their votes and responded to by legislatures and by the administrators and judges who carry out legislative policy. Systems theory, the most fashionable metaphor for explaining government, portrays public demands and support as the "inputs" of the system and legislative, executive, and judicial policy as the "outputs." Both systems theory and the traditional outlook are highly reassuring and justify the status quo, for they tell us that governmental action reflects what the people want.

The student of symbolism knows that this is often true, but does not avoid the less reassuring aspect of the political process: that government can often shape people's wants before it reflects them. To the extent that governmental actions create popular beliefs and wants, the political process is not democratic, but rather potentially antidemocratic, for policies are not always based on the people's will, even when they seem to be. It is tempting to take the appearance for the reality. This is true whether the manipulation of public opinion by governmental officials is deliberate or unintentional. For this reason the symbolic perspective often raises questions about the legitimacy of political regimes, the obligation to support them, and the desirability of their policies.

Symbolic Politics and Political Quiescence

■ *Legitimacy and Support.* Why is there so little resistance to, and such overwhelming support from all strata of the population for, a political system that yields the substantial inequalities in wealth, power, status, and sacrifice examined in the earlier chapters of this book? Support for the system and belief in its legitimacy are all the more striking in view of the fact that Americans are taught early that all people are created equal and that they live in a land of equal opportunity.

Many governmental processes inculcate both generalized support for the political system and acquiescence to particular policies. Such processes are symbolic in character, for they create meanings and influence states of mind. If they also allocate values, they are both symbolic and instrumental.

The symbols that most powerfully inculcate support for the political system are those institutions we are taught to think of as the core of the democratic state — those that give the people control over the government. Probably the most reassuring are elections. Americans learn early in life to doubt that any state can be democratic without free elections, and they are inclined to assume that a country that holds elections must be democratic. Whatever else they accomplish, elections help create a belief in the reality of popular participation in government and popular control over policy. For the individual voter, elections also create a sense of personal participation and influence in government.

The belief is crucial whether or not it is accurate. Research discussed in Chapter 19 raises doubts that belief in popular control through elections is fully warranted. There is evidence that much of the electorate is neither especially interested in issues nor well informed about them and that votes are often cast on the basis of other considerations.[4] On the other hand, issues apparently do sometimes make a difference.[5] But if elections powerfully legitimate the political system and the regime, whether or not they are responsive to people's wants and demands, the realistic political analyst must recognize legitimation as one of their functions, sometimes the major one.

Similarly, other institutions we are socialized to consider fundamental to democracy help inculcate broad support for the system and acquiescence in policies, even from those who do not like them. The publicized functioning of legislatures and courts promotes widespread confidence that majority will is reflected in the law, which is applied expertly and impartially to people who may have violated it. Here again, there is evidence that such belief is often not warranted. Legislative bodies reflect chiefly the needs of organized interests and strong pressure groups, and courts are more sensitive to the interests of some groups than to those of others — regardless of the "mandate" of the voters in the last election.[6]

Besides legitimizing the political system, governmental actions also create support for or acquiescence in particular policies. A wide range of devices is used to evoke such acceptable responses to controversial government acts. It is a challenging exercise to identify them and to learn to recognize new ones, for the analyst usually has to overcome his or her own identification with their popular or conventional meanings in order to recognize their symbolic functions.

■ *Reassurance: Protection Against Threats.* Some types of governmental action create the belief that government is providing effective protection against widely feared threats or undesirable developments. One policy area in which this effect is especially dramatic is government regulation of business to protect the consumer against high prices. We have antitrust laws to ensure that businesses compete, rather than conspire to concentrate economic power and charge what the traffic will bear. We have many laws

---

[4] See especially Angus Campbell, Philip Converse, Warren Miller, and Donald Stokes, *The American Voter* (New York: Wiley, 1960); Philip Converse, "The Nature of Belief Systems in Mass Publics," in *Ideology and Discontent*, ed. David Apter (New York: Free Press, 1964); Angus Campbell et al., *Elections and the Political Order* (New York: Wiley, 1966).

[5] For a study that tries to specify the conditions under which issues matter and for a review of the previous literature, see Gerald M. Pomper, "From Confusion to Clarity: Issues and American Voters, 1956–1968," *American Political Science Review* 66 (June 1972), pp. 415–428.

[6] For an exposition of the pertinent evidence and theory, see David B. Truman, *The Governmental Process* (New York: Knopf, 1951), chs. 11–15.

to prevent corporations that enjoy monopolies or special licenses in such fields as telephone, gas, electricity, and radio broadcasting from using their economic power to gouge the consumer with high prices or shoddy service. Antitrust actions are frequently in the news, as are the actions of public utility commissions, and politicians often declare their zeal to increase the effectiveness of protective legislation of this sort. Yet for many decades studies by economists and political scientists have shown that these laws and the agencies that administer them typically offer very little protection. They are usually highly sensitive to the economic interests of the businesses they "regulate" and far less so to the interests of consumers. The studies conclude that the agencies become captives of these businesses, rationalizing rate increases while ostensibly protecting the consumer.[7]

If the regulatory laws and commissions come close to reversing the economic function they are established to perform, why are they not abolished? They clearly serve political and psychological functions, both for politicians and for the mass public; politicians find that support for them or for strengthening them still brings in votes. Those who fear the concentration of economic power are reassured when the government responds to their anxiety by setting up an agency to keep prices fair or to regulate product quality. It is rarely clear to consumers just which price ceilings and product standards protect them and which exploit them. In short, the issues are ambiguous and complex. This combination of ambiguity and widespread public anxiety is precisely the climate in which people are eager for reassurance that they are being protected and therefore eager to believe that publicized governmental actions have the effects they are supposed to have.

In many other fields of governmental action the same conditions prevail; public policies are partly, perhaps often chiefly, symbolic in character. New civil rights laws reassure liberals that progress is being made. But police officers and courts can still ignore the laws or interpret them to permit the very denials of civil liberties they were intended to prevent. And many among the poor and minorities lack the knowledge and legal counsel to assert their rights. The civil rights laws serve as reassuring symbols for affluent liberals, whose own civil rights are fairly well protected. But for the black or radical who is beaten up after being arrested on false charges, there is no ambiguity and no symbolic reassurance. For those who are worried about ecological catastrophe, the passage of laws against water and air pollution brings reassurance and a sense of victory. But again, it is usually far from clear that such laws provide the money or the capacity to act against influential industrial and governmental polluters. Nonetheless, such statutes and clean-up, paint-up, and antilitter campaigns reassure many who would otherwise be aroused. Tokenism is

---

[7] See Chapter 16 for references to these studies and an analysis of the impact of regulatory agencies on power centers.

a classic device for taking advantage of ambiguity and conveying a false sense of reassurance.

■ *Reassurance: The Deprived Deserve Their Fate.* Governmental or elitist actions also reassure people about worrisome conditions by instilling a conviction that the deprived deserve their fate and are personally benefiting from it. It is comforting to believe that those who are denied the good things of life suffer from personal pathology, deviance, or delinquency and that they must be controlled, guided, or incarcerated as a form of "correction" or "rehabilitation." Such a rehabilitative and psychiatric ideology has increasingly dominated the laws, rhetoric, and bureaucracies of all the public institutions that have the power to impose severe penalties on the wayward and the dependent: prisons, mental hospitals, schools, and welfare departments. This is a "liberal" view, but its effects have been severely repressive, especially for the poor.[8] In this view the person who steals is reacting not to poverty or alienating institutions, but to psychopathic tendencies. The child who resists the school bureaucracy and its rules is "hostile" and must acquire "insight" by learning how inadequate he or she is. The person who is depressed or will not play conventional roles in life is a psychopath or schizophrenic who must be controlled and possibly locked up until he or she learns to behave in conventional ways. The welfare recipient is suffering less from lack of money than from personal inadequacies for which he or she needs counseling and control.

Because the staffs of these institutions enjoy wide latitude in defining deviance, the tendency is strong to perceive any behavior they dislike or that is uncommon in their own social circles as pathological and in need of "correction." Many people are unhappy or maladjusted; the problem lies in assuming that they themselves, rather than social institutions, are at fault.

For elites this way of defining the behavior of the poor and the unconventional has many advantages. It diverts attention from social and economic problems. It justifies repression of those who deviate from middle-class standards of behavior. It defines such repression as "rehabilitation," thereby enhancing the self-concepts of conservatives, liberals, professionals, and the administrative staff, who see themselves as altruistic. Finally, this ideology is accepted by many of the deprived themselves, making them docile and submissive. Docility and submission to authority are generously rewarded in schools, prisons, mental hospitals,

---

8 Cf. *Struggle for Justice: A Report on Crime and Punishment in America*, prepared for the American Friends Service Committee (New York: Hill and Wang, 1971); August Hollingshead and Frederick C. Redlich, *Social Class and Mental Illness* (New York: Wiley, 1958); Gideon Sjoberg, Richard A. Brymer, and Buford Farris, "Bureaucracy and the Lower Class," in *The National Administrative System*, ed. Dean A. Yarwood (New York: Wiley, 1971), pp. 369–377; Aaron Cicourel and John I. Kitsuse, *The Educational Decision-Makers* (Indianapolis: Bobbs-Merrill, 1963).

and welfare agencies, while independence, insistence on personal dignity, and imagination are usually penalized, often severely.

Dissemination of the belief that the deprived are less deserving than others and must be controlled for their own good is a common and potent form of symbolic political action. Such labeling becomes a self-fulfilling prophecy, subtly or coercively requiring people to act as they are defined[9] and making it more likely that they will become recidivists — that they will revert to the behavior that got them into trouble in the first place. In a society in which economic and social rewards are very unevenly distributed, such social-psychological control supplements the use of coercive police powers and is more effective than naked coercion in maintaining quiescence. It minimizes resistance, maximizes support from the general public, and soothes people's consciences.

The confusion between psychological help and political repression that is characteristic of the definition and treatment of "deviance" takes still another form, with even more far-reaching political consequences. The sociologists who study deviance have come to recognize that the person who is labeled an offender against morality or normality is sometimes more useful to society as a deviant (sick, delinquent, psychopathic) than as a nondeviant. He or she serves as a reference point, defining what behavior is acceptable and what is unacceptable and also making it clear that deviants are segregated and penalized. Consequently, institutions that keep people deviant by labeling them and then forcing them to maintain a pathological role are doing what many demand that they do to preserve the common conventions.[10] Repression of a conspicuous group of people in the name of "help," "rehabilitation," or "correction" powerfully shapes the beliefs and behavior of mass publics. Here we have one of the most striking, significant, and least obvious uses of political symbolism.

Summary

Ideology and symbolism have much in common as ways of justifying and defending the status quo in the face of policies that do not give priority to majority interests. Both are partly in our minds and partly in the actions and rhetoric of leaders. Both shape wants and needs in the image of what it is possible or convenient to deliver. Both divert attention and energy away from the actual consequences of public policies and provide layers of legitimacy for government action.

---

9 In addition to the studies cited in footnote 8, see Erving Goffman, *Asylums* (Garden City, N.Y.: Doubleday, 1961).

10 Lewis A. Coser, "Some Functions of Deviant Behavior and Normative Flexibility," *American Journal of Sociology* 68 (September 1962), pp. 172–174; Robert A. Dentler and Kai T. Erikson, "The Functions of Deviance in Groups," *Social Problems* 7 (1959), pp. 98–107.

Ideology is grounded in basic political values such as individualism, natural rights, limited government, materialism and the business ethic, and racism. The first four have a hallowed history and are seen as operative throughout our political institutions and practices today. They help us to understand that whatever our system does is (1) based on compromise among all interested groups, (2) democratic, and (3) the best possible accommodation under all the circumstances. Racism is unacknowledged and sometimes denied.

Symbolism is the process of creating images in people's minds that call forth approval or revulsion (in part by fulfilling inherent needs in people) and then invoking such reactions to build support or acquiescence for elite action. Much use of symbolism surrounds the legitimacy of government institutions and policies and converts natural fears or unserved needs into forms of reassurance.

THE CHALLENGE OF
THE 1980S

9

In response to the massive protests of the 1960s, government policies shifted somewhat toward social programs benefiting minorities and the poor. New policies also provided for greater safety at work, protection of the environment, limiting nuclear hazards, and "affirmative action" in the hiring and promotion of women and minorities. The idea of equality seemed to expand and to promise a variety of new opportunities to new categories of people — not just women and minorities, but also the handicapped, the aged, the retarded, and others. But then the American economy ran into the troubles described in Chapters 3 and 4, and suddenly frustration and discord spread across the political spectrum.

Some people felt that society had made only minimal or token changes in long overdue directions and/or was bent on "disciplining" working people again. Criticism from the left sharpened, and there was continuing pressure from the feminist movement. Others blamed the changes in policy and values that marked the 1960s and early 1970s for the social pressures, economic decline, and loss of national prestige that troubled them. Such a backlash might have been inevitable, but it was surely exacerbated by economic difficulties. The conflict between these reactions and between each of them and the liberal orthodoxy that remains dominant, if increasingly beleaguered and unsure of itself, accounts for much of the current turbulence surrounding American politics. We will take up each of these reactions in turn.

The Radical Left

Radicalism is the belief that drastic change is necessary at the roots of the social order. Radicalism of the left seeks change toward more egalitarian (equal) distribution of wealth, status, and power, while radicalism of the right defends inequalities in these respects and seeks to restore the values and traditions that support them. Each form of radicalism also holds contrasting images of *human nature* and of the amount of coercive *order* necessary to maintain social harmony. According to the left radicalism on which we focus here, humans are essentially good and cooperative and should enjoy a maximum of civil liberties and individual freedom. In contrast, conservatives generally hold a pessimistic view of human nature as selfish and aggressive, in need of restraint.

Radicalism, in eclipse during the 1940s and 1950s as a result of war, repression, and general social mobilization in support of the cold war, was reborn in the mid-1960s. Blacks' struggle for basic civil rights quickly reignited similar undertakings by Chicanos, Puerto Ricans, American Indians, Asians, and other minorities. The efforts of white college students, directed at first to the civil rights movement, soon shifted to opposition to the Vietnam War and then to community organizing, citizen participation, and efforts to change universities. This collection of activities, so much in contrast with that of earlier decades, soon became known as the "New Left." Lacking a fundamental critique of American society, it lost much of its momentum with the end of the Vietnam War. But the more theoretical and dedicated radicals among its ranks moved on to develop fuller critiques and a variety of alternative models for the future. Some sought to make links with working people, others to find new movements (antinuclear, environmental, minorities, feminist) that would join the effort toward large-scale social change.

The American left, however, remains characterized by division rather than coherence in either critique or program. Not counting radical demands made by nationalists in every major minority group, three major strains of radical thought currently pose serious opposition to American liberal orthodoxy: reformism, anticapitalism, and extreme individualism. These will be discussed on the next few pages.

Reformism

This primary strain of radicalism best illustrates the nature and consequences of the radical commitment to equality. Much of the history of tension between radicalism and the dominant orthodoxy can be attributed to the conflict between the values of equality and property as they are understood by the respective ideologies. The argument has involved both the *definition* and the *priority* attached to equality. Radicalism of this kind defines equality in broad and steadily expanding terms, proceeding from equality of opportunity to equality in the actual conditions of people's lives. And it gives full priority to equality, elevating it above all other political values when they come into conflict.

But it is easy to exaggerate the "radicalness" of this radical argument. For example, at no time in American history did any significant number of these radicals call for the abolition of private property as such or for drastic action to equalize the conditions of people's lives. They asked only for somewhat greater emphasis on equality in the context of competitive individualism and respect for property rights. Starting from the acknowledged principle of political equality, in the sense of voting rights and majoritarianism, they gradually caused restrictions inconsistent with such principles, such as those involving property, sex, and race, to be removed.

Increasingly in the twentieth century, however, sources of power other than government and other socially produced limitations appear to have prevented individuals from attaining their ends. Radicals, therefore, have sought to expand the implications of equality to legitimize government action to preserve opportunity and the provision of sufficient education and social status to enable individuals to compete more equally. Once again, there has been strong resistance on the part of those holding more restrictive definitions of equality. Thus, though equality is symbolically unchallenged, its political and socioeconomic effectuation has been tentative and controversial.

By contrast, attachment to property as a legitimate and paramount value has been widely shared and rarely challenged. No major American thinker, including Jefferson (supposed by some of his contemporaries to have been unsympathetic to the wealthy and propertied), has failed to support strongly the individual's right to whatever land, goods, and money he or she could amass. Hamilton and some other Federalists considered these the central goals of human motivations and sought to construct a government to serve these ends. Men like Adams and Jefferson believed that property gives people political independence, a stake in the society, and the capacity and right to judge — which in turn leads to wise public decisionmaking.

It should be clear that reformism historically affirmed other traditional values as well as property rights. The concepts of individualism, materialism, natural rights, limited government, and legalism were all taken for granted in the effort to expand and enhance equality. The same is true today: what this form of radicalism seeks is a reality that conforms to orthodox American rhetoric, providing greater opportunity for individuals to compete more successfully and to amass larger amounts of the material rewards of the American system.

To some extent, reformists do see flaws and limitations in the existing values and would repair these deficiencies. The principle of limited government, for example, though still considered valid in the abstract because people should be free to attain their individual ends, is seen as much violated in practice. In this view, the worst violations are subsidies, price supports, and other financial benefits for those very economic interests most likely to use the principle of limited government as a defense against proposed policies that would benefit ordinary people. Individualism is considered to have humanistic and esthetic, as well as material, dimensions. Material aspirations, however, are still taken to be the primary motivation of "human nature" and the basic dynamic of social life. Racism is acknowledged and condemned, but the chief remedy proposed is laws to prevent discrimination.

Black liberation, however, will not come about solely through the activities of black people. Black America cannot be genuinely liberated until white America is transformed into a humanistic society free of exploitation and class division. The black and white worlds, although separate and distinct, are too closely intertwined — geographically, politically, and economically — for the social maladies of one not to affect the other. Both must change if either is to progress to new and liberating social forms.

From Robert L. Allen, *Black Awakening in Capitalist America: An Analytic History* (New York: Doubleday, 1970), p. 281.

Reform ideology thus contains a profound ambivalence. On the one hand, it brusquely rejects the orthodoxy's claim that present policies must be appropriate because they are enacted by a system in which rules and widespread participation ensure outcomes that reflect a democratic consensus. Economic and social conditions, readily visible to all who are willing to look, completely rebut the claims of American orthodoxy and must be corrected. Concentrations of economic power must be prevented from continuing their exploitation, and ordinary citizens must recapture power over the circumstances of their lives. On the other hand, reformism holds that these goals can be achieved if more people become involved, reopen the political processes, and "throw the rascals out." By reforming certain aspects of politics, installing better people in office, and thus rearranging the priorities of government and society, the conditions of the mass of the people can be dramatically improved. In short, things are very bad, but it won't take much to set them right.

The fight against this concentration of privilege — open and covert, legal and illegal — is, we believe, the most important political question of this decade. Its goal is a more equitable distribution of wealth and power; its enemy is the entire arrangement of privileges, exemptions, and free rides that has narrowed the opportunity of most Americans to control their own destiny. This fight for fairness is political; it can be won only by organizing a new political majority in America.

From Jack Newfield and Jeff Greenfield, A Populist Manifesto: The Making of a New Majority (New York: Warner Paperback Library, 1972), p. 17.

This ambivalence has its roots in acceptance of most of the orthodox political values "as is" and in the effects of orthodox political ideology. Accepting the values of competitive individualism and materialism, reformism can say only that the "problem" is the unfair distribution of rewards — not the wrongness of the nature or workings of the economy as a whole. Thinking within the framework of American political ideology and therefore convinced of the rightness and legitimacy of the political system as a whole, it can say only that there must be something temporarily wrong. If corrected through the sincere efforts of the people, the national government could again become the agent of the people and the instrument of economic opportunity for all. For these reasons, reformism remains principally a protest movement, demanding reform and opportunity *within* the existing system.

Anticapitalism

Though not yet primary, the anticapitalist version of contemporary radicalism has grown in proportion to the failure of reformist radicalism to achieve real success for more than a few sectors of the population. It holds that the traditional American values are not just in need of redefinition and reordering, but are themselves the cause of current problems. In particular, anticapitalist radicalism rejects individualism in the orthodox sense. Human nature is not necessarily competitive and self-aggrandizing, such radicals argue; people can learn to share and to cooperate for the betterment of their mutual condition. When they do, a true sense of community will emerge. Justice in the form of roughly equal distribution of rewards will be available for all.

The key to achieving such results is seen as abolition of the private ownership of productive machinery and resources and the profit-maximizing use that necessarily results. As long as such private ownership and profit orientation exist, masses of people must be exploited. Thus, anticapitalist radicalism must reject the value of property rights, not as to personal property or home ownership, but as to large private holdings of land, capital, securities, and other forms of wealth.

The concept of limited government must also be abandoned, because government must serve as a central planning agency on behalf of the society as a whole. In order to provide enough goods and services for qualitative improvement of the lives of millions of ordinary American citizens and to discharge obligations to the rest of humanity, it will be necessary to employ the society's productive resources in an efficient manner. Central planning is thus required to determine at least what is to be done where. Local organizations of workers or others may then assume responsibility for deciding how each goal will be reached and by whom.

Materialism is not entirely rejected, for it will be crucial to raise the material standard of living for most Americans as well as for other people in the world. This is a prerequisite to the opportunity to enjoy other aspects of life and to develop the creative, esthetic, and other human potential that exists in all persons. But materialism will not be the principal motivating force in people's lives, because they will not seek to amass things for themselves. They will be assured of enough to serve their needs and instead will work out of a commitment to bettering the lives of others.

Anticapitalist radical values are clearly fundamentally different from those held by most Americans. The ideology derived from such values sees the American system today as fundamentally irrational. Private ownership and the profit motive lead inexorably to exploitation, widespread misery, and a sharply stratified class system with a very few powerful individuals at the top. There is a continued need for manipulation of the masses by the ruling capitalist class and its agents. Because the ruling class controls the nation's wealth, it also controls the government and, through it, the educational system and the political process generally. The major means of manipulation is inculcation of the ideology we have been calling American orthodoxy. Once fixed in the minds of the people, it makes social control possible with a minimum of conscious effort. Aspiring and competent people are induced to become agents of the ruling class because the ruling class controls the rewards and opportunities they seek.

In this self-reinforcing and self-perpetuating way, the system operates relatively smoothly. The problems that exist arise out of the characteristics of capitalism, but people recognize only their surface manifestations and not their causes. The financial problems of cities, for example, result not from the lack of a tax base or too much spending on education or welfare, but rather from the vast sums being spent to pay the interest and principal on loans from capitalist bankers. Because so many people are seen as hopelessly trapped in the orthodox values and ideology, anticapitalist radicals face a serious dilemma. Either they must commit themselves to trying to transform the system through revolutionary action with the conscious support of only a minority of the people, or they must await a change of mind on the part of a decisive majority of the people, through events or persuasion or both. Understandably, this issue remains a subject of vigorous debate within this strain of radicalism.

Individualism

Reformist radicalism accepts orthodox values and ideology and asks that rhetoric be made reality. Anticapitalist radicalism requires sweeping value changes and a sharp rupture with orthodox ideology. But both of these strains have in mind an ideal social system, in which aggregations of people do certain things in accordance with specific principles, thereby producing a pattern of rewards for individuals. If the rewards or satisfactions are not

---

It is plain that the goal of revolution today must be the liberation of daily life. . . . Revolutionary liberation must be a self-liberation that reaches social dimensions, not "mass liberation" or "class liberation" behind which lurks the rule of an elite, a hierarchy and a state. . . . Out of the revolution must emerge a self that takes full possession of daily life, not a daily life that takes full possession of the self. . . .

If for this reason alone, the revolutionary movement is profoundly concerned with lifestyle. It must try to live the revolution in all its totality, not only participate in it. . . . The revolutionary group must clearly see that its goal is not the seizure of power but the dissolution of power — indeed, it must see that the entire problem of power, of control from below and control from above, can be solved only if there is no above or below.

From Murray Bookchin, Post-Scarcity Anarchism (Berkeley: Ramparts Press, 1971), pp. 44–47.

just or desirable, the remedy is to change the way the social system operates. But the individualist form of radicalism rejects the idea that a large-scale social system can provide what individuals really need: such nonmaterial things as understanding of life and its meaning, harmony with nature and other people, love, and other forms of personal growth and fulfillment.

Thus, the individualist rejection of what it sees as a corruptly commercialized and destructive world is a personal, not a social, form of radicalism. Emphasis on individualism is greatly expanded and turned inward, away from material acquisitiveness and from the great mass of other people. The more limited government is, the better, for each individual must seek his or her own solution; real help can come only from the very small number of other persons with whom one has established special relationships.

This form of radicalism can be reached by a direct route from American orthodoxy or from reformist radicalism because it does not require extensive value change. Its emphasis on individualism and withdrawal makes it intellectually accessible to those who tire of struggling against large and impersonal social forces and to those who conclude that all large-scale social organizations are equally destructive of human freedom and potential. Unless vast numbers of people suddenly embrace the same personalized form of radicalism, it poses no serious threat to the continued operation of the American system or its orthodoxy. Power and its capabilities in a society are unaffected by the withdrawal of a few persons, particularly when their withdrawal is consciously based on the conviction that social efforts toward change are by definition undesirable or impossible. Nevertheless, this form of radicalism is gaining adherents, perhaps because the other two forms of radicalism are frustrating and (in the case of anti-capitalism) require greater value change than people can or want to achieve.

Summary

Table 9.1 summarizes these three viewpoints, all of which have run throughout American history. Reformism is probably the most conspicuous, for it has taken many forms and has led to changes in the character of capitalism itself. The Jacksonian, Populist, Progressive, and New Deal periods were all characterized by such protests and by the ultimate transformation of capitalism from one form to another. In effect, the dominant system was able to blunt, absorb, and convert such demands into forms that could serve its own needs because their basic nature was not antagonistic to the principles of capitalism. Direct challenges to capitalism itself were first made by late-nineteenth-century socialists and have continued to the present. They have been notably unsuccessful to date, because of the strength of American orthodoxy and attacks on those who hold such views by governments and others. Individualist withdrawal began with the transcendental individualists' attacks on the commercial society in the early nineteenth century. Today it takes the forms of a kind of liber-

Table 9.1

Characteristics of the Major Strains of American Radicalism

Ideology	Attitude Toward Basic American Values	Approach to U.S. Economic System	Major Goals
Reformist	Accepts all; seeks realization in practice, putting equality foremost	Accepts basic structure and dynamics, seeks greater opportunities for all and some redistribution of wealth and income	More humane welfare capitalism, with greater participation by all people
Anticapitalist	Rejects most, particularly individualism, but endorses greatly expanded equality and community	Rejects it as unjust and exploitative	Socialism, usually in decentralized egalitarian form, with all civil liberties
Individualist	Accepts all, but in original form, emphasizing freedom of individual and rights to property	Rejects it as too big, stifling to individuals, bureaucratic, and no longer true free enterprise	Individualist anarchist society via withdrawal or small-scale units

tarian anarchism and of certain versions of countercultural withdrawal. Because it has never been a serious threat, it has never been repressed, as have direct challenges to capitalism.

Thus, radicalism is neither a single coherent system of thought nor the rallying point of a unified social movement. Instead, it is a collection of different (and sometimes conflicting) beliefs, whose adherents chiefly share the conviction that they are deprived, powerless, and victimized by the dominant system. Radicalism begins as a set of reactions against contemporary conditions and against the values and ideology that rationalize and justify them. Ultimately, it takes the form of an alternative ideology.

People can and do move from one strand of radical thought to another. In the 1970s radicals tended to shift from demands for participation and reform to rejection of the existing system. Such rejection takes the form either of calls for the replacement of capitalism or of withdrawal into highly individualistic anarchism or countercultural lifestyles. At any given moment, of course, some people are sincerely hoping and working for reforms that will make the system more just in their eyes, while others, who have despaired of this approach, are either attacking capitalism itself or abandoning politics and social life to find solace by themselves. The developing economic crisis spurs each of these various currents in radical thought.

Feminism

Although women make up about 53 percent of the population, they suffer from some of the same forms of discrimination and bias as do racial minorities. Women are typically expected to take care of the housework or to fill low-status, low-wage jobs outside the home. Many people have been socialized to believe that women are less creative, less independent, and less capable than men of exercising independent judgment about business or governmental decisions. Men often seem to address women principally as sexual objects, to the point of oral or physical harassment and assault. The depths of women's resentment, fear, and anger may not be grasped even by normally sensitive men. Clearly, just as the problem in the case of minorities is starting to be recognized as a *white* problem, the feminist problem is at least as much a *male* problem as a *female* problem.

In the 1960s and 1970s a growing feminist movement tried to counter these demeaning attitudes regarding the capabilities and roles of women, to work for equality for women, and to raise the consciousness of both men and women about gender roles. While many premises and goals were shared within this movement, there were differences of analysis and prescriptions among groups of feminists. We distinguish these as equal rights feminism, radical feminism, and socialist feminism.

Types of Feminism

■ *Equal Rights Feminism.* This brand of feminism, of which the National Organization of Women (NOW) is an example, calls for the status and opportunity for women to be equal to those for men in every aspect of social, economic, and political life, but does not seek to otherwise change those systems. Women should be able to have a chance for professional careers or other jobs, just as men do, free of household or family responsibilities. To this end, NOW supports state- or employer-provided child-care facilities, the sharing of housework or hiring of outside help, and the rights of women to family-planning assistance and abortion. NOW also insists upon equality in the workplace. This means opening up traditionally male occupations, such as the military, to women, "affirmative action" to employ qualified women, and above all equal compensation.

Equal rights feminism seeks the opportunity for women to compete equally with men for the rewards that society has to offer. These opportunities are to be ensured through expanded participation in politics by women — a role aimed at obtaining legislation to protect and advance such opportunities. Although these goals do not fundamentally challenge the family or the socioeconomic system, they generate substantial reaction from men and often from other women as well. The idea of women's having independent lives and needs clearly contains serious threats to others' self-conceptions.

■ *Radical Feminism.* This version of feminism sees the world in more clear-cut class terms, with the classes being males as the oppressors and females as the oppressed. The biological nature of males and females is more important than race or wealth or economics in any form. The fact that women are the reproducers of the species makes them objects to be owned as property or targets to be possessed. Men become obsessed with power and the manipulation of others, while women learn to be far more sensitive, intuitive, and emotionally developed. A strong separatist current flows within radical feminism: women are nicer people and before all else should come to appreciate their qualities and enjoy one another.

The remedy that radical feminists see, therefore, focuses on the way that the society shapes sexual attitudes and seeks basic changes in such cultural concepts. Some believe that the society can be restructured from within by learning to accept homosexuality and bisexuality and/or by recognizing expanded and more flexible versions of the family than the traditional nuclear family. Others think that only a social revolution can accomplish liberation of women and that such an upheaval must focus on sexism and patriarchy *first* and economics or politics only secondarily. All radical feminists identify male domination as *the* problem, although their prescriptions then vary sharply.

■ *Socialist Feminism.* This approach to feminism combines the socialist critique of class-based exploitation with the feminist critique of male domination. It holds that neither can be eliminated without the other and that total social reconstruction must be accomplished. Socialists are charged with having failed to give sexism and racism equal status with the class struggle, but the socialist analytical framework is accepted as the only one comprehensive enough to include both an explanation and a prescription for the oppression of women. Sexism predated capitalism, but has grown together with it so that the two are now mutually supportive, and effective action to liberate women requires a strategy to deal with both at the same time.

Socialist feminists believe that they have much to offer a socialist movement. Paramount is the insight that the *personal* is *political* — that is, everyday life and intimate personal relationships are often shaped by the larger society, its values, social formations, power relationships, and the like. In turn, those everyday life and personal-identity factors *reproduce themselves* in people, thus preparing them to accept those same values, power relationships, and so forth in the future. If the personal-political link is recognized, therefore, it is within the power of every person to initiate the process of social change in his or her own life. And only in this way (accompanied, of course, by action to change the world) will the really desirable kind of change eventuate — a change that addresses both capitalism and patriarchy simultaneously not only for men, but for women as well.

The mainstream, or equal rights, feminists (clearly dominant within the movement) have gained some legitimacy from their moderation in contrast with the latter two, more radical, versions. Despite being charged with some such radical intentions, NOW and its supporters have achieved some real progress to which they are entitled to point with pride.

Accomplishments of the Feminist Movement

The most impressive accomplishments in changing women's roles have come in the economic marketplace. In the 1950s women began working outside their homes in increasing numbers, and in the 1970s the trend became a floodtide. By September 1977, 48.9 percent of women over sixteen years old held paid jobs, and 41 percent of *all* workers were women. But the median earnings of women were less than $7,000 per year, compared to roughly $12,000 for men, and men's incomes were rising at a more rapid rate.[1] College enrollments of women have also spurted, with women outnumbering men in undergraduate colleges and making up one-quarter of the students in law and medical schools. In at least some social circles there is a new awareness of sexism in everyday language and in everyday assumptions about who should do what kinds of work, and many cities and states have made it illegal to discriminate on the basis of sex in hiring or pay.

Still, the feminist movement has experienced serious setbacks as well as some successes, and it is not clear that significant gains can be expected in the future. Although a small number of women have become executives or have achieved high status in prestigious professions, most are still finding low-status, low-paying, dead-end jobs. Because child-care facilities are often inadequate or nonexistent, many women cannot go to school or seek work in industry. The opposition to equality has remained strong and in the late 1970s seemed to be mounting as part of an upsurge of conservative lobbying. Many men also seem immune to the new awareness of sexism, though the feminist movement cannot be successful unless men's consciousness of the inequity and the pathology of inequality in gender roles is also raised.

Probably the most publicized goal of the feminist movement has been ratification of the Equal Rights Amendment (ERA), an objective it has found extremely difficult to achieve. The Equal Rights Amendment is a short, simple statement declaring that there shall be no discrimination on the basis of sex. It was sought as one of the early goals of NOW. In March 1972 the Congress passed the amendment and referred it to the states, with the usual stipulation that unless ratification by the necessary

---

[1] *New York Times,* 29 November 1977, pp. 1, 28.

two-thirds of state legislatures occurred within seven years, the amendment would be void. Several states immediately ratified the amendment, some in such a hurry to be among the first to do so that charges later arose that they had not carefully considered its implications. But then a reaction set in, an active group of women began to oppose ratification, and the approval by states came only slowly and after protracted debate. In some states the amendment was defeated.

The reasons for the opposition reflected some misconceptions, some consequences of changes and tensions within American society, and a good deal of symbolism. In what would have fit well with Justice Holmes's famous description of a "parade of imaginary horrors," opponents of the amendment dreamed up all manner of possible changes and disruptions of social life that would follow upon ratification. It was said that women would be forced into military combat roles, that all bathrooms would have to be "unisex," that alimony and child support would be abolished, that the traditional role of housewife would be altered beyond recognition, and so forth. What lay behind these exaggerated fears in many cases were feelings of pressure from changes in social values and practices and particularly a sense of threat to the family from a variety of sources. The ERA seemed to its opponents to be a symbolic endorsement of all these changes and threats. To its supporters, on the other hand, the ERA seemed like simple justice.

The campaign for ratification was hard fought for several years. Supporters of ERA sought to get professional and other organizations that hold annual conventions to boycott states refusing to ratify the amendment, hoping that economic pressure involved in lost revenue from convention-goers would work where moral persuasion had not. Opponents sought to have states that had previously ratified act again to rescind their ratifications, which would have thrown the whole process into chaos. Supreme Court precedents and congressional opinion, however, seemed to be clear that once a state had ratified the proposed amendment, it could not later change its mind.

By mid-1978, three more states' ratifications were still needed to make the ERA part of the Constitution. But the time limit would expire in March 1979, before some state legislatures would be able to consider ratification (in some cases for the second or third time). Supporters therefore mounted a campaign to get the Congress to extend the deadline for another three years. Marches were conducted in localities around the nation and in Washington, and a lobbying group made up of nearly eighty sons and daughters of members of Congress issued an appeal to their fathers to extend the time limit. In October the Senate joined the House in granting a three-year extension, and supporters of ERA began a renewed campaign for ratification. But progress was very slow, and ultimate ratification remains very much in doubt.

The New Right

Any process of social change, particularly one with the media visibility of the equality-expanding efforts of the 1960s and early 1970s, is likely to produce a countering reaction. Such a backlash was already developing when the economic decline of the mid- to late-1970s set in, and the combined effect was soon certified by those same media as "the new conservative mood" of the country. The growing sense of military confrontation with the Soviet Union also was welcomed by some as helping to reduce the priority given to all other issues.

The "new conservatism" is actually a collection of several different types of reaction to previous changes and present conditions, some of them not new at all and most not conservative. (By "conservative," we mean a view that holds that people are fundamentally unequal in talent or wisdom and that the better-endowed should prescribe for the rest.) Two major themes seem to underlie much of this activity. One is an effort enjoying significant popular support to restore older values, particularly those surrounding the family. The other is the attempt by a defensive and profit-squeezed business community to reduce costs by eliminating regulation, increasing tax advantages, and rolling back the welfare state with its taxing, services, and minimum wage standards. We will touch briefly on some campaigns with popular appeal and on the business counterattack, before concluding with an assessment of the conservative intellectual component associated with these reactions.

Conservative Themes

■ *Popular Movements.* One cause that has enlisted substantial numbers of people working to limit abortions is the Right to Life movement. While opposition to abortion was led by the Catholic Church, many supporters from other faiths opposed abortions as well. Opposition took the form of (1) seeking the reversal of the Supreme Court's 1973 opinion holding that states could not constitutionally interfere with women's freedom of choice in early pregnancy or utterly forbid abortion in later pregnancy; (2) attempting to prevent the use of public funds for abortions on the part of poor or welfare women; and (3) running candidates against, or otherwise taking electoral action to punish, officeholders who supported abortion rights. In some states with third-party traditions, such as New York, a Right to Life party became a serious factor in state politics.

Related to the Right to Life movement are other campaigns that often draw support from the same or similarly minded people. One is the effort to block the expansion of homosexual rights, which has taken the form of electoral referenda in several communities. Gay men and lesbian women were in several instances able to win nondiscrimination ordinances or pledges so that they could be employed by governments or schools on an open and nondiscriminatory basis. In almost every case, however, counter-pressure has been brought to bear, and where elections were forced, the principle of such homosexual rights was defeated. National visibility was gained for this campaign by the efforts of singer Anita Bryant. Another campaign with national visibility is that mounted against the Equal Rights Amendment and the feminist cause generally. As noted earlier, organized pressure was mounted on state legislatures by means of highlighting a variety of undesirable consequences said to follow from ERA ratification.

One factor underlying the wide appeal of each of these movements may be the sense that the traditional family unit is threatened. Although (or perhaps because) a relatively small and declining proportion of families consist of the stereotyped mother, father (both married only once — to each other) and two children, this model has great symbolic weight. Divorce, abortion, homosexuality, and feminism all seem to pose dangers to the ideal, and some people feel that their own self-worth, or perhaps their last refuge in a high-pressure world, is being undermined.

Another popular movement focuses on taxation. Known as the "tax revolt," it charges government at all levels with waste and corruption and particularly with profligate welfare expenditures. It took the form in 1978 of a statewide referendum in California that reduced the state property tax, the principal source of state aid to local governments, by about 60 percent. In other states different forms of tax or expenditure limitations were pressed, often successfully. At the national level many state legis-latures asked Congress to call a constitutional convention to propose a constitutional amendment to limit federal taxation.

The roots of the tax revolt are not difficult to understand. As our earlier analyses show, the tax system as a whole places its heaviest burden upon middle- and low-income groups, and in the 1970s these same people were squeezed even harder by prices that rose faster than most of their incomes. At the same time, the welfare system must support two kinds of casualties of the economic system: millions of unemployed people (a 6 percent unemployment level has come to be regarded as "normal") and millions of the working poor. In effect, industry is relying on government, through the welfare system, to compensate for the inability of the economic system to provide jobs for all who are able and willing to work and to provide incomes that are adequate to support a family.

Still, the stark reality to the individual taxpayer is an increasingly tight family budget, higher taxes, higher prices, and constant claims of governmental waste and fraud, especially in administering welfare pro-grams. He or she is understandably troubled, resentful, and easy to per-suade that the tax burden is due chiefly to welfare and governmental waste, which are easier targets than price increases for which specific people cannot be blamed or defense expenditures the public is socialized to accept as necessary for national security. In California conservative groups played on these feelings, for the affluent are the chief beneficiaries of tax cuts of the Proposition 13 type, while they would be the chief losers if there were serious tax reform that eliminated loopholes.

About two-thirds of the tax savings in California go to the corporations that own apartment houses and commercial property rather than to the individual homeowners who provided strong support for Proposition 13. Nor do the cutbacks in public services apply chiefly to welfare programs, which are funded largely by the federal government, although there will be some effect on them. Most cutbacks are felt in the budgets for schools, police and fire protection, health, and recreation — services of great value to the lower class and the middle class. Initially, however, surpluses in the state treasury cushioned some of the impact.

Businesses are not only principal beneficiaries of antitax campaigns, but also leading sponsors. In several instances corporate financial support has combined with popular energies to bring about reductions in government expenditures and limitations on revenue raising.

A final category of popular movements — the fundamentalist religious groups — has a long history. These groups simultaneously advocate traditional religious values, laissez-faire economics, and vigorous anticommunism. Often supported by very wealthy individuals, themselves frequently self-made millionaires or more, such groups maintain a highly visible radio and television presence and appear to enjoy substantial popular followings.

■ *Business Counterattacks.* Although business often feels itself unappreciated, the sense among businesspeople that the corporate economy and free enterprise itself were under attack probably reached a height in the early 1970s. Consumer groups, ecology and environmental groups, muckraking journalists, and a veritable army of government regulators and inspectors seemed bent on eliminating profitability. Business reaction took several forms, from reconstructing public attitudes to extensive financial participation in electoral campaigns to active lobbying in Congress and the executive branch. Much of this activity will be described in Chapters 18 and 19, and we shall sketch only an outline here.

Perhaps the most immediately visible business response was the formation of a major new lobbying-and-educating arm in 1973, the Business Roundtable. The chief executives of the nation's largest corporations, already organized in the Business Council, a semiofficial body enjoying regular and close advisory contact with the highest officials in the executive branch, decided to form a more open organization to serve lobbying needs with Congress and educating functions with the public. In 1976, thirty-three of the forty-five leaders of the Business Roundtable were also members of the Business Council.[2] The Roundtable originally merged three

---

[2] G. William Domhoff, *The Powers that Be* (New York: Vintage Books, 1979), p. 79.

other business committees engaged in lobbying or public education in order to generate more impact. It is supported by 150 member companies that supply a $2.5 million annual budget. According to a leading business journal, the Business Roundtable has, in the short time since its creation, become "business' most powerful lobby in Washington,"[3] credited with having blocked several proconsumer and prolabor bills in the mid- and late-1970s.

The public-education activities of business groups have also been extensive. The themes articulated by the Roundtable and in corporate "institutional" advertising are deregulation, increase in productivity, reduction of government services (and hence taxation and the general wage level), the need for new tax advantages (depreciation, investment incentives), and the imperative of controlling inflation by means of eliminating federal budget deficits. A vital new component of the business effort has been the funding of new "think tanks" to provide business-oriented answers to others' proposals and a rationale for the basic themes of the business campaign. Such independent organizations as the American Enterprise Institute in Washington, the Hoover Institute in Stanford, and several business policy centers at major universities have begun to receive support now totaling more than $20 million per year from corporations or their foundations.

One of the most active entrepreneurs of the new corporate-to-business-oriented-think-tank contribution system is millionaire and former Secretary of the Treasury William Simon, whose book, *A Time for Truth*, was on the best-seller list for six months in 1979.[4] He may be the most visible spokesperson for the free-enterprise cause today. Among other things, Simon calls for the withdrawal of funding from universities that foster ideas such as egalitarianism or collectivism and the creation of a new intelligentsia to counter them. And he has organized a clearinghouse for corporate giving, the Institute for Educational Affairs, to maximize the impact of corporate contributions by concentrating on timely projects.

Neoconservative Intellectuals

In part inspired by the new corporate funding, but also in part (as befits the intellectual role) critically reacting against the conventional wisdom, a number of intellectuals have been in the forefront of the new-right reaction. Many of them were, in the later 1950s or early 1960s, mainstream liberals who apparently came to believe that too much was being attempted by government. Their view of human nature and the limited possibility of its improvement led to the conviction that the policies of the late 1960s were romantic and impractical. Some even concluded that

---

[3] *Business Week*, 20 December 1976, p. 63.
[4] William Simon, *A Time for Truth* (New York: McGraw-Hill, 1978).

a new class of impractical elitist intellectuals was seeking to remake the country against the interests and preferences of the majority of lower- and middle-class people. Such leaders of opinion as Irving Kristol, Daniel Patrick Moynihan, Edward Banfield, James Q. Wilson, Seymour Lipset, and others of similar age and experience mounted a campaign to relegitimate a conservative approach to social policy.

Another category of intellectuals promptly rallying to the cause of arresting the trends of the 1960s and early 1970s was a group that was soon labeled "the new economists." Starting from the premise that a free market is the source of all other freedoms, they provided a variety of arguments for ending government regulation and other attempts to moderate the harshness of the business cycle. While the apparent failure of Keynesian theory (as described in Chapter 3) led some economists to the left and Marxism, it seemed to lead many more to neoclassical views much more congenial to the business community.

By the early 1980s, business seemed to be well on its way to repairing the policy damage wrought earlier. Economic decline made the business case appear more compelling, at least in the eyes of policymakers. The social policy advances of the 1960s and early 1970s were being criticized from all points on the political spectrum: they were not enough and/or badly administered — or they were badly conceived and/or far too much — depending on the source. The conflict produced a significant amount of debate and captured such attention as was allowed for domestic issues after foreign policy crises received their priority.

PART
4

INSTITUTIONS
AND PROCESSES:
THE ROLE OF ELITES

MANAGING THE
POLITICAL AGENDA

We now begin a series of seven chapters that describe how decisions are made in governmental institutions. Some very important things happen before anybody in government drafts legislation or proposes action and long before hearings are held or lobbying starts. A *context of understanding* has somehow arisen, in which shared values and assumptions lead to a generally accepted framework for interpreting new events. Some things are taken for granted; memories, fears, and expectations are aroused; and an agreed-upon definition of the situation seems to take shape. Together these constitute a coherent perspective through which people see and interpret the rising issue or problem. A *political agenda* has also developed: some issues seem to have high priority, and policy solutions that have somehow emerged appear to be the "sensible" way of coping with the most pressing problems. Such policies recommend themselves in part because they "fit" with today's structures and values and in part because no other alternatives have emerged that so fully respond to problems as forecast and understood.

Our first task, therefore, is to try to see how this context of understanding and political agenda has arisen. In particular we want to know to what extent those who are advantaged by the basic pattern of public policies may have taken part in bringing about the understanding and agenda that created such results. This question boils down to one that has challenged and seriously divided contemporary social scientists: Do great wealth and high status[1] translate in some direct way into political power in the United States? If so, how? In this chapter we will present evidence and interpretations that strongly suggest that the owners, managers, and supporters of the corporate-banking sector shape the context and manage the agenda. But first we will look at the way contemporary social scientists have addressed these questions.

The Role of Wealth and Status in Political Power

For some who are ideologically insistent upon seeing the United States as a democracy in which power is equalized along the lines of the "one-person, one-vote" principle, wealth and status do not translate directly into political power. One way or another, they must deny that wealth and status are meaningful determinants of public policy outcomes. But others stand on apparently "objective" grounds, saying only that the role of wealth and status in shaping the policy product of government has never been empirically demonstrated. What they usually insist upon is proof of a direct relationship between holders of wealth and status and compliant decisionmakers who consistently follow their dictates. Such evidence is, of course, very difficult to find, if only because neither side would want such a relationship known.

We think that the problem is both interesting and complicated, yet capable of being resolved. This view is supported by two very recent and exhaustive studies. Undertaken with sharply contrasting ideological perspectives and methods, these studies nevertheless arrive at nearly identical conclusions. Both G. William Domhoff, a radical sociologist, and Thomas R. Dye, a conservative political scientist, studied the highest wealth and status strata of American society and how (or if) they controlled the government. Both find powerful evidence that they do, but not directly in the sense of issuing daily conference-call instructions to decisionmakers. Instead, both find systematic shaping of general public understanding and construction of the immediate political agenda as the principal means of managing the government's actions, together with powerful influence over decisionmakers, many of whom are members or eager supporters of the

---

[1] We use "status" as a summary term encompassing both *prestige* from whatever source derived and *position* of leadership in major national social and economic institutions.

same small circle of powerholders. We shall first compare these key studies and then, adding some supportive materials from other scholarly sources, examine how both understanding and agenda are actually shaped.

Domhoff is the author of several books analyzing aspects of upper-class life in the United States. He began with *Who Rules America?* (1967) and went on to examine upper-class lifestyles, clubs, recreational retreats, class cohesion and consciousness, and control of the two major political parties.[2] His most recent work, *The Powers that Be: Processes of Ruling Class Domination in America*,[3] summarizes much of his earlier research and applies it squarely to the question we have posed. His method is a combination of social and economic background analysis (wealth, family origins, places of education, types of occupation, intermarriages, and so on) and in-depth biographies and case studies. His premises and conclusions are that a governing class[4] can be identified in this way, that it can be shown to control the government, and that the dominance of such a class is profoundly undemocratic and undesirable.

Domhoff begins by focusing on that 0.5 percent of Americans who hold great wealth, totaling together about 25 percent of all the wealth in the country. He shows that these people have continuing school, business, and social relationships and that they therefore constitute a cohesive class with a high degree of class consciousness (awareness of their values and interests and how distinct they are from that of the rest of the population). He then identifies "four general processes through which economically and politically active members of the ruling class, working with the aid of highly trained and carefully selected employees, are able to dominate the United States at all levels."[5] These processes are:

1. The special-interest process (the way that individuals and corporations serve their short-term needs).
2. The policy-formulation process (the way that basic policy directions are set in the interest of the ruling class).
3. The candidate-selection process (how the ruling class ensures that
   the right politicians get elected).
4. The ideology process (the way that the general context of public
   understanding is shaped so that ruling-class interests are served).

Domhoff then presents extensive evidence to show how in each of these

[2] G. William Domhoff, *Who Rules America?* (Englewood Cliffs, N.J.: Prentice-Hall, 1967). See also *The Bohemian Grove and Other Retreats* (New York: Harper & Row, 1974); *Fat Cats and Democrats* (Englewood Cliffs, N.J.: Prentice-Hall, 1972) and *Who Really Rules?* (San Francisco: Goodyear, 1978).

[3] G. William Domhoff, *The Powers that Be: Processes of Ruling Class Domination in America* (New York: Random House/Vintage Books, 1978).

[4] See G. William Domhoff, *The Higher Circles: The Governing Class in America* (New York: Random House/Vintage Books, 1970).

[5] Domhoff, *The Powers that Be*, p. 10.

processes the politically active arm of the ruling class (the "power elite") operates to see that ruling-class interests are served.

Thomas Dye is the author of several books analyzing public policy in the United States and how it came to be that way. He has examined policies produced in the states and in the national government in a variety of ways. His major work, for our purposes, is *Who's Running America? The Carter Years*.[6] This book focuses on the characteristics and relationships of elites occupying the key positions of institutional leadership (economy, society, government) in the United States. His method is to start with the institutions in which key decisions are made and to identify all the people who held the important positions in them — a total of 5,416 persons. The institutions he includes are the largest corporations and banks (3,572 people), the three branches of government (286 people), the media (213 people), the prestigious colleges (656 people), the major foundations (121 people), the most powerful law firms (176 people), and leading civic and cultural organizations (392 people). He then explores the social and economic backgrounds of these people, how they obtained their positions, how they are connected with one another, and how they shape public policy. His premises and conclusions are that elites are inevitable in any society, that these people *do* constitute a dominant elite controlling the government, and that they are, on the whole, a socially responsible group whom the majority of people might well be glad to have managing the country.

Dye starts with recognition of the concentration of economic power in the United States, in which the presidents and directors of the one hundred largest corporations (two one-thousandths of 1 percent of the population) control about half of all U.S. assets. He argues that this control, because of institutional position, is more significant than the holding of great personal wealth and that analysis will yield sounder results throughout if it remains fixed on the levers of institutional control. For our purposes, his most interesting findings are that (1) most people at the top come from upper-class or upper-middle-class families; (2) many top elites have also held several top positions in their own or other fields; and (3) major public-policy directions are set by elites operating through identifiable "policy planning groups."

Of special interest to us is the fact that these two leading scholars, with very different political perspectives and methods, identify essentially the same process of elite management of the political agenda. Indeed, they both use the same term ("policy planning groups") and specify the same elite organizations as such planners and managers of policymaking. Domhoff names the Council on Foreign Relations, the Committee for Economic Development, the Conference Board, and the Business Council as his "Big Four," aided by think tanks, such as the Brookings Institution,

---

[6] Thomas R. Dye, *Who's Running America? The Carter Years*, 2nd ed. (Englewood Cliffs, N.J.: Prentice-Hall, 1979).

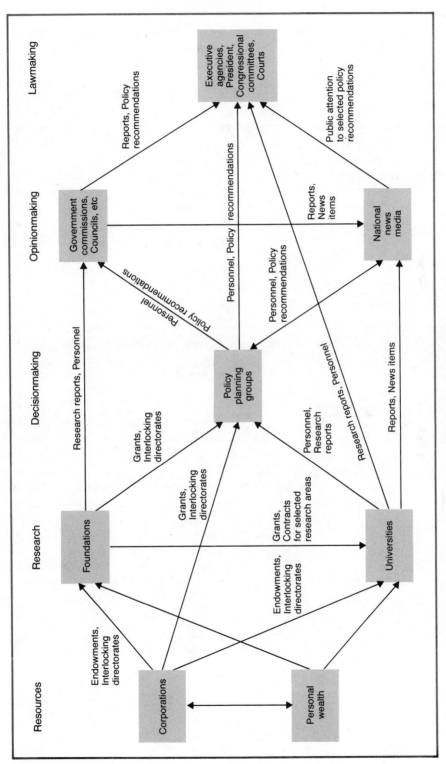

Figure 10.1 The policy process: The view from the top. (*Source:* From Thomas R. Dye, *Who's Running America? The Carter Years,* 2nd ed., © 1979, p. 212. Reprinted by permission of Prentice-Hall, Inc., Englewood Cliffs, N.J.)

that provide research and policy discussion. Dye names the Council on Foreign Relations, the Committee for Economic Development, and the Brookings Institution and concurs in the important role of the same think tanks that Domhoff lists. Their sections on this elite policy-managing process are almost interchangeable, and both employ the same summary diagram (reproduced here as Figure 10.1) to illustrate the total process of elite consensus shaping around its preferred policies.[7] We will return to this figure at the close of the chapter.

In the following sections we will draw on these different but concurring sources and other materials to sketch the way in which the context and the agenda for decisionmaking are shaped in the interest of the corporate-banking sector. Readers should keep in mind that we have not yet begun to analyze government institutions or decisionmaking within them, but are still looking at processes that are *prior to*, and perhaps *determinative of*, all that goes on within them.

Shaping the Context of Public Understanding

By "context of understanding" we mean (1) the orthodox liberal values and ideology (see Chapter 8) plus specific beliefs supplementing them, and (2) the assumptions, perceptions, and expectations about a particular subject area or problem. If the problem developing is that of staffing an expanding military force at minimal costs, for example, the context of understanding created probably will be one of growing threat from perceived enemies and unworkability and/or excessive cost of a volunteer military, against a background of the historical and democratic character of "citizen armies" winning past wars. The context of understanding operates to make some actions or policies seem natural or necessary at a particular time; some alternatives as "far out" or literally unthinkable.

The context of understanding is shaped by such social institutions as colleges and universities, the foundations, and the media (a subcategory of which is the advertising industry) and by such groups as higher professionals (doctors, scientists, engineers, and particularly lawyers) and visible intellectuals. We shall touch on what each does and how each is influenced by the highest elite strata, spending more time on universities than on the others because that is where both authors and readers spend most of their time.

Social Institutions

■ *Universities.* The roughly 2,500 public and private institutions of higher education in the United States, ranging from junior colleges to

---

[7] Ibid., p. 212. Domhoff acknowledges use of Dye's diagram, *The Powers that Be,* p. 126.

universities with 50,000 students and several graduate and professional schools, now enroll nearly 9 million students. These institutions are governed by trustees drawn chiefly from the upper classes; they are also linked closely to federal and state governments and perform several vital political functions.

Dye focuses on the trustees of the twelve private universities with the largest endowments, a group that together controls more than half of all the assets available to private education.[8] He looks particularly closely at these trustees for the additional reasons that these prestigious universities are where many, if not most, of the nation's future leaders receive their schooling and because these institutions often serve as models for the kind of education that will be provided elsewhere in the higher-education system. He finds that the trustees include many of the topmost leaders in business and government and that in general, such trustees hold several key positions at the same time.

A more wide-ranging study of trustees and regents of all colleges and universities was conducted in 1967 by the Educational Testing Service.[9] The researchers subclassified colleges and universities as "selective" private institutions (selective in admissions, meaning the Ivy League and similar schools, a list slightly larger than Dye's) and public universities, thus enabling separate analysis. They compared the trustees of these selective schools with those of all U.S. colleges and universities. They found that nearly two-thirds of all college and university trustees in the nation are in the top 1 percent in income level; in the case of the selective private universities, 43 percent earn more than $100,000 per year. The occupations of trustees are nearly all the highest-status ones, with business executives making up 35 percent of the total. The prevalence of businessmen helps to explain the fact that 20 percent of all trustees — including all the trustees or regents of junior colleges, community colleges, and small private colleges — are members of the boards of directors of one or more corporations whose stock is traded on a stock exchange. A total of 46 percent of the trustees of the selective private universities overlap with boards of directors of these major corporations, and 18 percent serve on three or more such corporate boards. In general, the selective private universities tend to have the wealthiest, highest-status trustees, perhaps partly because board positions are filled chiefly by the boards themselves on a kind of self-perpetuating basis. But state universities are not far behind. In a study focused chiefly on the California system, appointed regents were found to average three major corporate board directorates.[10]

---

[8] Dye, *Who's Running America*, pp. 133–136. The universities, predictably, are Harvard, Yale, Chicago, Stanford, Columbia, MIT, Cornell, Northwestern, Princeton, Johns Hopkins, Pennsylvania, and Dartmouth.

[9] Rodney T. Hartnett, *College and University Trustees: Their Backgrounds, Roles, and Educational Attitudes* (Princeton, N.J.: Educational Testing Service, 1969).

[10] David N. Smith, *Who Rules the Universities?* (New York: Monthly Review Press, 1974).

Trustees' political attitudes may be determined from their political-party identifications and self-described ideological orientations. Of all trustees, 58 percent were Republicans and 33 percent Democrats; 21 percent described themselves as conservatives, 15 percent as liberal, and the remainder as "moderate." [11] The proportion of each was roughly constant among the various types of institutions. The age of trustees may also be worth noting: 88 percent of the trustees of selective private universities and 74 percent of state universities were over fifty years of age; 46 and 40 percent, respectively, were over sixty.

The financing of most institutions of higher education is a major link to the more formal governing structures of both federal and state governments — and, presumably, to those dominant in such circles. Public institutions, of course, receive most of their financial support from state (or, in some cases, local) governments. They characteristically charge relatively low tuitions, with the deficit made up from public tax revenues. (A provocative and carefully detailed analysis of the sources of revenue and actual recipients points out that overall, this process amounts to working-class financing of low-cost educations for middle-class youth.[12]) The dependence of these institutions on the largesse of state legislatures makes them especially eager to serve the needs and preferences of individual state legislators and the interests dominant in the state generally. Thus, there is a strong desire to be "useful," as defined by key businesses and industries, and to avoid the taint of unorthodox political ideas or behavior that might antagonize established powers in the state. Despite these pressures, of course, tensions between the larger state universities and their legislatures are frequently high.

Both public and private universities also rely heavily on financial assistance in various forms from the federal government. Prestigious public universities, such as the University of Michigan and the University of California, receive about 50 percent and 40 percent, respectively, of their annual budgets from the federal government. At private universities, such as the University of Chicago and Harvard, the totals averaged roughly 65 percent and 40 percent, respectively. Federal assistance takes many forms: loans and grants to students, financing for buildings and equipment, performance of research and teaching functions (ROTC, for example) on the campus, and provision of contract services. In the latter case the university in effect acts as a direct arm of the U.S. government, whether in experimental programs of crime control or poverty amelioration in the United States or in the development of agriculture or training of police and bureaucrats in developing countries. In every case these funds are valued by universities, and a major university must place and keep itself in a position to

---

[11] Hartnett, College and University Trustees, p. 65.
[12] Lee Hansen and Burton A. Weisbrod, Benefits, Costs and Finance of Public Higher Education (Chicago: Markham, 1969).

compete successfully for such grants if it is to retain its status. Not only does the capacity to hire and provide research opportunities for well-reputed faculty members depend on funds of this type, but a substantial share of the operating budget of the university is also contributed in this way. Some university administrators see this process as a welcome opportunity to be of service to the society; others are less enthusiastic, but none deny the reality of the pressure.

Three basic purposes of both public and private universities may be identified, though how most universities rank them in terms of priority may be disputed. First is the purpose of providing social mobility for students and well-trained functionaries for the economy and society. These goals are complementary: students and their parents visualize college education principally as a means of getting a good job, and the economy and society require alert, aspiring, adaptable men and women to perform a multitude of tasks. The result is a vocationally oriented program of instruction whose chief criterion of success is the student's acquisition of a job offering prospects of income and status. To prepare students for such jobs, the current structure of the economic and social order must be taken as a given, its needs assessed and extended into the future, and students shown how to adapt to and fulfill those needs.

Second is the purpose of providing knowledge that will help solve problems facing the society. To be of assistance, the definitions of such problems must be similar to those of the relevant policymakers; otherwise, the results of research will not be used and this purpose will not be served. Thus, much research effort is devoted to finding ways for those who are currently dominant to carry out their policies. In seeking to solve problems of social disharmony, this purpose may lead to defining as "maladjusted" or "criminal" those who for one reason or another do not accept orthodox standards of behavior and lifestyles and to developing techniques for better controlling such "deviants." In the case of problems perceived by private industry, university efforts amount to socializing the sometimes high costs of research and development, while benefits accrue chiefly to the user industries.

Third is the intellectual purpose of the university — to transmit the culture and wisdom of the past, to adapt it to the needs of the present and the future, and to help students develop the capacity to think critically and independently about themselves, their society, and the world. This is the most difficult, least accepted, and least accomplished of the university's purposes. To think critically and evaluatively about oneself and one's surroundings requires great effort and self-discipline and the destruction of a lifetime's complacent assumptions. It provokes sharp reaction from an insecure but financially vital outside world. And so it does not often occur, and if it does, it is not often sustained long.

The faculty must operate within the context defined by these various factors. Men and women who teach, let us assume, seek advancement and security as much as do others in society. To be well regarded in one's own institution and profession, to do the research that makes for visibility and mobility, and to avoid the controversies that spell an end to advancement, faculty members must accept the basic standards that trustees, financial sources, and accepted university purposes have set for them. The real deviants soon become uncomfortably visible, pressures focus on them, and they either return to their accepted role or lose their university status. Nor is this established role uncongenial to many university faculty members. Their class origins; identification with a prestigious profession; need for access to people of knowledge, money, and power; and current positions of authority lead them to adopt the perspective of the "is." Their task is to explain, rationalize, and project the present into the future.

What is the impact of these various forces on the students who pass through American institutions of higher education? In general, survey evidence suggests that the long-term effect has been to induce them to trust and support the acts of government more fully than do ordinary citizens. College graduates are better informed, take part in politics more, and are more fully imbued with orthodox ideology than are those of comparable age and life experience who do not attend college. To some extent, the effects of college education may be mistakenly attributed to the effects of either youth (the proportion of college-educated people is higher in each new generation and age group) or economic status (college students come from wealthier families and earn more income after college). The autonomous influences of these separate factors are seldom made distinct. College education has repeatedly been shown to have an independent effect, aside from the fact that it usually coincides with both youth and wealth. Taken by itself, it correlates with greater confidence in the established political system and its current policies. Nor is the reaction to the Vietnam War really an exception to these general propositions. College graduates at first supported the war more strongly than others did and shifted to greater conviction that the United States had made a mistake only *after* President Nixon began to withdraw troops. The campus-based dissent against the war began as a very small movement; its escalation took several years and repeated provocations and even then seemed in many cases to be limited exclusively to the single policy of war in Southeast Asia.

It is clear, therefore, that the universities serve elites as a major means of developing long-term influence, both by shaping vocational orientations and skills and by instilling the political ideology and broad behavioral cues that will lead to later support. Nevertheless, some universities, some faculty members, and some students do not fit these general descriptions.

■ *Foundations.* Foundations are tax-exempt organizations that use the income from their invested assets to sponsor research or to promote programs in fields of their choice. Foundations are established by wealthy people or corporations that provide the original assets, prescribe the purposes, and establish a governing body that then takes charge. The

largest foundations are listed in *The Foundation Directory*,[13] which finds
that more than 2,500 have at least $1 million in assets or distribute more
than $500,000 annually. The very largest foundations are, of course, the
most engaged in deliberate efforts to shape public understanding and public
policy. Thirty-eight foundations had more than $100 million in assets in
1975, or slightly more than 44 percent of all foundation assets. Most of
these were originally established by powerful and wealthy families (Carnegie, Danforth, Ford, Kellogg, Lilly, Mellon, Rockefeller, and so on) and
often still have family members on their boards of directors. These largest
foundations' boards of directors are drawn almost exclusively from the
highest ranks of the society. Dye finds that the directors of the top twelve
foundations held an *average of eleven* other top leadership positions as
well.[14]

Three of the largest foundations that direct their efforts at shaping
national policy in several areas are the Carnegie, Ford, and Rockefeller
foundations. Each is governed by a board made up of well-known national
leaders, and each carefully selects the purposes for which it will sponsor
research or develop programs. By looking five or more years ahead and
giving researchers the necessary cues about foundation goals and then investing millions of dollars, such foundations can profoundly shape what is
known and what seem to be the alternatives as a problem rises to public
awareness. Dye presents as a case study the manner in which the Rockefeller Foundation initiated the study of population expansion and control.
In six pages he shows how grants to universities, subsidized books and
newspaper advertising, and lobbying led to the development of a national
population policy. From its inception in 1952 by John D. Rockefeller III,
the Population Council dispensed more than $100 million and in the
process succeeded in creating a whole new area for government and public
action along the lines it sought.[15] Not incidentally, as Dye notes, it also
affixed a particular understanding upon the plight of Third World people,
as follows:

> By focusing on population growth as the obstacle to improving the quality
> of life of the world's population, the more threatening question of *in-
> equalities in the distribution of wealth* between rich and poor nations and
> peoples can be bypassed. Hunger, disease, and violence are portrayed as
> a product of too many people rather than of inequality in the distribution
> of resources among people.[16]

■ *The Media.* Much has been written about the impact of mass media,
particularly television, on the shaping of public understanding in the

---

[13] *The Foundation Directory*, 5th ed. (New York: Russell Sage Foundation, 1976),
from which all data in this paragraph are drawn.
[14] Dye, *Who's Running America*, p. 152.
[15] Ibid., pp. 226–232.
[16] Ibid., p. 231.

United States.[17] Because television emphasizes what is dramatic and because it is far and away the leading source of information for most Americans, it is capable of massive impact in a very short time. One or two poignant pictures and three or four descriptive adjectives, and the terms within which an issue is to be understood have been set. For the fewer people who read newspapers and/or news magazines, the cues to interpretation are subtler, but no less effective. Nor is a particular understanding of events all that the media communicate: a good part of their impact comes in the form of the values stressed, explicitly and implicitly, by the commercials or advertising that accompany "objective" information.[18] Comedies or dramatic shows on television or the comics in the newspapers often contain not-so-hidden cultural values and political messages.

There is no area of American life in which control over such potential power is so tightly concentrated in a few hands. Only three television networks send news out to nearly all the major television stations in the country, and only two wire services send their version of the news out to thousands of radio stations and newspapers. Four or five "independent" newspapers (and nine chains of newspapers) and their associated news services account for most of what news presentation remains. And none of these is subject to government regulation; only the potential withdrawal of advertising by the businesses that buy time or space operates as a constraint on media policies or interpretations of the news.

Every one of these enterprises is among the largest and most profitable American corporations. Some of them own several different components of the media system. The Washington Post Company, for example, owns not only the newspaper of the same name, but also a radio station, a television station, a news magazine, and a news service. CBS owns, at last count, five television stations, fourteen radio stations, twenty-two magazines, and Columbia Records. The presidents and members of the boards of directors are, of course, drawn from high social origins and have the same backgrounds and relationships with other elites as do other top leadership people.[19]

Professional Groups

Because it is less explicit and less visible than many other activities, the political role of professionals is often ignored or vastly underestimated in analyses of American politics. The status that holding the credentials of

---

[17] Perhaps the best recent work is Edward J. Epstein, *News From Nowhere* (New York: Random House, 1973). For an effort at suggesting alternatives, see Bernard Rubin, *Media, Politics and Democracy* (New York: Oxford University Press, 1977).

[18] Even "public service" advertising may amount to blatant endorsement of corporate values and priorities; see the analysis in Domhoff, *The Powers that Be*, pp. 183–191.

[19] Dye, *Who's Running America*, Chapter 4.

doctor, scientist, engineer, or lawyer carries with it, however, means that such persons have special credibility, particularly in areas of their expertise and in a society that reveres science, technology, and practical capabilities. Professionals define what is "normal" and what is "deviant" or "insane." They prescribe for the "rehabilitation" of individuals who are "maladjusted" to society. All these terms are value judgments with vast significance for millions of people. This credibility is increased when the profession appears to be united and speaking with one voice, as when the official governing bodies (the American Medical Association or the American Bar Association, for example) take stands on issues, thereby legitimating or condemning policies or alternatives.

Formal action may be quite unnecessary if there appears to be general professional approval for a principle or program. A dramatic example of the latter was the widespread popularity and implementation of the "scientific management" doctrine developed by Frederick W. Taylor, an engineer, in the early decades of the twentieth century. Taylor combined the cultural fascination with science and progress with some very practical measures to control workers and to reduce wages, actions that were much appreciated by the business community of the time. Scientific management as developed by Taylor was a set of ways to reorganize work by eliminating the most skilled workers, breaking down their operations into components that could be done by less skilled (and less expensive) workers, maximizing the speed with which they did it, and introducing management supervision into every stage in the process. It was not necessarily more efficient, but it cost less and made the management of the work force much easier. Because it was labeled scientific and was presented by a professional engineer, it did not seem to most people to be controversial or political. And yet it served quite well the needs of the big corporations for control of workers. Furthermore, it is still having an effect today on the actual organization of work and on the cultural understanding of what is required for "efficiency." [20]

This example also suggests some subtler aspects of the political role of professionals. The skills or knowledge that make up the expertise of a professional must be skills or knowledge that are useful *to somebody* or *for something*. Both the need for such services and the money to pay for them (mainly from anticipated profits) are found chiefly in the corporate-banking sector. The ties between the two are likely to be many, therefore, and those professionals not already linked to the corporate money-and-status system may be trying via actions and rhetoric to connect themselves. Moreover, the acquisition of professional credentials is usually from skilled predecessors or graduate-level training programs. In both cases the new generation of professionals learns skills and ways of thinking that fit with

---

[20] For a full description of the nature and effects of scientific management in the United States and in other countries, including the Soviet Union, see Judith Merkle, *Management and Ideology* (Berkeley: University of California Press, 1980).

the social and economic status quo and that are *useful* — not at all times, places, and circumstances, but here and now — in the values and circumstances of American capitalist society. Some skills may be transferable elsewhere, but they come surrounded by and mixed with a variety of assumptions about the propriety and inevitability of what *is* today. They are internalized as such and are reproduced in the behavior of the professional.

Part of being a professional involves asserting the right to control the admission of others to that profession, ostensibly to assure the public that they are well qualified, but perhaps also to limit the number of persons who will enjoy the economic opportunities available. Sometimes it is the state that officially licenses newcomers, but the judgments involved in each case are made by professionals. In order to manage the instruction and credentialing of newcomers, to advance the profession's image and interests, to speak for the profession as a whole, and sometimes to establish ethical standards within the profession, most professions have an association to which almost all belong. The association has a governing body constituted in a more or less representative way. The professionals who have time and the inclination to serve on such bodies tend to be the elite of the elite — that is, the wealthier and better connected of a group already distinguished by greater education, wealth, and status than the rest of the population. Moreover, this governing body tends to cultivate connections of the same sort as its members enjoy — with the larger and more powerful corporations and banks and the top leadership positions in all areas — so as to advance the interests of the profession still further. Deviants *within* the profession are censured or otherwise constrained so that the status quo–supporting role of the profession is maintained.

Perhaps the most obviously significant profession for politics is the law. More than half of all top government positions and many corporate presidencies and directorships are filled by lawyers. But this is only the beginning. The most prestigious Wall Street and Washington law firms are daily participants in making public policy, serving the interests of their clients (the largest corporations and banks) and governing the legal profession through the American Bar Association. Dye identifies twenty top firms in New York City and five in Washington at the apex of the profession. Eighty-four percent of the 176 senior partners attended one of the prestige universities, and the *average* number of other top leadership positions they have held is nine.[21] None of them is a woman.

The governing body of the American Bar Association is its House of Delegates and below it the committees that study problems or proposed legislation and make recommendations on them. The ABA also asserts the right to screen and to make recommendations on all federal judicial appointments. Two recent scholarly studies deserve notice for their persua-

---

[21] Dye, *Who's Running America*, p. 152.

sive characterizations of the ABA. One shows that the ABA role is closely supportive of other elites' interests, particularly that of the largest corporations and banks. With or without specific authorization by the membership, ABA officials regularly lobby in the name of the profession for the interests of their client businesses before Congress and federal agencies.[22] The other study shows that throughout its history, the ABA systematically sought to prevent the admission to the bar and to inhibit the later legal practice of immigrants, minorities, and women. This was done through changing standards for legal education, managing ethical criteria, and exercising various social exclusions and pressures. At the same time, the ABA was acting on behalf of railroad and banking interests and justifying the various legal steps being taken to crush the World War I antiwar movement.[23]

Intellectuals

The political role of intellectuals is similar to, but of course less formally organized than, that of the professionals. Intellectuals who wish to be heard by more than academic colleagues usually write articles for relatively small-circulation (but highly influential) magazines or books for somewhat larger audiences. Some are critical of established institutions and practices, often in a moderate tone of reform. Not many can sustain themselves for long if they are too critical, for they will have to depend for support on that small slice of the population that is receptive to such ideas and has the money to keep buying books. Most intellectuals are drawn to thinking and writing in ways that support and justify the status quo by the fact that they seek and/or depend upon approval, support, and money from those who have such things to bestow. By and large, that means other intellectuals who have "made it" or the business, social, and political leadership in power. Intellectuals themselves are somewhat lower in social origins and current income than other elites and somewhat more liberal, but unless they are university-based, they are under continuing pressure to gain the support that only existing elites can provide.

An interesting fusion of the professional and intellectual functions in maintaining a context of understanding that supports the status quo may be found in the multilevel teaching of economics. By "economics," of course, is meant the virtues of the free-market economy. Domhoff reports on the activities of the Joint Council on Economic Education, which was started in 1949 by the Committee for Economic Development. Initially supported by the Committee for Economic Development and the Ford Foundation, the council eventually acquired enough corporate support to

---

[22] Albert P. Melone, *Lawyers, Public Policy and Interest Group Politics* (Washington, D.C.: University Press of America, 1979).

[23] Jerold S. Auerbach, *Unequal Justice: Lawyers and Social Change in Modern America* (New York: Oxford University Press, 1976), particularly Chapters 2 and 4.

publish books and pamphlets, introduce elementary and secondary school courses, provide adult workshops, shape college teacher training, and so on. Related councils were formed in all but three states to press these causes on all fronts.[24]

Another form of the same activity may be seen in the frequently repeated two-week seminars for federal court judges at the corporate-financed Law and Economics Center of the University of Miami Law School. Here free-market economists from the University of Chicago, University of California at Los Angeles, and Harvard educate twenty or so federal judges at a time on the world as they understand it.[25]

The Process of Forming Public Policy

All the activity discussed so far is directed at creating and maintaining a context of public understanding favorable to corporate-banking interests and priorities. We come now to the process by which the same interests and priorities are translated into public policies to meet specific problems. We shall look at the activities of three policy planning groups, all named by both Domhoff and Dye as major instruments in this process.

In so doing, it is worth noting immediately that we are not examining some new or hidden phenomenon. In an important study of the first two decades of the twentieth century, historian James Weinstein explored the makeup and activities of the National Civic Federation (NCF), the precursor and perhaps a model for today's policy planning groups.[26] The National Civic Federation was formed by big business so that different sectors could understand one another's needs, devise solutions that all could accept, and coordinate their strategy to have public policies enacted and implemented accordingly. The American Federation of Labor was represented as a means of muting labor opposition; several prestigious lawyers, academics, and a few politicians and social notables were also included. But the basic makeup was the presidents and directors of the largest corporations and banks. The National Civic Federation was successful: every major statute of that "reform" period was drafted or approved and ultimately supported by the NCF.

Nor are the three policy planning groups on which we will focus the only major participants in this process. Domhoff also includes the Conference Board and the Business Council in his "Big Four" and stresses the effective lobbying role of the more recently created Business Roundtable.[27]

---

[24] Domhoff, *The Powers that Be*, pp. 179–183.

[25] "Judges Discover the World of Economics," *Fortune*, 21 May 1979, pp. 58–66.

[26] James Weinstein, *The Corporate Ideal in the Liberal State, 1900–1918* (Boston: Beacon Press, 1968).

[27] Domhoff, *The Powers that Be*, pp. 69–75, 79–81. Other sources analyzing one or more of these groups include David Eakins, "The Development of Corporate Liberal Policy Research in the United States, 1885–1965," Ph.D. diss., University of Wisconsin, 1966; Hobart Rowen, *The Free Enterprisers* (New York: G. P. Putnam's Sons, 1964); and Floyd Hunter, *Top Leadership USA* (Chapel Hill: University of North Carolina Press, 1959).

But both Domhoff and Dye concur on the three, and other studies support their judgments. We may take, therefore, the Council on Foreign Relations (CFR), the Committee for Economic Development (CED), and the Brookings Institution as examples characteristic of the larger process we seek to analyze.

■ *The Council on Foreign Relations.* The CFR was founded shortly after World War I by a group of wealthy New York lawyers, bankers, and academics.[28] It was funded initially by personal contributions and later by grants from the Rockefeller, Carnegie, and Ford foundations. Its journal, *Foreign Affairs,* was established in 1922 and soon became the authoritative voice of American opinion on international relations. The CFR is made up of about 1,500 bankers, lawyers, and corporate executives, plus several journalists and subject-area experts from government and the universities. Half of the members are from the New York–Washington area; half from the rest of the country. It is entirely accurate to say that no major figure in the shaping of American foreign policy over the last half century has *not* been a CFR member, and normally they were members long before they were actually engaged in making foreign policy. Henry Kissinger, for example, got his start by performing well on assignments by the CFR and is reported to have told one of its leaders, "You invented me."[29]

The purpose of the Council on Foreign Relations was to bring together the leading men of American finance and industry to discuss world problems and alternative foreign policies and to reach a consensus that could be communicated to the government. Studies are commissioned with the aid of foundation support, and their analyses are discussed in small sessions with government and military leaders. Recommendations are then made the basis of larger sessions, and a final consensus is reached. This process takes place entirely off the public record, and members do not discuss the sessions. From time to time, books that embody CFR conclusions are published.[30] More often, CFR decisions are implemented directly as government policy. The council has been notably successful in this regard, having been generally credited with designing (1) every major part of the peace settlement after World War II, including the monetary plan that placed the U.S. dollar in a commanding position; (2) the Marshall Plan for the reconstruction of Europe; (3) the containment policy with respect to the Soviet Union; and (4) the subnuclear force strategies that led to the Vietnam War. As that war escalated,

---

[28] The indispensable resource for the origins, activities, and impact of the Council on Foreign Relations is the meticulously researched volume by Lawrence Shoup and William Minter, *Imperial Brain Trust: The Council on Foreign Relations and United States Foreign Policy* (New York: Monthly Review Press, 1977), from which all data in these paragraphs are drawn, unless otherwise noted.

[29] Ibid., p. 5, citing *Newsweek*, 2 October 1972, p. 40.

[30] One such book is Henry Kissinger's *Nuclear Weapons and Foreign Policy* (New York: W. W. Norton, 1969).

President Johnson appointed a fourteen-member Senior Advisory Group to advise him with respect to American strategy. Twelve of those fourteen were CFR members; when five of them withdrew their support for the war, in March 1968, Johnson announced his decisions to de-escalate the war and to retire from the presidency.

The Council on Foreign Relations is now engaged in a series of studies of future world problems, collectively known as "The 1980s Project." Several study recommendations have already been published, and some of these are being implemented by the Carter administration, most of whose leading foreign policy officials are CFR members. (See also the case study of the Trilateral Commission, created by CFR members in 1973, later in this chapter.)

■ *The Committee for Economic Development.* A somewhat less decisive force in domestic policymaking than the CFR is in foreign affairs, the CED is nonetheless the single most important policy planning group in domestic affairs.[31] It was created in 1942, by executives of the larger corporations, with two primary purposes: to prevent recurrence of the depression once the war ended and to give voice to an enlightened capitalist perspective so that other views (reactionary small business on the right, liberals and socialists on the left) would not preempt the field. Many of the initial 200 executives were drawn from the Business Council, originally linked to the Department of Commerce. Although considerably expanded, it has gone outside of the business world only in the case of some university presidents and some economists. Many of its members, however, are also members of the CFR.

The CED operates in much the same way as the CFR does, with foundation-financed study groups presenting recommendations on a wide range of problems. Its primary interests, however, lie with policies bearing on general levels of profitability, such as fiscal and monetary issues, inflation, unemployment, and trade. CED decisions are issued regularly as pamphlets, and its success in shaping policy is only slightly less than that of the CFR. The Employment Act of 1946, which created the Council of Economic Advisers, was in effect the CED's reconstruction of an earlier bill designed to put the federal government much more decisively into the business of managing the economy. In the 1970s the Carter energy program looked very much like CED recommendations, as did trade and welfare-reform proposals.

The CED has also been successful in placing its members in executive-branch positions in both Republican and Democratic administrations. One study reports that of the 150 men who were CED trustees between

---

[31] There is no source on the Committee for Economic Development equivalent to Shoup and Minter on the Council on Foreign Relations. This account draws on Dye, *Who's Running America*, pp. 218–220; Domhoff, *The Powers that Be*, pp. 67–69 and 109–116, and analysis of Committee for Economic Development reports.

1942 and 1957, 38 served in the national government.[32] The practice continued in similar fashion in the Carter administration, as it did in the Nixon and Ford administrations.[33]

■ *The Brookings Institution.* Dye calls Brookings "the foremost policy-planning group in domestic affairs" and its directors "as impressive a group of top elites as assembled anywhere."[34] It is certainly true that the quality of the research done at Brookings, particularly with respect to taxation, welfare, poverty, defense, and the national budget generally, is the best in the nation. And its personnel move back and forth to the executive branch of the government, though more often *into* Democratic and *out of* Republican administrations and, on the whole, at considerably lower levels than CFR or CED members do.

Brookings began in 1916 as the "Institute of Government Research," designed to promote economy and efficiency in government. It worked closely with the National Civic Federation, the precursor of today's policy planning groups. Major Brookings successes include the development of an integrated federal government budget in 1921, income maintenance and social security reform, and more recently the establishment of a congressional budget office and modifications of defense policy. During the Nixon years, Brookings published a series of counterbudgets. During the Carter administration, however, this task was abandoned to the left-wing think tanks.[35]

From the start, Brookings' trustees have included people at the pinnacle of the corporate, banking, and academic worlds. They remain so today and have extensive overlapping relationships with corporations, universities, and government. Table 10.1 is a composite sketch of the trustees or directors of Brookings, CFR, and CED as of 1976. Note that Brookings' trustees hold even *more* corporate directorships and university trusteeships than do the leaders of CFR and CED. As a group, Dye notes, these managers of the core policy planning groups are closely linked to the corporate world and have extensive governmental experience. *All* CFR directors had government experience at some time; the *average* for all these leaders was *more than twelve* such top leadership positions! The largest share by far came from a very few prestigious universities, and they are characterized further by the nearly complete absence of blacks and women.

Dye's table represents the clearest demonstration yet, or perhaps possible, of the integration of the highest echelon of the corporate-banking

---

[32] Karl Schriftgiesser, *Business Comes of Age* (New York: Harper & Row, 1960), p. 162. Cited in Domhoff, *The Powers that Be*, p. 68.

[33] Ibid., p. 69.

[34] Dye, *Who's Running America*, p. 131.

[35] See, for example, *The Federal Budget and Social Reconstruction* (Washington, D.C.: Institute for Policy Studies, 1978). It should also be noted that the director of Brookings, Dr. Gilbert Steiner, vigorously challenged Dye's interpretations when they were first made. See the *Journal of Politics* (Spring 1975), p. 26.

Table 10.1

The Policy-Planning Directors: A Collective Portrait, 1976

	CFR N = 25	CED N = 22	Brookings N = 20	Total N = 67
Interlocking				
Corporate directorships				
Average number	3.7	3.8	4.6	3.9
(% with none)	(28%)	(4%)	(10%)	(16%)
Government offices				
Average number	4.6	2.8	3.0	3.5
(% with none)	(0%)	(50%)	(20%)	(22%)
University trusteeships				
Average number	1.7	1.5	2.3	1.8
(% with none)	(16%)	(36%)	(20%)	(22%)
Civic association offices				
Average number	2.2	3.8	3.0	3.0
(% with none)	(20%)	(14%)	(25%)	(19%)
Total institutional affiliations				
(average)	12.0%	11.8%	12.9%	12.2%
Education				
Percent private prep school[a]	16.0%	17.4%	5.0%	11.9%
Percent college education	100.0%	100.0%	100.0%	100.0%
Percent prestigious university[b]	86.4%	63.6%	80.0%	76.1%
Percent with law degree	52.0%	18.0%	30.0%	34.3%
Percent graduate degree,				
including law	92.0%	72.7%	90.0%	85.0%
Social character				
Percent female (number)	4%(1)	0	15%(3)	6.0(4)
Percent black (number)	4%(1)	0	5%(1)	3.0(2)
Average age	58.8	59.0	59.5	59.0
Private club membership				
Average number	1.8	1.5	1.5	1.6
(% with none)	(36%)	(41%)	(30%)	(35%)

Sources: Marquis Who's Who Inc. *Who's Who in America*, 41st Edition, 1980–1981. Data on six directors were not available. Cited in Thomas R. Dye, *Who's Running America? The Carter Years*, 2nd ed. (Englewood Cliffs, N.J.: Prentice-Hall, 1979), p. 223.

[a] Andover, Buckley, Cate, Catlin, Choate, Country Day, Cranbrook, Deerfield, Episcopal, Exeter, Gilman, Groton, Hill Hotchkiss, Kingswood, Kent, Lakeside, Lawrenceville, Lincoln, Loomis, Middlesex, Milton, St. Andrew's, St. Christopher's, St. George's, St. Mark's, St. Paul's, Shattuck, Taft, Thatcher, Webb, Westminster, Woodbury.

[b] Harvard, Yale, Chicago, Stanford, Columbia, M.I.T., Cornell, Northwestern, Princeton, Johns Hopkins, Pennsylvania, and Dartmouth.

sector with the process of policymaking in the United States. But let us add a case study of our own that brings the story up to date — a brief analysis of the makeup and program of the Trilateral Commission.

The Trilateral Commission: A Case Study
of the Newest Policy Planning Group

In August 1971 President Nixon suddenly reversed long-standing U.S. policies and devalued the dollar, imposed surcharges on imports, and established wage-price controls. In this typically secretive yet drastic action, Nixon violated every major tenet of the Atlanticist (U.S.–Western Europe) corporate-banking establishment code: stable monetary relations, free trade, and coordination among multinational business, finance, and national governments in all important matters. The pressures to which Nixon reacted had been building for years and still characterize the world economy — high but uneven inflation rates, balance-of-payments problems, currency fluctuation, widespread unemployment, and so on. But that was all the more reason to proceed cautiously, with careful attention to the fragile and interdependent web of trading and investment relationships that characterize multinational capitalism today. Instead, Nixon abruptly asserted nationalist and protectionist principles and sent shock waves through the financial houses and corporate headquarters of multinational enterprises.

At the time, the chairman of the Council on Foreign Relations was David Rockefeller, also president of the Chase Manhattan Bank and manager of the Rockfeller family enterprises.[36] Working closely with other Council on Foreign Relations members, particularly Zbigniew Brzezinski (who later became executive director), Rockefeller gathered support and members during 1972 for an international version of the council, to be called the Trilateral Commission. "Trilateral" here refers to the three areas of the world in which industrial capitalist societies dominate: Western Europe, North America, and Japan. The goal of the new organization was to provide a forum for private international consultation and agreement on basic policies to be followed and coordination of influence on national governments to act accordingly. Operations formally began in 1973, and several studies with recommendations about world problems have been made the subject of discussion at semiannual plenary sessions or the more frequent executive committee meetings, with recommendations regularly forwarded (often in person) to affected governments and international institutions.

The makeup of the commission emphasizes the globally oriented sectors of contemporary capitalism, particularly banking and export-dependent multinational corporations. There are roughly 260 members, of whom about 60 are from the United States; many of the latter are also members of the Council on Foreign Relations, and some are members of the Committee for Economic Development. Nine of the world's fifteen largest

---

[36] Dye, *Who's Running America?* contains a profile of David Rockefeller and an important analysis of the Rockefeller interlocking relationships with major New York banks, oil companies, and insurance companies; see pp. 153–157, 157–161. In all other respects this case study rests on our own original research, primarily from the Trilateral Commission's own *Triangle Papers* and its quarterly newsletter, *Trialogue*.

banks are represented, including two of Europe's top three, the five largest in Japan (seven of the largest nine), and two of the three largest in the United States.[37] The leading European and Japanese industrial corporations, nearly all active exporters, are also well represented; executives of the four top Japanese firms, Italy's top two, and the top British, German, and Dutch corporations are members. But bankers and corporate executives are in every case supplemented by media owners and executives, politicians, prominent academics, and a scattering of trade union leaders.

The American contingent differs slightly from this pattern, perhaps because the close relationship with the CFR provides a dual representation system and/or the need for a somewhat different pool of resources to manage the American government. Except for the Bank of America, Chase-Manhattan, Exxon, and Shell, the American banks and corporations represented are ranked, but are not the largest in assets or sales, and there are proportionately many more professional politicians and academics.[38] In all, the commission in 1977 included representatives of seven leading banks or brokerage houses, nine major corporations, four key law firms, and the steel and auto unions, as well as the AFL-CIO. The twelve American politicians selected (two governors, four representatives, four senators, two executive appointees) were almost uniformly aspiring younger men, technically oriented systems thinkers intelligently responsive to research and recommendation in a global framework — essentially, a new generation of the "best and the brightest" in their commitments to rationalization and to social and economic engineering. The ten American academics selected included many with government experience, and most were engaged in some form of applied policy research and recommendation.[39]

At its inception, the Trilateral Commission included several members of the Nixon-Ford administration, even though its basic commitment to

---

[37] Banks are ranked by assets, industrial corporations by sales, both for 1975, as reported in *Fortune*, May and August 1976. The figure for Italy in the next sentence is based on private firms only.

[38] It may be more important to note what types of corporations are *not* included. Absentees include heavy industry (particularly steel and auto), the defense industry, and non-Rockefeller oil (Gulf, Texaco). Heartland older industries, those threatened by imports, and businesses by their nature national in character are barely involved.

[39] Perhaps the character of both politicians and academics is best summarized in the close relationship between the Trilateral Commission and the Brookings Institution. Brookings provided candidates for commission membership and a stable of experienced researchers as well. Only certain kinds of politicians are receptive to data-laden analyses and detailed managerial solutions, and only certain academics work well within the pragmatic political-economic framework of policymakers and produce "practical" recommendations. Trilateral-Brookings is the marriage of these: each has some of the other in its makeup, communication is easy, and agreed-upon ends are coherently pursued. As if to celebrate the marriage, the new president of Brookings, Bruce McLaury, is a prototypical Trilateralite: Harvard Ph.D., Trilateral Executive Committee member, former head of the Federal Reserve Bank of Minneapolis, and associate of Trilateral-CFR member Robert V. Roosa when the latter was under secretary of the treasury for monetary affairs; almost redundantly, Roosa also serves as chairman of the Brookings board of trustees.

international consultation and cooperation was so flagrantly violated in those years. Nelson Rockefeller was hardly unaware of its interests, and many of its members and staff had worked with him at some time. And Henry Kissinger, long a Rockefeller associate, was close enough in substance, though sharply contrasting in his "Lone Ranger" (Brzezinski's term) style; in confirmation he too became a member, shortly after leaving office.

It is not clear at what point Jimmy Carter, the former governor of Georgia and an original Trilateral Commission member, decided or was encouraged to announce his candidacy for President. No study has explored the Trilateral Commission's contribution to his rise through the primaries, though money and connections probably played a significant role. Certainly member Leonard Woodcock's timely endorsement before the Michigan primary helped some, and Executive Director Brzezinski served as foreign policy adviser and speechwriter throughout the campaign. After Carter had chosen fellow Trilateral Commission member Walter Mondale as his running mate, the two were repeatedly briefed by teams of experts in various fields, more than half of whom were Trilateral members or staff or associated with the Brookings Institution.

But it was only after Carter's election that the Trilateral connection became increasingly visible, as appointment after appointment went to Trilateral members and staff or to Brookings associates. Granting that this is a noteworthy talent pool, it is still remarkable to find that by June 1977, twenty-two present or former Trilateral members or staff and Brookings people closely associated with Trilateral work held positions at the assistant secretary level or above. Included were all the top foreign and economic policy-making positions: in addition to the President and Vice-President, the secretaries of state, defense, and treasury (plus four high offices in state, two in treasury, and two in defense); the national security adviser (Brzezinski); the chairman of the Council of Economic Advisers; deputy director of the Central Intelligence Agency; and seven key ambassadors or special representatives (among them the United Nations, Peking, the Panama Canal Treaty, and Nuclear Arrangements). Not included in this list are appointments declined (at least two cabinet secretaries) or the former executives of the Atlanta-based Coca-Cola Company (two high offices in defense plus the secretary of energy) and whose Trilateralist president, J. Paul Austin, remained a close personal adviser to Carter.

By 1980, the normal turnover in government had resulted in some change of responsibilities, but no less of a Trilateral presence. When the Trilateral secretary of treasury was replaced by the former head of the Federal Reserve Board (himself only a director of the Council on Economic Development), the appointee to chair the Federal Reserve Board was the Trilateralist president of the New York Reserve Bank; in turn, the latter was replaced by the Trilateralist former under secretary of the treasury for monetary affairs. The special representative for the Panama Canal negotiation, his job complete, was sent to the Middle East as special representative; and the special representative to Peking became the first U.S. ambassador to the People's Republic of China.

The commission sees a world undergoing severe crises (of various kinds of resources, including political will) and a process of fundamental change, such that either a new world order will emerge or we shall descend into chaos, conflict, and catastrophe. To achieve the former, a new and pervasive integration or rationalization on a world scale must be accomplished, particularly with regard to monetary and trade relations, and new international institutions developed appropriate to this goal. The Third World is and will continue to be a major problem arena, requiring special and coordinated attention. And there must be substantial change in the domestic economies and governing practices of the trilateral societies themselves. In every case, of course, the prescription for taking charge of ongoing change is intended to shape the future in a manner congenial to the commission's dominant interests — that is, finance capital and multinational and export-oriented enterprises.

The international goals of the Trilateral Commission lead to some clear priorities for foreign policy: elimination of military confrontations, stabilization of currencies, control of inflation, expansion of trade, and assurance of Third World debt repayment. To accomplish these ends, certain international institutions are marked for development. The institutions of greatest potential, given Trilateral Commission orientations, are the International Monetary Fund (IMF), the Organization for Economic Cooperation and Development (OECD), and the International Energy Administration (IEA).[40] The IMF is already assuming a policeman role in international lending and proving to be more successful than private banks or creditor governments at enforcing wage and services cuts or other conditions ensuring readier repayment upon debtor nations. The OECD, with its twenty-four industrial member nations and background of experience, is viewed as ripe for development into the primary coordinating body for the industrialized world, of which the trilateral societies are, of course, the core. The IEA, too, is marked for an expanded role as a potentially effective vehicle through which relatively indirect control can be exercised.

But what is perhaps most original and important about the advent of the Trilateral Commission among policy planning groups is its conscious use of the international agenda to manage domestic programs and populations. One controlling premise is that the trilateral societies are all suffering from an excess of democracy and the pervasive negative influence of hypercritical intellectuals and headline-hunting reporters. *Triangle Paper #8*, entitled "The Crisis of Democracy," summarizes this view. The introduction (author unspecified) sketches major parts of the problem:

> The advanced industrial societies have spawned a stratum of value-oriented intellectuals who often devote themselves to the derogation of leadership, the challenging of authority, and the unmasking and delegitimation of

---

[40] See *Triangle Paper #11*, "The Reform of International Institutions."

established institutions. . . . This development constitutes a challenge to democratic government which is, potentially at least, as serious as those posed in the past by the aristocratic cliques, fascist movements, and communist parties.[41]

The operations of the democratic process do indeed appear to have generated a breakdown of traditional means of social control, a delegitimation of political and other forms of authority, and an overload of demands on government, exceeding its capacity to respond.[42]

With respect to the United States, Brzezinski's regular collaborator, Samuel Huntington of Harvard, emphasizes a recurring Trilateral theme:

A government which lacks authority and which is committed to substantial domestic programs will have little ability, short of a cataclysmic crisis, to impose on its people the sacrifices which may be necessary to deal with foreign policy problems and defense.[43]

The solution, it is clearly intimated, lies in detaching government from the people so that responsible and knowledgeable elites can act as their wisdom dictates. In the context of multiple crises, the first casualty acknowledged by the Trilateral Commission is political democracy.[44]

The revitalization process prescribed for trilateral societies involves a struggle against ourselves in which the people must make sacrifices, and governing elites must regain their confidence and political will. This theme runs through several *Triangle* papers:

The real challenge of the energy problem is not a struggle with outside adversaries, as in most great crises of the past, but within and among our respective societies. Our governments must provide bold and far-sighted leadership in their domestic and foreign policies to face this challenge. Our peoples need a wartime psychology to fight this war against ourselves. They should be prepared to tighten their belts and to share sacrifices among themselves.[45]

It is a real question whether the necessary sacrifices will in fact be accepted by powerful elements in the body politic. . . . Do governments have the political will to face the truth and act, and if so, will their peoples give them the power to act?[46]

The goal of this restored authority in government is to maximize profit while maintaining social control. Mobilization of the population by a variety of means, including confrontation with the Soviet Union and the real threat of war, is quite likely. An associated approach is national eco-

---

[41] Michel Crozier, Samuel Huntington, and Joji Watanuki, The Crisis of Democracy (New York: New York University Press, 1975), p. 7.
[42] Ibid., p. 8.
[43] Ibid., p. 105.
[44] See Samuel Bowles's analysis on this point in The Progressive, May 28, 1977.
[45] Triangle Paper #5, "Energy: The Imperative for a Trilateral Approach," p. 30.
[46] Triangle Paper #6, "Energy: A Strategy for International Action," pp. 8, 10.

nomic planning, perhaps approximated at first by a comprehensive program for controlling the use of energy. Other goals are reduction of competition, greater efficiency in the use of resources, reduced taxes (achieved particularly by cutting government services), and reduced real wages (by increasing productivity, holding wage increases below the inflation rate, limiting welfare and unemployment, providing government-paid labor, and so forth). In all of these measures industrial working classes pay the price of restored profitability, and the great international engine of upward redistribution that is world capitalism spurts forward once again.

But the Trilateral Commission design faces at least three major obstacles. One is the sheer complexity of the organizational task involved, including intractable governments, unforeseeable events, and a variety of economic or other pressures that might fragment the currently supportive coalition. Another is the continued growth of a reactionary movement in the United States; protectionists, hard-liners, and a significant sector of the American economy have already organized and scored some early victories, such as forcing expansion of military budgets. Finally, there is the more remote possibility, as yet realized only in Third World settings, of popular movements' effective resistance and ultimate conversion of the world crisis into a democratic opportunity.

The pattern of mounting reactionary opposition has been well characterized by Michael Klare in a brief but insightful essay entitled "The Traders versus the Prussians."[47] Refining the cruder "Yankees versus cowboys" thesis of conflict between elements of the corporate-banking sector (roughly the liberal bankers and multinational corporations of the Northeast versus the aerospace, oil, and nationalist interests of the Southwest), Klare substitutes ideology and character of multinational interests for geography and economic sector. The "traders" are those committed to world-scale finance and trade and a relatively soft ideological line, while the "Prussians" are nationalist, protectionist, hard-line, and military-oriented.

The former are essentially the interests represented in the Trilateral Commission, and they are most effective when they can work through the international institutions (chiefly financial) that they dominate to shape the context and agenda of national governments. The latter group is much less cohesive in its economic base and is united as much by its opposition to internationalist finance and the Atlanticist establishment as by any other factor. The defense and aerospace industries are clearly visible, and one may assume that auto, steel, and other heartland industry will be supportive. The automobile industry, for example, has provided some of the leading opposition to even tentative steps toward national economic planning, a Trilateral Commission cornerstone. Some Prussians have found one another in the "Committee on the Present Danger," an American

---

[47] Michael Klare, "The Traders versus the Prussians," *Seven Days*, 28 March 1977, pp. 32–33.

organization of businessmen, retired military officers, former government officials, and intellectual "hard-liners." Many Reagan supporters were among its founding members (although a number of Trilateral members also supported Reagan in the 1980 election), and four received major appointments early in the Reagan administration.

If the Trilateral Commission is unable to work its will by subtler means, the prospect is for a trader-Prussian contest for public support — and consequent return of the ideological center to something approaching that of the late 1950s. What the larger analysis here implies, of course, is that the real conflict in American politics is between these two great power blocs, both of which are well represented in both major political parties. When danger threatens the basic structure of the system, however, such divisions may quickly disappear. In neither case have majorities of the population played much of a part in making choices between alternative policy directions.

Summary

We have combined the remarkably convergent conclusions of a radical sociologist and a conservative political scientist, who each used quite different methods, with several other sources to sketch the manner in which a *context of understanding is created* and the *political agenda is managed* before any government action occurs. All these sources point to the corporate-banking sector as the leading force in both of these processes. Some of the institutions or groups of people shaping the context of understanding are the universities, the foundations, the media, the higher professions, and the intellectuals. In each case, we sought to detail ways in which corporate-banking perceptions and priorities were absorbed and passed on to the public.

The actual managing of the political agenda so that the preferences of the corporate-banking sector are implemented as public policy is accomplished by an array of policy planning groups. We briefly described three that observers agree are among the most influential: the Council on Foreign Relations, the Committee for Economic Development, and the Brookings Institution. We saw that they are all tightly interlocked at the very top leadership level, that they are successful in having their recommendations adopted by the government, and that they serve as a personnel pool from which many government positions are filled.[48]

---

[48] Despite their obvious importance, however, they are noticed only rarely by political scientists, a fact that should generate curiosity. We surveyed twelve textbooks in American government bearing copyright dates of 1979 and 1980. Not one of them had index references for all three of the major groups reported here (Council on Foreign Relations, Committee for Economic Development, and Trilateral Commission), and each group was the subject of a reference only twice among all twelve books!

Perhaps the best summary of this chapter is found in Figure 10.1. This diagram, developed by Dye, but endorsed and used by Domhoff as well, shows the process of policyshaping moving from left to right. First, corporations and wealthy individuals endow and control foundations and universities. The latter study coming issues and problems in depth, beginning to shape the context of understanding and providing specific recommendations. The policy planning groups occupy the central role in refining studies and recommendations and in transforming them into government policies, often by directly staffing the relevant government positions themselves. Public acquiescence is promoted by the news media and the legitimating actions of presidential commissions. Finally, the government makes the policies for which the way has been so carefully prepared. In the next several chapters we turn to that stage of the process.

ELITE ANALYSIS: APPROACHES AND IMPLICATIONS

Chapter 11 analyzes elites in two different ways. The first section analyzes the assumptions involved in various methods of collecting evidence about power and who holds it. In other words, it asks questions about the questions analysts ask and what the answers will mean. We return to the basic question of "Who rules?" and to the alternative models of the American power structure posed in Chapter 2, and we try to frame narrower specific issues to be explored in the chapters of Part 4. Necessarily, this effort requires us to examine some scholarly controversy, but this should help the reader to understand why social scientists of equally high standing fundamentally disagree on who rules in the United States.[1]

---

[1] We think that careful clarification of the questions to be asked is a vital prerequisite to analysis of evidence and subsequent judgment about the nature of the American power structure. Those to whom the latter goal is less important or who do not read the book in sequence of chapters may wish to omit this first section entirely.

In the second section we move to an analytic survey of data about elites. We look chiefly at *socioeconomic background* data (evidence about age, family origins, occupations, education, social class, and so forth) and quickly at *attitudinal* data (evidence about how people think about principles or issues) about people in the institutions of the national government. This information will give us a general picture of who the people are who run the government. It will also help to refine what we want to keep asking as we proceed through the chapters of Part 4.

Questions and Approaches in Elite Analysis

In Chapter 2 we noted that in response to the question "Who rules?" three alternative models — the pluralist, the establishment, and the ruling class — of the American power structure were often urged. We suggested then that a responsible inquiry seeking to determine which version is substantially correct required a framework and approach broad enough and skeptical enough to permit each of these models to be tested against the evidence. This was because the approach to inquiry may well *suggest* or *contain* conclusions in one or the other direction.

At this point, we will examine three quite different approaches to seeking and using evidence about who rules in the United States. We call these the *systemic*, the *policy-consequences*, and the *governing-elites* approaches. Each has certain strengths and problems, but when these are understood, each has something distinct to offer us for the ultimate (Chapter 20) purpose of choosing which model is correct.

The Systemic Approach

This approach looks at an integrated political economy (much as we did in Chapter 2) and tries to identify the most fundamental sources of its dynamics. The most favored place to look is usually at the needs and circumstances of the economy, but basic cultural values, social conflicts, and external pressures also play important parts. The most basic factors, such as societal values or economic imperatives, are the tools for explanation in this approach, rather than personalities or characteristics of institutions. The systemic approach argues, for example, that government, *no matter who the people holding office may be,* has no alternative but to act in ways that serve the needs of the dominant units of the economic system. Whatever the social origins and political beliefs of officeholders, they *must* act to defend investments and to open up markets abroad. At home, they *must* encourage profitability, defend inequality of wealth and income, and prevent social unrest — whether accomplished by diversion, manipulation, or coercion.

According to the systemic approach, the answer to the question "Who holds power?" is not to be found by analyzing government officeholders or even their policies. Instead, it lies in the structure of ownership and control of the major units of the corporate-banking sector and identification of those whose interests are served by the workings of the total system. For many years, very little evidence was available to connect the interests of the owners and managers of the corporate-banking sector immediately with the actual decisionmaking of government officials. This lack of evidence did not prevent some observers from arriving directly at the conclusion that a tiny ruling class dominates all major actions in the economy, society, and government, but it did make their argument empirically weak. However, recent studies of the agenda-shaping role of prestigious policy planning groups, such as those examined in the preceding chapter, have gone a long way toward filling this gap.

One weakness of the systemic approach is that it may seem to explain things too mechanically or "deterministically" (*everything* happens because the needs of the economic system dictate it). After all, there is much conflict about proposed government actions, and at times the policies implemented appear to be at odds with the interests of the corporate-banking sector. Three observations need to be offered here. First, much of what government does is not of fundamental importance to the maintenance of the economic system itself, to its major imperatives, or to the basic pattern of burdens and benefits that it generates. Such nonfundamental issues may well be subjects of controversy among components of the corporate-banking sector or among groups emerging from the competitive business sector and the population generally (consumers, environmentalists, and the like).

Second, the shared commitment of all sectors to the maintenance and continued profitability of the total system should not obscure the existence of ongoing rivalries among component elements. The oil industry's success in increasing its profitability in the 1970s, for example, cost other major industries. They may in turn be expected to resist policies intended to consolidate the oil industry's gains and/or to seek ways of passing their new costs on to others; inevitably, considerable political conflict will result.

Finally, policies that appear to be contrary to the immediate interests of dominant elements of the corporate-banking sector may actually serve their long-range interests. The federal income tax is a celebrated example: rather than redistributing wealth, it appears to serve the function of assuring people that the tax system is progressive and fair while actually preserving the preexisting pattern of unequal distribution. The Marshall Plan, through which the United States invested tens of billions of dollars in the reconstruction of European industries after World War II, is often cited as an example of American generosity. But U.S. industries *required* export markets and trading opportunities, and the only possible market of the necessary size and scope was a revived Europe. Moreover, the investment of vast public funds provided many opportunities for profitable investment of private funds. And the American investment was provided by tax revenues from the entire population, not just from the corporate-banking beneficiaries of a revived Europe.

These observations make the systemic approach appear less mechanical and more open to contending forces whose efforts often succeed in shaping particular outcomes. All such conflict, however, can be seen as occurring within the basic framework created by the structure and imperatives of the total political economy. Where fundamental questions are concerned, the range of choice is very narrow, and whoever occupies positions of responsibility (in government, the corporate-banking sector, the media, schools, foundations, and the like) must act to preserve the mutual enterprise — the American economic system and its associated social structure.

The strengths of the systemic approach lie in its scope and its search for the most fundamental causes and explanations. When filled in evidentially, it provides a satisfyingly comprehensive interpretation of what is happening and why. There are still many problems in amassing a sufficient body of evidence to document every step (evidence of that sort is very difficult to develop), but informed inferences can help toward understanding.

The Policy-Consequences Approach

In this approach no particular elegance of conceptualization is required, nor need the analyst amass a great deal of detailed evidence about who makes decisions and on what basis. All that need be done is to specify who gains — and who either gains less or loses — from the actions of government over time. If regular patterns of consequences can be identified and if such patterns are found to recur in various areas, one may plausibly infer that those who benefit most have played a part in bringing about such results. Constant and recurring patterns are highly unlikely to be the result of sheer coincidence; their sources are to be found in structural factors or the power and influence of those who benefit most. People who are regularly on the losing side undoubtedly do not seek or prefer to be; something or someone has caused them to be losers. And where the majority of people appear to be systematically less favored, analysis points to a relative few as the key holders of power.

What is difficult about this approach is to say exactly what the consequences of particular government policies are. It is often difficult to tell what has resulted from which government actions and how the operation of the "private" economy may have affected final outcomes. This problem is partially solved by looking at large-scale and aggregate patterns of consequences over long periods of time. And where "public" and "private" sources of power are seen as related parts of one coherent whole, the problem is minimized still further.

The policy-consequences approach is at its best in raising questions that demand explanation. If the same small group of people win and the same great majority of the people lose as the result of policy after policy over a long period of time, the burden of proof is shifted to those who argue that majorities control policymaking through elections. The most plausible inference, of course, is that the political system responds to the power and preferences of the few who are so regularly favored. But there is a nagging lack of closure about this approach: by itself, it does not identify powerholders precisely, nor does it show how they go about achieving their ends in the face of a contrary majority preference. It leaves open the outside possibility that there may be other explanations (flaws in the machinery or failures on the part of majorities to assert their preferences, for example) for the systematic advantages gained by the favored few.

So far, we have employed both the systemic and the policy-consequences approaches in our analysis of power in the United States. Chapters 2, 3, 8, 9, and 10 are primarily systemic; they see everything in total context and search for the most fundamental explanations of why things happen as they do. Chapters 4, 5, 6, and 7 are primarily assessments of policy consequences; we looked at the nature of problems involved and tried to find patterns of who won and who lost as the result of government policies. From both kinds of approaches, we have seen strong evidence that power is concentrated in a relatively few hands and used for their benefit. Although both approaches permit any one of the three alternative models of power structure to be proved correct, in neither case did pluralism seem to be indicated. Instead, either establishment or ruling-class models seemed more plausible.

But we are now shifting to a focus on the institutions of government themselves, and a different approach becomes necessary. Our previous analyses should be valuable as *setting the context* in which government institutions function and as *raising questions* for us to ask as we study these institutions. Our findings, however, must be set aside for the moment, along with the systemic and policy-consequences approaches, to be picked up again when we try to bring *all* the evidence together for judgment in Chapter 20. To focus on institutions and decisionmaking within them, we need an approach appropriate to that purpose.

The Governing-Elites Approach

This approach is narrower than the others, in that it looks only at government institutions and the people who hold office in them. (We have broadened it here, as is customary in the study of political institutions, to take up also the constitutional structure, powers, rules, and practices within institutions that have so much to do with what policies are produced.) Strictly speaking, the governing-elites approach asks *who government officials are* (in terms of socioeconomic backgrounds) and/or *how they act in office.* Application of this approach has led analysts to one of two conflicting conclusions and has set off a scholarly controversy that still rages today.

The first school of analysis (the "power elite" viewpoint, roughly consistent in its conclusions with our two latter models) looks almost exclusively at the social backgrounds (family origin, income level, education, occupation, and the like) of key decisionmakers — chiefly in government, but also in the economy, media, and elsewhere. It finds them representative almost entirely of the upper class and concludes that government actions reflect the interests and preferences of that class. The other school of analysis (the "democratic pluralists") focuses on the actual decisionmaking of government officials, insisting that this is where the reality of policymaking is to be found. Proponents of this view deny that one can make the inference from social-background characteristics that the power elitists do, because upper-class people in government may act in the majority interest or in response to the interplay of group pressures in the policy-making process. It is how they *act* that counts, and the process of decisionmaking on various real issues is therefore what should be studied. Doing so reveals many sources of influence, an arbiter's role for public officials, and results that generally reflect compromises in the public interest.

Clearly, we shall want to use *both* foci of analysis to avoid being captured by either school. But there are still other ways to improve the quality of our analysis and to try to rise above this controversy. For example, we should be clear about definitions of "elites," the questions to which we seek answers, and what is at stake in the inquiry.

Elites are those people who hold more of the resources of power than do others, whom we term *nonelites* or, to avoid repetitiveness, *masses*. Where one draws the line between elites and nonelites is not crucial, as long as there is a clear basis for this necessarily arbitrary distinction. Everybody has *some* power, of course, but at some point the disparity between a member of Congress, corporation president, or newspaper editor on the one hand and a steelworker, welfare mother, or student on the other becomes quite obvious.

Elite status may flow from the mere possession of disproportionate wealth, status, knowledge, or any other power-yielding resource, held as a *personal attribute*. Persons in this general category are more capable of exercising influence over public policy than is the ordinary citizen, if they choose to so apply their resources. Or elite status may be bestowed on a person who holds an *institutional position* that confers the capacity to control or affect the lives of others, such as an officer or director of a major corporation or an official of government. In the latter case both the voluntary compliance granted to legitimate authority and the availability of means of coercion contribute to the official's potential power. Thus, most of our analysis will be directed at governmental elites.

We have data on the social makeup of governmental elites, but only incomplete evidence about their behavior. By looking at their age, sex, race, education, income, and occupation, we shall gain a sense of the kinds of people who staff and manage the government. We can also characterize the route by which they obtained their elections or appointments, which will help determine whether elite positions are owed to the choices of already existing elites and/or how much they depend on nonelite actions. We shall also consider how elites actually make decisions, on the evidence of their own explanations and the reported observations of others. Unfortunately, such sources are often only the tip of the iceberg and can be misleading when they are not just incomplete.

These data should be reviewed, therefore, with some caution and continuing concern for corroboration. Proof of the upper-class social origins of government decisionmakers, for example, is not proof that they act accordingly; the latter is only an inference. Perhaps they actually respond to nonelite preferences or interests; we need to know what those preferences or interests were on a given issue, if and how they were expressed, and what happened. Thus, we must undertake several steps and examine a variety of evidence before we can reach conclusions. We must look not only at who elites are and how they act in the various institutions of government, but also at the *relationship* between elites in government and nonelites outside. This will be the task not only of this and the next six chapters, but also Part 5, on nonelite attitudes and behavior.

Power involves a kind of transaction between two or more people, in which the greater resources of one cause the other(s) to act in certain ways. Similarly, leadership implies followership; one cannot be a leader unless others more or less willingly follow. Institutional elites and masses thus have a reciprocal relationship; initiatives and constraints flow back and forth between them. The actions of elites, taken with a view to probable mass reactions, are perceived by masses, whose responses in turn either suggest new actions to elites or cause them to recognize new limits on their action. Or mass demands, conceived in a context of perceived limits, are acknowledged by elites, who act to contain or promote them as their own interests and expectations of probable mass responses dictate.

Let us reiterate what is at stake in this inquiry. Neither masses nor elites are powerless. We know that each can initiate change and constrain the other under particular circumstances. Our question presses further: How much power of initiative and constraint characteristically lies on each side, and under what conditions is the normal balance disrupted? When and how can elites impose their preferences on unwilling masses? When and how can masses force elites to change their policies or to institute new ones? This phrasing of the question lacks subtlety, but it will serve to guide us on the path toward greater understanding of the real structure of power in the United States.

Not all of these questions can be answered, even when the chapters on nonelite attitudes and demands are combined with the coming series on institutions and decisionmaking within them. But they suggest the direction and goals of our inquiry, and they will help to remind us that this focus on governmental elites is narrow, omitting much more than it includes. It omits, for example, at least three-quarters of the kinds of evidence that would test the establishment or ruling-class models; it favors a pluralist interpretation because of the exclusivity of its focus on government alone. We can escape the effects of the premise that everything important is encompassed within the institutions of government by constantly recognizing it as a form of tunnel vision. With that recognition, however, we have much to gain from understanding the part played by governmental institutions in the total process of managing the American political economy. In effect, we shall add another important body of evidence and considerable subtlety to the data already accumulated and be on the verge of reaching defensible judgments about our system.

Elites in Government

The social backgrounds of people in major governmental positions have always been highly unrepresentative of the population as a whole.[2] Despite notable exceptions, the historical pattern has been for key governmental positions to be filled by upper-status people. This assertion is confirmed by a variety of empirical studies. They show that political decisionmakers are quite disproportionately white Anglo-Saxon Protestants with high incomes, many of whose families have been active in politics for generations. Their occupations are almost entirely the upper-status ones, principally the law. Although they account for less than 1 percent of the adult population, lawyers usually constitute about 60 percent of the two houses of Congress and the entire Supreme Court. Lawyers constituted 70 percent of all presidents, vice-presidents, and cabinet members between 1877 and 1934. And such lawyers are far from representative even of their own profession: in most cases wealth, family political involvement, or a large corporate law practice (or some combination of these) also prefigure high political position. Nearly half of all decisionmakers were educated in Ivy League schools — chiefly Harvard, Yale, and Princeton — or in the small, elite eastern colleges modeled on them. What emerges from this body of research is a composite picture of government conducted by a narrow slice of the population — and reflecting the very characteristics of income, status, and education we have described as elite.

A particularly good analysis illustrating these general propositions is Donald Matthews's study of members of the U.S. Senate during the period 1947–1957.[3] Matthews found that 84 percent of the 180 senators

---

[2] The major source of the data in this paragraph is Donald Matthews, *The Social Background of Political Decision Makers* (New York: Random House, 1955).

[3] Donald Matthews, *U.S. Senators and Their World* (Chapel Hill: University of North Carolina Press, 1960). Page citations are from the Vintage Books edition (New York: Random House); educational and occupational data, from pages 26–36.

Table 11.1

Occupational Distribution of Members of Senate Committees

	Occupations (in percentages)					
Committees	LAWYERS	BUSINESS-MEN	FARMERS	PRO-FESSORS	OTHER PRO-FESSIONALS	
Foreign Relations	59	16	6	16	4	= 100 (38)
Appropriations	55	27	12	0	5	= 100 (31)
Finance	46	36	11	4	4	= 100 (28)
Armed Services	55	32	6	3	3	= 100 (31)
Agriculture and Forestry	50	19	27	4	0	= 100 (26)
Judiciary	81	6	6	6	0	= 100 (31)
Interstate and Foreign Commerce	60	29	6	0	6	= 100 (35)
Banking and Currency	28	55	3	10	3	= 100 (29)
Interior	52	27	14	0	7	= 100 (29)
Public Works	50	35	6	3	6	= 100 (34)
Labor and Public Welfare	50	25	4	14	7	= 100 (28)
Government Operations	53	26	8	3	10	= 100 (38)
Rules and Administration	51	29	8	3	8	= 100 (38)
Post Office and Civil Service	56	20	13	4	7	= 100 (45)
District of Columbia	62	27	4	2	4	= 100 (48)
All Senators	54	27	7	5	7	= 100 (167)

Source: From *United States Senators and Their World* by Donald R. Matthews. Copyright 1960, The University of North Carolina Press. Used by permission.

Note: Data represent the 80th through 84th Congresses. Committee assignments of less than one year's duration are omitted.

had attended college (at a time when only 14 percent of the white population over twenty-five had done so) and that 53 percent had been to law school. Sixty-three percent of the Democrats and 45 percent of the Republicans were lawyers; 17 percent of the Democrats and 45 percent of the Republicans were businessmen. The other occupations represented were those of farmer, professor, and such other professionals as minister and physician. There were no representatives of any blue-collar occupation, only one woman, and no blacks. The senators came from upper- and middle-class families, as measured by their fathers' occupations; Matthews notes that "the children of low-salaried workers, wage earners, servants, and farm laborers, which together comprised 66 percent of the gainfully employed in 1900, contributed only 7 percent of the postwar senators."[4]

The implications of such a pattern of origins and occupations for the operation of the Senate as an institution are apparent in Table 11.1, which shows the occupational makeup of Senate committees. All pro-

---

[4] Ibid., p. 19.

posals for constitutional amendments and all nominations for the Supreme Court, for example, must pass the scrutiny of the Judiciary Committee, 81 percent of whom were lawyers. Businessmen accounted for more than half the membership of the Banking and Currency Committee, even though they constituted only about a quarter of all senators. The pattern is that each occupational grouping asserts control over governmental action in the areas of special concern to it. We shall see further implications in a later chapter.

The Senate, of course, is only one institution of government. Its counterpart, the House of Representatives, is somewhat — but only somewhat — less aristocratic in origins and occupations. Although it normally includes a few low-status occupations, it frequently has a higher proportion of lawyers. In general, it displays essentially the same income, status, and occupational characteristics as the Senate. The Supreme Court reflects a greater preponderance of high-status backgrounds, in part because it is made up of the upper echelons of the legal profession.

The executive branch, which most analysts see as possessing the important initiative and decision-making capacity within the federal government, displays some variations of the same basic characteristics. A major study of 1,041 individuals who held 1,567 executive appointments from March 1933 through April 1965 was published in 1967 by the Brookings Institution.[5] The study reports that 39 percent of these leaders had gone to private school; the total for the Department of State was 60 percent. Upper-status origins are also indicated by the fact that 26 percent of all appointees were lawyers and 24 percent were businessmen at the time of appointment. Sixty-three percent of all cabinet secretaries (86 percent of the military secretaries), 66 percent of all under secretaries, and 50 percent of all assistant secretaries were either businessmen or lawyers at the time of appointment.[6]

These findings are confirmed and highlighted in political scientist Thomas Dye's 1970 study of the recruitment of 227 top government officials in all three branches. He found that an absolute majority identified themselves as lawyers (56 percent), more than three times as many as those who came from the corporate or government worlds. For the most part, their legal education was in one of the prestigious Ivy League law schools and their current affiliation with one of the major New York or Washington law firms.[7]

When analysis turns to the very top positions in the executive branch, social origins and occupational backgrounds are even more upper class.

[5] David T. Stanley, Dean E. Mann, and Jameson W. Doig, *Men Who Govern* (Washington, D.C.: Brookings Institution, 1967).

[6] These are apparently recalculations by Gabriel Kolko, in *The Roots of American Foreign Policy* (Boston: Beacon Press, 1969), note 6, p. 141.

[7] Thomas Dye, *Who's Running America?* (Englewood Cliffs, N.J.: Prentice-Hall, 1979), p. 179.

Table 11.2

Career Occupations of Major Department Secretaries, 1953–1980

	Defense	State	Treasury
President, top bank or corporation	3	0	4
New York or Washington law firm	1	3	0
Investment firm	0	0	2
Education, science, foundation	2	2	0
Politics and government	1	1	1

Source: Who's Who in America, various years.

Table 11.2 shows the career occupations of the secretaries of the three major departments in the U.S. government between 1953 and 1980. The particular occupations indicated may be of less significance than the fact that each provides an opportunity for the holder to grasp the nature and needs of the interdependent American system and to understand how to serve them.

Patterns of Circulation

Other studies, focusing on smaller numbers of strategically located decision-makers, have produced findings that shed more light on the social backgrounds of executive officials. For one thing, a pattern of circulation appears to be developing in which decisionmakers are neither pursuing lifelong careers in government service nor close associates of the President. Instead, they are people who move back and forth between the upper echelons of business or law and government. Historian Gabriel Kolko studied the backgrounds and career patterns of 234 major decision-makers in the foreign policy field during 1944–1960.[8] He found that individuals whose career origins were in big business, investment banking, or law held 60 percent of the positions studied. Table 11.3, drawn from this study, shows that individuals with such origins held many more foreign policy positions than did those who rose through the ranks of government service. This table deserves careful study. First, Kolko has separated key officeholders into those who have held *four or more* high positions and those with *fewer than four*. He finds that 63 percent of these positions were filled by people in the first category, which indicates a great deal of "circulation" from office to office (and back and forth to the "private"

---

[8] Gabriel Kolko, *The Roots of American Foreign Policy* (Boston: Beacon Press, 1969).

Table 11.3

Occupational Origin of Individuals, by Number of Government Posts Held, 1944–1960

Occupational Origin	Individuals with Four or More Posts				Individuals with Less Than Four Posts			
	NUMBER OF INDIVIDUALS	PERCENT OF ALL INDIVIDUALS	NUMBER OF POSTS HELD	PERCENT OF ALL POSTS STUDIED	NUMBER OF INDIVIDUALS	PERCENT OF ALL INDIVIDUALS	NUMBER OF POSTS HELD	PERCENT OF ALL POSTS STUDIED
Law firms	12	5.1	55	8.1	33	14.1	72	10.6
Banking and investment firms	18	7.7	94	13.9	24	10.3	24	3.5
Industrial corporations	8	3.4	39	5.8	31	13.2	49	7.2
Public utilities and transportation companies	0	.0	0	.0	4	1.7	4	.6
Miscellaneous business and commercial firms	7	3.0	32	4.7	17	7.3	35	5.2
Nonprofit corporations, public service, universities, etc.	7	3.0	37	5.5	7	3.0	12	1.8
Career government officials (no subsequent nongovernment post)	15	6.4	85	12.5	11	4.7	19	2.8
Career government officials (subsequent nongovernment post)	8	3.4	38	5.6	12	5.1	13	1.9
Career government officials (subsequent nongovernment post and return to government post)	8	3.4	45	6.6	6	2.6	15	2.2
Unidentified	1	.4	5	.7	5	2.1	5	.7
Totals	84	35.8	430	63.4	150	64.1	248	36.5

Source: From Gabriel Kolko, *The Roots of American Foreign Policy* (Boston: Beacon Press, 1969), p. 18. Copyright © 1969 by Gabriel Kolko. Reprinted by permission of Beacon Press.

("The Wizard of Id" by permission of Johnny Hart and Field Enterprises, Inc.)

sector) by a quite small group of influential men. Second, Kolko has explored the occupational origins from which these decisionmakers came. He finds that the largest law firms, banks, investment firms, and corporations provide almost half of this crucial group. Counting both those who held more and fewer than four positions, these sources account for well over half of the incumbents in high positions. Kolko concludes that an overlap of attitudes and interests can hardly fail to arise under circumstances of circulation back and forth between business or law and government.

Nor is the convergence of upper-echelon personnel in government, business, banking, and law at any point a product of electoral decisions. Another study of top political decisionmakers found that only 28 percent of the more prominent politicians in 1933–1953 rose largely through elective office; 62 percent were *appointed* to all or most of their political jobs before reaching top positions.[9] These findings imply that the executive branch represents an even higher-status echelon than does the Congress, one that is even further detached and insulated from popular electoral control. This situation may be due in part to the increasing need for expert knowledge in the generation and implementation of governmental programs. But the apparent circulation of decisionmakers between government and high-status specialized occupations in the corporate, legal, and financial worlds occurs under both political parties and seems to imply at least an opportunity for certain "private" preferences to exert significant influence.

Social Background and the Elitist-Pluralist Debate

What have we gleaned from this analysis of the social backgrounds of elites? The existence of a relatively small group of people especially favored with the resources of power seems undeniable, as does the fact that those

---

[9] C. Wright Mills, *The Power Elite* (New York: Oxford University Press, 1956), p. 230.

in the major positions of government are drawn chiefly from this group. We may infer, though it has by no means been established, that people in the general category of elite share some values and interests that are distinct from those of the majority of the people and that governmental elites may also have such commitments or unconscious perceptions. A shared high level of income, wealth, and status — and, most likely, family histories of similar standing — does not necessarily mean that even governmental elites will hold similar views on all matters. Indeed, at times their economic interests or conceptions of the public interest may be diametrically opposed. The occasions and nature of the conflicts that result constitute one of the crucial issues of political analysis.

The pluralist view holds that conflicts among institutional elites are frequent and that the basic directions of public policy are determined by the people in elections. Supporting this view is evidence of distinctive social backgrounds among subgroups of elites. For example, Andrew Hacker surveyed the backgrounds of the presidents (as of 1959) of the one hundred largest industrial corporations, and compared them with the backgrounds of the one hundred senators in 1959.[10] Presidents were somewhat more likely to have gone to private school (28 percent to 15 percent) and an Ivy League college (29 percent to 15 percent) than were senators and to have exchanged their town and state of origin for metropolitan residence and national mobility. Hacker concluded that these and other similar findings helped to explain the existence of significant tensions between the major economic and political institutions.

A more focused analysis might suggest that such differences would be more likely to take the form of conflict between the executive and legislative branches. The upper echelons of the business world are well represented in the executive branch, as we have seen. And a good share of the larger, eastern, financial-international sector of the business community is concerned about "socially responsible" government. The reason often given is that public outrage will otherwise demand more far-reaching government measures, as in the following speech by a president of IBM:

> Much as we may dislike it, I think we've got to realize that in our kind of society there are times when government has to step in and help people with some of their more difficult problems. Programs which assist Americans by reducing the hazards of a free market system without damaging the system itself are necessary, I believe, to its survival. . . .
>
> To be sure, the rights and guarantees that the average man believes in and insists upon may interfere, to some degree, with our ability to manage our enterprises with complete freedom of action. As a result, there are businessmen who either ignore or deny these claims. They then justify their views by contending that if we were to recognize or grant them, the whole system of free enterprise would be endangered.

---

10 Andrew Hacker, "The Elected and the Anointed: Two American Elites," *American Political Science Review* 55 (1961), pp. 539–549.

> This, it would seem to me, amounts to an open invitation to exactly the kind of government intervention that businessmen are trying to avoid. For if we businessmen insist that free enterprise permits us to be indifferent to those things on which people put high value, then the people will quite naturally assume that free enterprise has too much freedom.[11]

This sector of the business community frequently encounters opposition from small business, which is much better represented in the Congress. But again, on major questions about the nature of the economy or the distribution of income, serious controversy would be unlikely.

The extent to which values and interests are in fact shared among elites and the differences between such values and interests and those of the masses of nonelite people are empirical questions. Inference from the existence of similar and distinctive social-background characteristics, while suggestive, is not conclusive. Similarly, the existence of internal conflicts between subgroups of elites can only be inferred from differences in social background. On larger questions, their essential homogeneity and difference from the mass public may be more determinative.

The Attitudes and Behavior of Government Elites

The attitudes of government officials have never been adequately characterized in any systematic way. The reasons may be obvious: their attitudes are too complex for understanding through survey questionnaires, government elites are naturally reticent on such subjects, and issues and alternatives change so rapidly that positions are quickly outdated. Inference (only) may be drawn from data about the attitudes of people in the *general* category of elites (the upper strata of the population from which government elites are drawn), but such inference is very inconclusive. The fact of being (and wanting to be) charged with governmental responsibility may convert governmental officials' attitudes from their "normal" class biases to something more responsive to wider perspectives.

One fact we do know on the basis of solid evidence is that institutional elites tend to be distinctly well informed, issue-oriented, ideological, and self-confident about their ability to influence political outcomes. Institutional elites also appear to reflect concern about the issues of the day much more than ordinary citizens do, again hardly a surprising finding. A celebrated study conducted at the height of Senator Joseph McCarthy's anti-Communist activity in the 1950s sampled a national cross section and selected community leaders in small cities across the country. The community leaders, local rather than national institutional elites, nevertheless saw communism as a more pressing problem and a greater threat than did

---

[11] Thomas B. Watson, cited in Robert Heilbroner, *The Limits of Capitalism* (New York: Harper & Row, 1966), p. 34.

ordinary citizens, very few of whom considered it a threat at all. By a nearly two-to-one majority, they expected communism to be rooted in the lower classes and the less educated. And they were much more likely than average citizens to view Communists as "crackpots," "queer people," or "warped personalities."[12]

But the most salient finding of the study, and one that is reinforced wherever a similar investigation is made, is that institutional elites appear more tolerant of unorthodoxy and more supportive of the democratic liberties of free speech and assembly than do ordinary citizens.[13] This finding may be attributable merely to a quicker recognition of the relation between hypothetical situations and standards of civil liberty, more elaborate ideology, greater confidence in their capacity to manage events, or a sense of responsibility as public officials. Or it may be that education and socialization in the life of politics have promoted genuine respect for the rules of the game of democratic politics. In any event, elites uniformly endorse the traditional civil liberties more emphatically than do nonelites; what they *do* in particular circumstances is, of course, another question.

But how does all this bear upon what government officials actually *do*? What priorities dominate in the decision-making process? These are the key questions emphasized by pluralist analysts. Socioeconomic backgrounds and attitudes are interesting subjects, but the payoff in regard to the nature of the system — the power structure laid bare — is found in what decision-makers *do*. This can be understood only in the context of what the powers and internal practices of institutions are. But by examining institutional characteristics and decisional processes together, we shall gain some sense of the mix of forces to which government officials respond. We should ask in every chapter not only *why officeholders did what they did*, but also *what needs or goals were served thereby and what that implies in the way of power structure.*

Summary

In the first section we examined three approaches to the analysis of power structure: the systemic, the policy-consequences, and the governing-elites approaches. The first is the most comprehensive and fundamental; the second, most effective for raising insistent questions about the patterns of distribution of burdens and benefits from government policies. By employing these questions in different chapters so far, we have developed evidence of concentration of power in the hands of the corporate-banking

---

[12] Samuel A. Stouffer, *Communism, Conformity, and Civil Liberties* (New York: Doubleday, 1955), pp. 172–175. Page citations are from the Science Editions paperback (New York: Wiley, 1966).
[13] Ibid., Chapter 2.

sector of the economy. But the narrower focus of the governing-elites approach on the institutions of government requires only that we put these findings aside for the moment and devise a new set of questions. We did so with the realization that the exclusivity of the focus on government institutions should be tempered by awareness of its narrowness and its tendency to suggest pluralist interpretations of the American power structure. With such recognition, we can add subtlety to our growing body of evidence by understanding the part played by constitutional structure, institutional rules and practices, and the behavior of elites within them.

In the second section we reviewed several studies of the socioeconomic backgrounds of people in government institutions. In general, those people were found to be drawn from the higher levels of the social pyramid: the higher one's position in government, the more likely it is that origin and occupation will be from the upper class. Moreover, there is considerable circulation between business or law and the highest government positions, with more than half of all key positions held by men who held four or more such positions during their careers. We noted the limits of social-background analysis and acknowledged the pluralist point that the real payoff would come when the actual policy-making behavior of elites was understood.

THE CONSTITUTION

Understanding the political and social implications of the American Constitution is no small task. Generations of historians have battled over the proper interpretation of the Constitutional Convention and the goals and purposes of the men who attended. To some, it was a conservative counterrevolution in reaction to the excesses of liberalism inherent in the Declaration of Independence. To others, it was a far-sighted, bold experiment in expanding the frontiers of democracy. Politicians disagreed from the very moment the veil of secrecy was lifted from the proceedings of the convention; Patrick Henry, for example, declared that he had "smelled a rat." James Madison, the chief note-taker at the convention, did not publish his records until more than fifty years later, and he has been accused of polishing them to ensure that they lent support to his changing views.[1]

---

[1] For a thoroughly revisionist view that is very hard on both Madison and Marshall, see William Crosskey, *Politics and the Constitution in the History of the United States* (Chicago: University of Chicago Press, 1953).

271

Nineteenth-century historians, perhaps sympathetic to Federalist principles, tended to be especially struck by the framers' accomplishments, occasionally implying that they were divinely inspired. In reaction to this school of Constitution-worship, Charles Beard lent support to Progressive Movement realism in 1913 with the publication of his *Economic Interpretation of the Constitution*.[2] Beard very nearly turned American history upside down by arguing that the framers were men who had acquired vast holdings of bonds and scrip (issued by the Continental Congress during the Revolutionary War) at low values, low because of the inability of the Congress to pay its debts. He implied that the framers then constructed a powerful government that could raise revenue and pay off the bonds at full value — to their great personal profit. This debunking was viewed by some as in very bad taste, but it helped others to look at the Constitution as a value-laden document with quite human strengths and weaknesses. Not for four decades did scholars seek to verify Beard's allegations, and when they did, it appeared that he had at the very least overstated his argument.[3] But few now deny that there was at least a shared upper-class ethos among the framers and that economic interests played some part in shaping the Constitution.

Against this general background of shared political values, the Constitution reflects several compromises among divergent interests that existed among the framers. Men from small states resisted exclusively population-based representation in the legislature and managed to secure equal status in the Senate. Southerners extracted a prohibition against interference with the importation of slaves for a fixed period of time. And the electoral college was constructed to balance the respective weights of the small and large states in selecting the President. Because of these and other differences among some of the framers, the document is not logically consistent or precisely symmetrical, and it has often been called a "bundle of compromises." But it is easy to overestimate the extent of conflict and the scope and difficulty of compromise at the Constitutional Convention. Much was shared in the way of political values, and the framers had very definite convictions about certain critical principles of government — all of which made compromise on the limited differences of interest among them more attainable.

This chapter analyzes the Constitution in three steps. We look first at what it *says*, then at *why* it says such things, and finally at *what it means* for American politics after nearly two centuries.

---

[2] Charles Beard, *An Economic Interpretation of the Constitution* (New York: Macmillan, 1913).

[3] The leading counter to Beard is Robert Brown, *Charles Beard and the Constitution* (Princeton, N.J.: Princeton University Press, 1956).

The Constitution: The Substance of the Document

After independence was declared, the American states needed some basis for cooperation in the war against England and for the conduct of foreign affairs generally. The Articles of Confederation were drawn up shortly after the Declaration of Independence was issued and performed this function until supplanted by the Constitution of 1787. Under the articles, the states retained all governing powers within their boundaries. The Congress was the only institution of the general government, but it had few powers and no capacity to enforce those it had.

The Revolutionary War was followed by a period of economic decline, and financial and commercial interests took the lead in calling for a stronger central government. Alexander Hamilton used a poorly attended meeting called for commercial purposes (the Annapolis Convention) to issue a call in 1786 for the states to send delegates to a convention in Philadelphia in 1787 to revise the articles. The convention met in June, and the delegates immediately decided to violate their instructions by embarking on consideration of an entirely new plan of government; they also prudently decided to keep their proceedings secret. They finished their work in September — a new Constitution for state ratification.

After protracted debate in key states such as Massachusetts, New York, and Virginia, the Constitution was finally accepted by narrow margins, but only after its supporters agreed to sponsor several amendments in the first Congress. It is difficult to recapture the bitterness of the opposition, but it was apparently chiefly from poor debtors, small farmers, some conservatives in New York, and a number of people who simply distrusted a potentially strong central government. We shall briefly analyze the document as it might have appeared to people at the time, emphasizing the scope and implications of the powers granted to the new government. We shall do so on an article-by-article basis, and we ask that this section be read along with the provisions of the Constitution as set forth in the Appendix.

■ *The Preamble.* The initial sentence ("We the people . . .") has been taken as an indication that the Constitution, and the government it creates, is the act of the people as a whole rather than that of the states in their separate sovereign capacities. The Articles of Confederation, of course, were explicitly a league of such sovereign states. But from the very start, the nationalists among the framers (soon to call themselves the Federalists) sought to reduce the part played by the states in forming or controlling the new government.

■ *Article I.* This article creates the legislative branch, consisting of two houses (one based on population, one on equal representation of the states) instead of the old one-house Congress in which each state had one vote. After providing for the election of each body and the manner of conducting business, the article grants powers (section 8), sets limits to powers (section 9), and sets limits on state powers (section 10). The powers granted are broad in scope, particularly in contrast to the powers of Congress under the articles. Now, Congress has power to raise revenue, to regulate interstate commerce, and to maintain national armed forces. Moreover, the final paragraph of Article I grants to Congress an indeterminate power to make all laws "necessary and proper" to carrying the others into effect. The limits on powers granted protect the importation of slaves for twenty years, require uniformity in economic legislation, and seek to prevent some of the too familiar excesses of British royalty. The states are excluded from foreign relations and from interfering with the creation of a national market with a single stable currency.

■ *Article II.* This article creates the new executive branch and boldly (in the light of pre-Revolutionary experience with British kings) grants the President broad power to be: commander-in-chief of the armed forces, voice of the nation in foreign affairs, and enforcer of the laws. The scope of powers granted here probably reflects the prospect that George Washington, having chaired the Constitutional Convention, would now accept office as the first President in the new government. Nearly the entire nation felt that Washington could be trusted and that conversely, he would be unlikely to accept any merely ceremonial post.

■ *Article III.* This article creates the new judicial branch in the form of the Supreme Court, whose justices are to hold office "during good behavior" — that is, for life. The jurisdiction of the Court extends to all those "cases or controversies" arising out of the existence of the new government: the Constitution, federal laws, and treaties. It has *no* power over matters of state law or practice, except as such actions might be in conflict with provisions of the Constitution or valid federal laws. Nor is there any mention of the power of *judicial review*, the power that the Court now enjoys of declaring acts of the Congress or the President void because it does not consider them authorized by the Constitution.

■ *Article IV.* This article prescribes certain relationships among the states. Each state must accept the validity of the governmental actions of other states, such as by enforcing debts for which court judgments have been obtained in other states. States cannot grant haven to persons accused of crimes in another state or do anything for escaped slaves except return them to their owners. And states must permit citizens of other states to do business within their borders on the same basis as their own citizens. Finally, the U.S. government gains power to help maintain existing state governments against the threat of rebellion by their own citizens. The latter provision was aimed at preventing incidents such as the farmers' rebellion against mortgage foreclosures in Massachusetts in 1786–1787 ("Shays's Rebellion").

■ *Article V.* This article prescribes two ways to amend the Constitution: by two-thirds vote of both houses of Congress or by a convention called by the Congress when requested by the legislatures of two-thirds of the states, followed in either case by ratification by the legislatures of three-quarters of the states. Only the first route has even been taken, but a call for a convention to propose an amendment to require a balanced national budget has recently come very close to the required two-thirds of the states.

■ *Article VI.* This article accomplishes two things of vital importance to the development of the nation: the assumption of the debts of the Congress under the articles and the assertion of the supremacy of the Constitution and laws of the United States over the constitutions, laws, and judicial proceedings of the states. The first of these was used by Alexander Hamilton to build the credit of the U.S. government and to gain the loyal support of bankers and other creditors who held the bonds and other obligations issued by the Congress. The second is the controversial "supremacy clause," which has finally been accepted as putting the laws and actions of the supposedly sovereign states into a secondary status, where they can be displaced by federal laws or court interpretations.

■ *Article VII.* This article provides for ratification by specially called conventions in the states rather than existing state legislatures. It hints, as does the Preamble, that the Constitution creates a new and direct relationship between the people as a whole and the U.S. government, one in which the state governments as such play no part.

■ *The Bill of Rights.* The first ten amendments, known collectively as the Bill of Rights, were an essential part of the agreement struck by the framers to gain ratification in the state conventions. As such, they may be considered part of the original Constitution, although one might ask why the framers thought it unnecessary to include such provisions in the original document itself. The amendments prohibit Congress specifically or the national government generally from interfering with some of the traditional civil liberties, hard-won over centuries, that had been part of the reason for the earlier movement for independence. As they stand, these amendments limit *only* the federal government, not the states.

Subsequent amendments are noted at other points in the book, where appropriate.

Principles and Purposes Underlying the Constitution

What the Constitution *says* takes on greater meaning when it is placed in the context of *why* such provisions were included in the way they were. In some cases the framers were implementing established principles of government organization that they considered necessary or desirable. In others they went a little further to advance values or goals that were more specific to their class or group interests. In both sets of cases time has endorsed some of their intentions and modified others. We shall look first at four principles of government organization evident in the Constitution and then at two more themes that seem to mark the framers' intentions. In each case we shall point to developments surrounding such principles or purposes in the two centuries of experience under the Constitution.

Limited Government

The U.S. government is a government of limited powers; it has only those powers, expressed or implied, *granted* to it in the Constitution and can exercise them only in ways not *prohibited* by the Constitution. For every action it takes, the U.S. government must find authorization somewhere in the Constitution *and* act without violating any of the limits contained in that document. Its judgment in both matters is continually subject to challenge in the courts. This is just the reverse of the situation for most governments, which are assumed to have all the powers that are or might conceivably be exercised by any government at any time, *except* as limited by a constitution. But it is quite consistent with the basic American political value that governments should be restricted in their scope and activities so that individuals can be as free as possible to seek their own goals without interference. And it reflects the American confidence in contracts that spell out in detail what the parties' respective powers, limitations, and responsibilities shall be.

Several important implications flow from the principle of limited government and its implementation in the constitutional contract here. One is that interpretation of the contract becomes vital to the day-to-day actions of government and itself the focus of political struggle. Another is that lawyers, the skill group with the greatest claim to interpreting contracts — particularly those that declare themselves to be law (the "supremacy clause" again) — rise to a special governing role in the society. Finally, the apparent lack of power to achieve a desired goal may lead to some very awkward situations and in some cases to strange uses of accepted powers.

Let's look at two examples of this last implication. The U.S. government has no power to make purely local acts (murder, assault, robbery, and so forth) crimes punishable by federal authorities. During the height of the civil rights movement of the 1960s, blacks in the South could be assaulted in the presence of FBI agents, who remained powerless until *federal* rights or laws had been violated. A particularly bizarre case developed a decade earlier when the federal government sought to eliminate organized gambling, often condoned by local police. Gambling is a local act, and there is no federal power to act on that subject. But the constitutional power to raise revenue was used to levy a $50 tax on all bookmakers in the country. Those who paid the tax and filed an address to which to send the revenue stamp were promptly reported to the local police, and a follow-up was made to see whether the local police had acted or not. A bookmaker who elected not to pay the tax, of course, was in default of a legal obligation to the federal government. The violater could then legitimately be made the subject of direct FBI investigation and ultimately prosecuted — not for bookmaking, but for failure to pay the tax and obtain the stamp.[4]

Even a limited government can expand its powers, however, as we know from the twentieth-century American experience. The process may be awkward, as we saw above. Or it may be awkward and time-consuming and dependent on the political makeup of the interpreters of the Constitution, as in the following example.

In the early years of the twentieth century one of the major goals of social-welfare advocates was the elimination of child labor. Efforts to obtain prohibitory laws from the states, which had clear constitutional power to legislate such statutes, were generally unavailing. Some state legislatures were under the influence of the very industries over which regulation was sought. Others were reluctant to put their industries at a competitive disadvantage by forcing them to pay higher wages than companies in other states.

The movement therefore turned to the national government, but found that the only pertinent federal power was that of regulating interstate commerce. Under then current Supreme Court definitions of "interstate commerce" (the framers having failed to provide any clues to the meaning of the term), the mere production of goods was not sufficient to define a factory as "in commerce"; the issue was therefore outside the scope of federal power. But a resourceful Congress nevertheless enacted a law forbidding the shipment across state lines of any goods made with child labor, thereby achieving nearly the same ends as if it had possessed the power to eradicate child labor in the first place. An equally resourceful Supreme Court, however, held that the statute was too palpable in its intent — that is, a subterfuge intended to achieve prohibited ends — and was therefore void as being in excess of congressional powers.[5]

And so the matter rested[6] — the political system being legally powerless to eliminate the practice of child labor — until a new and bolder Congress enacted an analogous statute to regulate labor relations in factories. A newly chastened Supreme Court then reversed past precedent and upheld such regulations as a legitimate aspect of the power to regulate commerce.[7] Since then, the congressional imagination and the Supreme

---

[4] *United States* v. *Kahriger,* 345 US 22 (1952), is the Supreme Court decision that upheld this arrangement.

[5] The case was *Hammer* v. *Dagenhart,* 247 US 251 (1918).

[6] A constitutional amendment to authorize child labor laws was passed by the Congress, but it was not ratified by a sufficient number of states to become effective.

[7] *National Labor Relations Board* v. *Jones & Laughlin Steel Corporation,* 301 US 1 (1937).

Court's acquiescence have enlarged the definition of commerce to the point that Congress can now constitutionally require little luncheonettes in the backwoods of Georgia to serve blacks, even if the luncheonette never sees a person traveling in interstate commerce and never buys supplies from another state. The supporting argument is that even though the luncheonette itself is not "in commerce," it has "an effect" on commerce because people who eat in the luncheonette do not go to eat in restaurants that are in commerce.[8]

If this sounds like an elaborate way to say that the Supreme Court is currently unwilling to limit congressional power to regulate commerce, consider the case that provided the basis for the decision just described. A farmer who was growing his full quota of grain under federal crop limitations (an exercise of the power to regulate commerce) decided to grow more, solely to feed his chickens and not for sale. He was nevertheless held to be in violation of the limitations on growing, because the grain he grew himself he would not buy in commerce; he thereby had "an effect" on commerce and was subject to congressional power.[9]

Federalism

Federalism is the division of powers between constituent units (the states) and a single central unit (the national government) such that each has defined powers and is supreme in its own allotted sphere. It implies a balance and a certain amount of tension between the two, with the deliberate purpose of permitting local majorities, or other interests not dominant in the central government, a base of power from which to seek their own ends. Although the Constitution does not expressly provide for federalism as such, it does confirm it as a fact of life (indeed, the framers had no choice, given the independence and power of the states in 1787) and specifies the powers and obligations of each level of government to the other. A *federal* system is to be distinguished from a *national* system, in which the central unit has ultimate control over the powers or actions of the states, and a *confederacy* (such as the United States under the Articles of Confederacy), in which the states hold the balance of power and can frustrate or defy the central government.

Federalism obviously involves a delicate balancing so that neither unit gains the upper hand. In the early decades of the Republic the states seemed to be in fact the more active and important units of government. But due partly to Supreme Court decisions favoring national power, the central government began to acquire greater leverage. The Civil War and the postwar amendments to the Constitution (the Fourteenth and Fifteenth Amendments, discussed in Chapter 14) confirmed national suprem-

---

[8] *Heart of Atlanta Motel* v. *Maddox*, 379 US 241 (1964).
[9] *Wickard* v. *Filburn*, 317 US 111 (1942).

acy. There was a period, from the 1890s through the early decades of the twentieth century, when the Supreme Court sought to revive the idea of inviolable state sovereignty as a rationale for limiting national power. Sometimes known as "dual federalism," this principle held that if a matter were subject to state power, it was therefore not subject to national power. In the example above of child labor, the first Court opinion held that local production was not subject to congressional regulation for that reason. When the Court reversed itself in 1937, it effectively inaugurated the current period of "cooperative federalism," in which both the states and the nation may regulate the same activity (provided they do not conflict). Since then, national power has expanded rapidly.

Part of the impetus for the expansion of national power has come from an ironic reversal of the framers' intentions regarding revenue-raising powers of the states and the nation. The most available source of revenue for governments at the time of the Constitutional Convention was property, particularly land. The Constitution provided (Art. I, Section 9, Para. 4) that *federal* property taxes must be apportioned by population, a requirement so cumbersome in practice that it effectively precluded the federal government from using that tax and forced it to rely on duties and excises (taxes on imports or the doing of certain acts) instead. But as the need for governmental revenue grew and the states encountered severe resistance from property-taxed citizens, the national government's end of the bargain began to look better. The income tax provided a means for acquiring revenue sufficiently remote from the taxpayer to be relatively immune to resistance. Further, the national government ran none of the risks a state did when it sought access to taxable resources within its boundaries. States, on the other hand, were constantly faced with a situation in which tax benefits were offered by competing states to encourage industries to move from one state to another. Many states, therefore, were naturally reluctant to take full advantage of the available resources lest a company move elsewhere. Thus, a provision originally designed to prevent the federal government from garnering enough revenue to overawe the states ultimately had the reverse effect, due to changed economic conditions.

By the midtwentieth century, the federal revenue-raising capacity was so much greater and more efficient than that of the states that some form of centralization was practically necessitated. Even with grants-in-aid to the states and other, more drastic revenue-sharing practices, it was clear that revenue-raising capacity alone would make possible federal involvement in (if not control over) the activities of state and local governments for the foreseeable future. What had begun as a deliberate scheme to promote decentralized government had become a powerful inducement to centralization. In this and other ways economic developments have outdated and reversed precise constitutional provisions. The provisions themselves are faithfully observed, but the consequences are far from what the framers intended.

But federalism remains real, and its effects are felt every day in the halls of the national government and particularly within the political parties. The existence of real power to do important things at the state level means that those who seek the benefits of governmental action, as well as those who seek power, must focus on the states. Those who successfully control or influence the actions of a state government for their own ends have a strong vested interest in maintaining and defending that control. Therefore, the political parties in each state may well become more concerned with state affairs than with national affairs. State elections and the subsequent uses of state patronage (both jobs and contracts) are frequently more vital to political party activists than are national issues, candidates, or policies.

Because each state party has a distinctive set of interests and priorities, the national party is not much more than a very loose coalition of fifty state parties, each with a unique view of what the national party should do and why. Party activists, accustomed to a local struggle for control of their major source of rewards and benefits, retain their localism and private-interest attitudes even when they enter the national political arena. Federalism almost by itself mandates internal divisions and conflict within the major political parties and ensures a decentralized and locally oriented ethos as well.

Separation of Powers

The idea of separation of powers says that governments exercise legislative, executive, and judicial powers and that these should be placed in the hands of different officials (separated) to guard against unification of all powers in a single person or body. In the latter case, it was assumed, all limits would be violated, and tyranny would inevitably ensue. The American Constitution implements this principle by creating separate institutions to exercise each power (Articles I, II, and III, respectively). But none of these institutions has full possession of all the government's powers in its area; separation of powers can be understood only in connection with the principle of *checks and balances* and both of them together in terms of the older idea of "mixed government."

Checks and Balances

"Checks and balances" is the term applied to the various opportunities given to each branch to affirmatively "check" the others, as distinguished from merely refusing to cooperate in carrying out a policy (as would be the case under strict separation of powers). Each branch of the American government has powers that under strict separation of powers would belong to another branch. The President, for example, has the (legislative) power of veto, and the Senate has the (executive) power of confirming appointments of ambassadors and department heads. Of course, most of the legislative powers of the national government are located in the Congress, most of the judicial powers in the Supreme Court, and so on. It has been well said, however, that the American system consists of "separated institutions sharing powers."[10]

The underlying idea behind both separation of powers and checks and balances is that of "mixed government," a principle that goes back at least to Greek city-state times. This idea, as developed in the British constitution that served as the model for most American thinking, held that the three major estates, or classes of society, must all be represented in the government ("mixed") in such a way that no action seriously against the interest of any could be taken. The three classes effectively mixed in the British constitution (at least in the eyes of John Adams, the leading American constitutional theorist) were the king, the aristocracy, and the commons (everybody else). Each was dominant in one institution and could, if necessary, prevent the others from acting. According to Adams, this was the genius of the British system that had led to the highest level of liberty yet known in the world. But in the United States, there was no king and no aristocracy — only an excess of commoners. Tyranny at the hands of the masses thus seemed inevitable.[11]

The solution to this prospect was to separate the powers of government, in order to divide the body of commoners against itself. To promote this possibility still further, powers to check and balance other branches were given to each branch. What the separation of powers does is to ensure that the power of government is placed in several hands, each with a distinctive constituency. The probability is high that the several constituencies represented will not share the same values or priorities and that conflict will result over all but the most innocuous questions. Political parties were particularly feared by the framers as agents of majority will, and they worked hard to prevent parties from becoming accepted or effective. Thus, although many people in government belong to the same political party, the fact that they are associated with different institutions and respond to distinctive constituencies leads them to disagree with one another.

In this way a political party is divided, and not even its national office-holders share a clear position on its programs. Instead, each fragment of the party claims that its views are representative of the entire party and then proceeds to seek allies within the other party who share its views on a given issue. Separation of powers in effect ensures internal conflict among

---

[10] This apt phrase was coined by Richard Neustadt in his *Presidential Power: The Politics of Leadership* (New York: Wiley, 1960).

[11] For a full discussion, see Bernard Bailyn, *The Ideological Origins of The American Revolution* (Cambridge, Mass.: Harvard University Press, 1967), Chapter 6.

both majority and minority officeholders in the national government and encourages attempts at temporary alliances between like-minded elements across party lines.

Protection for Property Rights

Much of the motivation for the Annapolis Convention, which preceded the call to revise the Articles of Confederation, and for the latter as well, was dissatisfaction on the part of businessmen with the protectionism of the states and the tendency of some state and lower units of government to promote both inflation and the avoidance of debts. For financial and creditor interests, the Constitution was a triumph. Businessmen gained:

1. Prohibitions on state import restrictions and taxation.
2. A prohibition on state impairment of the obligations of contracts, which meant that states could not legislate the postponement of debt repayment or prevent the foreclosure of mortgages.
3. A single central agency to coin money and regulate its value.
4. A prohibition on state use of paper money or other legal tender.
5. A system of courts operated by the central government, so that they did not have to take chances with locally run courts in states to which their debtors had fled.
6. A guarantee of full faith and credit in one state to the acts and judgments of another, so that they could pursue their debtors more effectively.
7. A guarantee of a republican form of government for the states as well as provisions for suppressing domestic insurrections so that they need fear no further incidents such as Shays's Rebellion.

In all these respects, the framers acted consistently to promote the enforcement of contracts, the collection of debts, the maintenance of stable valuation for money, and the promotion of a national economy. These are surely economy-building goals, at least under the conditions of the times, but they were implemented in the new Constitution at the expense of many small farmers and artisans. In this respect the Constitution favored the interests of one class over those of another. Nor was the desire of some small farmers to promote inflation, avoid debts, or protect their local industries merely an ungrateful rejection of contractual obligation. In their eyes, and perhaps objectively, the eastern financiers and business-men were profiting unconscionably from exorbitant interest rates and other forms of economic exploitation of the hapless and frequently penniless farmers and artisans. Shays's Rebellion, and such other west-east tensions as the Whiskey Rebellion, grew out of the perception by western working-men that they were being exploited by urban financiers. In their eyes the Constitution was another means of furthering this exploitation.

Antimajoritarianism

Consistent with the desire to protect property rights, but drawing more specifically on their anticipation of redistribution of property by the masses, the framers built into the Constitution layer upon layer of obstacles to simple majority rule. It may be instructive to see how fully almost every one of these restrictions has been moderated in subsequent years. If it had not been possible to find ways around these limitations, the Constitution would probably have aroused more criticism in recent decades.

The major limitations on majority rule and the means found to circumvent them are as follows:

1. Amendment to the Constitution is very difficult, requiring a vote of two-thirds of both houses of Congress and ratification by three-quarters of the states. But informal means of amendment have been developed, such as the shifting interpretations of the Supreme Court.

2. The electoral college is a device designed to give discretionary power to the elected delegates and to deny the people direct choice of the President. But delegates to the electoral college run on a pledged basis and virtually never violate their pledges; ballots list the names of the presidential candidates, and most voters do not realize that an intermediate step is involved at all.

3. Separation of powers prevents the people (supposedly represented in the Congress) from working their will in the government as a whole. But the President, too, claims to represent majority will, and the party system cuts across the separation of powers to induce some degree of cooperation between the branches.

4. Senators were originally selected by the state legislatures. But direct election of senators was accomplished by constitutional amendment in 1917, and for decades before that state legislators had run for election on the basis of pledges to vote for one or another senatorial candidate.

5. Judicial review is a means of applying restraints to the legislature, supposedly the representatives of the people. But Congress and the President together have shown imagination in pressuring the Court or avoiding the implications of its decisions.

6. The division of the legislature into two houses was an attempt to introduce institutional jealousies and constituency rivals into the popular branch and thereby to reduce coherent action. But the party system and presidential leadership have promoted some degree of unity between the two houses.

This catalog might be expanded, but the point should be clear: this impressive list of conscious efforts to fragment, divide, and neutralize the will of the people cannot be coincidental, nor is it likely that a government thus paralyzed in practice could have long endured. What has sustained the American political system is perhaps not so much the quality of its Constitution as the capacity of political elites to generate a style of political behavior that satisfies the different demands of the major economic and social interests and of the masses of average citizens.

The Impact of the Constitution Today

So far we have seen that the original provisions are only the beginning. They reflect the framers' values, assumptions, and goals — some of which have been implemented in practice much as they intended, and some of which have been frustrated or changed in basic ways. Both circumstances and the determined actions of governing elites have played a part in shaping the Constitution's ultimate meaning today.

This is not to say that the provisions of the Constitution are *merely* instruments to be used by various political activists as they see fit. There are traditions and expectations surrounding many specific provisions, and these traditions and expectations are felt very strongly by political elites whose careers and prospects are deeply committed to the need for consistent and predictable behavior on the part of other men and women in government. As a result, many provisions take on an independent status and meaning, which *in the absence of compelling reasons to the contrary* will probably control the outcome in any given case. When determined and powerful people or groups seek particular goals, however, constitutional words are not likely to prevent them from attaining their ends. In time (if they are successful), their preferences will become the new and accepted interpretation of the Constitution's meaning, and new generations will begin their political goal seeking from this new point of departure.

The most vital single point to be made when considering the implications of the American Constitution is thus implicit in these illustrations: there is simply no mechanical inevitability about American politics inherent in the Constitution. Nothing *necessarily* follows because of the wording of the document, and *everything* depends to a greater or lesser degree on the preferences and priorities of the more powerful political activists of the period. This realization lends crucial significance to the process by which the Constitution is interpreted and applied to contemporary politics. Whoever manages to interpret the Constitution acquires the aura of legitimacy and traditionalism the Constitution evokes from others in government and the general public. It is not a matter of indifference to most people whether the Constitution is or is not interpreted to permit abortion, busing, or sex discrimination.

Who interprets the Constitution is therefore a more important issue than *what the document says*. Nor is it clear in any given instance which institution or other participant will win the battle to establish the authoritative constitutional interpretation. There are many participants in the grim and sometimes invisible struggle within the national government for power to determine what the Constitution "requires" on any particular issue, and much is at stake in each of these contests. As we examine this struggle and the stakes involved in it in succeeding chapters, it will become clear that the Supreme Court is an intensely politicized organ of government — and by no means the only interpreter of the Constitution.

Despite — or perhaps in part because of — this continuing political struggle, the Constitution has continued to perform some very significant functions in the American system. We will consider two of these — *stability*, or continuity, and political *style*. As we shall see, the two are closely related and are mutually supporting.

Stability

The Constitution both conditions elite behavior and legitimizes acts of elites in the eyes of the general public. Officials in government internalize the precedents and traditions surrounding particular provisions and so enable one another to understand and predict official behavior. People outside of government revere the Constitution and apparently desire the sense of continuity and propriety it radiates, and so they seek assurance that new actions are consistent with it. Officials in government compete with one another for the power to interpret the Constitution as favoring their own positions in political controversies and thereby to gain the acquiescence of those less involved. To all political activists, apparently, there is a potential payoff in promoting and sustaining the idea that the Constitution contains all necessary answers to public problems if only we adhere to its principles.

In one important respect the Constitution itself promotes this continuity-symbolizing role. Some of its provisions are eminently precise, leaving little to chance. But in other respects it is almost unconscionably vague and indeterminate ("the President shall take care that the laws be faithfully executed . . ."). Careful analysis indicates that the *precise* provisions have to do principally with the manner in which elections are to be conducted and with the question of who is to hold office. The *vague and ambiguous* provisions, for the most part, have to do with the powers of officeholders, or, in other words, with what they are to do with their powers once they are in office. Political elites, therefore, may have confidence that officials are duly elected, for there is very little uncertainty about such matters. But the directions in which officeholders may lead the nation are very marginally circumscribed (except for a few specific prohibitions); they are practically free to do whatever they can justify by their political mandate and circumstances.

Continuity and symbolic reassurance are also furthered by the fact that contention over the meaning of particular phrases in the Constitution translates political controversies into the less heated arena of legal debate. It also simultaneously reminds both participants and the public of what they share — acceptance of the same Constitution and the accumulated political association it represents. The stifling of political controversy in this fashion has not led to later upheavals, perhaps because differences over division of the economic product were more frequent than differences over such fundamental matters as how the political or economic systems should be organized. Indeed, the reduction of tensions by translating them into legalistic debates has probably contributed to the tradition of non-fundamental political debates that is now part of the American political style. But more tangible ways of promoting stability are still to be examined before we get to the related matter of political style.

The Constitution, as we have seen, scatters official power across a wide spectrum of positions within the governments of the United States. First, it divides power between the national government and the various state governments and further fragments the power of the national government among the three major branches. Subsequent developments have extended this fragmentation well beyond the framers' intentions, so that significant portions of the capacity to govern are today located (due to a combination of tradition, necessity, and aggrandizement) in, for example, the committees of the Congress, the Joint Chiefs of Staff, and the middle ranges of the executive bureaucracy.

As has often been noted, this pattern of power distribution creates a multitude of pressure points (sometimes less neutrally characterized as veto points) scattered across the map of American government. Not surprisingly, what results is a political system highly sensitive to the status quo — one that does not readily produce new policies that would tend to destroy established relationships. Usually, it takes a wide-ranging and determined effort to neutralize all these veto points, to reach some form of accommodation with their preferences, so that a broadly supported new policy can be instituted.

There is nothing casual about the status quo–enforcing consequences of the Constitution's dispersal of power. It is entirely consistent with the framers' antigovernment biases. It conforms completely to their (and their successors') views on the need for private freedom of action: the only way that individuals can be sure of complete freedom to pursue their own ends as they see fit is through the reduction of governmental action to a "lowest common denominator." Moreover, it follows the more fully articulated political principles of James Madison, often termed the "father of the Constitution," in every basic feature.

■ *The Madisonian Approach.* Madison, perhaps the most scholarly of the framers and at the same time completely attuned to their concern for the threat of majoritarian redistribution of property, provided an intellectual framework for the simpler value preferences of his colleagues. He argued that the dangers of a rampant popular majority could be effectively checked by enlarging the scope of the republic to create so many special interests within the potential "majority" that no single, coherent majority could stay united long enough to do real damage to the status quo. By giving each special interest within the potential "majority" a selection of possible power points within the governmental structure at which to aim, their potential for mutual cancellation would be realized while nonetheless furthering pluralism.

The Constitution thus not only facilitates the realization of the pluralist (many groups, many veto points) image of how government does and should work, but also is itself based on a belief in the desirability of such a process. It should be clear that the creation of substantial and necessary units of power at a multitude of points within the political system invites (if it does not impel) various groups to seek to control those that happen to be most available to them. This inducement to group activity is not coincidental. It is instead the fruition of Madison's hopes for institutionalizing the social process, which he believed would permit the people to take part in government, but would also ensure that the government was still able to do the right thing — that is, what the better-informed and generally wealthier people thought was best.

Madison's thesis is sometimes known as the principle of "natural limits to numerical majorities." This means that when a majority in favor of an action becomes sufficiently large to have a chance of achieving its goals, its internal diversities will be so great as to fragment it. This prospect is made more likely by districting systems that require a very large (and nationwide) majority and result in election of its most moderate representatives. It is aided by multiple power points within the governmental structure that enable each divergent interest to make its opposition felt. And it is supplemented by division of the national government into branches, providing a further level of opportunity for opposition and disabling internal tensions. In this manner, argued Madison, ill-intentioned majorities would be held in check. So would "well-intentioned" majorities, of course, but Madison was arguing to the propertied upper classes of his day. His readers were not democrats, but aristocrats who favored more direct and explicit limitations on popular influence over governmental policies. Madison carried the day because he convinced some of them that he had devised a subtler and less provocative means to their goals than they had thought possible.

The pluralist characterization of politics and government in the United States thus has a long and respectable intellectual history. It begins with the intentions and achievements of the framers of the Constitution and is carried into effect today by the provisions of the document they produced. It is little wonder that this image should have such ideological power by now or that it should be effective in shaping the American political style.

Political Style: The Rules of the Game

American politicians tend to engage in a balancing act, in which they measure the weight, determination, and potential governmental access of groups that seek something from government and act according to this calculus rather than on the merits of the claim. Officeholders assume the posture of referees, despite the fact that they too are products of the system's power equations. As referees, they uphold "the rules of the game" — the specified ways in which groups seeking influence are supposed to go about their efforts. Theoretically, at least, fairness, hearings, due process, and tolerance of opposing positions are part of these rules of the game.

Concentration on the rules of the game, however, may obscure two crucial aspects of the process of politics. The nature of the rules is to allow certain kinds of competition among certain established players and also to foreclose and illegitimize some other kinds of conflicts. Bargaining, negotiation, compromise — the leading characteristics of the American political style — are possible only when the "antagonists" share certain assumptions about what the game is about and how it should be played. Management and labor can agree to submit issues to arbitration only when the issues at stake are sufficiently confined within shared value premises to be soluble by factual analysis or compromises that do not deprive either side of its essential holdings. Wages or specific assembly-line grievances have this potential, but the nationalization of the factory or the workers' right to hire the company president do not. Similarly, the rules of the game of politics allow only those types of disagreements that acknowledge shared value premises. These are disagreements within the basic framework of the status quo — disagreements about who gets how much of a particular economic product, for example, or the application of an accepted rule. To play by these rules, in other words, is to acknowledge the premises and continuity of the basic economic and political structure of the American social order.

The rules shape not only the validity of those premises, but also the kinds of results that can be obtained. Behind the rules lies a particular status quo, not an ideal form of political order. When the rules limit the scope of challenge, they eliminate much of the possible range of alternatives and specify that the status quo can be changed only a certain degree. Thus, if only limited changes are possible, the rules become part of the means of maintaining the status quo. To defend the rules as if they were neutral is really to defend the substance of the status quo. This gives new significance to the American penchant for concentration on procedure — how things are done — rather than on substance. It is as if it were more important that all the established procedures were followed than that the right thing were done. Countless tragedies have been written about this dilemma, from classic drama to contemporary works, but the issue has not yet been widely recognized as relevant to American political principles.

The inducements to engage in politics under the essentially pluralist rules of the game are very strong. The Constitution's structure and intentions and current political styles all militate in this direction. Just as there are strong attractions, however, there are strong auxiliary coercions for those who do not comply. The widely shared popular commitment to the established rules — which usually overlooks the fact that such rules shape what can be done — first creates a social support for such behavior. Next, a reputation for breaking the rules may lead to social or economic sanctions — ostracism from established society, exclusion from economic opportunities, loss of a job. If deviant behavior persists, legal reprisals are likely to be followed (or perhaps augmented) by physical coercions such as jail or other injuries. Those who seek substantial change in the policies of government may thus appear to be nothing but rule-breakers and may well suffer serious punishments in the bargain.

Conflict and the "American Way"

We cannot conclude this discussion without commenting on the way the rules and the American political style have labeled conflict. We have seen how the rules and the style combine to discourage behavior inconsistent with the premises behind the rules. Action at odds with the rules — in short, provoking serious conflicts of values or challenging behavioral norms — is deplored as violating "the American way." But there is nothing inherently immoral or socially reprehensible about conflict as such. Conflict of a fundamental kind (that is, conflict over ends and not just over means) may sometimes be essential to release constructive forces in a society and to remove restraints that simply will not eliminate themselves.

Nor is the distinction between nonviolent and violent conflict sufficient to permit moral or historical judgments. To take a very obvious example, slavery would not have been eliminated in the United States without violent conflict — unless one wishes to argue that blacks should have been willing to wait another two centuries until white plantation owners were persuaded of their own immorality so strongly as to overcome their economic interests. Conflict, in short, must be judged not on the basis of its existence and not on the basis of its nonviolent or violent nature, but in light of the entire context in which it takes place. If, on balance, it serves to further social and humanitarian progress, and if other means toward these ends are blocked by dominant forces within the society, disapproval of conflict is essentially a vote on behalf of one's private interest in maintaining the status quo. Widespread consensus within a society may be similarly good or bad, depending on what the consensus supports and how general are the interests that profit from it. If consensus maintains conditions or policies that are in the special interest of a few and not in the general interest, it is surely undesirable. A broadly shared consensus on either goals or methods that most of the society conceives to be in its interest would be valuable.

This argument is not intended as an unequivocal call for conflict instead of consensus. It is meant simply to point up the fact that political systems can find both functional at different stages in their development and that too much of either is likely to be destructive. In the American case, at least for the past decades, both the rules of the game and the general political style have strongly insisted on consensus and denigrated or repressed conflict.

The American style of not facing issues — of insistence instead on following the rules and letting the results fall where they may — has the merit of reducing conflict. Some conflicts may be potentially disastrous: they may be of such a fundamental nature as to be insoluble without mass violence. Where this is the case, the prospect of seriously self-destructive mass violence may suggest that the avoidance of issues and deflection of attention is morally and politically preferable. The crucial variable is the nature of the context: neither conflict nor consensus has meaning except in terms of goals and existing conditions, and what is useful and desirable in one setting may be disastrous in another. For the present, of course, we operate with the political style and the rules we have been describing.

LAW AND
THE SUPREME COURT

Law takes many forms, from constitutional and statutory provisions through regulations and ordinances to court decisions. Law originates in a variety of institutions: legislatures, administrative bodies, executives, the people, courts, and accumulated social practices. It serves multiple functions, from resolution of the most fundamental (or *constitutional*) questions to the day-to-day management of thousands of routine economic and political transactions between individuals, corporations, and governments. All are politically significant, for in many respects law is merely politics by another name.

At the apex of the American legal system sits the Supreme Court; the scope of its powers gives it a unique governmental role. In this chapter we explore the law and the Supreme Court's operating characteristics. We start with the question of interpreting the Constitution and then analyze the Supreme Court as a political institution. In an extended case study of the Court in action (with respect to the abortion cases of 1973), we see how cases arise and how the justices handle them.

Finally, we look at some current issues and the part played by law in the process of social control.

In general, we shall see that the workings of law are closely bound up with the values and goals that are dominant within the society, normally those of its more powerful members. Law and the legal order are the vehicles by which the relatively powerful effectively establish their values and priorities as controlling factors within the society. Almost by definition, law must be nonneutral — it is a conserving force that works in a wide variety of ways to sustain the established social order. Its principal task, after all, is to maintain order — that is, continuity of the existing structures and procedures, which has the effect of helping some people far more than others. But both the law and its applications are usually strongly supported by the great bulk of the people for whom they may also serve important, though different, needs.

Interpreting the Constitution

Law plays a larger role in organizing the basic structures and procedures of government in the United States than it does in most political systems. This is so because the Constitution is a written document and by its own declaration the supreme *law* of the land. Fundamental — constitutional — issues are thus removed at the start from the realm of open value choices made according to their merits and the felt needs of the times. They are translated into the language and procedures of the law as *it* exists at the time. Thus, issues must be articulated in terms of the concepts and forms the law happens to make available and entrusted to a particular (generally upper-class) skill group, lawyers. In the American system this means that a powerful role is played by preexisting contractual obligations, property rights, and precedent — the decisions and practices of a perhaps irrelevant past. It also makes for a contest over the right to say what the law "really" means — a contest which, however vital to all, must be decided only by the backward-looking professionals and methods of the law. In particular, as we noted earlier, this contest focuses on the capacity to authoritatively interpret the Constitution. Whoever succeeds in doing so gains real advantage in shaping the future policies and practices of government.

Most Americans, if pressed, would probably say that the Supreme Court is the proper vehicle for interpretation of the Constitution. Moreover, it would be difficult for them to imagine a basis for challenging the right and power of the Court to do so. Such is the triumph of Alexander Hamilton's argument, written into constitutional doctrine by the adroit opportunism of Chief Justice John Marshall. The complete acceptance of Hamilton's argument today, however, should not obscure the bitter clash of values and competing philosophies between Hamilton and Jefferson over the question of who was to interpret the Constitution. Hamilton's total victory brought with it mixed costs and benefits and has had fundamental consequences for the nature of the American system of government. We shall first review the stakes in the conflict and then examine the effects of Hamilton's victory.

The Hamilton-Jefferson Positions

At the Constitutional Convention, Hamilton had argued for a limited monarchy, but supported the final product as acceptable for the economy-developing purposes he had in mind. Together with John Jay and James Madison, he authored several essays, known collectively as the *Federalist Papers*, designed to promote ratification of the Constitution in New York. For the most part, Hamilton stressed the utility of union and the need for a strong central government as reasons for accepting the document. But he saved his special enthusiasm for two innovations in the Constitution that improved on the old Articles of Confederation: a strong and vigorous executive to administer the laws with force where necessary and an independent judiciary with the power of judicial review (the power to declare acts of Congress unconstitutional).

Some perplexity respecting the rights of the courts to pronounce legislative acts void, because contrary to the Constitution, has arisen from an imagination that the doctrine would imply a superiority of the judiciary to the legislative power. It is urged that the authority which can declare the acts of another void, must necessarily be superior to the one whose acts may be declared void. . . .

The interpretation of the laws is the proper and peculiar province of the courts. A constitution is, in fact, and must be regarded by the judges, as a fundamental law. It therefore belongs to them to ascertain its meaning as well as the meaning of any particular act proceeding from the legislative body. If there should happen to be an irreconcilable variance between the two, that which has the superior obligation and validity ought, of course, to be preferred; or, in other words, the Constitution ought to be preferred to the statute, the intention of the people to the intention of their agents.

Nor does this conclusion by any means suppose a superiority of the judicial to the legislative power. It only supposes that the power of the people is superior to both; and that where the will of the legislature, declared in its statutes, stands in opposition to that of the people, declared in the Constitution, the judges ought to be governed by the latter rather than by the former.

Alexander Hamilton, *Federalist Papers*, Number 78, 1788.

In arguing for judicial power to declare acts of the other branches unconstitutional and therefore void, Hamilton employed the legal analogy of the relationship between principal and agent.[1] The people (the principal) having granted the agent (the national government) certain powers and not others, Hamilton argued, any act in excess of those granted powers must be void. But this position raised the problem of how invalidity was to be determined: How does anybody know when an act of a legislature is in excess of the powers granted to it? Certainly sincere and knowledgeable legislators had decided that the act was within their powers, or they would have chosen another means of attaining the end they had in mind. Hamilton argued that these determinations were questions of law (again, the Constitution conveniently *declares* that it is the law of the land) and as such ought to be decided by the Court.

Jefferson, by contrast, insisted that the question of whether the principal had delegated a particular power to the agent ought to be decided by the principal and certainly not by the agent. In other words, he wanted the people to determine in every instance whether the act of the legislature was authorized or not. The Constitution itself does not specify by what means its provisions are to be interpreted, and so the issue evolved into a test of logic, persuasiveness, and power between the two positions. Analysis of the debate suggests that two major disagreements divided the parties and that both of these disagreements were rooted in the same conflict of values.

First, Hamilton and Jefferson had quite different views of the nature of a constitution. To Jefferson, it was a fundamental allocation of the people's powers, superior to the ongoing acts of government. For these reasons, it was not law in the ordinary sense of a statute or code, but rather the people's instructions to their government about the goals and purposes it should pursue. These goals and purposes would be changeable over time, of course, as circumstances changed, and Jefferson insisted on the right of the people to change their Constitution regularly. Hamilton, on the other hand, saw the Constitution as a technical legal document with more or less fixed meaning, requiring legal expertise for interpretation. He argued that the Court was more likely than the people to possess the expertise and wisdom necessary to divine the meaning of the document's words. Although he acknowledged that the Constitution flowed from the people, he insisted that their ratification had carried with it authorization of the Court as interpreter.

Second, the two men disagreed over the nature of the act of interpretation. Since Jefferson viewed interpretation as requiring value-based choices, it followed that the choice should be made by the people themselves. If that was not feasible, it should be made by the institution closest to the people — normally their elected representatives in either state or

---

[1] See essay number 78 of the *Federalist Papers*. (Its essence is contained in the brief excerpt.)

national legislatures. He was particularly unwilling to be subjected to the value choices of a body of judges not elected, but appointed (and for life terms) by members of the very national government whose exercise of powers was being questioned. Hamilton blandly declared that there was no act of choice involved in interpretation of the Constitution. He argued that it was simply a matter of comparing the statute with the words of the Constitution and registering the mechanical judgment that would be apparent from the comparison. He expressed confidence that the independence and life terms of judges would enable them to rise above the petty strifes of the day and to render decisions true to the basic intent of the document.

What really divides the antagonists in this debate is their respective value premises and priorities. Jefferson feared the self-serving tendencies of the financiers and businessmen represented by Hamilton and the Federalist party. Thus, he sought to prevent them from staffing and using the Supreme Court to legitimate their aggrandizing schemes. His trust in the people was by no means complete, but he preferred their judgments to those of any self-selected elite. Hamilton feared the property-redistributing tendencies of the masses and so sought to keep control over the scope of legislative powers in the hands of a trustworthy body sympathetic to property rights. Lawyers, already accustomed to reverence for the traditions and practices of the past, would be — particularly if well selected — another bulwark in defense of the Constitution's protections for the established order.

In principle, Jefferson's position appears the more logical and democratic. If, as seems evident, the act of interpretation involves value choices, choices by the people or their recently elected representatives seems more democratic than choice by an appointed body that is not accountable to

---

I ask for no straining of words against the General Government, nor yet against the States. . . .

But the Chief Justice says, "There must be an ultimate arbiter somewhere." True, there must; but does that prove it is either party? The ultimate arbiter is the people of the Union, assembled by their deputies in convention, at the call of the Congress, or of two-thirds of the States. Let them decide to which they mean to give an authority claimed by two of their organs. And it has been the peculiar wisdom and felicity of our constitution, to have provided this peaceable appeal, where that of other nations is at once to force.

Thomas Jefferson, in a letter to Justice William Johnson, June 1823.

the people in any way. But Hamilton's view was made into authoritative doctrine by Chief Justice John Marshall in the case of *Marbury v. Madison* in 1803.[2] To add insult to injury, Marshall accomplished his feat while Jefferson was President, with a Republican majority backing him in the

---

It is emphatically the province and duty of the judicial department to say what the law is. Those who apply the law to particular cases, must of necessity expound and interpret that rule. If two laws conflict with each other, the courts must decide on the operation of each.

So if a law be in opposition to the constitution; if both the law and the constitution apply to a particular case, so that the court must decide that case conformably to the law, disregarding the constitution; or conformably to the constitution, disregarding the law; the court must determine which of these conflicting rules governs each case. This is the very essence of judicial duty.

If, then, the courts are to regard the constitution, and the constitution is superior to any ordinary act of the legislature, the constitution, and not such ordinary act, must govern the case to which they both apply.

Chief Justice John Marshall in *Marbury v. Madison* (1803).

The Constitution and the right of the legislature to pass the Act, may be in collision. But is that a legitimate subject for judicial determination? If it be, the judiciary must be a peculiar organ, to revise the proceedings of the legislature, and to correct its mistakes; And in what part of the Constitution are we to look for this proud pre-eminence? Viewing the matter in the opposite direction, what would be thought of an Act of Assembly in which it should be declared that the Supreme Court had, in a particular case, put a wrong construction of the Constitution of the United States, and that the judgment should therefore be reversed? It would doubtless be thought a usurpation of judicial power. But it is by no means clear, that to declare a law void which has been enacted according to the forms prescribed in the Constitution, is not a usurpation of legislative power. It is an act of sovereignty. . . . It is the business of the judiciary to interpret the laws, not scan the authority of the lawgiver; and without the latter, it cannot take cognizance of a collision between a law and the Constitution.

Chief Justice Gibson of the Pennsylvania Supreme Court, in *Eakin v. Raub* (1825).

---

[2] *Marbury v. Madison*, 1 Branch. 137 (1803).

House of Representatives. He did it by declaring that an act of Congress was contrary to the Constitution. The institution restrained by the declaration of unconstitutionality was the Court itself, so Marshall faced no problem of failure to comply.

Despite some wavering in the face of Jefferson's pressures, Marshall stuck to the principle of the Court's power of judicial review throughout the remaining thirty years of his term on the Court. He had the political sophistication not to exercise the power, however, and it was not until 1857 and the *Dred Scott* case[3] that the second test of judicial review occurred. This case, too, met with strong political reaction, and the principle of judicial review did not become firmly established in practice until after the Civil War. By then, the Court had proved to be an effective defense against several states' experiments with social legislation, but the acceptance of the Hamiltonian position was nevertheless widespread.

The Hamilton Victory

Why did Hamilton win the argument so fully that it is now difficult to convey the significance of the choice that was unconsciously made? Surely the American penchant for legalism and the law is both cause and effect here. Americans were a receptive audience for Hamilton's legalistic approach to political problems. Further, the group to which Hamilton first appealed was made up chiefly of the upper and upper-middle classes of propertied people. They may have perceived the same advantages in the prospective role of the Court as he did. Business and wealthier interests consistently supported the Court's power of judicial review right up through the famous Court-packing conflicts of the New Deal period.

The latter event suggests another reason why Hamilton's argument may have succeeded in the long run. There is nothing inevitable about the Court's decision in any given situation, for the real determinant of a decision is less the power of the Court than the preferences of the judges who happen to be sitting on the Court at the time. The presence of liberal judges leads to liberal decisions, as the Warren Court era demonstrated; thus, the Court may become a Hamiltonian instrument that acts on behalf of Jefferson's ideals. This realization may lead to acceptance of the Court's power of judicial review by *all* political activists, each of whom hopes to control the presidency and thus appointments to the Court. Careful choice of appointees to the Court — and longevity on their part — may permit greater impact on the directions of public policy than some Presidents generate in four years in the White House.

There seems little doubt, however, that the bestowal of the power of judicial review on the Supreme Court adds an important dimension to the

---

[3] *Dred Scott* v. *Sanford*, 19 Howard 393 (1857).

character of American politics. For one thing, it tends to depoliticize some issues and to convert them into a form in which only some people — lawyers and their clients — rather than the entire citizenry, are the relevant decisionmakers. Taking some of the great value conflicts of the society to the Supreme Court for resolution probably siphons off some tensions and bitterness from our politics and perhaps renders the nation more stable. But this can be a mixed blessing, for people probably *ought* sometimes to become engaged in vital questions affecting their futures.

The Supreme Court is not the final authority on any question about which a large number of people care strongly. There are many ways to combat or circumvent a single decision. It is, nevertheless, even as a contingent decisionmaker, able to structure public understanding of some issues and to resolve many others without much public attention. Again, the desirability of this situation depends on one's attitude toward popular participation and the need for a preliminary decisionmaker in a large society with many public issues of considerable complexity.

Nonjudicial Factors in Interpretation

In any event, the Supreme Court does not perform the task of constitutional interpretation by itself. Many other institutions and political participants take part in shaping the meaning of the Constitution in any particular situation. The Court is, after all, an essentially passive institution, requiring several prior decisions by a variety of interested parties before a case even reaches it. Why and under what circumstances do some people or interests decide to sue others? Litigation is not the most direct and sure way of gaining one's political ends and therefore must be utilized because other routes appear blocked or unpromising. The courts thus become a kind of supplementary political level — a means of impelling other institutions to action or occasionally a route to limited, specific ends. Other choices within the legal arena include decisions to or not to appeal, decisions by the Department of Justice as to the position it wishes to take on cases appealed to the Supreme Court, and all the decisions of trial and lower appellate court judges on aspects of a case both before and after the Supreme Court decides it.

The many participants in the legal process are not allowed to decide important questions through interaction alone. Neither the Congress nor the President has been submissive to the Supreme Court in American history. Both have reacted strongly to decisions they considered inappropriate or undesirable. Congress can pass a new statute only marginally different from one ruled unconstitutional. It can initiate constitutional amendments to overrule decisions. And it can and does express its displeasure by modifying the Court's jurisdiction or by severely challenging and perhaps rejecting confirmation of newly appointed justices.

Because the President's cooperation is usually necessary to enforce Court decisions, he is often in an even stronger immediate position to prevent the Court's interpretation of the Constitution from becoming definitive or final. Presidents have ignored the Court, flatly refused to obey its decisions, or simply nominated judges with totally different views from those that previously prevailed. Thus, even when the Court does receive and decide a case in such a way as to assert a particular interpretation of the Constitution, the other institutions may reverse, modify, or ignore its determination.

Much of the time, questions about the Constitution's meaning are resolved without the involvement of the Court at all, such as when the President, the Congress, the political parties, and others establish precedents and traditions that are unchallenged or unchallengeable in courts. For example, the President is solely responsible for determining when the Constitution's guarantee to the states against domestic insurrection should be invoked. The political parties decide in light of their accumulated years of practice how the electoral college shall work, and so forth. Thousands of lower court opinions generate a wide variety of constitutional interpretations. In addition, statutes and regulations specify the jurisdictional boundaries of courts and agencies, particularize the generalities of the Constitution in an infinite number of ways, and authorize or preclude the bringing of claims to enforce constitutional "rights."

The history of interactions among the many participants in American politics suggests that interpretation of the Constitution is considered too important an act to be left to the Supreme Court. Even if it were capable in practice of hearing cases on all the disputed aspects of the Constitution, the other political participants are too vitally concerned about gaining their ends to defer to the preferences of the judges. The contest over whose preferences shall be asserted as the established meaning of the Constitution involves great stakes — perhaps the winning or losing of major prizes of politics — and so is on occasion bitterly fought. The final, authoritative meaning of the Constitution (assuming one ever finally emerges) is thus more a product of relative political power than of legalistic analysis alone.

Even if the Supreme Court is only a preliminary, or contingent, authority on the meaning of the Constitution, its role remains a powerful one. In analyzing the Court as an institution, we shall interpret it in political terms. For example, we shall examine the internal distribution of power and influence in order to come to grips with the reality of its operation.

The Supreme Court as a Political Institution

After two decades in which the Supreme Court has had major impact on a wide range of public matters — segregation, political freedoms, defendants' rights in criminal cases, and state legislative and congressional districting, to mention only a few — it hardly seems necessary to stress that it plays a major policy-making role within the national government. Although it can make decisions only on cases brought before it, the Court's powers to interpret the Constitution and to judge the acts of other branches render it an integral part of the political process. In order to decide what a statute or an executive regulation means, whether an act by a government official is consistent with authorizing legislation, or whether either is consistent with the Constitution, the justices must make choices. These choices are inevitably based, at least in part, on their personal values, preferences, and goals. It is no coincidence that the same issues that have been before the Congress or the executive branch are also brought before the Supreme Court. Thus, the Court is different from the other institutions in form, but not in political character or impact on the society.

The Supreme Court consists of only nine persons, all of whose votes are of equal weight. It has no committees, and (with rare exceptions) all the justices personally hear arguments on, discuss, and vote on every case. Nevertheless, there are ways in which influence becomes concentrated within the Court. Not all justices are equally determinative of the Court's policy positions. Official status, the division of labor among the justices, and their reputations, personalities, and styles as individuals are the chief reasons for sometimes sharp differences in their real power.

The Chief Justice

The position of chief justice offers the principal opportunity within the Court to affect the nature of its decisionmaking. In nearly two centuries under the present Constitution, there have been only fifteen chief justices, as compared with thirty-nine presidents. A politically astute person who becomes chief justice at a relatively early age and enjoys a long life may leave a more lasting imprint on the public policies of the nation than some presidents. Chief Justice John Marshall (1801–1835), for example, probably had considerably more effect on the development of the United States than did several of the presidents who held office during the nineteenth century. Not all chief justices have left the mark of a Marshall, a Hughes, or a Warren. Some have found the tasks of the office, the strongmindedness of other justices, or the issues of the times to be more than they could manage. To be effective, a chief justice must employ the political skills of bargaining and accommodation and must develop and use the formal powers of the office in harmony with the more personal techniques of small-group leadership in order to bring a majority of the justices into agreement with the positions he favors.

The formal powers of the chief justice are few. But tradition and practice have combined with an increasing caseload to make them important sources of leverage within the Court. For example, the chief justice presides over the conferences at which the justices select the cases on which they will hear arguments and write opinions expressing new or clarified rules of law. Of the many thousands of cases appealed every year, the Court must of necessity decline to hear the great majority and allocate its time to the 150 to 200 cases involving what the justices see as the most important issues. Although each justice has the right to review all these potential cases, the chief justice has a larger staff and therefore takes responsibility for seeing that all appeals are reviewed. In addition, the chief justice suggests the cases that should be selected for further hearings and those that should be rejected. Discussion at these conferences thus proceeds according to an agenda and a preliminary selection set by the chief justice, whose original list, if the work has been done carefully, will closely resemble the cases actually chosen for the Court's subsequent calendars.

The Court's practice is to hear oral arguments on cases for two-week periods and then to devote the next two weeks to research, decisions, and opinion writing. Decisions on cases are made at regular conferences of all justices, again presided over by the chief justice. At these conferences, the chief justice normally articulates the issues for resolution in each case and then opens the floor for discussion among the justices.

Perhaps more important, when in the majority the chief justice has the power to decide who will write the majority opinion in the case. A chief justice who wants to state the rule of law applicable to the case in terms consistent with personal policy preferences may either write the opinion or assign it to another justice of similar views. Exercising either power in this way, the chief justice controls the writing of the opinion and thus prevents the dissemination of an extreme, opposing view.

Writing the Majority Opinion

The writing of the majority opinion is a crucial stage in the Court's work. Through this opinion, other political activists and the public will learn of the Court's position and its reasoning, and a new bit of substance will be added to the body of law and precedent that supposedly guides or controls behavior in the nation. The scope and nature of the rule asserted by the Court in an opinion is normally more important than who wins or loses the case itself. The opinion exercises the justices' broad discretion as to whether their decision will be grounded in a new, perhaps drastic, interpretation of the Constitution or in a narrow interpretation of a statute or minor omission by one of the figures in the case. Further, the author of the opinion can write it in such a way that the reasoning behind the decision appears to apply to many similar or analogous situations. Or the opinion can be confined so strictly that no other cases or behavior need be affected.

The justice who is chosen to write the opinion in a crucial case thus acquires substantial influence within the Court, at least in that subject area. (Such justices also achieve public and professional visibility and the satisfaction of the judicial ego, a fact that gives the politically astute chief justice a kind of patronage to bestow on favored associate justices.) There are limits to this power, of course. If an opinion writer seriously misrepresents the views of the other justices who voted with the majority, one or more of them may decline to join in the opinion. In some cases this may mean loss of the vote(s) necessary to make up a majority. Drafts of the opinions are circulated within the Court for comments by the other justices, and the process of negotiation and compromise over the wording may take weeks. In some instances the majority-uniting solution is an opinion in which conflicting or ambiguous positions are taken — in effect, postponing precise formulation of new rules of law to some future time or other institution.

The chief justice has other powers, mostly of a housekeeping nature — such as assigning tasks and making clerks and secretaries available — which can be used to make the daily routines of the other justices relatively more pleasant. As head of various bodies having administrative responsibilities over the lower federal courts, the chief justice has opportunity to influence the opinions of lower federal court judges in a number of issue areas. Within the Supreme Court, however, the chief justice must rely for further influence on the personal support and regard of the other justices.

The only other institutional positions of importance within the Court derive from seniority relationships among the associate justices. When the chief justice votes with the minority in a case, the senior associate justice in the majority chooses the writer of the opinion. As the one most likely to select opinion writers when the chief justice votes in the minority, the justice with the longest tenure on the Court may acquire some added prestige, but rises above the other justices only slightly by virtue of such prerogatives.

Influence of the Justices

This analysis is not intended to suggest that the other Supreme Court justices are without means of developing significant influence as individuals. Instead, we stress that power within the nine-member Supreme Court is very much the product of individual reputation, effort, personality, and style. Justices can maximize their influence in many ways. By developing expertise in difficult subject areas, for example, or by earning a reputation for hard and effective work on the Court, justices may end up writing far more than their share of opinions. Or by joining with other justices through preconference "caucuses" or simple trading of votes, justices may help form coalitions that establish Court policy positions of great significance. Four votes are required to select a case to be heard on appeal, for example. Justices convinced that particular aspects of existing law should be changed may simply vote to hear any cases raising such issues, regardless of the chief justice's suggestions. The history of the Court's decisions shows that justices have frequently coalesced to form blocs for or against certain national policy developments. During some such periods, one or two "independent" justices have shifted back and forth between the blocs, casting the deciding votes first on one side and then on the other.

Extra-Court prestige, such as intimacy with the President, may contribute to a justice's capacity to exercise influence on the Court. More often, real power depends on the persuasiveness with which a justice argues cases among the other members of the Court and their personal regard. A justice who is almost always accurate, incisive, and unabrasive in intellectual discourse, tolerant of the views and mistakes of others, able to combine disagreement over policy with personal friendship, and understands what is possible and practical for the Court, and does not seek decisions that are inconsistent with the underlying nature of the system may become highly influential. In short, the Court places a premium on an accepted political style in much the same way as do the two houses of Congress. Though here it is much influenced by the language and techniques of legal scholarship, it is as well formed and as institutionally defensive as elsewhere in government. Mavericks who challenge the long-established operating procedures of the Court, who fail to do their share of the work, or who advocate actions that are "far out" in the eyes of their fellows are not likely to be effective.

Because of the relatively small number of men who have served as chief justice, or even as justices of the Supreme Court, it is difficult to generalize about the types of men and political preferences that have been dominant. The makeup of the present Court is shown in Table 13.1. All the justices have had legal training, and most have been prominent in the law or in political life. The President consistently nominates men likely to share his policy preferences, and senators just as consistently resist confirmation when a nominee holds views contrary to their preferences. Republican presidents tend to nominate men from the ranks of the federal and state judiciary or from large private law firms; Democrats are more likely to nominate men from political life, such as the Congress or the cabinet. (The Court is still awaiting appointment of its first woman justice.)

Presidents have occasionally guessed wrong about a nominee's probable actions on the Court or have paid political debts instead of seeking policy support. Eisenhower's nomination of former Chief Justice Earl Warren and Kennedy's appointment of Justice Byron White are only the latest in a series of such examples. But by and large, the best cues to the political preferences of the chief justice and the other members of the Court are

Table 13.1
Supreme Court Justices, 1981 (in order of seniority)

Name	Year of Birth	Home State	Law School	Prior Experience	Appointed by	Year of Appointment
Warren Burger	1907	Minnesota	St. Paul College of Law	Assistant attorney general, Federal judge	Nixon	1969
William Brennan	1906	New Jersey	Harvard	State judge	Eisenhower	1956
Potter Stewart	1915	Ohio	Yale	Federal judge	Eisenhower	1958
Byron White	1918	Colorado	Yale	Deputy attorney general	Kennedy	1962
Thurgood Marshall	1908	Maryland	Howard	Counsel to NAACP, Federal judge	Johnson	1967
Harry Blackmun	1908	Minnesota	Harvard	Federal judge	Nixon	1970
Lewis Powell	1907	Virginia	Washington & Lee	President, American Bar Association, Federal judge	Nixon	1972
William Rehnquist	1924	Arizona	Stanford	Assistant attorney general	Nixon	1972
John P. Stevens	1916	Illinois	Chicago	Federal judge	Ford	1975

the goals of the presidents who appointed them. Since Roosevelt appointees gained full control of the Court in 1941, it has been generally liberal, with the exception of a short period of Truman-appointee dominance in the late 1940s and early 1950s. The character of four Nixon administration appointees changed the Court toward a more conservative stance. Carter made no appointments, but several openings appeared likely during President Reagan's term.

The Federal and State Court Systems

One of the most conspicuous illustrations of American federalism is the dual court system. The national and state governments each maintain distinct and complete court systems with separate jurisdictions and powers. Both are hierarchically organized — that is, trial courts are superseded by a series of appeals courts rising to a single authoritative highest court. Each set of courts has both civil and criminal jurisdictions — that is, they hear and decide cases involving disputes between private persons, corporations, and governments *and* prosecutions by governments of those who are alleged to have violated criminal statutes.

The Federal System

The federal court system consists of more than ninety district courts, at least one in each state. These are the trial courts of the federal system, and they hear both civil and criminal cases. The kinds of civil cases that are brought to such courts involve federal laws, such as antitrust issues, or suits between citizens of different states. The criminal cases in their jurisdiction involve violations of federal statutes, such as income tax fraud or transporting narcotics across state lines, in which the federal government is the prosecutor. A single judge presides in such district court trials, although many judges are normally assigned to each district to keep up with the volume of business. Juries are a regular feature of such trials only in criminal cases. In roughly two-thirds of all civil trials, the litigants waive their right to a jury trial, but only one-third of criminal defendants do so.

The federal government also has several specialized trial courts to hear income tax questions, claims against the federal government, and customs or patent cases. For certain constitutional issues involving state or federal statutes, three judges are convened to form another special kind of court. This procedure is designed to speed the hearing of important constitutional questions; direct routes of appeal to the U.S. Supreme Court are available after their decisions.

Above the district and specialized courts in the federal system are the federal courts of appeal. Eleven such courts exist in the country, each in a separate geographic "circuit," from which trial-court cases may be appealed to them by losing litigants. Not all issues may be reexamined at this level; only matters of law that have been specifically raised at the trial-court level may be raised on appeal. This means, for example, that a question of fact (such as whether or not the defendant performed a particular act), once decided by a jury, is forever conclusive except under very special circumstances. The kinds of questions that can be raised involve such issues as whether the judge correctly instructed the jury as to the applicable law in the case, whether certain evidence was or was not lawfully admitted into the case, and so on. No new evidence may be presented on appeal; nor does an appellate court listen to any of the parties to the case. It may not even hear their attorneys, but may limit itself instead to reading the "briefs" they are required to file on the disputed points of law.

The highest federal court is, of course, the U.S. Supreme Court. It exercises supervisory authority over all federal courts, seeking to standardize their actions and procedures across the country. It also hears appeals from losing litigants in the courts of appeals. It should be obvious that several screening procedures operate to make it unlikely that any given case will ever reach the Supreme Court. First, only losing litigants can appeal and then only on points of law they have explicitly raised at the trial-court level. Second, the appeals process is very costly, because skilled attorneys must be retained and expensive briefs prepared; only wealthy or broadly supported litigants can normally afford to carry an appeal to the Supreme Court. Finally, as we have already noted, the Supreme Court does not have to hear every case appealed to it. It uses its right to choose the cases it will consider to select those involving serious constitutional questions, interpretation of key sections of federal statutes or of the powers or procedures of federal administrative bodies, or those in which two federal courts of appeal have ruled differently on the same issue.

The State Systems

Each state's court system has certain distinctive features; very few state systems are alike. In general, however, they parallel the federal system. At the trial-court level, states tend to maintain a great variety of courts with varying names. In some cases local magistrates or justice of the peace courts handle such minor matters as traffic offenses. Another set of trial courts hears more serious matters, such as felony cases (violations of the criminal laws involving possible jail sentences of more than a year). In some states civil and criminal courts are combined, as in the federal system; in most states there are separate courts and judges for the two types of cases. Specialized courts for such matters as domestic relations also exist in many states.

Only twenty-two states have intermediate appellate courts similar to the federal courts of appeal. In the majority of cases appeals from the major trial courts go directly to the state's highest court. Generally, the criteria for the right to appeal are the same as in the federal court system — only losing litigants can appeal and only on matters of law they raised at the trial-court level. Each state's highest court fully controls all matters of state law, just as the U.S. Supreme Court does in the federal system. In other words, once the highest court of the state has declared the proper interpretation of a state statute, no other court (including the U.S. Supreme Court) can modify that interpretation. The judgments of such courts are therefore final, and all matters of state law are determined solely within the legal system of that state. As a result, the laws and practices of the fifty states vary greatly; acts that are crimes in some states are not in others, and the rights of defendants or others in the various states also differ greatly.

If a question of federal law or a constitutional issue is raised in a state case, however, there is a possibility of an ultimate appeal to the U.S. Supreme Court. In these areas only the U.S. Supreme Court is superior to the highest courts of the states, since there must be a single authority to interpret the meaning of federal laws and of the Constitution. Once again, however, the Supreme Court decides whether the constitutional or other federal question raised in a case appealed to it is important enough for it to hear. If it does decide to hear the case, it considers only federal questions. Of course, state statutes or practices may be alleged to be contrary to the Constitution; if the Court agrees and declares them void, there is considerable opportunity for conflict between the Court and the state or states involved.

The Supreme Court in Action: The Abortion Case

In this case study we see how cases arise out of a historical and social context, how they are presented to the Court, and how the justices decide them. Then we look at an edited version of the text of the formal opinion written for the Court to explain the majority's reasoning and the legal-constitutional principles being laid down. Finally, we survey some of the reactions, effects, and continuing controversy that have followed the announcement of the Court's decision. The case selected for this purpose is the famous (or infamous) 1973 case of Roe v. Wade (and its companion case, Doe v. Bolton), in which the Court held certain state laws prohibiting abortions unconstitutional. Although this was (and is) a highly controversial decision, it is otherwise entirely typical of the Supreme Court's decisionmaking and role in the larger system; we chose it for both of these reasons.

The Case Comes to the Court

Statutes prohibiting abortions were part of the criminal law in most states during the first half of this century. Abortions were forbidden chiefly because they were dangerous to women under then existing medical procedures and particularly because they were often done secretly, by unskilled persons under unsanitary conditions. By the 1960s, however, there was a strong movement for repeal of these statutes. Birth control procedures had become widely accepted, medical capabilities had improved greatly, and social attitudes generally (and the growing feminist movement particularly) had helped raise the issue to the level of public controversy. Individual doctors began deliberately violating the prohibitions, and there were several well-publicized cases in which women had sought to have abortions rather than give birth to babies who were likely to be deformed. In 1970 the American Medical Association passed resolutions endorsing abortion when it was in accord with the best interests of the patient and sound medical judgment. The American Law Institute had also developed for possible adoption by state legislatures a model statute that provided for abortions under certain medical circumstances. About a fourth of the states had enacted laws of this sort by 1973; some states had gone even further in the way of liberalizing opportunities for abortions.

The Supreme Court had decided in 1965, in the case of *Griswold* v. *Connecticut*,[4] that the Constitution included a right to privacy, such that a Connecticut law preventing a married couple from access to birth control information and devices was unconstitutional. Later, in another opinion, the Court intimated that the vagueness of some abortion statutes might make them unconstitutional. Two cases soon presented the question directly to the Court.

Early in 1970 a single woman (given the pseudonym "Jane Roe" in the law's effort to protect her identity) began a challenge to the criminal abortion law of Texas. Joining her were a Texas doctor who had been arrested for violating the statute, a married couple, and "all others similarly situated," which is the way that a litigant seeks to argue as representative of a class of persons. The way in which the suit was initiated is important for what it shows of the relations between the federal and state court systems and because it was crucial to the Supreme Court's decision to hear the case. The case was brought against the district attorney of Dallas County, Texas, in the federal district court, on the grounds that Roe's constitutional rights had been denied by the Texas prohibition of a safe, medically performed abortion. In other words, Roe went directly to a federal court to challenge a state law on constitutional grounds. The Texas statute had been enacted in 1854 and was typical of the "old style" laws prohibiting abortion at any time and without exceptions.

---

[4] 381 U.S. 479 (1965).

At about the same time, a similar challenge, based on the American Law Institute's suggested version, was raised by a woman and her doctor to a Georgia statute. Georgia's "modern statute" required that abortions be performed only when necessary to preserve the life of the woman and then only in certain approved hospitals when a hospital abortion committee approved and the judgment of two physicians confirmed the attending physician's diagnosis. As in *Roe*, the *Doe* (equally pseudonymous) case was brought directly in the federal district court. (Because the Court ultimately resolved the major abortion issues in its opinion in the *Roe* case, *Doe* is relegated to a secondary status. The Court's opinion in *Doe* follows immediately after the opinions in *Roe* and merely applies the reasoning in *Roe* to the different nature of the Georgia statute. We shall concentrate on *Roe*, as did the Court.)

The federal district court in Texas upheld the state statute in *Roe*, as did the federal district court in Georgia. Both cases were carried to the Supreme Court on a "writ of *certiorari*," a procedure under which the Court itself has discretion to decide whether or not to hear the case. Four votes are required to hear such a case, and apparently these cases were accepted by the necessary four justices[5] because of the jurisdictional issue they presented — that is, whether federal courts should accept all or most cases challenging state laws as violating the U.S. Constitution before those laws had been actually applied to the people challenging them. If the Court were to rule against such openness on the part of the lower federal courts, it would both lighten the federal courts' workload and strike a blow for states' rights. This was the issue under which the abortion cases were first understood by the Court, and apparently the intent of the accepting justices was to prevent the federal courts from taking such cases except in the most extreme circumstances.

Roe's attorney in the Supreme Court was Sarah Weddington, whose 145-page "brief" in her behalf argued that: (1) the right to seek and receive medical care is a fundamental personal liberty secured by the Ninth and Fourteenth amendments; (2) the Texas law violated the right to privacy included as a personal right in the due-process clause of the Fourteenth Amendment as well as via the Ninth Amendment; (3) the Texas law was unconstitutionally vague; and (4) there was no compelling state interest sufficient to justify such a burden on either Roe or her doctor. Included with the brief were almost 500 pages of medical, social-scientific, and other evidence in support of her claim. A number of other parties and

---

[5] All characterizations of the justices' attitudes and actions in this and the next several paragraphs are drawn from Bob Woodward and Scott Armstrong, *The Brethren: Inside the Supreme Court* (New York: Simon & Schuster, 1979), pp. 165–177, 182–189, 229–240, and 413–416. Readers should keep in mind that investigative reporting in such a sensitive, complex, and unverifiable area may include serious errors of fact and interpretation. We have tried to avoid the more sensational and doubtful assertions by the authors and have employed only those that fit with other evidence.

organized groups filed *amicus curiae* ("friend of the court") briefs to urge the Court to strike down the statutes.

When the cases were argued before the Court in the fall of 1971, Justices Powell and Rehnquist had been nominated, but not yet confirmed, and so only seven justices were involved. Justices Douglas, Brennan, and Marshall were favorable to the rights of women to have abortions; Chief Justice Burger and Justice White were opposed. Justices Blackmun and Stewart were generally known to be conservative supporters of state legislative prerogatives, but each was also aware of women's issues and responsive to the informed opinion of the medical profession. Blackmun had been counsel for the famous Mayo Clinic in his home state of Minnesota and was particularly sensitive to the burdens placed on doctors by the statutes.

At the mid-December conference to decide the abortion cases, a prior case presenting the same jurisdictional issue was decided in favor of allowing the federal courts to hear constitutional challenges to state laws. Justice Stewart unexpectedly joined Justices Douglas, Brennan, and Marshall to make a 4-to-3 majority. But in effect this vote also resolved the jurisdictional question in the abortion cases, and so the justices had to take up the merits of the women's claims in each case.

Justices Douglas, Brennan, and Marshall took broad constitutional ground and were joined by Stewart and Blackmun on much narrower grounds to make five votes against the statutes, with White voting in support of the state laws. Burger's practice was to argue his position, in this case in favor of the statutes, but then to reserve his vote until the other justices had voted. In this way he could join a majority and exercise his privilege as senior justice to assign the writing of the Court's opinion to the justice of his choice. This enabled him to exercise some control over the legal principles enunciated by the Court, if necessary by assigning the opinion to himself. But it violated traditional procedures and created tensions on the Court, with Douglas particularly (who, as the most senior associate justice, would otherwise have made many of the assignments).

In these cases Burger, despite arguing for the state statutes, later assigned the opinions to Blackmun, known to be the slowest draftsman of the justices. Some of the justices believed that Burger was stalling, hoping to delay the decision so that it did not come down during the election year 1972 and/or so that it would be reargued after the two new Nixon appointees had joined the Court. Blackmun realized the importance of the case and wanted to write an opinion that would withstand all the criticism likely to be directed at it; the grounds he sought particularly to master were the medical ones. For all these reasons his progress on the opinion was even slower than usual.

In January 1972, with Justices Powell and Rehnquist now present, Chief Justice Burger suggested that all cases with a vote of 4 to 3 be reargued the next year before the full Court. He included on his list both the earlier case that had settled the jurisdictional question and the abortion cases. He argued further that the new justices should also vote on whether the cases should be reargued. But the new justices refused to vote on the question, and the antiabortion majority held on both the jurisdictional issue and the need to issue opinions on decided cases. Blackmun was still working on his first draft of the opinion, however, and did not circulate it until mid-May. Even then, it was an unfinished version that drew criticism from the majority and a vigorous dissent from White. Finally, after an extended conference with Burger, Blackmun suggested that his draft be withdrawn and the case put over to the next session (fall 1972). Reluctantly, the majority justices agreed.

Blackmun worked on his draft over the summer, developing the medical rationale carefully. It was circulated early in the fall, and a number of suggestions from justices in the majority (particularly Brennan) were incorporated. One issue of concern to Douglas and Stewart was whether the grounds of the decision were the (new) right to privacy (Douglas) or just one dimension of the substantive meaning of the due-process clause (Stewart). Reargument changed no positions, but allowed Powell to join the majority and Rehnquist the minority.

The majority and two concurring opinions and the two dissents were all ready by early December 1972, but nothing came from Chief Justice Burger. By early January 1973, the other justices were growing impatient about these and other cases that all seemed to be unnecessarily delayed. Burger resisted their suggestions that the decision be announced on Monday, January 15, and/or that he let the announcement be made without his vote. Instead, he said that he would vote with the majority, but needed time to add his own concurrence. The other justices concluded that Burger was insisting on one final bit of delay, to put off the historic and inevitably controversial decision until after he had sworn in antiabortion President Richard Nixon on Inaugural Day, January 20, 1973. In any event, Burger did write a three-paragraph "concurrence," in which he denied much of what the majority opinion held.

The Text of the Supreme Court's Opinion[6]

MR. JUSTICE BLACKMUN delivered the opinion of the Court [in Roe]: . . .
We forthwith acknowledge our awareness of the sensitive and emotional nature of the abortion controversy, of the vigorous opposing views, even among physicians, and of the deep and seemingly absolute convictions that the subject inspires. One's philosophy, one's experiences, one's expo-

---

[6] Roe v. Wade, 410 U.S. 113; 93 Sup. Ct. 705; 35 L. Ed. 2d 147 (1973); Doe v. Bolton, 410 U.S. 179; 93 Sup. Ct. 739; 35 L. Ed. 2d 201 (1973).

sure to the raw edges of human existence, one's religious training, one's attitudes toward life and family and their values, and the moral standards one establishes and seeks to observe, are all likely to influence and to color one's thinking and conclusions about abortion. In addition, population growth, pollution, poverty, and racial overtones tend to complicate and not to simplify the problem.

Our task, of course, is to resolve the issue by constitutional measurement free of emotion and of predilection. We seek earnestly to do this, and, because we do, we have inquired into, and in this opinion place some emphasis upon, medical and medical-legal history and what that history reveals about man's attitudes toward the abortive procedure over the centuries. We bear in mind, too, Mr. Justice Holmes' admonition in his now vindicated dissent in *Lochner v. New York*, 198 U.S. 45, 76 (1905):

"It [the Constitution] is made for people of fundamentally differing views, and the accident of our finding certain opinions natural and familiar or novel and even shocking ought not to conclude our judgment upon the question whether statutes embodying them conflict with the Constitution of the United States." . . .

The principal thrust of appellant's attack on the Texas statutes is that they improperly invade a right, said to be possessed by the pregnant woman, to choose to terminate her pregnancy. . . . Before addressing this claim, we feel it desirable briefly to survey, in several aspects, the history of abortion, for such insight as that history may afford us. . . .

The Constitution does not explicitly mention any right of privacy. . . . the Court has recognized that a right of personal privacy, or a guarantee of certain areas or zones of privacy, does exist under the Constitution. In varying contexts the Court or individual Justices have indeed found at least the roots of that right in the First Amendment [*Stanley v. Georgia*]; in the Fourth and Fifth Amendments [e.g., *Terry v. Ohio*]; in the penumbras of the Bill of Rights [*Griswold v. Connecticut*]; in the Ninth Amendment [id.]; or in the concept of liberty guaranteed by the first section of the Fourteenth Amendment, see [*Meyer v. Nebraska*]. These decisions make it clear that only personal rights that can be deemed "fundamental" or "implicit in the concept of ordered liberty" [*Palko v. Connecticut*] are included in this guarantee of personal privacy. They also make it clear that the right has some extension to activities relating to marriage [*Loving v. Virginia*], procreation [*Skinner v. Oklahoma*], contraception [*Eisenstadt v. Baird*], family relationships [*Prince v. Massachusetts*], and child rearing and education [*Pierce v. Society of Sisters; Meyer v. Nebraska*].

The right of privacy, whether it be founded in the Fourteenth Amendment's concept of personal liberty and restrictions upon state action, as we feel it is, or, as the District Court determined, in the Ninth Amendment's reservation of rights to the people, is broad enough to encompass a woman's decision whether or not to terminate her pregnancy. The detriment that the State would impose upon the pregnant woman by denying this choice altogether is apparent. Specific and direct harm medically diagnosable even in early pregnancy may be involved. Maternity, or additional offspring, may force upon the woman a distressful life and future. Psychological harm may be imminent. Mental and physical health may be taxed by child care. There is also the distress, for all concerned, associated with the unwanted child, and there is the problem of bringing a child into a family already unable, psychologically and otherwise, to care for it. In other cases, as in this one, the additional difficulties and continuing stigma of unwed motherhood may be involved. All these factors the woman and her responsible physician necessarily will consider in consultation.

On the basis of elements such as these, appellants and some *amici* argue that the woman's right is absolute and that she is entitled to terminate her pregnancy at whatever time, in whatever way, and for whatever reason she alone chooses. With this we do not agree. . . . The Court's decisions recognizing a right of privacy also acknowledge that some state regulation in areas protected by that right is appropriate. [A] state may properly assert important interests in safeguarding health, in maintaining medical standards, and in protecting potential life. At some point in pregnancy, these respective interests become sufficiently compelling to sustain regulation of the factors that govern the abortio ι decision. . . . In fact, it is not clear to us that the claim asserted by ꜱome *amici* that one has an unlimited right to do with one's body as one pleases bears a close relationship to the right of privacy previously articulated in the Court's decisions. The Court has refused to recognize an unlimited right of this kind in the past. [*Jacobson* v. *Massachusetts*] (vaccination); [*Buck* v. *Bell*] (sterilization).

We therefore conclude that the right of personal privacy includes the abortion decision, but that this right is not unqualified and must be considered against important state interests in regulation. . . .

Where certain "fundamental rights" are involved, the Court has held that regulation limiting these rights may be justified only by a "compelling state interest" . . . and that legislative enactments must be narrowly drawn to express only the legitimate state interests at stake. . . .

A.

The appellee and certain *amici* argue that the fetus is a "person" within the language and meaning of the Fourteenth Amendment. In support of this they outline at length and in detail the well-known facts of fetal development. If this suggestion of personhood is established, the appellant's case of course, collapses, for the fetus' right to life is then guaranteed specifically by the Amendment. . . . On the other hand, the appellee conceded on reargument that no case could be cited that holds that a fetus is a person within the meaning of the Fourteenth Amendment.

The Constitution does not define "person" in so many words. . . . In nearly all these instances, [in which the Constitution employs the word] the use of the word is such that it has application only postnatally. None indicates, with any assurance, that it has any possible prenatal application.

All this, together with our observation . . . that throughout the major portion of the nineteenth century prevailing legal abortion practices

were far freer than they are today, persuades us that the word *person*,
as used in the Fourteenth Amendment, does not include the unborn. . . .
This conclusion, however, does not of itself fully answer the contentions
raised by Texas, and we pass on to other considerations.

B.

. . . Texas urges that, apart from the Fourteenth Amendment, life
begins at conception and is present throughout pregnancy, and that, therefore, the State has a compelling interest in protecting that life from and
after conception. We need not resolve the difficult question of when life
begins. When those trained in the respective disciplines of medicine,
philosophy, and theology are unable to arrive at any consensus, the judiciary, at this point in the development of man's knowledge, is not in a
position to speculate as to the answer. It should be sufficient to note
briefly the wide divergence of thinking on this most sensitive and difficult
question. . . .

In areas other than criminal abortion the law has been reluctant to
endorse any theory that life, as we recognize it, begins before live birth or
to accord legal rights to the unborn except in narrowly defined situations
and except when the rights are contingent upon live birth. . . . In short,
the unborn have never been recognized in the law as persons in the whole
sense. In view of all this, we do not agree that, by adopting one theory
of life, Texas may override the rights of the pregnant woman that are at
stake. We repeat, however, that the State does have an important and
legitimate interest in preserving and protecting the health of the pregnant
woman, whether she be a resident of the State or a nonresident who seeks
medical consultation and treatment there, and that it has still *another*
important and legitimate interest in protecting the potentiality of human
life. These interests are separate and distinct. Each grows in substantiality
as the woman approaches term and, at a point during pregnancy, each
becomes "compelling."

With respect to the State's important and legitimate interest in the
health of the mother, the "compelling" point, in the light of present medical knowledge, is at approximately the end of the first trimester. This
is so because of the now established medical fact . . . that until the end
of the first trimester mortality in abortion is less than mortality in normal
childbirth. It follows that, from and after this point, a State may regulate
the abortion procedure to the extent that the regulation reasonably relates
to the preservation and protection of maternal health. Examples of per-
missible state regulation in this area are requirements as to the qualifications of the person who is to perform the abortion; as to the licensure
of that person; as to the facility in which the procedure is to be performed,
that is, whether it must be a hospital or may be a clinic or some other
place of less-than-hospital status; as to the licensing of the facility; and
the like.

This means, on the other hand, that, for the period of pregnancy
prior to this "compelling" point, the attending physician, in consultation
with his patient, is free to determine, without regulation by the State,

that in his medical judgment the patient's pregnancy should be terminated. If that decision is reached, the judgment may be effectuated by an abortion free of interference by the State.

With respect to the State's important and legitimate interest in potential life, the "compelling" point is at viability. This is so because the fetus then presumably has the capability of meaningful life outside the mother's womb. State regulation protective of fetal life after viability thus has both logical and biological justifications. If the State is interested in protecting fetal life after viability, it may go so far as to proscribe abortion during that period except when it is necessary to preserve the life or health of the mother.

Measured against these standards, [the law] sweeps too broadly. The statute makes no distinction between abortions performed early in pregnancy and those performed later, and it limits to a single reason, "saving" the mother's life, the legal justification for the procedure. . . .

To summarize and to repeat:

1. A state criminal statute of the current Texas type, that excepts from criminality only a *life-saving* procedure on behalf of the mother, without regard to pregnancy stage and without recognition of the other interests involved, is violative of the Due Process Clause of the Fourteenth Amendment.

a. For the stage prior to approximately the end of the first trimester, the abortion decision and its effectuation must be left to the medical judgment of the pregnant woman's attending physician.

b. For the stage subsequent to approximately the end of the first trimester, the State, in promoting its interest in the health of the mother, may, if it chooses, regulate the abortion procedure in ways that are reasonably related to maternal health.

c. For the stage subsequent to viability the State, in promoting its interest in the potentiality of human life, may, if it chooses, regulate, and even proscribe abortion except where it is necessary in appropriate medical judgment, for the preservation of the life or health of the mother.

2. The State may define the term *physician* . . . to mean only a physician currently licensed by the State, and may proscribe any abortion by a person who is not a physician as so defined.

In *Doe* v. *Bolton*, post, procedural requirements contained in one of the modern abortion statutes are considered. That opinion and this one, of course, are to be read together.

This holding, we feel, is consistent with the relative weights of the respective interests involved, with the lessons and example of medical and legal history, with the lenity of the common law, and with the demands of the profound problems of the present day. The decision leaves the State free to place increasing restrictions on abortion as the period of pregnancy lengthens, so long as those restrictions are tailored to the recognized state interests. The decision vindicates the right of the physician to administer medical treatment according to his professional judgment up to the points where important state interests provide compelling justifications for intervention. Up to those points the abortion decision in all its aspects is inherently, and primarily, a medical decision, and basic responsibility for it must rest with the physician. If an individual practitioner abuses the privilege of exercising proper medical judgment, the usual remedies, judicial and intra-professional, are available. . . .

It is so ordered.

MR. JUSTICE STEWART, concurring: . . .

Several decisions of this Court make clear that freedom of personal choice in matters of marriage and family life is one of the liberties protected by the Due Process Clause of the Fourteenth Amendment. . . . As recently as last Term, in [*Eisenstadt v. Baird*], we recognized "the right of the *individual*, married or single, to be free from unwarranted governmental intrusion into matters so fundamentally affecting a person as the decision whether to bear or beget a child." That right necessarily includes the right of a woman to decide whether or not to terminate her pregnancy. . . .

It is evident that the Texas abortion statute infringes that right directly. . . . The question then becomes whether the state interests advanced to justify this abridgment can survive the "particularly careful scrutiny" that the Fourteenth Amendment here requires.

The asserted state interests . . . are legitimate objectives, amply sufficient to permit a State to regulate abortions as it does other surgical procedures, and perhaps sufficient to permit a State to regulate abortions more stringently or even to prohibit them in the late stages of pregnancy. But such legislation is not before us, and I think the Court today has thoroughly demonstrated that these state interests cannot constitutionally support the broad abridgment of personal liberty worked by the existing Texas law. Accordingly, I join the Court's opinion holding that that law is invalid under the Due Process Clause of the Fourteenth Amendment.

MR. JUSTICE DOUGLAS, concurring [in *Doe v. Bolton* as well as in *Roe v. Wade*]:

While I join the opinion of the Court [except as to the dismissal of Dr. Hallford's complaint in the *Roe* case], I add a few words.

The questions presented [in these cases] involve the right of privacy, one aspect of which we considered in [*Griswold v. Connecticut*], when we held that various guarantees in the Bill of Rights create zones of privacy. . . .

The Ninth Amendment obviously does not create federally enforceable rights. It merely says, "The enumeration in the Constitution of certain rights shall not be construed to deny or disparage others retained by the people." But a catalogue of these rights includes customary, traditional, and time-honored rights, amenities, privileges, and immunities that come within the sweep of "the Blessings of Liberty" mentioned in the preamble to the Constitution. Many of them in my view come within the meaning of the term "liberty" as used in the Fourteenth Amendment.

First is the autonomous control over the development and expression of one's intellect, interests, tastes, and personality.

These are rights protected by the First Amendment and in my view they are absolute, permitting of no exception: . . .

Second is freedom of choice in the basic decisions of one's life respecting marriage, divorce, procreation, contraception, and the education and upbringing of children.

These ["fundamental"] rights, unlike those protected by the First Amendment, are subject to some control by the police power. . . .

Third is the freedom to care for one's health and person, freedom from bodily restraint or compulsion, freedom to walk, stroll, or loaf.

These rights, though fundamental, are likewise subject to regulation on a showing of "compelling state interest." . . .

[A] woman is free to make the basic decision whether to bear an unwanted child. Elaborate argument is hardly necessary to demonstrate that childbirth may deprive a woman of her preferred life style and force upon her a radically different and undesired future. Such a holding is, however, only the beginning of the problem. The State has interests to protect. . . . While childbirth endangers the lives of some women, voluntary abortion at any time and place regardless of medical standards would impinge on a rightful concern of society. The woman's health is part of that concern; as is the life of the fetus after quickening. These concerns justify the State in treating the procedure as a medical one. . . .

MR. JUSTICE WHITE, with whom MR. JUSTICE REHNQUIST joins, dissenting [in Doe v. Bolton as well as in Roe v. Wade]:

At the heart of the controversy in these cases are those recurring pregnancies that pose no danger whatsoever to the life or health of the mother but are nevertheless unwanted for any one or more of a variety of reasons — convenience, family planning, economics, dislike of children, the embarrassment of illegitimacy, etc. The common claim before us is that for any one of such reasons, or for no reason at all, and without asserting or claiming any threat to life or health, any woman is entitled to an abortion at her request if she is able to find a medical advisor willing to undertake the procedure.

The Court for the most part sustains this position. During the period prior to the time the fetus becomes viable, the Constitution of the United States values the convenience, whim or caprice of the putative mother more than the life or potential life of the fetus; the Constitution, therefore, guarantees the right to an abortion as against any state law or policy seeking to protect the fetus from an abortion not prompted by more compelling reasons of the mother.

With all due respect, I dissent. I find nothing in the language or history of the Constitution to support the Court's judgment. The Court simply fashions and announces a new constitutional right for pregnant mothers and, with scarcely any reason or authority for its action, invests that right with sufficient substance to override most existing state abortion statutes. The upshot is that the people and the legislatures of the fifty States are constitutionally disentitled to weigh the relative importance of the continued existence and development of the fetus on the one hand against a spectrum of possible impacts on the mother on the other hand. As an exercise of raw judicial power, the Court perhaps has authority to do what it does today; but in my view its judgment is an improvident and extravagant exercise of the power of judicial review which the Constitution extends to this Court.

The Court apparently values the convenience of the pregnant mother more than the continued existence and development of the life or potential life which she carries. Whether or not I might agree with that marshalling of values, I can in no event join the Court's judgment because I find no constitutional warrant for imposing such an order of priorities on the people and legislatures of the States. In a sensitive area such as this, involving as it does issues over which reasonable men may easily and heatedly differ, I cannot accept the Court's exercise of its clear power of choice by interposing a constitutional barrier to state efforts to protect human life and by investing mothers and doctors with the constitutionally protected right to exterminate it. This issue, for the most part, should be left with the people and to the political processes the people have devised to govern their affairs.

It is my view, therefore, that the Texas statute is not constitutionally infirm because it denies abortions to those who seek to serve only their convenience rather than to protect their life or health. . . .

[Mr. Justice Rehnquist's dissent, as well as Mr. Justice Blackmun's opinion for the Court in *Doe* v. *Bolton*, are omitted. In the latter, the Georgia statute's requirement that abortions be performed only under strictly limited circumstances was voided.]

MR. CHIEF JUSTICE BURGER concurring in both cases:

I agree that, under the Fourteenth Amendment to the Constitution, the abortion statutes of Georgia and Texas impermissibly limit the performance of abortions necessary to protect the health of pregnant women, using the term health in its broadest medical context. . . . I am somewhat troubled that the Court has taken notice of various scientific and medical data in reaching its conclusion; however, I do not believe that the Court has exceeded the scope of judicial notice accepted in other contexts.

In oral argument, counsel for the State of Texas informed the Court that early abortive procedures were routinely permitted in certain exceptional cases, such as nonconsensual pregnancies resulting from rape and incest. In the face of a rigid and narrow statute, such as that of Texas, no one in these circumstances should be placed in a posture of dependence on a prosecutorial policy or prosecutorial discretion. Of course, States must have broad power, within the limits indicated in the opinions, to regulate the subject of abortions, but where the consequences of state intervention are so severe, uncertainty must be avoided as much as possible. For my part, I would be inclined to allow a State to require the certification of two physicians to support an abortion, but the Court holds otherwise. I do not believe that such a procedure is unduly burdensome, as are the complex steps of the Georgia statute, which require as many as six doctors and the use of a hospital certified by the JCAH.

I do not read the Court holding today as having the sweeping consequences attributed to it by the dissenting Justices; the dissenting views discount the reality that the vast majority of physicians observe the

standards of their profession, and act only on the basis of carefully de-
liberated medical judgments relating to life and health. Plainly, the Court
today rejects any claim that the Constitution requires abortion on demand.

After the Decision: Reactions, Effects, Continuing Controversy

As expected, the announcement of the Court's decision was greeted with
both delight and denunciation. Right to Life and other antiabortion
groups mobilized and sought to have the decision reversed by means of
a constitutional amendment and/or new restrictions on abortions enacted
by Congress and the state legislatures. Right to Choose groups sought to
keep the momentum going toward making the rights of women to abortions more and more complete.

The Supreme Court's opinions in *Roe* and *Doe* distinguished between
trimesters of pregnancy, allowing the state a successively greater role in
controlling abortions with each three-month period. Several states tried
to place requirements for the consent of husbands, parents, medical boards,
and the like on abortions during the first trimester. But these were held
unconstitutional in lower courts. The refusal of public hospitals to conduct
abortions was also held unconstitutional. States were successful, however,
in setting stiff standards for demonstrating the woman's "knowing and
intelligent consent." Additional restrictions on second-trimester abortions
have been accepted by the courts, but generally the federal and state court
systems have faithfully implemented the basic principles of the original
Supreme Court decision.

Antiabortion forces have been much more successful in Congress and
in state legislatures. Although the Congress has never passed a constitutional amendment prohibiting abortion, it has enacted several limitations
on the uses of federal funds or agencies regarding abortions. The overall
effect is to make it difficult for poor women (who depend on public
hospitals, Medicaid, or the Legal Services Corporation's help) to obtain
abortions consistently with the Court's view of their constitutional rights.
A large number of restrictions probing every possibility remaining after
the *Roe* and *Doe* decisions have been passed by the various state legislatures, and several have added prohibitions against the use of public money
for abortions on the part of Medicaid or welfare recipients or even state
employees covered by state-paid health insurance.

The issue has generated such visibility, and groups on either side are
so well organized, that some legislative elections are regularly decided by
the candidates' positions for or against abortions. A formal Right to Life
political party has arisen in some states and has acquired continuing status
on the ballot. In other states organization has been less formal, but no less
potent. The issue will not go away and appears likely to be one of the
major factors in American politics for the foreseeable future.

Law, Political Freedom, and Social Control

Law and Political Rights

Citizens' basic political rights are set forth in the first ten amendments to the Constitution, known as the Bill of Rights, and particularly in the first six. They provide that the U.S. government shall not do certain things. In particular, it "shall make no law . . . abridging the freedom of speech, or of the press; or the right of the people peaceably to assemble, and to petition the Government for a redress of grievances." This sounds absolute — it seems to say that there can be no law abridging the freedom of speech or assembly and thus no instance in which government could legally prevent speech or assembly, of any kind. But in a series of decisions from the early days to the present, the Supreme Court has interpreted the First Amendment to guarantee only the limited form of freedom of speech and assembly protected by law in 1789 when the amendment was adopted. Thus, the Congress is free to adopt such limitations as it sees fit, provided they meet the Court's standards of reasonableness — which the Court derives from its view of the proper combination of eighteenth-century precedent and current circumstances and necessities. In practice, only twice in its history has the Court declared a congressional statute void on the grounds that it violated the First Amendment.

Notice that these political rights exist only as limitations on the U.S. government. In other words, they do not protect citizens against one another's actions. If a gang of hoodlums prevents a person from speaking in a private auditorium, for example, no constitutional rights have been violated; the crimes of assault or trespass may have been committed, but the Constitution provides guarantees only against the acts of government. As originally written, the Constitution did not provide these protections against state governments: in an early case the Court held that citizens must look to their state constitutions for such protections. In the 1920s the Supreme Court decided that at least some of these guarantees do apply to the states, and since that time it has in a series of decisions added one after another of the guarantees of the Bill of Rights to the list of individual rights that are protected against state action. The Court did so on its own initiative, holding that the Fourteenth Amendment's provision that the states not deny their citizens "due process of law" made the guarantees of the Bill of Rights applicable to the states. Not all of them are thus applicable, the Court has held, but only those that the Court deems fundamental to the concept of due process.

In practice, the protection of political rights presents serious problems for many elements of the judicial process. The Supreme Court has declared that speech is to be protected up until the time it presents a "clear and present danger of bringing about an act which government has a right to prevent." This means that if armed insurrection or rioting is

. . . the character of every act depends upon the circumstances in which it is done. . . . The most stringent protection of free speech would not protect a man in falsely shouting fire in a theater and causing a panic. . . . The question in every case is whether the words used are in such circumstances and are of such a nature as to create a clear and present danger that they will bring about the substantive evils that Congress has a right to prevent. It is a question of proximity and degree.

Justice Oliver Wendell Holmes, in *Schenck v. United States* (1919).

about to break out, police officers may legally restrain a speaker, and/or the speaker may be prosecuted for such words and/or action. The operative principle is that no one should be prevented from speaking or publishing something, no matter how unpopular it might be, but that he or she must bear responsibility for such acts afterwards, such as in suits for libel or slander.

But from the perspectives of both governments and dissenters, afterwards may be too late. Police may unreasonably foresee riots resulting from provocative speeches; licensing authorities may fear that granting a parade permit will make demonstrators vulnerable to attack by a hostile crowd, and either or both may act to prevent speech or assembly. Those who seek to exercise their rights in such circumstances must find an attorney willing to suffer public disapproval for representing their cause, and they must try to convince the courts to order the authorities to permit them their rights. Local judges do not willingly expose themselves to popular disapproval either, and so appeals to higher courts may be necessary. By the time all these procedures are concluded, of course, the occasion for exercising one's political rights may be long past. Thus, important discretion remains with local authorities who are often subject to popular pressures — and perhaps only too willing to support or help generate such pressures themselves.

The courts' record in defense of the exercise of the political rights supposedly guaranteed by the Bill of Rights has not been particularly aggressive or distinguished. Most of the time, courts side with legislative or administrative authorities. They typically consider claims made by unpopular people, parties, or causes only to conclude that the established authorities were exercising their constitutional powers in imposing limitations on political activity. Rights to dissent, assembly, and the like for purposes not favored by governments are far more firmly established in legal theory than in actual practice.

Table 13.2

Willingness to Grant First Amendment Rights

Type of Freedom	Year	Admitted Communist	Against Religion	For Governmental Ownership	Homosexual
To speak	1954	27	37	58	
	1972	52	65	77	
	1974	58	62	75	62
To have	1954	27	35	52	
book in	1972	53	60	67	
library	1974	58	60	69	55
To teach	1954	6	12	33	
	1972	32	40	56	
	1974	42	42	57	50

Source: Hazel Erskine and Richard L. Siegel, "Civil Liberties and the American Public," *Journal of Social Issues* 31, 2 (1975) Table 1 on p. 15. Used by permission.

Note: The questions were as follows: "There are always some people whose ideas are considered bad or dangerous by other people. For instance, somebody who is against all churches and religion. If such a person wanted to make a speech in your city (town, community) against churches and religion, should he be allowed to speak, or not? Should such a person be allowed to teach in a college or university, or not? If some people in your community suggested that a book he wrote against churches and religion be taken out of your public library, would you favor removing this book, or not?" The same questions were asked about the other "extremists."

A similar pattern is apparent among the general public. When contrasted to the theory of the Bill of Rights, popular support for political freedoms seems low. This may be attributable to the continuing barrage of criticism and condemnation directed by political and other opinion-makers at "deviants," "extremists," and others who do not think and act in orthodox ways. Or it may represent recognition by ordinary people that leaders' endorsement of political freedoms is more rhetoric than reality and hence may be a more honest response.

In any event, one of the interesting developments of the 1970s was a distinct rise in political tolerance and support for political liberties relative to the 1950s. This contrast is shown in Table 13.2. The questions asked (listed below the table) were the same in all cases. Levels of support for political freedoms may not seem high, but they are clearly rising in significant ways.

Observers might well have seen this development as a welcome step toward greater freedom and a more open political process. But instead, the major issue of the late 1970s was the extent of official governmental violation of political freedoms. In a series of lawsuits, citizens' demands for information, and subsequent congressional investigations, an extensive pattern of provocation and promotion of crimes, surveillance, wiretapping, burglaries, and other crimes on the part of governmental agencies was steadily documented. Many agencies, up to and including the National Security Council, the Defense Department, and the White House itself, were shown to have condoned, authorized, and participated in theft, burglaries, and wiretapping. The FBI acknowledged an extensive program of infiltration of legal organizations, use of informers and provocateurs to instigate or commit crimes, and a general pattern of harassment of civil rights leaders. The CIA had an analogous program of surveillance, provocation, and disruption. All these and other acts were extensively documented in the official reports of both House and Senate investigating committees.

Each revelation was matched by a sober report from the admittedly guilty agency that the illegal activities in question had been terminated. In some cases, however, agencies used such occasions to suggest "guidelines" that would authorize heretofore illegal activities at their discretion; Attorney General Levi, for example, proposed in 1976 to impose just such a set of guidelines on the FBI. And at the same time, the Congress began considering a revision of the federal criminal law that would, in its draft form at least, make legal many previously illegal actions, including many of those for which Watergate-related defendants were convicted. In the aftermath of the Watergate confessions and convictions, there remained a serious question as to where trustworthy support for political freedoms could be found. Clearly, executive agencies themselves had been the lawbreakers, and elected officials in all branches had inspired, authorized, or condoned their activities for a long time. The Nixon Supreme Court indicated in a series of decisions that it would not stand by the principles of constitutional law established by the Warren Court of the 1950s and 1960s. In one case, for example, it held that not even a demonstrated pattern of violation of constitutional rights by the Philadelphia police department created any right of redress for citizens. In another, it drastically cut back limits on the power of police to arrest people without warrants.

Crime and Punishment

The incidence of crime in the United States in the late 1970s seemed high to most people. Crime statistics are notoriously unreliable, both because the numbers reported can be manipulated in various ways and because people often fail to report crimes that are embarrassing or that they believe the police unable to do anything about. But crime was undeniably increasing, and fear of crime was rising even more sharply. Crime most often victimizes poor people in large cities, but fear radiates out to grip middle- and upper-class people as well — the people who have the most to lose and more political power to do something about it.

One manifestation of such dissatisfaction was hostility toward the Supreme Court. Many advocates of "law and order" alleged that the Supreme Court and other judges were "coddling criminals." The observance of defendants' constitutional rights may make convictions of guilty persons more difficult, but it may also protect the innocent and serve as a measure of a humane civilization. It is easier to condemn the courts, however, than to create a social order in which crime is not necessary or encouraged or even to pay for adequate policing and corrections facilities. In any event, the net result in the 1970s was a distinctly unfavorable attitude toward the Supreme Court and a strong desire for more conservative judges in the future.[7] As noted earlier, the Nixon Supreme Court responded to this preference by cutting back the rights accused defendants had gained in earlier decades.

There is considerable controversy in the United States over the effectiveness and uses of punishment. Some argue that crime is caused by an unjust society, whose reform should be the primary goal of social efforts. Others believe in the rehabilitation of individual criminals, to help them adapt to the society as it is. But many people, perhaps the majority, resist both these strategies, preferring instead to increase punishment for crimes as a means of deterring all future crimes. Despite considerable historical evidence that even such drastic punishments as torture and death did not prevent crime, moves have been made in several states to restore the death penalty and to impose harsher sentences. Such arguments received support from some arithmetically inclined economists, one of whose correlations indicated that every execution prevents seventeen murders. These findings were disputed by others, who stressed that the period of the study (the mid-1960s) was a time of social unrest and that the validity of any gross correlation characterized by so many other variables is questionable.[8]

Both issues we have been examining involve social control. Preservation of the status quo is one of the major goals of any governing elite. So is the use of the criminal law to enforce the present (unequal) distribution of wealth, property, and other benefits of the society. Let us grant immediately that any society must have some means of restraining people who wantonly assault or endanger others. But from that point forward, the values and characteristics of the society shape the nature of its approach to restraint. What acts are to be defined as crimes? If it is "legal" to charge 20 percent interest rates for necessities of life, why should it be "criminal" to keep such goods after missing an installment payment? What shall be done to those who break such rules — should they be helped in any of several possible ways, or should the society exact retribution by killing, confining, or otherwise punishing them? In every case, judgments are made consistent with the values of those who are

---

[7] *Gallup Opinion Index*, August 1973, p. 16.
[8] *Business Week*, 15 September 1975, p. 97.

(*Source*: By permission of Jules Feiffer © 1971. Dist. Field Newspaper Syndicate.)

favored by the existing system, and those who are not favored are limited (or perhaps, in their own eyes, exploited) by the provisions of the criminal laws.

Thus, the enforcers of these laws may come to be viewed as the agents of a repressive or exploitative system. Where it also appears that they enjoy broad discretion, serious tensions may result. This is particularly true in the case of minorities, who are likely to feel the restraint of criminal laws far out of proportion to their numbers or to the actual incidence of violation of such laws. Most large-city police forces are quite disproportionately made up of members of the dominant society. In no major city does the proportion of nonwhite police officers approach that of the nonwhite population. It is not surprising, therefore, that in some cities the police are looked on as an occupying army by ghetto residents.

The arbitrariness and variability that characterize the protection of political freedoms and the enforcement of criminal law create demonstrable patterns of injustice and serious tensions within American society today. Dominant groups are clearly advantaged by the character and actual uses of the law and the courts. The reasons for this situation include the makeup and backgrounds of those who apply the law, unequal access of legal services, and the exaggeration of certain structural characteristics of the law itself by the American emphasis on legalism as a political value. In the courts as well, a number of factors ensure that elite interests will be accorded great weight in decisionmaking. The nation's judges and lawyers are drawn disproportionately from the prosperous and high-status groups in the population. Law school education, like public education generally, consists in part at least of the inculcation of elitist values. Accused persons with money and social status are far more likely than those without these advantages to benefit from competent legal advice and defense. Finally, the elaborate legal code and the established processes for interpreting and enforcing it work in the interests of the advantaged.

The last of these factors is both more subtle and more potent than the others and in turn underlies and bolsters them. Americans have always been proud to say that we have "a government of laws, not of men." That belief stems from our development of an elaborate code of legal rules that are relied on to settle conflicts and to determine guilt or innocence, with a theoretical minimum of human arbitrariness and a maximum of impersonal "equality before the law." Justice is portrayed as blind — blind, it is alleged, to differences among litigants in income, color, race, education, social position, and so on.

In a crucial sense this very blindness to real differences means that the legal code repeatedly offers justifications for dealing harshly with the disadvantaged and leniently with the elite. In the trenchant words of Anatole France: "The law in its splendid impartiality prosecutes both the rich and the poor for stealing a loaf of bread or sleeping under bridges."

THE CONGRESS

14

The Constitution appears to envision the Congress as the nation's chief policy-making body, the arena in which national issues would be debated and basic decisions made. Article I, which is nearly three times longer than the next longest article (that regarding the presidency), creates and empowers the Congress and alone accounts for more than half of the Constitution. All the legislative powers of the U.S. government are given to the Congress; among them are the powers to tax and spend, to regulate commerce, to declare war and maintain the armed forces, and to "make all laws which shall be necessary and proper" to exercise the various powers granted to the national government. This is a sweeping grant of power and authority, and one might expect the Congress to be the decisive source of policymaking within the government.

But it has not worked out that way. At least in the twentieth century, Congress is much more an after-the-fact critic and modifier of policy initiatives taken by the other branches, particularly the President and the executive bureaus. Not even the crucial power to tax and spend has enabled the Congress to assert independent policy-making capacity over the vast federal bureaucracy. The reasons for this situation have been the subject of much debate, and answers range from the visibility and decisiveness of the presidency in an age of emergencies to the character and internal procedures of the two houses themselves. In any event, the tragic Vietnam War and the revelations of Watergate and its aftermath led to a major effort on the part of the Congress to reassert its policy-making powers in the 1970s. In this chapter we first look closely at the personnel and procedures of the two houses and then at the steps they have taken to regain initiative within the government.

The House of Representatives

The House of Representatives has 435 members. This fact, no doubt familiar from sixth-grade civics, has profound significance for the distribution of power and operating procedures within the House. The 435 representatives face a bewildering array of complex problems, a vast national budget, and a sprawling federal bureaucracy. Few of them come to Congress with any special expertise or experience that would enable them to cope effectively with such problems. Their time to acquire such knowledge is limited, both by the demands of service to their constituents and by the imminence of the next election. What little staff they have must devote most of its time to mail, errands, and, again, the forthcoming election.

Even, or perhaps particularly, for representatives with the sincerest intentions of translating constituents' wishes into governmental action, the task is extremely difficult, if not impossible. They must develop two types of capabilities: a subject-area expertise in order to know what should be done and administrative sophistication to enable them to recognize whether or not executive-branch employees are acting (and spending authorized funds) to administer congressional policies in the manner prescribed. In both areas they can act as independent policymakers only if they are able to acquire knowledge on their own, not if their knowledge depends on inevitably self-serving voluntary disclosures by the executive branch or private power centers.

For all these reasons, they have little choice but to divide their governmental responsibilities among individuals or committees formed from the House membership. Through specialization, at least some of the members will have a chance to develop the expertise and managerial capacity to make independent policymaking possible. Presumably, members will exercise such capabilities in accordance with the will of the majority of the House. But when there is a division of labor, a stratification of power results. Special knowledge or responsibility in a subject area gives the possessor the tools and prestige to cause others to go along with his or her views. Formation of a task group implies leadership within it, and whoever chairs a committee may come to exercise disproportionate influence over its work. To a considerable extent, these are the inevitable costs of a necessary division of labor.

It is a mistake, however, to take for granted that the members of Congress with the greatest knowledge of an area necessarily have the greatest influence on policy. Values play at least as great a part as do facts; indeed, the two are not really separable. If a particular set of values or ideology dominates a committee or a house of Congress, it is likely to be a more important shaper of policy than is expertise.

Before the reforms of the 1970s, the House of Representatives had evolved a unique manner of dividing its labor, such that most of its capacity to act lay in the hands of about twenty-five individuals occupying its key positions. Moreover, such individuals were chosen solely by virtue of their "seniority" (length of service). Although this may appear a mechanical, and therefore politically neutral, means of selection, it in fact placed power in the hands of older, usually more conservative, individuals: longevity in the House depends on having a relatively "safe" electoral district. Many such districts are found in the rural South and Midwest, usually the more conservative parts of the nation. Some districts in the more liberal large cities regularly return candidates of a single political party, but the availability of alternative political careers and the volatility of city districts tend to eliminate any given representative before he or she reaches the higher levels of seniority.

The overall effect of this House system was to create a highly structured game. In this "game" only the oldest members actually held power; members on the next level had invested many years in moving up the ladder and were more or less patiently awaiting the death or retirement of their elders, and the newest and youngest members were close to impotent. The House has roughly coequal hierarchies of leadership positions, both reflecting this principle clearly; this pattern has survived the recent reforms. The first type of position involves leadership of committees, each of which has responsibility for the actions of the House in a particular policy area; the major position is that of chairman, with secondary status for the ranking member of the minority party. The second type is leadership in the management of the House itself; these positions include the Speaker of the House, the majority and minority leaders (and their "whips," or assistants), and the Rules Committee. Let us briefly examine the powers of these offices and the characteristics of their occupants.

Policy-Area Committees

There are twenty-two standing committees in the House, ranging in importance and prestige from Civil Service and Post Office to Armed Services, Ways and Means, and Appropriations. Most committees have twenty to twenty-five members (Appropriations has fifty), appointed from each party roughly according to the partisan ratio in the House. Each representative usually serves on two committees. Although they naturally seek assignment to committees whose work will be of importance to their home districts, representatives have no way to ensure this. There are only so many choice assignments, and it takes a certain amount of seniority to lay claim to them. The two most sought-after policy committees are those dealing with money matters — Ways and Means (taxation, social security, and Medicare, for example) and Appropriations (all expenditures). Raising and spending money, absolutely crucial to the operation of the government, is the route by which Congress has the greatest chance to influence the conduct of the rest of the government.

Though, as we have said, the key position on a committee is that of chairman, the recent reforms have parceled out some authority to the chairmen of subcommittees. The division of power between the chairman of the full committee and the chairmen of subcommittees tends to vary with each committee, depending in part on the political skills and personalities of the incumbents. These powers include setting the agenda for the committee or subcommittee, controlling hearings and executive sessions, choosing witnesses, managing the actual drafting of legislation, and shepherding a bill through floor debate and possible later conferences with a Senate committee to work out the bill's final version. In all these actions, the chairman's personal preferences can play a crucial role in determining the final provisions of laws.

Chairmen are not autonomous, of course. The President and the House or party leadership may bring pressure on them, and members of the committee may bring concerted influence to bear. But chairmen have defenses at their command. Neither the President nor the leadership wants to incur their opposition, for they know that chairmen can cause delay, drastic revision, or even destruction of legislation they dislike. Nor do the members of committees wish to lose either opportunities to obtain special provisions in legislation that chairmen can grant them or the public visibility that their goodwill makes possible. At all times, chairmen also have on their side the traditions of the House, which call for action only in accordance with duly established procedures — in this case with the recommendations of the standing committee having jurisdiction over the subject area of the bill. The House almost never considers, and even more rarely enacts, legislation that is completely opposed by the chairman of the applicable committee. In part, this is because alert chairmen know when to join a majority position; even when they do so, however, they leave the clear mark of their preferences on the final product.

The ranking member of the minority party on a committee gains some leverage from representing his or her party and mobilizing other party members on behalf of specific positions. He or she becomes the chairman of the committee when the party wins control of the House.

Frequently, this prospect generates a friendly modus vivendi with the chairman, for both have served on the committee for a long time and know that they may be destined to alternate in the chairmanship for the rest of their political careers. Having served together for some time, the two probably also share a strong concern for the "proper" working of the House itself and for the efficient discharge of their committee's responsibilities to the House. In many ways, therefore, the two positions complement each other, rather than serving as opposing correctives.

House Leadership Positions

The major leadership positions within the House itself are filled by the majority political party, usually through application of the seniority principle. The key position is that of Speaker of the House. The Speaker presides over House debates on bills and recognizes — by prearrangement or preference — speakers considered appropriate. The Speaker also shapes the House agenda, deciding which bills will receive priority, designates the members of the "conference committees" who will represent the House in negotiations with the Senate, and makes public visibility possible for, or ignores, fellow members. In addition, the Speaker is privy to the President's preferences and intentions regarding the legislative program for that session of Congress and can (if desired) work in harmony with the President to schedule and obtain passage of desired legislation.

The majority and minority leaders within the House are party leaders. In both cases seniority is a major factor, but policy views representative of the mainstream of the party are also influential in determining election by the party's caucus. The duties of these leaders, who are assisted by their elected "whips," are to mobilize party members behind legislative positions the leadership has decided are in the party's interest. Members of the House are often under pressure to support the position of the President when he is of their party or to join with other members of their party in opposition to a President of the other party. (Many measures before the House are not made matters of party discipline, of course, and in such cases members are free of all pressures to vote with the leadership.)

Another group of positions of crucial importance to the management of the business of the House is membership on the Rules Committee. These are among the most coveted committee positions in the House and are filled, predictably, with its most senior members. All proposed legislation must go through the Rules Committee en route to the floor of the House. The function of the Rules Committee is to set specific rules for debate and voting on each piece of business, in order to conserve the time and to order the transactions of that unwieldy body. In practice, this means that the Rules Committee exercises an important influence over the form in which a given bill will be presented and the real prospects for its passage. Particularly at the close of congressional sessions, the Rules Committee (frequently in the person of its chairman) may prevent legislation from reaching the floor. Or it may attach rules for debate and voting calculated to ensure its defeat, such as permitting unlimited amendments to a tax bill that represents a number of delicate compromises. At other times, the Rules Committee may content itself with making clear to the chairman of a policy-area committee that certain provisions must not be included in prospective legislation.

The formal powers of the party leadership in the House were first reduced and then augmented by recent reforms; the leadership nonetheless remains capable of making a member's political life much easier or more difficult — depending on his or her willingness to abide by the informal rules and traditions of the House. For those who "go along" and demonstrate the proper respect for the institution and its elder members, there are special opportunities for public visibility and status, which are often the keys to reelection. The party leadership is also one of the major sources of information for ordinary members, most of whom would otherwise have no better sources than the daily newspapers. Party leaders provide knowledge about the President's plans and make arrangements for joint action by all party members in response to those intentions. Representatives cannot be successful by themselves; they must have the support of many other representatives, and the political party machinery is the most promising means to secure it. Thus, the party leadership gains an important kind of leverage within the institution.

Why do the other members usually acquiesce in the dominance of these two types of leadership positions? The simple answer is that as a practical matter, there is very little they can do about it. Communication among the balance of the 435 members is very difficult and is inhibited by party and ideological differences. Even if they could agree on measures to redirect or unseat the leadership, the total control of the parliamentary machinery by the established leaders would make such action very complicated, requiring a degree of perception, trust, skill, and discipline not likely to exist in any large body. If they did replace the leadership, moreover, the new leaders might be even less desirable than the old ones.

A more sophisticated answer would point out that most members do not even want to extricate themselves from the web of seniority-based leadership and management. Representatives depend for reelection on achieving visibility in the home district, preferably by accomplishing some tangible benefit for constituents. They can do so in their early terms in the House, when need is greatest, only through the assistance of established members — such as the chairmen of committees and subcommittees or the party leadership. Almost before they realize it, they have incurred debts to senior colleagues. And as soon as they acquire a degree of seniority themselves, the system begins to look better. Representatives, finding that there are payoffs in the established operating procedures, begin to identify with the House as an institution and the accommodating, bargaining sys-

Table 14.1

Biographical Survey of Political Leaders and Key Committee Chairmen
of the House of Representatives, 97th Congress, 1981–1983

Position	Name	Age (as of 1981)	Occupation or Profession	Year Entered Congress	State
Political leadership					
Speaker	Thomas O'Neill	68	Insurance	1953	Massachusetts
Minority Leader	Robert H. Michel	58	Businessman	1956	Illinois
Chairmen of major committees					
Agriculture	Thomas Foley	52	Lawyer	1962	Washington
Appropriations	Jamie Whitten	71	Lawyer	1941	Mississippi
Armed Services	Melvin Price	76	Journalist	1945	Illinois
Banking and Currency	Henry Reuss	69	Lawyer	1955	Wisconsin
Education and Labor	Carl Perkins	69	Lawyer	1948	Kentucky
International Relations	Clement Zablocki	69	Teacher	1948	Wisconsin
Judiciary	Peter Rodino	72	Lawyer	1949	New Jersey
Rules	Richard Bolling	65	Teacher	1948	Missouri
Ways and Means	Dan Rostenkowski	50	Businessman	1959	Illinois

tem to which it is committed. Some naturally begin to give higher priority to maintaining harmonious relationships among members than to the merits of the great issues of national policy.

Table 14.1 provides some basic data about the incumbents of the major positions in the House of Representatives of 1981–1983. In addition to the personal backgrounds of these individuals, it is noteworthy that most of them are relatively older people who have been in Congress for some time. This does not necessarily mean that they are conservative or out of touch with current thinking, but it does raise such questions. We shall explore the matter of age, ideology, and committee/subcommittee chairmanships further when we examine the progress of reform efforts in our final section.

The Senate

The Senate has only one hundred members and prides itself on dispensing with the many formal rules and procedures that characterize the House. In contrast to what it views as "the lower house," the Senate tries to operate with a minimum of organization and a maximum of "courteous" agreement, which allows for the objection of one senator to prevent or delay the transaction of crucial business. In fact, the Senate has evolved an elaborate set of rules and traditions governing the behavior of members.

These standards are maintained by an institutional establishment — an informal group of usually senior senators distinguished principally by their commitment to the Senate as an institution. This group asserts authority not only over internal procedures, but also on occasion over the policy positions assumed by the Senate as a body. Membership in the inner circle of the Senate is personal rather than institutionally based. Supplementing this form of leadership is a division of labor characterized by many of the same benefits and costs as is that of the House of Representatives. Again, the types of positions may be divided between policy areas and Senate leadership.

Policy-Area Committees

The differences between House and Senate committee structure and operation are minor, reflecting chiefly the difference in size of the respective houses. The Senate has fewer, smaller committees, ranked somewhat differently in terms of prestige. Finance and Appropriations, which deal with revenue and expenditures, respectively, are (despite the Senate's secondary role in House-initiated money matters) probably the most important committees. The Foreign Relations Committee, because of the Senate's special powers in that field, is more visible than many others and so attracts many senators, but its impact on policy is not great. Judiciary, because of its power to confirm or reject Supreme Court nominees and the Senate's special concern for proposed constitutional amendments, is also a high-status committee. Armed Services and Agriculture follow, and the remainder are reserved for specialists and newcomers.

The formal powers of a Senate committee chairman are much the same as those of a House chairman, but in practice they fall short of the autocracy of the House model. Operating with smaller numbers and a more relaxed, cordial ethos — perhaps abetted by the relative length of their six-year terms — the Senate chairmen tend to consult more with their members, grant them more visibility and influence within the committee, and proceed on the basis of a general consensus. The chairman is clearly the leader, and no junior senator would be unaware of or dare to ignore that fact, but the operation of the committee is normally more harmonious than in the House.

The Senate's traditions of elaborate courtesy among members extend to the manner in which pressure is applied to chairmen to consider legislation and to the relationship between the ranking minority member of a committee and its chairman. Rising to the chairmanship of a Senate committee implies not only substantial seniority, but also commitment to the Senate as an institution and to its "proper" functioning within the system. No President or party leader would insult the dignity of the Senate by making brash or blatant attempts to coerce a committee chairman. And party differences ordinarily play a small part in the deliberations of senior members of a committee. In short, in the Senate there is at least the appearance of greater consideration of the merits of issues and a smaller organizing role for the political party.

Senate Leadership Positions

Although the position of President Pro Tem of the Senate corresponds in form to that of Speaker of the House, it is in practice no more than an honorific title bestowed on a very senior member. The actual managerial functions performed by the Speaker in the House are in the hands of the Senate majority leader. This officer is elected by the senators of the majority party at the outset of each session; once chosen, of course, a senator usually remains majority leader until death, retirement, or election defeat. The choice is influenced, but not controlled, by relative seniority among senators of the majority party. But more important is a reputation for commitment to the protection and furtherance of the Senate as an institution, a mainstream position within the party on major issues, adherence to traditional rules and procedures, a sense of fair play, and parliamentary skills. Choice of the minority leader by the minority party is based on similar criteria.

The majority and minority leaders serve informing, scheduling, and unifying functions for their respective parties, in effect combining the duties of Speaker, party leader, and Rules Committee in the House. The majority leader (1) coordinates the activities of Senate committees and seeks to bring bills to the floor in accordance with his or her view of the proper priorities for that session, (2) selects members of the conference committees that negotiate differences between House and Senate versions of enacted legislation, (3) is the chief source of information for other senators as well as the dispenser of public visibility, additional institutional responsibilities, and improved committee status, and (4) consults regularly with the minority leader so that most of the Senate's business can proceed with the support of a broad consensus. Both leaders are normally consulted and kept informed of major developments by the President, although matters of party strategy or program are reserved for the leader of the President's party.

Behind the two leaders of the Senate is the inner "establishment," or "club," of generally senior senators. This group has no precise boundaries, but some senators are clearly inside and some just as clearly outside. Membership is personal, based in part on acceptance of the Senate's traditional ways and in part on the senators' political skills and style. Senators who work hard and effectively on committees and other tasks assigned by the leadership, thereby contributing to the work of the Senate, are soon marked as potential members. If they continue to show tolerance and respect for other senators, demonstrate a strong concern for the harmonious transaction of the Senate's business and the preservation of its reputation, and are not too "far out" on issues, they may be consulted more and more often about important matters of Senate policy. In time, they will be fully socialized and eventually integrated into the social grouping within which most of the major decisions of the Senate are made.

The individual senator, whether a member of the inner group or not, is somewhat more capable of being heard within the institution than is a member of the House. Such a senator is no more likely to be able to redirect or unseat the leadership, nor is he or she likely to want to try. But he or she can count on being able to gain the floor and address the Senate, which a representative may not be able to do. Further, the Senate's tradition of operating on the basis of unanimous consent means that the objection of a single senator can delay or, in some cases, prevent action on matters to which one senator is opposed. The Senate's famous filibuster rule, for example, permits any senator or group of senators to talk for as long as they are physically capable, and some have held the floor in excess of twenty-four hours. Toward the close of a legislative session, a filibuster or even the threat of one by one or more senators can result in a leadership decision to abandon proposed legislation. Thus, the individual resources of senators are substantial, though it is questionable whether they can have any greater ultimate impact on policies than their counterparts in the House. In both cases the leadership's grip on the machinery of the institution is very strong.

Table 14.2 shows the backgrounds of the leaders of the Senate during the 97th Congress (1981–1983). These senators are somewhat older than their counterparts in the House, and some of them were once members of

Table 14.2

Biographical Survey of Political Leaders and Key Committee
Chairmen of the Senate, 97th Congress (1981–1983)

Position	Name	Age (as of 1981)	Occupation or Profession	Year Entered Congress and/or Year Entered Senate	State
Political leadership					
Majority Leader	Howard H. Baker, Jr.	56	Lawyer	1966	Tennessee
Minority Leader	Robert C. Byrd	63	Lawyer	1952, 1959	West Virginia
Chairmen of major committees					
Appropriations	Mark Hatfield	59	Professor	1967	Oregon
Armed Services	John Tower	56	Professor	1961	Texas
Banking	Jake Garn	49	Businessman	1975	Utah
Finance	Robert Dole	58	Lawyer	1961, 1969	Kansas
Foreign Relations	Charles Percy	62	Businessman	1967	Illinois
Judiciary	Strom Thurmond	79	Lawyer	1954	South Carolina

that body. The key committees are chaired by men whose terms in the Senate average 19 years (as of 1981, not counting House service). Not surprisingly, lawyers predominate among the leadership, even more completely than in the Congress as a whole.

The Legislative Process

The Role of Congressional Operations

What do these patterns of power distribution and incumbency mean for the overall operation of the Congress? Clearly the most powerful individuals are far from representative of the nation's population. They are much older, probably much more conservative, and motivated by long-established traditions that impose additional restrictions on what they can seriously consider or hope to accomplish in the way of legislation. Because such individuals are rarely challenged effectively in elections, they do not feel pressures for change within the society unless the interests and people with whom they have close contact happen to present such problems to them. Under these conditions, the Congress is normally likely to be responsive to developments in the economy or society chiefly in arbitrary, unpredictable, and conservative ways. Further, what appear to be challenges to the system itself are likely to be met with lack of understanding and severe reaction. On such matters, nearly all men and women of power are likely to be of a single mind.

A second major consequence of the existing pattern of power in the Congress is its great dependence on effective leadership. Unless the President and the party leaders within the two houses are able to establish clear and agreed priorities and to work effectively to coordinate committee actions and floor debates, very little legislation will be produced. At best, the Congress is an institution that operates on a fits-and-starts basis; the number of powerful individuals who must be convinced of the necessity of a particular action, the difficulty of persuading them, and the multitude of public problems on which action of some kind must be taken mean that a given subject comes before the Congress for serious consideration only once every few years. Unless the leadership does its job well, the opportunity for action will pass, having given rise to the enactment of a halfway or patchwork measure that makes conditions worse instead of better.

Finally, the decentralization of power in the hands of a relatively few members of Congress means that many veto points are created from which the positions and prerogatives of well-established groups can be defended even against the wishes of a large majority. Because it is so easy for one or two key members to block legislative action and so difficult for the leadership to mobilize support at all the necessary points in the legislative process, inaction (and advantage to those favored by the status quo) is a frequent result. The other likely result is legislation of the "lowest common denominator" kind — legislation that offends few, usually because it has no serious effect on the status quo. One may well ask, of course, whether such legislation is capable of solving problems.

Authorization and Appropriation

The legislative process has two major parts: authorization and appropriation. At the authorization stage, a bill proposing a new policy or activity for the national government is submitted; if ultimately passed in some form, it becomes in effect a commitment by the government to execute that policy. If new funding is required to launch such a program, as is often the case, all costs must be inserted in the budget proposed to the Congress the next year, which in effect subjects the matter to a second consideration. If it successfully emerges from the latter (appropriations) stage, during which an entirely different set of committees and interest groups is able to affect the outcome, the new program takes its place among the activities of the national government.

Both stages are long and difficult. Thousands of bills are submitted during each session of the Congress, but only a relative handful are enacted into law. If a bill is to be taken seriously, special attention must be called to it. Such special treatment usually comes about because it is part of "the President's program" (the list of legislation the President tells the Congress is desirable that year) or by decision of the majority party leadership in the Congress.

The first step in the passage of a bill is referral to the appropriate policy-area committee and then to the relevant subcommittee in each house. After several weeks or months of hearings, lobbying, bargaining, compromising, and the like, the subcommittee addresses itself to the task of drafting the actual provisions of the bill. Formal votes are not usually taken until the final draft is considered by the committee as a whole, by which time many trade-offs and amendments have already been made. When the bill has finally been passed by the standing committee, it is ready for consideration on the floor of the House or Senate. In the House of Representatives, as we have said, the Rules Committee determines when and how the bill will be debated.

If the bill is passed in both houses, a conference committee is ordinarily required to iron out the differences in the bills passed by the two houses. Usually made up of key members of the relevant policy-area committees of each house, the conference committee is the real source of the final version of the bill. In some cases influential members wait until this point to shape the bill to their liking. Often the final bill resembles the earlier versions only vaguely. Both houses must pass the bill in the same final version.

If the President signs the bill, it becomes law. If the President vetoes it, but both houses pass it again by two-thirds majorities, it becomes law.

The influence of the threat of a presidential veto can be substantial: all it takes is one-third of the votes plus one in one house to thwart the work of weeks or months by both houses. This threat and the use of the news media to put public pressure on the Congress enable the President to shape legislation.

But enactment into law may be only the beginning. Relatively few statutes are "self-executing" in the sense that they can immediately be put into effect by existing agencies. Many require funding, if only in the form of new personnel to perform the investigation, services, or enforcement called for in the statute. In such cases the appropriations process following submission of the next year's budget serves as the second consideration of the issues addressed by the statute; the arena is not the policy-area committees, but rather subcommittees of the appropriations committees. When a budget has been passed by each house, differences are settled by an appropriations conference committee.

The allied processes of logrolling and coalition building are basic to legislative policymaking. Only a rare issue, such as a declaration of war or a strong civil rights bill, arouses a fairly strong interest, pro or con, in virtually all members of the legislative body. When this happens, it is because there is widespread concern or controversy over the issue in the country at large. Only a relatively small proportion of the members take an active interest in most issues that come before a legislative body. Most have a mild concern or none at all, largely reflecting the degree of interest or lack of it among their constituents. A proposal to raise the tariff on foreign coal imports will certainly evoke strong interest in the coal-producing areas of Pennsylvania, West Virginia, and Illinois and thus in legislators representing these areas. But most other members of Congress are not likely to be strongly aroused, even though some of their constituents use coal to heat their homes or factories. A proposal to appropriate federal funds to redirect the flow of the Colorado River will certainly awaken hopes or anxieties in legislators from the states bordering the river, but will probably not deeply stir legislators from Georgia, Alaska, or New Jersey.

Where this combination of strong interest among a few legislators and apathy among most prevails, conditions are ripe for bargaining, logrolling, and coalition building. A representative from Pennsylvania who wants support for a higher tariff on coal knows that supporting votes from unconcerned colleagues can probably be obtained in return for his or her goodwill and the resulting expectation of support for them in the future on some issue on which *they* badly need support. The representative may have an understanding with representatives from cotton-growing states to vote for higher price supports for cotton, an issue in which he and his Pennsylvania constituents have relatively little interest. It is more likely that there will be no such explicit understanding about vote trading at all, but rather a political recognition that a favor rendered today deserves a return favor in the future.

Appropriations in Action: The Military Orchestrates Pressure

Each year, the President submits to the Congress a budget that reflects his judgments and preferences on national priorities for the coming fiscal year. The Congress then reviews the proposed funding for each department and activity of the government and modifies allocations in accordance with its own priorities before appropriating the money. Underlying this formal description, of course, are some hard realities: each year, bitter contests take place, first within the executive branch and then in the Congress. In relation to military spending, there is conflict among the armed services themselves and also between the military and its supporters and those seeking other priorities for governmental action. Each service naturally believes that its needs are paramount and that with new weaponry it can make an even greater contribution to national security. The cumulative effect of sincere and persuasive arguments for the pressing needs of the air force, army, navy, and marine corps is to force other governmental departments and functions to defend themselves or be content with what is left over. In this competitive process three factors work to the advantage of the military services.

1. As large and complex organizations, the military services constantly need increased funds merely for self-maintenance. Over the years they have perfected tactics for effectively influencing the Congress and the public. In this they have been aided by a general aura of patriotic necessity and selfless sacrifice in the struggle against communism. Not surprisingly, in their testimony before Congress, in speeches, and in books generals and admirals consistently endorse the doctrine that only superior military power can keep the peace and ensure the security of the United States and the free world. When budget-cutting pressures build, they are likely to report new advances by Soviet military forces and to predict dire consequences unless our own appropriations are increased. We may be sure that they are sincere in reporting conditions as they perceive them. They believe that it is part of their job, if not their duty, to proceed in this fashion. At some point, however, natural enthusiasm and confidence in the importance of one's lifework are likely to produce claims that are, from the broader perspective of all national needs and resources, out of proportion. But it is not easy for either a citizen or a member of Congress to resist when confronted by a high-ranking military officer's expert testimony that national security will be endangered unless another $5 billion is provided for a new defense system. Nor do members of Congress relish hearing their opponents at the next election attack their records on the ground that they have been "penny-pinching with the nation's security" or "advocating unilateral disarmament."

Below the level of patriotic publicity and exhortation, the military services make effective use of the pressure tactics familiar to American politics. They regularly lobby supporters and potential supporters in the

Congress and explain in detail the economic benefits to districts and regions that can result from new defense contracts and rewarding their friends
with free air transportation or round-the-world trips. Because the Armed
Services and Appropriations committees of the two houses are so crucial to
approval of new spending programs, the military services pay special attention to them. They lobby on behalf of their friends for appointment to
these cherished positions, and they build new bases in, and direct defense
contracts toward, the districts represented by such members.

The armed services are also able to call on powerful allies in their
efforts to influence decisionmakers. Private associations closely aligned with
each service bear much of the burden of lobbying, particularly in ways that
might seem improper for military officers on active duty. These associations
are made up of former military officers and reservists, contractors and suppliers who do business with that service, and some interested citizens. By
holding conventions, issuing statements, visiting members of Congress, and
otherwise engaging in pressure tactics, these associations serve as nongov-
ernmental extensions of the various services. A second and growing body
of allies is that segment of the scientific community engaged in research
and development work for the military services and NASA. Some scientists
have left universities to set up businesses to provide skills and products for
the services, while others retain their university positions. In both cases
their prestige and seeming independence lend useful support to the military
argument.

2. The military services can count on powerful and closely coordinated support from major defense suppliers who stand to gain or lose
large sums as a result of budgetary decisions. It seems fair to conclude
that these companies have a vital interest in the outcome of military
appropriations controversies, some because of near complete dependence
and others because of the profitability of this portion of their business.
Nor are these companies reluctant to press their efforts to acquire contracts: frank statements of determination to secure shares of this business
lie behind extensive lobbying, contributions to the services' associations,
and institutional advertising in national magazines and scientific and engineering journals. Coordinated lobbying campaigns as well as close contacts for the purpose of securing contracts and administering them smoothly
are achieved through the contractors' well-established pattern of employing
high-ranking retired military officers with procurement experience. Senator
William Proxmire of Wisconsin released figures in 1970 showing that as
of February 1969, 2,124 former high-ranking officers were employed by
the one hundred largest military contractors.[1] The ten largest suppliers
employed 1,065 of these retired officers: Lockheed had 210; Boeing, 169;
General Dynamics, 113; North American Rockwell, 194; and General

---

[1] William Proxmire, *Report from Wasteland* (New York: Praeger, 1970), pp. 153–154.

Electric, 89. As a group, the top ten suppliers employed about three times as many ex-high-ranking officers in 1969 as they had a decade earlier. The same rate of increase applies to the top one hundred defense contractors.

3. The key members of Congress are strong supporters of the military services, and most others are vulnerable to the economic opportunities for their districts represented by military contracts. The members of the Armed Services committees of the two houses and their counterparts on the Appropriations committees enjoy a virtual monopoly of influence over the substance of military authorizations and appropriations. They have the time and opportunity to become informed about the details of military activities and expenditures. In past decades they have usually been willing to appropriate more than the services requested. The ordinary member of Congress is habituated to take the word of colleagues who are specialists in a subject area, unable to acquire the inside knowledge that permits informed challenge or preparation of sensible alternatives, and vulnerable to the economic needs of his or her district. This dependence on the evaluations and recommendations of others has several implications.

The geographic concentration of defense business creates both strong defensiveness on the part of members of Congress who want to maintain business for their districts and strong acquisitiveness on the part of others who want to share it more widely. Defense business is monopolized by a few states. Others, chiefly in the Midwest, are especially low in defense business. Although the lack of any real opposition to military budget appropriations makes analysis of congressional voting patterns on this issue meaningless, it is clear that what opposition exists comes quite dispropor-tionately from the Midwest and urban areas where the level of defense business is particularly low.

For many members of Congress, defense contracts have become an-other (and larger) "pork barrel" like public works. A politician's constant need to be able to show constituents that he or she is working effectively on their behalf is fulfilled by the announcement of new defense contracts, even if he or she had little or nothing to do with securing them. The military and the White House have contributed to the gamesmanship and spoils-system aspects of defense contracting by helping to make members of Congress "look good" in this respect — by arranging for them to make public announcement of contract awards, for example. The question of who has done or who can do most for the district by obtaining contracts is regularly an issue in many congressional campaigns.

What does this mean? To what extent can it be said that Congress controls the appropriations process, let alone the various other activities of the far-flung federal government? In effect the division of labor into committees that is necessary to transact business at all has caused the Congress to parcel out vital power to a few members — who then become as much advocates as overseers of the agencies under their jurisdiction.

Only rarely does the Congress rise to the level of independent policy-maker. For the most part, the sheer volume and complexity of issues force it into secondary, modifying-ratifying roles. And, as we have just seen, it has difficulty performing even these functions rationally and consistently.

Congressional Developments and Reforms in the 1970s

The Vietnam War, followed by the Watergate scandals, led to demands, and resultant opportunities, for efforts to check the President's steadily increasing power and discretion and to reassert and reclaim the role of Congress. The most obvious means of providing for such a check on the presidency is to restore the power of Congress to establish the policy it believes to best serve the national interest and to exercise constant oversight of the acts of the executive branch. But this outcome requires that the Congress itself be ready and able to act, which would represent a major deviation from past experience. We will look first at the efforts made in each house to reform its rules and procedures to enable it to act more effectively and democratically. Then we will examine the changes in makeup of the two houses that both *made possible* the reform of rules and procedures and *were one of the results* of those reforms. Finally, we will try to assess the implications of both types of change for the role of Congress in the national policy-making system.

The House of Representatives' rules and procedures were changed in several ways through actions by the Democratic caucus (the Democratic members meeting together and then voting as the majority in the House). Major changes included the following:

1. No House member can chair more than one legislative subcommittee. Adopted in 1971, this rule resulted in the rise to subcommittee chairmanships of several younger Democrats. Changes in 1979 reduced the number of subcommittee positions members could hold and set up procedures whereby junior members could get better assignments.
2. Subcommittee members have a kind of "bill of rights" that assures them of real influence and consideration throughout the committee process. The power of committee chairmen has been reduced and is now more broadly shared with members of subcommittees. In the larger committees the formation of subcommittees was mandated, and subcommittees were authorized to hire their own staffs.
3. Committees were required to have written rules, again reducing the capacity of chairmen for arbitrary action.
4. In late 1974 the Democratic caucus limited senior Democrats to two subcommittee positions and effectively diminished conserva-

tives' power on the Appropriations Committee. It also required that the chairmen of such subcommittees be elected by the caucus; it subsequently unseated the chairmen of three key committees and replaced them with younger and presumably more active members.

5. Committee meetings, including actual bill-drafting sessions, were required to be open to the public (and thus to reporters and lobbyists) except under limited circumstances. Even joint House-Senate conference committee sessions, the most sensitive of all such meetings, were included.

6. A series of changes culminating in 1979 reduced opportunities for members to block floor debate or otherwise tie up the entire House to prevent or delay votes on bills. Many of these placed additional powers in the hands of the House leadership.

The Senate began the change process somewhat more slowly than did the House, in part because its smaller size and more open floor procedures already enabled members to have more committee opportunities and floor impact. But by 1980, several important changes had been made:

1. The celebrated filibuster rule, which made it possible for a small number of senators to prevent legislation from being enacted at times, was loosened. Instead of requiring the votes of two-thirds of senators present and voting to shut off debate and bring a bill to a vote, the rule now requires only three-fifths of the full Senate, or sixty votes when there are no vacancies. In 1979 new limits were set on postcloture delaying tactics.

2. Committee meetings, including bill-drafting sessions, were required to be open to the public (and reporters and lobbyists) except under limited circumstances.

3. Committee chairmen were to be elected by secret ballot in the Democratic caucus whenever one-fifth of the caucus requested.

4. A number of committees and subcommittees were eliminated, and the number of such positions that senators could hold reduced proportionately. The resulting streamlined committee system had fifteen standing committees and eleven special, select, joint, or temporary committees. The number of chairmanships that any senator could hold was also reduced.

The Changing Makeup of Congress

At one time the Congress deserved the stereotypical image of a body of elderly men grimly surviving until the seniority system granted them autocratic powers in their seventies and eighties. But this is no longer the case. In the 96th Congress (1979–1981) the average age was below fifty, the lowest in more than thirty years. More than half of all representatives had served four years or less, and more than half of all senators had served six years or less. These reductions in average age and length of service were consistent with ten-year trends, apparently because service in Congress was highly demanding, frustrating, and unrewarding.

The prime movers toward regeneration of the Congress from within have been the Democratic members of the House. An unusually large number of new Democratic members entered the House in the 1960s, and they began to use the Democratic party caucus as a vehicle for pressuring standing committee chairmen and party leaders to share power more broadly. Between 1958 and 1970, for example, 293 new Democrats entered the House; between 1971 and 1975, another 150 came to the House for the first time. The advent of 75 new "freshmen" in early 1975 tipped the balance and enabled these generally younger and more liberal members to institute several reforms.

At the same time the new Democrats were entering the House, an unusually large number of older and senior members were retiring. This trend began in 1972 and 1974, with thirty-five and forty-four members retiring, and peaked (to date) in 1978, when a record forty-nine members did not run for reelection. One result was that fewer members of the House held high seniority, and there was thus greater opportunity for newer members. But the large proportion of junior and inexperienced members also led to concern for the capacity of Congress to work its will amidst the more permanent bureaucracy and the more powerful President. Indeed, in 1978 much attention was drawn to the fact that members of the House seemed to be retiring out of frustration with their inability to get things done and the growing demands of their constituents. The results of the 1980 congressional elections are shown in Table 14.3.

Turnover in the Senate, initially slower than in the House, also began to pick up in 1978. A total of twenty new senators entered the 96th Congress, which convened in 1979: ten replacements were due to retire-

Table 14.3

The Results of the 1980 Election — Summary of Congressional Results

The Senate (Republicans, 53; Democrats, 47*; net change, +12 Republicans)	
Seats Democrat to Republican	12
Seats Republican to Democrat	0
Total new senators	12
The House (Democrats, 243†; Republicans, 192; net change, +33 Republicans)	
Seats Democrat to Republican	37
Seats Republican to Democrat	4
Total new representatives	41

* Includes Harry F. Byrd, Jr., of Virginia, elected as Independent.
† Includes Representative Thomas Foglietta of Pennsylvania, elected as Independent.

ments, the most in the post–World War II era; three incumbents were defeated in primary elections, the most in a decade; and seven more were defeated in the November general election. The latter figure had been exceeded only once in twenty years, and then in 1976 when nine incumbents lost. There has been nothing comparable in the Senate to the rules changes accomplished in the House, but some of the same forces seem to be at work. That is, committee chairmen act less arbitrarily, power is more decentralized, increasing proportions of new senators make for inexperience, and frustration among members runs high.

Some share of responsibility for the increasing rate of turnover in both the House and the Senate must be assigned to the new rules and practices. Seniority no longer carries the power or prestige that it once did, and it is now more difficult to get agreement on legislation from so many independent-minded members. With lobbyists watching every move and constituency demands multiplying, some members feel that there is little time or space for independent judgment or creative policymaking.

Thus, the advent of new representatives and senators made possible the reforms of the 1970s, and in turn those reforms speeded up the process of bringing new people into each house (and for shorter terms). Other factors were at work too, of course, such as the unsettled mood of the electorate and the growing militancy of such single-issue groups as anti-abortion and anti-gun-control organizations. Together, these factors seemed to be creating a new Congress.

The Consequences of the Changes

Observers differed sharply as to the significance of the Watergate aftermath, rules changes, and membership changes for the Congress. According to *Business Week*, for example, the Congress of the 1970s was engaged in a "Great Congressional Power Grab," particularly noticeable in 1977–1978: "The overwhelmingly Democratic 95th Congress has wrested policy control from the executive over energy and taxes, interferes more than ever in foreign policy, and is openly contemptuous of executive leadership."[2] But the Congress, because of turnover, lack of party discipline, the dominance of special interests, and the like, has been unable to exercise its power constructively. Instead, it essentially blocks presidential leadership while falling more out of touch with the need for decisive action every day.

Others disagree with the idea that Congress is newly powerful, at least as far as exercising continuing purposeful control over the national government is concerned. In a series of postelection articles in November 1978, for example, the *New York Times* stressed the new emphasis among members of Congress on "service to the District" and the increasingly

---

[2] *Business Week*, 11 September 1978, p. 90.

powerful role of special-interest groups.[3] Both of these developments suggest less sustained, policy-oriented power in Congress as a whole and more specialized efforts by various members toward self-interested ends.

The issue seems to boil down to the question of what one thinks the Congress *should* be doing. It clearly has not shown the capacity to provide steady or sustained direction for the basic course of American public policy, but it has on occasion blocked important presidential or other policy initiatives, and it reserves its systematic attention to the needs of local interests — or at least those represented by members of Congress with power in their respective houses. Reform has not worked to achieve the former capability, but it probably has enhanced the latter.

The Election of 1980

The election of 1980 brought significant changes to both houses of Congress. The change was most dramatic in the Senate, where Republicans gained twelve seats and became the majority party, but there was also substantial change in the House, where Republicans gained thirty-three seats. Although there was still a fifty-one-vote Democratic majority in the House, many of these were conservative southerners who might vote with the Republicans on a variety of issues. It is possible to exaggerate the extent to which the election of 1980 really represented a conservative movement on the part of the electorate, because turnout was very low, and many voters apparently just thought that it was "time for a change" from Jimmy Carter. The result in Congress, however, was that many liberals and southern moderates went down with the President, and more conservative members took their places (see Table 14.3).

In the Senate the Republican victory meant the elimination of several prominent liberals and the transfer of committee chairmanships to substantially more conservative Republicans. With some important assistance from well-funded and organized groups of the New Right, Republican candidates defeated such powerful senators as McGovern of South Dakota, Church of Idaho, Bayh of Indiana, Nelson of Wisconsin, Culver of Iowa, and Magnuson of Washington. Moreover, by gaining a majority, the Republicans were able to organize the Senate with full control, including Vice-President Bush as presiding officer, for the first time since 1952. This meant organizing not only the leadership positions, crucial in gaining support for President Reagan's initiatives (treaties, Supreme Court nominations, and so on) that require Senate approval, but also committee chairs.

In most cases the new chairpersons were very different from their predecessors. In a transfer between polar opposites Senator Thurmond of

---

[3] *New York Times*, 13 November 1978, p. B9.

South Carolina replaced Senator Kennedy of Massachusetts as chairperson of the Judiciary Committee. Senator Garn of Utah, the new chairperson of the Banking Committee, was a long-time foe of aid to financially troubled cities like New York. Senator Helms of North Carolina, the new chairperson of the Agriculture Committee, was a dedicated opponent of the food stamp program.

In ideology and policy preference the shift was great. But whether it would translate into actual policy changes was much less certain. Many programs operate on the basis of fixed "entitlements" that give recipients rights to federal funds under certain specified conditions (social security, agricultural subsidies), and the federal government has a legal obligation to continue funding them. Substantial tax cuts in the face of steep budget deficits present real difficulties to inflation-conscious conservatives. The general commitment to increased military spending also places a constraint on fiscal policy.

In the House Republicans defeated several committee and subcommittee chairpersons, as well as the third-ranking party leader. The balance within the Democratic Party was thus tilted toward its more conservative members, although there was still quite a gap between the majority party in the House and that in the new Senate. The actual policy performance of the House would be likely to depend on the character of presidential leadership and the success of the newly expanded Republican membership in drawing Democratic support for the President's program.

Members of both parties also promptly began looking ahead to the elections of 1982. In the Senate another thirty-four senators' terms would be expiring, two-thirds of them Democrats. Those who sought reelection might face a continuing conservative trend and New Right organizational power, and new gains would give the Republicans commanding dominance for years to come. In the House the Republicans were clearly within striking distance of obtaining a majority. But without the popularity of President Reagan to draw voters to the Republican ticket, such gains might be more difficult.

THE PRESIDENCY

15

Presidential Power

In the early 1960s Americans accorded the presidency "great respect," and most children regarded the President as a "benevolent leader."[1] In 1968 President Lyndon Johnson, who had won a landslide victory four years earlier, was forced to withdraw from office without seeking reelection because the public distrusted him and his Vietnam War policies. Six years later President Richard Nixon was forced to resign the presidency under threat of impeachment for abuses of power and serious violations of the law. Americans had lost much of their earlier confidence in the presidency.

Was it just personal defects that led President Johnson and Nixon into serious trouble? That is part of the story, but only a small part. The President stands at the head of a rapidly growing executive branch that employs more than 2 million people and that affects the

---

[1] Fred I. Greenstein, "What the President Means to Americans," in *Choosing the President*, ed. James David Barber (Englewood Cliffs, N.J.: Prentice-Hall, 1974), p. 125.

lives of Americans and other people all over the world. As the powers of the office increase, opportunities for mistakes and abuse grow. Late-twentieth-century presidents can act without public knowledge in ways that their predecessors could not, and they can take advantage of the attention focused on them to *create* public opinion in ways that were impossible before the advent of television and radio networks and instantaneous worldwide communications.

The modern presidency is a very different institution from what it was before World War II and the Great Depression. In 1932 there were three people on the White House staff; in 1979 there were 379 (see Figure 15.1), though the numbers are now only suggestive, because presidents borrow staff members who are counted on the staffs of other departments and because the White House Office is part of a larger, ever changing Executive Office of the President, as explained below. In 1930, 601,319 people administered all the functions of the federal government; in 1975 the number was 2,835,348. Throughout most of American history, including the first third of the twentieth century, Congress dominated the government, though an occasional "strong" President was able to have his way

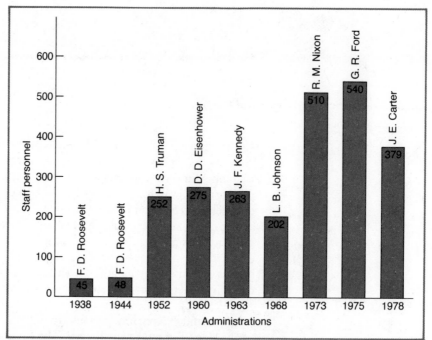

Since every president "borrows" employees from the departments, one should generally add 20 percent to these official figures drawn from the Budget of the United States.

Figure 15.1 Growth of the White House staff, 1938–1978. [*Source*: Thomas E. Cronin, *The State of the Presidency* (Boston: Little, Brown and Company, 1975), p. 119. Adapted by permission from Howard E. McCurdy, "The Physical Manifestations of an Expanded Presidency," paper delivered at the 1974 Annual Meeting of the American Political Science Association, Chicago, 1 September 1974.]

for a short time. Now every President is "strong," suggesting that the office has changed more than the personalities of the men who have occupied it.

Though the powers of and checks on the President specified by the Constitution have hardly changed, what is being done with the powers has changed enormously. To understand the place of the President in American government today, we must look not only at the person who lives in the White House, but also at power centers and tensions in the society as a whole, what a President can do to shape them, and what *they* can do to shape a President. In a sense, therefore, this entire book describes the forces that make the presidency what it is; in this chapter we focus directly on what the President can do and how the President does it.

The Sources of Presidential Power

The President's power is of a kind that no other government official has at his or her disposal: that power derives from being the executive head of the nation and the symbol of the United States to Americans and to citizens of other countries. The Constitution, the laws, and court decisions confer particular powers on public officials: a general can decide where to attack; the secretary of agriculture can ban contaminated wheat from the market. The most important powers of the President, by contrast, depend less on specific provisions of the laws than on presidential influence over public opinion. No citizen can have direct knowledge of more than a tiny fraction of the thousands of issues on which the government acts every day, and few can or want to spend all their time keeping informed. It is chiefly what the President and White House staff say publicly and tell reporters that causes the average citizen to worry about a military threat from Russia or Vietnam, to believe that the steep increases in food bills are due to union pressure for higher wages, or to conclude that it is patriotic to save oil by driving more slowly. The President, far more than anyone else, can make large numbers of people worry about alleged threats to their welfare, lead them to accept sacrifices for "the common good," or reassure them that the government is solving the problems that concern them. By shaping people's hopes and fears, the President can usually do a great deal to influence what people support and what they oppose.

This is especially true of issues of foreign policy, internal security, and other matters that have a deep impact on our lives, but depend on actions over which most of us have little control. When President Lyndon Johnson told the country in August 1964 that the North Vietnamese had fired on two harmless American ships in the Tonkin Gulf, he immediately created overwhelming public and congressional support for sending American troops into Vietnam. No one was in a position to question his claim, and the President himself may not have known that he was distorting the facts, though it later became clear that he had. Johnson had been planning for at least several months to ask the Senate for a resolution that could be used to authorize military intervention, and his administration helped

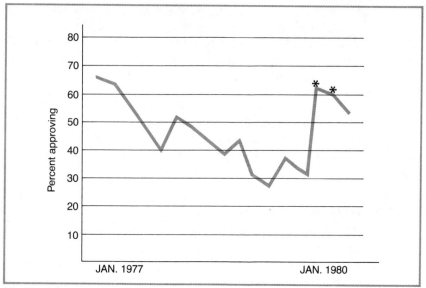

*Data from Gallup

Figure 15.2 Approval of Carter's handling of the presidency. (*Source: New York Times*, 16 January 1980, p. A18. © 1972/79/80 by The New York Times Company. Reprinted by permission.)

create an incident that would arouse public opinion in support of such intervention.

Members of trade associations, labor unions, and other organizations that try to influence many policies are less likely than other citizens to be influenced by the President on such issues. They have strong interests in profits or wage increases regardless of what the President says. But even in such cases the President can exercise a great deal of power over public opinion generally by linking economic interests to national security — by urging, for example, that wage restraint or limits on prices are necessary to keep the United States strong.

Most countries have a head of state (like the English queen or the president of Israel), who symbolizes the nation, and a prime minister, who is the executive in charge of day-to-day affairs. Combining both roles, American presidents are in a unique position to shape their own powers by creating and guiding the very public opinion to which they respond.

The President benefits in personal popularity from any development that increases patriotic or nationalist feeling. Threatening events abroad have this effect, whether or not the President had any role in them. Figure 15.2 shows that President Carter's popularity shot up sharply after the takeover of the American embassy in Iran in 1979 and the holding of its staff as hostages. This steep rise in popularity ran counter to the usual trend, for virtually every President loses popularity in the first several years of his term, as Figure 15.3 indicates. Even when a President's foreign

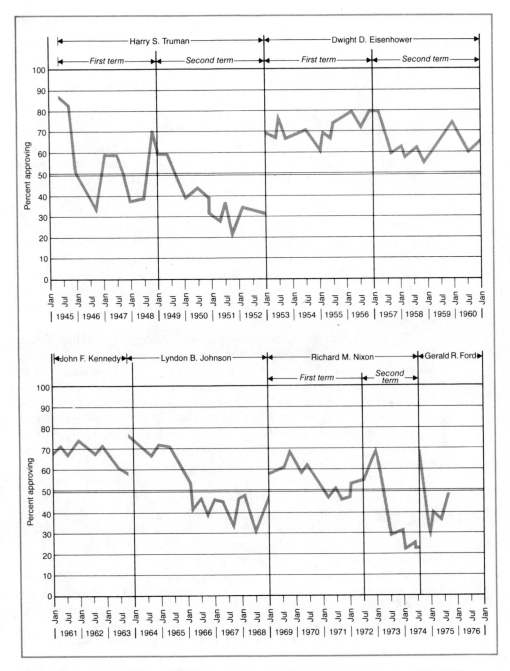

Figure 15.3 Presidential popularity (assessed at 3–5-month intervals, June 1945–1975).
(*Question*: "Do you approve of the way _____ is handling his job as president?")
[*Source*: From Thomas E. Cronin, *The State of the Presidency*, pp. 110–111. Copyright ©
1975 by Little, Brown and Company (Inc.) Reprinted by permission].

actions have been unsuccessful, they increased his popularity if they were dramatic. In 1962, for example, President John Kennedy's unsuccessful effort to invade Cuba at the Bay of Pigs brought an increase in his popular support. Foreign policy decisions are undertaken with at least one eye on domestic politics, a factor that sometimes tempts presidents into dramatic or bold actions.

The President can increase presidential powers by *ignoring* the public as well as by influencing what it believes. During Harry Truman's presidency, the CIA apparently provided arms for Chinese Nationalist troops in Burma, and under Dwight Eisenhower it helped bring down governments in Iran and Guatemala. Richard Nixon ordered the secret bombing of Cambodia, a country with which the United States was not at war. Lyndon Johnson received FBI reports on secret telephone taps of the conversations of public officials and political opponents. Nixon or his staff did the same and also brought pressure on the Internal Revenue Service to be especially severe in auditing the tax returns of opponents of the Vietnam War. The White House pursued these and similar actions for long periods without the knowledge or approval of the public, the Congress, or the courts. In most cases they would certainly have met with far more popular disapproval than support.

Concentrations of economic power flow more directly than before from public policies, as described in Chapters 4 and 6. The President, through the Office of Management and Budget, serves as the coordinating instrument for elite power and is therefore in much closer touch with key decisions and private and public decisionmakers than Congress or the courts can be. And in the years after World War II, the secrecy that had long characterized some aspects of the conduct of foreign affairs became far more pervasive in that field and began to creep into some domestic governmental activities. It is always the alleged need for security — from criminals, subversives, and foreign foes — that justifies secrecy, abroad and at home. The creation of an expanded intelligence establishment went hand in hand with the cold war against communism that dominated American foreign policy from the late 1940s until the 1970s, the suspicion of internal subversion that characterized "McCarthyism" in the 1950s, and the hot wars in Korea (1949–1952) and Southeast Asia (1965–1972). Secrecy, public concern for national security, and presidential oversight of intelligence feed one another and together make it easier for presidents to extend their controls over public and private life, with public support and sometimes without it. But the ability of presidents and of executive agencies to conceal much of what they do also permits them to act on behalf of powerful economic and social interests without arousing public criticism or the threat of political challenge to their actions.

The President's Formal Powers

The Constitution and the hundreds of laws Congress has enacted over the years confer formal powers on the President. What such provisions mean is never fully apparent from the legal language in which they are stated; their meaning resides in the actions of particular presidents and court decisions interpreting them — which is another way of saying that such meanings change continuously and usually in the direction of wider presidential powers.

According to the Constitution, the President is commander in chief of the armed forces, while Congress has the power to declare war. But many presidents have waged wars without congressional approval, and some have created situations that left Congress little choice. During the first twenty-five years of American history, presidents waged three undeclared naval wars. In 1846 President James Polk ordered troops into territory claimed by Mexico, provoking a war that Congress then had to declare. Presidents Johnson and Nixon later waged wars in foreign countries without formal declarations by Congress.

The Constitution also authorizes the President to make treaties, which must then be ratified by a two-thirds vote in the Senate, but recent presidents have increasingly evaded the requirement of Senate approval by entering into "executive agreements," in effect making treaties without regard for the "advise and consent" role of the Senate provided for in the Constitution.

The most general grant of power in the Constitution directs the President to "take care that the laws be faithfully executed," a provision whose meaning depends on what presidents actually do as well as on occasional reviews of their authority by the courts. After America's entry into World War II, President Franklin Roosevelt imposed far-reaching economic controls by *executive order*, without waiting for Congress to pass laws authorizing such controls. These measures included nationwide price, wage, and rent ceilings, limits on the use and export of raw materials, and curbs on employment practices that discriminated against blacks.

A great many laws also confer powers on the President. The Communications Act of 1934, for example, authorizes the President to allocate radio frequencies for use by federal government agencies in their own operations — a matter of considerable importance to the armed forces, the Commerce Department, the Civil Aviation Agency, manufacturers of communications equipment, and commercial radio and television stations, which get their licenses to broadcast from the Federal Communications Commission. In allocating frequencies, the President relies on an Interdepartment Radio Advisory Committee, but can intervene personally when the agencies concerned do not agree among themselves. Another example is the tariff laws, which allow the President to raise or lower tariffs on some imported goods within specified limits; this power strengthens the President's hand in negotiations on trade matters with foreign countries.

Restrictions on the President

Sensitive to the abuse of power by eighteenth-century European monarchs, the framers of the Constitution were careful to provide for curbs on the President. The courts and the Congress can check some of the President's actions; in addition, the President's need to maintain broad political support imposes other restraints. As we have seen, these checks worked well for about a century and a half. Some historians believe that they worked too well, often creating impasses among the three branches of the government that prevented effective governmental action. These restraints are far less effective now, and the predominant criticism of the "balance of powers" among the branches of government in the 1970s was that the presidency had grown too powerful, "imperial," and capable of the kind of abuse of executive power the delegates to the Constitutional Convention of 1787 tried to prevent. Developments in the next several decades will reveal just how effective the checks still are; meanwhile, it is impossible to understand the presidency without knowing what these checks are and how they are being weakened or ignored.

Legal restrictions on the President, in which the Founding Fathers and early constitutional lawyers placed most of their faith, today seem to be in jeopardy. Determined presidents have found ways to circumvent some of the most important congressional powers, including the power to declare war and the power to approve treaties. And, as we shall see, presidents have found devices to evade other powers of the Congress, including its powers to direct the President to carry out particular laws and to override presidential vetoes by a two-thirds vote of both houses. Even the power of Congress to act as the chief legislative branch is no longer clear-cut, for recent presidents have devised programs and made policy themselves. Yet congressional prerogatives remain important as long as presidents are subjected to criticism for bypassing them and are forced to justify actions some see as exceeding their powers.

The requirement that the Senate confirm presidential appointments of federal judges and high officials in the executive branch of government is not easily evaded. The occasional rejection of a nominee makes presidents think twice about ignoring popular values (or ignoring senators from the nominee's home state, who are usually supported by their Senate colleagues if they ask for rejection on the ground that the nominee is "personally obnoxious" to them). President Kennedy's nomination of Francis X. Morrissey to a district judgeship and President Nixon's nomination of Clement F. Haynsworth and G. Harrold Carswell to the Supreme Court were rejected because the nominees' competence or fairness were in serious doubt.

In all but the rare case, however, presidential appointments win routine approval and are the White House's major means of exerting influence on the executive and judicial branches. Occasionally presidents use the power of appointment for ends that would be politically harmful if they avowed them openly or asked for legislation to accomplish them. Senator John Kennedy, for example, won wide support from liberals for his strong stand on civil rights, but as President he appointed a large number of district judges in the South whose decisions crippled much of the civil rights legislation he had initiated or publicly supported. In this way the President paid debts to powerful Democrats in the South who were less than enthusiastic about his rhetorical stance on civil rights. Richard Nixon appointed a director of the Office of Economic Opportunity, Howard Phillips, who disapproved of the programs to help the poor that agency was administering. Phillips succeeded in virtually killing the agency by dismantling its programs and replacing or firing many members of the staff who tried to take their duties seriously.

Informal Restrictions on the President

Though it is supposed to be subject to presidential orders, the federal bureaucracy is a tough obstacle for every President. The bureaucracy, which is considered in detail in Chapter 16, restricts the President simply because agencies develop their own ways of doing things, beliefs about what is or is not desirable, and devices for ignoring or sabotaging directives from above that they do not like. The prevailing attitude is that presidents, cabinet secretaries, and assistant secretaries come and go, while the real work is done by experts who will still be around after the political guard has changed. For this reason, political scientist Richard Neustadt has argued that the only way for presidents to be influential is to persuade others to go along.[2] Otherwise, they may issue orders only to realize later that little or nothing has happened in spite of them.

The power of the bureaucracy to drag its feet is important chiefly with regard to long-established domestic programs supported by influential pressure groups. Franklin Roosevelt's effort to make the Federal Trade Commission and the Antitrust Division of the Justice Department effective watchdogs of business by means of appointments to their top positions did not succeed, for the permanent staffs of both agencies and organized business groups proved more effective in defending established postures than did the unorganized consumers who would benefit from revitalized regulation, even when the consumers were supported by the President of the United States.

---

[2] Richard E. Neustadt, *Presidential Power* (New York: New American Library, 1960), pp. 42–63.

Presidents have much less reason to fear this form of restraint from subordinates when they are launching new programs or dealing with foreign policy or national security. In these cases public opinion and patterns of pressure are more volatile and easier for them to manipulate through actions and rhetoric that make people fear foreign or internal threats.

No list or chart of influences and restrictions on the President can present a sufficiently *dynamic* picture of how these pressures operate. In areas of policymaking in which prosperous industries have built close alliances with administrative agencies and congressional committees, the most eloquent and popular President can do little except go along. But it must be remembered that some of the most affluent industries achieved wealth and power in the first place due to government contracts, subsidies, and tax breaks that were publicly supported because a President helped arouse such support. The cold war psychology that all the presidents of the 1950s and 1960s did their best to promote led to a level of spending on armaments that made corporations like Lockheed, General Dynamics, and McDonnell-Douglas formidable political forces. Allied as they are with the congressional military affairs committees and the Defense Department, no President can ignore them. Kennedy's touting of space exploration helped create a potent aerospace industry, and Nixon and Ford did a great deal to expand the nuclear energy industry by playing on fears of oil shortages. The Congress, the courts, the political parties, the press, public opinion, and foreign governments all influence the President, but such influence flows in both directions. The astute analyst of public affairs must calculate under what conditions and in what policy areas the President has the advantage. If the President either reflects the interests of powerful groups or wins over a supportive public, other elites usually go along with the President rather than serving as checks and balances.

Presidents and their staffs often feel frustrated by the need to take account of other powerful groups, but cannot arbitrarily ignore them. Some illegal actions of the Nixon administration to increase its own powers in the early 1970s led to the only resignation of an American President in history. The Nixon White House tried to ensure its own continuation in office and to weaken political opposition by means of various unlawful actions and attempts to politicize a number of key federal agencies to cause them to act in the political interests of the President. The unlawful acts included a break-in at the office of a psychiatrist whose patient, Daniel Ellsberg, the administration wanted to discredit for having made public the "Pentagon Papers," a set of documents that raised serious questions about the justification for waging the Vietnam War. Break-ins were also staged at the headquarters of the Democratic National Committee as part of a more general plan, approved by the President in 1969, for widespread spying and harassment of people the administration distrusted. During the 1972 campaign the White House supervised "dirty tricks" against Democratic aspirants the administration feared, planting embarrassing phony letters and disrupting some campaign appearances. And fund raisers for the President put strong pressure on corporations to make large secret campaign contributions of doubtful legality.

The administration also brought pressure on the Internal Revenue Service to make special audits of the income tax returns of leading political adversaries and opponents of the Vietnam War and encouraged the FBI to spy on the same kinds of domestic "enemies."

The Watergate affair, as this series of events is called, seemed to be aimed at expanding personal power for Nixon and his top aides, not at presidential power in the interest of dominant economic and social groups. These groups and governmental agencies that reflect their interests helped bring down the President who tried it. Enterprising reporters for the *Washington Post* were helped by people inside the bureaucracy to expose the illegal White House actions; the exposure, in turn, brought popular outrage, recommendations for impeachment from the Judiciary Committee of the House of Representatives, and, ultimately, Nixon's resignation. For students of American government, the Watergate affair illustrates both the possibility of abuse of presidential power and the checks that other governmental organs, the media, and corporations can bring to bear when they perceive the President as a threat to established power centers.

The Organization of the Presidency

The presidency is really a group of organizations rather than an individual person. The thousands of agencies, bureaus, and other subunits of the federal government represent the interests of many different and often conflicting groups, some with enormous economic and social power and others with very little. Because presidents must try to prevent open and serious conflict among the complex set of interests in American society, they cannot rely only on the established departments of the government for information or estimates of the extent of public support for their programs. Increasingly, presidents have had to create organizations under their own control, partly duplicating the functions of many of the regular administrative agencies, such as defense, foreign policy, telecommunications, and energy. As is so often true in politics, the same conflict expresses itself in several forms and can be interpreted in alternative ways. The competing interests of unions and employers, for example, may take the form of conflicting policy recommendations from the Labor and Commerce departments; the same conflict may also be reflected in personal infighting between the secretaries of those departments or between other officials responsive to the two interests. The student interested in personal sparring for position will find it, and so will the student interested in conflicts over value allocations; they will typically be seeing different aspects of the same battle.

To collect reliable information and to exercise control, modern presidents work through a set of concentric organizations with themselves at the center. Trusted assistants who comprise the White House Office channel information to the Oval Office, but shield the President from far more information than they transmit. In this respect presidential styles have differed. Franklin Roosevelt liked to know about serious conflicts, was relatively open to reports from the various agencies, and appointed trusted people to subordinate positions in key departments as sources of information and advice. Roosevelt sometimes assigned two different agencies overlapping responsibility for the same controversial program. Thus, if serious problems arose, conflict between the two organizations would make him aware of such problems and allow him to step in if he chose to do so. At the other extreme, Lyndon Johnson and Richard Nixon tended to be isolated by their staffs, who shielded them from unwelcome information and advice. Screening is obviously necessary, but the temptation every White House staff feels to minimize criticism reaching the Oval Office and to tell the President what he wants to hear can hurt the President and the country, as was the case with both Johnson and Nixon.

The White House Office is part of the Executive Office of the President, whose composition varies somewhat depending on prevailing national problems. One of its key units is the Office of Management and Budget (OMB), which carries out the responsibility of the President to prepare

"And put in a higher fence too." (*Source*: From *Herblock Special Report*, W. W. Norton & Co., Inc., 1974).

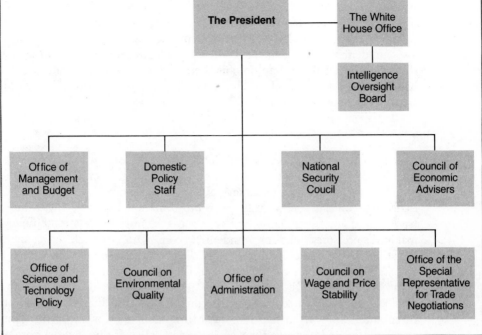

Figure 15.4 Executive Office of the President. [*Source: U.S. Government Manual, 1978–1979* (Washington, D.C.: U.S. Government Printing Office, 1979), p. 90.]

the federal budget. Its staff of more than 600 people reviews the annual budget requests of all executive departments and agencies and all legislation such agencies would like to recommend to Congress. This is a critical form of presidential control, since an agency's effectiveness depends on its appropriation and the statutes that pertain to its policy area. The OMB typically trims agency appropriation requests somewhat. Some agencies have enough private backing and influence in Congress to push legislation through (surreptitiously) even if the OMB refuses to make it part of the President's program. Such occasional "end runs" around the OMB in effect tell the President that the current strength of the interest group that accomplishes them has been underestimated.

Other agencies in the Executive Office — notably the Council of Economic Advisers, the Council on International Economic Policy, and the Council on Environmental Quality — help presidents keep abreast of economic trends (see Figure 15.4). In conjunction with the budgetary and legislative powers of the OMB, these agencies contribute to a trend toward White House coordination of the broad policies of the entire executive branch. It is important to remember, however, that an organizational structure that permits presidents to coordinate the policies of other agencies does not free them from the need to be sensitive to politically powerful groups. Neither does it allow presidents to do whatever they please on behalf of the poor, consumers, or other groups with little political power of their own, though liberal presidents are expected to try to, and usually do, advance measures advantageous to such groups in symbolic or short-term ways. Legislation to protect environmental quality, for example, lost presidential support in the 1970s when widespread belief in an energy shortage allowed oil and automobile companies to claim that the country had to choose between clean air on one hand and adequate heating and transportation on the other.

The Cabinet

The term cabinet has been used since George Washington's administration to refer to the heads of the large executive departments, whom the president appoints and can remove at pleasure. Though the term implies that these officials collectively plan broad national policy, the cabinet has never done so regularly, and it engages in less and less joint policy-making as pressures build for presidential coordination through the agencies in the Executive Office that are under direct White House control.

Cabinet members can be useful to the President in a variety of ways. Some are appointed because of their political appeal to a wing of the President's party or a segment of the public. Because Presidents Hoover, Eisenhower, and Nixon had few ties to the labor movement, all of them appointed labor leaders as their secretaries of labor during at least part of their administrations; Presidents Roosevelt and Kennedy, who had prolabor reputations, did not feel it necessary to make that gesture. Some cabinet members have reputations as experts on the matters for which their departments are responsible. Some have done political favors for the President. Others have followings in regions of the country where the administration is politically weak. Several recent presidents have appointed women to cabinet posts, with at least one eye on the fact that more than half of all eligible voters are women.

The same qualities that make cabinet members valuable politically give them some independence from the President and incline them to represent particular interests rather than to work together. So do the pressures on them to promote the objectives of the groups that influence the departments they head, whether farm organizations, defense contractors, or advertisers interested in low postal rates for "junk mail."

One student of the presidency makes a useful distinction between the "inner" cabinet — the heads of the Defense, State, Justice, and Treasury departments and a few high-level White House staff members — and the "outer" cabinet — the heads of the departments dealing with domestic affairs: Interior, Agriculture, Commerce, Labor, Education, HUD (Urban Development), Transportation, and Health and Human Services.[3] Mem-

---

[3] Thomas E. Cronin, *The State of the Presidency* (Boston: Little, Brown, 1975), pp. 190–191.

bers of the inner cabinet, as individuals if not collectively, enjoy close ties to modern presidents, for their departments deal with matters that enable presidents to appeal powerfully to broad public opinion by invoking national security and internal security.

Increasingly, presidents pay little personal attention to the outer cabinet members, delegating this function to White House aides and to the director of the OMB. The departments they head deal primarily with the problems of groups possessing few political resources (welfare recipients, students, Indians, railroad passengers) and with the interests of organized groups whose well-established influence presidents could not change substantially even if they wanted to try (large manufacturers, corporate farmers, organized labor, cattle grazers). Because these circumstances leave little room or reason for dramatic maneuvering, the problems addressed by these departments tend to involve relatively small changes in existing policies and conflicting demands that are often politically embarrassing. Understandably, tension is constant between cabinet secretaries under pressure to make concessions to one or another group and White House aides eager to minimize domestic spending and to avoid politically harmful publicity. In the Nixon White House, for example, the authoritarian style of the President's chief assistants, H. R. Haldeman and John Ehrlichmann, exacerbated relations with the inner cabinet, and in the Carter White House tension between the President's chief assistants and many of his cabinet members led to the firing of five of them in July 1979 (see Table 15.1). But such conflict transcends personalities in that it involves basically incompatible roles: the White House is subjected to a wider range of political pressures than is the secretary of a cabinet department and so must resist his or her demands and recommendations much of the time.

The President's Daily Activities

A letter by President Dwight Eisenhower,'s secretary, Ann Whitman, on how the President spent his time is probably fairly representative of the workload of other recent presidents as well.

Regular Weekly Meetings:

1. The National Security Council seems to be the most time-consuming, from the standpoint of number of hours *in* the actual meeting, the briefing before the meeting that has seemed to become a routine, and the time that the President must give, occasionally, to be sure that the meetings reflect exactly the decisions reached. . . . [Mrs. Whitman thought that frequently the President was already well informed on the substance of the prior briefings and of the meetings themselves. She noted "he himself complains that he knows every word of the presentations as they are to be made. However, he feels that to maintain the interest and attention of every member of the NSC, he must sit through each meeting. . . ."]

Table 15.1
President Carter's Inner Cabinet, January 1980

Name	Position	Age	Occupation	Previous Governmental or Political Position
Cabinet members				
Cyrus R. Vance	Secretary of State	63	Lawyer	General Counsel, Department of Defense, 1961, 1962; Secretary of the Army, 1962–1964; Deputy Secretary of Defense, 1964–1967; Special Representative of the President in Cyprus crisis, 1967–1968; U.S. negotiator at Paris Peace Conference on Vietnam, 1968–1969
Harold Brown	Secretary of Defense	53	Research scientist and physics lecturer	Scientific adviser to several defense-related officials; Delegate to the Strategic Arms Limitation Talks in Helsinki, Geneva, and Vienna, 1969; Secretary of Air Force, 1965–1969
Benjamin R. Civiletti	Attorney General	45	Lawyer	Assistant U.S. Attorney, 1962–1964; Assistant Attorney, General Criminal Division, Department of Justice, 1964–1977
G. William Miller	Secretary of Treasury	55	Lawyer	Board Chairman, Textron, Inc.; Director, Federal Reserve Bank of Boston; Chairman, Federal Reserve Board, 1977–1978
Charles W. Duncan Jr.	Secretary of Energy	56	Industrial executive	President, Coca Cola, Foods Division, 1964–1967; Executive Vice President, Coca Cola, 1970–1971; Deputy Secretary of Defense, 1977–1979

Table 15.1
President Carter's Inner Cabinet, January 1980 (continued)

Name	Position	Age	Occupation	Previous Governmental or Political Position
Executive Office staff				
Lloyd N. Cutler	Counsel to President	62	Lawyer	Director, Kaiser Industries Corp, 1962–1979
Hamilton Jordan	White House Chief of Staff	35	Social worker	Executive Secretary to Governor Carter Manager, Jimmy Carter campaign committee
Zbigniew K. Brzezinski	Assistant to the President for National Security Affairs	52	Professor	Member, Policy Planning Staff, Department of State, 1966–1968
Jody Powell	Press Secretary to the President	37	Insurance adjuster	Personal aide to the gubernatorial campaign of Jimmy Carter, 1970 Press Secretary to Governor Carter, 1971–1975 Press Secretary for Jimmy Carter Campaign Committee, 1975–1976
James T. McIntyre	Director of the Office of Management and Budget	39	Lawyer	Director, Georgia Office of Planning and Budget, 1974–1976 Deputy Director, Office of Management and Budget, 1977
Charles R. Schultze	Chairman, Council of Economic Advisers	56	Economist	Staff Economist, Council of Economic Advisers, 1952–1953 Assistant Director, U.S. Bureau of the Budget, 1962–1965 Director, Budget Bureau, 1965–1968
Stuart E. Eizenstat	Assistant to the President for Domestic Affairs and Policy	37	Lawyer	Political adviser to Carter gubernatorial and presidential campaigns Political adviser to political campaigns of Andrew Young, 1970–1976
James M. Fallows	Chief Speechwriter	31	Editor	Member, Democratic National Committee, 1979 None

2. The Cabinet meetings are not usually so long as NSC, but the President feels in some instances that to fill out an agenda, items are included that are not necessarily of the caliber that should come before the Cabinet. . . .

3. The Press Conferences. These meetings are preceded by a half to three-quarter hour briefing by staff members. [Mrs. Whitman felt that in most cases Eisenhower was already sufficiently informed to meet the press without briefings, but added "the meetings do serve the purpose of letting him know how various members of the staff are thinking. . . ."]

4. Legislative Leaders Meetings. When the Congress is in session, these are held weekly but do not last, on the average, more than an hour and a half and only about five minutes' preparation is required.

5. The President has a weekly meeting with the Secretary of Defense.

6. The President usually has a half-hour meeting with [Economic Advisers] Dr. [Gabriel] Hauge and Dr. [Arthur] Burns. I think he finds these meetings valuable and do not believe the sessions are unduly prolonged.[4]

Besides these regular meetings, the President has daily intelligence briefings, and there are other demands on his time, some of them largely ceremonial.

How to Become President

Presidential Elections: A Constraint or a Springboard to Power?

The framers of the Constitution thought that providing for presidential elections every four years was a useful device to ensure that presidents could not abuse their powers without being called to account for such actions. Yet like most efforts to limit the President, this has been a two-edged sword: our system of presidential nominations and elections has also served to ensure that only people with certain social characteristics can become President and to enable incumbent presidents to dominate their parties, future elections, and public opinion.

■ Nomination. The choice of presidential nominees by the two major political parties is more critical than the general election, since it eliminates all but two people from any chance of becoming President. And though millions of people meet the constitutional requirements for serving as President — native-born citizens at least thirty-five years old — only a very small number are ever seriously considered as nominees who might attract a large popular vote. In the thirty-six years between 1936 and 1972,

---

[4] Quoted in Fred I. Greenstein, "The Modern Presidency," in Anthony King, ed., *The New American Political System* (Washington, D.C.: American Enterprise Institute, 1978), pp. 60–61. Used by permission.

only sixty-two Democrats and forty-seven Republicans won the support of as much as 1 percent of members of their own parties in Gallup polls on candidate preferences.

The narrowing-down process is neither a lottery in which everyone starts with an equal chance nor a rigorous screening to find the best or most popular candidate. Only aspirants whom newspapers and television news programs have mentioned frequently are regarded as serious contenders, and publicity as a serious contender in turn gives an aspirant a public following.

This kind of self-fulfilling prophecy seems to pervade the nominating process. An aspirant who makes a good early showing in the polls and the primaries finds it much easier to raise the millions of dollars necessary to continue to look popular. Even the "fat cats" and corporations that make large contributions, directly or indirectly, want a winner as well as a candidate who will support their interests. Names familiar from previous contests for the nomination are most often mentioned in conjecture about future ones. Because past winners have virtually all been male, white, Protestant, Anglo-Saxon, public officeholders, fairly wealthy, and fairly old, the overwhelming majority of the eligible population has little chance of being taken seriously. A rigid informal barrier confronts women, blacks, Jews, people whose ancestors emigrated from any part of the world other than Northern and Western Europe, and probably Catholics as well, even now; it is assumed that large numbers of voters are prejudiced against these groups.[5]

There are other limits on eligibility for the nomination. First-term presidents can normally have their party's nomination for a second term if they want it; they usually do. Victorious generals are the chief exception to the practice of nominating only individuals who have held elective office before, especially as vice-president or senator. An impressive military record has helped nominate and elect seven presidents, though it is hardly likely that the same qualities make for success in both jobs. Figure 15.5 shows the public offices presidential nominees have held.

The tests that are all-important in choosing nominees come partly from presidential primary elections held in a number of states in the early months of election years and partly from the preferences of local party officials and activists. Thirty-four states conduct primaries in which voters may express a preference for one of the aspirants or actually select delegates to their party's nominating convention; approximately two-thirds of the convention delegates are chosen in primaries. The presidential primaries receive a lot of publicity, but their chief consequences are to encourage intraparty competition and divisiveness, to increase the cost of the election process substantially, and to create the often illusory

---

[5] Donald R. Matthews, "Presidential Nominations," in Choosing the President, ed. James David Barber (Englewood Cliffs, N.J.: Prentice-Hall, 1974), pp. 39–40.

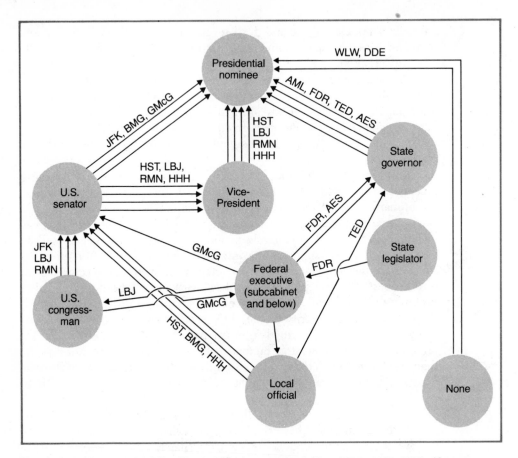

Figure 15.5 Pattern of public office holding by presidential nominees, 1936–1972. (*Source*: Donald R. Matthews, "Presidential Nominations: Process and Outcomes," p. 46 in *Choosing the President*, edited by James David Barber, © 1974. The American Assembly, Columbia University. Reprinted by permission of Prentice-Hall, Inc., Englewood Cliffs, New Jersey.)

impression that "the people" have a major voice in the selection of nominees. Convention delegates do not always support the candidate who won their state's primary; the convention may choose a candidate who did not even enter the primaries, as the Democrats did when they nominated Hubert Humphrey in 1968. The aspirant who leads the field in the early polls almost always wins. Presidential nominating conventions serve more as occasions for hoopla, party propaganda, and the *legitimization* of choices made earlier than for key decisionmaking.

■ *Advantages of Incumbents.* Let us consider some features of election campaigns that are distinctive to presidential elections. The general account of elections in Chapter 19 is also pertinent. Incumbent presidents enjoy an advantage. For one thing, they can use press releases and other reports by the entire executive branch to create an impression of accomplishment and help for citizens with all sorts of problems. Recent presidents have increasingly done so. During the Nixon administration approximately 60 people in the White House and 6,144 people in the executive branch worked on public relation, at a cost of $161,000,000 a year.[6] An Associated Press survey in 1975 found 6,391 full- and part-time officials of the federal government dealing with public relations and information.[7]

Incumbent presidents have also spent federal funds to help them win renomination and reelection. In an effort to meet a challenge to his renomination, President Carter allocated $24.8 million in discretionary highway funds to Chicago in 1979. This was $7.8 million more than a presidential candidate is allowed to spend for the entire primary campaign.

The needs of news reporters make it all the easier for the incumbent regime to tout its activities — and to manage the news, if it wants to do so. Public affairs are so wide ranging that even the wealthiest and most conscientious newspaper, television network, or wire service must rely on official releases for most of its information. Table 15.2 shows that the *New York Times* and the *Washington Post* do so, even though they have far better means of independent news gathering than do most other newspapers, which draw heavily on them as sources and as models of how to treat current news stories.

Psychological needs on the part of the public also help the incumbent President. People who are worried about foreign or domestic threats they cannot deal with themselves tend to want to believe that the President

Table 15.2
Sources of Information in the *Times* and the *Post* — All Stories
($N = 2,850$)

	% of Total Sources
U.S. officials, agencies	46.5
Foreign, international officials, agencies	27.5
American state, local government officials	4.1
Other news organizations	3.2
Nongovernmental foreigners	2.1
Nongovernmental Americans	14.4
Not ascertainable*	2.4

Source: The table, reprinted by permission of the publisher, it taken from Leon Sigal, *Reporters and Officials* (Lexington, Mass.: D. C. Heath, 1973), p. 124. It is based on a count of a sample of stories in the two newspapers over the years 1949 to 1969.

* Not ascertainable includes stories in which the channel was a spontaneous event or the reporter's own analysis.

[6] David Wise, *The Politics of Lying* (New York: Random House, 1973), pp. 188–213.
[7] *Wisconsin State Journal*, 5 October 1975.

can cope with them, and so they cooperate in creating an image of presidential competence. Asked in one study what they looked for in a President, people seemed concerned primarily with strength and toughness. Compassion was hardly mentioned.[8] It is also striking that every landslide presidential victory since Roosevelt's in 1936 was won by an incumbent who had coped or seemed to cope resolutely with a major crisis: Roosevelt with the Great Depression; Eisenhower in 1956 with the ending of the Korean War; Johnson in 1964 with the War on Poverty and the aftermath of the Kennedy assassination; and Nixon in 1972 with the ending of the Vietnam War and détente with Russia and China. Their opponents, by contrast, were reputed to be indecisive or inconsistent (Landon, Stevenson, McGovern) or wild, trigger-happy, and therefore unreliable (Goldwater). In the very close elections of the same period (1960, 1968), on the other hand, no incumbent was running, and neither candidate had built a reputation for toughness and decisiveness.

Until 1940 no President ever sought a third term, though no constitutional provision prevented it. Franklin Roosevelt ran for a third term that year and was elected to a fourth term in 1944. This precedent might have enhanced the advantages of incumbency considerably, but the Twenty-second Amendment, ratified in 1951, forbids election to the presidency more than twice.

■ *Candidates and Their Parties.* A presidential candidate or incumbent is supposed to be the party leader as well, and Presidents Thomas Jefferson, Abraham Lincoln, both Roosevelts, and Woodrow Wilson certainly were that. From the point of view of local leaders of the Republican and Democratic parties, the main use of the name at the top of the ticket is to carry into office hundreds of candidates for lesser offices from the same party; even so, this "coattail effect" often does not work, and there is some question whether any candidate can lend popularity to others.

Some recent presidents and candidates have paid little attention to their regular party organizations. Many local Democratic leaders refused to cooperate with George McGovern, the presidential nominee in 1972, because they resented his attempts to weaken their positions by bringing higher proportions of young people and women into party and campaign activities. In the same campaign Richard Nixon, virtually ignoring the regular Republican party organization, set up the separate Committee to Reelect the President (CREEP) dominated by White House aides loyal to him personally, but uninterested in the party as a whole. The regular party workhorses found this arrangement frustrating because it denied them both funds and presidential cooperation. They liked it even less when Republican candidates for governorships and Congress did quite poorly

---

[8] Doris A. Graber, "Personal Qualities in Presidential Images: The Contribution of the Press," *Midwest Journal of Political Science* 16 (February 1972), pp. 54–55.

on election day while Nixon won reelection by an enormous majority and still less when it became known that CREEP had engaged in unlawful activities and "dirty tricks" that hurt the Republican party badly in the 1974 congressional election.

■ *News Management by Candidates.* Presidential incumbents can take advantage of newsmaking resources and of popular trust in the office to create exaggerated or misleading impressions of their competence and achievements. They would be less than human if they failed to do so, though some incumbents and candidates have shown far more interest in and skill at news management than others. A favorite device is the "pseudoevent," an incident that seems to occur naturally, but is deliberately contrived to make an impression on an audience: the "crowd" that is concentrated at one point so as to appear large on television as the candidate drives by; the crowd recruited to insult a candidate or to act violently in order to win sympathy for him; the planted question or the planted group of "representative Americans" who chat with the candidate on TV, leading to a display of rapport with many elements in American society and knowledgeable treatment of complex issues. Trips to foreign countries, and especially to trouble spots, are a classic strategy by means of which presidential candidates display their interest in and mastery of foreign affairs.

The Vice-President and Succession

The vice-presidency is a key office in the federal government, but only because there is a very good chance of the incumbent's becoming President either due to the death of the President or by election at a later time.

The Twenty-fifth Amendment, ratified in 1967, ensures that there will be no lengthy period without a Vice-President, by authorizing the President to respond to a vacancy in the vice-presidency by nominating a candidate, who then takes office if confirmed by majority vote of both houses of Congress. Vice-President Spiro Agnew's resignation in 1973 brought this provision into play, and President Nixon appointed Gerald Ford to the office. Ford became President upon Nixon's resignation in August 1974 and in turn invoked the Twenty-fifth Amendment to appoint Nelson Rockefeller Vice-President. This exceptional sequence of events meant that for several years, neither the President nor the Vice-President had been elected to their offices, a state of affairs that has aroused some criticism of the Twenty-fifth Amendment.

Another part of the same amendment provides for the Vice-President to serve as Acting President if the President is unable to perform the presidential duties. In case of the death or disability of the President and Vice-President, the Speaker of the House of Representatives is next in line, followed by the President Pro Tem of the Senate (a senator elected by the other senators to that post) and then by the members of the cabinet in the order in which their departments were established historically.

The Vice-President is formally the presiding officer of the Senate and may vote only on the rare occasions when there is a tie vote, though this sometimes constitutes an important power. Vice-presidents have traditionally not been given important functions in the executive branch, although most presidents make some pretense of doing so. John Nance Garner, who served as Vice-President during Roosevelt's first two terms, considered the administration much too liberal and was hardly on speaking terms with the President. President Eisenhower, asked near the end of his term to name a key administration policy in which Vice-President Richard Nixon had played an important role, replied, "Give me a week and maybe I'll think of one." As Gerald Ford's Vice-President, Nelson Rockefeller tried very hard to exert some influence on domestic energy policy, but had to employ a large private staff and the resources of the Rockefeller family in the effort.

The 1980 Presidential Election

The result of the 1980 presidential campaign was dramatic — a landslide victory for the Republican candidate, Ronald Reagan, who carried forty-four states with 489 electoral votes; Jimmy Carter, by contrast carried only six states and the District of Columbia, for a total of 49 electoral votes. Figure 15.6 shows the Reagan-Carter outcome; Table 15.3, the vote among all candidates. The deeper meaning of the campaign lay in its showing that a large part of the public was alienated from the electoral process, its encouragement of groups favoring conservative causes, and its discouragement of people advocating policy changes to help the disadvantaged and the minorities and to reduce the burdens and the dangers of large military expenditures.

The Nominating Process

The state caucuses and primaries and the national nominating conventions foreshadowed these outcomes. On the Republican side all the leading contenders for the nomination were conservative in their ideology except Congressman John Anderson, whose lackluster showing in most of the early primaries forced him out of contention; he chose to run as an independent candidate. The leader of the Republican Party's right wing, Ronald Reagan, emerged early as the front runner and had the nomination secured long before the convention. Men like Gerald Ford and George Bush, long labeled "conservative," were now called "moderate," signaling a shift in the party's locus of power. Reagan chose Bush as his running mate to "balance the ticket."

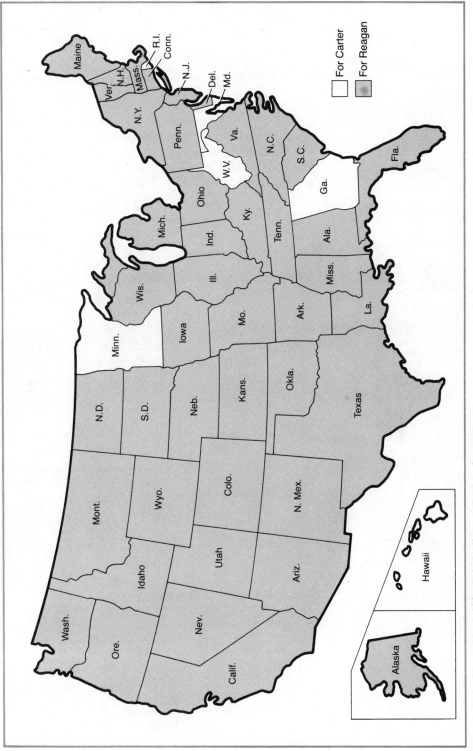

Figure 15.6 The 1980 presidential election — the vote by states.

Table 15.3 Vote for President by States

State	EV[a]	PR[b]	Jimmy Carter	Ronald Reagan	John Anderson	Ed Clark	Barry Commoner
Alabama	8	100	627,808	641,609	15,855	12,002	538
Alaska	3	86	31,408	66,874	8,091	14,495	—[c]
Arizona	6	100	243,498	523,124	75,805	18,570	—
Arkansas	6	99	392,404	396,689	21,057	8,638	2,237
California	45	100	3,040,600	4,447,266	727,871	146,780	60,072
Colorado	7	100	367,966	650,786	130,579	25,628	5,608
Connecticut	8	100	537,407	672,648	168,260	8,272	5,956
Delaware	3	100	106,650	111,631	16,344	1,986	—
District of Columbia	3	100	124,376	21,765	14,971	1,037	1,686
Florida	17	100	1,369,120	1,943,989	178,483	29,322	—
Georgia	12	100	882,785	644,691	34,912	15,261	—
Hawaii	4	100	135,879	130,112	32,021	3,269	1,548
Idaho	4	100	109,410	289,789	27,142	8,482	—
Illinois	26	99	1,951,073	2,335,806	344,836	23,604	4,117
Indiana	13	99	832,213	1,232,764	107,729	17,776	4,522
Iowa	8	100	508,735	676,556	114,589	12,324	2,191
Kansas	7	100	324,974	562,848	67,535	14,089	—
Kentucky	9	99	605,876	626,072	29,428	5,427	1,242
Louisiana	10	100	707,981	796,240	26,198	8,247	1,698
Maine	4	100	220,387	238,156	53,450	5,087	4,491
Maryland	10	100	706,327	656,255	113,452	13,924	—
Massachusetts	14	100	1,051,104	1,054,562	382,044	21,170	3,146
Michigan	21	100	1,659,208	1,914,559	272,948	41,060	12,089
Minnesota	10	99	924,770	844,459	169,960	30,375	8,202
Mississippi	7	100	429,988	440,747	11,871	4,651	—
Missouri	12	100	917,663	1,055,355	76,488	14,135	—
Montana	4	99	111,972	195,108	27,919	9,536	—
Nebraska	5	100	164,276	413,401	44,025	8,920	—
Nevada	3	100	66,468	154,570	17,580	4,346	—

Table 15.3 Vote for President by States (continued)

State	EV[a]	PR[b]	Jimmy Carter	Ronald Reagan	John Anderson	Ed Clark	Barry Commoner
New Hampshire	4	100	109,080	221,771	49,295	2,063	1,276
New Jersey	17	100	1,119,576	1,506,437	224,173	20,094	7,765
New Mexico	4	100	165,054	245,433	28,404	4,348	2,359
New York	41	99	2,632,099	2,797,684	440,480	51,280	19,410
North Carolina	13	100	875,776	913,898	52,364	9,866	2,341
North Dakota	3	98	76,533	187,483	22,390	3,498	417
Ohio	25	100	1,743,829	2,201,864	255,521	49,543	8,888
Oklahoma	8	100	399,292	683,807	38,051	15,642	13,362
Oregon	6	100	446,721	557,381	109,621	25,407	10,760
Pennsylvania	27	100	1,932,336	2,252,260	288,704	31,118	—
Rhode Island	4	100	185,319	145,576	56,213	2,411	—
South Carolina	8	99	417,633	421,117	13,990	4,919	—
South Dakota	4	100	103,909	198,102	21,342	3,839	—
Tennessee	10	100	781,512	787,244	35,921	6,784	1,099
Texas	26	100	1,844,349	2,539,144	109,707	36,825	—
Utah	4	100	123,447	435,839	30,191	7,193	1,844
Vermont	3	100	81,421	93,554	31,671	1,861	2,315
Virginia	12	100	748,638	983,311	93,813	12,462	13,761
Washington	9	100	583,596	764,393	165,443	25,848	8,442
West Virginia	6	97	353,508	326,645	30,499	4,259	—
Wisconsin	11	100	988,255	1,089,750	159,793	29,245	7,701
Wyoming	3	100	49,123	110,096	12,350	4,694	—
Total	538		34,913,332	43,201,220	5,581,379	881,612	221,083

Source: *New York Times*, 6 November 1980, p. A28. Reprinted by permission of The Associated Press.

[a] Electoral vote.
[b] Percentage of precincts reporting.
[c] Candidate not on ballot.

On the Democratic side Senator Edward Kennedy, at first more popular than President Carter in the opinion polls, challenged the President for the nomination, appealing to the liberal wing of the party. The taking of American hostages in Iran in November 1979 bolstered the President's popularity markedly, as foreign crises often do, and Kennedy never regained his lead, although he did retain an ardent following of liberals. A substantial majority of the delegates to the Democratic National Convention were formally pledged to Carter, who stamped out a movement to dump him by accepting some liberal platform planks, chiefly on economic issues, that he did not favor.

The General Election Campaign

From the start of the campaign, it was clear that a great many voters were unhappy with the electoral choices available to them. Even close to election day the number of undecided people was far larger than usual, and all three candidates played heavily on popular doubts and anxieties regarding their opponents. The indecisiveness was not due to apathy. There was deep popular discontent with high prices, high unemployment levels, and ineffectiveness in foreign policy, together with widespread doubts about the competence of Jimmy Carter and fears that Ronald Reagan might act rashly, become embroiled in nuclear war, and remain indifferent to the country's social problems.

John Anderson steadily lost support throughout the campaign. Many people thought it pointless to vote for a sure loser; others found Anderson's voting record in Congress to be inconsistent with his liberal campaign positions.

Both major-party candidates favored substantial increases in the military budget, tax cuts, and nuclear power. Reagan had the strong support of right-wing groups, including some that ordinarily see both major parties as too liberal. An important bloc of his supporters were religious fundamentalists who defined rightist politics as the "moral" course of action. The Democratic platform was more liberal on most social and economic issues than either the Republican platform or Carter's record, creating a dilemma for those who favored change in administration policy.

For advocates of help for the disadvantaged and a less militant foreign policy, there seemed to be no viable choice, resulting in their disaffection, waffling, and nonvoting. The National Organization of Women announced before the campaign started that it would not support Carter, who had made some important appointments of women to judicial and administrative offices, but had opposed publicly funded abortions and had rudely dismissed some forthright feminists from advisory positions. But Reagan's opposition to the ERA as well as to abortions drove many feminists to support Carter anyway. The women's vote ultimately split about evenly between the two candidates. Similarly, many blacks were bitterly disappointed with Carter's record on urban, racial, and economic issues, but most were even more fearful of Reagan's policies. Jewish voters who disliked the administration's tilt toward the Arab countries and wavering support for Israel were for the most part even more concerned about Reagan's ties to Protestant fundamentalism. For many such groups, the campaign served chiefly to dampen hopes and expectations. Table 15.4 shows that with the exception of blacks, there were substantial defections to Reagan from the groups that have been the mainstays of Democratic support in most elections since the 1930s.

A revealing aspect of the campaign was a marked last-minute shift of a great many voters against Carter. Until two days before the election, the polls showed the two major candidates very close, with Reagan holding a lead smaller than the margin of error. In a televised debate a few days before the election Reagan apparently dispelled many people's fears that he was trigger-happy; he also seemed to show a more pleasing personality than his opponent. Shortly before election day Iran announced its conditions for freeing the fifty-two American hostages held there for a year: news that for many apparently became a symbol of the Carter administration's failure in many policy areas. The undecided vote went heavily to Reagan, some Carter supporters switched, and many people did not vote at all. This was the fifth successive presidential election in which voter turnout declined, falling to about 52 percent of the eligible population.

The wholesale last-minute switching, the large number of undecided people, and especially the upturn in nonvoting may in the long run be a more significant political development than the Republican victory. These are probably signs of voter alienation. They call into question the effectiveness of voting as a legitimizer of the regime for a great many Americans. They suggest that many people now doubt that elections give them a significant voice in a polity in which severe economic and social problems persist and inequalities largely perpetuate themselves. From one perspective the 1980 election was a mandate for conservative policy directions. From another perspective it was a signal of popular discouragement and anger.

Summary

This chapter has examined the place of the presidency in the American political system. Through symbolic importance, ability to define issues, problems, and crises, and discretionary spending powers, the President is an enormously powerful figure. Yet there are other economic and social power centers as well, and even the President cannot flout them arbitrarily. More often the President responds to them by coordinating

Table 15.4

The New York Times/CBS News Poll — How Different Groups Voted for President*

	Carter	Reagan	Anderson	Carter-Ford in 1976
Democrats (43%)	66	26	6	77–22
Independents (23%)	30	54	12	43–54
Republicans (28%)	11	84	4	9–90
East (32%)	43	47	8	51–47
South (27%)	44	51	3	54–45
Midwest (20%)	41	51	6	48–50
West (11%)	35	52	10	46–51
Blacks (10%)	82	14	3	82–16
Hispanics (2%)	54	36	7	75–24
Whites (88%)	36	55	8	47–52
Female (49%)	45	46	7	50–48
Male (51%)	37	54	7	50–48
Female, favors equal rights amendment (22%)	54	32	11	—
Female, opposes equal rights amendment (15%)	29	66	4	—
Catholic (25%)	40	51	7	54–44
Jewish (5%)	45	39	14	64–34
Protestant (46%)	37	56	6	44–55
Born-again white Protestant (17%)	34	61	4	—
18–21 years old (6%)	44	43	11	48–50
22–29 years old (17%)	43	43	11	51–46
30–44 years old (31%)	37	54	7	49–49
45–59 years old (23%)	39	55	6	47–52
60 years or older (18%)	40	54	4	47–52
Family income:				
Less than $10,000 (13%)	50	41	6	58–40
$10,000–$14,999 (14%)	47	42	8	55–43
$15,000–$24,999 (30%)	38	53	7	48–50
$25,000–$50,000 (24%)	32	58	8	36–62
Over $50,000 (5%)	25	65	8	—
Professional or manager (40%)	33	56	9	41–57
Clerical, sales or other white-collar (11%)	42	48	8	46–53
Blue-collar worker (17%)	46	47	5	57–41
Agriculture (3%)	29	66	3	—
Looking for work (3%)	55	35	7	65–34
Education:				
High school or less (39%)	46	48	4	57–43
Some college (28%)	35	55	8	51–49
College graduate (27%)	35	51	11	45–55

Source: 1976 and 1980 election day surveys by The New York Times/CBS News Poll and 1976 election day survey by NBC News. © 1980 by The New York Times Company. Reprinted by permission.

* Based on 12,782 interviews with voters at their polling places. Shown is how each group divided its vote for President and, in parentheses, the percentage of the electorate belonging to each group.

governmental, corporate, and military activities and goals and by maintaining public support in the best way possible for the policies that further that objective. Sometimes this means concessions to public groups that can bring pressure. Sometimes it means explaining problems. Sometimes it means secret operations. And sometimes it means using public fears of foreign threats to win over public opinion.

THE BUREAUCRACY

16

The Nature, Growth, and Influence of the Bureaucracy

Though the President, representatives, senators, cabinet members, and Supreme Court justices often appear in the headlines, what they do rarely has a direct effect on people's everyday lives. It is police officers, income tax auditors, welfare department caseworkers, field examiners for the National Labor Relations Board, customs officers, FBI agents, army sergeants, wheat inspectors for the Department of Agriculture, and thousands of other public employees, often in relatively lowly positions, who decide whether individuals and groups of individuals will be helped or hurt by the statutes, court decisions, and executive orders they apply and interpret. Not even a congressional declaration of war, to take an especially dramatic example, affects the daily lives of citizens until draft boards decide whether they can remain civilians; a rationing board decides how much meat, sugar, and ketchup they can buy; wage and price boards determine how well they can afford to live; and a war production board determines which industrial products will be manufactured and which will be scarce. It is at the level of administration that the political system pays off for the man and woman in the street.

Bureaucrats Make Public Policies

Nor is it true, as primary school textbooks sometimes assert, that administrators only "carry out" decisions made at the higher levels of the government. It is seldom possible for a President, legislature, or high court to make policies that take effect automatically and do not need to be interpreted in the course of application to a specific case. For example, Congress has directed the Federal Communications Commission (FCC) to grant and renew radio and television licenses so as to promote "the public interest, convenience, or necessity." But this legal phrase hardly specifies who gets licenses or what types of applicants are favored in grants of a scarce, influential, and very lucrative public resource. The real policymakers include FCC accountants who decide whether applicants have adequate financial resources, FCC engineers who decide whether a proposed station will interfere excessively with other stations, FCC lawyers and other employees who decide whether proposed programs meet standards of fairness and balance, and so on.

A 55-mile-per-hour speed limit posted on a highway does not mean what it says if the highway police never issue tickets to anyone traveling less than 60 miles per hour, as is often the case; it means whatever the police officer chooses to do about it. An applicant for welfare benefits who is turned away by a caseworker at the welfare office does not benefit from the words in the law, even though a different caseworker might have interpreted those words in his or her favor.

Public administration, in short, involves discretion, and it involves politics as well, for administrators have a great deal to do with determining who gets what, when, and how. Administrators' decisions reflect the conflicts of interest that divide people. Should TV and radio licenses be awarded to applicants with ample financial resources to ensure the use of good equipment, or should they be awarded to applicants who represent diverse economic and social groups and diverse ideologies? How much weight should a draft board give to the value of letting a student finish college and how much to the value of making young people from middle-class families just as susceptible to the draft as young people who cannot afford to go to college? In deciding thousands of such matters, administrators are making critical choices on politically divisive issues.

Bureaucrats are embroiled in politics in another way as well: their actions and the language in which they describe their policies create public opinion at least as much as they reflect what the public already thinks. Citizens are typically unaware of an issue until news media bring it to their attention. It is often news about administrative actions that shapes what large numbers of people recognize as a problem and what they then think about it. A welfare administrator quoted as declaring it necessary to clear the chiselers off the welfare rolls is obviously creating the belief in many people's minds that many welfare recipients have no legal or ethical right to their benefits. He or she is intensifying conflict between resentful taxpayers and those who need or favor the current level, or higher levels, of welfare payments. Nor is the public's attention directed to related public issues: whether, for example, people legally entitled to benefits are being denied them and whether welfare payments amount to a significant or a minimal drain on the public treasury relative to other politically controversial costs, such as armaments or space research. What the public statement implies may be accurate or inaccurate, but few who hear and react to it have access to any source of information other than the statement of a supposed authority on the subject.

Because of their concern with public opinion, agencies maintain public relations staffs. Table 16.1 gives some information about the public relations resources of the cabinet departments.

Administrative *actions* often create public beliefs even more effectively than does language, since their effect is more subtle. The sudden mobilization of troops or a military alert awakens fears that a hostile country is about to attack and so musters support for a larger armaments budget and greater influence on the part of military experts in foreign policy decisions. When the Department of Labor undertakes retraining programs to help the unemployed, its action encourages the belief that unemployment is due largely to the failure to match vacant jobs with those who have the skills to perform them. Though this belief is partly valid, it points to a

Table 16.1
Public Relations Resources of the Federal Agencies, 1977

	Public Relations Staff	1977 P.R. Budget (in millions)
Department of Defense	1,740	$24.0
Department of State	204	5.1
Department of Health, Education and Welfare	396	22.9
Department of the Treasury	252	4.3
Department of Interior	195	1.0
Department of Commerce	170	5.2
Department of Agriculture	763	24.7
Department of Labor	200	6.5
Department of Housing and Urban Development	39	1.2
Department of Transportation	300	9.1
United States Information Agency	8,374	263.0

Source: Reprinted with permission from National Journal (23 July 1977), p. 1142.

relatively minor cause of unemployment and so may awaken false hopes in many trainees and false beliefs in the public generally.

Still another reason that administrative actions are a form of politics is that they are closely linked to outside pressure groups and to the opinions and demands of influential people. In favoring radio and TV license applicants with large financial resources, the FCC is taking a position that pleases the National Association of Broadcasters. When a state public utilities commission allows gas and electric companies to raise their rates several times in a single year, as many have in recent years, it is responding to pressure from the utilities and recognizing that the people who must pay the higher bills are neither organized to protect their interests nor able to refuse to pay. Decisions on controversial matters made inside a public administrative agency reflect the political clout of groups outside the agency that are helped or hurt by what it does; in turn, the agency's policies often *contribute* to the political power or weakness of outside groups.

The result is that administrative agencies are bound to reflect and also to *strengthen* the interests of groups that are already powerful. Though public bureaucracies maintain public support by claiming impartiality and expert knowledge, they use that support — with few exceptions — to further the goals of elites. That is the common theme of analyses of bureaucratic growth, structure, decisionmaking, and impact. Administrative agencies' claims that they simply "carry out" policies made by representatives of the people can be understood largely as a way of legitimizing administrative actions that further the goals of the economically and politically powerful. It will be clear from our analysis that many of the actions of the most controversial administrative agencies are taken without the knowledge or direction of legislative or executive superiors. In some cases they *violate* the law. To understand and predict such actions, a realistic analysis must focus on the groups with the power to influence the thinking, careers, and budgets of the agencies.

The Growth of the Bureaucracy

Throughout most of the nineteenth century, American federal, state, and local governments dealt chiefly with foreign relations and national defense, the prevention of crime, delivery of the mail, public schooling (especially in the primary grades), and the use and disposal of public lands. Governmental functions were few and simple relative to today, costs were relatively low, and the number of people needed to administer the laws was small.

The big increases in the number of people employed in government occurred in the second third of the twentieth century, when all levels of government acquired new functions made necessary by the development of an extremely complex industrialized economy, sharp increases in population, and a large shift of population from rural to urban areas. These changes brought about pressures on government to help both those who were benefiting from such changes and those who were suffering from the social problems that had become serious and chronic in the twentieth century: poverty, health problems, emotional disturbance, bad housing, and monotonous and unsatisfying work.

As a result, public employees today perform just about every kind of work found in private industry as well as some types only governments undertake. Every professional, scientific, and managerial skill is represented, as is every form of unskilled labor. Public administrative activities include regulating and aiding industries, fighting wars, performing scientific research, running hospitals, prisons, and schools, and building roads.

Employees of the federal government account for only a small fraction of the number who perform these diverse governmental functions: there are close to 2.8 million civilian federal employees and well over 11 million employees of state and local governments. At least 7 million more work for private firms hired by governmental agencies to build highways and public buildings, manufacture equipment for the armed forces and space exploration, undertake research, and execute other public contracts (see Table 16.2).

Table 16.2
Paid Civilian Employment in the Federal Government 1816–1978

Year	Total	Executive Branch	Legislative Branch	Judicial Branch
1816	4,837	4,479	243	115
1851	26,274	25,713	384	177
1881	100,020	94,679	2,579	2,762
1901	239,476	231,056	5,690	2,730
1921[a]	561,142	550,020	9,202	1,920
1930	601,319	588,951	10,620	1,748
1940	1,042,420	1,022,853	17,099	2,468
1945	3,816,310	3,786,645	26,959	2,706
1950	1,960,708	1,934,040	22,896	3,772
1955	2,397,309	2,371,462	21,711	4,136
1960	2,398,704	2,370,826	22,886	4,996
1965[b]	2,527,915	2,496,064	25,947	5,904
1970	2,921,909	2,884,307	30,715	6,887
1975[c]	2,850,448	2,803,678	36,851	9,919
1978	2,838,806	2,786,873	39,148	12,785

Source: U.S. Bureau of the Census, *Historical Statistics of the United States: Colonial Times to 1957* (Washington, D.C.: U.S. Government Printing Office, 1957), p. 710; *Statistical Abstract of U.S.*, 1975, p. 243; and 1978, p. 278.

a As of July 31.
b Includes 33,480 appointments under Youth Opportunity Company.
c As of January 31.

The Structure of the Federal Bureaucracy

Organizational charts, like Figure 16.1, call attention to the many different kinds of organizations in the executive branch and also depict legal and formal lines of authority; they tell us who can give orders to whom. Such charts are useful as long as the reader remembers that formal legal authority sometimes has very little bearing on real influence in the day-to-day operations of a governmental bureaucracy. As we have already noticed, an outside pressure group is often the key influence on a particular administrative agency, though it does not appear on the organization chart at all. And, as we will see in more detail later, subordinates often wield more real power than their superiors.

Organization charts also oversimplify by making it look as though each governmental function is neatly assigned to a particular agency or subunit within an agency. In practice, governmental organizations' functions often overlap. Consider, for example, responsibility for keeping track of the activities of labor unions in foreign countries. The labor attaché assigned to each major American embassy, though formally under the authority of the State Department, is chosen largely by the Department of Labor, with the understanding that the AFL-CIO can veto choices it does not like. The attachés have frequently been CIA agents as well, and their reports and activities are often influenced by the concerns of the Department of Commerce, the Department of Labor, the Department of Defense, or the Council on International Economic Policy in the Executive Office of the President. When the British Labour party won an election in 1946 and unexpectedly came into power, the labor attaché in our London embassy was for a time the most influential member of its staff: he had already developed close ties with key people in the new Clement Atlee government, many of whom had trade union backgrounds, while senior embassy officials hardly knew them. Organizations must have formal and legal structures, but it is necessary to examine each situation to learn who calls the shots and how often.

Links to the President and Congress

Administrative agencies have various sorts of formal ties to the President and Congress. The President can remove heads of the cabinet departments at will, but members of independent regulatory agencies, like the Interstate Commerce Commission, can be dismissed only for such specific causes as misuse of their official positions. The Federal Bureau of Investigation is a subdivision of the Justice Department, but its popularity and strong support on Capitol Hill have rendered it quite independent of its nominal superior, the attorney general, and to some extent even of the President. The Army Corps of Engineers, though officially subject to the Defense Department, enjoys similar independence because of the strong

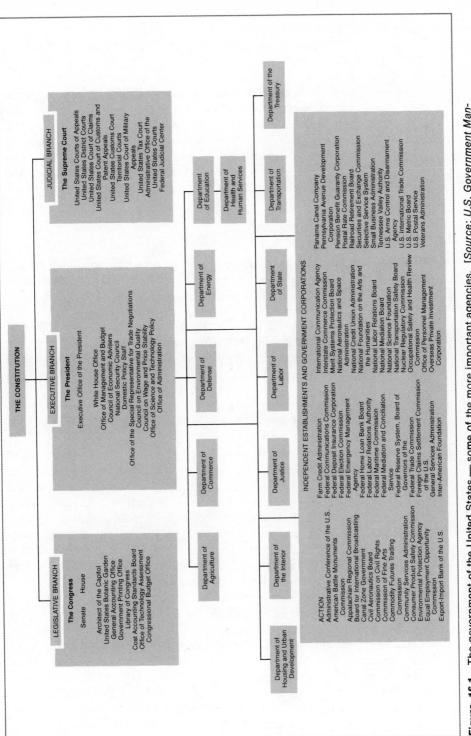

Figure 16.1 The government of the United States — some of the more important agencies. [*Source: U.S. Government Manual, 1978–1979* (Washington, D.C.: U.S. Government Printing Office, 1979), p. 28.]

support of localities in which it can create jobs by building bridges, dredging rivers, and granting other favors that also win it independent congressional backing.

Some executive branch agencies are corporations owned by the government; one such is the Tennessee Valley Authority, which generates and sells electric power, guards against flooding by means of an intricate system of dams in seven southeastern states; manufactures fertilizers, and demonstrates good farming practices. Some are service organizations, like the General Services Administration, which performs housekeeping jobs (purchasing, building, storage of equipment) for other agencies. And there are research organizations, like the National Institutes of Health.

The Civil Service System

Government jobs can be dispensed to serve a number of different purposes. Until late in the nineteenth century, federal jobs were awarded to people who had actively supported victorious political parties and candidates. Jobs were part of the spoils of office, but the spoils system also encouraged people to work for political parties, which play an important part in any government. In 1882 Congress passed the Pendleton Act, which was intended to make ability rather than party or personal loyalty the criterion for choosing federal workers. The act established a Civil Service Commission to draw up detailed rules and regulations, and Congress gradually extended the merit system to cover more employees. By 1938, 80 percent of all federal employees were covered; in 1940, 95 percent were covered.

The top officials in each agency and those on whom the President relies for general policy advice are not regarded as part of the civil service. They are ordinarily chosen because the President likes their political beliefs or because their appointment to high posts is politically advantageous for the administration — not necessarily because of skill or expertise and certainly not because they score high on a competitive examination. Cabinet secretaries and assistant secretaries, commissioners in the regulatory agencies, top White House aides, ambassadors, and some other leading figures in the executive branch fall into this group.

There have been exceptions to the merit principle. Veterans, for example, receive preference for federal employment, as a result of lobbying by the American Legion. Some agencies, such as the CIA, are exempt from hiring by civil service criteria because they claim to have special requirements. The National Labor Relations Board, established in the 1930s to prevent employers from interfering with labor unions, was allowed in its early years to discriminate in hiring in favor of people who believed in the principle of union organization. A trend toward more comprehensive application of the merit principle has been apparent, however, even in many state and city governments.

Decisionmaking in Bureaucratic Organizations

Each administrative agency is formally charged with achieving some goal the legislature has decided the people want: regulating public utility rates, ensuring that food and drugs are not contaminated, defending the nation, protecting citizens against crime, protecting lakes and air against pollution, helping cities build airports, ensuring fair incomes for farmers, protecting the interests of Indians, and thousands of comparable objectives. Most of the tasks public administrative organizations undertake involve assembling complicated facts and deciding among the claims of people with diverse personal interests and conflicting values.

Such agencies, organized in a pattern we call "bureaucratic," are basically similar regardless of field of operation. For one thing, they are hierarchical, which means that staff positions are ranked so that occupants of lower positions are formally subject to the authority of those in higher positions. The army, characterized by ranks running from commander in chief to private, is an especially clear example of a hierarchy.

The subunits into which a bureaucratic organization is divided are grouped so that each can devote its attention to a given topic and employ a staff qualified to deal with that topic. The Federal Communications Commission, for example, maintains a law department and an engineering department because every application for a broadcasting, telephone, or other communications license involves both legal and engineering questions. Sometimes an agency's organization reflects the variety of people or clients with whom it deals; thus, a welfare department may have separate subunits for the elderly, children, the handicapped, and so on. Specialization makes it possible to bring together staff members who supposedly have the skills to find the necessary facts and to interpret them.

But administrative decisions depend on more than facts. Values — judgments about what is good or bad, desirable or undesirable — also shape choices. It is commonly assumed that the laws an agency administers give it its values and that officials make judgments that will achieve those values in the particular policy areas for which they are responsible.

As an example, consider a typical National Labor Relations Board case in which an employer is charged with having fired a worker for taking an active role in a labor union. The law prohibits such a dismissal as an unfair labor practice. The employer admits firing the worker, but says that the person was a poor worker and that union activities had no part in the firing. A relatively low-level NLRB employee, called a field examiner, is sent out to find the facts. The field examiner probably interviews the employer, the discharged employee, and other workers; examines the past history of labor relations within the company; compares the work record of the fired employee with those of other workers; and looks into any other evidence he or she can turn up. The field examiner then files a report containing the "findings of fact." Other NLRB offices review the report and add their own comments. If the case is not settled by informal agreement, as are more than 80 percent of unfair labor practice charges, another NLRB official presides over a hearing at which all interested parties testify and are cross-examined. He or she then files a report, including a decision on the legality of the firing. This report is reviewed by the five-member board, which may uphold it or overturn it. Finally, the board issues a legally binding finding and order. It may, for example, find that the employer did indeed commit an unfair labor practice and order the employee reinstated, with or without retroactive pay. Or it may find that the firing was for incompetence and therefore did not violate the law.

Decision-making procedures vary in other kinds of NLRB cases and in other agencies. Some administrative decisions result not in judgments on the rights of particular individuals, but in general rules, such as a Department of Agriculture regulation specifying the proportion of adulterated matter allowed in grain intended for export. Both forms of administrative policymaking are based on the interpretation of facts in light of the values of those who make the decisions.

A realistic student of bureaucratic decisionmaking must realize that the values of an agency's staff members influence its policies no matter how high or low they rank in an organization. This is true even when administrators are supposed to limit themselves to finding facts. In the case just discussed, it is impossible for an NLRB field examiner to cast aside his or her own beliefs about unionism in deciding whether a complex set of acts in a plant amounts to antiunion discrimination; his or her conclusions are presented as facts and are bound to influence higher NLRB officials, who cannot reexamine every complaint themselves. Similarly, decisions by relatively low-level officials in American embassies are usually decisive in determining whether aliens wishing to come to the United States may do so. In making such decisions, the officials are supposed to consider the moral character of the applicant and any prior political activity potentially harmful to the United States. Obviously, no one can make such decisions except in the light of his or her own value judgments; the precedents of many such judgments influence general State Department rules about which aliens may be admitted to America and which must be kept out.

Facts are never completely objective; the values of the people who perceive them shape their meanings. Thus, administrative decisionmaking is never the wholly impersonal, expert, professional process bureaucrats often claim it is. The claim itself, however, is a way of mobilizing public opinion to support administrative policies. For example, people dislike paying higher rates for telephone service, but a public utility commission that lets the phone company increase its charges can assume that few citizens will seriously challenge its "findings of fact" about the company's need for higher earnings to cover higher production costs or future investments in equipment.

Though administrative agencies are therefore relatively free from strong pressures by consumers and unorganized clients, they must be responsive to pressures from interest groups whose resources give them political influence. Bureaucrats are in constant contact with the organized groups that have a stake in their policies. Many agency employees either begin their careers in such industries or are later employed by them. A congressional study released in September 1975 shows that 350 officials of federal regulatory agencies had once worked for the industries they were regulating; in the previous five years at least 41 high-level officials had accepted higher-paying jobs in companies they had previously regulated.[1] For these reasons it is only natural that the same goals and values are usually dominant in both the government agencies and the regulated industries, whether they are commercial airlines, television licensees, gas and electricity companies, railroads, or whatever. Such sharing of values and interests will be examined at greater length in the discussion of pressure groups in Chapter 19.

The typical result is that agency staff members come to see issues from the point of view of the groups they are supposed to regulate. It is never clear exactly how much such "regulation" is benefiting consumers and how much it simply authorizes industries to do what they would do anyway, legitimizing their actions with a governmental stamp of approval. Many studies of administrative regulation of business conclude that the second result is more common than the first.

Some bureaucratic organizations are established to help large groups of people who are politically and economically weak, rather than to regulate relatively small groups of people who are politically and economically strong. Welfare departments are set up to help the poor, public hospitals to help the sick, and education departments to help people get educations. The Bureau of Indian Affairs is supposed to protect the Indian population. These agencies do help, but they also control the politically powerless, making sure that they will not offend the economic interests, morals, and norms of the middle class.

Welfare agencies, for example, provide money to some who need it, offer counseling services that may assist people, and help clients find other governmental and private services that might be able to alleviate their problems. Yet the helping agencies regulate their clients as well. Welfare agencies are under constant pressure from conservatives and groups purporting to represent taxpayers to limit the money they give welfare recipients and to pressure them to take jobs, often on terms other workers will not accept. Welfare counseling consists largely of pressure on the poor to adopt middle-class patterns of living, raising children, keeping house, and working industriously. Most children acquire a basic education in school, and some schools provide liberating education, but virtually all schools indoctrinate their students to play the social roles that employers, the government, armed forces, and/or the middle class expect of them: to

---

[1] *Wisconsin State Journal*, 28 September 1975.

I'M STEPPING DOWN FROM THE REGULATORY COMMISSION AND GOING BACK TO THE PRESIDENCY OF MY OLD CORPORATION. THE CURRENT PRESIDENT--FRED FRIBLY-- WANTS OUT...

THAT'S TOO BAD. I DON'T KNOW WHERE WE'LL FIND A REPLACEMENT WITH YOUR DEEP UNDERSTANDING OF THE FIELD..

HAVE YOU THOUGHT OF FRED FRIBLY?

OH, GOOD IDEA!

Capitol Games. (*Source:* © by James Stevenson.)

work hard, to be loyal to superiors, and if necessary to sacrifice for the benefit of the state or the corporation. Hospitals and health departments help cure sick people, but in dealing with what they call "mental illness," they also regulate unconventional behavior, especially on the part of poor people, and drug or lock up nonconformists who resist efforts to make them conform.

This is, at least, the view of many critics. That supporters and critics of organizations to help the powerless see them so differently is itself an important political phenomenon: these agencies respond both to the groups they are established to help and to more powerful groups that want to be sure that such help is limited and accompanied by controls on unconventional and uncooperative behavior and rebelliousness. An agency head who is not sufficiently sensitive to such pressures becomes a target of public criticism and of budgetary cuts and is charged with coddling lazy people who refuse to work or failing to train students for practical work. Here again, the political analyst must be sensitive to the actual effects of administrative actions on people's lives, regardless of the formal goal of the agency in question.

Organizational Effectiveness

Every organization must adjust to the pressure groups concerned about its policies. This fact raises some important questions about administrative agencies' "effectiveness," suggesting that such judgments depend as much on the values of the student or observer of such organizations as on the agencies' acts. The Civil Aeronautics Board, for example, seems to be fairly effective at protecting the interests of the scheduled airlines, but how much protection it offers the airplane passenger and shipper is disputed. Whether it is judged a useful agency depends, therefore, on which of these goals is more important to the observer. In the same way, evaluations of a typical welfare agency depend on the relative importance to the observer of the various policies such an agency enforces. Administrative organizations reflect the values of the more powerful groups in the community and cannot survive for long if they try to do otherwise.

Bureaucratic organizations fall short of total effectiveness for another reason: they can almost never acquire enough information to make the best possible decision, no matter whose interpretation of "best" is applied. Consider the problem facing the Secret Service, which is charged with protecting the President. Such an objective is much more specific and more widely supported by public opinion than are those of most other governmental organizations; thus, it ought to be relatively easy to make the necessary policy decisions. But is it? The only way to give the President virtually complete protection from an assassination attempt is to prevent *all* public appearances. But all presidents resist such an edict and so does much of the public. So the Secret Service must adopt other strategies, all of which involve far more guessing than knowledge. How can people likely to try to shoot the President be identified in advance? How much public support and opposition will there be for detaining such people as a preventive measure when they have not committed any crime? In what cities and situations are assassination attempts most likely? What qualities are most desirable in Secret Service agents? In choosing among strategies, none of which is foolproof, which will minimize public criticism of the agency if it fails? These questions are a sample of those Secret Service policymakers must ask themselves; moreover, they must make policies without ever having definite answers. When dealing with complex issues involving economics, military planning, and social policy, the uncertainty is far greater.

■ *A Crackdown on Effectiveness: The Case of the Federal Trade Commission.* Administrative agencies that can help or hurt groups of people financially are naturally subjected to pressures that reflect the political clout of those groups. Such pressures explain administrative actions and inactions better than do the laws that create the agencies and give them their formal goals.

Congress established the Federal Trade Commission (FTC) in 1914 to protect consumers by encouraging business competition and by preventing misleading advertising. Throughout most of its history, the commission was known as a timid agency, contenting itself with token actions and wrist slaps against offending companies. But in 1975 Congress dramatically increased the commission's power. The Magnuson-Moss Act empowered the FTC to set standards for an entire industry rather than having to take on one firm at a time. At about the same time, some new appointments to the commission, especially that of Chairman Michael Pertschuk, infused the FTC with the willingness to enforce the laws effectively. During the next several years it issued regulations that required funeral home operators to disclose burial costs to grieving relatives; investigated suspected price fixing by some billion-dollar-a-year agricultural cooperatives; found some insurance companies guilty of selling millions of dollars worth of virtually worthless policies, especially to the poor and the elderly; proposed a rule that would give consumers information about major

(*Source*: From *Herblock on All Fronts,* New American Library, 1980.)

mechanical and safety defects in used cars; and proposed rules for other powerful industries as well.

The corporations affected by these actions charged that the FTC was engaging in "overregulation"; they brought pressure on Congress, which responded by considering a number of measures that would gut or kill the commission. The House of Representatives passed a bill in 1979 that would forbid the FTC from using its powers under the Magnuson-Moss Act. Other bills would prevent regulation of specific industries and would allow either house of Congress to veto an FTC rule.

These legislative threats, whether or not they become law, are clear messages that a regulatory agency should be wary about offending powerful interest groups by actually enforcing the laws it is supposed to enforce. They are also evidence that consumers have relatively little legislative influence, except in winning symbolic actions.

Bureaucratic Budgets and Policy Choices: Routines or Reassessments

Officials of any given administrative agency typically take it for granted that in the coming year the agency will continue to do as it has been doing, with minor changes that justify a somewhat higher budget. The previous year's appropriation is almost always the benchmark for deciding how much money the government will spend on the agency's programs. Reassessment of an established program seldom takes place to determine whether it ought to be drastically expanded, reduced in size, or eliminated entirely. To do so would require time and effort that are seldom available. Furthermore, administrators do not want to challenge the policies that give them their roles, jobs, and sense of accomplishment; also, they know that there is rarely any chance of winning executive and legislative support for drastic expansion. At best they can make a case for more funds to handle an increased workload, rising costs, or other relatively small additions — a budgeting strategy known as *incrementalism*.

The interest groups concerned with an agency's field of operations are a known political force with which the agency has established a more or less stable relationship; some of these groups, however, can be counted on to resist reductions in its program, while others are just as certain to resist expansion of its program. A proposal to halve the budget of the Food and Drug Administration, for example, might be welcomed by drug and food manufacturers, but would quickly elicit charges of a sellout from consumers and the opposition political party. Interest-group concern is therefore another reason why major changes in the scope of an ongoing program are rare. The expedient course for everybody concerned is to treat most budgetary decisions as routine.

That strategy is safe, easy, and almost always adopted, but it is by no means neutral with regard to who gets what. Supporters of incrementalism make the following kind of case for it. First, it is an efficient way of making most decisions, because it builds on past decisions; it would be wasteful — in fact, impossible — to reassess past decisions about the importance of each program every year or two. Second, it minimizes conflict. To accept last year's appropriation as generally appropriate means that conflicts over the basic worth of the program are not raised or fought repeatedly. Political argument is limited to marginal issues: whether, for example, the Federal Aviation Agency should be allowed to increase its spending somewhat for the improvement of electronic landing devices at commercial airports. Whether the government *should* be subsidizing commercial airlines by providing them with electronic landing devices is not raised as an issue. Decisions, in short, are made relatively easily and usually without divisive, bitter, or ideological disputes.

The opponents of incrementalism use the same observations to criticize it. It is, they say, a strategy for ignoring critical political issues while focusing on the relatively trivial ones with which incremental change is concerned. For this reason it is undemocratic and conservative in its consequences, while pretending to be democratic and liberal in its procedures and forms. Incrementalism also makes it likely that ineffective programs will continue and even expand so long as no powerful group has reason to attack them. And budget drafters' systematic focus on minor changes rather than basic programs makes it unlikely that administrators will evaluate their effectiveness either.

Regardless of the opposing arguments, incrementalism continues to be the characteristic strategy of the great majority of programs. The exceptions are chiefly emergency policies, such as those adopted in response to wartime needs, steep inflationary surges, or major depressions.

Even deliberate efforts to abandon the incremental strategy seem to have a way of flickering out. In the mid-1960s, for example, President Lyndon Johnson ordered that a system of evaluating administrative programs called Program Performance Budgeting (PPB) be adopted in all federal agencies. PPB emphasizes evaluation of the contribution of every expenditure to the achievement of specific objectives. It is designed, in short, to force administrative staffs to consider in a systematic way everything they do, rather than relying on routine incremental increases. But within a few years PPB was judged a failure and largely abandoned. It did require agencies to present their budgets in a new form, but the language used to present and justify such budgets changed more than did the agencies' acts or the care with which they assessed their goals and achievements. Here is added evidence that political pressures and values continue to influence administrative policies despite commands from on high.

Conflicts Among Powerful Interests

Agencies sometimes clash with one another over policy. The Department of Labor, for example, is traditionally sensitive to the concerns of unions and of the AFL-CIO leadership; the Department of Commerce, which maintains close ties with the National Association of Manufacturers, the U.S. Chamber of Commerce, and the Business Roundtable, can be counted on to reflect the concerns of businesspeople. When the President is considering measures to curb inflation, therefore, it can be taken for granted that the secretary of commerce will favor effective controls on wages, while the secretary of labor will be more sensitive to the political problems arising from the unions' distaste for tight wage controls, but the latter will be more willing than Commerce Department officials to support controls on industrial prices.

The Labor Department can do little to promote unions' interests with regard to many issues of grave concern to workers, because it has no jurisdiction over these issues. In a time of high unemployment, for example, the department has no power to expand the credit and money supply or otherwise encourage an upturn in business activity that would mean more jobs for the unemployed; the Federal Reserve Board, which does have such powers, includes no representatives of unions, though the law specifies that industry, banking, and agriculture must be represented on the board. The Federal Reserve Board is therefore bound to be more sensitive to businesses and banks' concerns about inflation and decline in the value of the dollar than to workers' concerns about unemployment, especially since the policies that cut unemployment sometimes promote inflation.

An especially dramatic example of infighting among administrative agencies responsive to conflicting interests was the War on Poverty in the 1960s. The Office of Economic Opportunity, established in 1964 to help the poor, was staffed largely by people dedicated to pursuing that goal with considerable zeal. In many cities agencies established by OEO aroused the opposition of local welfare departments, mayors, and other units of city and county government by bringing legal actions to force the latter to put more people on the welfare rolls and to end long-established policies that allegedly discriminated against the poor. Opponents of OEO eventually succeeded in dismantling some of its programs and in transferring others to different agencies.

Defense and Intelligence Bureaucracies

The Department of Defense

Since World War II, the Defense Department has grown so large that it dominates the federal bureaucracy, is the largest single influence on the American economy, and strongly influences public opinion. In size and influence it is hardly typical of other administrative agencies, but it *is* typical in its hierarchical organization, its close links to private interest groups, and its power to arouse popular fears and hopes.

■ *Influence and Policies.* The Department of Defense employs more than 1.3 million civilians; this figure represents about 40 percent of *all* federal government employees and substantially more workers than the largest private employer, General Motors, has on its payroll. The department spends about three-fifths of the budget of the entire executive branch, and additional large military expenditures are made by the CIA, the National Security Agency, the National Aeronautics and Space Administration, and the Department of Energy. American military spending remained fairly low throughout the nineteenth century; the sizable increases occurred at the time of World War I and especially during and after World War II.

Critics of government spending often pay little attention to the defense budget and concentrate instead on reducing appropriations for

Table 16.3

The Controllable Portion of the Federal Budget, Fiscal Year 1973
(departmental shares of the controllable budget)

Department, Agency, or Branch of Federal Government	Percent of Controllable Budget
Defense-Military	.62
Health, Education and Welfare	8
Agriculture	5
Treasury	4
Housing and Urban Development	3
Labor	3
Transportation	2
Veterans Administration	2
Commerce	1
Justice	1
State	*
Legislative	*
Judiciary	*
All other	8
Total	100

Source: M. L. Weidenbaum and D. Larkins, *The Federal Budget for 1973* (Washington, D.C.: American Enterprise Institute, 1972), p. 52. Used by permission.

* Less than 1 percent.

such functions as welfare and education. The fact is that a great many federal expenditures represent fixed obligations that cannot be controlled or changed. The people who have paid taxes into the social security system all their lives are legally entitled to the benefits they were promised. Interest on the national debt cannot be reduced by failing to appropriate it. If we focus our attention on *controllable* government outlays, it turns out that more than 60 percent of them are military expenditures, as Table 16.3 shows.

In 1947 Congress reorganized the old departments of war and navy into a new Department of Defense, though the secretaries of the army, navy, and air force remain members of the President's cabinet, along with the secretary of defense, who overshadows them. This organizational change occurred at a time when domestic shifts were also taking place in the nature and frequency of American involvement in wars and in the importance to the American economy of the production of goods for military use. Fear of attack from abroad and preparation for war are, of course, the justification for having a Department of Defense and the basis of popular support for the department and the armed forces. Since World War II, American involvement in wars has been more frequent, and such wars have lasted longer. Equally important, the definition of Russia, China, and other foreign countries as ideological threats to the United States has accustomed the American public to the idea of "cold war" — to the belief, that is, that very high levels of armament, tough military postures, resistance to diplomatic concessions, and readiness to go to war at any moment are necessary to prevent a Communist takeover of the free world. The cold war, interrupted by frequent shooting wars and American intervention in wars in various parts of the world, keeps the public anxious and supportive of the large defense budget and gives military considerations a dominant place in the formulation of all governmental policies. The department constantly publicizes foreign threats; critics charge that it helps create them by frightening potential adversaries into increasing their own military budgets so they will not fall too far behind the United States.

But the influence and policies of the Defense Department cannot be understood only as a response to military threats from abroad. The American economy has come to depend so heavily on military orders that such orders represent a major influence on economic prosperity and public economic policy. The armed forces annually buy weapons and equipment priced at an average of more than $40 billion, or about 15 percent of the goods manufactured in the United States.[2]

A number of the largest companies depend very heavily, or entirely, on military contracts, and the orders are highly concentrated. In 1971 the one hundred largest defense contractors accounted for 72 percent of the defense business.[3] Thousands of smaller firms also depend heavily on subcontracts for military goods; at least 20,000 firms do some manufacturing for the Pentagon.

Some sections of the country are especially dependent for their economic well-being on military orders. The South and California have been especially successful at attracting military orders and military bases, and the Middle West has been least successful at securing military contracts; this configuration may help explain the prominence of southerners among Pentagon supporters and of Wisconsin senators and representatives among Pentagon critics.

Foreign arms sales also cement the bond between the Pentagon and arms manufacturers, for there are both political and economic reasons to expand that trade. To the extent that a foreign country, such as Saudi Arabia, is dependent on American arms, it becomes a more reliable ally of America. And this political consideration is strengthened by several economic factors. The U.S. economy is increasingly dependent on military exports to improve its balance of trade and to provide a market for the aerospace industry. The Defense Department itself has a stake in expand-

---

[2] Tom Christoffel, David Finklehor, and Dan Gilbarg, *Up Against the American Myth* (New York: Holt, Rinehart and Winston, 1970).

[3] Murray L. Weidenbaum, *The Economics of Peacetime Defense* (New York: Praeger, 1974), p. 42.

ing the foreign market because American arms manufacturers can afford to keep more types of weapons in production and to sell them to the Pentagon more cheaply if they can sell the same weapons abroad. Little wonder, then, that U.S. foreign military sales amounted to $9.5 billion in the fiscal year ending 30 June 1975, having jumped from $3.9 billion two years earlier. These sales now account for almost a tenth of all American exports.[4]

■ *Military Expenditures.*   Probably the most salient fact of all is that truly awesome amounts of money have been invested in the pursuit of military supremacy: during the decade ending in the mid-1970s, the United States invested more than $800 billion in direct military expenditures. One critic of military spending summarized the situation this way:

> Each year the federal government spends more than 70 cents of every budget dollar on past, present, and future wars. The American people are devoting more resources to the war machine than is spent by all federal, state, and local governments on health and hospitals, education, old-age and retirement benefits, public assistance and relief, unemployment and social security, housing and community development, and the support of agriculture.[5]

Partly because the new weaponry is increasingly expensive and partly because of inflation, the military budget exceeded $130 billion in 1980 (see Figure 16.2). The United States spends one-third of the total world cost for war, though it has only 5 percent of the earth's population.

Expenditures of this size cannot help but have powerful effects throughout the economy. For one thing, an entire new industry has been created since the end of World War II. New companies, some of which do all or nearly all their business with the government, have been created to supply these needs. Fewer than thirty such companies received more than half of all defense dollars awarded in the mid-1970s.

The major defense contractors are located in two sections of the country: the aircraft and missile manufacturers and their related subcontractors tend to be centered in the Southwest and Florida, while the electronics industry is located chiefly in the northeastern states. In 1972, for example, California, Texas, and Florida received almost 34 percent of all defense expenditures. The northeastern states of New York, Connecticut, Massachusetts, New Jersey, and Pennsylvania received almost 20 percent. The other forty-two states shared the remaining 37 percent of the defense budget, none of them receiving as much as any one of the five leading companies doing business with the Defense Department. This concentration of expenditures in a few regions means that the impact of defense spending is greatly multiplied in those areas. One estimate holds, for ex-

---

[4] Emma Rothschild, "The Boom in the Death Business," *New York Review of Books* 14 (2 October 1975), pp. 7–12.
[5] Richard J. Barnet, *The Economy of Death* (New York: Atheneum, 1970), p. 5.

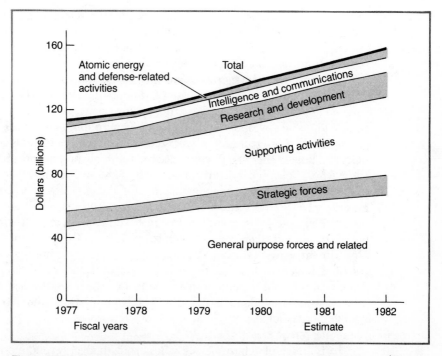

Figure 16.2 National defense programs (budget authority). [*Source*: U.S. Office of Management and Budget, *The Budget in Brief, 1980* (Washington, D.C.: U.S. Government Printing Office, 1979), p. 28.]

ample, that 43 percent of the economy of the Los Angeles area depends on direct defense expenditures and the jobs and other services they generate indirectly.[6] Cutbacks in Boeing's prime contracts in the 1969–1970 period led ultimately to unemployment levels approaching 20 percent in the Seattle area.

Though military spending creates jobs for some, it represents a substantial financial cost for most of the country. A recent study found that the Pentagon budget drains money out of 305 congressional districts and channels it into 130 districts.[7] More important, and contrary to general belief, increases in the military budget mean a decline in jobs. A study by Marion Anderson, a Michigan economist, analyzed the number of jobs created by military spending and the number that would be created by spending the same money in the civilian economy. He found that a military budget of $124 billion costs the jobs of 1,440,000 Americans, that every additional $1 billion of spending for the Pentagon costs the country 116,000

---

[6] Murray Weidenbaum, "Defense Expenditures and the Domestic Economy," in *Defense, Science, and Public Policy*, ed. Edwin Mansfield (New York: W. W. Norton, 1968), p. 25.

[7] *New York Times*, 19 November 1979, p. A18.

jobs, and that military spending is substantially more inflationary than is spending for civilian goods and services.[8]

It is difficult to imagine a more solid political base for a governmental organization than the Defense Department. The general public counts on it for security from foreign foes and ideologies, and the department maintains and intensifies that wide base of support each time it calls attention to a foreign threat, deploys troops to a "danger zone," or justifies a decision to develop a new weapons system. Underlying public opinion of this kind are politically powerful groups with economic incentive to press for a large defense budget: the largest corporations, the high proportion of the labor force whose jobs depend on military spending, and roughly two-thirds of university researchers. Few members of Congress are in a position to criticize the power generated by such an impressive bureaucracy, and presidents in the last quarter century all have made it part of their political appeal to support high levels of defense spending and expansion of Defense Department activities, even in some cases while decreasing federal appropriations for education, health, welfare, and other domestic governmental functions. Dwight Eisenhower, speaking in 1960, was the last President even to warn that dangers might be inherent in the "military-industrial complex" the defense program has brought into being as a political and economic force.

In the face of a bureaucracy whose staff, budget, economic influence, and political power are this large, the notion that administrative agencies only administer policies assigned to them by the Congress and the President becomes untenable. It is probably true enough that most people support the budget and activities of the Defense Department to the extent that they are aware of both. But it is also true that such support is elicited largely by the symbolism, public relations activities, and economic clout of the Defense Department itself. And, as was the case during the last four years of the Vietnam War, it is sometimes doubtful that there really is wide public support. Empirical research shows that most Americans opposed the war,[9] though the Nixon administration continued to claim that it was supported by a "silent majority."

■ *Personnel, Personality, and Ideology.* The Defense Department and the industries with which it does business constitute a "complex" for still another reason: many key staff members move back and forth between them, working as civilian employees of the department or as officers of the armed forces for part of their careers and as officials of large defense contractors after — or sometimes before — their stints in government. A number of secretaries of defense, army, navy, and air force previously

---

[8] Reported in *Madison Press Connection*, 8 February 1979, p. 7.
[9] John E. Mueller, *Wars, Presidents, and Public Opinion* (New York: John Wiley, 1973).

worked for major military suppliers. In 1974, 499 former Defense Department employees filed reports declaring that they were employed by major defense contractors.

An even more basic personnel link makes the boundary line between the Defense Department and the defense industry unclear. We noticed earlier that within any organization operating in a controversial policy area, the administrative staff tends to share common values and a common ideology: the values and ideology of the outside groups whose interests they reflect. This pattern is especially conspicuous in organizations responsible for military policy, a subject that elicits especially clear and strong ideological differences in the general population.

To take an extreme example, a pacifist is not likely to look for work in the Department of Defense or in a company that manufactures munitions; an employee of either organization who voices pacifist ideas will soon be made to feel unwelcome and will very likely be fired if he or she does not quit first. In the day-to-day course of a job in the Defense Department (involving, for example, planning military reactions to possible foreign threats, choosing weapons systems, lobbying Congress for higher defense appropriations, ordering equipment for the armed forces, maintaining housekeeping facilities and post exchanges at foreign and domestic military bases, or coordinating plans with the CIA), the bureaucrat's basic commitment to the ideology of military preparedness and to the possible need for military solutions to foreign problems is likely to be reinforced. People who work in defense industries, especially at the managerial level, are likely to be sympathetic to the same beliefs; if they were not, they would find it difficult to live with themselves and to work industriously at their jobs. The Defense Department is therefore the center of a defense community that reflects the society's concern with military defense and resists criticisms of militarism and of the concentration of power in a military-industrial complex.

For the same reason, the employees of any organization are typically called on to make use only of those skills and forms of thinking that contribute to the achievement of the organization's task. A lawyer for the Defense Department is expected to use his or her legal skills to make it possible for the department to do what its top officials want to do, not to criticize them. An air force deputy secretary for management systems, A. Ernest Fitzgerald, was fired for calling public attention to the contracting procedures by which the Pentagon had paid Lockheed $2 billion more than its initial estimate because costs had skyrocketed. The case was an example of *cost-plus contracting*, an arrangement under which the government pays the costs of manufacturing a product it has ordered plus a fixed profit, regardless of how high the costs turn out to be. This formula clearly rewards inefficiency. The Fitzgerald case illustrates one of the problems of bureaucracy: the pressure on people to play a narrow role in the interests of the organization, even if doing so means making inadequate use of their talents and suppressing their moral qualms. Such pressure is not always present, but it is a constant danger.

Intelligence, Spying, and Underground Operations

Like the Defense Department, the intelligence organizations became a major — and unique — feature of the federal bureaucracy only in the middle decades of the twentieth century. And like the Defense Department, they differ from conventional departments and agencies in their functions, relative freedom from congressional controls, and power.

The Federal Bureau of Investigation (FBI) was created within the Department of Justice after World War I to guard against threats to internal security from criminals and subversive political movements. Its long-time director, J. Edgar Hoover, achieved an early reputation for incorruptibility and dedication, but the FBI first won general popularity in the 1930s with its dramatic capture of John Dillinger and other colorful desperadoes. Continuous publicity for such operations and for the FBI director made the bureau a political force that was virtually untouchable on Capitol Hill and even by the President. The cold war and fear of subversion that characterized the 1950s further enhanced the FBI's political influence and budget, which has continued to grow in spite of recent criticisms.

The FBI has been charged with doing little to combat organized crime or white-collar crime, which are far more damaging to the country than are the individuals on its widely publicized list of the "Ten Most Wanted Criminals." The bureau has interfered with the civil rights of lawful dissenters, destroying reputations by reporting unverified rumors to employers and government agencies, taping tapped telephone conversations, and preventing people from exercising their rights of free speech and assembly by making them afraid of FBI harassment. It was learned in 1975 that over a period of twenty-six years, the FBI had illegally broken into several hundred houses in an effort to find evidence of subversion; these burglaries produced almost no evidence of the kind.

For the political observer or critic, such bureaucratic actions pose a question of values. In the minds of people for whom crime and subversion are overriding concerns, an agency that fights these evils deserves support even though it deprives some people of their civil rights. Many also take the position that a national police agency is justified in breaking the law in order to combat others who allegedly break the law. In the minds of those for whom civil liberties and the rights of the individual are overriding concerns, on the other hand, law enforcement as an end does not justify resorting to illegal means, especially when such tactics hurt the innocent and are typically ineffective.

While debate goes on, the FBI has continued to enjoy public, congressional, and presidential support well in excess of that given most agencies. Fear of crime and subversion runs strong and deep, and an organization widely believed to be curbing both is allowed a great deal of moral and legal leeway. Indeed, such an agency must justify its existence by discovering, or even creating, subversives.

Similar fears have given intelligence agencies a role in foreign policy that is even more powerful and independent of congressional control than that of the FBI at home. Congress created the Central Intelligence Agency (CIA) in 1947 to gather and evaluate foreign intelligence for the President under the direct supervision of the National Security Council (NSC). Almost at once, the CIA also undertook actual operations to influence the makeup, policies, and officials of governments in Western Europe, Iran, Guatemala, Greece, Cuba, Laos, Vietnam, and many other countries.

The annual budget for the CIA and for Defense Department intelligence activities is close to $10 billion. With agents in virtually every foreign capital, the CIA gathers information from public sources; operates secretly to buy information; tries to shape the activities of foreign labor, business, student, and other organizations; strengthens some foreign regimes and political parties and weakens others; and influences elections in foreign countries. It has helped overthrow lawfully chosen governments in a number of foreign countries, including Chile, Iran, and Guatemala, and has been accused of doing so — and even of plotting the assassination of foreign leaders — in many other countries. To accomplish its ends, the CIA has bought influence in foreign newspapers, circulated false rumors to embarrass political figures it opposes, and engaged directly in military operations.

Though the CIA is limited by law to foreign operations, it has for many years illegally spied on Americans at home, maintained files on U.S. citizens, opened their mail, infiltrated protest groups, tapped telephone conversations, and broken into homes.

The CIA is largely free to choose its own activities; there has been little oversight of its operations, and it is doubtful that effective limitations can be imposed on an agency that is allowed to engage in covert activities and to draw on a massive secret budget. The NSC gives the CIA formal instructions, but these inevitably allow for a great deal of discretion. And the same leeway applies within the CIA: former agents allege that even relatively low-level agents sometimes ignore limits and instructions from the director when they are convinced that a given action would be in the national interest.

The CIA's budget is hidden within that of other federal agencies, especially the Defense Department. A congressional "watchdog committee" has been able to exercise little surveillance or control, though it does serve as an assurance to the public that somebody is on the alert.

Though the CIA gathers a great deal of information, most of it from public sources, it is impossible to evaluate the agency's overall effectiveness. It failed to learn about the surprise installation of Russian ballistic missiles in Cuba in 1962 until after they were in place, failed to give adequate

"It's frightening the way some of those congressmen want to pry into our affairs." (Copyright 1975 by Herblock in *The Washington Post*.)

advance warning of the construction of the Berlin Wall in 1961, failed to warn of the impending outbreak of several wars of serious concern to U.S. interests, and was caught by surprise when a coup overthrew the Portuguese government in 1973. In 1975 the chairman of the House Select Committee on Intelligence declared that the CIA could not be counted on even to warn against a surprise military attack on the United States, a charge the CIA director vehemently denied.[10]

Whether an observer views the intelligence agencies as the bulwark against subversion or as threats to civil liberties, they are extraordinary organizations. In some respects they simply exaggerate trends displayed by all bureaucratic organizations, especially the tendency to make policy while claiming that they only administer it. The same claim is sometimes useful to the President and Congress, in that it lets them disown CIA and FBI actions that misfire or prove unpopular while allowing intelligence agencies to take covert risks and actions the government could not officially admit or defend.

---

[10] *New York Times*, 29 September 1975, p. 1. For some of our data on the CIA, we have relied on Harry Howe Ransom, *The Intelligence Establishment* (Cambridge, Mass.: Harvard University Press, 1970), and Philip Agee, *Inside the Company: CIA Diary* (New York: Penguin Books, 1975).

In sum, the Defense Department and the intelligence establishment are paramount influences on tensions abroad, economic conditions at home, and public fears and hopes. Once having acquired as much money and popular sentiment as they have, can their influence be reduced, or is it bound to grow still larger?

The Future of the Bureaucracy

Public attention is focused chiefly on the branches of government that have traditionally wielded power and made the key policy choices: the President, Congress, and the Supreme Court. But day-to-day decisions by administrative organizations seem to have an increasing impact on the quality of every citizen's life and also to predetermine a great deal of what the President, Congress, and the courts can do. Concern is widespread about the bureaucratization of society, and ever more insistent calls are heard for administrative accountability and for means by which individuals can insulate themselves from bureaucratic influence and controls.

Nonetheless, there is little reason to expect any lessening of bureaucratic power or slowing of its growth, short of holocaust. Administrative agencies have to respond to interests that can hurt them, and so they sometimes become instruments of groups that wield social and economic power. Though they combat such groups in token fashion, they also strengthen them. To survey American bureaucratic organizations is to identify the centers of power and the interests of Americans with influence; it is also to identify both the cutting edge and the cement of the contemporary governmental process.

PART
5

INSTITUTIONS
AND PROCESSES:
THE ROLES
OF NONELITES

THE POLITICAL
CONTEXT OF
NONELITES

17

The next three chapters deal with issues and relationships that stand in stark contrast to those examined in the last six chapters. Here we deal with nonelites, the overwhelming majority of relatively powerless people who have little or no wealth and no institutional positions. What are their lives like? How do their lives affect their beliefs, attitudes, and actions? How and where do the felt needs of nonelites have an impact on public policy? In short, what is the meaning — the political implications — of the context, attitudes, and actions of nonelites?

In a sense, we shall now look at the meaning and consequences of capitalism at the mass level; previously, we analyzed the workings of the major power units in the system. Immediately, we face the issues of (1) a satisfactory definition of the concept of social class, and (2) the political relevance of class and class consciousness in American politics. Our analysis begins in this chapter with an exploration of the objective conditions of nonelites' lives and certain of their subjective reactions, from which we conclude that many of the requisites of "class" and "class consciousness" are fulfilled in this country. In Chapter 18 we examine the values, ideology, and other attitudes of nonelites. We tentatively conclude that the dominant orthodoxy has diverted attention from objective circumstances and has blunted thrusts toward redress of those injustices that are perceived. Finally, in Chapter 19 we analyze the ways in which nonelites seek fulfillment of their perceived needs. For the most part, the orthodox channels — such as political parties — are managed by elites, and nonelites have only limited choices among their offerings. But alternative channels, such as strikes and demonstrations, also influence policy. Although they are costly, they can have powerful effects.

The overall thesis of these chapters is that (1) nonelites have real and unfulfilled needs, but that orthodox values and ideology inhibit recognition of the depth, scope, and shared nature of such needs ("class consciousness") and diffuse or deflect efforts to fulfill them; and (2) the orthodox channels of influence available to nonelites are arranged by elites and tend to absorb nonelites' thrusts or to convert them into harmless or mutually canceling forms. Thus, the status quo persists, and nonelites appear to generate little explicit or effective action to change it. Some observers are quick to say that they are satisfied and that the system has fulfilled all their real wants and needs. Let us examine this question step by step.

Social Context and Social Class

What is the political significance of the lives nonelites lead? In this chapter we try to understand what such lives are like and how they shape nonelite political ideas and actions. One of our focal points will be the economic status of nonelites. It is sometimes said that nonelites are becoming predominantly affluent and middle class in income and lifestyle and that this accounts for the lack of political militance on the part of working and lower classes. The weight of the evidence, however, suggests that nonelite economic status is insecure and marginal, that the gap in the quality of life between elites and nonelites does not narrow over long time periods, and that we must look elsewhere for explanations of their apparent quiescence. This issue leads to another set of questions: What needs really do exist at this level? How fully have nonelite needs actually been satisfied, and what kinds of wants that might be served through public policies still remain unfulfilled?

We also examine the extent to which nonelite life conditions justify thinking in class terms and search for indications of class consciousness among nonelites. In Chapter 11 we saw that the concept of class is meaningful for elites (that is, those who identify themselves as members of the "propertied class"). But it is much more difficult to give concrete meaning to the concept of class in the case of the much larger and less cohesive body of nonelites. If class consciousness were strong at this level, the political implications would be enormous: a powerful and cohesive force capable of significant impact on public policy would exist in the American political arena.

Definitions of Class

What do we mean by "class"? There are many definitions, some with long and emotional histories. Each definition carries a particular set of implications. Some refer only to objective characteristics of people, such as their income, education, occupational status, or relationship to the means of production (as either owners or nonowners). Others define class in subjective terms, arguing that classes exist only to the extent that people think of themselves as members of social classes, or are "class conscious." The first type of definition often amounts to no more than a set of convenient categories in the mind of the observer: such categories may have little meaning for the people involved and therefore do not say anything about their thoughts or actions. The second type of definition suggests that a class can come into existence only if people see themselves as privileged or disadvantaged, but do not connect such perceptions to any objective factors in their lives. According to this view, quite casual shared perceptions might be enough to create a "class," even if they are mistaken, or "classes" might never exist. In other words, each of these definitions requires supplementing by the other before it becomes useful.

A useful definition of class for purposes of political analysis adds to these two a third dimension — present or potential political power. The concept of class we shall use posits three conditions. First, a number of people are objectively affected in similar ways by some fundamental dynamic of the socioeconomic system. For example, wealth distribution is a fact of life, and it flows from the workings of the economic system.

Second, groups of people develop similar values, attitudes, and orientations toward the world, which are related to the objective conditions of their lives and distinguish them from other groups. For example, they have, and understand that they have, certain patterns of access to education, certain probabilities of future income or job satisfaction, and certain cultural experiences or interests related to amounts of wealth. If these first two conditions are met, a class exists. (Its members need not be conscious of how fully they share their particular situation with other people or of other factors to be noted.)

Third, for a class to have real political significance, its members must become aware that they share their situation and that the reason for their shared status is that they are similarly affected by the economic system. The realization that their status is systematically caused becomes the primary factor in their political orientation. It leads them to define their political goals and to mobilize their political power in order to defend or improve their relative positions. No other goals, interests, or loyalties take precedence over the desire to serve the class's needs in this manner. And people must (correctly) believe that political power can be mobilized for their advantage so that they are not, and do not see themselves, engaging in an empty exercise.

Political Class Consciousness

The third condition is what we mean by class consciousness in the political sense. It requires four elements: (1) recognition of a significant status shared with others, (2) identification of the systemic cause of this shared status, (3) commitment to group action with respect to this status and cause, and (4) perceived access to (real) sources of political power sufficient to make the group an effective force in politics. It is thus possible for a class to have much political significance as an independent force. But it is not possible for class consciousness to exist without the objective and subjective components of classhood to give it substance. Women will not constitute a class or its equivalent, for example, even if they all become conscious of what they share as women, unless they also perceive such characteristics as the most significant forces in their lives, define themselves politically in such terms, and find and apply political power toward sys- temic reconstruction.

We will use this concept of class to analyze the situation of nonelites and their political potential. If a class exists, there is always the possibility of class consciousness. But many forces work against it. If such forces are strong enough, and sustained enough, class consciousness may never develop. If class consciousness does develop, however, dramatic political consequences may follow. One of the continuing arguments in American politics, as we shall see, is over the existence and consciousness of an American "working class." Recently this debate has centered on the existence of a "new working class" made up of professional, technical, and other higher-level white-collar workers and students — and on the possibility that such a class might take over the historical role of the working class as an agent of change. Let us begin by describing some of the characteristics of nonelite life and work our way toward these more complex issues.

Economic and Social Conditions

Monetary and Occupational Circumstances

American affluence is celebrated and, in aggregate terms, is real. Per capita gross national product and real income are the highest in the world. Per capita personal income in 1970 was about four times higher than it was in 1900. But these figures represent averages; the high incomes of a small proportion of the population balance the low incomes of most. When the actual incomes of all families are examined, it becomes clear that the majority of Americans are either poor or economically marginal — that is, likely to drop into the ranks of the officially poor in the event of a layoff, illness, or accident.

The measurement and exact definition of economic marginality is difficult. One method is to compare income levels with the family budgets published regularly by the Bureau of Labor Statistics.[1] These are calculated for families of four living in urban areas and are set at "lower," "intermediate," and "higher" levels, according to prices of food and other goods and living standards thought to be common or appropriate to families at these levels. The intermediate budget (formerly termed the "modest but adequate" budget), for example, assumes careful shopping, modest apartment rental, and other frugal habits. And yet at no time since these budgets were first prepared in the mid-1960s had the income of any category of blue-collar worker, except certain skilled craftsmen and foremen, reached this level. Almost half of all employed males and the great majority of employed females earn incomes that fail to provide them with even "modest but adequate" standards of living. Life is far from affluent at this level, and those whose regular earnings do keep them above this line are in constant danger of dropping below it in the event of a recession or other financial reverse.

Some recurring myths about changes in the American occupational structure and about the identity of those who are poor or economically marginal might well be addressed at this point. Table 17.1 summarizes many of these changes, comparing the proportions of workers in each of the major categories in 1900, 1940, and 1970. It shows clearly, for example, that blue-collar workers are not disappearing from the labor force; to the contrary, the proportion of males in manual-work occupations has actually risen since 1900! In 1970 only half as many people were in the independent, entrepreneurial category of managers, proprietors, and farm owners as in 1900. In other words, more and more people are working for wages and salaries, and fewer own their own businesses. Long-term changes have drawn workers away from the farms and toward professional-technical and clerical-sales occupations. Women workers in particular have been concentrated in clerical positions. Black workers, who make up 11 percent of the labor force, are still most numerous in service jobs; the proportion of blacks in manual jobs is only slightly higher than the proportion for the labor force as a whole.

Financial standing is also measurable in terms of accumulated assets and liabilities. Annual surveys that measure both assets and liabilities regularly report that people have very limited funds on hand and exten-

---

[1] The basic source of data in this passage is Bureau of Labor Statistics, *Employment and Earnings*, January 1970, p. 67.

Table 17.1
Occupations of the U.S. Labor Force (percentages)

	1900			1940			1970			
	MALE	FEMALE	ALL	MALE	FEMALE	ALL	MALE	FEMALE	ALL	NONWHITE % OF ALL
Managers, officials, proprietors, farm owners	30	7	26	22	5	18	17	5	13	4
Professional-technical	3	8	4	6	13	8	14	15	14	7
Clerical and sales	7	8	8	12	29	16	13	42	24	7
Service workers	3	36	9	6	29	12	7	22	12	23
Manual workers	38	28	36	46	22	40	47	16	35	14
Farm workers	19	13	18	8	3	7	3	1	2	12
Total	100	100	100	100	100	100	100	100	100	100

Source:: *Historical Statistics of the United States; Statistical Abstract, 1970.* (Figures may not total 100%, due to rounding.)

sive debts for the purchase of cars and appliances. Sixteen percent of all families own no assets at all, and 42 percent have less than $500 in checking or saving accounts — and are thus only two or three paychecks away from public assistance of some kind.[2] Installment debts are steadily climbing, and the great majority of all families with incomes under $10,000 have debts requiring regular payments from current earnings.[3]

Many other factors enter into economic and occupational status. A major one is the prospect of unemployment. Manual workers and other lower-paid workers are most likely to be laid off during recessions or to work only intermittently at the best of times. Less educated and less skilled workers, particularly minorities, are likely to be the last hired and the first fired; economic fluctuations thus have exaggerated effects at these levels. Technological change works particular hardship on older workers, who may not be able to find alternative employment for which they are qualified. All workers who suffer intermittent unemployment risk losing such fringe benefits as medical and hospitalization insurance. In most cases, of course, the economic ups and downs of business firms occur for reasons unrelated to workers' efforts or competence, but workers nevertheless feel the effects.

Social Circumstances

Despite national affluence, the United States as a whole does not enjoy a particularly high level of social welfare. In many Western nations, for example, family allowances (payments to help support children) are a common means of sharing this financial burden and marginally redistributing income. Most have broader training and reemployment assistance programs than the United States does, and few either experience or (apparently) would tolerate the levels of unemployment that are standard in this country.

The general health conditions of Americans are not commensurate with national affluence either, and hardships are concentrated in the lower socioeconomic levels. Americans have lower life expectancies at birth than do the citizens of fifteen other nations of the world; infant mortality rates are higher than in fourteen countries, and rates of death from a variety of diseases are higher than in several other countries.[4] The lower classes, and particularly blacks, experience a higher incidence of infant mortality and higher death rates from infectious disease than do the middle and upper classes. For example, among employed males aged forty-five to sixty-

---

[2] George Katona, James N. Morgan, Joy Schmiedeskamp, and John A. Sundquist, *1967 Survey of Consumer Finances* (Ann Arbor: University of Michigan, 1967).

[3] *Statistical Abstract of the United States*, 1974, p. 397.

[4] U.S. Department of Health, Education, and Welfare, *Toward a Social Report* (Washington, D.C.: U.S. Government Printing Office, 1969), pp. 6–10. The data apply to the mid-1960s.

four, those with incomes of less than $2,000 have three-and-a-half times as many disability days as do those who earn over $7,000.

The living conditions of the working and lower classes also differ from those enjoyed by the more affluent. The most drastically substandard housing in the country is found in rural settings inhabited chiefly by the poor — and, again, principally by the black poor. Large city neighborhoods are normally crowded, and the cost per square foot of living space is frequently higher than in the suburbs. Blacks in particular have little choice over where they will live, as the nation's sharply (and in many cities, increasingly) segregated city ghettos attest.

Moreover, the incidence of crime is far higher in lower-class areas, and particularly in black neighborhoods, than elsewhere. Despite all the concern expressed by middle-class suburbanites about crime, it is the poor — and, again, the black poor — who experience most of the nation's personal crimes. Except for the theft of property, which naturally occurs more often among those who have property, the lower income levels experience more incidents of every kind of crime than do the higher levels. Whether due to the surroundings in which they live or the lack of effective police protection, crime is a condition poor people must live with to a degree unknown to the middle and upper classes.

The Persistence of Class Divisions and of Inequality

It is a striking fact about American society that disadvantaged groups as well as privileged groups are willing to accept large inequalities in wealth, income, status, and other basic values. Toleration of persisting inequality and class divisions is all the more impressive in view of the strong emphasis in American schooling and in patriotic oratory upon the United States as the land of opportunity where "all men are created equal." Objectively, classes exist and persist. Subjectively, many Americans fail to notice them, to define their own lives in terms of class, or to act politically so as to narrow or end class inequalities. The modern state allocates values unequally, while at the same time inducing people to live with the results. How does it do so?

A major part of the answer lies in the power of the most widely publicized and the most intensely debated governmental actions to create an impression of progress toward equality and of governmental sensitivity to the problems of nonelites — even when the progress is sometimes illusory and the sensitivity spotty and often nonexistent with regard to the most important forms of privilege and deprivation. The policies that are always in the news and always controversial are very largely those that promise to decrease inequalities: civil rights laws, welfare policies, affirmative action, and regulations of monopolies, public utilities, and other powerful business groups. But it is precisely these public policies that typically have little or no effect in reducing the inequalities with which they try to deal, according to the pertinent studies. They normally amount to the use of law as symbolism, tokenism, reassurance, or threat: governmental action influences mass beliefs and perceptions substantially, but changes conditions, solves problems, or meets the needs of nonelites only marginally or not at all.

The most widely publicized governmental programs, those that reassure nonelites and middle-class liberals, try to deal with inequalities by proclaiming that they will no longer be permitted to exist. Words used in this way amount to the invocation of magic to bring about a desired state of affairs; words do not solve problems simply because they are enacted into law. But they do reassure the public that progress is being made, which people very much want to believe. Such symbolic legislation lets both the privileged and the disadvantaged live with their situations and with themselves; such governmental programs do powerfully bolster the status quo, even while they promise to change it to benefit the disadvantaged.

The change such legislation brings about is typically minimal or nonexistent because it does not alter unequal resources in money, in organizational position, and in economic and social opportunities. Unequal ability to influence business, governmental, and social organizations yields still more unequal resources. Such structural inequalities are crucial. Neither political rhetoric nor legal rhetoric can make much headway against them.

By proclaiming that the interests of nonelites are protected and that the state is ensuring the fair operation of the system, the government encourages the disadvantaged to blame themselves for their misfortunes and the elite to attribute their good fortune to personal merit. The tendency to see failure and success in terms of individual choice also deters people from recognizing just how the social structure confers very different opportunities on individuals and how established inequalities perpetuate themselves.

A recently completed study of long-term trends in American wealth inequality shows substantial inequality since the seventeenth century, and it does not show a long-term trend toward greater equality.[5] The colonial era was followed by more than a century of steeply increasing concentration of wealth; by the early twentieth century, wealth concentration in the United States was as great as in France and Prussia. Equality did make significant headway during some periods, notably during World War I and between the late 1920s and midcentury — years that included the Great Depression and World War II. Since about 1950 there has been no significant change either in wealth or in income inequality, even though this thirty-year period has included the years of the War on Poverty and

---

[5] Peter H. Lindert and Jeffrey G. Williamson, "Long Term Trends in American Wealth Inequality," University of Wisconsin Institute for Research on Poverty, Discussion Paper No. 472, 1977.

a great many welfare and social programs. The study finds that "the inequality of wealthholding today resembles what it was on the eve of the Declaration of Independence."[6]

For the overwhelming majority who do not enjoy elite status, opportunities are very unequal and the quality of their lives likely to be the same as that of their parents. A new study of the relative chances of improving one's status in America shows dramatic evidence for these conclusions.[7] Consider two second graders, Bobby and Jimmy, both good students with high IQs and comparable reading skills. Bobby's father is a successful lawyer with an annual salary of more than $35,000, and Jimmy's father is a part-time messenger and janitor whose annual income is $4,800. Bobby's chance of finding a job that will put him in the top tenth of all incomes in the country is twenty-seven times as great as Jimmy's. The chances are greater than 8 to 1 that Jimmy will earn less than the median income for the population as a whole. It is family resources and status, not ability, that shape the odds a child will live well or poorly. "Class, race and sex are the most important factors in determining a child's future," according to this research. Efforts to improve the morality, character, skills, and intelligence of children do not improve equality of opportunity, for it is existing class resources that count, not individual abilities or moral traits.

Some individuals do dramatically improve their class position, of course, and others suffer declines in status and well-being, but such shifts are typically the result of individual good or bad luck, illegal or opportunistic actions, or extraordinary talent of a kind that brings high monetary rewards. They do not change economic inequality for the population as a whole, although they do partly reflect the greater willingness of some people to compete in a way that brings success in a capitalist society.

Virtually the entire American population enjoys some material and cultural benefits that were unknown in the colonial period or even seventy-five years ago. To some extent such progress comes from technological inventions and from the increased productivity of machines, but it has not reduced the gap in quality of life between elites and nonelites and in some ways has increased it. For one thing, the supply of shoddy and harmful goods and of environmental hazards has also increased.

Policy Implementation and the Persistence of Class Inequality

While public attention is focused on legislation and on the rhetoric of election campaigns and of top political executives, the governmental decisions that decisively influence how well people live usually take the form

---

[6] Ibid., p. 3.

[7] Richard DeLone, *Small Futures: Children, Inequality, and the Limits of Liberal Reform* (New York: Harcourt Brace Jovanovich, 1979). See also Christopher Jencks et al., *Inequality: A Reassessment of the Effect of Family and Schooling in America* (New York: Basic Books, 1972).

of unpublicized actions of administrators and policy implementers. This governmental activity normally receives little public attention or debate, for it is typically technical and complex, and people are taught to see it as simply the "carrying out" of the decisions of their elected representatives: the application of efficient and rational methods for accomplishing the goals reached by democratic procedures.

But these technical decisions are the critical ones, for the decisions that implementers judge to be "efficient" and "rational" usually maintain existing inequalities. When the Federal Reserve Board raises interest rates or requires banks to hold more money in their reserves in order to curb inflation, for example, the result is likely to be layoffs or poverty for thousands of people, though that result is not intentional. When the Federal Communications Commission favors an applicant for a television or radio frequency because that applicant commands large financial resources and can more credibly promise good programs and good equipment than can a struggling consumer group or minority group, the commission is being rational and efficient, but is also increasing the advantages of those who already have the most advantages. The point is that "efficiency" and "rationality" take on meaning in the context of the prevailing social and economic system. Administrators naturally look for courses of action that will preserve existing values and existing institutions, and that means the preservation of established inequalities as well. Though the statutes may declare that their goals are to protect the powerless or to benefit the deprived, these are empty words compared to the incentives administrators feel every day to respond to the groups that can help or hurt the agency's budget and their personal careers.

The public policies that matter most are shaped increasingly by networks of professionals, interest-group representatives, and administrators who work in the same policy area, such as health, energy, weapons procurement, or housing. People concerned with the same issues come to know one another, meet socially as well as in their work, and after a time learn one another's resources, tactics, and political clout. As a key result of this new importance of "issue networks," a small number of people dominate policymaking and develop a common interest in getting along with one another, even when they represent rank-and-file citizens with conflicting interests. Smoothly and subtly, therefore, policy reflects what these lobbyists, professionals, and bureaucrats believe to be the diverse resources of interest groups. For this reason as well, the gains of nonelites from public policy remain limited.[8]

The critical role of an active network of people concerned with the same issue excludes the public affected by the issue from not only involvement in policy formation, but also the kinds of information that enable

---

[8] Cf. Hugh Heclo, "Issue Networks and the Executive Establishment," in Anthony King, ed., *The New American Political System* (Washington, D.C.: American Enterprise Institute, 1978), pp. 87–124.

people to act effectively in behalf of their own interests. The public too often comes to be seen as a force to be manipulated in order to win its support rather than as people with a right to know the facts and to influence the governmental policies that affect their lives. Nuclear plant safety, the need for expensive weapons systems, the decision to close a neighborhood school, the policing of crime and of subversion, and thousands of other decisions come to be regarded as the province of experts, with the public the target of propaganda rather than the source of basic values. Policy implementers cannot survive if they do not respond to existing power concentrations; their inclination to do so is strengthened by their acceptance of prevailing beliefs that upper-class groups are respectable, meritorious, and competent and that low-status groups are often suspect, undeserving, immoral, or sick. In order to maximize economic productivity, military effectiveness, and other widely supported values, it is usually efficient to give additional resources to those who already have the largest technical resources and to impose controls on people whose role it is to provide labor, loyalty, and legitimacy for established institutions. In an environment marked by large inequalities, then, it is usually "efficient" and "rational" to perpetuate the inequalities unless the elimination of inequality is explicitly chosen as the paramount value. But the focus on technique expected of policy implementers typically means that they pay little attention to values, for the prevailing values of the society are taken for granted.

To preserve established values and institutions, it is sometimes necessary to make concessions to nonelites who resort to militant protest, riot, and disorder; such tactics by disadvantaged groups do win benefits, as our discussion of that topic in Chapter 19 demonstrates. But neither rhetoric about goals nor the promises of statutes is likely in itself to improve conditions for the disadvantaged substantially.

Social Structure or Individual Choice

We often assume that people can make choices, even when they cannot, or that elite or nonelite status is a result of conscious choice, even when it is not. In America today most people have little choice about whether to use an automobile to get to their jobs, to do their shopping, and for other necessary travel. Residential zoning, the rapid growth of suburban shopping centers and suburban factories, the decay of central cities, and the absence of public transportation have foreclosed that decision for a high proportion of the population. Yet people are urged to reduce their driving, and gasoline prices are deliberately increased to encourage the reductions. As few people have much choice, the result of such public policies has been some conservation of scarce fuel, but also a tighter financial squeeze on the poor and the working class, little inconvenience for the affluent, a spurt in oil company profits, and feelings of guilt by many who cannot reduce their gasoline use.

Poverty is similarly a condition that most poor people can do little to avoid, as the DeLone, Jencks, and other studies cited in this chapter make clear. Nonetheless, there is a strong tendency to blame all the poor for their own poverty and an equally strong tendency for the poor to blame themselves.

These examples should make it clear that the attitudes people voice and the opinions they express can often best be understood as systematically flowing from the social and economic situations in which they find themselves. Political attitudes help people to justify their own lives or to rationalize their willingness to accept a disadvantaged status without political resistance. As a part of such justifications, opinions about other social classes are also often rationalizations. Nonelites especially suffer from middle-class resentment of welfare costs; these resentments may take the form of blaming welfare recipients, whether or not the individual recipient had any choice about his or her unemployment or about receiving wages below the poverty level.

Is responsibility for either elite or nonelite status an individual decision, or is it the result of a social structure in which opportunities and advantages are very unequal? That is the critical question. Social scientists are aware that social structure is always critical, though individual decisions do account for some mobility upward and downward in the social scale. But in everyday political debate and in the minds of a large part of the population, it is far more common to blame or to praise the individual. To do so subtly excuses social and economic institutions from responsibility and implies that the ills of society can be cured if only every individual will adopt the proper attitude, work hard, and abide by the rules.

Nonelite Attitudes, Needs, and Wants Ignored by the Political System

Political analysts who call themselves "pluralists" assume that all segments of society concerned with public policy will be taken into account in a reasonably fair way. Much of our analysis in this and earlier chapters suggests that this is usually true in terms of formal procedures, but that the concerns and demands of nonelite groups are often reflected in policy largely in a tokenistic or symbolic sense. Thus, democratic forms are observed, but the promise of a fair allocation of values often is not. The political system consistently ignores two important issues involving several nonelite wants and needs: (1) those defined as subject to the decisions of private businesses rather than government, and (2) those involving such widely accepted norms that few raise them or take them seriously. Yet it is precisely these two issues that most effectively keep nonelites in their disadvantaged situations.

Voting and other means of popular influence upon governmental action have no more than the most marginal or trivial impact upon the kinds of goods and services available or the prices charged for them. If luxury goods are more profitable than necessities, as they usually are, private entrepreneurs will devote a disproportionate share of available capital and labor to the production and sale of luxuries, making it harder and more expensive for most of the population to obtain the goods and services they need. But since government interferes with such corporate decisions only in exceptional cases, this kind of policy does not appear as an issue for public choice or political discussion. To label some policy decisions that are important to how well people live as "private" and others as "governmental" is to legitimize the denial of many basic values of nonelites in a subtle but powerful way — and to do so without any public debate or discussion of the values that are produced and those that are denied.

The avoidance of public discussion about value allocations important to nonelites occurs through political socialization as well. We all learn early in life to take for granted that the fundamental value allocations to which we are accustomed will continue, with governmental decisions making only incremental changes in them. It therefore never becomes an issue for public choice or even political debate whether the basic inequalities in wealth and opportunities should be maintained or abolished: whether, for example, the distribution of income and wealth holding, described in Chapter 6, is the one Americans choose to maintain or to change substantially. Similarly, it never becomes a political issue whether the armed forces should be substantially cut or doubled in size, though we regularly (and somewhat ritualistically) increase them each year by increments in the range of 5 to 15 percent. Nor do we ever seriously consider or debate politically whether to abolish or to double social security or welfare benefits. Most of the poor and the middle class would no doubt like to become rich or more nearly equal through the same kinds of governmental subsidies, tax favors, and protections of sources of income that help the affluent, but only the affluent regularly make such demands on government because it is taken for granted that they have a good chance of winning such benefits.

Such subtle, usually unrecognized, highly effective limits on what people debate and what the government does are basic determinants of how well nonelites live. It is the underlying inequalities in value allocations, rather than the debated increments, that determine the quality of people's lives: the caliber of their education; their access to material goods and to economic, cultural, and political opportunities; and the norms by which they and their neighbors live their lives.

Symbolic Politics and Class Consciousness

People experience conflicting cues about the fairness of the advantages they enjoy and the deprivations they suffer. Clearly, working life is a source of discontent for many. But the political system helps to blur class consciousness and to justify disadvantages, partly by concessions to avoid protest and disorder, but even more important, by serving as a symbol of justice and of protection for all citizens.

Social workers who refuse to give destitute people their welfare checks unless they agree to "counseling" on how to spend their money, raise their children, and run their homes view counseling as help for the unfortunate. They refer to themselves as members of a "helping profession." Many of their clients, however, see "counseling" as demeaning and repressive interference in their private lives and as coercion to make them live by middle-class standards and values. The same phenomenon symbolizes very different things to the two groups most directly involved with it.

What counseling symbolizes for the general public determines which group has power, status, and public support. Because social workers have been able to get their perspective on this issue widely accepted by the general public, they wield the greater power. Their clients are generally perceived as people who have much more wrong with them than lack of money. The notion that they need counseling evokes a view of the poor as personally inadequate and incompetent, unable to cope with life in the way other people do and in need of guidance and even coercion to behave well. Most people do not even perceive counseling as a political issue, so completely are they "socialized" to see social work as a helping profession. Indeed, convincing the public to perceive the exercise of authority and the allocation of values as a "professional" rather than as a political issue is one of the most common and effective political techniques in contemporary society. Fortunately, beliefs and perceptions about the world and about ourselves are also often realistic and based on accurate observation. When people are directly and critically affected by readily observable political events, they are likely to base their beliefs on what they see rather than on symbolic cues. The poor in eighteenth- and nineteenth-century Europe rioted when food shortages occurred.[9] Peasants in Southeast Asia today riot or rebel when their patrons stop providing them with at least a subsistence level of food, clothing, and shelter.[10] Blacks in American urban ghettos typically base their beliefs about progress toward racial equality on what happens to them in their daily lives, not on the enactment of civil rights laws. In none of these cases is there much doubt or uncertainty about what is happening, and those most affected are realistic, though other groups may not be.

It is in ambiguous situations that evoke strong fears or hopes that symbolism becomes a powerful influence on what people believe and what they think is happening.[11] To upper-middle-class whites, the enactment

---

[9] George F. Rude, *The Crowd in History* (New York: Wiley, 1954).

[10] James Scott, "The Erosion of Patron-Client Bonds and Social Change in Rural Southeast Asia." Mimeographed.

[11] For a discussion and documentation of this point, see Murray Edelman, *Politics as Symbolic Action* (Chicago: Academic Press, 1971), pp. 19–20.

of civil rights laws is an encouraging signal that the lot of the ghetto black is improving, especially if there was a bitter struggle in Congress over passage of the law. Their evidence is news stories about the legislative outcome, not experience of life in the ghetto. For some lower-middle-class whites, the same news stories create a belief that blacks are progressing too quickly and are threatening their jobs. When hopes or fears are strong and political events cannot be observed directly, governmental acts become especially powerful symbols. But every political belief involves some mix of direct observation and symbolic cuing, although in greatly varying proportions. The hungry food rioter is close to the realistic end of the realism-symbolism scale. Close to the other end of the scale is the German in the 1930s who followed and obeyed Hitler because he or she believed Hitler's claim that the Nazis would create a glorious empire that would last a thousand years.

For most Americans most of the time, the belief that people are rewarded or deprived because of their class position rather than because of personal merit is held intermittently and is blurred. Political symbolism is a major contributor to the blurring.

What Does It Mean? The Subjective Side of Nonelite Life

This brief account of the major socieconomic and political facts of nonelite life is only part of the story. It says nothing about the feelings of people at this level about their lives, their jobs, and their prospects. And the latter may be more crucial to the actual lifestyles and potential class consciousness of such people than are the bare facts of income and job status.

People's status in their own eyes and in the opinion of others depends very largely on their jobs, their income, and their educational levels. A recent sociological study tried to learn just how each of these factors contributes to a person's social standing in America today. Figure 17.1 summarizes the findings. The arrows show what causes what, and the numbers show how great an effect each item has. The number 1.0, for example, means that income status, not surprisingly, depends entirely on income; the number 0.70 means that income status accounts for seven-tenths of a person's social standing. Figure 17.1 also shows, however, that schooling influences jobs and income directly as well as social standing indirectly; so all three factors are important to social standing.

From some other kinds of research, in which people were asked to talk about themselves, we get a deeper insight into how it feels to be a worker in a rather low-status job. In an account of her talks with General Motors auto workers at the Lordstown, Ohio, plant at a time when their union was threatening to strike, Barbara Garson paints a vivid picture of

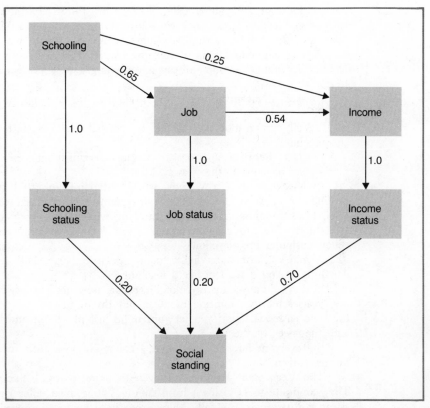

Figure 17.1 Schooling, job, and income effects on general social standing. (*Source*: Richard R. Coleman and Lee Rainwater, *Social Standing in America*, 1978, p. 282, © 1978 by Basic Books, Inc., Publishers, New York.)

how the workers see their everyday lives and especially the working conditions that dominate their lives.[12]

"My father worked in auto for thirty-five years," said a clean-cut lad, "and he never talked about the job. What's there to say? A car comes, I weld it; a car comes, I weld it; a car comes, I weld it. One hundred and one times an hour."

I asked a young wife, "What does your husband tell you about his work?"

"He doesn't say what he does. Only if something happened like 'My hair caught on fire' or 'Something fell in my face.' "

"There's a lot of variety in the paint shop," says a dapper twenty-two-year-old, up from West Virginia. "You clip on the color hose, bleed

---

[12] Extracted from *All the Livelong Day* by Barbara Garson. Copyright © 1972, 1973, 1974, 1975 by Barbara Garson. Reprinted by permission of Doubleday & Company, Inc.

out the old color, and squirt. Clip, bleed, squirt, think; clip, bleed, squirt, yawn; clip, bleed, squirt, scratch your nose. Only now the Gee-Mads have taken away the time to scratch your nose."

A long-hair reminisced, "Before the Gee-Mads, when I was on door handles, I could get a couple of cars ahead and get myself a whole minute to relax."

I asked about diversions. "What do you do to keep from going crazy?"

"Well, certain jobs like the pit you can light up a cigarette without them seeing."

"I go to the wastepaper basket. I wait a certain number of cars then find a piece of paper to throw away."

"I have fantasies. You know what I keep imagining? I see a car coming down. It's red. So I know it's gonna have a black seat, black dash, black interiors. But I keep thinking what if somebody up there sends down the wrong color interiors — like orange, and me putting in yellow cushions, bright yellow!"

"There's always water fights, paint fights, or laugh, talk, tell jokes. Anything so you don't feel like a machine."

"I don't do anything any more," says an old-timer (twenty-four with four years seniority, counting nineteen months in the Army). "I think the time passes fastest if you let your mind just phase out and blend in with the speed of the line."

But everyone has the same hope: "You're always waiting for the line to break down."

The Vega plant hires about seven thousand assembly-line workers. They commute to Lordstown from Akron, Youngstown, Cleveland, even as far as Pittsburgh. Actually, there is no Lordstown — just a plant and some trailer camps set among farmhouses. When the workers leave, they disperse throughout northern Ohio. GM presumably hoped that this location would help minimize labor troubles.

I took the guided tour of the plant. It's new, it's clean, it's well lit without windows and it's noisy. Hanging car bodies move past at the speed of a Coney Island ride slowing down. Most men work alongside the line but some stand in a man-sized pit craning their necks to work on the undersides of the cars.

I stopped to shout at a worker drinking coffee, "*Is there any quiet place to take a break?*" He shouted back, "*Can't hear you, ma'am. Too noisy to chat on a break.*" As a plant guard rushed over to separate us I spotted Duane, from Fort Lewis, shooting radios into cars with an air gun. Duane had been in the Army while I was working at a GI coffee-house. He slipped me a note with his address.

When I left the plant there were leafleteers at the gate distributing *Workers' Power*. Guards with binocular cameras closed in, snapping pictures; another guard checked everyone's ID. He copied down the names of leafleteers and workers who took papers. He took my name too.

That evening I visited Duane. He had rented a two-bedroom bungalow on the outskirts of a town that had no center. He had grown his hair a bit but, in fact, he looked neater and trimmer than when he'd been in the Army.

I told him about the incident at the gate. "Just like the Army," he said. He summarized life since his discharge: "Remember you guys gave me a giant banana split the day I ETSed [got out on schedule]? Well, it's been downhill since then. I came back to Cleveland; stayed with my dad, who was unemployed. Man, was that ever a downer. But I figured things would pick up if I got a car. But it turned out the car wasn't human and that was a problem. So I figured, 'What I need is a girl.' But it turned out the girl was human and that was a problem. So I wound up working at GM to pay off the car and the girl." And he introduced me to his lovely pregnant wife, of whom he seemed much fonder than it sounds.

A couple of Duane's high school friends, Stan and Eddie, wound up at Lordstown too. Stan at twenty-one was composed and placid, a married man with a child. Eddie at twenty-two was an excitable youth. Duane had invited them over to tell me what it's like working at the plant.

"I'll tell you what it's like," said Duane. "It's like the Army. They even use the same words, like *direct order*. Supposedly you have a contract so there's some things they just can't make you do. Except, if the foreman gives you a direct order, you do it, or you're out."

"Out?" I asked.

"Yeah, fired or else they give you a DLO — disciplinary layoff. Which means you're out without pay for however long they say. Like maybe it'll be a three-day DLO or a week DLO."

Eddie explained it further. "Like this new foreman comes up to me and says, 'Pick up that piece of paper.' Only he says it a little nastier with a few references to my race, creed, and length of hair. So I says, 'That's not my job.' He says, 'I'm giving you a direct order to pick up that piece of paper.' Finally he takes me up to the office. My committeeman comes over and tells me I could of lost my job because you can't refuse a direct order. You do it, and then you put in a grievance — HA!"

"Calling your committeeman," says Duane, "that's just like the Army too. If your CO [commanding officer] is harassing you, you can file a complaint with the IG [inspector general]. Only thing is you gotta go up to your CO and say, 'Sir, request permission to see the inspector general to tell him my commanding officer is a shit.' Same thing here. Before you can get your committeeman you got to tell the foreman exactly what your grievance is in detail. So meantime he's working out ways to tell the story different."

Here Stan took out an actual DLO form from his wallet. "Last week someone up the line put a stink bomb in a car. I do rear cushions and the foreman says, 'You get in that car.' We said, 'If you can put your head in that car we'll do the job.' So the foreman says, 'I'm giving you a direct order.' So I hold my breath and do it. My job is every other car so I let the next one pass. He gets on me and I say, 'Jack, it ain't my car. Please, I done your dirty work and the other one wasn't mine.' But he keeps at me and I wind up with a week off. Now, I got a hot committeeman who really stuck up for me. So you know what? They sent *him* home too. Gave the committeeman a DLO!

"Guy next to me, this boob Larry, he puts in alternators and they changed it to a one-man job. So he lets half the cars get away. Then he calls the committeeman and files a seventy-eight [a grievance claiming that the job can't be done in the allotted time]. I walk up to him afterwards and say, 'Look at you! Now you're smiling and you're doing the goddamn job. You can wipe your ass with that grievance.' Two months later he's still doing the job just like GM wants him to. The union is saying, 'Hang on fellah, we'll help you,' and he's still on the line like a fucking machine.

"See, just like the Army," Duane repeats. "No, it's worse cause you're welded to the line. You just about need a pass to piss."

"That ain't no joke," says Eddie. "You raise your little hand if you want to go wee-wee. Then wait maybe half an hour till they find a relief man. And they write it down every time too. 'Cause you're supposed to do it on your own time, not theirs. Try it too often and you'll get a week off."

"I'd rather work in a gas station," said Stan, wistfully. "That way you pump gas, then you patch a tire, then you go to the bathroom. You do what needs doing."

"Why don't you work in a gas station?" I asked.

"You know what they pay in a gas station? I got a kid. Besides, I couldn't even get a job in a gas station. Before I got in here I was so hard up I wound up selling vacuum cleaners — $297 door to door. In a month I earned exactly $10 selling one vacuum cleaner to a laid-off steel worker, for which I'll never forgive myself."

"No worse than making cars," Eddie comforted him. "Cars are your real trap, not vacuum cleaners. You need the car to keep the job and you need the job to keep the car. And don't think they don't know it. They give you just enough work to keep up the payments. They got it planned exactly, so you can't quit."

"He's a little paranoid," Duane cautioned me.

"Look-it," says the paranoid reasonably. "They give you fifty, fifty-five hours' work for a couple of weeks. So your typical boob buys a color TV. Then they cut you back to thirty hours. There's not a married man who doesn't have bills. And the company keeps it like that so there's no way out. You're stuck for life."

I asked about future plans.

Eddie was getting out as soon as he saved enough money to travel. He thought he might work for three more months. He'd said three months when he started and it was nine months already but, "Things came up."

Duane figured he'd stay till after his wife had the baby. That way he could use the hospital plan. After that? "Maybe we'll go live on the land. I don't know. I wish someone would hand me a discharge."

Stan was a reasonable man . . . or a boob, as Eddie might have it. He knew he was going to stay. "If I'm gonna do some dumb job the rest of my life, I might as well do one that pays."

Though none of them could afford to quit, they were all eager for a strike. They'd manage somehow. For Stan it was a good investment in his future job. The others just liked the idea of giving GM a kick in the ass from the inside.

AN AUTO WORKERS' COMMUNE

Later in the week I stayed at an auto workers' commune. Like so many other young people, they were trying to make a one generational family — a homestead. Life centered, as of old, around the hearth, which was a water pipe bubbling through Bourbon. The family Bibles were the Books of the Dead — both Tibetan and Egyptian. Throughout the evening six to ten people drifted through the old house waiting for Indian Nut (out working night shift at Lordstown) and his wife, Jane (out baby-sitting).

Jane returned at midnight to prepare dinner for her husband. By 2 A.M. she complained, "They can keep them two, three, four hours over." (Overtime is mandatory for auto workers and it's not as popular at Lordstown as it is among older workers at other plants.)

At two-thirty the Nut burst in, wild-haired, wild-eyed, and sweet-smiled. He had a mildly maniacal look because his glasses were speckled with welding spatter.

"New foreman, a real Gee-mad-man. Sent a guy home for farting in a car. And another one home for yodeling."

"Yodeling?" I asked.

"Yeah, you know — " And he yodeled.

(It's common in auto plants for men to break the monotony with noise, like the banging of tin cans in jail. Someone will drop something, his partner will yell "Whaa" and then "Whaa" gets transmitted all along the line.)

"I bet there's no shop rule against farting," the Nut conjectured. "You know those porkers have been getting their 101 off the line again, and not that many of them need repairs. It's the hillbillies. Those cats have no stamina. The union calls them to a meeting, says, 'Now don't you sabotage, but don't you run. Don't do more than you can do.' And everybody cheers. But in a few days it's back to where it was. Hillbillies working so fast they ain't got time to scratch their balls. Meantime those porkers is making money even faster than they're making cars."

I ask who he means by the hillbillies. "Hillbillies is the general Ohio term for assholes, except if you happen to be a hillbilly. Then you say Polack. Fact is everybody is a hillbilly out here except me and two other guys. And they must work day shift 'cause I never see them.

"Sabotage?" says the Nut. "Just a way of letting off steam. You can't keep up with the car so you scratch it on the way past. I once saw a hillbilly drop an ignition key down the gas tank. Last week I watched a guy light a glove and lock it in the trunk. We all waited to see how far down the line they'd discover it. If you miss a car they call that sabotage. They expect the sixty-second minute. Even a machine has to sneeze. Look how they call us in weekends, hold us extra, send us home early, give us layoffs. You'd think we were machines the way they turn us on and off."

I apologized for getting Indian Nut so steamed up and keeping him awake late. "No," sighed Jane. "It always takes a couple of hours to calm him down. We never get to bed before four."

The next morning, about 1 P.M., Indian Nut cooked breakfast for all of us (about ten). One nice thing about a working class commune — bacon and eggs and potatoes for breakfast — no Granola.

Another excerpt from Barbara Garson's book calls attention to some special problems of clerical workers.[13]

Probably the most up-to-date image of factory work has seeped into our consciousness from Charlie Chaplin's *Modern Times*. And it's fairly accurate.

Despite automation the places where workers still sit or stand doing the job have not changed much. As a matter of fact the principles of division of labor haven't basically advanced since Henry Ford. And the placement, use and control of the workers is more or less unchanged since the time-and-motion, carrot-and-stick studies of Frederick Taylor.

What little literary image we have of factory work, then, remains pretty much true.

Our image of office work, on the other hand, is as widespread as it is outdated.

All day on TV situation comedy stars hatch their plots on the office phone, while soap-opera heroines have time to undergo crisis and catharsis every fifteen minutes at work.

Faced with the image of the receptionist, the boss's secretary, the doctor's nurse, it is almost impossible for a keypuncher, a copy typist, a data-control clerk to explain what she does all day or even organize it into a coherent reality in her own head.

The methods of Ford and Taylor, division of labor and stop-watch supervision, which were applied to factories at the turn of the century are now being applied to offices.

At present a secretary is still somewhat master of her craft. "If you want the minutes and those three Letters of Agreement to go out by five o'clock, I won't be able to start on the Baum contract until tomorrow morning."

Word Processing and related new systems are designed to wrest this control away from secretarial workers. Letters will be dictated on tape and messengered or tubed to the typing pool. Each typist then receives a constant flow of work and can be held responsible for a specific number of lines a day. She will no longer be expected, or allowed, to schedule her own time.

In the most advanced form of Word Processing the tapes are transcribed onto paper automatically. So far these systems have produced disastrously or humorously absurd letters. Direct transcription only reveals how very much a live secretary edits illiterate dictation. But manuals are now being prepared to help executives standardize their dictation. Word Processing systems are actually aimed at controlling the output and reducing the skills of both secretaries and middle management.

Under these new systems the actual typing may not be faster but the company will be in a better position to control the pace and to hire less expensive workers. This is exactly the process that occurred when weavers or mechanics were first brought into factories.

---

[13] Excerpt from *All the Livelong Day* by Barbara Garson. Copyright © 1972, 1973, 1974, 1975 by Barbara Garson. Reprinted by permission of Doubleday & Company, Inc.

Even now the clerk-typist in the back room of an insurance company works at a superindustrial pace. Business machines control the operator's mind and motions more completely than in almost any factory situation. The repetitious processes of stamping, stapling, filing, coding are weirder and less accessible to our imagination than anything that goes on at Lordstown or Helena Rubenstein.

I interviewed articulate women who could talk for half an hour about what went on during their ten-minute break. But they could say nothing at all about what they did for the other seven hours.

These jobs are even more difficult to picture because of the prevalent false images of the "secretary" drinking coffee, answering the phone, flirting with the boss.

The work people do is typically their most important cue to their worth as human beings. It tells them whether others regard them as important people making a distinctive contribution to society or rather as replaceable objects to be used and controlled by their superiors. That theme of personal worth or lack of it is central in the talk of workers, in what they do not like to talk about, and in the social science studies of their problems and their reasons for dissatisfaction or gratification.

A high proportion of American workers are dissatisfied with their jobs. As Table 17.2 shows, satisfaction is very closely related to the level of skill a worker can bring to the job and to the prestige of the job. To realize oneself as a human being, a person must have some control over his or her own work, feel the gratification of doing it well or creatively, and be respected by others for this contribution to society. When manual work is challenging and allows the worker some independence, it can be fulfilling, as a skilled construction worker makes clear in the following statement, on page 434.

Table 17.2

Proportions in Various Occupations Who Would Choose Same Kind of Work If Beginning Career Again

Professional Occupations	Per-cent	Working-Class Occupations	Per-cent
Mathematicians	91	Skilled printers	52
Physicists	89	Paper workers	52
Biologists	89	Skilled automobile workers	41
Chemists	86	Skilled steelworkers	41
Lawyers	83	Textile workers	31
Journalists	82	Unskilled steelworkers	21
White-collar workers, cross section	43	Unskilled automobile workers	16

Source: Reprinted from Work in America: Report of a Special Task Force to the Secretary of Health, Education, and Welfare, 1972, p. 16, by permission of the MIT Press, Cambridge, Massachusetts.

I climb up on those beams every morning I'm working, and I like being way up there looking down at the world. It's a challenge up there, and the work's hardly ever routine. You have to pay attention and use your head, too, otherwise you can get into plenty of trouble in the kind of work I do. I'm a good man, and everybody on the job knows it.[14]

The talk of the Lordstown auto workers illustrates the deep resentments people feel when they are treated as children or as machines and thereby denied self-respect, the respect of others, the self-fulfillment that comes from independent exercise of their abilities. To these relatively well-paid workers, money is therefore less important than are working conditions. In their minds the job is not simply the exchange of work for pay, but subjection to demeaning controls by other people whose power comes from their ownership of the machines the workers operate.

Frustrations with discipline and with work that yields little gratification are sometimes expressed in sabotage of the employer's product. In this way, at least, a worker can exercise some autonomy, and one sensitive student of work experiences has pointed out that "being irresponsible is one of the few sources of power that lower participants have in an organization. At least they can exercise control by keeping quiet, slowing down, or not contributing when they should."[15] And, as one of the Lordstown workers points out, it is a way to slow down the line momentarily or to get a brief break when the work comes at you too quickly. To the workers the need for such measures comes from the uselessness of the channels that the corporation provides for dealing with grievances and often from the inadequacy of their union as well.

While the basic causes of job dissatisfaction are the same, white-collar workers experience some problems that blue-collar workers do not share, stemming from the romantic and false pictures of their opportunities and working conditions in the popular media and from the putdowns suffered by women. As is true of many blue-collar workers as well, the increasing automation and technical sophistication of the machines clerical workers operate has lowered the skills they need, increased managerial controls over them, and forced the workers to pay the costs of these changes both in low pay and in boredom. That work is changing in this way for many, at the same time that workers are better educated, increases their dissatisfaction both with jobs and with schooling.

Some Other Consequences of Job Dissatisfaction

The evidence that workers' subjective reactions to their jobs often influence their political beliefs is convincing. Some express them in attachments to "extremist" social and political movements and some in apathy toward

14 Lillian B. Rubin, *Worlds of Pain* (New York: Basic Books, 1976), p. 158.
15 Rosabeth Moss Kanter, *Life in Organizations* (New York: Basic Books, 1979), p. 185.

politics.[16] In both cases workers feel that they have little political efficacy, or influence, over the government and over their own lives. The appeal of charismatic religions and religious leaders, such as the "Moonies" or the Hare Krishna, to many young people in recent years may well be one expression of this tendency, especially as young workers are among the most dissatisfied with the conditions of their working lives.

Physical and mental health are closely related to working conditions as well. A careful, fifteen-year study of aging found that work satisfaction is the best predictor of how long people live, and the next best is overall "happiness."[17] Stress in one's occupation is closely associated with heart disease, peptic ulcers, arthritis, and other physical illnesses. Many studies have found a strong link between a low socioeconomic status and psychiatric symptoms and hospitalization. Lengthy unemployment is linked with high suicide rates. More generally, low status, little independence, rapid technological change, and associated problems help cause "psychosomatic illnesses, low self-esteem, anxiety, worry, tension, and impaired interpersonal relations."[18] Alcoholism, drug abuse, and suicide are common consequences.

Elements of Class and Class Consciousness

Clearly, the quality of people's lives and their satisfactions with their jobs and with themselves differ sharply with their income level and with the status and autonomy they enjoy in their occupations. In our society people are socialized to attribute such differences in socioeconomic status and "success" to personal merit or personal failings: to individual differences in ambition, intelligence, willingness to work, or natural talents. That view denies that class is a significant issue, and it implies that both the rich and the poor get pretty much what they deserve. Nonelites who are "class conscious" hold a very different value judgment: that it is systematic differences in opportunities and obstacles that account for whether people are well off, prestigious, and autonomous on the one hand or poor, demeaned, and controlled in their working lives on the other. As we have seen, some studies conclude that class differences persist over generations, but the rating of individuals that constantly goes on in schools, corporations, social welfare agencies, and psychiatric examinations reinforces the view that individual ability or disability is basic. In some degree and in some situations, everyone is likely to accept both of these views. Evidence from a study of a midwestern city in the late 1960s shows, however, that the prosperous are more inclined to focus on personal qualities as the explanation of success or failure and that the poor, especially the black

---

[16] *Work in America: Report of a Special Task Force to the Secretary of Health, Education and Welfare* (Cambridge, Mass.: MIT Press, 1972), p. 30.

[17] Ibid., p. 77.

[18] Ibid., pp. 81–91.

poor, are much more likely to attribute their low status to systematic economic social conditions.[19] This last view is a rough measure of class consciousness.

A sociologist who talked to a great many working-class people noticed that the working-class family subtly but powerfully socializes each generation to accept its class position:

> But those realities [of class] make us uncomfortable; they seem to call the lie to the mobility myth we cherish so dearly. Consequently we proliferate "people changing" programs — programs with which we hope to change the manners, the mores, and the lifeways of the poor and the working class. Then, we tell ourselves and them, they will be able to move into the more privileged sectors of the society. A comforting illusion! But one that avoids facing the structured reality that there's no room at the top and little room in the middle; that no matter what changes people or groups make in themselves, this industrial society requires a large work force to produce its goods and service its needs — a work force that generation after generation comes from working-class families. These families reproduce themselves not because they are somehow deficient or their culture aberrant, but because there are no alternatives for most of their children. Indeed, it may be the singular triumph of this industrial society — perhaps of any social order — that not only do we socialize people to their appropriate roles and stations, but that the process by which this occurs is so subtle that it is internalized and passed from parents to children by adults who honestly believe they are acting out of choices they have made in their own lifetime.[20]

Will class consciousness grow in the future, or will the better-educated middle class identify with the poor and the dissatisfied? The real question is whether, in the context of American orthodoxy, such middle-class and relatively affluent people can and will develop a sense of shared deprivation — fundamental, systemically caused — equivalent to class consciousness. Individualism is probably stronger at this level than at higher and lower levels, where class feelings have historically been more potent. It will be very difficult for such people to submerge their individualism in favor of shared class sensitivity.

In the meantime, it seems too soon to dismiss the traditional working class as a potential force for change. The manual worker has not disappeared, although the proportions of skilled workers are increasing. Blue-collar workers are for the most part poor or economically marginal. Inflation is rising, taxes are increasing, and little has been done to ease the burden on either blue- or white-collar lower-middle- or working-class people.

---

[19] William H. Form and Joan Huber (Rytina), "Ideological Beliefs on the Distribution of Power in the United States," *American Sociological Review* 34 (January 1969), p. 23.

[20] Lillian B. Rubin, *Worlds of Pain*, pp. 210–211.

But again, the basic issue is the extent to which people see their fundamental interests as shared and their plight as systemically caused and commit themselves to seeking remedies as a group. And it is at this point that the dominant orthodoxy enters in. In the next chapter we turn to the meaning of that ideology as it finds expression in the attitudes of nonelites.

Summary

The distribution of wealth, status, and influence in America is highly unequal and has been so for 250 years. Although individuals sometimes rise dramatically in socioeconomic status and others fall, the chances are overwhelming that any person born into the working class or into affluence will stay pretty much at the same level. In short, classes do exist and maintain themselves, and political influence is determined largely by the class structure.

But consciousness of class is blurred in the United States, though less so in the upper class than in the working class. Nonelites do not typically think of themselves as a class and do not often try to use political power to further their common class interests and needs. One reason for the acceptance of inequality is that governmental actions and language reassure people that their needs are being cared for and that progress is being made in removing discriminatory practices. Class consciousness is also blurred by an ideology of individualism that attributes success or deprivations to individual merit or inadequacies rather than to the systematic functioning of economic and social institutions, for it creates the belief that both elites and nonelites deserve their lot in life. A rising standard of living for many, based upon exploitation of the natural resources of the country, has also helped dim class differences as a political issue.

Yet for nonelites, working life and home life are often difficult, and the hardships are resented. They give rise to health problems; to family problems; to feelings of personal and political inadequacy; to industrial inefficiency; to hostilities based on race, sex, and color; and even to sabotage on the job. It remains to be seen whether the economic problems of the 1980s will create more awareness among nonelites of common needs and deprivations that are not the fault of individuals and that call for common political action.

PUBLIC OPINION AND ATTITUDE CHANGE

18

In this chapter we examine the nature of public opinion, how it forms, and how it changes. In so doing we see close ties with the pattern of class-related beliefs noted in the last chapter. We also consider some of the American people's basic beliefs and doubts. Confidence in government, and indeed in established leaders in many areas of life, has been declining in the past fifteen years, as Table 18.1 suggests. And yet most people still believe in the orthodox values and want to believe in and defend their government.

Another major focus in this chapter is an attempt to understand ambivalence in opinion, including this mixture of dissatisfaction and apparent support for the status quo. We will see that channels of communication are dominated by elites and that in many respects people have to depend on cues from above before they can respond to events. Finally, we analyze influences on opinion regarding one of the most controversial issues of the 1970s and 1980s, the building of nuclear power plants.

Table 18.1

Confidence in Leaders of Social Institutions (in percentages)

Institution	1966	1971	1974
Medicine	72	61	50
Military	62	27	33
Education[a]	61	37	40
Major U.S. companies	55	27	21
U.S. Supreme Court	51	23	40
Congress	42	19	18
Organized religion	41	27	32
Federal executive branch	41	23	28
Press	29	18	25
Television[b]	25	22	31
Organized labor	22	14	18

Source: Hazel Erskine and Richard L. Siegel, "Civil Liberties and the American Public," *Journal of Social Issues* 31, 2 (1975), Table 2 on p. 23. Used by permission. Notes in the original.

Question: "How much confidence do you feel in the people who are running [institution]: a great deal, only some, or hardly any?" Entries are percentages responding "a great deal."

[a] For 1974 the question specified "colleges."
[b] This question was asked about television news.

Public Opinion

Every government, even the most dictatorial or totalitarian one, must take account of public opinion, for people who feel strongly and act together can block public programs, give them the support they need to survive, or bring about the downfall of regimes. But governments take public opinion into account in many different ways. They may respond to it, as pluralists assume they do in democratic countries, or they may create it, as our analyses of symbolic politics show all branches of government do on some occasions. They may respond to the opinions of people who feel strongly about an issue even if they are a small minority, assuming that most of the general public, chiefly nonelites, will be uninformed, apathetic, unorganized, and therefore unable to act effectively in their own interests.

On controversial political issues there is no one public opinion, but rather many publics, and individuals are often torn or unsure where they stand. In this chapter we examine the complex nature of public opinion, the methods social scientists use to assess it and measure it, and the conditions under which it changes. To illustrate complexity and change in opinion as a combination of dependence on elites and reaction to events, we examine public attitudes toward nuclear power in the middle and later 1970s.

Key Characteristics of Public Opinion

Whatever else "democracy" means, the term suggests that government should be responsive to the interests and concerns of the people. But that idea is not as simple as it might first seem to be.

"Public opinion" is commonly spoken of as a force to which governments respond, an idea as misleading as it is reassuring. Politics involves controversy. On virtually every public issue there is a range of opinions and a range of interests among people rather than a common point of view. On the issue of whether to build the very expensive MX missile, for example, some people think that it is too costly, some doubt that it will work effectively, some maintain that it is a necessary deterrent to Soviet aggression, and some favor it because it will help win Senate support for an arms limitation treaty even if they doubt that it is needed. In addition, many other people have not heard of it, are not interested in it, or have no opinion. A news report of a Soviet buildup or a cut in the Soviet arms budget or a scientist's testimony about the MX missile's workability is likely, moreover, to shift many opinions. For every controversial issue, there are many opinions, often a substantial group with no opinion, and changes in opinion over time. Table 18.2, for example, illustrates some of the complexity of public opinion about American

Table 18.2

Popular Opinion on American Military Commitments

Attacked Nation	Send Troops	Send Supplies	Refuse to Get Involved	Don't Know
West Germany	27%	32%	33%	8%
Israel	12	42	37	9
Japan	16	35	40	9
England	37	30	24	9
India	7	34	47	12
Mexico	42	25	23	10
Thailand	10	32	46	12
Brazil	15	33	39	13
Nationalist China	8	27	54	11
Canada	57	19	14	10
Saudi Arabia	7	27	54	12
Philippines	29	34	26	11
Turkey	9	29	49	13

Source: *The Gallup Opinion Index*, Report No. 121 (July 1975), pp. 16–28. Used by permission. Cited in Dan Nimmo, *Political Communication and Public Opinion in America* (Santa Monica: Goodyear, 1978), p. 285.

Question: "In the event a nation is attacked by communist-backed forces, there are several things the U.S. can do about it—send American troops or send military supplies but not send American troops or refuse to get involved. What action would you want to see us take if _____ is attacked?"

military commitments. While it shows substantial differences in policy preferences, a more complete analysis of opinion on those issues would make it even more complicated. How many of the people who favored sending troops if West Germany were attacked would change their opinions if such an attack seemed to pose no threat to the United States? How many more would favor involvement if it did pose such a threat? How many of the opinions offered were "off the cuff" or tentative, and how many reflected strong and persisting feelings?

■ *Dimensions of Public Opinion.*   To get a useful picture of where people stand on an issue, an observer must consider a set of dimensions of opinion. One of these is *direction,* or whether people favor or oppose a particular policy proposal. A second dimension is *stability,* or how much or how little change there is in people's positions with the passage of time and with change in conditions. A third dimension is *intensity,* or how strongly people feel about their positions.

But the direction, stability, and intensity of a person's opinions about public issues are not embedded in his or her mind and personality; rather, they are created and changed by the people, events, and pressures one encounters in his or her daily activities. Some of these conditions remain largely unchanged for long periods or even for a person's lifetime. The great majority born into poverty, the working class, or affluence, respectively, will remain in the same social class, and that condition, in turn, will probably go far toward shaping their opinions on a wide range of public issues, such as attitudes toward labor unions, welfare policy, and regulation of corporate products and prices. Some opinions are linked fairly closely to specific occupations, regional locations, and other conditions that change more often than social class does but are still fairly stable. News reporters are more likely than FBI agents, for example, to rank freedom of the press high in their scale of values. People who live in the arid western states are more likely to favor federal programs to improve irrigation than are easterners who are not aware of such programs. A high proportion of hunters are likely to oppose gun control, but their ardor on that issue may cool if they give up hunting for skiing and bird watching. Social situations encourage opinions that may change in direction or in intensity as the situations change.

■ *Effect of Information.*   Opinions also depend on what information people have about public issues, and the amount and the nature of their information usually change faster than their social class or their occupations, regional location, or personal interests. As Table 18.3 dramatically shows, many people are poorly informed about political matters, but they may nonetheless hold opinions. Some who favor capital punishment may change their views after learning that being poor or black strongly increases a convicted criminal's chances of execution and that evidence of the inno-

Table 18.3

The Level of Political Information Among the Adult Public

		Year	Source
94%	Know the capital city of United States	1945	[AIPO]
94%	Know the president's term is four years	1951	[AIPO]
93%	Recognize photograph of the current president	1948	[AIPO]
89%	Can name governor of their home state	1973	[Harris]
80%	Know meaning of term "veto"	1947	[AIPO]
79%	Can name the current vice president	1978	[NORC]
78%	Know what initials "FBI" stand for	1949	[AIPO]
74%	Know meaning of the term "wiretapping"	1969	[AIPO]
70%	Can name their mayor	1967	[AIPO]
69%	Know which party has most members in U.S. House of Representatives	1978	[NORC]
68%	Know president limited to two terms	1970	[CPS]
63%	Know China to be Communist	1972	[CPS]
63%	Have some understanding of term "conservative"	1960	[SRC]
58%	Know meaning of term "open housing"	1967	[AIPO]
52%	Know that there are two U.S. senators from their state	1978	[NORC]
46%	Can name their congressman	1973	[Harris]
39%	Can name both U.S. senators from their state	1973	[Harris]
38%	Know Russia is not a NATO member	1964	[AIPO]
34%	Can name the current secretary of state	1978	[NORC]
30%	Know term of U.S. House member is two years	1978	[NORC]
31%	Know meaning of "no fault" insurance	1977	[AIPO]
28%	Can name their state senator	1967	[AIPO]
23%	Know which two nations involved in SALT	1979	[CBS/NYT]

Source: Robert S. Erikson, Norman R. Luttbeg, and Kent L. Tedin, *American Public Opinion: Its Origins, Content, and Impact*, 2d ed. (New York: Wiley, 1980), p. 19. Used by permission. Data from American Institute of Public Opinion (Gallup); Center for Political Studies; Lou Harris and Associates; National Opinion Research Center; CBS/NYT.

cence of an executed person occasionally comes to light too late. People may also misperceive facts in order to be able to retain opinions they cherish. As an extreme example, Nazi sympathizers today sometimes deny that there was any holocaust or genocide against Jews in Hitler's Germany. Or those who favor nuclear power plants are likely to interpret news about them, such as the Three Mile Island accident, as demonstrating that they are safe, while those who oppose them interpret the same news as proving that they are dangerous.

The popularity of political leaders is relatively unstable and is usually closely related to news developments that give them a chance to appear to be coping well or, by contrast, make them look ineffective. After the seizure of hostages in the American embassy in Iran in 1979, for example, the percentage of people who approved of President Carter's performance in office jumped from 32 percent to 61 percent in about three weeks.[1] In August 1980 the figure was down to 21 percent, after widespread publicity to information that the President's brother had received $220,000 from the government of Libya.

■ *Conflict and Consistency.* Still another key characteristic of a great deal of political opinion is ambivalence: the presence in a person's mind of two or more conflicting beliefs. This kind of internal conflict is a natural result of the fact that people respond to a range of other people and authorities who are often in disagreement. A great many see reports of crime in the streets as proving the need for enlarged police authority in order to maintain law and order, yet many of these same people are disturbed at reports of violations of the law and of people's civil rights by the FBI and local police departments. Whether they support one or the other of these divergent goals is likely to depend on the sympathies of those around them at the time, what news they have heard lately, or other passing cues. Reports of the results of opinion polls typically leave the impression that each human mind holds an opinion on each issue, so that supporters and opponents of a particular policy or candidate can be neatly counted as opposing forces. While that model helps to justify the results of elections and the actions of regimes, it grossly oversimplifies the human mind and its capacity for change, subtlety, complexity, and contradictory beliefs and actions.

An individual's continuing concerns often conflict with one another, producing what are sometimes called "overlapping interests" or "cross-pressures." A member of the United Automobile Workers who is prejudiced against blacks, for example, may be "cross-pressured" about the union's official stand in favor of fair employment practices. In an influential book, David Truman has argued that such overlapping interests moderate social conflict and promote stability; people who are opponents on some issues are allies on others, and such crisscrossing divisions of opinion help cement the society together.[2] If people who disagreed on foreign policy also disagreed on economic policy, educational policy, civil rights, and everything else, the society would be divided into two hostile camps, and civil war would probably be inevitable; because disagreements are moderated by cross-cutting agreements, however, we have moderation and stability.

This view is a reassuring one, and overlapping interests often do have that result, but the United States is in fact characterized by frequent out-

[1] *New York Times,* 10 December 1979, p. A22.
[2] David Truman, *The Governmental Process* (New York: Knopf, 1951).

breaks of violence, deep polarization of opinion, and occasional instances of riot and civil war. Critics of Truman's argument make several important points. First, it is not justifiable simply to assume that a person who holds membership in two groups with conflicting goals is in fact cross-pressured and therefore inhibited from taking a strong position. Cross-pressuring is a *subjective* condition and can be shown to exist only by empirical examination of people's actual behavior when pressured to act in inconsistent ways. Often they simply ignore one of the pressures. Furthermore, it is argued, people do not necessarily try to reduce tension in their lives; they often *seek out* tension-producing situations, including those produced by conflicting political pressures. There is evidence, for example, that voters often seek out conflicting opinions rather than selectively exposing themselves only to congenial views.[3] The implication of this finding is that cross-pressuring is not necessarily a moderating influence on pressure groups or on political conflict. It is also compatible with intense feelings, social tension, and the outbreak of political violence.

The apparent lack of consistency of many individual opinions is so striking and important and can be explained in so many different ways that it provides a useful example of the dependence of political analysis on the values and assumptions of the observer or analyst. One political scientist, Philip Converse, concluded from a study of successive opinions of the same individuals over time that "a mass public contains significant proportions of people who, for lack of information about a particular dimension of controversy, offer meaningless opinions that vary randomly in direction during repeated trials over time."[4] Converse found that the opinions of elites are more consistent because issues are more meaningful to them, so that his theory can be interpreted as a putdown of the logic or the seriousness of nonelites. But other studies challenge that conclusion. Norman Luttbeg analyzed the attitudes of "citizens" and of "community leaders" toward various local issues and found that *both* groups' opinions were organized in a logical way, though the leaders and the mass of citizens used different organizing principles.[5] How consistent a person's opinions seem to be, whether that person is an ordinary citizen or a member of an elite group, very likely turns on the reasons the issue is important or unimportant to him or her. Another political scientist, Lance Bennett, has contributed to this debate by suggesting that it is the range of social influences and pressures to which a person is subjected that determines how consistent or contradictory his or her opinions are. If Bennett is right, it does not make much sense to

---

3 Peter W. Sperlich, *Conflict and Harmony in Human Affairs: A Study of Crosspressures and Political Behavior* (Chicago: Rand McNally, 1971).

4 Philip E. Converse, "The Nature of Belief Systems in Mass Publics," in David E. Apter, ed., *Ideology and Discontent* (New York: The Free Press, 1964), p. 243.

5 Norman R. Luttbeg, "The Structure of Beliefs Among Leaders and the Public," *Public Opinion Quarterly* 32 (Fall 1968), pp. 398–409.

expect an outside observer's view of what is logical to fit people whose social situation is different from that of the observer.[6]

The Bennett view recognizes that people's opinions do not emerge from thinking machines isolated from the world, but rather from human beings in a particular class and social condition and that they are bound to reflect that condition. Opinions often serve to justify or rationalize people's high or low social status or the political actions they have supported in the past.

If opinions are responses to the past and current situations in which people find themselves, they do not necessarily tell us how people will act under circumstances different from the one in which they voiced their opinions, even though it is often assumed that responses to an opinion poll do predict future behavior. Because opinions help people accept the lives they can usually do little to change, expressions of satisfaction with political conditions are more likely to predict future behavior than are expressions of discontent. When large proportions of the American people voiced the suspicion in 1973, and again in 1979, that the very large oil price increases of those years were unnecessary and unjustified, it did not mean that there would be serious resistance to paying them or widespread demands to nationalize the oil companies or roll back the prices. People will usually accept a rationalization, such as allegations of an oil shortage, even if they feel strong ambivalence about it, rather than disrupt their lives to devote time to political action or resistance. Talk and action often serve different purposes in politics, so that the political opinions people express may not be a clue to how they will act. For this reason, as well as because opinions are often ambivalent, the results of polls must always be interpreted in the light of other information about people's social conditions and concerns.

■ *Intensity versus Numbers.* Another characteristic of public opinion is especially important to take into account in assessing the impact of opinion upon public policy. On most issues most of the public has no opinion or none that is strong enough to matter to a government agency charged with formulating policy. Farmers whose land and crops may be damaged by the path of a power line are likely to try to block the line by bringing pressure on the state public utility commission; in considering the question, however, the commission can take it for granted that most people in the state will have little interest in the question. The very nature of a great many policy proposals predetermines which groups will have strong opinions and in what direction, which will have weak opinions, and which will feel no concern. People in the first of these classes often comprise only a small minority, but if they have the incentive and the resources to act

---

[6] Lance Bennett, "Public Opinion: Problems of Description and Inference," in Susan Welch and John Comer, eds., *Public Opinion* (Palo Alto: Mayfield, 1975), pp. 117–131.

on their opinions, they are likely to be the most influential group. On issue after issue, organized and powerful elite groups therefore exert the key influence on policy, regardless of their small numbers.

On some political issues it is ideology rather than economic interest that makes the intense opinions of a small group more influential than the contrary opinions of most of the population. For a long time some 85 percent of the population has favored some form of gun control, but has had little success in achieving that goal because the small minority opposing gun control can be counted on to vote only on the basis of an official's record on that one issue, while the proponents are likely to forget that issue on election day in their concern with other matters. So far as influence on policy is concerned, intensity is often far more important than numbers.

The Mobilization of Intense Opinions in a Large Public

That people respond to different social pressures that are not necessarily logically consistent has still another important implication for policy formation. The responses that come from fears of external or internal threats can often be deliberately aroused by political leaders or interest groups and are likely to overshadow other opinions, even if the latter are more logical or more realistic. When the Johnson administration announced, misleadingly, in 1964 that American ships had been attacked while on a routine maneuver in the Tonkin Gulf, it was predictable that most Americans would respond by supporting military action against North Vietnam. More often the mobilization of intense opinions in a large part of the public depends less on deliberate lying than on the particular *interpretation* of a political development that comes to be widely accepted. When the government of Iran supported a takeover at the American embassy in Teheran by Iranian students in 1979 and the holding of 53 American hostages, many Americans responded with intense anger and favored military action or the internment of Iranians in the United States. Others saw the embassy takeover as a response to past American support for the brutal regime of the deposed Shah and so favored diplomatic negotiation. When the conflicting interpretations support alternative courses of action, a regime has the option of pursuing either course or some compromise, knowing that the action it takes is itself likely to create public support from the large number of spectators who are in conflict or are uncertain about what should be done.

Opinion Polls and Surveys

In the last forty years the taking and reporting of opinion polls has become a major influence in election campaigns and in governmental policymaking. Aspirants to public office win or lose financial backing according to how well they do in the polls, and some abandon their candidacies if they make a poor showing. Officials and candidates often shape their rhetoric and their policies to conform to what the polls say the public wants. Political spectators learn from the polls whether they are in the mainstream or are deviant. The effects of all this on who gets what from government and on the concentration or dispersal of power are substantial. Let us first examine how poll takers reach the conclusions they do and then consider their influence in contemporary politics.

Polls are based on interviews with only a small number of people. Presidential preference poll takers, for example, typically interview only 1,200 to 1,500 people, although they are usually fairly accurate in learning the preferences of the approximately 50 million who vote in presidential elections. This rather remarkable result is predictable if the respondents in the poll are so chosen that each person in the population has an equal chance to become part of the interviewed sample — that is, if the respondents are chosen in a truly random way. A sample of 1,500 respondents will produce responses that, 95 percent of the time, vary by no more than three percentage points from what the results would be if the entire population were interviewed. In a close election a 3 percent error may be enough to yield the wrong result, of course, but that outcome is not common in election polling.

The number of respondents, as well as the cost, can be reduced still further by "quota sampling" — that is, by choosing a sample that accurately reflects the various groups of the population that differ with respect to the questions asked. If it is believed that views on a controversial issue differ by religious preferences, age, and gender, for example, a sample representing the proper proportions of each of these groupings could be chosen, but there is no way to be certain which groups should be represented or to calculate the margin of error if quota sampling is used.

If we think of each citizen as a self-contained generator of opinions about candidates, issues, and causes, opinion polls are a valuable technique for making government more democratic. They might be thought of as supplementing elections by giving public officials and candidates a reading of public opinion regarding specific issues. That reassuring view of polling is in fact the view usually taken for granted when poll results are reported. It is assumed by the polling organizations and reinforced by the candidates and interest groups whose positions are supported by current poll results. There is an important sense in which polls do tell us what the people think when we might otherwise have no idea or a mistaken idea. If poll results are kept in the proper perspective and are considered in the light of everything else we know about opinion formation and change, they are certainly useful.

The proper interpretation of polls, however, is not always simple, and they easily yield misleading conclusions if they are accepted as the last word on what the public wants. The major reason is that individuals are not independent generators of their own opinions. Instead, we are all influenced by what we perceive happening around us and thus by the opinions of other people important to us.

Another, and more general, reason that the opinions individuals express cannot be taken as the only evidence of what the people want from government is that opinion polls not only reflect opinions, but also help shape them. It is not so much that they give people cues as to how to respond to specific questions, though they sometimes have that effect too. Rather, the more important function of the polls is to define for people who read them what *range* of views on public issues is realistic and respectable. What others are reported as thinking is shaped, as we have just seen, by existing conditions, and the polls in turn reinforce the same opinions by defining as extreme or as deviant views not in accord with them. As a result, the public usually supports only marginal policy changes on issue after issue.

There may be heated controversy over whether the arms budget should increase 5 percent or 15 percent, but the polls make it clear to the general public that an opinion in favor of substantially reducing the arms budget, or of tripling it, is wild and defines its holder as not to be taken seriously. In time of inflation people favor different degrees of tightness in monetary policy, but the polls constantly remind everyone that an opinion favoring the abolition of the Federal Reserve Board or a change in the board to make it reflect the interests of nonelites is deviant and not to be taken seriously. As a result, few opinions based on a vision of a different social order or political institutions different from those that exist ever appear. Polls intrigue people because they tell them what others are thinking, and in doing so they exert some democratic influence, but they are unquestionably a conservative influence as well.

The form of the question is important, for it may shape answers in several ways. A long checklist of possible answers may result in the impression that people have many strong opinions, though the checklist itself may have suggested them to the respondent. A "free-answer" question, requiring the respondent to come up with his or her own reply, may come closer to revealing real knowledge and concerns. A word or phrase in the question often taps associations that influence the response or distort it. Industrial psychologist Robert Kahn has suggested, for example, that a direct question about workers' satisfaction with their jobs strikes too close to the worker's self-esteem to be answered simply, and most workers do answer that kind of question by saying that they are moderately satisfied. According to Kahn, a worker

> tells us more only if the questions become more searching. Then we learn that he can order jobs clearly in terms of their status or desirability, wants his son to be employed differently from himself, and, if given a choice, would seek a different occupation.[7]

---

[7] Quoted in *Work in America: Report of a Special Task Force to the Secretary of Health, Education, and Welfare* (Cambridge, Mass.: MIT Press, 1972), p. 15.

Rather than asking a national sample a standardized set of questions, attitudes are sometimes probed by interviewing a group of people in depth regarding their views about issues of concern to them; this method provides a far more complete picture of opinion, but is more costly and calls for greater interviewing skill. In a subtle and revealing study of eighty-two poor men in a southern city, for example, Lewis Lipsitz sought to learn their opinions about priorities in government spending. He found that of those who thought that the government spent too much money, 79 percent identified the space program, military expenditures, or foreign aid as projects for which too much was spent; *none* named domestic welfare programs. Conversely, of those who thought that government was not spending enough money, only 5 percent said that more should be spent for space exploration, the military, or foreign aid, while 95 percent thought that domestic welfare programs should receive more funds. Summarizing his analysis, Lipsitz concludes:

> The dominant theme is the sense of being cheated: one's government is not concerned enough with one's well-being; one's government is willing to spend money on what appear to many of these men as frivolous or illegitimate enterprises while it fails to meet their own deeply felt day-to-day needs.
>
> In keeping with this sense of deprivation, we also found a desire among the poor for some sort of assistance from the government, and a series of dissatisfactions with the kind of work the government was engaged in. . . . We should acknowledge that poor people have many grievances concerning both what the government does and does not do.[8]

Lipsitz adds that in his view one of the reasons such grievances are not expressed more forcefully in politics is that political activists do not always take them up — that is, the elites who frame grievances into issues have not been concerned with these matters. Nor do poor people with grievances necessarily know how to carry them into the political arena by themselves, Lipsitz argues.

Conventional polls sometimes create the impression that the public has opinions, when it is doubtful that many people have thought about the issue or have crystallized their views except to the extent that the polls themselves have encouraged them to do so. One authority with long experience in conducting polls has cogently summarized several of our observations:

> We think of public opinion as polarized on great issues; we think of it as intense. . . . Because of the identification of public opinion with the measurements of surveys, the illusion is easily conveyed of a public which is "opinionated." . . . The public of opinion poll results no doubt acts

---

[8] Lewis Lipsitz, "On Political Belief: The Grievances of the Poor," in *Power and Community: Dissenting Essays in Political Science,* ed. Philip Green and Sanford Levinson (New York: Random House, 1970), pp. 165–167.

as a reinforcing agent in support of the public's consciousness of its own collective opinions as a definable, describable force. These published poll data may become reference points by which the individual formulates and expresses his opinions.[9]

A public that is apathetic or unsure can be made to seem "opinionated" because respondents feel some social pressure to have an answer when an interviewer for a polling organization asks a question. Nonetheless, public opinion and the polls that help us learn what it is are an important part of politics, for they influence what we know, what government does, and even what people think.

Basic Attitudes: Wants and Needs

Some Fundamental Wants and Needs

Some wants and needs are so fundamental that they barely change over time. For example, the same two responses have regularly prevailed about Americans in nearly three decades of polling. The two dominant personal hopes are good health for oneself and a better standard of living; the two dominant fears are ill health and a lower standard of living. War and peace usually rank next in each sequence. When the question is phrased in terms of hopes and fears for the country as a whole, war and peace far outdistance all others. Only economic stability ever challenges these responses.

These basic concerns seem to underlie broad support for governmental action in the social welfare field. Since responsible public opinion surveying began in the 1930s, large majorities have favored the basic social security and social assistance programs that were ultimately enacted. Public support often preceded enactment by several years or even decades, as in the case of medical care. The federal social welfare programs of the 1960s enjoyed no less support, two-thirds of the population favoring most aspects of the poverty program, aid to education, housing, the reduction of unemployment, and so forth. There can be little doubt about the strength of public demand and support for these "welfare state" policies.

But this desire for government to be of service in coping with the problems of daily living in an industrial society does not transcend some basic practical and ideological limits. Nearly equal majorities say that taxes are too high, and the lower income levels are usually most resistant to taxation. The latter fact is sometimes cited as an inconsistency on the part of those who are the probable beneficiaries of much of the social legislation to be funded by such taxes. But it may represent an insistence

---

[9] Leo Bogart, "No Opinion, Don't Know, and Maybe No Answer," *Public Opinion Quarterly* 31 (Fall 1967), p. 336.

that those who can better afford the burden of taxation should carry a larger share.

■ *Influence of the Media.* We know that Americans have a variety of attitudes and beliefs that more or less add up to an orthodoxy. What we are interested in here is the way in which these basic beliefs (unevenly distributed among different strata of the population, as we have seen) *interact* with events, perceptions, and experiences to generate a *process* of attitude formation and change that has political importance. We shall examine some characteristics of the way in which people learn about events and then try to explore the ambivalence generated as existing ideology and media-communicated cues interact with people's feelings.

One image of the communications process is that the media keep citizens informed and enable them to exercise influence over public policy. Another is that the media are a means by which elites derive support for their actions. There are ways in which the first image is correct, of course. Without information from newspapers, magazines, radio, and television, most people would have little chance of exercising influence on government at all or even of knowing when an issue of concern to them arises.

At the same time, studies of opinion formation and opinion change point unmistakably to a number of mechanisms through which mass publics are placed at a disadvantage and are subjected to both deliberate and unconscious influence by elites.[10] A substantial proportion of the people have relatively little interest in news of public affairs and do not especially try to expose themselves to it. One study, which questioned people about their knowledge and opinions on eight different public issues, found that from 22 to 55 percent of the population, depending on the issue, either had no opinion or had one but did not know what the government was doing.[11] Also relevant is the finding that much political information is "retailed" by opinion leaders to large audiences. Such a two-step flow of messages in the media gives elites, who are somewhat better educated and have somewhat higher status than the recipients of the messages, a disproportionate influence.[12]

People get most of their political information from television and radio stations that rely chiefly on a few networks to supply their news programs and from newspapers that rely heavily on a few wire services. Understandably, there is concern both about the possibility of mass manipulation and about the concentration of influence. As the late A. J. Liebling, a critic of American journalism, once remarked, "To have freedom of the press, you have to own one."

---

[10] Converse, "The Nature of Belief Systems in Mass Publics," pp. 206–261; see also Robert E. Lane and David O. Sears, *Public Opinion* (Englewood Cliffs, N.J.: Prentice-Hall, 1964), pp. 57–71.

[11] Lane and Sears, *Public Opinion*, pp. 59–60.

[12] Elihu Katz and Paul Lazarsfeld, *Personal Influence* (New York: Free Press, 1955).

On this issue, as on others we discuss, different levels of analysis yield somewhat different conclusions. Many of the major studies of mass communications conclude that the media can have only limited effect on opinions regarding political issues.[13] The human mind is not a blank slate on which those who control the media can write whatever they like. Female secretaries who are demeaned in the office will not be impressed by a television program proclaiming that the feminist movement has dramatically improved the status of women. A dedicated Republican is unlikely to change his vote even if he sees a Democratic spot commercial repeatedly. People's loyalties to their fellow workers, professions, ideologies, political parties, religions, and other beliefs are often stronger than the persuasive power of political rhetoric or drama. Studies of election campaigns typically find that they change the voting intentions of a relatively small proportion of the electorate (though that may be enough to change the result).

At another level, however, the mass media do have substantial effects by: publicizing and legitimizing established institutions, including the major political parties; justifying inequalities in power; and predetermining the political issues that people will regard as important. In other words, the very stability in opinion that some studies see as *limiting* the effects of the media is itself a significant result of media influence.

Those who want to influence the public go to great lengths to win media coverage for their points of view. The kidnapping of political figures and other violent actions of political dissenters are a dramatic way of ensuring media attention to their grievances. Opposition groups see desperate measures of this sort as sometimes necessary to win public notice, largely because the media so consistently reflect the positions of officials and other elites.[14]

In election campaigns media attention is similarly prized, and it is won increasingly by the efforts of professional campaign management firms that contrive impressions, events, and the candidates' personalities when they can. Most people, especially those with relatively low incomes and limited education, get most of their news from television. A recent study concluded that television news teaches viewers little about the issues and has no effect on voters' images of the candidates, but the same study found that viewers do learn about the issues from television commercials, including spot commercials, which therefore encourage rational voting.[15] Another

---

[13] Some studies that emphasize this conclusion are: David O. Sears and Richard E. Whitney, *Political Persuasion* (Morristown, N.J.: General Learning Press, 1973); Lee Becker et al., "The Development of Political Cognitions," in Steven H. Chaffee, ed., *Political Communication* (Beverly Hills: Sage Publications, 1975), pp. 21–64; Joseph T. Klapper, *The Effects of Mass Communication* (New York: Free Press, 1960).

[14] This point is discussed on pp. 235–236.

[15] Thomas E. Patterson and Robert D. McClure, *The Unseeing Eye* (New York: Putnam, 1976).

Table 18.4
Responses to Three Salience Measures: Fall 1974

	Issue Important Personally	Issue Talked About Most	Issue in the News
Inflation	68	67	63
Watergate	8	8	21
Other	24	24	17
Total (n = 339)	100%	99%	101%

Source: This table, drawn from "The Development of Political Cognitions" by L. B. Becker et al., is reprinted from *Political Communication* (Sage Annual Reviews of Communication Research, Vol. 4), Steven H. Chaffee, Editor, copyright 1975, p. 45 by permission of the Publisher, Sage Publications, Inc. (Beverly Hills/London).
Note: Respondents could select only one issue for each measure.

study concluded that the 1976 television debates between the presidential candidates also contributed to informed and issue-related voting.[16] These findings were based on interviews with voters. Some critics do not accept either the findings or the authors' interpretations.

Some other studies of the media analyze their long-term and more subtle effects and raise some questions about the findings just discussed. Television does have considerable influence on the issues people discuss and worry about. Table 18.4 shows a striking correlation between issues in the news and those seen as important and talked about most. The media therefore also influence the issues people forget or ignore. While crises, economic and social problems, and scandals are always in the news, the class distinctions and chronic inequalities in wealth and power that produce problems and crises are not likely to be. The media play an important part in perpetuating established conditions by shaping people's consciousness about what is inevitable, what is fair, who is meritorious, incompetent, or immoral. This result is not usually consciously planned, and it is not wholly effective, but it may well be the most important impact of the media in the second half of the twentieth century.

■ *The Basic Ideology.* One interesting illustration of the tension between felt needs and received ideology is provided by Lloyd Free and Hadley Cantril, professional students of American opinion.[17] Using the responses of a national cross section to a series of questions in 1964, they constructed

---

[16] Jack Dennis, "Impact of the Debates upon Partisan, Image and Issue Voting," in Sidney Kraus, ed., *The Great Debates 1976: Ford versus Carter* (Bloomington: Indiana University Press, 1979).

[17] Lloyd A. Free and Hadley Cantril, *The Political Beliefs of Americans* (New York: Simon & Schuster, 1968). The analysis in the following paragraphs is drawn from Chapter 3.

two "spectra" of opinion. One, called the "operational" spectrum, was composed of answers to questions regarding specific governmental actions or proposals in the areas of Medicare, poverty, housing, and aid to education. The other, labeled the "ideological" spectrum, was made up of answers to more abstract, less tangible questions about how problems ought to be solved and whether the government interferes too much in private and economic affairs. Those who consistently favored governmental assistance in the specific issue areas were labeled either strong liberals or predominantly liberal, depending on the number of affirmative responses they gave. Opposition to governmental assistance led to classification as predominantly conservative or strongly conservative. The same approach was applied to the ideological spectrum, with endorsement of governmental solutions and denial that the government interferes too much characterizing the liberal category.

When the two spectrums were compared, some very interesting and revealing findings emerged. In operational terms 65 percent of respondents were completely or predominantly liberal. But in ideological terms only 16 percent were. Fully 50 percent of respondents were ideologically conservative, compared to only 14 percent who were operationally conservative. This suggests that when it comes to a question of what government should do in a specific situation, people want action to solve problems. But when issues are cast in the form of abstract philosophies or basic values, people endorse the conservative and more traditional assumptions. In other words, the grip of ideology remains strong even in the face of specific needs and desires to the contrary. The questions that gained such support for the conservative side of the ideological spectrum involved standard American nostrums: the federal government is interfering too much — it is regulating business and interfering with the free-enterprise system; social problems could be solved if government would keep hands off and let people handle them themselves; anybody who wants work can find it; and we should rely more on individual initiative and not so much on welfare programs. No doubt some people can cheerfully voice such beliefs and can then endorse governmental action to solve problems; 46 percent of ideological conservatives were operational liberals. But people of conservative ideology gave only half as much support to liberal measures as did those of liberal ideology. And those who were conservative ideologically accounted for almost all those who were conservative operationally. Thus, the conservative nature of the ideology and its continuing strength appear to contribute importantly to resistance, even among the general public, to governmental social legislation.

■ *Implications of the Findings.* What are the implications of these findings? For one thing, they suggest a gap between rhetoric and performance. For another, they suggest that the ways in which people focus on politics and what they see as important may coincide with those differing dimensions. Those who think and perceive in ideological terms may care most about the abstract principles and rhetoric surrounding government. Those who are operationally oriented may be more concerned with solutions to concrete problems. This conjecture is confirmed by Free and Cantril's analysis of their respondents' ranking of public concerns. Ideological conservatives ranked such intangibles as preserving economic liberties and states' rights at the top of their list of concerns, while liberals gave first place to specific actions such as aid to education and ending unemployment. Thus, in addition to the familiar divisions among people along class, racial, religious, and other such lines, we must distinguish among them on the basis of perceptual orientation. The phenomenon is related to class status, but is not identical with it.

Diversions by Means of Racial Conflict and Scapegoating

Several kinds of diversions operate to deflect nonelites from making efforts to fulfill their wants and needs through coherent political action. War, which causes people to forget their differences and to unite in patriotic support for their government, is the classic example. Even if the war is unpopular, it serves as a focus for conflict that aligns people in ways other than the class-based contests that could bring fulfillment of nonelite wants and needs. Space programs, races to the moon, and other forms of international competition — particularly against communism — serve many of the same functions.

Other diversions divide groups of nonelites. Ethnic and religious conflicts and sex discrimination are examples. But the single most important diversion for all Americans is racism. Outbursts of racist violence have served to vent nonelite resentments throughout American history. Continuous systematic denigration of minority groups has provided satisfactions for those just above such minorities on the social ladder. In part, such continuing tensions are kept alive by the natural tendency of employers to seek the lowest possible labor costs. Historically, this has meant the use of minorities as cheap labor and as strikebreakers, to the detriment of white working-class wage levels. Aid to the poor has also been interpreted as aid to minorities, particularly blacks; as a result, whites have been less supportive than they might have been had they understood the potential recipients to be people like themselves.

Racism and racial tensions remain prominent focuses of nonelite attention today. Whites blame blacks for wanting too much too quickly and for not working hard enough to get it. Blacks see whites as unresponsive and racist. The more blacks seek equality, the more whites resent it, and the less either group sees its problems as caused by anything but the other. How rapidly white resistance stiffened in the 1960s is apparent in the shift in whites' opinions about whether blacks "have tried to move too fast."

Year	Yes: Too Fast	No: Not Fast Enough
1964	34%	32%
1965	49	19
1966	85	3

Reprinted by permission of the publisher from *Public Opinion Quarterly* 32 (Fall 1968), p. 522, citing a Louis Harris survey.

The differences of opinion that separated whites and blacks in the 1970s remained at the high levels to which they rose in reaction to the riots of the late 1960s. A Louis Harris national survey in 1972 showed, for example, that much of the gap still (or again) focused on integration of schools and the use of busing for the purpose.[18] Blacks wanted schools integrated by a 78 percent to 12 percent margin, compared to a 46 percent to 43 percent margin among whites. But whites opposed busing for that purpose by an overwhelming 81 percent to 14 percent margin, while blacks favored it by 50 percent to 36 percent. Similar but less dramatic differences were found in a series of other social welfare areas. Blacks also demonstrated lack of confidence in the Nixon administration's record on racial matters, while whites approved it solidly. The overall impression was one of dogged white resistance and black conviction that whites simply had no real interest in racial equality.

Other forms of scapegoating also frequently occur in American politics. Youth, protestors, and unorthodox or dissenting people have served from time to time as objects of such scapegoating. Hostility to protestors and to black demands tends to be highest among the lower echelons of nonelites. In 1971 one study found that twice as many blue-collar people expressed high hostility toward student demonstrators and black demands as did professional white-collar persons.[19]

Intolerance of dissent or unorthodoxy is a familiar feature of nonelite attitudes. It is sometimes argued that this finding means that nonelites are "undemocratic" or that elites' support for free speech and due process is the main pillar of democracy in the United States. We think it is better understood as evidence of a tendency to scapegoating, brought about by the unfulfilled wants and needs and other ambivalences we have explored.

[18] Louis Harris survey (November 1972).
[19] H. Edward Ransford, "Blue Collar Anger: Reactions to Student and Black Protest," *American Sociological Review* 37 (June 1972), p. 339.

Symbolic Politics and Public Opinion

Political Metaphors

Some of the most powerful influences on public opinion are more subtle than deliberate propaganda or dramatic news developments. The metaphors we use, usually unconsciously, to describe political events and issues also shape political thought. A metaphor describes the unknown by comparing it to something that is well known, and in doing so it highlights some features and conceals others. "A crusade for freedom" and "legalized murder" are two metaphoric descriptions of war that place it in quite different perspectives. A wage-control program can be viewed either as "a battle against inflation" or as "a subsidy to employers." Every controversial political development is described and perceived by the use of conflicting metaphors, not necessarily because of a deliberate effort to influence or to mislead (though that, of course, happens too), but because we cannot speak or think about any complex matter without resorting to metaphor. It permeates our language whether or not we are aware of it.

The particular metaphor that describes a political issue for a person reinforces the other symbolic processes. A person who works in a defense industry and fears Soviet aggression is likely to adopt the political role of defender against a foreign enemy and to see the cold war as a crusade for freedom; those who call war "legalized murder" will look like dupes or traitors. His or her beliefs, self-concept, and language reinforce one another and are, in fact, components of a single pattern of thought and behavior. They can be fully understood only as aspects of one another, and this is the important function of political language. It is always a vital part of a larger pattern of thought and action.

Political metaphors help shape both what we see as fact and how we *evaluate* political developments. Some think of abortion as a form of murder, and some think of it as a form of freedom. Whichever metaphor is in a person's mind influences what he or she imagines when reading a news story about an abortion clinic or about legalization of abortion. And, obviously, it influences whether he or she favors or opposes legal abortion.

The metaphoric mode in which people perceive complex political issues and events is an obstacle to complete understanding and to changes in perception and belief as new information becomes available. New information is ordinarily screened to conform to the metaphor, rather than allowed to change it. Two people with opposing views can read the same news about abortion clinics and both find that it confirms their earlier opinions. In this way metaphors become self-perpetuating. They are the patterns into which we fit our observations of the world. If, for example, army communiqués describe the bombing of "structures" in Southeast Asian villages, people feel better than they would if they were told that our bombs were destroying people's houses or huts; the word "structures" evokes an image of military installations rather than homes.

Political Arousal

The symbols that promote quiescence create the widespread conviction that people are being protected from the threats they fear or that those who behave unconventionally need to be restrained or punished for their own good and that of society. Protection of the public is the key symbolic theme in either case. The symbols that arouse mass publics to protest or to violence evoke the opposite expectation — that a widely feared threat to their interests is growing more ominous, that those who pose that threat are malevolent, and that these enemies must be resisted or, sometimes, exterminated. In the face of such a threat, people are generally likely to set aside the lesser conflicts that ordinarily divide them and to fight together against what they perceive as a more serious hazard to their common interests.

Political protest and militance are often based upon realistic recognition that some other group is threatening or oppressive. But mass arousal can be based upon symbolic cues when the facts are unclear, as they often are in politics. Nothing helps American "hawks" win support for larger military budgets and incursions into foreign countries as much as allegations that hawkish sentiment and action are growing in foreign countries commonly believed to be hostile. It is therefore hardly surprising that hawks in rival countries are careful to observe, publicize, and exaggerate the militaristic actions and rhetoric of their adversaries. As they observe and exaggerate their enemies' alleged escalations, rival hawks serve each others' interests; they win added public support for their opponents as well as for themselves. Nothing so powerfully contributes to antipolice sentiment and behavior in American cities or on college campuses as allegations or evidence that police are arbitrarily harassing, beating, or arresting the poor, black, or ideologically unconventional. Political conflicts of these kinds engage more people and greater passions on both sides as each adversary group comes to see the other as its enemy, bent on its repression or extermination. A new and sudden step-up in harassment typically arouses widespread fear and support for escalation on the other side. This is the general pattern of escalating political conflict on any issue that arises.

A central feature of this process is the personification of adversaries. Hostile or potentially hostile groups or nations are not seen as internally divided, though this is bound to be true of every formal organization or nation. Instead, the enemy is seen as monolithic and resolute: as loyal followers of the alien leader or oligarchy, who symbolizes evil. This view simplifies the situation, substituting a vision of malevolence for the more realistic recognition that there is a large measure of drift in policymaking, that people change their positions from time to time, and that political leaders must respond to contending groups within their own countries in order to retain their positions. Simplification promotes solidarity against, and eagerness to escalate attacks on, the enemy.

The Uses of Enemies

The choice or creation of political enemies is often a symbolic way of widening political support. Some political enemies are real enough. Migrant fruitpickers whose employer houses them and their families in shanties without sanitary facilities, underpays them, and overcharges them for necessities have a real adversary. So do prisoners arbitrarily thrown into solitary confinement because they displeased a guard. Jews in Nazi Germany had little doubt about who their enemies were. Those who have real enemies benefit from their elimination or loss of power.

There is another kind of political enemy, however, who *helps* his or her adversary politically by providing a purpose, a cherished self-concept, and political support. For the Nazis, the Jews served as a politically useful enemy. Hitler portrayed the Jews to the German people as the satanic force he had to fight to preserve the country. Without this enemy to arouse their passions, minimize their internal differences, and unite them behind him, Hitler could hardly have achieved power or maintained it as long as he did. The Americans, the Russians, and the Chinese served similar functions for one another during the cold war years. Without native radical movements, the FBI would win far less public support and far lower budgetary appropriations. In cases like these, the enemy is partly or entirely symbolic. The symbolic enemy looks the same to adversaries as real enemies do, but helps them as much as or more than hurts them. It is in the interest of such enemies not to eliminate one another, but to perpetuate one another — and to create a popular belief in the strength and aggressive plans, not vulnerability, of the enemy.

Belief in real enemies is based on empirical evidence and is relatively noncontroversial. Belief in symbolic enemies is based on rumor and social suggestion and is often highly controversial. Such beliefs tell us more about the believers than about the ostensible enemies, since they bring political and social benefits for those who hold them. For this reason, they are not easily challenged by facts incompatible with them. A group that is eager to marshal political support for its cause is likely to define as the enemy whatever adversary will most potently create and mobilize allies. A foreign country long regarded as hostile, heretics among true believers, anarchists in the early decades of the twentieth century, Communists after the Russian revolution, capitalists in the Soviet Union, the yellow peril, blacks — all have served such a political purpose.

Groups perceived as the enemy are consistently defined in ways that dehumanize them. They are seen as alien, strange, or subhuman, or a single feature or alleged mode of behavior is emphasized: their color, alleged lack of intelligence (or uncanny shrewdness), clannishness, and so on. This is politically effective because people can deliberately hurt or kill only those they do not acknowledge as sharing their own human qualities.

Political symbolism is a major influence upon public opinion because people look to politics not only for realistic understanding and control over their lives, but also for reassurance that their fears are unfounded and that their own political roles are not only justified but also noble. The language we speak and the process by which our minds accept or screen out information lend themselves both to remarkable creative accomplishments and to illusion and misperception. To recognize these dangers is not to grow cynical or to despair. It is a necessary step toward the realistic assessment of politics and an attempt to avoid its pitfalls and realize its promise. No analysis of the prospects for political change can fail to take these processes into account.

Public Opinion Formation and Change: The Case of Nuclear Power

Very likely the most critical set of governmental decisions this generation of Americans will make deals with the use of power generated by nuclear energy. The stakes are enormously high and dramatic; they involve money, safety, the quality of life, military power, and civil liberties. Little wonder that proponents and opponents of nuclear power are trying hard to mobilize public opinion.

The issue illustrates all the characteristics of public opinion we have described. Important and conflicting values are involved, as are decisions that help some people and hurt others and frequent new developments that change people's beliefs about how they will be helped or hurt. There is a great deal of uncertainty and many contradictory claims.

Let us outline some of the major influences on opinion, beginning with those that encourage people to favor nuclear power. After World War II, this technology was publicized as a plentiful new source of energy that would be cheap and that could be generated safely. This was the chief message from the Atomic Energy Commission and the power companies, and for a long time there were few rebuttals to it from authoritative sources. Whenever there is a monopoly of information on a subject, those who hold the monopoly are likely to have their views accepted. In this case a history of American confidence in technology and in engineers reinforced the early hopes for nuclear energy. The belief that nuclear power development would also increase national security through its link to the military uses of atomic energy (especially through the increased production of plutonium in a form needed both for power and for bombs) was an important consideration. Nuclear reactors were built — a step which created a large economic stake in nuclear power through jobs, stimulation of the economy in communities near the plants, and profits for stockholders throughout the country. By the late 1970s, some 12 percent of all power generated in the country was coming from nuclear plants, and many more reactors were under construction or being planned, representing large investments that generated still more pronuclear sentiment (see Figure 18.1).

Steep increases in oil prices in 1973–1974 and again in 1978–1979 and the accompanying warnings by government and industry officials of an "energy crisis" and of the economic and military dangers of American dependence on Middle Eastern oil all made nuclear energy look even more important, though many people were also skeptical, suspecting that the claims were excuses for arbitrary price increases. Economists, public officials, and others with a claim to authoritative knowledge offered conflicting views and analyses, which is frequently the case on controversial issues. On this point opinion shifted gradually toward a more serious view of the energy situation after President Carter called it the "moral equivalent of war" in April 1977, shortly after he took office. Table 18.5 shows the change in public opinion.

Groups with the strongest interest in nuclear power do everything they can through public statements, advertisements, editorials, and price increases to impress on the public the need for more nuclear plants. Their stakes are enormous. The major oil companies have bought up uranium reserves at home and abroad; 80 percent of America's uranium is owned by eight companies, five of which are oil companies. Westinghouse and General Electric together control 72 percent of the reactor market and have invested billions in nuclear technology. The director of the Westinghouse Power Systems Division estimated in 1973 that nuclear power would earn the company $300 billion by the year 2000. Utility companies expect high and continuing profits from nuclear power.

Though there were fears about nuclear reactors and opposition to them from the start, an antinuclear movement became a significant political force in the 1970s, due chiefly to disturbing information about health hazards, publicity about accidents at nuclear plants, and rising costs of nuclear energy. A public that had been sold on its benefits and reassured about its risks was now offered reasons to question both claims. Many people

Table 18.5
Seriousness of the Energy Situation

	Very Serious (%)	Fairly Serious (%)	Not at All Serious (%)	No Opinion (%)
(August 1979)	47	35	16	2
June 1979	37	36	24	3
February 1979	43	42	13	2
March/April 1978	41	39	15	5
November 1977	40	42	14	4

Source: The Gallup Poll, 2 September, 1979. Used by permission.

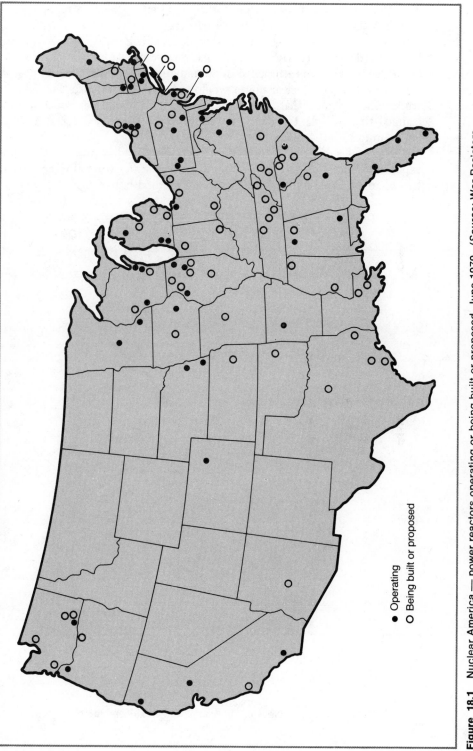

Figure 18.1 Nuclear America — power reactors operating or being built or proposed, June 1979. (*Source:* War Resisters League, 339 Lafayette Street, New York, New York 10012.)

● Operating
○ Being built or proposed

found ground for concern in news that children exposed to fallout from atomic tests in Utah during the 1950s developed leukemia at a rate 2.5 times the national average. Studies of people living near nuclear plants also showed a significantly increased incidence of cancer, which may appear as long as twenty years after exposure to radiation. Leading medical authorities predicted that nuclear power would substantially increase this hazard, while others denied that low-level radiation is a reason for concern and claimed that the plants were built to ensure the safety of workers and of communities near them.

News of accidents, of defects in the plants, and of workers ill from exposure to radiation appeared more often, sometimes years after accidents had occurred. The public learned that no method has yet been developed

(*Source*: From *Herblock on All Fronts*, New American Library, 1980.)

for safe storage of the thousands of pounds of radioactive waste materials — which remain highly toxic for thousands of years — the industry turns out every year. Protest meetings and demonstrations to prevent nuclear plant construction became more common. Evidence of efforts to suppress information about accidents, sloppy safety procedures, and illness began to surface, bringing charges of systematic attempts, in the name of plant "security," to suppress data the public needs to evaluate the issue. A popular movie, *The China Syndrome*, dramatized concern that a serious nuclear accident could kill millions of people and contaminate a large surrounding area.

These fears were crystallized in the spring of 1979, when a major accident occurred at a plant at Three Mile Island, near Harrisburg, Pennsylvania. For twelve days the country was glued to TV and radio, hearing of the possibility of serious radiation poisoning, of leaks that could not be controlled, of technological failures and "human error," of evacuation of children and pregnant women, and the possibility of more widespread evacuation. While plant and Nuclear Regulatory Commission officials assured the public that things were under control, minutes of the commission meetings released later showed that the commissioners had been far more concerned than they had told the public and that the commission had had inadequate knowledge of the facts and the dangers. Following the accident, the public was barraged with conflicting claims about how serious it had been, how much radiation had been released, and what the health hazards were, immediately and in the future. Conflicting claims about other pertinent considerations have continued to generate news stories and commentaries as well, especially the feasibility, costs, and effects on the environment of large-scale use of such alternative forms of energy as solar power, oil extracted from shale, and synthetic fuels.

In view of those contradictory pressures for and against nuclear power, what can we say about public opinion on the issue? Polls give us some information, but leave a great deal unclear, especially about the stability of opinion. A poll comparing attitudes before and immediately after the Three Mile Island accident showed a sharp drop in the percentage of the population favoring nuclear power. Table 18.6 reports responses to the question, "Would you approve or disapprove of building more nuclear

Table 18.6
Attitudes Toward Construction of More Nuclear Power Plants

	Approve	*Disapprove*
July 1977	69%	21%
April 1979	46%	41%

Source: New York Times–CBS Poll, reported in *New York Times*, 10 April 1979, p. 1. © 1972/79/80 by The New York Times Company. Reprinted by permission.

Table 18.7

Attitudes Toward Construction of Nuclear Power Plants
in Own Community

	Approve	Disapprove
July 1977	55%	33%
April 1979	36%	56%

Source: New York Times–CBS Poll, reported in *New York Times*, 10 April 1979, p. 1.
© 1972/79/80 by The New York Times Company. Reprinted by permission.

power plants?" When the question was worded to emphasize personal consequences for the respondent, approval rates dropped. Table 18.7 shows responses to the question, "Would you approve or disapprove of building more nuclear power plants in your community?"

Still, even after Three Mile Island, people apparently were more worried about an energy shortage than about safety considerations. In April 1979 the Gallup Poll put the following question to a national sample:

> Some people feel that nuclear power is essential to meet the energy needs of the nation in view of a dwindling supply of petroleum and the higher cost for this kind of fuel. Which do you think presents the greater risk to the nation — the presence of nuclear power plants or the energy shortage that might result if these plants were eliminated?

Fifty-six percent thought that an energy shortage was the greater risk; 31 percent, nuclear plants. There was little difference in opinion among geographical regions or people with different educational levels, but women were considerably more inclined than men to put safety factors ahead of economic considerations.[20]

The intensity of opinion on this issue has increased with rising fuel prices, news of an energy shortage, and fears of accidents and health hazards. But opinion has been unstable and will doubtless continue to be so because of conflicting information, conflicting interpretations of news developments, and changing perceptions of how the nuclear question is linked to other issues, such as national security and civil rights. One conclusion to be drawn from this example is that polls are bound to oversimplify the complexity and the subtlety of the human mind.

On issues that are important to people and unclear in their implications, as political issues typically are, opinions not only reflect views about public policy, but also help people to adjust to a complex and often threatening world and to justify their own roles, actions, and inactions.

---

[20] Gallup Poll release, 10 May 1979.

Summary

In a democracy governments must be responsive to what the people want, but public opinion on controversial issues is complicated. There are many publics, and they differ in what they believe, in how strongly they feel, and in how stable their opinions are. Many people have no opinion on current issues, and many are poorly informed. Individuals are often torn in their own minds about political issues, so that they may be inconsistent or shift with changes in the news or in the opinions of others.

Governments and pressure groups do a great deal to shape opinions and can often arouse intense feeling in a part of the population by appealing to fears and insecurities. In such instances a relatively small group that feels strongly may have more influence on policy than a larger public with less intense opinions.

Polls based on a small random sample can usually give a fairly accurate picture of the opinions of a much larger group. But the polls often create opinion as well as reflect it, and they rarely give an adequate picture of the complexity and ambivalence of public opinion.

People learn about political developments through the mass media, especially television. The media are limited in their influence because opinions are based to a considerable extent on people's place in the social structure, on their established loyalties, and on their economic and social roles. But the media do have a strong influence on what people pay attention to and think about, and they help legitimize established institutions.

For nonelites, and therefore for most Americans, the same basic wants and needs have remained stable over the thirty-year history of opinion polling. The dominant personal hopes are for good health and a better standard of living. The dominant hopes for the country as a whole are peace and economic stability.

PARTICIPATION:
VOTING AND
ALTERNATIVES

19

There are many forms of political participation. Most of the more effective forms — personal contact with decisionmakers, large contributions to political parties, lobbying, test cases before the Supreme Court, and extensive campaigns for or against contemplated legislation — are open chiefly to elites. Nonelites participation may take these forms, but it is for practical purposes limited to those activities in which a citizen may engage near home and with limited resources and time. Nonelite participation is distinctly low, whether measured in terms of the resources brought to bear by individuals or groups, the proportion of the people who actually use officially authorized channels, or the proportion who engage in other types of participation. Participation in the established channels, such as political parties and elections or interest groups, rises sharply with class status and varies directly with income, occupation, and education.

Political parties and interest groups tend to be both hierarchically organized and bureaucratic. Not surpris-

469

ingly, stable and self-perpetuating leadership elements develop arrangements for conducting business with one another. Often they pay more attention to their own needs or those of their leading supporters than to the interests of the mass of nonelites.

Alternative forms of participation — such as demonstrations, petitions, and ad hoc campaigns for particular goals — do arise from time to time and reveal demands for change that have gone unheeded within the established channels. But even participation in these informal processes is infrequent and low and often reflects the same class biases as do the official channels.

The reasons why nonelite political participation is both low and relatively ineffective have aroused much speculation since survey evidence first called attention to the problem. It may be that the lower classes are satisfied with the upper classes' management of the political system, that they have more economically productive uses for their time, or that they are simply uninformed or too apathetic to care about public affairs. Or they may have been convinced that their role is to accept what their betters achieve for them and that all works automatically for the best in this ingenious system. Perhaps they are too busy trying to make ends meet amid economic hardships, or they may know from past experience or intuition that it will do no good to press their goals through the established system because it is designed to permit elites to deflect, delay, and ultimately deny them. It is worth trying to resolve some of these issues. In this chapter we first explore the orthodox channels, looking particularly at the incidence and nature of participation and its meaning for the system as a whole. Then we examine some of the ways in which elites are able to manage these orthodox channels so that nonelite interests do not predominate. Finally, we look at some of the unorthodox means that have been used to express nonelite desires and demands more directly — and at some of the mixed reactions they have aroused.

Political Parties

Political parties help spectators of the political scene to make sense of the complexities of government by reducing them to a small number of key choices and by dramatizing the differences among party candidates and policies. Party organizations nominate candidates for public offices, draw up "platforms" to appeal for voter support, and so try to mobilize public opinion in order to elect their own candidates. In countries such as Italy and France, where fairly stable blocs of voters are divided on ideological grounds, usually five to eight parties regularly elect candidates to the national legislative bodies and to local offices; the various parties compete on the basis of differences in ideologies and specific issues as well as on the basis of candidates' personalities.

In the United States and in other countries with a two-party system, party competition is far less ideological, though there are sometimes differences on particular issues. The existence in any country of a two-party system has always been taken as evidence of a basic consensus in most of the population on central policy directions: that most public opinion lies in what is usually perceived as the center of the political spectrum, so that the major parties either have to appeal to that body of opinion or else keep their statements on controversial issues so fuzzy that voters will be able to read whatever they want into them. The Republicans and Democrats have usually followed that strategy, for it is the way to win votes.

Such a system has little need for policy consistency or clarity among the supporters or candidates of either party, and these qualities have seldom been conspicuous in the American major parties. Each party typically includes within its ranks a range of people from conservatives to liberals, with the center of gravity in the Democratic party usually somewhat more liberal than that in the Republican party in the last half century, except in the Deep South.

The relative unimportance of coherent policy stands in American parties is underlined by the slackness of party discipline. Only rarely and in the most flagrant cases have legislators been disciplined for opposing the positions the party has taken in its campaign platforms or in legislative caucuses, which means that the voters can have little confidence that the promises party leaders or organizations make in election campaigns will be carried out by candidates who win elections. At the same time, individual legislators are free under this party system to respond to the opinions of their constituents when they are strong or to follow their personal policy or ideological inclinations when those are strong. In the South, for example, Democratic candidates for Congress ignored the pro–civil rights positions of party platforms with impunity for many years because voter turnout was low on election day, and relatively few blacks or civil libertarians voted. With the increase in black voting and the influx of industry into the South in recent years, this situation has begun to change, resulting both in the election of Republicans from the once solidly Democratic South and in the beginning of greater Democratic responsiveness to these new constituents, at least in some districts.

Third Parties

For more than 150 years the United States has maintained the same basic two-party system. This means that with rare and temporary exceptions, only two parties have had any serious chance of winning the presidency or even a substantial minority in the Congress. A great many "third parties" have existed over the course of American history, and one of these, the Republican party, even managed to become a major party. Most American third parties (Know-Nothing, Prohibition, Populist, Greenback, Socialist, Communist, Progressive, Liberal, American Labor, Peace and Freedom, and others) have had relatively short lives. Third parties have occasionally elected candidates to public offices at every level of government except the presidency. They have chiefly espoused policy positions regarded in their times as more or less deviant or "extreme," though many of these positions gained broad popular support and eventually began to look quite conventional. The chief function of these parties for the political system has been to introduce policy innovations: to make it clear that a course of action earlier thought deviant was in fact widely supported and so to induce one or both major parties to espouse that position. Universal compulsory education for children, the progressive income tax, prohibition of the sale or use of intoxicating beverages, the Tennessee Valley Authority, governmental guarantees of the right of workers to organize labor unions, and many other policies first became live options because a third party made them campaign issues.

An idea that wins enough public support becomes attractive to the major parties. The Socialist party, for example, had favored unemployment insurance and federally financed old-age benefits long before the Democrats concluded in the middle 1930s that these programs would win more votes than they would lose. And today the Republican party, which opposed the Social Security Act of 1935, accepts it as necessary and desirable, partly because experience with the law has demonstrated that it benefits industry by providing pensions for workers financed so that the costs can be shifted to consumers and to the workers themselves. A policy innovation that appeals to a wide range of groups, even though it is for different reasons, is sure to be embraced in time by the major parties. In taking over such programs, the major parties keep third parties from benefiting from their own political proposals.

Party Organizations

The two major American parties do not have a base of dues-paying party members, as do most political parties in foreign countries with multiparty systems. Instead, they consist of a large number of voters with strong or weak loyalties to the Republicans or the Democrats and a relatively small cadre of activists who serve in the party organizations and work in political campaigns.

The organizations of such "cadre parties" are weak and perform only a limited set of functions. Laws of each of the fifty states provide for party committees, usually at the precinct, county, congressional district, and statewide levels, as illustrated in Figure 19.1. The committees usually play a role in finding candidates for elective offices at these various levels and in choosing delegates to the quadrennial national conventions, but in some states the party organization of one or the other major party does little or nothing, usually because it has little chance of winning elections.

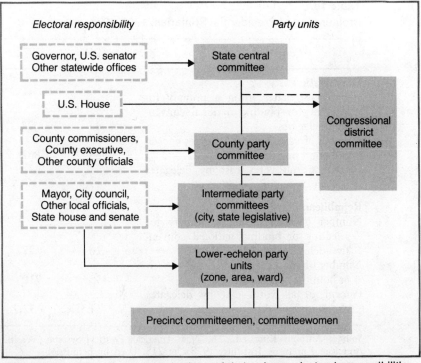

Figure 19.1 Units of party organization and their primary electoral responsibilities. (*Source*: Dennis S. Ippolito and Thomas G. Walker, *Political Parties, Interest Groups, and Public Policy: Group Influence in American Politics*, © 1980, p. 77. Reprinted by permission of Prentice-Hall, Inc., Englewood Cliffs, New Jersey.)

Each party also has a national committee, with representatives from every state. Its chief function is to arrange for the national nominating convention in presidential election years. Party committees also function in Congress and in the state legislatures to try to muster votes for or against measures favored by the President or governor. The congressional party committees also have a role in distributing campaign funds from the party coffers.

■ *Twenty Years of Party Decline.* The social unrest and disappointments of the 1960s and 1970s have led many Americans to question the ability of governmental institutions to cope with economic and social problems or to represent the population fairly. Even while politicians and public officials have become more self-conscious about public relations and symbolism in order to win votes and support, dramatic defeats and failures in both foreign and domestic policy have increased public skepticism. Political parties have been especially vulnerable to this decline in confidence in political institutions and have experienced some significant changes in the past fifteen years, thus reducing their importance and their functions.

Table 19.1

Proliferation of Presidential Primaries, 1968–1976

Party and Coverage	1968	1972	1976
Democratic Party			
Number of states using a primary for selecting or binding national convention delegates	17	23	29*
Number of votes cast by delegates chosen or bound by primaries	983	1,862	2,183
Percent of all votes cast by delegates chosen or bound by primaries	37.5	60.5	72.6
Republican Party			
Number of states using a primary for selecting or binding national convention delegates	16	22	28*
Number of votes cast by delegates chosen or bound by primaries	458	710	1,533
Percent of all votes cast by delegates chosen or bound by primaries	34.3	52.7	67.9

Source: Anthony King, ed., *The New American Political System* (Washington, D.C.: American Enterprise Institute, 1978), p. 218. Used by permission.

* Does not include Vermont, which held a nonbinding presidential-preference poll but chose all delegates of both parties by caucuses and conventions.

A key development of this kind has been a marked growth in the number and the importance of state presidential primaries and a corresponding decline in the role of party activists and national nominating conventions in choosing the major parties' presidential nominees. As shown in Table 19.1, between 1968 and 1976 the number of states holding such primaries to test the popularity of contenders for the nomination rose from seventeen to thirty.[1] In 1980 there were thirty-four. There has been a corresponding increase in the attention given to the state primaries, to state party caucuses, and to other early indications of the relative strength of aspirants for the presidential nomination.

As a result, contenders try hard to show unexpected strength in early primaries and caucuses in order to win financial and voting support in the later primaries. In 1976 the little-known Jimmy Carter gained national attention from publicity about his surprising show of strength in caucuses in Iowa. In 1972 Edmund Muskie came out first in the New Hampshire primary, but lost status and support because he had been *expected* to do even better in a state next door to his native Maine. In 1968 Lyndon

---

[1] Austin Ranney, "The Political Parties: Reform and Decline," in Anthony King, ed., *The New American Political System* (Washington, D.C.: American Enterprise Institute, 1978), p. 218.

Johnson similarly won the most votes in the New Hampshire primary, but shortly afterward withdrew from the race because Eugene McCarthy had shown surprising strength in New Hampshire while opposing Johnson's Vietnam War policy. It has, in fact, become less important to win these early tests than to do better than expected, with the result that aspirants devote almost as much attention to trying to shape public expectations as they do to winning votes. This strategy may have little to do with finding the candidate who will be the best, or even the most popular, President, but its successes in recent years have markedly increased the influence of the media and of public relations firms in the nomination process; that of party organizations and party leaders has declined correspondingly.

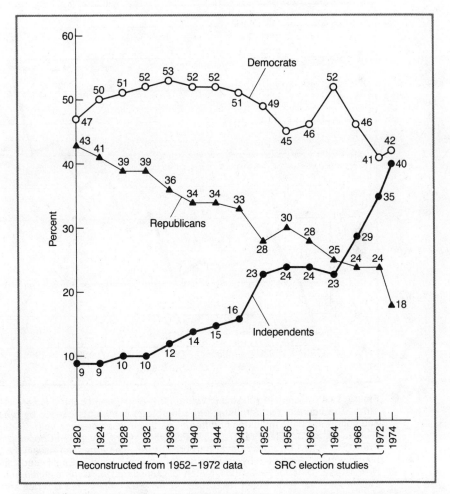

Figure 19.2 Party identification, 1920–1974. [*Source:* Reprinted by permission of the publishers from *The Changing American Voter*, by Norman H. Nie, Sidney Verba, and John R. Petrocik, p. 83. (Cambridge, Mass.: Harvard University Press © 1976, 1979 by the Twentieth Century Fund.)]

So too has the proportion of voters who identify themselves as Democrats or as Republicans declined, while the proportion of independents in the electorate almost doubled between 1964 and 1976 (see Figure 19.2). One reason for this trend was the lowering of the voting age to eighteen by the Twenty-sixth Amendment in 1971. Young people are less likely than older voters to have strong party loyalties, but that is clearly not the only explanation of the trend toward independence in voting, and probably not a major one.

A related sign of party decline has been a striking increase in the past twenty years in split-ticket voting. While 65 percent of the voters cast

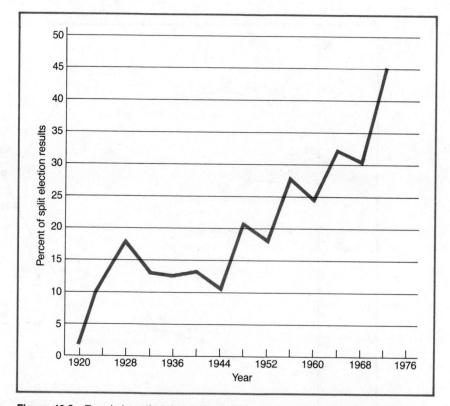

Figure 19.3 Trends in split-ticket voting for President and congressmen, 1920–1972. The figure is the percentage of congressional districts carried by presidential and congressional candidates of different parties in each election year. [*Sources:* Richard W. Boyd, "Electoral Trends in Postwar Politics," p. 185 in *Choosing the President*, edited by James David Barber, © 1974. The American Assembly, Columbia University. Reprinted by permission of Prentice-Hall, Inc., Englewood Cliffs, New Jersey. Data for 1920–1964, Milton C. Cummings, Jr., *Congressmen and the Electorate* (New York: Free Press, 1966), p. 32. For 1968, Walter DeVries and V. Lance Tarrance, Jr., *The Ticket-Splitter* (Grand Rapids: Eerdmans, 1972), p. 30. For 1972, the data are provided by Pierre M. Purves, director of statistical research, National Republican Congressional Committee, Washington, D.C., and by Michael Barone, Washington, D.C.]

straight party ballots in 1964, about 33 percent did so in 1976 — further evidence of the increased importance of individual candidate strategies and image building as compared to party identification (see Figure 19.3).

■ *Restrictions on the Party Organizations.* Throughout American history, the center of power in the major parties has been at the local and state levels. There has never been a national party boss or a national organization that was more than a loose confederation of state and local party leaders. While this is still true, public criticism of party leaders, especially of the minimal role given to women, minorities, and other nonelites in the national nominating conventions and other party organizations, produced some restrictions on state party organizations in the 1970s. New rules adopted by the Democratic and the Republican national committees called for increased participation in party activities by minority groups, Native Americans, women, and youth; abolished proxy voting and other practices that gave local party leaders much of their maneuverability; and required Democratic candidates for convention delegate to make their presidential preferences known. These rules have reduced the number of participants in the presidential nominating conventions who are male, middle-aged, white, and party regulars and have, especially in recent Democratic conventions, increased the proportions of female, black, and young delegates.

But the policy preferences of convention delegates are still not close to those of voters who identify with the party. A study of the 1972 conventions found that delegates to the Republican convention better represented the policies of state rank-and-file Democrats than Democratic delegates did.[2] This conclusion highlights both the overlap in appeal of the two major parties and the unrepresentative character of party conventions.

The conventions themselves have declined in importance, largely as a result of the new focus on presidential primaries and the restrictions on the state party organizations already discussed. Before these developments, the party national nominating conventions were settings for deals involving jobs in the new administration, the vice-presidential nomination, and policy directions and votes. Such bargains were usually struck after a first ballot in which nobody secured the necessary majority. Today, the primaries eliminate most of the contenders; there is usually a strong front-runner, and most delegates are publicly identified with an aspirant for the presidential nomination. Party "leaders," therefore, wield little power, and many are not even at the convention, which serves chiefly as an occasion to make the most of television and newspaper coverage in order to generate publicity for the ticket.

■ *Campaign Money.* The cost of political campaigning is high, and pressures to spend large sums of money have mounted dramatically as television has become the chief medium for reaching the public. In this crucial area

[2] Ranney, op. cit., p. 235.

as well, the role of political parties has declined, and that of individual candidates and campaign management organizations has dramatically increased. These developments stem mainly from changes in the federal election laws in 1971, 1974, and 1976 designed to end the serious abuses of the electoral process that marked the Watergate scandals of the early 1970s.

The new laws limit campaign contributions by an individual to a federal candidate to $1,000 in any one primary or general election. Individuals may contribute $5,000 to a committee and $25,000 to the national committee of a political party, but an individual's total contributions in any calendar year may not exceed $25,000. Organizations may not contribute more than $5,000 to any candidate.

There are also restrictions on expenditures. Contenders for a presidential nomination may spend up to $10,000,000, and candidates in a presidential election may spend $20,000,000. Party committees in a general election may spend two cents per voter, or about $3.5 million, the same amount on senatorial campaigns, and $10,00 on each House of Representatives campaign. Because these restrictions do not limit the total amount that can be spent by all organizations, such restrictions have encouraged interest groups to form new organizations to spend money, with some important consequences that we will examine later.

For the first time in American history, government money is being used to fund election campaigns. A candidate becomes eligible for federal money in a primary if he or she raises at least $5,000 in gifts of $250 or less in each of twenty states. But every candidate who accepts federal funds must limit his or her total spending to $10 million in a primary and to $20 million in a general election. A candidate who accepts federal funding in a general election may not raise funds privately. Major and minor parties receive money from the Federal Election Fund to pay for their national conventions, but minor-party candidates are not eligible for any governmental financing.

The 1971 law created a bipartisan Federal Elections Commission to interpret and administer the election laws; the later amendments increased its powers. These amendments are an effort to clean up federal election campaigns, ensure that they are conducted fairly, reduce candidates' dependence on large contributors, and strengthen the positions of candidates and parties through partial public financing.

Critics concerned about civil liberties and the rights of political independents and minorities charge that the new laws are having some undesirable effects. This legislation does not reduce the influence of wealthy contributors, in spite of its limits on contributions by individuals and special-interest groups. The American Civil Liberties Union (ACLU) explains how the law can be flouted:

> Ten executives at an oil company, for example, each contribute $25,000 to a voluntary political fund. The fund can then distribute $5000 apiece to the re-election campaigns of fifty favored congressmen and senators.

If ten oil companies each do the same thing, then those fifty congressmen and senators would receive a total of $50,000 each in perfectly lawful contributions from the oil industry, or a total of $2,500,000. However, if one well-to-do backer of a minority party wanted to give $1500 to its congressional candidate, the law makes that a crime.[3]

The ACLU further charges that the law will discourage small contributions and make it easy to harass dissenters. Contributions of less than $100 cannot be a corrupting influence, but by requiring that they be disclosed, the law subjects small contributors to penalties from employers or others who may not like their politics.

There is no question that money and the expectation of governmental favors can corrupt the political process. But the careful analyst of government must also consider the role of free public services, the free publicity available to incumbents, the ability of public officials to reward big contributors with governmental favors, and the fact that those who challenge such actions are limited in their contributions.

The new legislation on campaign financing strongly bolsters the trends already noted: party decline and an increase in the importance of individual campaign management and of interest-group support for candidates. All the federal matching funds for prenomination campaigns and 90 percent of the matching funds for general elections go to candidates directly, so that the party's role in allocating money has been sharply reduced. In 1972 many contributions to the major parties were in amounts of $10,000 or more, and these totaled $53 million. In 1976 the total was about $42 million; it came from federal money given to the two chief candidates.[4] Large sums were also spent by interest groups, as discussed below, but these were independent of party control.

Issue Voting

What is the relative influence of voters' choices, party affiliation, the candidates' personalities, and the issues? Studies of this question necessarily rely on surveys of voters' beliefs and behavior. They find that in the 1950s the issues were less important than either candidate images or party identification, which was by far the most important influence. But in the 1960s and 1970s issues grew in significance as parties declined. That was especially true in the two elections in which a major-party presidential candidate was widely perceived as "extreme" on the issues: Goldwater as a conservative in 1964 and McGovern as a liberal in 1972. The most thorough recent survey of voting behavior concludes: "If the public is faced with candidates distinguished from each other on the basis of the issues, it will vote on the issues. If the public is offered a more centrist choice, the vote will depend

---

[3] American Civil Liberties Union, *Civil Liberties* 308 (September 1975), p. 6.
[4] *Neil O. Staebler on the Campaign Finance Revolution* (Citizens' Research Foundation, Los Angeles, 1979).

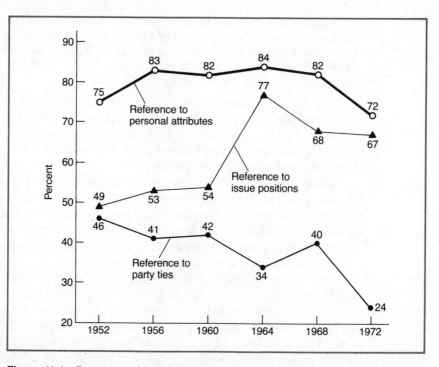

Figure 19.4 Frequency of evaluations of candidates in terms of party ties, personal attributes, and issue positions, 1952–1972. [*Source*: Reprinted by permission of the publishers from *The Changing American Voter* by Norman H. Nie, Sidney Verba, and John R. Petrocik, p. 167. (Cambridge, Mass.: Harvard University Press © 1976, 1979 by the Twentieth Century Fund.)]

much more heavily on partisan identification."[5] The same study finds that most voters prefer a candidate with a centrist position when the opponent takes an extreme position (see Figure 19.4).

At another level of analysis, these statements may look a little less like a law of human nature and more like a statement about symbolic politics. The labeling of some political positions as "centrist" and others as "extreme" is not an objective judgment, but a reflection of mainstream opinion, and such opinions change over time. To conclude that most voters take issues into account by choosing centrist rather than extreme positions is not very different from concluding that most voters choose the issue positions that most voters prefer, because that is how "centrist" is defined.

Nor are party identification, issue choices, and candidate preferences independent of one another. Voters are likely to assume that the parties and candidates they like will usually take the *positions* they like, especially when stands on issues are fuzzy. Issue voting is an important consideration,

---

[5] Norman H. Nie, Sidney Verba, and John R. Petrocik, *The Changing American Voter* (Cambridge, Mass.: Harvard University Press, 1976), p. 318.

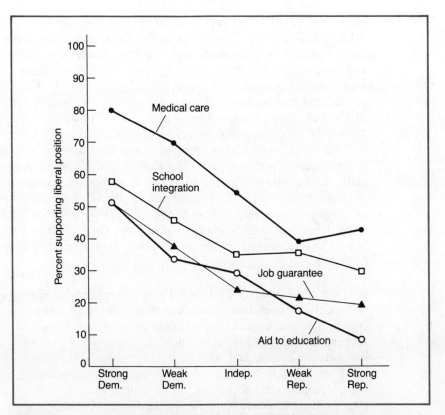

Figure 19.5 Party identification and policy beliefs, 1968. [*Source*: James David Barber, ed. *Choosing the President* (Englewood Cliffs, N.J.: Prentice-Hall, Inc., 1974), p. 193. Based on a table by Gerald M. Pomper, "From Confusion to Clarity: Issues and American Voters, 1956–1968," *American Political Science Review* 66 (June 1972), p. 417. Used by permission.]

but the perception of issues is limited by the perception of parties and of candidates and by the distribution of opinions in the population as a whole.

This increased concern for issues has also meant that Republican voters are more consistently conservative than Democrats, at least in their responses to opinion polls. In the 1950s supporters of the two major parties were equally inconsistent. Now, as Figure 19.5 demonstrates, Democrats are more likely than Republicans to say that they favor governmental support of medical care, school integration, governmental guarantees of jobs for the unemployed, and federal aid to education.[6] For reasons discussed in Chapters 8, 14, and 16, however, it is far from certain that such voter preferences will be translated into tangible policies.

The new emphasis on issues is also creating strains *within* the parties. The Democratic party relies in part on people interested chiefly in policies

---

[6] Gerald M. Pomper, "From Confusion to Clarity: Issues and American Voters, 1956–1968," *American Political Science Review* 66 (June 1972), p. 417.

friendly to labor unions and in social security benefits; these people often disagree with another component of the Democratic party's constituency: those favoring the encouragement of diverse lifestyles, rejection of racism and economic inequality, and a foreign policy that deemphasizes militarism, cold war, and support of despotic foreign governments. The party's 1968 presidential standardbearer, Hubert Humphrey, chiefly reflected the values of the first group; George McGovern, its 1972 nominee, more closely reflected the concerns of the second group.

For some of the same reasons, there have been recent geographic realignments in party support. The Deep South, which was solidly Democratic for a century following the Civil War, now shows considerable Republican strength due to Republican emphasis, since Goldwater's 1964 campaign, on opposing welfare benefits and civil rights for blacks and on identifying cities with crime and disorder. These themes have also cut heavily into Democratic strength among European ethnic groups and Catholics.

■ *Issues and Volunteer Campaign Help.*   People whose interest in politics springs chiefly from their concern with specific issues have in recent years been willing and eager to do volunteer work in campaigns: canvassing prospective voters, soliciting signatures on nominating petitions, delivering literature to homes, and working in campaign headquarters. Such work has been a highly significant form of campaign contribution, and it has been especially conspicuous in the campaigns of such issue-oriented aspirants as Eugene McCarthy, Barry Goldwater, George Wallace, George McGovern, and John Anderson.

Voting Patterns

The act of voting is closely related to intensity of preference for one or another candidate or party and in turn to class level and membership in active political groups. Nearly 90 percent of college-educated persons and nearly 80 percent of high school graduates vote in presidential elections, but only a little over half the eligible population with grade school educations does so. The dropoff in voting is constant all the way down the status ladder. Skilled workers, for example, vote with greater regularity than do unskilled workers. Union members vote with distinctly greater consistency than do similar workers who do not belong to unions. In general, members of organized groups are much more likely to vote than are people who are not members.

Other *demographic* characteristics are also associated with the disposition to vote. Men are more likely to vote than are women, a circumstance that almost certainly reflects widely held beliefs about the "proper" role of women in society; this is the case in almost all countries. The young are less likely to vote than are older people, partly because of residency requirements that discriminate against the mobile and partly because older people more often feel that they are part of the political system. Blacks are much less likely to vote than are whites, even when they are not legally barred from doing so or not intimidated. People who live in urban areas vote more frequently than do rural residents, probably because political life in the cities is more stimulating and there is more social pressure to vote. Voting-participation rates are far lower in the South than in other regions, chiefly because of the higher proportion of the southern population that is poor, black, and lacking much formal education.

The turnout of voters depends not only on these socioeconomic factors, but also on people's interest and involvement in party politics. That high-status voters go to the polls more often chiefly reflects their greater belief that it matters how they vote and who wins. Anyone who feels strongly that it makes a difference is obviously more likely to vote than is someone who does not.

If the act of voting gives people a feeling of identification with the state and of influence on government, the rather sharp decline in voting in the last twenty years points to growing alienation from the political system. This trend is linked to the others we have mentioned, and it may well be the most significant of them. As Figure 19.6 shows, there has been a steady and rather sharp decline since 1960 in voting turnout in both presidential and congressional elections.

For some, nonvoting is an expression of their rejection of the belief that voting makes a difference — of their assumption that the major parties present no real choice and that the voters have little influence on what government does. The proportion of nonvoters who consciously reject the electoral system in this way has probably always been small, but this phenomenon may be particularly significant because it occurs in the face of such an intense barrage of pressure and propaganda to take part. This pressure is, of course, intended to integrate people into the political system and to give them a greater stake in it. The extension of the right to vote — first to propertyless males, then to women, blacks, and finally to those aged eighteen to twenty-one — has never had any effect on government policy. But it does seem to have lessened the protests of such groups and to cause them to believe that remedies for their problems can be found within the orthodox political processes. The right to vote thus helps to commit people to the system and to legitimize governmental actions. Not to exercise that right requires strong resistance to American orthodoxy.

Power of the Vote

For most people, voting is the most potent of all symbols of popular rule and therefore a powerful ingredient in the legitimacy of a regime that holds public office. Whether a group of political participants wins or loses an election, the fact that it has supposedly been consulted evokes its support for the government. It may not like some policies the government

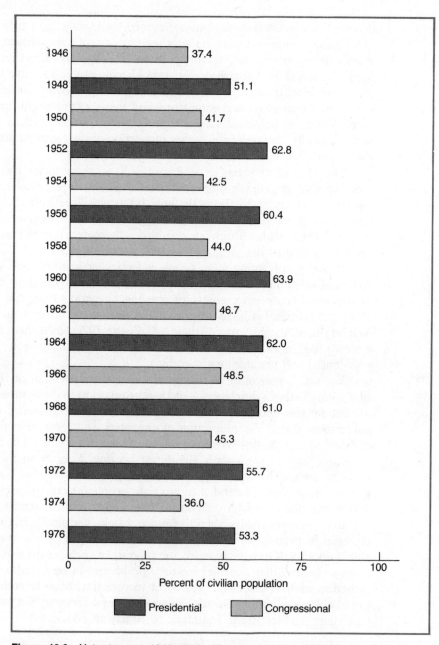

Figure 19.6 Voter turnout, 1946–1976. (*Source: AFL-CIO American Federationist* 83, December 1976, p. 7. Used by permission.)

pursues, but it is far less likely to challenge its right to pursue them than would be the case if the government had not been elected. In this critical sense elections lessen social tensions and inhibit potential civil strife. This is frequently, perhaps usually, the chief function they serve in the political system, though that hypothesis is debatable and not easily susceptible to rigorous testing. Provisions for compulsory voting in some countries, as well as social pressures to vote in order to prove that one is a "good citizen," doubtless reflect an awareness that people who vote are psychologically inoculated against fundamental resistance to the state.

It is even more clear that the use of elections in nondemocratic states reflects the same awareness. Some forms of election, such as the plebiscites of totalitarian countries, do not even offer the *possibility* of defeating unpopular candidates or policies, amounting only to ratification of actions already taken. It is in such rigged elections, nonetheless, that legal and social pressure to vote has been strongest. The citizen who fails to vote is suspect as a potentially disloyal person and can expect the kind of ostracism that would await a member of a primitive tribe who refused to participate in a communal fertility rite or war dance. Sometimes elections are rigged to eliminate candidates who stand for a genuine alternative on controversial issues, as is true of many elections in the Deep South, some in the North, and virtually all elections in one-party states. The results are nevertheless publicized as mandates for the government and fervently accepted by many as exactly that.

Apart from their uses in promoting and symbolizing social solidarity, to what degree do elections provide policy guidelines for public officials to follow? On the occasional major issue on which the two major parties disagree, they apparently do furnish a clear mandate, though historical examples warn against making this logical assumption without empirical evidence. In 1928 the Democratic platform favored repeal of the Eighteenth (Prohibition) Amendment, while the Republicans were "dry." A Republican victory did indeed delay repeal for four years, even though public sentiment increasingly favored repeal, and in 1932 both parties' platforms reflected that sentiment. In 1964 escalation of the Vietnam War, certainly a major issue, was favored by Barry Goldwater, the Republican candidate, and opposed by Lyndon Johnson, his Democratic opponent. Though Johnson won by a wide margin, he moved quickly after the election to escalate the war. Though this is by no means the only instance in which a major party disregarded what appeared to be a clear popular mandate, elections do in such instances provide a means for evaluating the performance of a regime. This can be an important factor in the following election, as it evidently was in 1968, but there is no guarantee that it will be.

Permanence of the Election Mandate

Even when elections do offer a real choice, however, they are not a sufficient condition of democracy. Election mandates are almost always unclear, and it is always possible to justify departures from them on the ground that conditions have changed since election day. Even when elected officials have every intention of heeding the voice of the people as they understand it, election mandates typically furnish only the vaguest kind of guide to administrative officials and judges who have to make decisions in particular cases. Does the fact that the winning political party promised to hold down prices mean that it should institute wage-and-price ceilings when some economists forecast rising prices and others disagree? Should officials elected on such a plank institute price controls after prices have risen 6 percent? 8 percent? 15 percent? What difference should it make if the winning political party also promised to avoid unnecessary governmental intervention in the economy?

Dilemmas like these face modern governments all the time. The decisions taken to resolve them are bound to reflect a complex set of group interests and guesses about the future political and economic effects of one or another course of action. They cannot be predetermined, or even guided very far, by the votes people cast in elections.

Because of the American parties' avoidance of clear stands on issues and the tendency of candidates (once elected) to act as they consider necessary under the circumstances, it is very difficult to say precisely what elections mean in the United States. We have no doubt that it sometimes makes a difference which party or candidate wins an election, at least in the general approach to problems of governing, if not in specific policies. But the permanence of the basic social coalitions underlying the parties and the arbitrariness of both parties' internal processes preceding nominations preclude exact definition of the role of elections. Events can split the basic social coalitions. But in the past, only the Civil War and the Great Depression of the 1930s were of sufficient magnitude to realign the major social blocs and to redirect the party system. After the Civil War, the Republicans were dominant for nearly seventy years, with only two Democratic intrusions (Cleveland and Wilson). After the Depression, the Democrats took over and remained in office, with the exception of Eisenhower, until 1968.

Interest Groups

Between two-thirds and three-quarters of the American people belong to voluntary organizations to further interests they hold in common.[7] Directly or indirectly, virtually all these interests involve stands on some political issues. Table 19.2 shows the types of interests represented by the more than 13,000 voluntary associations that are national in their scope; many more are local or regional.

People tend to join groups to express interests that are stable and fairly strong. The doctor who joins the county medical society, the worker who

---

[7] Verba and Nie estimate the figure at 62 percent; Salisbury, at 74.5 percent. Cf. Sidney Verba and Norman H. Nie, *Participation in America* (New York: Harper & Row, 1972), p. 176; Robert Salisbury, "Overlapping Memberships, Organizational Interactions, and Interest Group Theory" (paper presented at the annual meeting of the American Political Science Association, 1976).

Table 19.2
Voluntary Associations of National Scope in the United States

Type of Organization	Number	Percent
Business, trade or commercial	2,992	22.0
Cultural and educational	2,188	16.1
Health and medical	1,278	9.4
Scientific, engineering, technical	932	6.9
Public affairs	913	6.7
Social welfare	848	6.2
Religious	772	5.7
Hobby	759	5.6
Agricultural	640	4.7
Legal, governmental, military	479	3.5
Fraternal, nationality, ethnic	448	3.3
Athletic, sports	476	3.5
Greek letter societies	320	2.4
Labor	230	1.7
Veteran, patriotic	211	1.6
Chamber of commerce	103	0.8
Totals	13,589	100.1

Source: Nancy Yakes and Denise Akey (editors), *Encyclopedia of Associations*—Vol. 1 (Detroit: Gale Research Company, 14th edition, 1980). Used by permission.

joins a union, the factory owner who joins a trade association, and the hunter who joins the National Rifle Association all have other interests that do not give rise to organizational membership, chiefly because they are not as important or continuous as these. Many people do not join organizations, in spite of stable and strong economic interests, because they enjoy the benefits of relevant pressure groups' activities anyway. Businesspeople benefit from the probusiness lobbying of the chamber of commerce whether or not they are members; similarly, workers often win higher wages because employers want to *discourage* them from joining unions. One astute analyst has suggested that membership in interest groups is often dependent either on coercion (such as a requirement that lawyers join the state bar association in order to practice law) or on incidental benefits (such as a union pension plan or a malpractice insurance plan available only to members of a medical association).[8] It is chiefly middle-class and upper-middle-class people who join the interest groups that most actively try to influence governmental policy, for this class has solid economic and social roots and is likely to be conscious of its joint interests.

Some people have strong common interests, but are not brought together in a way that makes organization likely. This is true of the poor,

---

[8] Mancur Olson, *The Logic of Collective Action* (New York: Schocken Books, 1968).

the unemployed, the workers who work intermittently or are very poorly paid, and consumers. It cannot be taken for granted, therefore, that every interest will have its organized "watchdog." The oil and natural gas companies will lobby effectively through their trade associations, but the people who buy heating oil and gasoline are unlikely to organize at all.

Some interest groups represent stable and continuing concerns of those who belong to them or support them, and so they remain active indefinitely or for long periods of time. Trade associations that represent businesspeople in the same industry, labor unions, farm organizations, medical and other professional associations, and churches are examples. Some voluntary groups spring up as a reaction to a political issue that arouses wide or passionate attention. Examples are "prolife" groups that oppose abortion, organizations to advocate or oppose amnesty for Vietnam War draft evaders, and organizations to oppose nuclear power. Groups of these kinds survive as long as the issue they espouse remains controversial, which may be for a year or two or for decades or longer. Because such politically active groups are always concerned with controversial policies, they make claims that conflict with the claims of other groups.

Other kinds of interest groups are sometimes influential in contemporary government. Public-interest organizations try to protect the interests of people who are unorganized or have few financial resources with which to protect themselves, such as consumers, the poor, victims of environmental pollution, prisoners, and mental patients. Leading examples of public-interest groups are Ralph Nader's Center for the Study of Responsive Law, the League of Women Voters, Common Cause, Consumers Union, and public-interest law firms. Though such organizations represent interests shared by large numbers of people, they are not typically the concerns many people feel intensely, so that legislators and administrators are tempted to pay less attention to them than to smaller groups with financial resources, skilled lawyers, and professional lobbyists at their disposal.

Local and state governmental organizations are an increasingly important kind of interest group, for they depend to a considerable extent on federal money and federal laws and regulations to carry on their functions. Individual cities and states lobby with Congress and executive agencies; so also do such organizations as the Council of State Governments, the National League of Cities, and the Conference of Chief Justices.

Still another kind of organization exists to promote an ideological cause. Some examples are the John Birch Society on the far right, the Committee to Restore the Constitution almost as far in the same direction, and Americans for Democratic Action in the liberal center and moderate left. The Committee on the Present Danger lobbies for larger arms expenditures and a more militant stance toward the Soviet Union.

Interest groups play a part in all phases of the political process. They lobby to shape legislation, employ various tactics to influence executive and administrative actions, and appear before state and federal courts. They play a role in election campaigns to try to elect sympathetic officials, thereby increasing their effectiveness in all the other governmental forums.

The Spurt in Political Action Committees in the 1970s

The decline in public support and in financial resources of political parties has made it necessary that other institutions perform some of their functions, especially mobilizing public opinion behind policies and candidates and providing funds for campaigns. Interest groups have, accordingly, become far more active in elections, chiefly through political action committees (PACs).

Labor groups began forming such committees in the 1940s because of laws prohibiting unions from spending money in elections; the committees could do so from funds contributed by individual union members rather than from the union treasuries. Large gifts from individual corporate officials to the political parties were still possible until the 1974 election law amendments, so that corporations saw little need for political action committees before that time. But since the imposition of relatively small limits on individual contributions, corporations and other interest groups have vigorously been following the union lead, with results that are rapidly changing the electoral landscape. In 1974 there were only 89 corporate PACs, but in September 1979 there were 1,938 — more than twenty-one times as many. Ideological groups, especially conservative and right-wing groups, have also been forming PACs at a rapid rate (see Figure 19.7).

Except for federal contributions to candidates, PACs are now the major source of campaign money. In the period between 1 January 1977 and 31 December 1978, they contributed $35.1 million to federal candidates, nearly triple the PAC spending in 1974. Seventy-one percent of these funds went to incumbents. Challengers received only 12 percent, and the rest went to candidates for open seats.

Candidates in primaries and general elections must now try to get support from this new source of money that has gone a long way toward replacing political-party disbursements and large individual contributions. In 1977 Ronald Reagan, a contender for the Republican presidential nomination, created his own off-season political action committee, Citizens for the Republic, one of the most successful of the PACs in attracting contributions.

Some of the more successful committees concentrate on a single emotional issue and raise large amounts of money, often defeating candidates for their positions on that issue regardless of their records otherwise. Examples of such single-issue groups are the Gun Owners of America, the National Rifle Association, PACs opposing abortion, and those advocating large increases in the arms budget.

Mailing lists and computers are crucial to the new financial politics. People who subscribe to a magazine with a particular ideological bent,

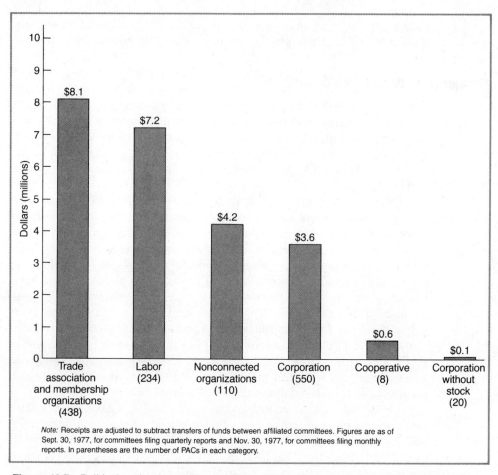

Figure 19.7 Political action committee receipts, 1977. [*Source*: Federal Election Commission; *Congressional Quarterly Almanac* 34 (1978), p. 770. Used by permission.]

contribute money to an ideological cause, or have particular economic, ethnic, or other traits can be identified by computers as likely prospects for related causes. Such pinpointing of prospects for PAC solicitations has been enormously successful, especially as employed by the developer of the technique, Richard A. Viguerie, who concentrates on raising money for conservative causes and has helped create more than a dozen new-right organizations. His computer stores more than 200 mailing lists that are broken down by issues and include 10 to 20 million contributors to right-wing causes.

It appears, then, that a major result of the changes we have described in political parties, nominating procedures, interest-group activities, and campaign financing has been sharply increased influence for groups with strong positions on a small set of issues and sharply reduced importance of identification with a political party. The influence of the single-issue, ideological, and economic groups comes much less from their numbers than from effective deployment of their financial resources.

A revealing example of substantial spending by a coalition of groups with a common interest in an issue is the campaign contributions connected to the Cargo Preference Bill of 1977, which gave American merchant ships preferential treatment and raised shipping costs. Shipping interests and unions interested in this bill contributed $100,000 to President Carter in the primary, $450,000 to congressional campaigns, and $100,000 to members of the committees responsible for the bill.[9] While campaign contributions are unlikely to buy legislative votes or presidential support, they do make it easier to gain entry and to win a sympathetic hearing. On most issues legislative and executive officials will not have strong personal positions or knowledge; thus, financial support is likely to make the official receptive to the information and arguments of those who supply it. That is why interest groups find it helpful to support incumbents. An officer of one major national corporation doubtless reflected these assumptions when he told an acquaintance asking for a political contribution: "If you're an incumbent, we give $1,000, and if you beat an incumbent, we give $1,000 to retire your debt."[10]

Interest groups play a part in election campaigns in other ways as well. Some rate legislators according to their votes on issues of concern to the group. Environmental Action, Inc., publicizes its "Dirty Dozen" list of members of Congress who take antienvironmental positions, and the Consumer Federation of America lists "Consumer Heros" and "Consumer Zeros." Such ratings amount to indirect endorsements and denunciations, and some interest groups endorse candidates directly as well. Ratings and endorsements are not major influences on votes.

Lobbying in All Three Branches

Pressure groups that lobby for favorable legislation are most effective when they can be helpful to the legislators they try to influence. Buttonholing a member of Congress at a cocktail party is not likely to be very useful to a lobbyist, nor is an organized letter-writing campaign. The most effective lobbyists are those who regularly provide useful information to legislators and so come to be trusted. A legislator often needs accurate information about both technical matters and the strength of various groups' feelings about an issue; thus, the lobbyist who gains a reputation for accurate reporting on such matters wins goodwill and influence for his or her group.[11] In 1977 there were more than 5,000 persons engaged in lobbying with Con-

---

[9] Letter to the New York Times, 3 October 1979, p. A26, from Millicent Fenwick, Member of Congress, 5th District, New Jersey.
[10] New York Times, 30 May 1979, p. A23.
[11] For a good account of legislative lobbying, see Lester Milbrath, The Washington Lobbyists (Chicago: Rand McNally, 1963).

gress, though many of them were not registered, because of loopholes in the 1946 Federal Regulation of Lobbying Act.[12]

Bringing pressure on legislators indirectly through the arousal of sentiment in their home districts, either among the public generally or among sympathetic groups, is a common and effective lobbying ploy. Lobbyists often help draft bills of interest to the groups they represent. Because a bill must hurdle many obstacles as it goes through subcommittees, committees, votes on the floor, and amendments, lobbyists trying to kill a proposal are usually in a better tactical position than are those pushing for new legislation.

Like legislators themselves, lobbyists form alliances with one another when they can. Though business and labor groups are typically on opposite sides on bills to encourage or discourage collective bargaining or increase minimum wages, they work as allies on bills to restrict auto emissions or to restrict the importation of competing foreign products.

Many interest groups devote more attention to administrative than to legislative bodies, though these efforts are less widely recognized and publicized. As we noted in Chapter 16, it is chiefly administrative rules and decisions that allocate tangible values. Some administrative agencies continuously reflect particular economic or social interests, as in the cases of the Commerce and Labor departments. Others do pretty much the same, while symbolically reflecting a different or wider range of interests, as in the case of regulatory commissions that are consistently sensitive to the interests of the industries they are supposed to control. A growing number of Washington, D.C., law firms specialize in such fields as radio, health, or environmental law and become practiced lobbyists before the appropriate governmental agencies for interest groups and corporations that hire them. In the 1970s the number of trade and professional associations with headquarters in Washington exceeded the number in New York City for the first time. In 1977, 1,800 organizations, well over half of those with annual budgets of more than a million dollars, were located in the Washington metropolitan area to facilitate administrative and legislative lobbying.[13]

Interest groups can sometimes be more effective through court action than through legislative or administrative lobbying. The National Association for the Advancement of Colored People has relied heavily on the courts to protect blacks' civil and economic rights. Environmental groups often resort to the courts as well. When possible, groups representing the disadvantaged have brought "class action suits," a way of protecting the interests of all people suffering the same infringement of their rights even if they are not actively associated with the lawsuit. The Supreme Court

---

[12] Carol S. Greenwald, *Group Power* (New York: Praeger, 1977), p. 191.

[13] Hugh Heclo, "Issue Networks and the Executive Establishment," in Anthony King, ed., *The New American Political System* (Washington, D.C.: American Enterprise Institute, 1978), p. 97.

severely limited the use of such actions in a 1974 decision.[14] Interest groups also try to influence judicial policies by filing "friend of the court" briefs in cases that, although they are not party to, nonetheless affect their interests. Because the law places considerable emphasis on the protection of property rights and because it offers numerous procedural devices for blocking change, the courts are also a valuable recourse for business groups. Interest groups often have some leeway in the choice of the court in which they file an action and so can shop around for a sympathetic one. More generally, the courts provide an alternative channel to interest groups for winning benefits they are denied in the legislative, executive, or administrative arenas.

Popular Support and Opposition to Interest Groups

Though organized groups lobby and spend money to advance their objectives, their success depends heavily on how a much wider body of public opinion responds to their activities. They need either sympathizers or apathy, and they need to minimize popular opposition to their goals. In general, pressure groups try to avoid publicity and to work through ongoing governmental contacts when they are getting what they want and the issues are technical or complex. This strategy prevents potential opposition from being awakened to action. Groups that are losing under existing arrangements, on the other hand, usually gain more by publicizing an issue in the hope that a larger public will support them. Paper mills in Wisconsin are not likely to appeal for public support of their right to pollute rivers with contaminating chemicals as long as they are allowed to do so without interference, but environmental groups are sure to try to arouse as wide a public as possible to the dangers of pollution. "Fellow travelers" who are not themselves members of interest groups often make a critical difference in determining policy outcomes.

Alternative Forms of Political Participation

The alternative forms of participation span a wide range of activities. Some are as authorized and accepted as, though less formalized than, elections or interest-group actions. Others are discouraged or forcefully repressed, but nevertheless represent means by which some nonelites participate in politics and may influence policy. In general, although the alternative forms are frequently efforts to bypass the established channels, they exhibit many of the same class biases as do parties, elections, and interest-group activity.

One of the most obvious and accepted modes of communication and "pressure" from nonelites to decision-making elites is the simple act of writ-

---

[14] *Eisen* v. *Carlisle and Jacquelin,* 417 U.S. 156 (1974).

ing a letter or signing a petition to be sent to an official or a newspaper. Legislators are sometimes said to "wait for the mail" before making up their minds how to vote on an issue. But there are several problems with this assumption. One is that people tend to write or petition those they have reason to believe are on their side or at least on the fence. This means that letter writers favoring a proposal write to decisionmakers who favor it, and those against write to those who oppose it. The net result, even if the decisionmakers take their mail seriously, is no change in positions. Another problem is that decisionmakers become impervious to pressure campaigns organized by small interest groups.

Even more important is the fact that writing letters, and to a lesser extent carrying and signing petitions, is more likely to be undertaken by people who are relatively well educated and upper class. Even within class and education levels, it is an act more likely to be undertaken by conservatives than by liberals. In an effort to find out why the 1964 Republican strategists thought there was a "hidden" conservative vote, the Michigan Survey Research Center compared the political preferences of those who wrote letters to officials or newspapers with those who did not.[15] The researchers found that only 15 percent of the population had ever written a letter to a public official and that two-thirds of all letters were written by a total of 3 percent of the population. The 3 percent was distinctly conservative in every ideological dimension; by "vote" of letter writers, Goldwater would have been elected by a comfortable majority. Thus, if decisionmakers took guidance, or if officials sought to measure the mood of the country, from the views expressed in the mail to officials and newspapers, they would acquire a very skewed image.

Citizen Participation

Some alternative forms of participation are built into the process of administering and implementing laws. Juries, for instance, place a significant function in the hands of citizens and might well serve as a means of communicating citizens' dissatisfaction with law or with their circumstances. But juries are drawn from lists of voters or property owners (or, in the case of grand juries, from "blue-ribbon" panels) and thus reflect class orientations. Nevertheless, juries in many cases involving political figures and issues (Black Panthers, draft resisters, the Chicago 7 trial, and others) have refused to convict or been relatively lenient, suggesting that some potential prosecutions may have been discouraged by these results.

In many areas of governmental activity advisory boards of citizens are required by law. Urban renewal, selective service, and other agencies deliberately engage citizens in the implementation of their programs. But they

---

[15] These data are drawn from Philip Converse, Warren Miller, Jerold G. Rusk, and Arthur C. Wolfe, "Continuity and Change in American Politics: Parties and Issues in the 1968 Election," *American Political Science Review* 63 (1969), p. 333.

accomplish relatively little for ordinary citizens, because participants in these programs are drawn from the higher echelons of nonelites. Business-people, local leaders, and higher-status people generally dominate these positions. Only in the Community Action Agencies of the poverty program has there been a real contest over who is to shape a governmental program. Lower-class citizens did begin to take part, and the result was first an amendment to the law that gave local governments control over the local aspects of such programs and then such controversy that the funding for many local units was sharply cut back or eliminated.

In general, formal participation by nonelites in policy-making bodies is bound to be largely ritual unless it is accompanied by a form of power nonelites can assert, such as a strike, boycott, or disruption of programs important to elites. The chance to participate is often regarded as a concession, but it is more often a way of making sure that a low-status group will not resort to effective protest or resistance. Participation is so effective a way of diverting discontented people from disorder that it is often required of low-status groups in totalitarian settings: in prisons, mental hospitals, schools, and totalitarian states, where it serves as a form of pseudodemocracy.

A much less institutionalized form of participation that has arisen from time to time in American history, and particularly during the 1960s, is the protest demonstration, sit-in, disruption, or deliberate refusal to obey rules. Those who have been unable to make themselves heard through the established channels have resorted to these tactics, often with great success, when their claims were consistent with generally shared values and not at extreme odds with the basic features of the political system. But when they have been unable to find allies or have been seen as dangerously at variance with established values or familiar political practices, rejection and repression have been very harsh. Successful protest-type activity requires allies, or at the very least inaction on the part of those who might oppose the protesters. It involves risks of a personal kind for the participants and is difficult to keep up for a long period of time without a supportive environment. Thus, it depends on achieving some tangible goal, usually from an existing political structure.

Another, even less institutionalized alternative form of participation is the spontaneous riot. Although clearly grounded in the circumstances of ghetto existence, the riots of the 1960s and those in Miami in 1980 were spontaneous, in contrast to deliberate obstructive sit-ins or other protest tactics. Touched off by one or another form of provocation, riots may engage thousands of participants for days at a time. The immediate consequences are destruction of millions of dollars' worth of property and the deaths of many ghetto residents at the hands of police and national guard forces. Subsequently, governmental assistance to ghetto residents and other poor people may increase, as it did in the aftermath of the 1960s riots, but so too did some popular support for repressive measures and for political candidates who stood for such action.

■ *Riot and Demonstration Patterns.* Patterns of participation in riots offer some insight into these alternative forms of participation. In the case of the widespread ghetto riots of 1967, for example, it is clear that substantial proportions of each community were involved. Supplemental studies undertaken for the National Commission on Civil Disorders estimate that participants represented from 11 to 35 percent of residents of the riot areas in major cities (Detroit, Newark, New Haven) where riots occurred.[16] The composition of the rioters was roughly representative of the occupational makeup of the ghetto population, with a slight emphasis on the less skilled and the unemployed. Nearly all of those arrested during the riots were residents of the neighborhoods involved.[17] The riots were thus fairly broad-based actions by cross sections of the area populations. They were not caused by the "criminal elements," by "outside agitators," or by a tiny minority of militants. They were, it seems fair to say, genuine expressions of community protest of an essentially political kind. Certainly they were perceived as such by most blacks; indeed, several surveys have shown that while most blacks do not approve of rioting, they see it in many cases as necessary and helpful toward achieving black goals.[18] Younger blacks in particular tend to believe that violence will be necessary before such objectives are attained.

But the same riots were perceived quite differently by whites. We have already seen the electoral consequences of these riots and other race problems. National elites, with limited exceptions, tended to emphasize theories that outside agitators, a few militants, or habitual troublemakers had caused the riots. Only the Kerner Report blamed "white racism"; it went largely unheard.

■ *The Aftermath of the Riots of the 1960s.* Eruptions in the black ghettos of a large number of major cities in the 1960s almost certainly helped keep welfare rolls high by frightening the middle class into liberalizing eligibility and benefits, at least for a time.[19] But it is already clear that the riots have not significantly changed the social or economic conditions of the poor and/or black population. Each wave of riots in American history has produced commissions and recommendations for reform in employment practices, city services to the poor, housing, transportation, and racist attitudes, but such recommendations yield few lasting results. The accompanying

---

[16] Robert M. Fogelson and Robert B. Hill, "Who Riots? A Study of Participation in the 1967 Riots," *Supplemental Studies for the National Advisory Commission on Civil Disorders* (Washington, D.C.: U.S. Government Printing Office, 1968), p. 231.

[17] Ibid., pp. 236, 237.

[18] Opinion data in this section are drawn from Angus Campbell and Howard Schuman, "Racial Attitudes in Fifteen American Cities," in Fogelson and Hill, *Supplemental Studies*, pp. 48–52.

[19] Frances F. Piven and Richard A. Cloward, *Regulating the Poor* (New York: Random House, 1971).

account of the situation in Watts — a black suburb of Los Angeles that experienced one of the earliest, most publicized, and most studied riots of the 1960s — is typical: it describes a relapse into acceptance of high unemployment, endemic crime, poverty, and hopelessness.

IN WATTS A DECADE LATER: POVERTY IN ASHES OF RIOTS

By Jon Nordheimer

LOS ANGELES, Aug. 6. — *Ten years after the fires of the era of the long hot summer were kindled in Watts, the black ghetto on the south side of Los Angeles has lapsed into a cold autumn of desperation.*

Watts, for a while, became a workshop for new ideas and bold invention — a laboratory for social theory and strategies financed by the foundations and the universities and the Federal Government.

But the money and manpower dried up, so did the programs and the will of those who felt that individual risk and sacrifice could make the difference. Like a great wave that surged forth in full flood, it eventually retreated under resistance, carrying away with it the elements not irretrievably rooted there.

Compared with the economic and spiritual desolation that exists today, the conditions that sparked six days of looting and burning a decade ago now seem almost salubrious.

For Watts today is a community that has been left behind in the advancement of those who by luck or pluck were able to take advantage of the gains won by black Americans in the intervening years.

Watts today, in the view of those inside and outside the community, is a compendium of urban failure, a nesting place of the social and racial ills that represent the nation's retreat from the challenge of finding effective measures to deal with its most intractable problems.

Like scores of other black, central-city ghettos, Watts in the summer of 1975 has been further devastated by high unemployment and other ills of the national recession, yet so far there has been no sign of a renewal of mass violence.

It is an area stripped of stable leadership, for those who can escape Watts depart at the first opportunity, leaving behind a paralyzed society of welfare mothers, street gangs and the elderly. Unemployment is running about 50 percent among those who can work, breeding hard-core social dependence and crime.

Source: *New York Times*, 7 August 1975, p. 1. © 1980 by The New York Times Company. Reprinted by permission.

The white-owned shops and small plants that were burned out or closed by the rioting have never reopened. Houses that were removed by renewal projects were not replaced. Economic conditions that created a recession elsewhere fell with a hammer blow here.

"This whole environment is designed for failure," says Gregory Welch, a 25-year-old ex-convict, as he stands at the intersection of Central Avenue and 103d Street, the epicenter of the 1965 riots. "Watts is all negative with very few positives."

There are few who dispute that assessment. "What we are seeing today is an overwhelming mental depression, particularly among the young, that life holds no promise of opportunity for them," say Dr. Roland Jefferson, a black psychiatrist who is a consultant at the Watts Health Center.

Consequently, Dr. Jefferson notes, ghetto youths in recent years have moved deeper into self-destructive pursuits, turning aggression inward through a variety of forms such as drug addiction, alcoholism or suicide, a pattern he describes as "ominous."

"The increase in the number of black alcoholics, particularly among the young, is phenomenal," he says. "Even more frightening is the sharp rise in young black suicides, where black males under the age of 25 now have the highest suicide rate of any group in the country."

Technically, Watts is a three-square-mile community of about 28,000 residents in the southwestern corner of Los Angeles, a palm-lined ghetto of one-family cottages and sun-splashed public housing projects that appear benign compared to the festering tenements of New York's Harlem or the Chicago South Side.

But emotionally Watts represents the broader, predominantly south-central corridor of the city that fell under curfew during the 1965 riots that resulted in 34 deaths, more than 1,000 injured, and property damage estimated at $40 million.

Median family income in Watts is about $6,000, a figure that includes welfare benefits. Increasingly, it has become a community of welfare mothers and children, unemployed young blacks and the elderly. The group between 25 and 50 has become the vanishing generation of Watts.

Since the riots, Watts has become one of the most analyzed communities in America, yet the only tangible product of all the research and all the reports is a dust-gathering pile of paperwork and the corrosive emotion of failure.

Watts today is not typical of anything except a community where the cycle of poverty, promises and a new decline has exhausted the energy of change and hope. Conditions are not quite that bad for poor blacks in other areas of Los Angeles, but some other areas come close to Watts.

The city of Compton to the south, for example, is a community with black political control where conditions were recently described by a recent special report of the Los Angeles grand jury as "worse than at the time of the Watts revolt."

As in Watts, unemployment in Compton is running about 50 percent, and an estimated 60 percent of the population there is receiving some form of public assistance, compared to 24 percent in Watts 10 years ago.

And almost no one knows what to do about these conditions. For the most part — with few skills, money or other resources — there is little that the people of Watts can do outside of trying to survive one day at a time. Even the threat of rioting has little support, though each summer day still holds the potential for a spontaneous outburst.

"The cops got all the power," say Robert Searles, a lounger outside a Central Avenue barbecue stand. "Rocks ain't much good against tanks."

The Impact of Nonelites on Policy

Elections are an uncertain vehicle of political participation. Interest groups are highly specialized. The alternative forms of participation are erratic and even counterproductive. And yet needs, claims, and demands are introduced into the political arena by the actions of segments of nonelites. At least to some extent, elites feel obliged, or are forced, to respond. Their response may be merely symbolic, negative, or marginal, but there is nevertheless often some response and sometimes one consistent with nonelite demands.

Frequently, a fully satisfactory "solution" is impossible because of perceived conditions, opposition from other segments of nonelites, or elites' priorities and preferences. These determinations are made by elites, of course. Their power, status, and legitimacy enable them to decide how to fit demands that are strongly pressed and supported by established values into the mix of policy and practice that characterizes the political system. Other demands can normally be deflected or dismissed. In this process elites are aided by the screening effect of the greater participation and efficacy of the better-educated and higher-status members of nonelites. They cushion or absorb much of the thrust of deviant, minority, or lower-class demands before such demands emerge into the national political arena and begin to induce elite response.

In many instances at least some members of elites want to respond; they may even have been waiting for a chance to do so. Elites may support mass demands because they expect to benefit from doing so. Free universal public education is a case in point. Before the Industrial Revolution, free public education was an issue that divided Americans along economic class lines. It was a major plank in the platform of one of our earliest third parties, the Workingmen's Party, which gained considerable support among wage earners in Philadelphia between 1828 and 1832. The issue grew less and less controversial as industrial technologies required that a larger proportion of the work force be literate and possess elementary skills in arithmetic and what were called the "agricultural, industrial, and mechanic arts." Indeed, many states began establishing normal schools, state colleges, and universities around the middle of the nineteenth century, and in the Morrill Act of 1862 the federal government helped them to do so. As industry and agriculture have required work forces with increasingly complex skills, elite support for education at all levels has also increased. To some degree, this trend has been further bolstered by the fact that methods of financing state universities provide a direct subsidy to the largely middle-class students who attend them.

Sometimes elites have even more pressing and immediate economic reasons to support mass demands. In the early years of the twentieth century, a growing number of states enacted minimum-wage laws. It was widely acknowledged that if workers were unable to live on their earnings, they should be entitled to a wage that would at least support their families at a subsistence level. This policy was supported both on a moral basis and because it was recognized that people could not work efficiently when undernourished. A chief reason for the enactment of the first federal minimum-wage law in 1938 was its support by some powerful industrial groups, especially New England textile manufacturers. Forced by unions of their workers to pay higher wages than their unorganized southern competitors, the New England mill owners saw in the minimum wage a device to increase their competitors' labor cost to the level of their own, thereby improving their competitive position.

Social security legislation, certainly a significant benefit to a large part of the public, has also enjoyed substantial elite support, for economic and other reasons. Growing worker demands for industrial pension plans, backed by the right to strike, put employers under strong pressure to make some concessions. Governmental old-age benefits, financed by regressive payroll taxes paid chiefly by the workers and by consumers, represented an economical solution. Consequently, frequent improvements in the benefits and coverage of American social security legislation have been relatively uncontroversial since the basic federal law was enacted in 1935.

Elite Fear of Public Restiveness

This discussion has deliberately moved from a consideration of such routine channels of influence as voting and legislative bargaining to those some regard as illegitimate, such as civil disobedience. The analysis and illustrations should make it obvious that there is no clear dividing line between legitimate and illegitimate tactics. Similarly, there is no clear empirical distinction, but only an analytically useful one, between people who feel relatively gratified and those who feel relatively deprived. It is the relatively deprived who are most likely to support political strikes, boycotts, riots, civil disobedience, or civil war as channels of influence.

It is tempting but misleading to classify people neatly as content or dissatisfied, as exhibiting a sense of gratification or a sense of deprivation, as perceiving the political system as legitimate or illegitimate, or as believing that they are efficacious or politically powerless. Test results do, of course, categorize people in these ways, but there is also clear evidence, some of which we have already cited, that people's feelings may vary over time, by issue, and according to the social context in which the question is presented to them. How stable and how consistent any individual or social group is in these respects is an empirical question, to be answered by observation and research. To take stability and consistency for granted is to underestimate human complexity and to guarantee that some of the most significant political phenomena will not be investigated or fully understood.

In spite of great inequalities in wealth, power, and dignity, the mass of the population rarely makes demands for basic changes in who gets what. People usually accept their lot, partly because of the legitimizing and symbolic actions discussed earlier and partly because it is rarely clear how to organize common action among people who share the same grievances. Only when conditions become desperate or intolerable is common protest action likely, not simply when people come to expect a better life. Rising expectations alone do not bring serious political restiveness.

Sometimes public officials and the general public fail to recognize protest activities for what they are. A sharp increase in delinquent rent or tax payments, in truancy from school, or in welfare applications signals massive discontent, but because it is usually not organized or publicized, people see it only as individual delinquency, not as political action, so that it is more likely to result in repression than in responsiveness to people's grievances.

In the face of disorder or civil disobedience, however, there is sure to be some kind of elite response. Sometimes there are significant concessions. All industrialized countries, for example, have established social security systems, almost all of them instituted earlier and extending wider protection than the American system does. In Germany Bismarck's highly elitist and authoritarian government provided extensive social security protections as early as the 1880s.

Similarly, the civil rights demonstrations and boycotts led by Martin Luther King in the late 1950s and early 1960s brought wider awareness of discriminatory practices and of denials of civil liberties. Figure 19.8 shows that Congress passed the civil rights laws of 1964 and 1965 when demonstrations were most frequent. Though it is impossible to prove a direct causal connection, this study and others make it reasonable to conclude that the demonstrations were responsible both for a rise in public concern about civil rights and for congressional actions, which continued for a time even after the demonstrations began to wane. But the *enforcement* of the voting rights and open-housing laws Congress passed in those years is itself

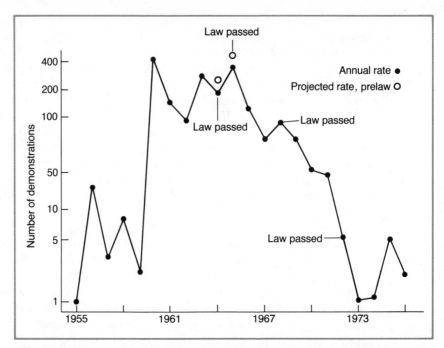

Figure 19.8 Number of civil rights demonstrations and passage of civil rights laws. (*Source*: Reprinted by permission of the publisher from "Public Opinion, Demonstration, and the Passage of Antidiscrimination Legislation," by Paul Burstein, *Public Opinion Quarterly* 43, Fall 1979, p. 169.)

responsive to public concern and so is likely to lapse with a decline in that concern.

Fear of mass restiveness or violence has been a major reason for the enactment of other governmental programs benefiting nonelites. For example, large-scale strikes, rural violence to protest the taking of land from farmers who could not make payments on their mortgages, and the spread of radical ideology helped win wide support for the New Deal reforms of the 1930s.

Though mass defiance is one of the few ways the poor and the disadvantaged have been able to achieve some political impact, the gains this tactic has won for them have usually been quite limited. While such legislative victories as those just mentioned are seen as major breakthroughs, their administrative enforcement tends to become half-hearted after a time, and symbolic results are more common than tangible ones. As protest fades, established inequalities often reappear, and concessions may be withdrawn.

The rise and demise of the National Welfare Rights Organization (NWRO) offers some insight into the uses and limits of disruption as a political strategy for disadvantaged groups. Founded in 1966 to promote the rights of welfare applicants and recipients, the NWRO relied during its first few years on mobilizing the poor to demonstrate against specific grievances. Though it had little money in its treasury and only a skeletal organization, NWRO repeatedly forced welfare office staff members to grant applicants the benefits to which they were legally entitled by informing them of their rights and helping them file claims, by staging demonstrations outside and inside the offices, picketing, demanding hearings, and encouraging a national campaign for special grants for hardship cases. This militancy not only won welfare rights for individuals and groups, but also contributed to support for the antipoverty program in general by reminding officials and the general public of the risks of disorder. The very success and prominence of the NWRO began to bring it legitimacy, substantial funds from private foundations and from the public treasury, and formal representation on governmental committees. By the early 1970s, it was functioning largely through the conventional lobbying channels of bureaucratic and legislative politics and abandoning its earlier reliance on demonstrations and disruption of established routines. As it became respectable, the NWRO, paradoxically, lost its effectiveness and gradually faded from the scene. Its demise was due not only to its change in tactics and status, but also to the ebbing of black protest generally.[20]

Militance and Popular Support

The efficacy of civil disobedience and militance in winning benefits for the masses depends ultimately on how much popular support these tactics stimulate for their cause. When they serve dramatically to call attention to deprivations widely regarded as shocking and unfair, they are effective in rallying such support. Until the civil disobedience campaigns of the early 1960s and the riots of the middle 1960s, a large segment of the American people was blissfully unaware of the "other America" living in poverty and denied basic civil rights. Increasingly militant demonstrations against the Vietnam War awakened many Americans to the dubious grounds on which the Johnson administration had justified escalation of the war, its high toll in civilian and military casualties, and the corruption and unpopularity of the Saigon regime.

Civil disobedience and violence do, as we have seen, create a "backlash" and so damage the political position of those who engage in them. Militance unquestionably antagonizes some people and evokes repression. The historical record leaves no doubt, however, that it also wins support for righting genuine wrongs. If such real deprivations can be dramatically brought to public attention, militant tactics are the most potent political device in the meager arsenal of tactics available to nonelites.

---

[20] Cf. Frances F. Piven and Richard A. Cloward, *Poor People's Movements* (New York: Pantheon Books, 1977), pp. 264–362.

Summary

Every government distributes or redistributes the benefits that people value and also tries to maintain its legitimacy: its public support and loyalty. Political parties and elections have always been the chief legitimizers of American government and its policies. Though they still serve that function, they are less effective legitimizers than they were twenty years ago, while some other political institutions are becoming much more effective.

Fewer people now identify themselves as Republicans or as Democrats, and the major parties have lost much of their historic role as raisers and spenders of funds in political campaigns. At the same time, more people call themselves independents, fewer vote on election day, fewer vote straight party tickets, and the lack of party discipline over public officials that has always been characteristic of American politics continues.

Single-issue groups and political action committees, especially on the right, have become more numerous and far more significant than they once were: in election financing, in lobbying, and in influencing public opinion. Interest groups act directly in election campaigns and in legislative, administrative, and judicial lobbying, largely filling the vacuum left by the reduced role of the parties. Aspirants for public office depend heavily on campaign management firms and public relations firms. The federal government has become the most important single source of campaign money. Through these developments, incumbents and groups with large financial and other resources have augmented their political clout.

Those who find it difficult or impossible to organize and those with little money or specialized skills at their disposal find this new political landscape threatening. Their most effective tactic is the kind of protest or disruption that makes elites willing to yield concessions, but such militance is necessarily sporadic, and its successes are often only temporary. Political participation, like economic participation in a capitalist state, remains very uneven in its forms and in its benefits.

PART
6

POWER STRUCTURE AND POLITICAL CHANGE

THE AMERICAN POWER STRUCTURE

It is now time to draw conclusions about the American power structure and to move on to what those conclusions mean for the character of American democracy and the prospect of change. We first summarize the evidence developed in this book and next explain (and elaborate upon) our choice among the models posed. Then we comment upon the implications for democracy. The issue of possible directions for change is left for Chapter 21.

A Summary of the Evidence

In Chapter 2 we described the models of power structure most often put forward: the pluralist, the establishment, and the ruling-class versions. In Chapter 11 we evaluated three different analytical approaches: systemic, policy consequences, and governing elites. We argued that the goal should be to apply a framework/approach that would permit any one of the three models of power structure to be proved correct if it conformed to the kinds of evidence developed in each approach. The first nine chapters of the book employed either the systemic or the policy-consequences approach, both of which substantially met our criteria; the evidence suggested either the establishment or the ruling-class model of power structure. Chapters 10–19, however, concentrated on elites in institutions and their relationship with nonelites. Of necessity, we used the governing-elites approach, which in this case involved considering (1) social background data, (2) actual decisionmaking, and (3) the part played by constitutional structure and the powers, rules, and practices of institutions. The relatively narrow focus on government institutions gave substantial advantage to the pluralist model, because it omitted many of the questions and much of the evidence on which the others depend. But we tried to correct for this potential tunnel vision by remaining aware of the total context in which institutional decisionmaking occurs.

In Chapters 2 and 3 we conceptualized and characterized an integrated political economy dominated by a relative handful of giant corporations and banks. We began to see that the structure and needs of this sector of the economy serve as a set of parameters — the taken-for-granted "givens" — for the making of all other major public policies. This corporate-banking dominance, moreover, reproduces itself in the social pyramid: the wealth, status, and leadership positions of the owners and managers of the biggest corporations and banks far outdistance the wealth, status, and leadership positions of ordinary citizens. In Chapter 10 we saw that this dominance is used to shape general public opinion and, through several key policy planning groups, to manage the political agenda. Overall, our application of the systemic approach showed clearly the control of major government actions by the concentrated power of the corporate-banking world.

In Chapters 4 and 5 we saw that both energy and military policies are based primarily on the needs of the corporate-banking sector for profitability, stability, and predictability. In Chapters 6 and 7 we saw that income distribution, taxation, welfare, and minorities policies have, over time and despite some recent efforts, done more to hold workers, women, and minorities at the bottom of the social pyramid than to help them. Sharp disparities in the pattern of burdens and benefits allocated by government policies were found, and they almost always favor the wealthier few in the society. The policy-consequences approach thus established a clear case of winners and losers from public policies and pointed to the probability that these same winners are indeed the powerholders of the society.

Chapters 8 and 9 sought to sketch the reactions of people to the economic and social pressures they experience and to the pattern of policies described. They address the extent to which people generally are dissatisfied with their government's performance and what, if anything, they want to do about it. We saw that there are many forces at work to build support for or acquiescence in the status quo, even when it does not serve a person's needs or interests. While there are significant movements seeking change, the most recent development is a powerful movement to defend the status quo and/or to do away with recent policy changes. The conflicts generated by these contrasting reactions, movements, and ideologies account for much of the dynamics of our politics today and are an important part of the total context.

In Chapters 12 through 16 we explored the constitutional structure, institutions, and traditions of the national government and the behavior of elites within them. We saw that these elites are drawn quite disproportionately from the upper classes and that the influences on them are also disproportionately from the corporate-banking sector or other wealthy sources. Constitutional structure and institutional rules and practices also favor the status quo and contain within acceptable limits whatever impulse toward change might be present. Size, scale, and inertia in the bureaucracy help the same cause. While this application of the governing-elites approach is somewhat more congenial to the pluralist interpretation of the American power structure, there appear to be clear and consistent biases directed toward policymaking in the interest of the upper echelons of the society and the corporate-banking sector in particular.

In Chapters 17 through 19, we saw that there are many unfulfilled wants and needs on the part of nonelites, but that it is very difficult for them to mobilize their power resources to achieve them. Much of their energy is spent in sheer economic survival or personal activities. Political parties are dominated by the wealthy, and elections become in many respects meaningless rituals. Other forms of pressing political goals are tried as a result, but with very mixed success. The overall picture that emerged was of a population undergoing substantial pressures and experiencing real needs, but lacking the mechanisms to translate demands into responsive public policies.

All these pieces of evidence seem to add up and to form themselves into some coherent themes about public policies, political values, and governmental structures and processes — and finally, power structure itself. The theme about public policies is by now tiresome: *Government policies assume that the existing organization, operations, motivations, and perceived needs of the American economic system must be preserved and furthered in every practical way.* No other premises or motivations evident in U.S. public policies effectively displace this basic assumption. Nor can any goal, however desirable in the abstract, be implemented effectively if it conflicts with this presupposition. Given this basic premise, governmental actions and their consequences may be understood as a coherent, integrated, and purposeful package. Without such recognition, they can only be described, with puzzlement at apparent contradictions and chagrin at the mixture of successes and failures, hopes and frustrations.

The needs of the economic order are expressly addressed in the area of economic stability and growth. They are evident in development policies and again in military expenditures. The military establishment and the space program are also vital to such foreign policy goals as limiting Communist expansion and inducing developing nations to adapt their economies to ours and to reach more harmonious long-term relationships. Anticommunism itself rests heavily on the desire to protect the existing economic order and the values surrounding it. Policies to combat poverty encounter resistance because they conflict with values that bolster the economic system (such as self-reliance and rewards according to effort and talent) and because they threaten the distribution of wealth and power that system creates. Racism lingers in part because stronger measures to enforce desegregation and equal opportunity would run counter to economic values (such as freedom to sell property or hire workers) and perhaps disrupt the current operations of the economic system. In short, although the policy areas we have examined were chosen only because of their diversity and continuing social importance, actual governmental policies in each area seem to flow from the same economic premises. What appeared to be isolated, independent problem areas, each with a distinctive set of characteristics and relevant political forces, now appear to be overlapping, integrated extensions of a single set of priorities and limitations.

The theme with respect to political values is closely related: *in practice, economic values and property rights take precedence over any other values, such as equality or community.* The rights to a return on invested capital, protection of that return by armed force if necessary, and the unrestricted use and secure enjoyment of one's property converge to impose imperatives for governmental action abroad. They also create imperatives for, and erect barriers against, governmental action in domestic affairs. The United States must stand firm against communism and in favor of an open door to developing nations. It must maximize economic growth, but tread lightly in combating poverty and racism because of these strong commitments. Associated with property rights are the allied economic values of materialism and profit maximization and the exaltation of productivity as a sufficient measure of societal achievement. Below this upper echelon of values are some with lower priority but more general applicability, such as anticommunism and the tendency to resort to military force if the dominant economic values are not being adequately served by other means. Still lower on the scale, and subject to a strong general commitment to the existing distribution of wealth and racial status, is the value of equality. Centuries of much rhetoric and some action have given equality real stature as a principle, though it remains subject to the higher priority of other values.

This rough ordering is an operational (as distinguished from historically received, rhetorical, or symbolic) ranking of American political values and goals. The central economic values we have identified and ranked as paramount need not have been explicit in the minds of policymakers. But they are evident in several apparently independent policy areas and over lengthy time periods. Whether implicit or explicit in the minds of policymakers, they seem to have been prime factors in the shaping of policies.

These chiefly economic values and goals may serve as an initial framework for understanding the relative weights given to other political values. The latter must be assigned lesser status in the hierarchy, according to the extent to which they are in harmony with and serve to further the paramount values and goals. Ultimately, we emerge with a serviceable and historically grounded image of the priority ranking of political values that currently animates the American political system. In brief, it amounts to the protection and promotion of the American economic system and the distribution patterns it has established by various means, culminating in military force.

The theme with regard to *government structures and processes* is that *they are anything but neutral; instead, they limit majorities, systematically favor the status quo, and protect the opportunity of those with private power resources to gain their ends without "interference."* The constitutional structure and institutional arrangement of American government, for example, limit the legal capacities of national, state, and local governments and disperse the total governing power across a wide landscape of levels and branches. The effect is to ensure primacy for the private sphere on most questions. Those who are able to generate the greatest power out of private sources can shape basic patterns of thought and behavior, because government is unable to act coherently in majoritarian interests. Instead, government is open to penetration by major private interests, which use its many veto points to establish defenses against the threat of change in economic and social life. Majorities of people are delayed, if not prevented, from achieving their common goals by their internal divisions and by the complex procedures and limitations that must be transcended. For decisive governmental action to occur, it must be entirely consistent with the limits and goals of external powerholders, or there must be some highly unusual organizing force (such as an extreme emergency or a charismatic leader, or both) operating to unify its dispersed powers.

Similarly, decision-making persons and processes operate with a set of imperatives and constraints that combine to reinforce the economic priorities. To begin with, many offices are filled by persons who have previously risen to high positions in the legal, banking, or business communities. Their orthodoxy seems assured. Even persons who achieve high official status from extraestablishment positions experience powerful inducements to adhere to accepted priorities. They are normally appointed to governmental offices only because they have acted out their commitments to established values in some way. After doing so for some time, they may find it natural and congenial and a way to avoid a rash of complaints from others in high places. More important, nearly every officeholder shrinks from the prospect of national unemployment or depression and thus becomes committed almost by default to maintaining the growth and prosperity of the existing economy as a (if not *the*) major priority of government.

Many officeholders are thoroughly familiar with the need for good relations with major sources of wealth. Both political parties, and nearly all candidates for nominations within them, are able to compete effectively only with the support of large contributors. Access to the mass media, if not the official support of those who own them, is essential to winning office. Officeholders thus learn the importance of economics early and in a multitude of ways. Under these circumstances, their decisionmaking cannot help but reflect the priorities of the established economic system. In short, neither structures nor processes are neutral in the sense of giving rise equally to any number of different patterns of policy. Instead, they contribute to reinforcement of the standards that yield this particular set of results.

At every major stage of analysis, this review suggests that the policy consequences we have examined are not the product of accident or coincidence. They reflect a consistent relationship among policies, values, institutional structures, and the officials and processes by which decisions are made. Each of these political factors independently contributes to, and in effect reinforces, the primacy of property rights and the protection and promotion of the economic system as the basis of policymaking.

The American Power Structure

The evidence has cumulated into a single coherent package; no major component is at odds with any of the others. There seems little doubt that the pluralist interpretation must be rejected on the grounds that it (1) ignores much of the evidence and (2) is simply wrong in its many assumptions. We have already noted the narrowness of an exclusive focus on government institutions and need not belabor that point further. We will expand on the second as a means of making clear why pluralism is unacceptable as an interpretation of the power structure in the United States.

Part of the problem with the pluralist model lies with an ideological premise — the extraempirical conviction that the United States is an open, democratic political system in which all citizens play roughly equal parts in shaping governmental policy — and it strains to interpret events to conform to this optimistic assumption. It never asks, for example, to what extent the American political parties actually present the electorate with the full range of possible policy choices at elections or to what extent both parties are controlled by factors other than popular preferences.

But let us go on to state two even more serious problems: one of commission and one of omission. First is the charge that nearly every major assumption the pluralist view makes about the economic and social structures of the United States is wrong. And second, it is argued that this view fails to explain why a consistent pattern of policy consequences and operative values exists — unless one makes some very agile intellectual leaps or some very unlikely assumptions about the society we live in. The latter criticism interests us more, for the former has been made often and with little effect on those who choose to adhere to this interpretation. But let us consider each in turn.

First, there seem to be solid grounds for challenging almost every assumption about the American social and economic structure that underlies this interpretation of the structure of power. The social and economic systems are not separate from, but intimately integrated with, the political system. One cannot rise to the top in the former without both acquiring the capacity to, and experiencing the necessity of, exerting power in the latter.[1] Inequalities of social status and economic possessions (and hence of the major resources of power) in the United States are too obvious and too widely documented to require much elaboration. Wealth, whether measured by income or by property holdings, is heavily concentrated in the upper twentieth of the population, with severe deprivation in the lowest third. Vast accumulations of economic power in the great corporations are under the control of a relative handful of owners and managers.

The social structure clearly represents these facts of economic life: a small upper class dominates the major institutions and controls the corporate economy, while a large middle class takes its cues from this upper class. More than half of the population, however, consists of blue-collar workers, low-salaried office personnel (particularly women), and the unemployed and unemployable. This large proportion of the society is divided against itself — whites resisting the progress of blacks, and men defending their "prerogatives" against women — so that the upper echelon's preponderance of effective power is even greater than its share of wealth and official positions would suggest. Although each system — economic, social, and political — is "open" in the sense that some members of each rising generation are able to penetrate or be co-opted into the upper reaches, the general patterns are continuity (those on top stay there) and concentration and overlap (those on top in one system merge with those on top in the others). "One man, one vote" thus evokes a democratic illusion: power flows from many sources other than votes, and concentrations of power of various kinds regularly move into government and work their will through government.

Readily documentable social and economic realities suggest much less benign and self-congratulatory value judgments about its operation than those implied by the pluralistic interpretation. At the very least, there are substantial grounds to doubt the propriety of terming this system "democratic." More important for our analysis, the crucial assumptions of the pluralist model about social and economic structure seem seriously to lack

---

[1] In part, this is a matter of defining what constitutes "power" and what activities are "political." The reader should recognize by now that we are committed to broad definitions of both and should choose the definitions that seem most reasonable under the circumstances. But we do not stand solely on our definition: the empirical verification is also extensive and, we think, persuasive.

empirical accuracy. And if it is factually invalid in these important respects, as well as dubious in its accompanying value judgments, the model itself appears to be undermined.

The second criticism of the pluralistic interpretation is that the consistent pattern of policy consequences and operative values we have identified is left completely unexplained. This is a crucial point, with profound implications for the validity of the pluralist model. The first criticism, examined above, has been made regularly, exhaustively, and with considerable evidential support. But it has not been accepted by most political scientists, because the link between social and economic inequalities of power and the actions of government has not been demonstrated to their satisfaction. It is not enough, in the eyes of those who subscribe to the pluralist model, to show that inequalities result in concentrations of power in the upper echelons of the population and that these same people hold a very high proportion of the key positions in government. It must also be shown that such people *actually use their power* to cause government to act in ways that are *not only in accordance with their own interests, but also opposed to the public interest.* This is a high standard of proof, perhaps insisted on out of the deep desire to believe in a relatively democratic interpretation of power. It is not an illogical standard, but is a very difficult one to meet, given the understandable limitations on acquiring accurate evidence about the motivations of decisionmakers.

The evidence we have developed, however, circumvents this difficulty and addresses the issue of whether governmental action is shaped according to the preferences of private powerholders. We have seen the consequences of government policies, and we have extrapolated the value priorities that actually dominate governmental action. The central theme is action on behalf of the preservation and promotion of the economic order, frequently at the cost of personal deprivations for many millions of people and denial of values that are rhetorically exalted. Such actions are, however, entirely consistent with the interests and power of the upper echelons of the overlapping social and economic structures of the United States.

In the light of such evidence, it seems fair to infer that the patterns we discerned were brought about by *some* consistent and purposeful force operating through the government. We may then demand that alternative interpretations attempt to explain *how* this consistent pattern may have been produced. The pluralist model offers only happenstance, coincidence, or determinism by way of explanation. We think that there must be more plausible explanations. We have seen solid evidence of the manner in which major powerholders go about the task of shaping public opinion, managing the political agenda, and exercising the powers of public office to achieve their ends. Accordingly, we shall reject the pluralist model ex-*cept with regard to minor decisions* and shall concentrate on the search for more plausible interpretations of the structure of power as it applies to the fundamental issues of politics.

Our problem now is to choose between the establishment and the rul-ing-class models. In at least one important respect, the two interpretations agree that on all fundamental questions, a unified power structure is ready and determined to defend the status quo in drastic and effective ways. But in most other respects, the two models are quite distinctive. The ruling-class model in effect abstracts one dimension — the economic — out of the establishment model and makes of it a simpler, harsher characterization of the structure of power. The economic dimension is surely central to the establishment model and is the proper one to build on if only one theme is to dominate. But doing so posits not only a different basis of power, but also a distinctive set of implications for the various prospects and tactics of change.

The ruling-class model sees power arising from economic holdings, tightly concentrated in private hands, and using government as a tool. The establishment model sees power flowing from several resources (of which economic strength is a major one) and thus spread more broadly within the upper echelons of the society. Decisive power in any situation may rest with an ad hoc coalition of establishment members, depending on the subject area, the dynamics of specific events and social conditions, the skills of strategically located individuals, and the particular configuration of popu-lar attitudes toward the government and the issue. Private power merges subtly with government's independent powers after an exchange in which people at the top act and elicit symbol- and ideology-induced support for that action from key segments of the general public. Again, the result may be the same, but the process is different. The establishment model envi-sions a somewhat more open process, characterized by interchangeable roles for a larger number of top figures, greater mutual dependence between individuals in and out of government, and greater reliance on more or less "voluntary" popular support.

The ruling-class model emphasizes economic sources of power and economic motivations on the part of the ruling elite, with capitalism as the source of the values and ideology that facilitate their management of the system. The establishment model not only is multicausal, but also sees an independently generated set of values as more important than economic interests on at least some decision-making occasions. This belief system, perhaps originally influenced quite strongly by the nature of the economic system, is seen as now self-perpetuating. Although it has a strong economic component, it is made up also of the heritage of Anglo-American legal thought, Judaeo-Christian religious postulates, and such values as national-ism, patriotism, and equality. When the establishment acts, it does so on the basis of one or a combination of these received values and beliefs. There is thus more room for uncertainty on its part and greater need for confidence that key segments of the population concur and support it. To state the point from the perspective of nonelites, the establishment is more vulnerable to popular demands.

The ruling-class model assumes a greater divergence of interests be-tween upper and lower classes and a more distinctive set of values and ideology among those lower classes. Accordingly, although it too sees ideology-based manipulation as a convenient means of managing the masses, physical coercion plays a greater part in maintaining elite governance. In part because coercion is employed so regularly, the lower classes are kept aware of their different interests. Of course, the middle and upper classes are not normally cognizant of such violence and would probably assume it to be necessary and justified if they were. The establishment model tends to see lower classes as more fully captured by the values and ideology pro-mulgated by the establishment, so that they do not clearly recognize the divergence of their interests from the middle and upper levels. Thus, man-agement of popular preferences is easier. The underlying value system contributes massively to the stability of the economic and political order because it teaches the population to "genuinely" want, accept, and defend what is in the establishment's interest. Physical coercion, though necessary at times, is a last resort. Further, indiscriminate use of physical coercion raises the risk of loss of support (and bestowed "legitimacy") by a people who have been taught to revere due process.

The ruling-class model has the virtue of zeroing in on the central theme of power and presenting a clear and coherent interpretation of the Ameri-can power structure. It permits clearer assignment of motivation and much greater apparent predictability of future elite behavior. The establishment model, although it posits the same results in crisis situations, envisions those results as flowing from a distinctly more complex structure and process. The differences are not insignificant, in light of our concern for the prospects of change. Stated briefly, the most crucial issues are (1) the relative solidarity and single-mindedness of decisive elites and the extent to which they are able to command, as opposed to being obliged to seek to acquire and de-velop, the power resources of government; and (2) the extent to which their management of the polity is accomplished through consent or quies-cence manipulated or coerced from the lower classes, as opposed to drawing more on apparently "voluntary" support. These are open questions, for which conclusive evidence is still lacking. And much is at stake in the answers tentatively chosen.

Implications for Change

The implications for change may already be obvious. If the ruling-class model is correct, elites are largely impenetrable by nonelites; nor is govern-ment a significant means of nonelite access to a share of power. But at the same time, there is greater consciousness of divergence of interest and dep-rivation among the lowest classes. Under these conditions, there may be a continuing tension between the desire for change below and the rigid structure of power above. For change to occur, however, drastic reconstruction of the social order from below — by forceful means — may be the only route. However unlikely, and perhaps unattractive to contemplate, no other method of change is in keeping with this interpretation.

If the establishment model is correct, elites' incomplete domination of government and their need for its legitimating power open an aperture for nonelite penetration. If representatives of such nonelites are successful at acquiring key offices and at resisting coming to serve as establishment agents, they may succeed in short-circuiting accepted practices or even in introducing new priorities. Because the underlying values generate broad and "voluntary" support for the existing economic and political order and the establishment is genuinely dependent on this support for effective management of the system, two paradoxical results follow. The establishment recognizes that it must at least appear to satisfy changing demands among the major segments of the population, and may even be led by such changes to adopt new policies. But changes in values and ideology require long periods of education, among the principal devices for which is the behavior of leading establishment figures themselves. One implication of the mutually reinforcing situation is that power relationships may remain apparently stable for some time, while shifts in underlying values are actually steadily eroding the bases of that power. When a dramatic event or condition sparks bold action by some establishment figure, he or she may encounter widespread approval and acceptance, much to the surprise of all who remain steeped in the conventional wisdom.

Thus, with the establishment model, relatively peaceful change seems somewhat more possible. It does require a special convergence of people, events, and conditions, and even then it is likely to proceed only to modest lengths before enough popular demands are satisfied to reduce the situation to a manageable level again. Further, it requires a period of value change to bring broad segments of the population to the point where their desires induce some establishment members to act boldly in unprecedented directions. The few truly change-oriented representatives of nonelites who penetrate the establishment and remain unco-opted are not able to do more than raise issues. Although this is a major means through which segments of the public can adopt new priorities, only determined mass insistence on doing so will cause the establishment to agree to the wholesale modification of governmental policies.

Which of these two interpretations of the structure of power is the more accurate? As may be clear from our analysis, we tentatively accept the more complex establishment interpretation. We acknowledge the revealing thrust of the ruling-class version and view it as an often accurate portrait; we are also aware of the utility of clear and direct answers to "Who rules?" But there seem to us to be more currents of power at work, greater uncertainty in the ways power is mobilized and applied, and more (though by no means direct) influence by popular attitudes. For these reasons, our image of the American power structure is essentially that of the establishment model. Perhaps we are also affected by the contrasting implications for the nature and prospects of change; discouraging as it is, the establishment model nevertheless holds out some hope for a process of change that falls short of full-scale revolution.

The Nature of the American Establishment

Let us expand a bit on the nature and operating style of the American establishment as a preliminary to full analysis of the prospects of change. The concept of an *establishment*, though vague and subject on occasion to overtones of conspiracy, has an expressiveness that justifies its use. For us the term encompasses individuals holding positions of power (in government *and* private affairs) who have come to share roughly the same values, interests, political ideology, and sense of priorities about what government should be doing. Most of all, it denotes a shared proprietary concern for the continued success of the enterprise — meaning the American system in its familiar social, economic, and political dimensions. Admission to the establishment is not easy, and it is never automatic. It is contingent first on possession of some distinct power resource, such as institutional position (in politics, business, education, or other fields), talent, money, family status, and so forth. Among the many men and women with such resources, some are distinguished by their concern for the success of the enterprise, their willingness to play by the familiar rules, and their talent for finding and articulating the compromise or making the sacrifice that ensures conflict reduction. These are the crucial attributes. It is such people whom established leaders will invite into the loose and highly informal establishment. Members recognize one another not by labels or lapel pins, but by the orthodoxy they share — for example, the readiness with which they can negotiate with one another, even across class lines or occupational boundaries. Establishment types are "regular guys" who try to understand the other fellow's problems, avoid "rocking the boat" publicly, and instead do what they can to reach accommodations in which all end up better off than when they started. Mutual trust, mutual support, and mutual advantage knit the establishment together, but it is never so self-conscious and coherent as when challenges arise to the very system that has made possible this relaxed and congenial arrangement.

The establishment recognizes its antagonists on both left and right, uses their complaints to demonstrate its own middle-road propriety, but acts against them only when they "go too far." In part, this is because the establishment has loose margins at either side, some useful part-time members moving back and forth, and it prefers to act only at such late stages that practically all its members and supporters will concur that "something must be done." (This was true, for example, when conservatives took the lead in the late stages of undermining Senator Joseph McCarthy in the 1950s and again when liberals formed the cutting edge of prosecution of radicals and peace movement leaders in the 1960s.) Within the establishment itself, consensus is highly valued. Members may disagree on occasion, particularly over the *best* means by which to preserve the system in times of crisis, without risking their membership unless their convictions lead them to take antisystem instead of system-preserving actions.

Thus, our concept of establishment does not suggest that a unified upper social class totally and automatically dominates the nation's political structure, though great wealth and upper-class connections serve many as platforms from which they can achieve such a status. Nor do we see economic imperatives as the sole determinants of establishment actions, though in the absence of compelling reasons to the contrary, they will often be the "natural" principles of behavior. We do not even envision much explicit consultation among establishment members about positions on issues, partly because none is necessary. Our concept of an establishment is not a tight ruling class, but neither is it the benevolent representative statesmen envisioned by some democratic pluralists. Our establishment ranges between the two, depending on the type of issue involved. On most routine issues and decisions, it may function much as the latter view suggests. But on fundamental questions or when the system itself is threatened, it acts in ways characteristic of the former.

Social background and shared responsibility for the management of public affairs are not the only factors operating to cause decisionmakers at this level to see issues from a single perspective. Most people in key positions are of roughly the same generation and thus became politically "aware" at the same period in American history. All of us tend to be structured permanently by what was happening in politics at the time we happened to tune in to such matters. For one generation, Vietnam meant opposition to a callous and wasteful foreign policy. For many of their teachers, however, political socialization occurred during the early days of the cold war or the late years of World War II, when one did not question the need to defend the "free world" and to resist the spread of communism. For those who made up the establishment in the 1960s, the structuring experiences dated back to pre–World War II failures to contain Hitler, and they showed that they remembered those lessons. The analogy to Munich and the inevitable failure of appeasement was offered again and again as a rationale for American policy in Vietnam.

The image of international communism as a unified, monolithic force was shared by most decisionmakers. Thus, wherever trouble broke out in the world, including the United States, the guiding hand of Moscow was discerned. An oft-cited classic example is the allegation by Dean Rusk, made two years after the Chinese Revolution, while he was in charge of Far East operations for the State Department, that Mao Tse-tung was a

Russian agent. Mao's regime, he asserted, was "a colonial Russian government — a Slavic Manchukuo on a large scale — it is not the government
of China. It does not pass the first test. It is not Chinese."[2] The point is
not that anyone can be wrong on occasion. It is that each generation shares
a basic image of what is going on in politics and what is likely to happen,
created largely by the lessons its members have drawn from experiences at
the outset of their careers. As such, today's establishment shares an understanding of the world derived from the 1940s and before.

The Establishment View of the World

The convergence and rigidification of beliefs and principles of action among
the top echelon of decisionmakers is further aided by some characteristic
features of large-scale organizations. Once a position has been taken and
the organization has become committed to it in terms of allocation of resources and the career investments of personnel, it is very difficult to modify
its methods, purposes, or actions. Many large agencies of the national government, such as the FBI and the State Department, are now committed
to a view of the world, a set of procedures, and an understanding of how
things should work that reflect and support the establishment's principles.
They see, and report to their superiors, what is consistent with their expectations and career aspirations. One classic example of the triumph of
organizational commitments over evidence is the experience of strategic
bombing during World War II.[3] The Air Force and its supporters had
insisted for years that bombing alone could destroy German war production,
cripple the armed forces, and eliminate the German people's will to fight.
The U.S. Air Force accordingly had been designed and trained for strategic
bombing, which was carried out with high optimism and massive loads of
explosives. But according to the careful postwar Strategic Bombing Survey
undertaken by the air force itself, strategic bombing never seriously affected
war production, had little or no effect on the capacity of the armed forces or
the will of the population, and incurred heavy losses in the bargain. Intelligence failures, equipment failures, and faulty analysis of the German
economy and society were also to blame, but the chief explanation was
simply the incapacity of bombing to accomplish the goals set for it. The
same conclusion was arrived at by a similar official study in Japan at the
end of hostilities there. But the Vietnamese experience suggests that lessons about the limited capabilities of air power have still not been learned.

An establishment of relatively small size thus receives many self-
confirming and supporting messages from its environment. Its approach

---

[2] Dean Rusk, as quoted in Ronald Steel, *Pax Americana* (New York: Viking, 1967),
p. 129. In 1961 Rusk became secretary of state, serving in that capacity until 1969.
[3] This account is drawn from Herbert Wilensky, *Organizational Intelligence: Knowledge
and Policy in Government and Industry* (New York: Basic Books, 1967), pp. 24–34.

to politics and its view of the world are validated by almost every trusted source — in bureaucratic memoranda, in the communications media, and at the country club. Attitudes and practices may, under such circumstances, become hardened. Supported by belief in the rightness of their actions, and even in the sacred nature of their responsibility to defend the system against those who would undermine it, members of the establishment may become highly resistant to basic change.

But this does not mean that they are insensitive or inflexible. Indeed, long-term stability is promoted by short-term flexibility (within limits) and adroit channeling of thrusts toward change — in part through judicious use of available coercive power. Although one major characteristic of the establishment is its shared basic beliefs and principles of political action, it would be a gross misinterpretation to see such agreement extending to rigidity of *membership* or of *specific policies*. Indeed, one of the most stability-producing features of American ideology and practice — of the American system, in other words — is its flexibility. By opening itself to new members, new ideas, and new policies, the American system incorporates thrusts toward change into its upper-level consensus. *Such new members, ideas, and policies must, however, accept the basic framework of political values, ideology, structure, and style on which that system is based.* To the extent that they do, of course, extrasystemic movements for change are effectively blunted. Popular movements lose their leaders and their platforms. New governmental policies include enough of their proposals to give the appearance of progress — and reasons for unusual political activity no longer exist.

Co-optation, Flexibility, and Stability

The process by which rising leaders with new ideas or programs are drawn into the establishment is known as *co-optation*. Many aspiring young men and women seek leadership positions and try to display their ideas and talents in such a way as to make themselves candidates for co-optation. Others find that their efforts on behalf of a particular constituency gain attention and produce opportunities to take on governmental responsibility and carry out some of the programs they have been urging. In both cases, establishment-arranged appointments to offices or aid in electoral advancement lead to rises in stature and responsibility. The sobering consequences of responsibility then combine with the real difficulties of achieving goals through the complex political process to induce the candidate to practice the skills of accommodation and mutual support that are the hallmark of the establishment. A candidate who demonstrates these skills and concern for the maintenance of the essential outlines of the system will rise further; one who does not will soon decide to leave government, thereby losing prospective establishment status.

Co-optation does not mean that new leaders give up their independence, ideas, or program entirely. They retain substantial proportions of each, but learn to adapt them to the framework of the established system so that they are compatible with it. They frequently do succeed in changing things, if they are skillful advocates of their causes, but not as much as they might originally have wished (and for reasons that they — and we — might rightly consider fully persuasive). The directions of public policy may shift in response to such initiatives after strenuous efforts by their new leaders, their supporters, and the new allies their establishment status has made available to them. When the process has run its course, some new policies have been instituted, the basic complaints against the system have been reduced, the establishment has absorbed new members, and the system has acquired new defenders. The basic outlines of the system have again survived. Flexibility in the short run, in other words, means permanence in the long run.

Other types of flexibility also contribute to the stability of the American political system. Many layers of government make for many alternative ways to achieve particular goals, and people who seek ends unacceptable to those in power may be directed from one government to another, from one type of approach to another, or from one branch, committee, or department to another. Demands that at first seem indigestible or extreme may be converted into another form and thereby rendered satisfiable. A minority group's demand for status and recognition may be salved by appointing a prominent leader to a visible position or by naming a public monument or park in the group's honor. Or, if not quieted by such costless tactics, the group may be diverted by channeling its claims into aggression against another minority religious or racial group. Some claims can be converted into economic demands or settled largely on such terms.

The materialistic orientation of the people and the abundance of the economy have made this a recurring tactic throughout American history. By merely increasing the size of the total economic product and directing the new surplus toward the demanding group, its claims could be satisfied without depriving those who were already advantaged of any of their possessions or expectations. In the history of labor-management conflicts, for example, an increase in total production and therefore total profits (or an increase in price to the consumer) made it possible to grant higher wages without reducing owners' returns. Workers, for their part, tended to be satisfied by higher wages and to abandon other goals, such as control over the means of production.

Flexibility is thus a means of absorbing, blunting, and deflecting thrusts toward change. But flexibility does not operate alone to promote stability. It functions in tandem with other factors to induce or compel behavior into the established channels. American political ideology emphasizes procedural regularity and insists on working through the means provided for the attainment of political goals. The "law-and-order" ethic legitimates action against those who do not follow such prescribed procedures. And under the conditions of the late twentieth century, the official agencies of law enforcement have a vast monopoly over the power that is necessary to compel obedience. Thus, there is a considerable array of inducements at work to direct political activity into forms that can be dealt with by the established order without serious threat.

Over the years, these factors have helped to render the American system stable — in itself a desirable characteristic for a political system to enjoy. Most people probably would assess the costs of this stability (in terms of lost opportunities, unfulfilled aspirations, poverty for some, and the like) as entirely tolerable. To many, stability is the highest priority in politics. Whether stability continues to be equally desirable today, measured against possibly greater costs and more challenging conditions, is a more acute and more controversial question. After an extended period of stability, unabsorbed pressures for change may build to explosive potential. Or issues may arise that even the most flexible system will have difficulty containing.

Implications for Democracy

How is it that so many Americans can so firmly believe that the United States is a democracy, when the evidence so clearly points to rule by the establishment on behalf of the corporate-banking sector of the economy? Part of the answer must lie with the power of ideology and symbolism, described in Chapter 8. But part may also be found in the way democracy has come to be defined in the United States. We understand democracy entirely in terms that are compatible with capitalism and its associated structure of power; in other words, we know only *liberal democracy*. This is a kind of democracy that emphasizes the participation of citizens in elections and in communications to their government (writing letters, lobbying, and the like), stresses the availability of civil liberties, and endorses regular procedures for elite decisionmaking. Freedom means only the absence of government interference, and equality means only the opportunity to take part in economic and social life. It is a *procedural* definition of democracy, one that ignores as much about the world as does the pluralists' exclusive focus on governmental institutions.

A contrasting definition of democracy would be *substantive* in character — that is, it would emphasize the *content* of public policies, the *conditions* of people's lives, and the *quality* of their daily experiences. Substantive democracy would compare people's wants and needs with what the government was actually doing and measure the extent of democracy by what that government *did* rather than merely by the fact that people were able to vote for decisionmakers. Substantive democracy would focus on the conditions of people's lives and insist that equality should have social and economic dimensions and that people therefore should be roughly equal in wealth, status, and power. Only that way can they be truly equal politically.

Freedom would become the ability to do things, which would require the removal of constraints flowing from private power and vast development of people's human talents and potential. And substantive democracy would be concerned for people's relationships with other people, their sense of dignity and happiness.

If most Americans accepted the substantive definition of democracy, they would not so readily describe the United States as a democracy. It is crucial to governance by the few in the United States that most people accept the procedural definition of democracy, and it is a major ideological achievement that they have been led to do so. Definitions are by no means unimportant, and much intense political struggle takes place in a very quiet way over what definitions are to be inculcated in people. There *have* been advocates of the substantive definition of democracy in our history: some abolitionists, some black thinkers, some populists, some socialists, some feminists. And part of the radical left today seeks to raise just this issue. Whether they can successfully put the question of change into the form of an effort to fully realize democracy in its substantive sense may be the real key to progressive change in the future.

POLITICAL CHANGE

This chapter addresses the most crucial questions about the future of the American political system. Will there be change? What kind? What kind of change *should* there be? How may such change come about? These questions force us to try to say how political change does and can occur, given the current political power structure and associated social and economic order of the United States. Applying this general framework to circumstances as they develop, we can generate some sense of the types of change that are most likely to occur.

We will first speculate about when and how change occurs and what determines the form such change will take. We will specify factors and relationships among factors that make change of various kinds either more or less, likely. Then we will apply this framework to contemporary events in the United States in an effort to assess the probable outcome of the forces now operating in this country.

The Analysis of Political Change: A Framework

At the outset, we should recognize that there is often no direct, logical, or "rational" relationship between events or conditions and perceptions or consequences of them. The central theme of symbolic analysis of politics is the *gap* between perceptions or beliefs on the one hand and actual gains or losses in money, power, status, or tangible goods on the other. As political conflict escalates, this gap becomes wider.

The winner of symbolic victories may not be the winner of tangible victories. As an international war or "police action" escalates, the low- and middle-income citizens of the country that is victorious on the battlefield may find their taxes far more burdensome, their lives more regimented, their sons and relatives killed or wounded. But they are "the winners." Defenders of civil rights who win a court decision guaranteeing that accused persons be provided with lawyers and information about their procedural rights may later learn that actual practices in the stationhouse have changed little or not at all. Citizens whose outcries against arbitrary rate increases and poor service by a public utility bring about legislation to protect consumer interests have won a symbolic victory. But this form of political triumph rarely brings about lower rates or better service for long. The regulatory agency often makes it easier for the utility to raise rates.

Other disparities between perceived and real changes in policy consequences become evident as political conflict widens and intensifies. Benefits often come to be perceived as deprivations and vice versa. As international conflict grows hotter, the armed forces gain larger appropriations for weapons, new powers to draft soldiers, higher status, and more influence on governmental decisions. It is chiefly the poor and the lower middle class whose sons are drafted to fight, whose incomes are disproportionately taxed, and whose influence on governmental decisions is least. Rather than appearing as real benefits and losses for a specific group of people, however, these changes are perceived and publicized as "costs" of defense, sacrifices the nation as a whole must valiantly assume to combat its enemies.

Even the identification of enemies and allies becomes confused and uncertain and may fail to correspond to observable reality as conflict escalates. Such confusion is not accidental, but a consistent and systematic aspect of political conflict. It is important to create perceptions that induce people to fight, and to sacrifice if necessary, to serve a noble cause and to defeat an evil one. In international conflict the belief is fostered that the country is uniting to defeat a common enemy. In fact, there are always internal divisions about whether and how seriously the fight should be waged and whether the enemy is really harmful or malevolent. These internal divisions partly reflect the differences in interest noted above. Escalation means that the more hawkish or militant groups are winning more support than their dovish rivals. As already noted, hawkish groups win support for their foreign counterparts as they win it for themselves, though this tacit cooperation is systematically masked by belief in the implacable hostility of the two countries.

As civil rights conflict escalates, the same ambiguities appear. Here the symbolic conflict is between believers in "the rights of minorities" and believers in "law and order." These symbols unite people on both sides and bolster political support. At the same time, there are tangible gains and losses for both supporters and opponents of civil rights that do not correspond to the symbolic definition of the situation. As civil rights conflict grows more intense, the more militant groups on both sides win tangible benefits and the less militant ones lose. White supremacists and civil libertarians win followings and money as public opinion is polarized. The police get larger appropriations for personnel and weapons, higher status and more influence for top police officials, and greater authority over others. The more militant black groups gain moral and financial support at the expense of the Urban League and white liberals. To make this point is to recognize both that there is competition for tangible benefits within groups of symbolic allies and that escalation benefits militants, whereas détente benefits moderates and compromisers. There is, then, a systematic link between symbol and fact, but it is a link that conceals or distorts the facts and thus can evoke political support for self-defeating policies.

Most political conflict is ritualistic. It is confined within narrow limits and pursued through mutually accepted routines; furthermore, it serves more to justify than to determine outcomes, for they are largely predetermined by long-standing differences in bargaining resources. Election campaigns (especially in a two-party system), the procedures of regulatory administrative agencies, and most international arms and trade negotiations are examples of such ritualized conflict. To the minor degree that they bring about policy changes, their functions are generally recognized and reported in the news. Insofar as they serve to promote wide public acceptance of leaders and of policy outcomes (that is, serve symbolic functions), news reports typically miss their significance.

Political leaders retain followings (which are, of course, what makes them leaders) by means of a number of devices that are basically symbolic in character. We ordinarily think of leaders as people who point the way for others through unusual abilities, wisdom, courage, or force of personality. But leaders can often retain their positions, whether or not they have these qualities, by creating in their followers a belief in their ability to cope. We have just seen that ritualized conflict creates such a belief. Other common political actions do so as well. Leaders who are resolute and forceful and seem confident in a situation that makes most people anxious and uncertain reassure the public and create a following, whether their actions succeed or fail. Those who are bewildered want very much to believe that their political leaders can cope. President Kennedy's seemingly resolute action in the disastrous Bay of Pigs invasion of Cuba in 1961 and President Carter's stern warnings and firm posture during the crises in Iran and Afghanistan during 1979 and 1980 illustrate the point. Survey data show that presidential popularity consistently rises after such dramatic actions, whether they succeed or fail or are ambiguous in their consequences. Clearly, it is less the leader's skills, courage, and effectiveness that bring political success in such cases than his or her dramaturgy and the anxieties of mass publics.

When is change likely to occur in the structure of policies of the American political system? What circumstances determine the form it will take? Our approach is based on the premise that certain preconditions cause pressure to be exerted on the fundamental aspects of the political system. If they are strong enough, modifications of both mass and elite behavior follow, and — depending on the particular configuration of factors, forces, behavior, and events — political change of various kinds and directions then occurs. We shall take up three areas in which the preconditions of change are likely to be generated and then identify some of the major factors that determine the degree and kind of effect such conditions will have on the political system. We shall then consider four alternative types of political change possible in the United States and the prerequisites and processes associated with each of them.

The Preconditions of Change

In one sense political change is continuous. Governing elites regularly make adjustments in established policies or undertake major policy initiatives in response to changing conditions. Such changes may, and often do, result in alterations in domestic economic or social relationships or in international affairs. One example is the emergence of cold war foreign policy and the related evolution of massive defense and space programs. Another is the decision to institute a "war on poverty." But these changes we term *marginal* because their essential effect is to defend and to promote the established economic and political structures and the existing patterns of distribution of wealth and status within the society. We shall reserve the term *fundamental* for instances of substantial alteration in the economic or political power structures or in key governmental policies bearing on distribution of wealth and status. Fundamental change is drastic in character; it may come about, however, through either violent or relatively peaceful means.

Our approach to the analysis of political change should permit us to distinguish between these two types of change and to acknowledge the relative improbability of the more fundamental type. *Marginal* change is frequent, requiring few preconditions. But *fundamental* change is infrequent and is unlikely to occur without severe pressures on the central concerns of politics that are widely perceived and acted on by masses and elites alike. We would expect fundamental change only when the preconditions begin to disrupt or to seriously threaten the basic organization and operation of the economy, the class structure, existing control over the uses of government's coercive powers, or the established patterns of distribution of wealth and status. The more preconditions generate such effects, the more probable are changes in the structure and uses of political power, the character of political institutions, and the key policies of government. In short, the severity of dislocations in closely related policy areas determines the probability of fundamental *political* change; we shall consider three such areas in the order of their importance for political change.

■ *Changes in the Level and Distribution of Economic Prosperity.* The most powerful source of pressure on the political system is the state of the economic system, for the obvious reason that it affects first the very survival and then other avidly sought goals of people in all social settings. Despite its image of stability, American politics has always been highly sensitive to fluctuations and dislocations in the economy. When the economy is stable and unemployment limited, the political system is normally free of strain, even though distribution of economic rewards is very unequal. But if either inflation or recession occurs, pressures begin to build up, and distribution differences become salient and provocative. If a depression develops, pressures may become truly explosive.

■ *Social Tensions and Underlying Value Changes.* A second — and potentially quite independent — major source of pressure on the political system is the rise of tensions and open conflict among major segments of the society. Such conflict is often associated with, and normally exacerbated by, rapid changes in the level and distribution of economic prosperity or other major technological changes. But it can also be generated by noneconomic factors and can culminate in deep and widely felt animosities even during periods of economic affluence.

Deep social divisions exist within the United States, rhetorical calls for solidarity and assertions of consensus notwithstanding. The most visible, long-standing, and deeply rooted of these is race. The extent to which racism is entrenched in the psychological makeup, political values, and institutional practices of white America may never be fully understood. But white-black/brown/red tensions escalate with every new assertion of the right to equal status.

More likely to produce fundamental change than the tensions created by the demands of relatively small and containable racial minorities are those grounded in class consciousness. Suppose that most blue-collar workers and other wage earners — black and white, men and women — should come to perceive themselves as jointly exploited for the benefit of a small group of owners and managers who already hold the vast majority of the nation's wealth. Justice, in their eyes, entitles them to a much larger share of the economic product. Their numbers alone would ensure great impact, if their power could be organized and applied — though that is difficult.

Other sources of tension exist, though none compares with race and class as long-established antagonisms with continuing raw edges. Religious, regional, and rural-urban conflicts remain real and could exert pressure on the political system if particular issues again raise perceptions of deprivation or create frustrations. But new forms of tension unrooted in old divisions also exist. One is the general lack of a sense of personal satisfaction that seemed to pervade the United States in the 1970s. Despite such achievements as moon landings and the highest standard of living in the world, many observers saw Americans as lacking contentment, self-confidence, and a sense of purpose. Work seemed to be providing a less meaningful rationale for life and to be less a source of pride than in previous decades. Individuals seemed to be aware of their apparent powerlessness to affect the course of events or even matters touching their own lives.

In the late 1960s and early 1970s, much of the pressure for change in the United States came from the new values developed by young people. Some of these changes emphasized egalitarianism, humanism, participation, and self-fulfillment through a wide variety of individual activities. Their contrast with the materialism, nationalism, conformity, and support for the economic and political status quo of their elders was so sharp that these values together came to be known as a "counterculture." Some young people went beyond the counterculture to join with left intellectuals and trade unionists in a sustained left political movement. Parallel pressures were generated by a growing women's liberation movement that pressed for change that reached deep into the personal relationships and public roles of men and women and potentially into the most basic societal values. But all these movements ultimately provoked a vigorous backlash in the form of the New Right, a loose coalition of interests seeking to restore the values and government practices of the 1950s. Conditions, particularly the apparent return to the cold war and military preparedness of that period, seemed to give the latter group greater prospect of success in the 1980s.

■ *International Tensions and Events.* The obvious interdependence of international and domestic affairs means that events overseas often spark economic and social tensions at home. Such developments may serve either to generate massive new pressure on the political system or to deflect already powerful pressures away from it.

The most obvious source of restructured domestic relationships is war or the immediately perceived threat of war. A relatively small, festering war in a distant place, such as Korea or Vietnam, is likely to create new social divisions or to exacerbate tension between left and right; at the same time, it promotes economic well-being and then inflation. A full-scale war or even a small war close to home tends to draw wider support and to eclipse all other issues that might otherwise divide people. More complex effects derive from the threat of armed conflict and from a posture and ideology that support constant readiness for nuclear war. This atmosphere creates underlying tensions while it legitimates many actions and diverts attention from others in the name of patriotism and national security.

But war and the threat of war are only the most obvious sources of disruptive tensions and the prospect of political change. Sharp changes overseas — such as an oil embargo, nationalization, or severance of trade relations — may reverberate throughout segments of the U.S. economy and induce shortages, diplomatic pressure, or military intervention to restore American advantage. International developments of a noneconomic nature may also have an impact on American life. The increasing militance among American blacks during the 1950s and 1960s was due in part to the example of newly independent African and Asian nations whose nonwhite leaders acquired power and led their countries effectively and with great pride.

This brief analysis of some sources of intrasocietal tensions and conflicts sufficient to raise the possibility of fundamental political change is merely illustrative, not comprehensive. No doubt there are many other causes of pressure on the political system. But our point is that substantial pressures must be generated from some source before established econo-political relationships are likely to undergo change of a fundamental kind. If there are several such pressures, and if they converge or overlap in such a way as to be mutually reinforcing (rather than pitting different groups against one another in a self-canceling and immobilizing fashion), the prospect of such change is greater.

The Political Impact of the Preconditions of Change

Preconditions are thus necessary, but not sufficient, causes of fundamental change. What is crucial for our purposes is the manner in which such preconditions become translated into effects on the political system. Multiple sources of tension clearly exist, some of them deep and others worsening. But there have always been some such tensions, and fundamental political change has not occurred in more than a century. Depressions and severe social tensions have given rise to militant parties and movements seeking fundamental change, but they have failed to achieve their goals. (Sometimes, of course, depression and serious social tensions do not inspire action at all. They may send people into withdrawal, apathy, or destructive scapegoating; or, they may redouble support for the status quo through the helpless conviction that "happiness is just around the corner.") Social tensions must not only produce converging and mutually reinforcing perceptions of deprivation, but must also be translated into politics in particular ways before they are likely to generate fundamental change. We can identify several prerequisites that if fulfilled, will make fundamental change more likely. Again, we do not see it as necessary or inevitable that all these political effects be present in order for change to take place, but the prospect of change will increase as each is fulfilled. We shall frame the conditions as three basic questions.

1. How fully do existing dislocations, tensions, and underlying value changes disrupt established patterns of distribution and detach masses of people from their previous commitments to the dominant political values, ideology, and behavior? *For fundamental change to occur, there must be a decrease in the supportive attitudes of people toward their government; its legitimacy must be eroded, and a vacuum of authority must develop.* This is a long-term process, of course, and must be deep-seated enough to counteract the best efforts of the major socializing and interpreting agents (schools, mass media) of the existing system. It also requires visible, legitimate leadership, but leaders are not likely to arise until the trend of popular change is already under way. Thus, the impetus toward change in values must be self-generated. Social and economic conditions, international events, or personal experience must create perceptions of serious personal deprivation that call into question the legitimacy or propriety of established political values and practices. Such perceptions of contradiction or unworkability in the present system must be strong enough to survive such explanations and diversions as the alleged failure of individuals, racial antagonisms, symbolic appeals, anticommunism, and so forth. Not just one or two such perceptions, but rather an extended and cumulating series of them are probably necessary to drive people to develop new priorities for political action and to seriously consider alternatives to the present system. Without deep doubts about established values, at the very least, proposals or movements for change will be ignored, dismissed, or resisted by the very people who constitute an almost irreplaceable component in the process.

2. How much (and what kind of) power can be mobilized by change-oriented elements within the society, and how does such power relate to elites' power resources? Almost by definition, those who feel personal deprivation in such a way as to commit themselves to fundamental change do not possess large or immediately effective power resources. A few wealthy, well-connected, or strategically located persons may identify with the causes of the deprived and serve as leaders or key supporters. But most persons with access to major power resources are probably either already members of the establishment or at least persuaded that the basic structures and values are acceptable and that only marginal change is required. *Fundamental change thus normally requires the mobilization of the latent power resources of the currently powerless.* Numbers become crucial. Regardless of how slight their individual power, if a substantial segment of the population becomes committed to unified action in support of fundamental change, their joint power is immense. Strategic location within the economy or society is also important. Effective strikes in vital service-providing fields (governmental functions, transportation, and the like) greatly multiply the power of relatively small numbers of people.

But the most crucial factors for mobilizing the powerless into a potentially successful force for fundamental change are *organization* and *communication*. Organization means the emergence of groups of people whose commitment is so complete that they subordinate all economic and other personal goals and make single-minded efforts to awaken numbers of other people to the need for (and prepare them for the action necessary to) achieving fundamental change. Organization building requires a supportive environment for group members so that their commitments are regularly reinforced and new members are recruited. And it requires substantial agreement on (or at least only limited conflict over) the basic strategy by which change is to be accomplished.

The need for communication has both internal and external dimensions. There must be regular exchanges of information and effective coordination between the geographically (and perhaps in some ways ideologically) separated units of the growing organization. And there must be communication between the organizers and the people whom they seek to mobilize. Unless numbers of people can be brought to support the organized movement, or at least detached from their support of established ways and thus neutralized, the movement has little real prospect for success. It will either gradually become aware of its failure and dissipate or be forced into isolation and resort to indiscriminate terrorism or other desperate and self-destructive measures.

The task of mobilizing numbers of people into a unified, change-seeking force is very difficult. Previously inert individuals must acquire a sense of political efficacy and hope strong enough to impel them to action. Various means of attracting attention and reaching people in terms they can readily identify with and understand are necessary: action, deliberate self-sacrifice, rational persuasion, and blatant propaganda all play parts at various stages. As organization progresses, a series of minor skirmishes in which victories over established institutions or procedures are scored probably contributes to awakening self-confidence and determination. The bases of solidarity among people must be developed over time and against a background of deep-seated suspicions, divisions, prejudices, and misunderstandings. Without the development of such organization and its promotion of broad support, fundamental change seems unlikely.

3. How do established elites react to forces seeking fundamental change? Because they hold the initiative and have a responsibility to act in response to events, existing elites' behavior plays a vital role in the evolving process of change. They may act to promote divisions and hostility within the population and/or to isolate and discredit groups seeking change, thereby making mobilization difficult or impossible. They may appear to institute, or actually make, marginal changes in policies in order to reduce popular perceptions of deprivation, thereby undercutting (or, in some circumstances, promoting) the thrust toward fundamental change. They may introduce wholly new issues or appeals, such as space exploration, war, or the threat of war, which redirect attention or mobilize support for the existing order. They may also engage in active repression of change-seeking groups. If done with sophistication and restraint, this may help to solve

their problem. But if handled crudely, it can provide the movement with substantial new constituencies.

In each case, it is clear that elite response shapes the opportunities and problems of change seekers. What determines how elites act? In part it depends on which segment of the establishment is currently dominant within the executive branch. The eastern upper class, the managers of the great corporations, and welfare-state liberals tend to react with modest policy changes, deflection, and sophisticated repression. Those newer to real power and more steeped in the ideology than the practice of American government, such as the southern and southwestern individualist-conservatives, are more likely to react by exaggerating the threat, appealing to popular fears and prejudices, and escalating open repression.

Neither set of behaviors by itself determines whether the movement for change will gain or lose momentum as a result. What it does, essentially, is to shape the degree of polarization in the society. When accompanied by the disaffection, tensions, and loss of legitimacy described earlier, and when there is a cohesive organization ready to act with substantial popular support, a highly polarized situation ripe for fundamental change may be created. What is then required is a spark — the fortuitous event that creates the opportunity for the movement to cross the threshold to real and sweeping impact of some kind. Then, if the existing organization has the skill (or the sheer determination, which may often overcome lack of skill or the absence of some important conditions) to apply its power decisively, the whole structure of power may be sharply altered. Violent revolution need not occur, although violence undoubtedly plays a major role in promoting change of a fundamental nature. Established elites are quite unlikely to release their grip on governmental power unless convinced that it is necessary or inevitable that they do so. Often the escalation of the stakes that results from serious and repeated mutual violence has created such conviction. A relatively low level of violence, if sustained and accompanied by credible threats of more to follow, has sometimes induced elites to acquiesce in, or even to institute, major changes sought in a relatively peaceful manner. Once the process of change has reached this point, developments are no longer even crudely predictable. The outcome depends on such factors as key individuals' personalities and chance.

We can summarize these general observations about the politics of change in terms of a contrast between top-down and bottom-up processes of change. Thus far, we have been speaking chiefly of fundamental change and its prerequisites; marginal change is almost always possible, at the almost exclusive option of establishment elites. To be sure, there are limits within which such elites must select their policy options, but these are chiefly of their own making and only partially subject to popular preferences. In a fundamental change situation, however, elites have lost their predominance. They are either fragmented and beginning to contend with one another or struggling to maintain themselves against the demands of a newly powerful antagonist arising from outside their ambit. Clearly, we are dealing with two contrasting levels and processes of change. Change initiated from the top down by established elites occurs because of their perceptions and needs, or perhaps through gradual changes in their membership. Such changes are likely to affect only minor policies, well within the established power system — or, in short, to be *incremental* changes. Only when a thrust from outside the establishment (that is, from below) begins to have an impact on elites' power and status does fundamental change become a possibility. The agency of change must be created by the previously powerless and must build on deep social tensions and/or value changes to force its way into the political arena. The more such thrust is generated from below, the more the system itself is the target, and the more likely is fundamental change.

Levels and Directions of Change: Four Scenarios

We have said nothing about the *direction* that either marginal or fundamental change may take. Clearly, either may go to the *left*, in the direction of wider distribution of power, wealth, and status within the society, or to the *right*, toward rigid insistence on the status quo or even narrower and more restrictive distribution. A nearly infinite number of combinations of possible factors in the total political context could give rise to either marginal or fundamental changes in either direction. We shall reduce this wide range of possibilities to four, briefly describe the features of each, and try to specify what determines the direction they may take. In what seems to us their order of probability in the United States today, we shall discuss (1) erratic marginal change — perpetuation of the status quo with slight changes vacillating left and right, but tending ultimately to an integrated and corporate-dominated econopolitical system; (2) reactionary marginal change culminating relatively promptly (in, say, ten to fifteen years) in nearly fundamental change to a system best termed totalitarian electoral fascism; (3) sustained marginal change with a reformist emphasis, resulting after a longer time span in something like welfare-state capitalism; and (4) revolution, generated by a left-oriented movement, which would result in a more rapid arrival of *either* fascism or socialism, depending on unforeseeable circumstances developing as the revolution took place. In each case, we shall highlight those conditions and processes that our previous analysis suggests are of key importance.

■ *Erratic Marginal Change, Culminating in a Corporate-Dominated System.* This scenario assumes that no major depression develops. Race conflict remains salient, but more or less effectively suppressed through the isolation and containment of black/brown/red peoples. Class consciousness remains low, and radicalism proves to be a minor and transitory phenomenon, genuinely rejected by workers and middle class alike and ultimately dissipated or suppressed. Threats of nuclear war continue, but no major land war is fought outside the Western Hemisphere. In short, basic conditions create no major new dislocations and leave established elites entrenched and with full capacity to orchestrate popular support for their decisions.

Under these conditions, the level of perceived deprivation remains not much higher than it is at present, the government retains its legitimacy and authority, and established values are not seriously challenged. Racial tensions continue to be the chief source of social conflict, and the mass of relatively powerless people is thus divided and distracted. Established elites are relatively unthreatened and thus able to respond to what seem to them the most important needs of the nation. Their concerns center on the continued stability and growth of the economy. More and more, the continued success of the dominant large corporations (and thus full employment and continued prosperity for most) depends on the use of government power. Hence, government undertakes management of the basic conditions of social life, financing of research and development, underwriting of major risks through subsidies and guarantees, and military protection of overseas activities. And it repels all efforts to change such priorities.

Thus, elites perceive no acceptable alternatives to the growing (and, in the eyes of most, welcome) domination of both the society and the polity by the major corporations. Greater and greater integration between business and government occurs, until the two are nearly indistinguishable. Because established values remain unchanged, economic attainments are the principal measure of progress, and in any event a steadily rising standard of living remains an unchallenged necessity. Existing social problems will also be dealt with, but only when serious incidents occur; even then, they will be second-priority, and remedies will be applied to their symptoms rather than to their causes. Occasionally, special efforts will be made to elicit popular support for space exploits, threats of nuclear war, or domestic "crusades" against the surface manifestations of problems that annoy many people. But the basic line of development will be an extension of the status quo, to the point that a corporate-managed society evolves. Conditions of life will not appear unfree or distasteful to most people, though to a small and permanent minority, life will appear intolerably structured by the technological monsters of our own creation.

■ *Marginal Reactionary Change, Culminating in Fascism.* In this scenario a stagnating economy causes inflation and unemployment to remain high and forces governments to cut back on services. The lowest levels of the white working class and all minorities feel the pinch quite seriously, though most of the middle class remains relatively affluent. Racial conflict is exacerbated by such conditions, and class consciousness is commensurately retarded. Social tensions multiply, there appear to be many severe problems but no solutions, and no clear moral or spiritual principles, except militant anticommunism, seem applicable. Amid this general social fragmentation and purposelessness, various militant protest movements gain adherents. Some call for a general redistribution of wealth, others for a "return to fundamentals"; all are impatient with the continuing claims of minorities for equal status and opportunity. Governing elites, particularly those with roots in the corporate and financial world, grow alarmed at the obviously decaying social situation and worsening condition of the economy. They use international tensions to mobilize popular support for drastic controls and general militarization of the society.

A disorganized left offers little serious resistance, manifesting itself chiefly in isolated strikes and occasional terrorism. The new government uses the latter to justify exaggerated public attacks on minorities, the left, and all forms of unorthodoxy and un-Americanism. Infiltration and surveillance are used in a broad campaign of intimidation. The general public, genuinely alarmed by the apparent reality of the alleged threat to national security, supports vigorous repression as necessary and justifiable.

Swept along by the hysteria, courts and juries find the means to jail people suspected of unorthodox actions or intentions. The Supreme Court, staffed by the nominees of the same elites, approves (and thereby legitimates) such uses of the police and judicial systems. The acknowledged vulnerability of the society appears to justify far-reaching supervision and control over behavior to prevent outbreaks.

At the same time, established elites recognize the necessity of promoting economic well-being, by which they mean serving the needs and preferences of various segments of the economy as fully as possible. Accordingly, they proceed much further than in the preceding scenario, regimenting the domestic working population, actively insisting on opportunities for American investment and trade in various parts of the world, and employing American military power freely on behalf of both ends.

Political opposition begins to fade at the same time. Because of their similar perceptions of social conditions, as well as trends among those in authority and among voters, few recognized political leaders seriously dispute the propriety of existing public policy. Elections thus become contests between candidates who share a commitment to repression of dissent and promotion of the needs of the economy at practically any cost. Regardless of the winning political party and because of the widespread inability to perceive any alternative to surveillance and repression, such policies, once undertaken, become fixed and can only intensify. In this manner — by the steady erosion of fixed standards of due process and fair procedures, coupled with rigid insistence on the status quo — a police state evolves. The American version of fascism, well grounded in popular support, is complete.

■ *Marginal Reformist Change, Culminating in Welfare Capitalism.* This scenario posits visible and continuing economic dislocation sufficient to convince a sizable segment of the population — not just intellectuals and leftist organizers — that something is wrong with the economic order. It could be a mild depression or a continued recession that affects more than the lowest levels of workers. What is crucial is that it provide a basis for some degree of class consciousness or other shared consciousness of joint deprivation sufficient to overcome the divisiveness of group or racial conflicts. The latter, though unlikely to mellow substantially, could become somewhat less divisive if black/brown/red leaders began to interpret their plight in class-based or economic, rather than exclusively racial, terms. Young people would continue to be a source of new, more egalitarian, and humanistic values. For ever increasing numbers of them, the older priorities would simply lack validity. Vitally important to the convergence of these conditions is the absence of war, for war would inject new obstacles into the path of a growing but fragile coalition seeking to span class, age, racial, and sexual divisions.

Considerable value change, gaining momentum continually as new waves of young people enter the society's mainstream, would make for a temporarily severe "generation gap." Before very long, however, elites themselves would be penetrated by the new standards, and key personnel at middle-management levels would begin to see like-minded persons permeating their areas of activity — including politics. Organizations of change-seeking persons would proliferate, venting their impatience with the stubbornness of the established procedures in repeated outbreaks of violence. Unions in particular would regain their old militance as younger workers reinvigorated them, and waves of strikes demanding greater control over the conditions of work (not just higher wages and benefits) would take place.

Widening agreement among both elites and the general public on the justice of such causes would inhibit, but not entirely preclude, elite repression. Elites, perceiving themselves as severely threatened, would seek to undercut the new thrust by making marginal concessions to demands. In time, as each adjustment granted new legitimacy to the rationale underlying the demands and as more and more elites became committed to the new values, a major turning point would occur. The most likely would seem to be a sweeping victory for the more progressive political party in an election posing clear-cut alternatives between the new and the old values. After that, major institutional changes (such as the elimination of conservative rules in the Congress) would be possible, and fundamental change could then ensue.

The change would involve implementation of new value priorities: community, human rights, and esthetic concerns would replace competition, property rights, and materialism. Structural manifestations would include effective political control and direction of the corporate economy, decentralized management of most governmental and productive functions, and widespread participation by ordinary citizens in various stages of policy-making and its implementation. Technological developments would be subordinated to questions about the desirability of their impact. Economic "progress" would be viewed in terms of worldwide, rather than domestic, circumstances. Redistribution of wealth within the United States would be steadily extended, until resources and productivity were shared with other nations generally.

■ *Immediate Fundamental Change by Revolution, Leading to Fascism or Socialism.* Revolution, though difficult to contemplate in a heretofore highly stable, advanced industrial nation where the means of large-scale violence are thoroughly monopolized by government, is nevertheless a possibility that must be considered. Revolution requires substantial economic crisis, such as a severe depression, which would create wide unrest. Change in consciousness is thus not limited to the young. But there must be a united cadre group to serve as the principal moving force. Social tensions that place militants, black and white, in a position to join together, accompanied by at least some organized workers, are essential. The crucial factor is a continuing source of provocation that overrides racial suspicions and class differences and brings youth and workers together to serve as the nucleus of the instrument of change.

For such people, and for those similarly affected by economic, social, or world conditions, value shifts are drastic. The government soon loses all legitimacy and with it the power to restrain behavior. In response to militant behavior, polarization becomes sharp. Conditions nevertheless make a substantial segment of the population responsive to well-framed appeals by organizations of militants. Major strikes in key industries and occasional victories in local conflicts mark their growing power and capability. Elite repression adds to the organizations' constituencies. At this point the situation is ripe for the final spark that can — if the organizations' leaders are perceptive and determined enough — eventuate in revolution. The spark would have to be so dramatic and the response of major leaders and groups so indecisive or mutually conflicting that an impasse would be apparent and police and military forces divided or immobilized. A hopelessly deadlocked presidential election, savage repression of a major strike, or the imminent prospect of nuclear war might be capable of providing such a spark.

If a total effort to seize power in the national government is made, with no limitations on the means or sacrifice involved, it might succeed. Actions limited to what is perceived as possible rarely exceed such bounds; those based on "impractical" aspirations sometimes achieve most of them, much to everyone's surprise. Once the attempt at revolution begins, of course, uncontrollable forces are set in motion. An effort undertaken in the absence of the conditions necessary to success can be totally self-destructive. Whoever mobilizes the means of violence most effectively emerges the winner. Their goals could be the faintly concealed fascism that appeals to many of the powers on the American right or the democratic socialism that motivates the left. But revolutionary processes ensure only that the old order will not survive, and there is no guarantee that what results will be an improvement on it. The result *might* be either fascism or democratic socialism. But there is no way to foresee the outcome until after the revolution has run its course.

Prospects for Change in the American Political System

These four scenarios suggest the range of possibility that lies before us. Difficult as it is to see ahead, this is exactly what we must try to do if we are to play any significant part in helping to shape events. Let us speculate a bit about the American future.

We are confident of our basic premise: the United States and the world are experiencing an unprecedented era of transformation from which shall emerge a different economic and social order. One thing of which we can be sure is that the society we have known is in the process of being replaced by something different. Obvious preconditions of that change are visible in the economic pressures of the early 1980s and the ongoing social disintegration and underlying value change that have marked the last decade.

But the nature of the change we are experiencing is far less clear than is its existence. Multiple possibilities are open, each of them prefigured in part by our present circumstances. This brings us to our second major point: the eventual outcome will depend on what *people* do and think and seek in the next years. History often seems inexorable and predetermined. But there also occur times of change and multiple possibility when the actions of knowledgeable and determined people shape the future, and this is surely one of those times.

The four scenarios just described are listed in what we consider the order of their likelihood. The first two are almost interchangeable, and the events of the late 1970s may make the second the more probable. But these are only probabilities, not inevitabilities. Many people consider themselves helpless to affect the outcome of such momentous issues, of course. As we have seen, there is good reason for them to feel thus — at least as far as acting within the established ideological and political channels is concerned. That very helplessness, however, should be recognized as an outcome of the teachings of the American ideology: we are taught first that we must use only the established channels to seek political goals and then that we are powerless anyhow.

Both of these self-imposed limits must be challenged, if people seek to avoid the worst of the prospective futures and to make something better. To withdraw into individual isolation or to go along because everyone else seems to be accepting whatever happens is to contribute personally to the likelihood that the worst possible future will come about. What is required instead is a reexamination of who we are as people and what kinds of people we want to be — and then of the kinds of social relations and institutions that would be necessary to enable us to become such people. Just as our present circumstances are forcing change, some of which may well be very dangerous and undesirable, so do they bring opportunities to create a far more satisfying society and life. Free of the limitations of our present ideology and the narrow forms of political activity it prescribes for us and possessing images of the social orders we *do not* and *do* want, Americans might well reconstruct their society. The first steps are the crucial ones, however, and those to which this book has been addressed: we must free ourselves from the grip of unexamined orthodoxy, see our present conditions and practices clearly, and recognize the pressing need to reshape them to serve our needs.

THE CONSTITUTION OF THE UNITED STATES OF AMERICA

We the People of the United States, in Order to form a more perfect Union, establish Justice, insure domestic Tranquility, provide for the common defence, promote the general Welfare, and secure the Blessings of Liberty to ourselves and our Posterity, do ordain and establish this Constitution for the United States of America.

Article I

Section 1. All legislative Powers herein granted shall be vested in a Congress of the United States, which shall consist of a Senate and House of Representatives.

Section 2. The House of Representatives shall be composed of Members chosen every second Year by the People of the several States, and the Electors in each State shall have the Qualifications requisite for Electors of the most numerous Branch of the State Legislature.

No Person shall be a Representative who shall not have attained to the age of twenty five Years, and been seven Years a Citizen of the United States, and who shall not, when elected, be an Inhabitant of that State in which he shall be chosen.

Representatives and direct Taxes shall be apportioned among the several States which may be included within this Union, according to their respective Numbers, *which shall be determined by adding to the whole Number of free Persons, including those bound to Service for a Term of Years,* and excluding Indians not taxed, *three fifths of all other persons.*[1] The actual Enumeration shall be made within three Years after the first Meeting of the Congress of the United States, and within every subsequent Term of ten Years, in such Manner as they shall by Law direct. The Number of Representatives shall not exceed one for every thirty Thousand, but each State shall have at Least one Representative; and until such enumeration shall be made, the State of New Hampshire shall be entitled to chuse three, Massachusetts eight, Rhode-Island and Providence Plantations one, Connecticut five, New-York six, New Jersey four, Pennsylvania eight, Delaware one, Maryland six, Virginia ten, North Carolina five, South Carolina five, and Georgia three.

When vacancies happen in the Representation from any State, the Executive Authority thereof shall issue Writs of Election to fill such Vacancies.

The House of Representatives shall chuse their Speaker and other Officers; and shall have the sole Power of Impeachment.

Section 3. The Senate of the United States shall be composed of two Senators from each State, *chosen by the Legislature thereof,*[2] for six Years; and each Senator shall have one Vote.

Immediately after they shall be assembled in Consequence of the first Election, they shall be divided as equally as may be into three Classes. The Seats of the Senators of the first Class shall be vacated at the Expiration of the second Year, of the second Class at the Expiration of the fourth Year, and of the third Class at the Expiration of the sixth Year, so that one third may be chosen every second Year; *and if Vacancies happen by Resignation, or otherwise, during the Recess of the Legislature of any State, the Executive thereof may make temporary Appointments until the next Meeting of the Legislature, which shall then fill such Vacancies.*[3]

No Person shall be a Senator who shall not have attained to the Age of thirty Years, and been nine Years a Citizen of the United States, and who shall not, when elected, be an Inhabitant of that State for which he shall be chosen.

The Vice President of the United States shall be President of the Senate, but shall have no Vote, unless they be equally divided.

The Senate shall chuse their other Officers, and also a President pro tempore, in the Absence of the Vice President, or when he shall exercise the Office of President of the United States.

---

[1] Italics are used throughout to indicate passages that have been altered by subsequent amendments. In this case, see Amendment XIV.

[2] See Amendment XVII.

[3] Ibid.

The Senate shall have the sole Power to try all Impeachments. When sitting for that Purpose, they shall be on Oath or Affirmation. When the President of the United States is tried, the Chief Justice shall preside: And no Person shall be convicted without the Concurrence of two thirds of the Members present.

Judgment in Cases of Impeachment shall not extend further than to removal from Office, and disqualification to hold and enjoy any Office of honor, Trust or Profit under the United States: but the Party convicted shall nevertheless be liable and subject to Indictment, Trial, Judgment and Punishment, according to Law.

Section 4. The Times, Places and Manner of holding Elections for Senators and Representatives, shall be prescribed in each State by the Legislature thereof; but the Congress may at any time by Law make or alter such Regulations, except as to the Places of chusing Senators.

The Congress shall assemble at least once in every Year, and such Meeting shall be on the first Monday in December, unless they shall by Law appoint a different Day.[4]

Section 5. Each House shall be the Judge of the Elections, Returns and Qualifications of its own Members, and a Majority of each shall constitute a Quorum to do Business; but a smaller Number may adjourn from day to day, and may be authorized to compel the Attendance of absent Members, in such Manner, and under such Penalties as each House may provide.

Each House may determine the Rules of its Proceedings, punish its Members for disorderly Behavior, and, with the Concurrence of two thirds, expel a Member.

Each House shall keep a journal of its Proceedings, and from time to time publish the same, excepting such Parts as may in their Judgment require Secrecy; and the Yeas and Nays of the Members of either House on any question shall, at the Desire of one fifth of those Present, be entered on the Journal.

Neither House, during the Session of Congress, shall, without the Consent of the other, adjourn for more than three days, nor to any other Place than that in which the two Houses shall be sitting.

Section 6. The Senators and Representatives shall receive a Compensation for their Services, to be ascertained by Law, and paid out of the Treasury of the United States. They shall in all Cases, except Treason, Felony and Breach of the Peace, be privileged from Arrest during their Attendance at the Session of their respective Houses, and in going to and returning from the same; and for any Speech or Debate in either House, they shall not be questioned in any other Place.

No Senator or Representative shall, during the Time for which he was elected, be appointed to any civil Office under the Authority of

4 See Amendment XX.

the United States, which shall have been created, or the Emoluments whereof shall have been encreased during such time; and no Person holding any Office under the United States, shall be a Member of either House during his Continuance in Office.

Section 7. All Bills for raising Revenue shall originate in the House of Representatives; but the Senate may propose or concur with Amendments as on other Bills.

Every Bill which shall have passed the House of Representatives and the Senate, shall, before it become a Law, be presented to the President of the United States; if he approve he shall sign it, but if not he shall return it, with his Objections to that House in which it shall have originated, who shall enter the Objections at large on their Journal, and proceed to reconsider it. If after such Reconsideration two thirds of that House shall agree to pass the Bill, it shall be sent, together with the Objections, to the other House, by which it shall likewise be reconsidered, and if approved by two thirds of that House, it shall become a Law. But in all such Cases the Votes of both Houses shall be determined by Yeas and Nays, and the Names of the Persons voting for and against the Bill shall be entered on the Journal of each House respectively. If any Bill shall not be returned by the President within ten Days (Sundays excepted) after it shall have been presented to him, the Same shall be a Law, in like Manner as if he had signed it, unless Congress by their Adjournment prevent its Return, in which Case it shall not be a Law.

Every Order, Resolution, or Vote to which the Concurrence of the Senate and House of Representatives may be necessary (except on a question of Adjournment) shall be presented to the President of the United States; and before the Same shall take Effect, shall be approved by him, or being disapproved by him, shall be repassed by two thirds of the Senate and House of Representatives, according to the Rules and Limitations prescribed in the Case of a Bill.

Section 8. The Congress shall have Power To lay and collect Taxes, Duties, Imposts and Excises, to pay the Debts and provide for the common Defence and general Welfare of the United States; but all Duties, Imposts and Excises shall be uniform throughout the United States;

To borrow Money on the credit of the United States;

To regulate Commerce with foreign Nations, and among the several States, and with the Indian Tribes;

To establish an uniform Rule of Naturalization, and uniform Laws on the subject of Bankruptcies throughout the United States;

To coin Money, regulate the Value thereof, and of foreign Coin, and fix the Standard of Weights and Measures;

To provide for the Punishment of counterfeiting the Securities and Current Coin of the United States;

To establish Post Offices and post Roads;

To promote the Progress of Science and useful Arts, by securing for limited Times to Authors and Inventors the exclusive Right to their respective Writings and Discoveries;

To constitute Tribunals inferior to the Supreme Court;

To define and punish Piracies and Felonies committed on the high Seas, and Offences against the Law of Nations;

To declare War, grant Letters of Marque and Reprisal, and make Rules concerning Captures on Land and Water;

To raise and support Armies, but no Appropriation of Money to that Use shall be for a longer Term than two Years;

To provide and maintain a Navy;

To make Rules for the Government and Regulation of the land and naval Forces;

To provide for calling forth the Militia to execute the Laws of the Union, suppress Insurrections and repel Invasions;

To provide for organizing, arming, and disciplining, the Militia, and for governing such Part of them as may be employed in the Service of the United States, reserving to the States respectively, the Appointment of the Officers, and the Authority of training the Militia according to the discipline prescribed by Congress;

To exercise exclusive Legislation in all Cases whatsoever, over such District (not exceeding ten Miles square) as may, by Cession of particular States, and the Acceptance of Congress, become the Seat of the Government of the United States, and to exercise like Authority over all Places purchased by the Consent of the Legislature of the State in which the Same shall be, for the Erection of Forts, Magazines, Arsenals, dock-Yards, and other needful Buildings;—And

To make all Laws which shall be necessary and proper for carrying into Execution the foregoing Powers, and all other Powers vested by this Constitution in the Government of the United States, or in any Department or Officer thereof.

Section 9. The Migration or Importation of such Persons as any of the States now existing shall think proper to admit, shall not be prohibited by the Congress prior to the Year one thousand eight hundred and eight, but a Tax or duty may be imposed on such Importation, not exceeding ten dollars for each Person.

The Privilege of the Writ of Habeas Corpus shall not be suspended, unless when in Cases of Rebellion or Invasion the public Safety may require it.

No Bill of Attainder or ex post facto Law shall be passed.

No Capitation, or other direct, Tax shall be laid, unless in Proportion to the Census or Enumeration herein before directed to be taken.

No Tax or Duty shall be laid on Articles exported from any State.

No Preference shall be given by any Regulation of Commerce or Revenue to the Ports of one State over those of another: nor shall Vessels bound to, or from, one State, be obliged to enter, clear, or pay Duties in another.

No Money shall be drawn from the Treasury, but in Consequence of Appropriations made by Law; and a regular Statement and Account of the Receipts and Expenditures of all public Money shall be published from time to time.

No title of Nobility shall be granted by the United States: And no Person holding any Office of Profit or Trust under them, shall, without the Consent of the Congress, accept of any present, Emolument, Office, or Title, of any kind whatever, from any King, Prince, or foreign State.

Section 10. No State shall enter into any Treaty, Alliance, or Confederation; grant Letters of Marque and Reprisal; coin Money; emit Bills of Credit; make any Thing but gold and silver Coin a Tender in Payment of Debts; pass any Bill of Attainder, ex post facto Law, or Law impairing the Obligation of Contracts, or Grant any Title of Nobility.

No State shall, without the Consent of the Congress, lay any Imposts or Duties on Imports or Exports, except what may be absolutely necessary for executing its inspection Laws: and the net Produce of all Duties and Imposts, laid by any State on Imports or Exports, shall be for the Use of the Treasury of the United States; and all such Laws be subject to the Revision and Control of the Congress.

No State shall, without the Consent of Congress, lay any Duty of Tonnage, keep Troops, or Ships of War in time of Peace, enter into any Agreement or Compact with another State, or with a foreign Power, or engage in War, unless actually invaded, or in such imminent Danger as will not admit of delay.

Article II

Section 1. The executive Power shall be vested in a President of the United States of America. He shall hold his Office during the Term of four Years, and, together with the Vice President, chosen for the same Term be elected as follows:

Each State shall appoint, in such Manner as the Legislature thereof may direct, a Number of Electors, equal to the whole Number of Senators and Representatives to which the State may be entitled in the Congress: but no Senator or Representative, or Person holding an Office of Trust or Profit under the United States, shall be appointed an Elector.

The Electors shall meet in their respective States, and vote by Ballot for two Persons, of whom one at least shall not be an Inhabitant of the same State with themselves. And they shall make a List of all the Persons voted for, and of the Number of Votes for each; which List they shall sign and certify, and transmit sealed to the Seat of the Government of the United States, directed to the President of the Senate. The President of the Senate shall, in the Presence of the Senate and

House of Representatives, open all the Certificates, and the Votes shall then be counted. The Person having the greatest Number of Votes shall be the President, if such Number be a Majority of the whole Number of Electors appointed; and if there be more than one who have such Majority, and have an equal Number of Votes, then the House of Representatives shall immediately chuse by Ballot one of them for President; and if no Person have a Majority, then from the five highest on the List the said House shall in like Manner chuse the President. But in chusing the President, the votes shall be taken by States, the Representation from each State having one Vote; A quorum for this purpose shall consist of a Member or Members from two thirds of the States, and a Majority of all the States shall be necessary to a Choice. In every Case, after the Choice of the President, the Person having the Greatest Number of Votes of the Electors shall be the Vice President. But if there should remain two or more who have equal Votes, the Senate shall chuse from them by Ballot the Vice President.[5]

The Congress may determine the Time of chusing the Electors, and the Day on which they shall give their Votes; which Day shall be the same throughout the United States.

No Person except a natural born Citizen, or a Citizen of the United States, at the time of the Adoption of this Constitution, shall be eligible to the Office of President; neither shall any Person be eligible to that Office who shall not have attained to the Age of thirty five Years, and been fourteen Years a Resident within the United States.

The Case of the Removal of the President from Office, or of his Death, Resignation, or Inability to discharge the Powers and Duties of the said Office, the Same shall devolve on the Vice President, and the Congress may by Law provide for the Case of Removal, Death, Resignation or Inability, both of the President and Vice President, declaring what Officer shall then act as President, and such Officer shall act accordingly, until the Disability be removed, or a President shall be elected.

The President shall, at stated Times, receive for his Services, a Compensation which shall neither be increased nor diminished during the Period for which he shall have been elected, and he shall not receive within that Period any other Emolument from the United States, or any of them.

Before he enter on the Execution of his Office, he shall take the following Oath or Affirmation:—"I do solemnly swear (or affirm) that I will faithfully execute the Office of President of the United States, and will to the best of my Ability, preserve, protect, and defend the Constitution of the United States."

Section 2. The President shall be Commander in Chief of the Army and Navy of the United States, and of the Militia of the several States,

[5] See Amendment XII.

when called into the actual service of the United States; he may require the Opinion, in writing, of the prinicpal Officer in each of the executive Departments, upon any Subject relating to the Duties of their respective Offices, and he shall have Power to grant Reprieves and Pardons for Offences against the United States, except in Case of Impeachment.

He shall have Power, by and with the Advice and Consent of the Senate, to make Treaties, provided two thirds of the Senators present concur; and he shall nominate, and by and with the Advice and Consent of the Senate, shall appoint Ambassadors, and other public Ministers and Consuls, Judges of the supreme Court, and all other Officers of the United States, whose Appointments are not herein otherwise provided for, and which shall be established by Law; but the Congress may by Law vest the Appointment of such inferior Officers, as they think proper, in the President alone, in the Courts of Law, or in the Heads of Departments.

The President shall have Power to fill up all Vacancies that may happen during the Recess of the Senate, by granting Commissions which shall expire at the End of their next Session.

Section 3. He shall from time to time give to the Congress Information of the State of the Union, and recommend to their Consideration such Measures as he shall judge necessary and expedient; he may, on extraordinary Occasions, convene both Houses, or either of them, and in Case of Disagreement between them, with Respect to the Time of Adjournment, he may adjourn them to such Time as he shall think proper; he shall receive Ambassadors and other public Ministers, he shall take Care that the Laws be faithfully executed, and shall Commission all the Officers of the United States.

Section 4. The President, Vice President, and all civil Officers of the United States, shall be removed from Office on Impeachment for, and Conviction of, Treason, Bribery, or other high Crimes and Misdemeanors.

Article III

Section 1. The judicial Power of the United States, shall be vested in one supreme Court and in such inferior Courts as the Congress may from time to time ordain and establish. The Judges, both of the supreme and inferior Courts, shall hold their Offices during good Behavior, and shall, at stated Times, receive for their Services, a Compensation, which shall not be diminished during their Continuance in Office.

Section 2. The Judicial Power shall extend to all Cases, in Law and Equity, arising under this Constitution, the Laws of the United States, and Treaties made, or which shall be made, under their Authority;—to all Cases affecting Ambassadors, other public Ministers and Consuls;—to all Cases of admiralty and maritime Jurisdiction;—to Controversies to which the United States shall be a Party;—to Controversies between two or more States;—*between a State and Citizens of another State;* [6]—between Citizens of different States;—between Citizens of the same State claiming Lands under Grants of different states, *and between a State, or the Citizens thereof, and foreign States, Citizens, or Subjects.* [7]

In all cases affecting Ambassadors, other public Ministers and Consuls, and those in which a State shall be Party, the supreme Court shall have original Jurisdiction. In all the other Cases before mentioned, the supreme Court shall have appellate Jurisdiction, both as to Law and Fact, with such Exceptions, and under such Regulations as the Congress shall make.

The Trial of all Crimes, except in Cases of Impeachment, shall be by Jury; and such Trial shall be held in the State where the said Crimes shall have been committed; but when not committed within any State, the Trial shall be at such Place or Places as the Congress may by Law have directed.

Section 3. Treason against the United States, shall consist only in levying War against them, or in adhering to their Enemies, giving them Aid and Comfort. No person shall be convicted of Treason unless on the Testimony of two Witnesses to the same overt Act, or on Confession in open Court.

The Congress shall have Power to declare the Punishment of Treason, but no Attainder of Treason shall work Corruption of Blood, or Forfeiture except during the Life of the Person attainted.

Article IV

Section 1. Full Faith and Credit shall be given in each State to the public Acts, Records, and judicial Proceedings of every other State. And the Congress may by general Laws prescribe the Manner in which such Acts, Records, and Proceedings shall be proved, and the Effect thereof.

Section 2. The Citizens of each State shall be entitled to all Privileges and Immunities of Citizens in the several States.

A Person charged in any State with Treason, Felony, or other Crime, who shall flee from Justice, and be found in another State, shall on Demand of the executive Authority of the State from which he fled, be delivered up, to be removed to the State having jurisdiction of the Crime.

No Person held to Service or Labour in one State, under the Laws thereof, escaping into another, shall, in Consequence of any Law or Regulation therein, be discharged from such Service or Labour, but shall be delivered up on Claim of the Party to whom such Service or Labour may be due. [8]

[6] See Amendment XI.
[7] Ibid.
[8] See Amendment XIII.

Section 3. New States may be admitted by the Congress into this Union; but no new State shall be formed or erected within the Jurisdiction of any other State; nor any State be formed by the Junction of two or more States, or Parts of States, without the Consent of the Legislatures of the States concerned as well as of the Congress.

The Congress shall have Power to dispose of and make all needful Rules and Regulations respecting the Territory or other Property belonging to the United States; and nothing in this Constitution shall be so construed as to Prejudice any claims of the United States, or of any particular State.

Section 4. The United States shall guarantee to every State in this Union a Republican Form of Government, and shall protect each of them against Invasion; and on Application of the Legislature, or of the Executive (when the Legislature cannot be convened) against domestic Violence.

Article V

The Congress, whenever two thirds of both Houses shall deem it necessary, shall propose Amendments to this Constitution, or, on the Application of the Legislatures of two thirds of the several States, shall call a Convention for proposing Amendments, which, in either Case, shall be valid to all Intents and Purposes, as Part of this Constitution, when ratified by the Legislatures of three fourths of the several States, or by Conventions in three fourths thereof, as the one or the other Mode of Ratification may be proposed by the Congress; Provided that no Amendment which may be made prior to the Year One thousand eight hundred and eight shall in any Manner affect the first and fourth Clauses in the Ninth Section of the first Article; and that no State, without its Consent, shall be deprived of its equal Suffrage in the Senate.

Article VI

All Debts contracted and Engagements entered into, before the Adoption of this Constitution shall be as valid against the United States under this Constitution, as under the Confederation.

This Constitution, and the Laws of the United States which shall be made in Pursuance thereof; and all Treaties made, or which shall be made, under the Authority of the United States, shall be the supreme Law of the Land; and the Judges in every State shall be bound thereby, any Thing in the Constitution or Laws of any State to the Contrary notwithstanding.

The Senators and Representatives before mentioned, and the Members of the several State Legislatures, and all executive and judicial Officers, both of the United States and of the several States, shall be bound by Oath or Affirmation, to support this Constitution; but no religious Test shall ever be required as a Qualification to any Office or public Trust under the United States.

Article VII

The Ratification of the Conventions of nine States, shall be sufficient for the Establishment of this Constitution between the States so ratifying the Same.

Done in Convention by the Unanimous Consent of the States present the Seventeenth Day of September in the Year of our Lord one thousand seven hundred and eighty seven and of the Independence of the United States of America the twelfth. In witness whereof We have hereunto subscribed our Names.

*　*　*

Articles in addition to, and amendment of, the Constitution of the United States of America, proposed by Congress, and ratified by the several States, pursuant to the Fifth Article of the original Constitution.

Amendment I

[Ratification of the first ten amendments was completed December 15, 1791]

Congress shall make no law respecting an establishment of religion, or prohibiting the free exercise thereof; or abridging the freedom of speech, or of the press; or the right of the people peaceably to assemble, and to petition the Government for a redress of grievances.

Amendment II

A well regulated Militia, being necessary to the security of a free State, the right of the people to keep and bear Arms, shall not be infringed.

Amendment III

No Soldier shall, in time of peace be quartered in any house, without the consent of the Owner, nor in time of war, but in a manner to be prescribed by law.

Amendment IV

The right of the people to be secure in their persons, houses, papers, and effects, against unreasonable searches and seizures, shall not be violated, and no Warrants shall issue, but upon probable cause, supported by Oath or affirmation, and particularly describing the place to be searched, and the persons or things to be seized.

Amendment V

No person shall be held to answer for a capital, or otherwise infamous crime, unless on a presentment or indictment of a Grand Jury, except in cases arising in the land or naval forces, or in the Militia, when an actual service in time of War or public danger; nor shall any person be subject for the same offence to be twice put in jeopardy of life or limb; nor shall be compelled in any criminal case to be a witness against himself, nor be deprived of life, liberty, or property, without due process of law; nor shall private property be taken for public use, without just compensation.

Amendment VI

In all criminal prosecutions, the accused shall enjoy the right to a speedy and public trial, by an impartial jury of the State and district wherein the crime shall have been committed, which district shall have been previously ascertained by law, and to be informed of the nature and cause of the accusation; to be confronted with the witness against him; to have compulsory process for obtaining witness in his favor, and to have the Assistance of Counsel for his defence.

Amendment VII

In Suits at common law, where the value in controversy shall exceed twenty dollars, the right of trial by jury shall be preserved, and no fact tried by a jury, shall be otherwise re-examined in any Court of the United States, than according to the rules of the common law.

Amendment VIII

Excessive bail shall not be required, nor excessive fines imposed, nor cruel and unusual punishments inflicted.

Amendment IX

The enumeration in the Constitution, of certain rights, shall not be construed to deny or disparage others retained by the people.

Amendment X

The powers not delegated to the United States by the Constitution, nor prohibited by it to the States, are reserved to the States respectively, or to the people.

Amendment XI

[*January 8, 1798*]

The Judicial power of the United States shall not be construed to extend to any suit in law or equity, commenced or prosecuted against one of the United States by Citizens of another State, or by Citizens or Subjects of any Foreign State.

Amendment XII

[September 25, 1804]

The Electors shall meet in their respective states and vote by ballot for President and Vice President, one of whom, at least, shall not be an inhabitant of the same state with themselves; they shall name in their ballots the person voted for as President, and in distinct ballots the person voted for as Vice President, and they shall make distinct lists of all persons voted for as President, and of all persons voted for as Vice President, and of the number of votes for each, which lists they shall sign and certify, and transmit sealed to the seat of the government of the United States, directed to the President of the Senate;—The President of the Senate shall, in the presence of the Senate and House of Representatives, open all the certificates and the votes shall then be counted;—The person having the greatest number of votes for President, shall be the President, if such number be a majority of the whole number of Electors appointed; and if no person have such majority, then from the persons having the highest numbers not exceeding three on the list of those voted for as President, the House of Representatives shall choose immediately, by ballot, the President. But in choosing the President, the votes shall be taken by states, the representation from each state having one vote; a quorum for this purpose shall consist of a member or members from two thirds of the states, and a majority of all the states shall be necessary to a choice. And if the House of Representatives shall not choose a President whenever the right of choice shall devolve upon them, *before the fourth day of March next following,*[9] then the Vice President shall act as President as in the case of the death or other constitutional disability of the President.—The person having the greatest number of votes as Vice President, shall be the Vice President, if such number be a majority of the whole number of Electors appointed, and if no person have a majority, then from the two highest numbers on the list, the Senate shall choose the Vice President; a quorum for the purpose shall consist of two-thirds of the whole number of Senators, and a majority of the whole number shall be necessary to a choice. But no person constitutionally ineligible to the office of President shall be eligible to that of Vice President of the United States.

Amendment XIII

[December 18, 1865]

Section 1. Neither slavery nor involuntary servitude, except as a punish-

---

[9] See Amendment XX.

ment for crime whereof the party shall have been duly convicted, shall exist within the United States, or any place subject to their jurisdiction.

Section 2. Congress shall have power to enforce this article by appropriate legislation.

Amendment XIV

[July 28, 1868]

Section 1. All persons born or naturalized in the United States, and subject to the jurisdiction thereof, are citizens of the United States and of the State wherein they reside. No State shall make or enforce any law which shall abridge the privileges or immunities of citizens of the United States; nor shall any state deprive any person of life, liberty, or property, without due process of law; nor deny to any person, within its jurisdiction the equal protection of the laws.

Section 2. Representatives shall be apportioned among the several States according to their respective numbers, counting the whole number of persons in each State, excluding Indians not taxed. But when the right to vote at any election for the choice of electors for President and Vice President of the United States, Representatives in Congress, the Executive and Judicial officers of a State, or the members of the Legislature thereof, is denied to any of the male inhabitants of such State, being twenty one years of age, and citizens of the United States, or in any way abridged, except for participation in rebellion, or other crime, the basis of representation therein shall be reduced in the proportion which the number of such male citizens shall bear to the whole number of male citizens twenty one years of age in such State.

Section 3. No person shall be a Senator or Representative in Congress, or elector of President and Vice President, or hold any office, civil or military, under the United States, or under any State, who, having previously taken an oath, as a member of Congress, or as an officer of the United States, or as a member of any State legislature, or as an executive or judicial officer of any State, to support the Constitution of the United States, shall have engaged in insurrection or rebellion against the same, or given aid or comfort to the enemies thereof. But Congress may by a vote of two thirds of each House, remove such disability.

Section 4. The validity of the public debt of the United States, authorized by law, including debts incurred for payment of pensions and bounties for services in suppressing insurrection or rebellion, shall not be questioned. But neither the United States nor any State shall assume or pay any debt or obligation incurred in aid of insurrection or rebellion against the United States, or any claim for the loss or emancipation of any slave; but all such debts, obligations, and claims shall be held illegal and void.

Section 5. The Congress shall have power to enforce, by appropriate legislation, the provisions of this article.

Amendment XV

[March 30, 1870]

Section 1. The right of citizens of the United States to vote shall not be denied or abridged by the United States or by any State on account of race, color, or previous condition of servitude.

Section 2. The Congress shall have power to enforce this article by appropriate legislation.

Amendment XVI

[February 25, 1913]

The Congress shall have power to lay and collect taxes on incomes, from whatever source derived, without apportionment among the several States, and without regard to any census or enumeration.

Amendment XVII

[May 31, 1913]

The Senate of the United States shall be composed of two Senators from each State, elected by the people thereof, for six years; and each Senator shall have one vote. The electors in each State shall have the qualifications requisite for electors of the most numerous branch of the State legislatures.

When vacancies happen in the representation of any State in the Senate, the executive authority of such State shall issue writs of election to fill such vacancies: *Provided,* That the legislature of any State may empower the executive thereof to make temporary appointments until the people fill the vacancies by election as the legislature may direct.

This amendment shall not be so construed as to affect the election or term of any Senator chosen before it becomes valid as part of the Constitution.

Amendment XVIII

[January 29, 1919]

Section 1. *After one year from the ratification of this article the manufacture, sale, or transportation of intoxicating liquors within, the importa-*

tion thereof into, or the exportation thereof from the United States and all territory subject to the jurisdiction thereof for beverage purposes is hereby prohibited.

Section 2. *The Congress and the several States shall have concurrent power to enforce this article by appropriate legislation.*

Section 3. *This article shall be inoperative unless it shall have been ratified as an amendment to the Constitution by the legislatures of the several States, as provided in the Constitution, within seven years from the date of submission hereof to the States by the Congress.*[10]

Amendment XIX

[*August 26, 1920*]

The right of citizens of the United States to vote shall not be denied or abridged by the United States or by any State on account of sex.

Congress shall have power to enforce this article by appropriate legislation.

Amendment XX

[*February 6, 1933*]

Section 1. The terms of the President and Vice President shall end at noon on the 20th day of January, and the terms of Senators and Representatives at noon on the 3rd day of January, of the years in which such terms would have ended if this article had not been ratified; and the terms of their successors shall then begin.

Section 2. The Congress shall assemble at least once in every year, and such meeting shall begin at noon on the 3rd day of January, unless they shall by law appoint a different day.

Section 3. If, at the time fixed for the beginning of the term of the President, the President elect shall have died, the Vice President elect shall become President. If a President shall not have been chosen before the time fixed for the beginning of his term, or if the President elect shall have failed to qualify, then the Vice President elect shall act as President until a President shall have qualified; and the Congress may by law provide for the case wherein neither a President elect nor a Vice President elect shall have qualified, declaring who shall then act as President, or the manner in which one who is to act shall be selected, and such person shall act accordingly until a President or Vice President shall have qualified.

---

[10] Repealed by Amendment XXI.

Section 4. The Congress may by law provide for the case of the death of any of the persons from whom the House of Representatives may choose a President whenever the right of choice shall have devolved upon them, and for the case of the death of any of the persons from whom the Senate may choose a Vice President whenever the right of choice shall have devolved upon them.

Section 5. Sections 1 and 2 shall take effect on the 15th day of October following the ratification of this article.

Section 6. This article shall be inoperative unless it shall have been ratified as an amendment to the Constitution by the legislatures of three fourths of the several States within seven years from the date of its submission.

Amendment XXI

[December 5, 1933]

Section 1. The eighteenth article of amendment to the Constitution of the United States is hereby repealed.

Section 2. The transportation or importation into any State, Territory, or possession of the United States for delivery or use therein of intoxicating liquors, in violation of the laws thereof, is hereby prohibited.

Section 3. This article shall be inoperative unless it shall have been ratified as an amendment to the Constitution by conventions in the several States, as provided in the Constitution, within seven years from the date of the submission hereof to the States by the Congress.

Amendment XXII

[February 26, 1951]

Section 1. No person shall be elected to the office of the President more than twice, and no person who has held the office of President, or acted as President, for more than two years of a term to which some other person was elected President shall be elected to the office of President more than once. But this Article shall not apply to any person holding the office of President when this Article was proposed by the Congress, and shall not prevent any person who may be holding the office of President, or acting as President, during the term within which this Article becomes operative from holding the office of President or acting as President during the remainder of such term.

Section 2. This article shall be inoperative unless it shall have been ratified as an amendment to the Constitution by the legislatures of three fourths of the several States within seven years from the date of its submission to the States by the Congress.

Amendment XXIII

[March 29, 1961]

Section 1. The District constituting the seat of Government of the United States shall appoint in such manner as the Congress may direct:

A number of electors of President and Vice President equal to the whole number of Senators and Representatives in Congress to which the district would be entitled if it were a State, but in no event more than the least populous State; they shall be in addition to those appointed by the States, but they shall be considered, for the purposes of the election of President and Vice President, to be electors appointed by a State; and they shall meet in the District and perform such duties as provided by the twelfth article of amendment.

Section 2. The Congress shall have power to enforce this article by appropriate legislation.

Amendment XXIV

[January 23, 1964]

Section 1. The right of citizens of the United States to vote in any primary or other election for President or Vice President, for electors for President or Vice President, or for Senator or Representative in Congress, shall not be denied or abridged by the United States or any state by reason of failure to pay any poll tax or other tax.

Section 2. The Congress shall have power to enforce this article by appropriate legislation.

Amendment XXV

[February 10, 1967]

Section 1. In case of the removal of the President from office or of his death or resignation, the Vice President shall become President.

Section 2. Whenever there is a vacancy in the office of the Vice President, the President shall nominate a Vice President who shall take office upon confirmation by a majority vote of both Houses of Congress.

Section 3. Whenever the President transmits to the President pro tempore of the Senate and the Speaker of the House of Representatives his written declaration that he is unable to discharge the powers and duties of his office, and until he transmits to them a written declaration to the contrary, such powers and duties shall be discharged by the Vice President as Acting President.

Section 4. Whenever the Vice President and a majority of either the principal officers of the executive departments or of such other body as Congress may by law provide, transmit to the President pro tempore of the Senate and the Speaker of the House of Representatives their written declaration that the President is unable to discharge the powers and duties of his office, the Vice President shall immediately assume the powers and duties of the office as Acting President.

Thereafter, when the President transmits to the President pro tempore of the Senate and the Speaker of the House of Representatives his written declaration that no inability exists, he shall resume the powers and duties of his office unless the Vice President and a majority of either the principal officers of the executive department[s] or of such other body as Congress may by law provide, transmit within four days to the President pro tempore of the Senate and the Speaker of the House of Representatives their written declaration that the President is unable to discharge the powers and duties of his office. Thereupon Congress shall decide the issue, assembling within forty-eight hours for that purpose if not in session. If the Congress, within twenty-one days after receipt of the latter written declaration, or, if Congress is not in session, within twenty-one days after Congress is required to assemble, determines by two-thirds vote of both Houses that the President is unable to discharge the powers and duties of his office, the Vice President shall continue to discharge the same as Acting President; otherwise, the President shall resume the powers and duties of his office.

Amendment XXVI

[*June 30, 1971*]

Section 1. The right of citizens of the United States, who are 18 years of age or older, to vote shall not be denied or abridged by the United States or by any state on account of age.

Section 2. The Congress shall have power to enforce this article by appropriate legislation.

Proposed Amendment (XXVII) — Equal Rights for Men and Women

[Passed by Congress on March 22, 1972, and submitted to the state legislatures for ratification]

Resolved by the Senate and House of Representatives of the United States of America in Congress assembled (two-thirds of each House con-

curring therein), That the following article is proposed as an amendment to the Constitution of the United States, which shall be valid to all intents and purposes as part of the Constitution when ratified by the legislatures of three-fourths of the several States [within seven years from the date of its submission by the Congress:][11]

Article

Section 1. Equality of rights under the law shall not be denied or abridged by the United States or by any State on account of sex.

Section 2. The Congress shall have the power to enforce, by appropriate legislation, the provisions of this article.

Section 3. This amendment shall take effect two years after the date of ratification.

Proposed Amendment (XXVIII) — Treatment of the District of Columbia

[Passed by Congress on August 22, 1978, and submitted to the state legislatures for ratification]

Article

Section 1. For purposes of representation in the Congress, election of the President and Vice President, and article V of this Constitution, the District constituting the seat of government of the United States shall be treated as though it were a State.

Section 2. The exercise of the rights and powers conferred under this article shall be by the people of the District constituting the seat of government, and as shall be provided by the Congress.

Section 3. The twenty-third article of amendment to the Constitution of the United States is hereby repealed.

Section 4. This article shall be inoperative, unless it shall have been ratified as an amendment to the Constitution by the legislatures of three-fourths of the several States within seven years from the date of its submission.

---

[11] In 1978 Congress extended the deadline for ratification of the ERA to June 30, 1982.

GLOSSARY

agribusiness The term used to denote large-scale food and/or crop production as opposed to "farming" or "agriculture" as small-scale enterprise. It may be either a vertical industry — production through manufacture and marketing — or the overall controller of a series of small farms that contract their individual production to a single entity.

anarchism Usually refers to the doctrine that government in any form is oppressive and should be abolished. It comes from a long-standing philosophical tradition, the core of which is an aversion to any kind of institutional management of people's lives. There are two main strands: communal and individual. The most common American version tends toward individualistic, or libertarian, anarchism; the main emphasis is the removal of all external restraints of any kind on the individual.

Annapolis Convention The precursor to the Constitutional Convention, it was called together in 1786 by Alexander Hamilton. Its purported purpose was to discuss the economic problems merchants were encountering due to state and local particularism in credit laws, tariff policies, and so on. These conditions were perceived to be "chaotic" by middle and upper classes.

Articles of Confederation The document on which the government of matters of general concern to the newly independent colonies was based prior to the framing of the Constitution. In it, each state had an equal vote.

authoritarian A term, usually pejorative, used to imply that an entity is *too* controlling. When used in connection with a government, it implies that there is too much ordering of citizens' lives.

authority That which is generally accepted as having the deciding voice — that is, governmental authority would be that person and/or institution which is accepted as the controlling voice of the government.

business cycle An assumption that the economy will expand and contract in a regular, predictable fashion. It is a *normal* aspect of capitalist society and assumed to be healthy as long as one or the other aspect of the cycle does not swing too widely.

capital Money or property available for use to produce more wealth.

capital gain Profit from the sale of capital.

capitalism An economic system wherein production of goods and services is for *private* profit.

> **capitalism/liberalism** The American combination of economic/government ideology and practice.

> **capitalist countries** Those countries whose economic system is devoted to *private* profit and production or at least whose main emphasis is private profit.

> **world capitalism** The capitalist economic system that covers and crosses several national boundaries.

caucus An informal group of like-minded and/or like-labeled persons who meet to devise common strategies and/or policies so as to present as united a front as possible.

change Alterations within the political system:

> **fundamental** Those instances of substantial alteration in the economic or political power structures or in key governmental policies bearing upon distribution of wealth and status.

> **incremental** Alterations in minor policies, well within established power systems.

> **marginal** Alterations whose essential effect is to defend and promote established economic and political structures and existing patterns of distribution of wealth and status within the society.

> **political** Alterations in the economic or governmental structures and/or policies.

> **process of** *How* alterations occur.

> **theory of** Beliefs regarding how and types of alterations possible and/or probable.

class A concept covering socioeconomic status:

> **class consciousness** *Awareness* of the arbitrary nature of socioeconomic status and of one's place within it. Unlike most definitions, which rely on the objective indicators, this one incorporates the subjective parameters included in distinctions of wealth, status, and so on.

> **class system** Existing patterns of distribution of socioeconomic status so that differences are apparent.

> **middle class** Those whose socioeconomic indicators place them above poverty and below wealth.

> **ruling class** Major owners of key banks and corporations.

> **working class** Those who sell their labor power.

communism A belief system whose end goal is the elimination of class distinctions and private profit enterprise so that all persons share in basic necessities and no one is in need; also a pejorative term used in the Western world to denigrate beliefs and/or nations which disagree with and/or challenge Western ideas, making "communism" something to be feared and destroyed by "anti-Communists."

community control The belief in the process of decentralization whereby local groups (from neighborhoods to cities) direct those policies and programs that affect them — for example, local participation in school boards, zoning, and police practice.

competitive sector That portion of the American economy composed of small businesses, mostly retail or services-providing, in which real competition still exists and market principles apply.

conceptual framework That set of basic, underlying premises and assumptions that provide the ordering for data, argument, research, and so on.

conservative A term used in a variety of ways in the American polity; originally, a distinctive ideology based on tradition and a notion of an organic society moving through time with societal interests paramount. In the United States (so strongly liberal in the classic mold), conservatives can be either those who draw on the original tradition or those who draw on classical, laissez-faire liberalism.

> **fiscal conservative** One who prefers that the government refrain from spending ("excessive spending") and manipulation of the economy thereby.

constituency A group of persons to which a representative is responsible, comprising the geographical area from which he or she is elected.

contractualism The belief in ordering all relationships — person to person, person to business, person to government, entity to entity, and so on — by means of written, delineated benefits and obligations, rights and responsibilities.

co-optation The process whereby a dissenter or protester becomes a supporter by being given a share of the pie and/or a position of status so that his or her criticisms are eroded (almost subconsciously).

corporate-banking sector That portion of the American economy composed of the largest, often multinational, productive and financial institutions.

cost of living A statistical measure of the amount required to sustain human life — that is, the cost of the basic necessities such as food, shelter, clothing, transportation, and so on.

counterculture See culture.

crisis A point at which a problem becomes critical; it can be "real," "imagined," and/or "manufactured."

> **energy crisis** An example of a "manufactured" crisis. When the oil companies discovered that their profits were dropping, they declared that natural resources are finite, the Arabs control the oil, demand outruns supply, and so on, so that prices must rise and supply be carefully controlled.

> **fiscal crisis** The financial condition in which tax revenues and other state or governmentally collected monies cannot meet the loan and bond obligations (and similar forms of long-term debt obligations), with

the result that the mutually supportive transfer of money between banks and governmental entities is in danger of collapsing.

population crisis The world condition believed and advertised by some that the number of people on earth is outstripping the capacity of the earth to support human life in terms of basics such as food, space, and so on. Those who argue that it is the way in which the earth's resources are distributed that causes the problem say that this crisis is ideologically based and thus "imagined."

culture The pattern of beliefs and institutions characteristic of a community or a population.

counterculture The term covering a wide variety of "isms," emphasizing values new and/or different from the standard pattern.

currency Paper money issued by national governments and supposedly backed by them.

devaluation A national policy whereby the currency value relative to other nations' is deliberately lowered.

exchange rate The value of the basic unit of currency of one nation relative to another's.

fixed exchange rate A ratio established and agreed to by nations for currency-exchange purposes.

floating exchange rate The ratio that fluctuates according to the buying and selling of currency by those speculating in national currency value.

deflation The economic condition in which money buys more. See **inflation**.

democracy In popular terms, "the people's rule"; when examined more closely, it covers many different ideas and is used when someone wishes to label a certain practice, institution, policy, and so on, as "good."

democratic pluralism The generally accepted view of the American political process whereby negotiation and compromise among many factions and groups result in a product that is a reasonable approximation of both democracy and the public interest.

demography The study of such characteristics of human populations as geographic distribution, size, growth, age distribution, birth rates, and death rates.

depression An extended period of decline in gross national product, industrial production, and employment.

détente An uneasy truce between the United States and the Soviet Union, including the attempt to warm the relationship.

developed countries Those nations whose economic base is industrial and technologically advanced. It carries an ideological bias so that economic imperialism can be promoted as aiding the "development" of "undeveloped countries" in order to enable them to grow up in the image of "developed" countries.

distribution The manner in which resources (national, world, and so forth) are shared and/or utilized.

maldistribution When some have more or less than their fair share.

redistribution To alter present patterns of resource usage and consumption.

dollar glut Overabundance of dollars held by the major banks of foreign countries, primarily Western Europe.

Dred Scott v. Sanford The case whereby the Missouri Compromise was declared unconstitutional as interfering with property rights without due process of law. A slave, Scott, had escaped from territory where slavery was permitted and had gone to territory declared "free" by the Compromise; therefore, he argued, he was now a free man. The Court declared him "property" that had to be returned and the Missouri Compromise, declaring such territory "free," unconstitutional, since it interfered with property rights.

due process The term covering the notion that governmental practices and implementation must be carried on by established procedures in a fair, reasonable, depersonalized, impartial, and neutral manner. See Amendment V to the U.S. Constitution.

economic security Steadily expanding opportunities for profitable investment and trade throughout the world so that constant growth is ensured.

economists Those who study and attempt to make policy for the economy.

    conservative economists Those who favor a return to a position of governmental hands off the economy.

    liberal economists Those who accept Keynesian notions of government/economy partnership in order to control and ameliorate the effects of business cycles, assuming that government can and is in control.

    radical economists Usually Marxian, those who perceive government as the servant of the major units of the economy, maintaining capitalism to the detriment of the people.

egalitarianism The belief system that emphasizes equality of all forms above all.

elite Those who hold more of the resources of power than others do.

    governing elite Those members in the upper class in public positions.

    nonelites The masses, those not in power and status positions.

    power elite Those members who have influence and power and can shape governmental events and policies for their benefit.

empiricism The way of thinking that bases truth only in tangible evidence, that which can be discovered through the use of the senses. The belief that there is a tangible world "out there" which can be discovered and defined.

energy crisis See **crisis.**

establishment That large proportion of individuals holding positions of power (in government *and* private affairs) who have come to share roughly the same values, interests, political ideology, and sense of priorities about what government should be doing and a shared proprietary concern for the continued success of the American system in its familiar social, economic, and political dimensions.

executive agreement An agreement made by the President, without senatorial ratification, with the head of a foreign state.

expropriation The takeover of a private economic enterprise by a governmental entity. Usually used when a new government comes to power and nationalizes all industry, which includes that of foreign nationals, and is then used as a term of approbation. See also **nationalization.**

fascism A governmental system wherein economic and governmental spheres are merged and social control of all aspects of an individual's life is achieved, usually accompanied by police state apparatus to ensure compliance at all levels and to repress any and all dissent.

economic fascism That system wherein government and economy are merged for the benefit of private profits, and the population, as workers, is controlled. But this system is not necessarily accompanied by the entire police state apparatus, compliance being more voluntary on the part of the citizenry.

Federal Reserve System The institutions and practices of the federal banks and management personnel (the Federal Reserve Board) that make and enforce national fiscal and monetary policy.

federalism The division of powers between constituent units (the states) and a single central unit (the national government) such that each has defined powers and is supreme in its own allotted sphere.

Federalist party The label for the group that, at the time of the drafting, ratification, and initial implementation of the U.S. Constitution, supported ratification and a subsequent policy of increasing utilization of national powers and centralization. Among the Federalists were James Madison, Alexander Hamilton, George Washington, and John Adams — but not Thomas Jefferson, a bitter enemy.

fiscal crisis See **crisis.**

fiscal year A twelve-month period for which a government or organization plans its revenues and expenditures.

framers Those men who drafted the body of the U.S. Constitution, in convention, in Philadelphia in 1787. Most of them remain unknown, but names such as Madison, Hamilton, Adams, and Franklin generally evoke the image of "framers."

freedom In American ideology, the absence of restraint on an individual. Since total absence of restraint would lead to chaos, it also usually implies only those restraints necessary and includes a procedure whereby those restraints can be tested, with full coverage afforded by the Bill of Rights.

full employment Originally, when the proportion of unemployed represented only those workers normally changing jobs or temporarily displaced by the advent of new technologies. It has shifted to mean the level of unemployment that would maintain price stability and hold inflation down.

futurists That group whose belief system emphasizes planning and preparing for the long term. Most, however, assume continuation of present policies, power structures, and so on, and simply project them into the future, planning in order to maintain them.

government The ongoing structure, institutions, and practices generally perceived to be public, carrying authority and granted legitimacy by its citizens.

gross national product The total value of the goods and services a nation produces during a specified period of time.

growth rate The proportion of increase or decrease in the gross national product from one year to the next.

hegemony Conformity. Usually refers to ideological conformity so that all agree, or at least publicly state that they agree, on goals, policies, and so on. The "party line."

Horatio Alger An author who wrote a series of books about poor boys who, through luck and hard work, became rich men — who went from "rags to riches." The name came to be synonymous with the American myth of the self-made person; the idea that anyone can make it by trying hard enough (the "luck" part of the original stories being forgotten).

hortatory language Language intended to persuade.

humanism The values based in the desire to improve the welfare and well-being of human beings as the end goal of any activity.

ideology That collection of beliefs that people in a society hold about how their government works, or should work, and why.

imperialism One nation's interference in the affairs of another. It can be through military dominance, economic capability, cultural arrogance, and so on and/or any combination so that the end result is that the dominant nation receives compliance from the subordinate.

incumbent Current officeholder.

industrialized countries Those whose economy is based on industry, as opposed to those based primarily on agricultural or raw materials.

    industrial capitalist countries Those that are industrialized and capitalist; usually means the "free world — that is, the United States, Canada, Western Europe, and so on.

inflation A general rise in the prices of goods and services such that the *real*, or purchasing power, value of money is reduced.

infrastructure Underlying but necessary building blocks.

institutions Identifiable, long-standing structures and/or associations.

    economic institutions Those structures involved with the production of goods and services, such as corporations and trade unions.

    political (public) institutions Those structures, such as Congress, the President, and political parties, that have open accountability and responsibility.

    private institutions Those structures, such as churches, the family, and corporations, with no governmental character.

interest A concern and /or need.

    public interest That which is of concern to *all* members of the polity.

    special interest That which concerns a certain segment and/or group and/or institution, often assumed to be in contrast to the public interest, though it is advertised to be congruent with it by the special interest.

investment guaranty contract Insurance underwritten by the U.S. government for private enterprise involved in ventures in foreign nations so that the risks of such economic involvement are lessened.

judicial review The power of the Supreme Court to declare acts of Congress unconstitutional and thus void; in other words, overseeing of "political" branches by "legal" branches.

laissez-faire Denotes the proponents and policies associated with the belief in "hands off" the economy by government. The belief that the government is best that governs least, especially with regard to property and economics.

law and order A catch phrase denoting the American ideological belief in the need for prescribed rules to which everyone must adhere so that anarchy or chaos will not prevail. It became a political slogan covering repression of dissent and protest by terming dissenters lawless (thus criminal) and thus capable of bringing on anarchy.

left Those who lean toward support of a wider distribution of power, wealth, and status within the society.

legalism Belief in procedural regularity and written rules for conduct and procedure as the best method of dispute settlement of any kind.

legitimacy 1. The quality of a government by virtue of which it is regarded as lawful or as entitled to compliance with its orders. 2. A status conferred by people generally upon the institutions, acts, and officials of their government by believing that their government is the right one, that it works properly and for desirable ends, so that they place their trust in it and grant it their obedience.

liberal Another word for the American ideology, but used popularly only for those on the left side of the American ideology.

> **liberal/capitalist** The peculiar interlocking combination of political and economic ideologies extant in the United States.

> **liberal economist** See **economists**.

libertarian anarchism See **anarchism**.

logrolling The exchanging of votes by legislators: "You vote for my locally oriented bill, and I'll vote for yours."

masses Those who hold little power — nonelites. See **elites**.

median (in statistics) The middle value in a distribution, with an equal number of values above and below it.

military-industrial complex The popular term for the interlocking and interchanging people and interests between the armed forces and the large private contractors and industries that benefit from arms and related production and require military protection for foreign investments.

multinationals Economic entities that exist in several nations and move easily through national boundaries, faithful only to themselves.

> **multinational banks** The financial institutions servicing and dealing with the multinational corporations.

> **multinational corporations** Multinational industries and productive enterprises — for example, the oil companies.

national economic planning The newest move to institute extensive government planning and controls to keep the economy running smoothly.

national income The sum of the income residents of a nation receive in profits, interest, pensions, and wages.

national security Originally, military supremacy over the Soviet Union and other Communist countries and now becoming expanded and controversial as interference in other countries takes on multiple dimensions.

national security managers American policymakers dealing with foreign affairs.

nationalization The taking over by the government or other public bodies of the management and interest in a previously privately owned and managed enterprise. A "good" term when it is either accepted or at least not opposed by the business community. See also **expropriation**.

norm A prescribed standard of acceptability, desirability, or typicality.

OPEC Organization of Petroleum Exporting Countries — the Third World organization of heads of state of those nations with oil resources and holding shares in multinational oil corporations, whose purpose is to unify and increase their bargaining power relative to the multinational American-dominated oil companies.

pluralist See **democratic pluralist.**

policy An established set of rules, written or unwritten, and procedures, either formal or informal.

fiscal policy Rules regarding government management of its own finances.

foreign policy Rules regarding relations with other nations.

incomes policy Rules regarding wages and prices.

monetary policy Rules regarding the money supply.

public policy Usually official, governmental rules and procedures (though it can be informal) regarding a certain subject area or areas.

political consciousness Awareness of and critical involvement and/or challenge of present ideological constraints and circumstances.

political economy The conceptual approach that sees economic and political life as an integrated whole, interpenetrating and mutually supportive.

political science That branch of study devoted to public institutions and relationships.

political socialization The process by which children become imbued with the values and assumptions supportive of the present governmental arrangements — schools, family, television, and so on — and of nationalism and patriotism.

politics The process by which power is employed to affect whether and how government will be used in any given area.

population crisis See **crisis.**

populist One critical of big government and big business and supportive of the "little people."

radical populist One who challenges the status quo on behalf of the "common person," emphasizing equality, democracy, and community.

pork barrel A piece of legislation that enriches a certain district and/or area, such as a defense contract, a highway project, or a new building.

power The possession of those resources, ranging from money and prestige to official authority, that causes others to modify their behavior and conform to what they perceive the possessor of the resources prefers.

power structure The relatively permanent distribution of power among people and institutions that serves to set the general direction of public opinion and public policy.

pragmatic A philosophy associated with William James, based on the "possible." The current American variant reduces it to the "possible" that is totally within present terms, usually meaning a continuation of what presently exists and acceptance of all those boundaries and constraints.

private enterprise The American ideological term for ownership and management and profits of production and other property uses adhering in individuals for individual benefit.

protectionism Belief in the use of governmental policy to shelter internal product prices from competitive pressure from the same or similar products from other localities.

public interest See **interest.**

radicalism The belief in the need for drastic change at the roots of the social order.

radical economist See **economist.**

radical populist See **populist.**

rationing A public policy of controlling production and consumption and enforcing it through control of amounts available to individuals and other entities by issuing certificates for the purchase of such commodities in limited quantities, requiring such certificates be presented before purchase is allowed.

real income The amount of money received, adjusted to take account of increases or decreases in prices: income adjusted to reflect change in purchasing power.

real wages See **wages.**

reality The "facts" and "laws" of the universe. Different ways of thinking pose different versions of what is "real" or "reality." American liberal empiricism's reality is that tangible world outside ourselves which can be discovered, measured, and defined through the use of the scientific method.

reality testing Examining for truth or actual existence.

recession A decline in economic activity, less severe and shorter than a depression; a temporary period of increase in unemployment and decline in investment and production.

republic That form of government in which the public has a voice but does not rule absolutely, not strict majority rule, but tempered, checked, and balanced in a variety of ways.

revolution A destruction of the old order and replacement with a new one. Debate continues on what deserves the name, ranging from seizure of governmental power to total transformation of values, institutions, culture, and so on.

right Those who lean toward insistence upon the status quo and/or even narrower and more restrictive distribution.

robber barons The name applied to the men who built vast economic empires by various and sundry not so legal or moral means during the turn of the century and into the 1920s.

separation of powers The division of specific national governmental powers among the institutions of the national government.

social legislation Those statutes enacted to further policies designed to promote the health and well-being of the populace.

socialism A philosophy, with many variants, centering on human beings as social beings (as opposed to self-sufficient individuals) whose minimal material needs can and should be met through cooperative and communal efforts, thus allowing social relationships to grow and develop.

socialist countries Those nations in opposition to the capitalism of the United States and its allies and/or that claim to be so. It is used in a variety of ways and for various countries by different people at different times, depending upon the immediate issue at hand.

spoils system The filling of governmental posts and bureaucratic positions by an incumbent (usually newly elected) as rewards for service rendered to the officeholder; supposedly replaced by the Civil Service system.

state The combined governmental units and practices of a nation.

status quo The present structure and distribution of power and resources.

SALT Strategic Arms Limitation Talks, ongoing negotiations between the United States and the Soviet Union regarding halting and/or limiting production and stockpiling of weapons of war.

system Related and connected series of institutions, practices, and/or policies mutually beneficial and reinforcing.

   class system A society wherein people occupy and possess differentiated material and status positions.

   economic system The private-enterprise connections.

   econopolitical system The combined governmental and economic enterprises.

   international monetary system The connections among world currencies that allow international trade to occur.

   political system The public-enterprise connections.

   "the" system A general term covering the institutionalized status quo.

tariff The taxes one has to pay in order to import articles.

Third World The term usually encompassing the "undeveloped" countries, those not firmly within the Western or the Soviet blocs, such as nations in Africa, the Middle East, and South America.

trade war The condition in which governmental policies are used to increase the advantage of home industries, and the competing governmental entity retaliates with its own import/export restrictions.

Trilateral Commission An international group of leading financiers and corporate executives, initiated by David Rockefeller of the Chase Manhattan Bank, which makes studies and proposals for economic coordination among capitalist countries.

tunnel vision The acceptance of an ideology so that one sees only within its confines and interprets everything within its terms.

vaccum of authority See **authority**.

wages Payment for services rendered.

   marginal wages Just enough payment to maintain life, sometimes a little more, but only so that the worker is in constant fear of any major or unforeseen expense.

   real wages The purchasing power of the payment.

Warren Court The term denoting the Supreme Court while Earl Warren was chief justice; actually came into widespread usage only as the Court's civil liberties decisions became more liberal and more controversial.

welfare capitalism The "humanizing" of capitalism through social services and income support for masses of people.

welfare state A term, often used pejoratively, to describe a government that aids its citizens through various programs supplementing income, such as unemployment compensation and Medicare.

workers Those who must sell their labor power in order to survive.

blue-collar workers Menial laborers, assembly-line folks; term derived from the dominant color of working clothes.

marginal workers Those who do not make enough to be secure and/or are part-time or temporary laborers, seasonal workers, and so on, so that survival is a constant problem.

World Bank The financial institution, created by the United Nations and dominated by the United States, that provides loans to developing nations, more affluent countries allowing their money to be loaned and used by less affluent ones.

world view The comprehensive and consistent manner of perceiving people and the natural world and their interrelationship, underlying and leading to more specific values, beliefs, ideologies, and so on.

zero growth The concept of limiting population and industrial and other kinds of expansion or increase to as close to a 0.0 percent growth rate for the world as possible.

BIBLIOGRAPHY

The selections that follow have been drawn from the vast and rapidly growing literature on American politics. We have sought to identify additional reading, usually available in paperback, that will fill out each chapter in some important way. Sometimes these selections contrast sharply with our interpretation; at other times they extend it beyond the point that we consider supported by available evidence; or they represent reflections on approaches or methods worth examining. In no case, of course, can our selections be taken as a comprehensive bibliography. They are a beginning — a highly diversified one.

CHAPTER 1 Why and How to Study Politics

Politics as an attempt to describe and explain:

Dahl, Robert A. *Modern Political Analysis*, 3rd ed., Englewood Cliffs, N.J.: Prentice-Hall, 1976.

Eulau, Heinz. *The Behavioral Persuasion in Politics*. New York: Random House, 1963.

Sorauf, Frank J. *Political Science: An Informal Overview*. Columbus, Ohio: Charles E. Merrill, 1965.

Politics as an extension of ethical concerns:

Kaplan, Abraham. *American Ethics and Public Policy.* New York: Oxford University Press, 1963.

Kariel, Henry S. *The Promise of Politics.* Englewood Cliffs, N.J.: Prentice-Hall, 1966.

Pranger, Robert J. *The Eclipse of Citizenship.* New York: Holt, Rinehart and Winston, 1968.

CHAPTER 2　The American Political Economy

Baran, Paul A., and Paul M. Sweezey. *Monopoly Capital.* New York: Monthly Review Press, 1966.

Best, Michael, and William E. Connolly. *The Politicized Economy.* Lexington, Mass.: D.C. Heath, 1976.

Friedman, Milton. *Capitalism and Freedom.* Chicago: University of Chicago Press, 1962.

Galbraith, John K. *American Capitalism — The Concept of Countervailing Power.* Boston: Houghton Mifflin, 1952.

———. *The Affluent Society.* New York: New American Library, 1958.

———. *The New Industrial State.* New York: New American Library, 1968.

Greenberg, Edward S. *Serving the Few: Corporate Capitalism and the Bias of Government Policy.* New York: Wiley, 1974.

Miliband, Ralph. *The State in Capitalist Society.* New York: Basic Books, 1969.

Musolf, Lloyd D. *Government and Economy.* Chicago: Scott, Foresman, 1965.

Potter, David M. *People of Plenty.* Chicago: Phoenix Books, 1954.

Reagan, Michael. *The Managed Economy.* New York: Oxford University Press, 1963.

Schur, Edwin M., ed. *The Poverty Establishment.* Englewood Cliffs, N.J.: Prentice-Hall, 1974.

CHAPTER 3　The World Context of U.S. Economic and Foreign Policy

Engler, Robert. *The Politics of Oil.* Chicago: The University of Chicago Press, 1969.

Galbraith, John Kenneth. *Economics and the Public Purpose.* Boston: Houghton Mifflin, 1973.

Kolko, Joyce. *America and the Crisis of World Capitalism.* Boston: Little, Brown, 1975.

Mermelstein, David, ed. *The Economic Crisis Reader.* New York: Vintage Books, 1975.

Pirages, Dennis, and Paul Ehrlich. *Ark II: Social Response to Environmental Imperatives.* San Francisco: W. H. Freeman, 1974.

Samuelson, Paul A. *Economics,* 9th ed. New York: McGraw-Hill, 1973.

Tanzer, Michael. *The Sick Society: An Economic Examination.* New York: Holt, Rinehart and Winston, 1971.

Zeitlin, Maurice, ed. *American Society, Inc.* Chicago: Markham, 1970.

CHAPTER 4 U.S. Economic Problems and Policies

Agee, Philip. *Inside the Company: CIA Diary.* New York: Stonehill Press, 1975.

Horowitz, David, ed. *Corporations and the Cold War.* New York: Monthly Review Press, 1969.

Jenkins, Robin. *Exploitation: The World Power Structure and the Inequality of Nations.* London: MacGibbon & Kee, 1970.

Magdoff, Harry. *The Age of Imperialism: The Economics of U.S. Foreign Policy.* New York: Monthly Review Press, 1969.

Parenti, Michael, ed. *Trends and Tragedies in American Foreign Policy.* Boston: Little, Brown, 1971.

Tanzer, Michael. *The Political Economy of International Oil and the Underdeveloped Countries.* Boston: Beacon Press, 1970.

Williams, William A. *The Tragedy of American Diplomacy.* New York: Delta, 1959.

CHAPTER 5 National Security: Issues, Policies, and Consequences

Barnet, Richard J. *The Roots of War.* New York: Atheneum, 1972.

————. *The Economy of Death.* New York: Atheneum, 1969.

Bloomfield, Lincoln P., et al. *Khrushchev and the Arms Race.* Cambridge, Mass.: M.I.T. Press, 1966.

Boulding, Kenneth. *Conflict and Defense: A General Theory.* New York: Harper & Row, 1963.

Clayton, James L. *The Economic Impact of the Cold War.* New York: Harcourt Brace Jovanovich, 1970.

Donovan, John C. *The Cold Warriors: A Policy-Making Elite.* Lexington, Mass.: D. C. Heath, 1974.

Huntington, Samuel. *The Common Defense.* New York: Columbia University Press, 1961.

Klare, Michael. *Supplying Repression.* Washington, D.C.: *Institute for Policy Studies,* 1980.

Lapp, Ralph E. *The Weapons Culture.* New York: W. W. Norton, 1968.

Marchetti, Victor, and John D. Marks. *The CIA and the Cult of Intelligence.* New York: Knopf, 1974.

Melman, Seymour. *Pentagon Capitalism.* New York: McGraw-Hill, 1970.

————, ed. *The War Economy of the United States.* New York: St. Martin's Press, 1971.

Neiburg, H. L. *In the Name of Science.* Chicago: Quadrangle Books, 1966.

Prouty, L. Fletcher. *The Secret Team: The CIA and Its Allies in Control of the United States and the World.* Englewood Cliffs, N.J.: Prentice-Hall, 1973.

Thayer, George. *The War Business.* New York: Simon & Schuster, 1969.

CHAPTER 6 Income Distribution: Inequality, Poverty, and Welfare

Bachrach, Peter, and Morton Baratz. *Power and Poverty.* New York: Oxford University Press, 1970.

Baltzell, E. Digby. *Philadelphia Gentlemen: The Making of a National Upper Class.* Glencoe, Ill.: The Free Press, 1958.

Bottomore, T. B. *Classes in Modern Society.* New York: Vintage Books, 1966.

Clark, Kenneth, and Jeanette Hopkins. *A Relevant War on Poverty.* New York: Harper & Row, 1969.

Cloward, Richard A., and Frances Fox Piven. *The Politics of Turmoil: Essays on Poverty, Race, and the Urban Crisis.* New York: Pantheon Books, 1974.

Dahrendorf, Ralf. *Class and Class Conflict in Industrial Societies.* Stanford, Cal.: Stanford University Press, 1959.

Donovan, John. *The Politics of Poverty.* New York: Pegasus, 1967.

Ferman, Louis, et al. *Poverty in America.* Ann Arbor: University of Michigan Press, 1965.

Harrington, Michael. *The Other America.* Baltimore: Penguin, 1967.

Haveman, Robert H., ed. *A Decade of Federal Antipoverty Programs.* New York: Academic Press, 1977.

Kolko, Gabriel. *Wealth and Power in America.* New York: Praeger, 1962.

Lampman, Robert J. *Ends and Means of Reducing Income Poverty.* New York: Academic Press, 1971.

————. *The Share of Top Wealth-Holders in National Wealth.* Princeton: Princeton University Press, 1962.

Lenski, Gerhard. *Power and Privilege.* New York: McGraw-Hill, 1966.

Matthews, Donald. *The Social Background of Political Decision-Makers.* New York: Random House, 1955.

Miller, S. M., and Pamela Roby. *The Future of Inequality.* New York: Basic Books, 1970.

Mills, C. Wright. *The Power Elite.* New York: Oxford University Press, 1956.

Plotnick, Robert D., and Felicity Skidmore. *Progress Against Poverty: A Review of the 1964–1974 Decade.* New York: Academic Press, 1975.

Rainwater, Lee, ed. *Inequality and Justice.* Chicago: Aldine, 1974.

Roby, Pamela, ed. *The Poverty Establishment.* Englewood Cliffs, N.J.: Prentice-Hall, 1974.

CHAPTER 7 The Status of Racial Minorities

Allen, Robert. *Black Awakening in Capitalist America.* New York: Doubleday, 1969.

Brown, Dee. *Bury My Heart at Wounded Knee.* New York: Holt, Rinehart and Winston, 1970.

Carmichael, Stokely, and Charles V. Hamilton. *Black Power: The Politics of Liberation in America.* New York: Vintage Books, 1967.

Clark, Kenneth B. *Dark Ghetto: Dilemmas of Social Power.* New York: Harper & Row, 1965.

Cleaver, Eldridge. *Soul on Ice.* New York: McGraw-Hill, 1968.

Coleman, James S., et al. *Equality of Educational Opportunity.* Washington, D.C.: U.S. Government Printing Office, 1966.

Coles, Robert. *Children of Crisis.* New York: Dell, 1964.

Friedman, Lawrence M. *Government and Slum Housing.* Chicago: Rand McNally, 1968.

Greenberg, Edward S., Neal Milner, and David J. Olson, eds. *Black Politics.* New York: Holt, Rinehart and Winston, 1971.

Herzog, Stephen J., ed. *Minority Group Politics.* New York: Holt, Rinehart and Winston, 1971.

Jencks, Christopher, et al. *Inequality.* New York: Basic Books, 1972.

Knowles, Louis L., and Kenneth Prewitt, eds. *Institutional Racism in America.* Englewood Cliffs, N.J.: Prentice-Hall, 1969.

Lewis, Oscar. *La Vida.* New York: Random House, 1966.

————. *The Children of Sanchez.* New York: Random House, 1961.

Liebow, Elliot. *Talley's Corner.* Boston: Little, Brown, 1967.

Malcolm X. *Autobiography.* New York: Grove Press, 1964.

Masters, Stanley H. *Black-White Income Differentials: Empirical Studies and Policy Implications.* New York: Academic Press, 1975.

Matthews, Donald R., and James W. Prothro. *Negroes and the New Southern Politics.* New York: Harcourt Brace Jovanovich, 1966.

Moynihan, Daniel. *Maximum Feasible Misunderstanding.* New York: The Free Press, 1969.

Parsons, Talcott, and Kenneth B. Clark, eds. *The Negro American.* Boston: Houghton Mifflin, 1966.

Rendon, Armando. *Chicano Manifesto.* New York: Macmillan, 1971.

Report of the Advisory Commission on Civil Disorders. New York: Bantam Books, 1968.

Shockley, John S. *Chicano Revolt in a Texas Town.* Notre Dame, Ind.: University of Notre Dame Press, 1974.

Van Den Berghe, Pierre L. *Race and Racism.* New York: Wiley, 1967.

Walker, Jack L., and Joel D. Aberbach. "The Meanings of Black Power: A Comparison of White and Black Interpretations of a Political Slogan," *American Political Science Review* 64 (June 1970): 367–388.

Zinn, Howard. *SNCC: The New Abolitionists.* Boston: Beacon Press, 1964.

CHAPTER 8 Justifying the Status Quo: Ideology and Symbolism

Banfield, Edward. *The Unheavenly City Revisited.* Boston: Little, Brown, 1974.

Becker, Carl. *Freedom and Responsibility in the American Way of Life.* New York: Vintage Books, 1960.

Boorstin, Daniel. *The Genius of American Politics.* Chicago: University of Chicago Press, 1960.

Devine, Donald. *The Political Culture of the United States.* Boston: Little, Brown, 1972.

Edelman, Murray. *The Symbolic Uses of Politics.* Urbana: University of Illinois Press, 1964.

————. *Political Language.* New York: Academic Press, 1977.

Girvetz, Harry. *The Evolution of Liberalism.* New York: Collier Books, 1963.

Grimes, Alan P. *American Political Thought.* New York: Holt, Rinehart and Winston, 1966.

Hartz, Louis M. *The Liberal Tradition in America.* New York: Harcourt Brace Jovanovich, 1955.

Kristol, Irving. *On the Democratic Idea in America*. New York: Harper & Row, 1972.

Lane, Robert. *Political Ideology: Why the American Common Man Believes What He Does*. New York: Free Press, 1962.

Rossiter, Clinton. *Conservatism in America: The Thankless Persuasion*. New York: Vintage Books, 1955.

CHAPTER 9   The Challenge of the 1980s

Allen, Robert L. *Black Awakening in Capitalist America*. New York: Doubleday, 1969.

Boggs, James, and Grace Lee Boggs. *Revolution and Evolution in the Twentieth Century*. New York: Monthly Review Press, 1974.

Carmichael, Stokely, and Charles V. Hamilton. *Black Power: The Politics of Liberation in America*. New York: Vintage Books, 1967.

Dolbeare, Kenneth M., and Patricia Dolbeare. *American Ideologies: The Competing Political Beliefs of the 1970's*. Chicago: Markham, 1971.

Jacobs, Paul, and Saul Landau, eds. *The New Radicals*. New York: Vintage Books, 1966.

Lowi, Theodore. *The End of Liberalism: Ideology, Policy and the Crisis of Authority*, 2nd ed. New York: W. W. Norton, 1978.

Newfield, Jack, and Jeff Greenfield. *A Populist Manifesto: The Making of a New Majority*. New York: Warner, 1972.

Sherman, Howard. *Radical Political Economy*. New York: Basic Books, 1972.

Theodori, Massimo, ed. *The New Left: A Documentary History*. Indianapolis: Bobbs-Merrill, 1969.

CHAPTER 10   Managing the Political Agenda

Bell, Daniel, and Irving Kristol, eds. *Capitalism Today*. New York: Mentor Books, 1971.

Cook, Fred J. *The Welfare State*. New York: Collier Books, 1962.

Domhoff, G. William. *Who Rules America?* Englewood Cliffs, N.J.: Prentice-Hall, 1967.

Dye, Thomas. *Who's Running America? The Carter Years*, 2nd ed. Englewood Cliffs, N.J.: Prentice-Hall, 1979.

Edelman, Murray. *The Symbolic Uses of Politics*. Champaign-Urbana: University of Illinois Press, 1964.

Kelley, Stanley. *Professional Public Relations and Political Power*. Baltimore: Johns Hopkins University Press, 1956.

Key, V. O. *Public Opinion and American Democracy*. New York: Knopf, 1961.

Klapp, Orrin. *Symbolic Leaders*. New York: Minerva Press, 1968.

Kolko, Gabriel. *Wealth and Power in the United States*. New York: Praeger, 1962.

Lang, Kurt, and Gladys Lang. *Politics and Television*. Chicago: Quadrangle Books, 1968.

Lasswell, Harold. *Politics: Who Gets What, When, How*. Cleveland: Meridian Books, 1958.

Lundberg, Ferdinand. *The Rich and the Super-Rich*. New York: Bantam Books, 1968.

Miliband, Ralph. *The State in Capitalist Society*. New York: Basic Books, 1969.

Mintz, Morton, and Jerry Cohen. *America Inc.: Who Owns and Operates the United States?* New York: Dell, 1971.

Schattschneider, E. E. *The Semi-Sovereign People*. New York: Holt, Rinehart and Winston, 1960.

CHAPTER 11   Elite Analysis: Approaches and Implications

Bauer, Raymond, Ithiel de Sola Pool, and Louis Anthony Dexter. *American Business and Public Policy*. New York: Atheneum Press, 1963.

Dahl, Robert A. *Who Governs?* New Haven, Conn.: Yale University Press, 1961.

Kariel, Henry S. *The Decline of American Pluralism*. Stanford, Cal.: Stanford University Press, 1961.

Key, V. O. *Southern Politics*. New York: Vintage Books, 1949.

Lens, Sidney. *The Military-Industrial Complex*. Philadelphia: Pilgrim Press, 1970.

Matthews, Donald R. *The Social Background of Political Decision Makers*. New York: Random House, 1955.

McConnell, Grant. *Private Power and American Democracy*. New York: Knopf, 1966.

Milbrath, Lester W. *The Washington Lobbyists*. Chicago: Rand McNally, 1963.

Mills, C. Wright. *The Power Elite*. New York: Oxford University Press, 1959.

Polsby, Nelson W. *Community Power and Political Theory*. New Haven, Conn.: Yale University Press, 1963.

Prewitt, Kenneth. *The Recruitment of Political Leaders*. Indianapolis: Bobbs-Merrill, 1970.

Rose, Arnold. *The Power Structure*. New York: Oxford University Press, 1967.

Zeigler, Harmon. *Interest Groups in American Society*. Englewood Cliffs, N.J.: Prentice-Hall, 1964.

CHAPTER 12   The Constitution

Andrews, William G. *Coordinate Magistrates: Constitutional Law by Congress and President*. New York: Van Nostrand, Reinhold, 1969.

Beard, Charles A. *An Economic Interpretation of the Constitution of the United States with New Introduction*. New York: Macmillan, 1954 (originally published in 1913).

Bickel, Alexander M. *The Least Dangerous Branch*. Indianapolis: Bobbs-Merrill, 1962.

Danelski, David J. *A Supreme Court Justice Is Appointed*. New York: Random House, 1964.

Krislov, Samuel. *The Supreme Court in the Political Process.* New York: Macmillan, 1965.

McCloskey, Robert G. *The American Supreme Court.* Chicago: University of Chicago Press, 1960.

Miller, Arthur S. *The Supreme Court and American Capitalism.* New York: The Free Press, 1968.

Mitau, G. Theodore. *Decade of Decision: The Supreme Court and the Constitutional Revolution, 1954–1964.* New York: Scribner's, 1967.

Pritchett, C. Herman. *The American Constitutional System,* 2nd ed. New York: McGraw-Hill, 1967.

Shapiro, Martin. *The Supreme Court and the Administrative Agencies.* New York: The Free Press, 1968.

Sutherland, Arthur E. *Constitution in America.* New York: Blaisdell, 1965.

CHAPTER 13   Law and the Supreme Court

Abraham, Henry J. *The Judicial Process,* 2nd ed. New York: Oxford University Press, 1968.

Becker, Theodore L., ed. *The Impact of Supreme Court Decisions.* New York: Oxford University Press, 1969.

Cardozo, Benjamin. *The Nature of the Judicial Process.* New Haven, Conn.: Yale University Press, 1921.

Casper, Jonathan D. *American Criminal Justice: The Defendant's Perspective.* Englewood Cliffs, N.J.: Prentice-Hall, 1972.

Cole, George F., ed. *Criminal Justice: Law and Politics.* Belmont, Cal.: Wadsworth, 1972.

Frank, Jerome. *Law and the Modern Mind.* New York: Doubleday, 1930.

Goldman, Sheldon, and Thomas P. Jahnige. *The Federal Courts as a Political System.* New York: Harper & Row, 1971.

Jacob, Herbert. *Justice in America,* 2nd ed. Boston: Little, Brown, 1972.

Lewis, Anthony. *Gideon's Trumpet.* New York: Vintage, 1964.

Murphy, Walter F., and Joseph Tanenhaus. *The Study of Public Law.* New York: Random House, 1972.

Rodgers, Harrell R., and Charles S. Bullock III. *Law and Social Change: Civil Rights Laws and Their Consequences.* New York: McGraw-Hill, 1972.

Scheingold, Stuart A. *The Politics of Rights: Lawyers, Public Policy, and Political Change.* New Haven, Conn.: Yale University Press, 1974.

Schmidhauser, John R. *The Supreme Court: Its Politics, Personalities, and Procedures.* New York: Holt, Rinehart and Winston, 1960.

CHAPTER 14   The Congress

Bailey, Stephen K. *The New Congress.* New York: St. Martin's Press, 1966.

Berman, Daniel M. *A Bill Becomes a Law: Congress Enacts Civil Rights Legislation,* 2nd ed. New York: Macmillan, 1966.

Bibby, John, and Roger Davidson. *On Capitol Hill: Studies in the Legislative Process.* New York: Holt, Rinehart and Winston, 1967.

Fenno, Richard F., Jr. *The Power of the Purse: Appropriations Politics in Congress.* Boston: Little, Brown, 1966.

Froman, Lewis A., Jr. *Congressmen and the Constituencies*. Chicago: Rand McNally, 1963.

Green, Mark, et al. (Ralph Nader Congress Project). *Who Runs Congress?* New York: Grossman, 1972.

Koenig, Louis W. *Congress and the President*. Chicago: Scott, Foresman, 1965.

Matthews, Donald R. *U.S. Senators and Their World*. Chapel Hill, N.C.: University of North Carolina Press, 1960.

Polsby, Nelson W. *Congress and the Presidency*. Englewood Cliffs, N.J.: Prentice-Hall, 1964.

CHAPTER 15   The Presidency

Barber, James David, ed. *Choosing the President*. Englewood Cliffs, N.J.: Prentice-Hall, 1974.

Bernstein, Carl, and Bob Woodward. *All the President's Men*. New York: Warner Books, 1975.

Cornwell, Elmer. *Presidential Leadership of Public Opinion*. Bloomington: Indiana University Press, 1965.

Corwin, Edward. *The President: Office and Powers*, 4th rev. ed. New York: New York University Press, 1974.

Cronin, Thomas E. *The State of the Presidency*. Boston: Little, Brown, 1975.

Dunn, Delmer. *Financing Presidential Campaigns*. Washington, D.C.: The Brookings Institution, 1972.

Fenno, Richard F. *The President's Cabinet*. Cambridge, Mass.: Harvard University Press, 1959.

Fisher, Louis. *President and Congress: Power and Policy*. New York: The Free Press, 1972.

Hargrove, Edwin C. *The Power of the Modern Presidency*. New York: Knopf, 1974.

McConnell, Grant. *The Modern Presidency*. New York: St. Martin's Press, 1976.

Mueller, John E. *War, Presidents and Public Opinion*. New York: Wiley, 1973.

Neustadt, Richard. *Presidential Power*. New York: Wiley, 1960.

Page, Benjamin I. *Choices and Echoes in Presidential Elections*. Chicago: University of Chicago Press, 1978.

Polsby, Nelson, and Aaron Wildavsky. *Presidential Elections*, 3rd ed. New York: Scribner's, 1972.

Schlesinger, Arthur M., Jr. *The Imperial Presidency*. Boston: Houghton Mifflin, 1973.

Sorenson, Theodore C. *Decision-Making in the White House*. New York: Columbia University Press, 1963.

CHAPTER 16   The Bureaucracy

Agee, Philip. *Inside the Company: CIA Diary*. Penguin Books, 1975.

Allison, Graham T. *Essence of Decision: Explaining the Cuban Missile Crisis*. Boston: Little, Brown, 1971.

Barnet, Richard J. *Roots of War*. New York: Atheneum, 1972.

Downs, Anthony. *Inside Bureaucracy*. Boston: Little, Brown, 1967.

Halperin, Morton H. *Bureaucratic Politics and Foreign Policy*. Washington, D.C.: The Brookings Institution, 1974.

Heclo, Hugh. *A Government of Strangers: Executive Politics in Washington*. Washington, D.C.: The Brookings Institution, 1977.

Janis, Irving L. *Victims of Groupthink*. Boston: Houghton Mifflin, 1972.

Melman, Seymour. *The Permanent War Economy*. New York: Simon & Schuster, 1974.

Perrow, Charles. *Complex Organizations*. Glenview: Scott, Foresman, 1972.

Pressman, Jeffrey, and Aaron Wildavsky. *Implementation*. Berkeley: University of California Press, 1973.

Rourke, Frances E., ed. *Bureaucracy, Politics, and Public Policy*, 2nd ed. Boston: Little, Brown, 1976.

Simon, Herbert A. *Administrative Behavior*, 3rd ed. New York: Free Press, 1976.

Wildavsky, Aaron. *The Politics of the Budgetary Process*. Boston: Little, Brown, 1964.

Wise, David. *The Politics of Lying*. New York: Random House, 1973.

CHAPTER 17 The Political Contest of Nonelites

Aronowitz, Stanley. *False Promises*. New York: McGraw-Hill, 1973.

Berelson, Bernard, Paul F. Lazarsfeld, and William N. McPhee. *Voting*. Chicago: University of Chicago Press, 1954.

Blauner, Robert. *Racial Oppression in America*. New York: Harper & Row, 1972.

Braverman, Harry. *Labor and Monopoly Capital*. New York: Monthly Review Press, 1974.

Campbell, Angus, et al. *Elections and the Political Order*. New York: Wiley, 1966.

Converse, Philip. "The Nature of Belief Systems in Mass Publics," in *Ideology and Discontent*, ed. David Apter. London: Free Press of Glencoe, 1964.

Converse, Philip, and Georges Dupeux. "The Politicization of the Electorate in France and the United States," *Public Opinion Quarterly* 26 (Spring 1962): 1–24.

Converse, Philip, et al. "Continuity and Change in American Politics: Parties and Issues in the 1968 Election," *American Political Science Review* 63 (December 1969): 1083–1105.

Downs, Anthony. *An Economic Theory of Democracy*. New York: Harper & Row, 1957.

Easton, David, and Jack Dennis. *Children in the Political System*. New York: McGraw-Hill, 1969.

Flanigan, William H. *Political Behavior of the American Electorate*. Boston: Allyn & Bacon, 1968.

Greenstein, Fred I. *Children and Politics*, rev. ed. New Haven, Conn.: Yale University Press, 1968.

Hartz, Louis. *The Liberal Tradition in America*. New York: Harcourt Brace Jovanovich, 1955.

Hess, Robert D., and Judith V. Torney. *The Development of Political Attitudes in Children*. Chicago: Aldine, 1967.

Huber, Joan, and William Form. *Income and Ideology: An Analysis of the American Political Formula*. New York: The Free Press, 1974.

Langton, Kenneth. *Political Socialization*. New York: Oxford University Press, 1969.

Marvick, Dwayne. "The Political Socialization of American Negroes," *Annals* 361 (September 1965): 112–127.

Raskin, Marcus G. *Being and Doing*. New York: Random House, 1971.

Rubin, Lillian B. *Worlds of Pain*. New York: Basic Books, 1976.

Skolnick, Jerome H. *The Politics of Protest*. New York: Ballantine Books, 1969.

U.S. Department of Health, Education, and Welfare. *Toward a Social Report*. Washington, D.C.: U.S. Government Printing Office, 1969.

Wolfenstein, Martha, and Gilbert Kliman, eds. *Children and the Death of the President*. Garden City, N.Y.: Doubleday, 1965.

CHAPTER 18   Public Opinion and Attitude Change

Aronowitz, Stanley. *False Promises: The Shaping of American Working-Class Consciousness*. New York: McGraw-Hill, 1973.

Cantril, Albert, and Charles Roll. *The Hopes and Fears of the American People*. New York: Universe Books, 1972.

Clausen, John A., ed. *Socialization and Society*. Boston: Little, Brown, 1968.

Dawson, Richard, and Kenneth Prewitt. *Political Socialization*. Boston: Little, Brown, 1969.

Devine, Donald. *The Political Culture of the United States*. Boston: Little, Brown, 1972.

Edelman, Murray. *Political Language*. New York: Academic Press, 1977.

Hamilton, Richard F. *Class and Politics in the United States*. New York: Wiley, 1972.

Lane, Robert E. *Political Ideology: Why the American Common Man Believes What He Does*. New York: The Free Press, 1962.

————. *Political Thinking and Consciousness*. Chicago: Markham, 1962.

Lane, Robert E., and David O. Sears. *Public Opinion*. Englewood Cliffs, N.J.: Prentice-Hall, 1964.

Marcuse, Herbert. *One-Dimensional Man*. Boston: Beacon Press, 1964.

Schoenberger, Robert A. *The American Right Wing: Readings in Political Behavior*. New York: Holt, Rinehart and Winston, 1969.

Stouffer, Samuel. *Communism, Conformity and Civil Liberties*. New York: John Wiley, 1966 (originally published in 1956).

Welch, Susan, and John Comer, eds. *Public Opinion: Its Formation, Measurement, and Impact*. Palo Alto, Cal.: Mayfield, 1975.

CHAPTER 19   Participation: Voting and Alternatives

Almond, Gabriel, and Sidney Verba. *The Civic Culture*. Princeton, N.J.: Princeton University Press, 1963.

Altshuler, Alan A. *Community Control: The Black Demand for Participation in Large American Cities.* New York: Pegasus, 1970.

Boyd, Richard W. "Electoral Trends in Postwar Politics," in David J. Barber, ed. *Choosing the President.* Englewood Cliffs, N.J.: Prentice-Hall, 1974.

Burnham, Walter Dean. *Critical Elections and the Mainsprings of American Politics.* New York: W. W. Norton, 1970.

Campbell, Angus, et al. *The American Voter.* New York: Wiley, 1960.

————. *Elections and the Political Order.* New York: Wiley, 1966.

Clark, Kenneth, and Jeanette Hopkins. *A Relevant War Against Poverty.* New York: Harper & Row, 1970.

Cloward, Richard A., and Frances Fox Piven. *The Politics of Turmoil.* New York: Pantheon Books, 1974.

Flanigan, William H. *Political Behavior of the American Electorate.* Boston: Allyn & Bacon, 1968.

Graham, Hugh Davis, and Ted Robert Gurr (Task Force to the President's Commission on Violence). *Violence in America.* New York: Signet Books, 1969.

Gurr, Ted Robert. *Why Men Rebel.* Princeton, N.J.: Princeton University Press, 1970.

Jennings, M. Kent, and Harmon Zeigler, eds. *The Electoral Process.* Englewood Cliffs, N.J.: Prentice-Hall, 1966.

Key, V. O. Jr. *The Responsible Electorate.* Cambridge, Mass.: Harvard University Press, 1966.

Kramer, Ralph M. *Participation of the Poor: Comparative Case Studies in the War on Poverty.* Englewood Cliffs, N.J.: Prentice-Hall, 1969.

Lipsky, Michael. *Protest in City Politics.* Chicago: Rand McNally, 1970.

Moynihan, Daniel P. *Maximum Feasible Misunderstanding.* New York: The Free Press, 1969.

National Advisory Commission on Civil Disorders. *Report.* New York: Bantam Books, 1968.

Nie, Norman H., Sidney Verba, and John R. Petrocik. *The Changing American Voter.* Cambridge, Mass.: Harvard University Press, 1976.

Piven, Frances Fox, and Richard A. Cloward. *Regulating the Poor.* New York: Vintage, 1971.

Roszak, Theodore. *The Making of a Counter Culture.* Garden City, N.Y.: Doubleday, 1969.

Rubinstein, Richard E. *Rebels in Eden: Mass Political Violence in the United States.* Boston: Little, Brown, 1970.

Sorauf, Frank J. *Party Politics in America,* 3rd ed. Boston: Little, Brown, 1976.

Sundquist, James. *Dynamics of the Party System: Alignment and Realignment of Political Parties in the United States.* Washington, D.C.: The Brookings Institution, 1973.

Zeigler, L. Harmon, and Wayne G. Peak. *Interest Groups in American Society,* 2nd ed. Englewood Cliffs, N.J.: Prentice-Hall, 1972.

CHAPTER 20   The American Power Structure

Barber, Richard J. *The American Corporation: Its Power, Its Money, Its Politics.* New York: E. P. Dutton, 1970.

Dahl, Robert A. *A Preface to Democratic Theory.* Chicago: University of Chicago Press, 1956.

————. *Who Governs? Democracy and Power in an American City.* New Haven, Conn.: Yale University Press, 1961.

Domhoff, G. William. *Bohemian Grove.* New York: Harper/Colophon Books, 1975.

————. *Who Rules America?* Englewood Cliffs, N.J.: Prentice-Hall, 1967.

Domhoff, G. William, and Hoyt B. Ballard. *C. Wright Mills and the Power Elite.* Boston: Beacon Press, 1968.

Kariel, Henry S. *The Decline of American Pluralism.* Stanford, Cal.: Stanford University Press, 1961.

Kaufman, Arnold S. *The Radical Liberal: New Man in American Politics.* New York: Atherton Press, 1968.

Polsby, Nelson W. *Community Power and Political Theory.* New Haven, Conn.: Yale University Press, 1963.

Rose, Arnold M. *The Power Structure: Political Process in American Society.* New York: Oxford University Press, 1967.

Rowen, Hobart. *The Free Enterprisers: Kennedy, Johnson and the Business Establishment.* New York: G. P. Putnam, 1964.

Weinstein, James. *The Corporate Ideal in the Liberal State.* Boston: Beacon Press, 1968.

CHAPTER 21   Political Change

Carnoy, Martin, and Derek Shearer. *Economic Democracy.* Washington, D.C.: Institute for Policy Studies, 1980.

Dolbeare, Kenneth M. *Political Change in the United States: A Framework for Analysis.* New York: McGraw-Hill, 1974.

Dowd, Douglas. *The Twisted Dream: Capitalist Development in the United States Since 1776.* Cambridge, Mass.: Winthrop, 1974.

Gross, Bertram. *Friendly Fascism: The New Face of Power in America.* New York: M. Evans, 1980.

Harrington, Michael. *The Twilight of Capitalism.* New York: Simon & Schuster, 1976.

Heilbroner, Robert. *An Inquiry Into the Human Prospect.* New York: W. W. Norton, 1975.

Marcuse, Herbert. *Essay on Liberation.* Boston: Beacon Press, 1969.

Schroyer, Trent. *The Critique of Domination.* New York: George Braziller, 1973.

INDEX